OXFORD EARLY CHRISTIAN STUDIES

General Editors

Henry Chadwick   Rowan Williams

THE OXFORD EARLY CHRISTIAN STUDIES series will include scholarly volumes on the thought and history of the early Christian centuries. Covering a wide range of Greek, Latin, and Oriental sources, the books will be of interest to theologians, ancient historians, and specialists in the classical and Jewish worlds.

HOLY CITY,
HOLY PLACES?

*Christian Attitudes to Jerusalem and the Holy Land
in the Fourth Century*

P. W. L. WALKER

CLARENDON PRESS · OXFORD
1990

Oxford University Press, Walton Street, Oxford ox2 6DP
Oxford New York Toronto
Delhi Bombay Calcutta Madras Karachi
Petaling Jaya Singapore Hong Kong Tokyo
Nairobi Dar es Salaam Cape Town
Melbourne Auckland
and associated companies in
Berlin Ibadan

Oxford is a trade mark of Oxford University Press

Published in the United States
by Oxford University Press, New York

British Library Cataloguing in Publication Data
Walker, Peter
Holy city, holy places?: Christian attitudes to
Jerusalem and the Holy land in the 4th century.
1. Christianity, history
I. Title
209
ISBN 0-19-814467-9

Library of Congress Cataloging in Publication Data
Walker, P. W. L. (Peter W. L.)
Holy city holy places: Christian attitudes to Jerusalem and the
Holy Land in the fourth century/ P.W.L. Walker.
(Oxford early Christian studies)
Revision of the author's thesis (Ph.D)—Cambridge University.
Bibliography: p.   Includes Indexes.
1. Jerusalem in Christianity—History of doctrines—Early church.
ca. 30-600.   2. Palestine in Christianity—History of doctrines-
Early church, ca. 30-600.   3. Eusebius, of Caesarea, Bishop of
Caesarea, ca. 260-ca. 340.   4. Cyril, Saint, Bishop of Jerusalem,
ca. 315-386.   I. Title.   II. Series.
BT93.5.W35 1989   263'.042569442'09015—dc20   89-9390
ISBN 0-19-814467-9

Set by Oxford Text System
Printed in Great Britain
Biddles Ltd., Guildford and King's Lynn

For Georgie, my wife,
and in memory of
Cyril, my father
(†14.2.89)

IX, 7, 17, 127, 129

PREFACE

Few lands can attract the attention of so many people with such a wide range of interests as does the land of Palestine.[1] It is a land of history, of pious devotion, of religious and political tension. It is a land dug up by archaeologists, prayed in by pilgrims, and often torn apart and fought over by religious opponents. A study such as ours, the chief purpose of which is to describe how Eusebius, himself a historian, a Christian and an important political statesman, would have assessed the land of Palestine, should therefore be of value to people with interests in each of these three areas. First, biblical historians or archaeologists, anxious to decide the authenticity of the various Gospel sites, may learn here how to evaluate the testimony of this ancient historian who, though he lived three hundred years after Christ, is in many cases our first available witness to the supposed location of Gospel events. Secondly, those concerned with Christian spirituality and the practice and theology of pilgrimage at the 'holy places' may learn in these pages how a local Christian came to assess the value of these historic sites and their role in the life of faith. Thirdly, those who are concerned with the history of religion in general, or more particularly with any issue which relates to the land of Palestine, may learn here how an important Church leader developed his own Christian understanding of Palestine and of Jerusalem at a pivotal moment in the history of this land. Finally, our study will naturally be of interest to those whose chief interest lies in the history and thought of the fourth century, one which marked such a watershed in Christian history and marked the beginning of the great patristic era of the Church.

Our subject matter therefore touches on many different fields of

---

[1] In today's heated political climate, much care is required even in one's choice of name for this land. Normally the 'Holy Land' has been used in Christian works as a convenient means of avoiding a reference to Palestine or Israel. Since, however, our enquiry raises the very question of whether Eusebius would have considered 'holy' to be a proper title for this land, it has been decided in the following to use 'Palestine', the name by which Eusebius and his contemporaries would have known it. This is therefore used strictly in its historical sense, though more modern overtones cannot be avoided entirely.

interest. Its own central focus, however, is quite specific. It concerns
just two questions, both of which (especially in the light of the
Crusades) are of vital importance within Palestine and indeed of
quite central importance within Christendom at large. First, how
should Christians view those places associated with the life of
Jesus? Secondly, what constitutes a Christian attitude to the city
of Jerusalem? Two concepts are thus being examined: that of 'holy
places' and that of a 'holy city'.

The phenomenon of 'holy places' raises some major questions
of theology and spirituality. What exactly are 'holy places' and what
is their role? Are they merely places of historical commemoration, or
do they have some deeper spiritual function, indeed some inherent
quality that makes them 'holy'? Do they threaten the spiritual
emphases of Christianity, or are they another valid example of the
sacramental approach to the physical? What exactly, within an
orthodox Christian framework, was the purpose of the Incarnation,
and how truly do 'holy places' reflect that purpose?

Meanwhile the phenomenon of a 'holy city' raises a different
set of questions, about biblical interpretation and about God's
supposed involvement with this city. In what sense, if any, can we
talk of Jerusalem having been 'special' to God in the Old Testament,
or having a distinctive theological status? Or is the city's holiness
in any age a merely human construct? However, if its affirmed that
there was indeed a divine involvement with Jerusalem during the
Old Testament period what is the relationship between it and
the Jerusalem of the New Testament? Should Christians understand
the crucifixion and then the fall of Jerusalem to have indicated a
divine judgement on the city which is final and irrevocable? Or
can they preserve their belief in the city's essential holiness and
specialness by emphasizing its privileged involvement with the
Incarnation and the Resurrection? Any such Christian evaluation
of Jerusalem as a 'holy city' inevitably then has a direct bearing
on any Christian encounter with Judaism or Islam, both of which
have similar, yet quite different, convictions that Jerusalem is
indeed a 'holy city'.[2]

Naturally therefore no simple solution is offered in these pages.
The task in hand is that of raising awareness, not providing

---

[2] For a useful modern survey of Jerusalem as the 'holy city' of three religions,
see Werblowsky (1973-4).

answers. For these two age-long questions, which raise so many issues, have been a source of Christian debate throughout much of the Church's life. What is offered instead is an analysis of the 'first round' of that debate.

The Peace of the Church in the fourth century provided the first real opportunity for Christians to express their natural interest in Palestine in both word and deed. It is therefore to the fourth century (and in particular to the debate observable between Eusebius and Cyril) that we have returned. It is hoped that, with a greater understanding of that debate in its earliest stages, we may be helped in our modern discussion concerning precisely the same issues.

Eusebius of Caesarea (*c.*260–339),[3] was probably the 'most learned man', the 'greatest scholar' and the 'most famous living writer' of his day.[4] 'He had a breadth of learning which is simply astonishing.'[5] Indeed he was perhaps the most accomplished and erudite Christian ever to have been born in the homeland of Jesus. He also had the privilege of living in that land at that singular moment when a Roman emperor who wished to espouse Christianity took power in the East. If the arrival of Constantine was an exciting moment for the Church at large, it was also a strategic moment for Palestine in particular. The tiny land that had experienced other major changes in such unforgettable years as 587 BC and AD 70 (and which would experience many more in the years to come, such as 638, 1099, 1948, and 1967) now experienced in 325 a further dramatic change: Palestine came under Christian rule.

This new involvement of the Church in Palestine had lasting effects, for good and for ill, on both the Church and the land. It was also something of particular concern to the elderly Eusebius, who since 313 had been the metropolitan bishop of the province. Now for the first time Jerusalem and the places associated with the life of Christ were securely in Christian hands. Thus Eusebius had the unique privilege and responsibility of establishing a Christian attitude to these historic entities. Eusebius thus lived in

---

[3] For dates, see Barnes (1981), 94, 263, and (for an outline chronology of Eusebius' life) 277–9.

[4] Levine (1975a), 126; Foakes–Jackson (1933), 44 and 133; Chesnut (1978), 245 respectively.

[5] Quasten, iii (1960), 311.

a strategic place at a strategic time—close both to Jerusalem and
to Constantine.[6]

However, though his attitudes to the emperor have been much
studied,[7] his attitudes to his own homeland have been comparatively
neglected. Many have noted that Eusebius probably had a natural
interest in the new opportunities of a Christian Palestine,[8] but
there has been little more detailed analysis.[9] As a result, Eusebius
has too often been portrayed as being fully behind all the new
expressions of Christian interest in the land, fully committed to all
the changes that these would involve in Christian practice and
thought. Yet it is our contention that this was not so. His experience
of that land naturally influenced his early thinking, and he could
draw on that extensive experience, whether as historian or apologist,
as theologian or bishop, to cope with the sudden changes of his
final years. Yet that experience gave him several strong reasons
for being cautious about this new development. A picture is
therefore offered in these pages of Eusebius' assessment of Palestine
and Jerusalem before and after the Peace of the Church in 325,
which will show how his attitudes were more complex and indeed
more negative than has commonly been supposed.

In recent years, for example, Eusebius has been depicted by
scholars as the founder of the Christian 'Holy Land' and as
Constantine's 'chief agent in its development.'[10] 'If the flowering
of . . . Palestine into a place of pilgrimage, the 'Holy Land', is to
be ascribed to a single man,' it is claimed, 'that man is certainly
Eusebius.'[11] Indeed it has been asserted that 'without Eusebius
devotion to the Holy Places might never have arisen'.[12] Such
presentations of Eusebius are far too simple. It is time to rescue
him from such caricatures.

For here were complex issues, liable to produce many changes,

---

[6] Even if not as close as Eusebius himself pretended: see Barnes (1981), 265 ff.,
and fn. 66.

[7] See esp. Barnes (1981), incl. extensive bibliography; also Winkelmann (1962).

[8] See Cross (1951), Telfer (1955a and b), Wallace-Hadrill (1960), 201–6, Cardman
(1979), 21 ff., Wilkinson (1981), 12, and Linder (1985), 2.

[9] This is confined, for example, to a single note in Barnes (1981), 391, fn. 31.
Groh (1983) gives the most comprehensive appraisal.

[10] Telfer (1955a), 20.

[11] Wilkinson (1981), 12 (though this clear-cut stance is noticeably softened in his
corrigenda, 311–12); cf. Linder (1985), 2.

[12] The conclusion of Cross (1951) in an extended note asserting the unique role
of Eusebius (p. xv, fn. 2).

and Eusebius was a deep enough thinker to sense the need for caution. Major changes, especially of the order which the Church and Palestine experienced in 325, are seldom countenanced by the learned and the elderly without some understandable qualms and questions, without a fear that something of essential value from the past might be in danger of being too quickly laid aside. Eusebius' response to a Christian Palestine was no exception.

By the end of that century the Church came to accept that the Gospel sites were truly to be deemed 'holy places' and that Jerusalem was indeed a 'holy city'. Eusebius, however, who really belonged to a former age when such ideas were little known, had some major questions about such developments. They were a far cry from what he had been proposing in the first years after 325. For he seems clearly to have denied that Jerusalem was a 'holy city' and to have approached the places of Christ primarily as a historian, not as a pilgrim, preserving his emphasis on the spiritual nature of Christianity which was the hallmark of all his earlier theology. It is our task therefore to discover afresh Eusebius' own response to our two questions: What was his attitude to the places of Christ? What was his attitude to Jerusalem? In particular, were they 'holy'? If so, in what sense?

Our understanding of Eusebius' thinking, however, will greatly be increased through having a contemporary voice with which to compare his thoughts. Cyril of Jerusalem (c.320-?386) provides us with an ideal comparative foil. Although he was strictly two generations younger than Eusebius, Cyril delivered his *Catechetical Lectures* within fifteen years of Eusebius's writing the *Life of Constantine*. Through a comparison of what these two men said concerning Jerusalem and the places of Christ in these and other works, we begin to sense the great movement that was already under way towards a far more developed theology of 'holy places' and an explicit belief in Jerusalem as a 'holy city'.

Too often it has been assumed that Eusebius would have concurred fully with these sentiments of Cyril, that Cyril was only making explicit what was implicit in Eusebius' thought. In this way Cyril's words are allowed to speak for Eusebius, while Eusebius' distinctive voice is hardly heard. In the following, by contrast, every effort has been made to let Eusebius speak for himself.

This has entailed a thorough reading of all Eusebius' surviving works in order that the whole flavour and structure of his theology

might be discerned. Too often his thought on these two questions
has been assessed merely through a study of a couple of his works
(especially the *Life of Constantine* and the *Onomasticon*), wrenched
from this wider theological context and read with seemingly too
much hindsight.[13] Instead, however, as the recent monumental
work of Barnes (1981) has shown concerning other Eusebian issues,
it is vital to study the whole of his thought, to find out those
convictions he held from his earliest years, and to establish the
proper background for those statements that he made towards the
end of his life.

The results are indeed worthwhile. For what is revealed is a far
more interesting picture, of a Palestinian Christian who yet found
himself committed to a theology that tended to play down the role
of such places and of Jerusalem, of a metropolitan bishop who
found himself on the losing side of an ecclesiastical struggle with
the bishop of that 'holy city', Jerusalem, and of an elderly theologian
who had thought deeply about these issues and who retained to
the end of his life certain convictions that others after him would
never share.

It will reveal too a probable discrepancy between Eusebius'
views and those of the enthusiastic new emperor. Above all,
however, it brings to light a sharp disagreement between Eusebius
and Cyril, a disagreement founded principally upon their divergent
theologies (partly, though not totally, caused by the different eras
in which they lived), but also upon the increasing ecclesiastical
tension between Caesarea and Jerusalem. Jerusalem and the 'holy
places' showed from the outset that, despite their capacity to be
focuses for Christian unity, they also had great potential for
division.

The relevance of this to any modern Christian assessment of
Jerusalem or the places of Christ should by now be more than
evident. Unfortunately, space will forbid anything more than a
cursory examination of these perennial questions in their modern
context. Yet it will be sensed that Eusebius' views could interreact
quite creatively with modern formulations. For example, his more
historical approach to the places of Christ might find a parallel
with those who see these places as only 'holy by historical
association' and to deny that they are 'holy' in any more inherent

[13] This seems to be the approach of Telfer (1955b) and Wallace-Hadrill (1960).

sense. Even more pointedly, his negative attitude towards Jerusalem, denying it the status of a 'holy city', runs directly counter to many modern Christian assessments which (either through emphasizing the New Testament and the Incarnation, or through emphasizing the Old Testament and God's unchanging purposes towards 'Sion') seek to defend in some sense the 'holiness' of this city.

Eusebius' attitudes may be questioned or ridiculed by many. Yet such critics will need to acknowledge, even if they disagree, that these attitudes are those of a man who, more than any other, was well qualified to speak on all these issues, a Palestinian who lived in the land all his life, an apologist who knew well the differences between Christianity and Judaism, a historian who was also a forceful theologian, indeed a bishop who played an important part in the very development of Christian Palestine. If therefore this man of all men had certain qualms and reservations about an over-enthusiastic appropriation of the 'Holy Land' by Christians, we would do well in our own far more troubled day not merely to note them, but perhaps even to heed them. 'A man of this breadth is not to be dismissed lightly.'[14]

Of our two areas of concern, that of Jerusalem is of course the one with the greater repercussions in our own day, as Jews, Muslims, and Christians all seek to define their religion's attachment and their political rights to this one city. The sudden events which overtook that historic land in Eusebius' lifetime may indeed now seem so much more straightforward than those which the same land has experienced in our own. Yet they were sufficient to cause Eusebius to wrestle hard with that enduring question concerning the status of Jerusalem which is now ours too. As such, this analysis of his wrestlings may serve as a useful instruction for those today who are called similarly to wrestle with the problems of that city. It is offered, not in the forlorn hope of answering those problems, but with the desire to set them in one of their many possible historical contexts, all of which can help Christians to make an intelligent stance in a situation now fraught with spiritual and political complexities.

It is six years since this work was first begun and two years since

[14] Wallace-Hadrill (1960), 8.

its first (very different) appearance as a doctoral thesis for Cambridge University. Over such a period there have naturally been numerous people to whom I am greatly indebted for advice and encouragement.

In those earliest days conversations with Stewart Perowne, John Wilkinson and Ted Todd did much to guide my initial interest. For four years that interest was sustained through the unfailing enthusiasm and timely suggestions of my supervisor, Dr Caroline Bammel. Fortunately, however, those years of research were punctuated by three valuable visits to Jerusalem, sponsored in part by the Cambridge Divinity Faculty and my college, Corpus Christi. In Jerusalem I had the privilege of staying at St George's College, the École Biblique, and Christ Church, each of which in their very different ways did so much to influence my thinking endeavours. More recently I am grateful to the staff (and friends) at both Christ Church, Abingdon, and Wycliffe Hall, Oxford, who have released me from other work to enable the task of publication to proceed; the Skinner's Company have also been generous in their financial support of this venture.

However, there are then all those scholars and friends who have patiently read portions of this book in its different stages and whose advice on all matters, whether historical, theological, archaeological or grammatical, has been so greatly appreciated; Professor Henry Chadwick and Professor Averil Cameron, Professor Rowan Williams and Bishop Kenneth Cragg, Professor Hal Drake, Professor Yoram Tsafrir and Professor Ze'ev Rubin, David Hunt and Gerald Bray, Ora Limor and Oded Irsai, Jerome Murphy-O'Connor and Justin Taylor, John Peterson and Gilbert Sinden, Eileen Fenton and Hilary Feldman, also my loyal friends, Robin, Steve, Graham, Andrew, Leslie, John, Tim, Stephen, Geoff, Colin, and Jonathan.

Finally, such a work would never have started and would have been quite impossible without the love, belief and patient support of my parents and family, who have often seen so little of me as a result. Georgie may not have been present when this project was first begun; but her arrival in mid-course gave it a valuable new lease of life at a critical time, and without her encouragement and patience its completion would have been quite impossible.

Wycliffe Hall, Oxford
25 January 1989

Peter Walker

CONTENTS

A NOTE ON THE CITATION OF PRIMARY
SOURCES

Throughout the volume the abbreviations listed below have been used for primary sources. References in the body of the text take the English titles of works; those in the footnotes use abbreviations of the Latin forms. Where a reference gives details in addition to the original book and section numbering of the work in question, the figure is in all cases the column or page (and line) number of the edition specified. The bibliographical details of the editions used for each patristic author are listed in the first section of the Bibliography.

The system adopted for biblical commentaries is somewhat different, but it is similar for all authors: *Title of commentary* [biblical chapter and verse, which may or may not be the author's method of structure], book and section numbers. In most cases this is considered sufficient for the reader. If, however, it is necessary to be very specific, column or page and line numbers of the edition cited in the Bibliography are also given; thus—Origen, *Comm. in Jo.* [1.1], 2.3, 56.29–57.7. The exception to this format is Origen's *Commentary on St Matthew* which in the Berlin corpus (GCS: *Die griechischen christlichen Schriftsteller der ersten drei Jahrhunderte*) covers three volumes (Origen, x–xii): the commentary itself, the *commentariorum series* [CS], and a volume of fragments [Fr.]. In references to these GCS volumes CS or Fr. details replace the book and section number. There is also a volume of Lucan fragments (Origen, ix).

References to the psalms, principally in Eusebius, are always to the Septuagint (LXX) numbering. Where a psalm number is cited in the text the Hebrew (Masoretic) alternative—with which modern English readers are familiar—is given in square brackets; thus— LXX Ps. 87 [88]. Unless the LXX is specified in the text all references are to the Hebrew numbering; all references in the footnotes are to the LXX.

(a) *Eusebius*

Adv. Marc.	*Against Marcellus*
Chron.	*Chronicle*
Comm. in Is.	*Commentary on Isaiah*
Comm. in Luc.	*Commentary on Luke*
Comm. in Ps.	*Commentary on the Psalms*
Dem. Ev.	*Proof of the Gospel*
Ep. Caes.	*Letter to the Church of Caesarea*
Ep. Const.	*Letter to Constantia Augusta*
Hist. Eccl.	*Ecclesiastical History*
L. Const.	*In Praise of Constantine*
Mart. Pal.	*The Martyrs of Palestine*
Onom.	*Onomasticon*
Pasch.	*On the Paschal Festival*
Praep. Ev.	*Preparation for the Gospel*
Proph. Eclg.	*Prophetic Eclogues*
QM/QS/QMS	*Gospel Questions and Solutions*
Sep. Chr.	*On Christ's Sepulchre*
Theol. Eccl.	*Ecclesiastical Theology*
Theoph.	*Theophany*
V. Const.	*Life of Constantine*

Translations that are abbreviated are as follows:
DPC Drake, H. A., 1976, *In Praise of Constantine*
FPG Ferrar, W. J., 1920, *The Proof of the Gospel*
LET Lee, S., 1843, *Eusebius on the Theophaneia*

The reader will find in the Appendix a discussion of matters of authenticity and dating in the works of Eusebius and Cyril. It is followed in section one of the Bibliography by a full listing of the texts and their appropriate modern editions.

(b) *Cyril*

Catech.	*Catechetical Lectures*
Ep. Const.	*Letter to Constantius*
Hom. para.	*Homily on the paralytic*

The translation used throughout (unless otherwise specified) is:
WCJ McCawley, L. P., and Stephenson, A. A., (1969–70). *The Works of St Cyril of Jerusalem*

(c) Origen

Cant.	*Commentary on the Song of Songs*
Comm. in Jo.	*Commentary on John*
Comm. in lib. Jes.	*Commentary on Joshua*
Comm. in Matt.	*Commentary on Matthew*
C. Cels.	*Against Celsus*
Hom. in Jer.	*Homilies on Jeremiah*
Mart.	*Exhortation to Martyrdom*

Unless otherwise specified the edition of Origen in the Berlin corpus has been used and references conform to the pattern outlined above.

(d) *Other authors*

The writings of Egeria [*Egeria*] and the Bordeaux Pilgrim [*BP*], of Josephus, Pliny, Sozomen, Theodoret, Jerome, Gregory of Nyssa, Epiphanius, and other patristic authors, are also treated as outlined above.

For further information see the general abbreviations list and Bibliography, §1.

LIST OF ILLUSTRATIONS

I

PROBLEMS AND PERSONALITIES

Fig. 1. Map of fourth-century Palestine

EUSEBIUS AND CYRIL:
THEIR LIFE AND TIMES

Eusebius and Cyril lived in a strategic place at a strategic time. Theirs was the task of speaking on behalf of the Church in the land of Jesus' birth in the early years of the Christian empire·in the fourth century. Theirs was the task of establishing how, in a time of great excitement and change, Christians should value the 'Holy Land' and Jerusalem.

Yet Palestine had not always been such a strategic place. Our enquiry must begin much further back by describing the Palestine into which Eusebius was born in the middle of the third century. Such a description will only reveal how great were the changes which came over Palestine as a result of Constantine's arrival in the East in 324/5. Palestine in the third century was quite different from the Palestine that would emerge in the fourth century.

1. THIRD-CENTURY PALESTINE

The Palestine into which Eusebius was born was of virtually no significance at all. Still suffering from the effects of two catastrophic revolts against Rome fought nearly two hundred years previously, in economic terms the province of Palestine fared worse than most in the depression throughout the empire in the third century.[1] In political terms Palestine's importance to the empire was simply strategic, as a buffer against the unpredictable movements of the peoples to the East. Rome had never quite forgotten the humiliating and disastrous defeat which Crassus had suffered three centuries before on the eastern frontier against the Parthians; for its part

---

[1] For discussion of the economic plight of third-century Palestine, see Avi–Yonah (1976), 89–136; Sperber (1978) and Smallwood (1976), 526–38.

4 Problems and personalities

Palestine was relearning that its fragile peace depended on the good will of world powers quite beyond its own control. In cultural and religious terms Palestine was well and truly mixed. There was no single language that could be understood throughout the province; the Greek of the empire mingled with the Latin of the military and civil administration, as well as with the local Aramaic.[2] Nor was the province any longer primarily Jewish. Although the Jews were still very much the majority in Galilee to the north, elsewhere the province was now predominantly pagan. Meanwhile Christians proved to be a tiny minority. Indeed the state of the Church in those days seemed only to endorse in a new and painful sense the prophetic dictum that Jesus had first spoken among the Jews of the Nazareth synagogue, to the effect that a 'prophet is not without honour except in his own country' (Luke, 4.24).[3] There were still some isolated groups of Jewish–Christians, perhaps especially in the Galilee area, who struggled to preserve their identity amid hostility—on one side from the Jews and on the other (increasingly) from the Gentile Church; although their numbers may therefore have been more than our Gentile sources suggest, they would still have been quite negligible within the overall population.[4] The majority of the Church in Palestine, however, was Gentile in background, the result of the steady influx of non-Jews from the rest of the empire after the overthrow of Judaea in AD 70 and 135. Yet there were not many Christians among them; of the many villages and towns scattered throughout the province, only three seem to have had a significant or predominant Christian presence.[5]

The strongest Christian presence was in Caesarea, the provincial capital, situated on the trade-routes between East and West, with

---

[2] See Bardy (1946), 11–18 and Telfer (1955a), 35, fn. 43 commenting on Eus. *Mart. Pal.*, 2.1 and *Egeria*, 47.3–4. The non-Hellenic element in Palestine throughout this period will have been far from negligible. Telfer even suggests that Cyril repeated each of his lectures on the following day in the vernacular Aramaic.

[3] For an outline of pre-Constantinian Christianity in Palestine, see Heyer (1984), 7–26.

[4] See below 5.2(c). The arguments of the Franciscan community in Jerusalem today—see esp. Bagatti (1971)—for a large number of such Jewish–Christian groups have yet to gain scholarly acceptance.

[5] Eusebius himself records this in *Onom.*, 26.13–14; 108.1–4; 112.14–17. For Eusebius' seeming acceptance of the idolatrous nature of Palestine, see *Comm. in Ps.* [75.2–4], 875b.

a superb Herodian harbour.[6] Here alone Christianity had put down firm roots.[7] Jews and Samaritans also made up considerable minorities in this prosperous city,[8] but for Christians this was the only effective centre of Christianity in the land of Jesus' birth.

What then of Jerusalem, the central city of the Bible? By the third century it could not truly claim any longer to be the centre of anything, whether religious or political. A shadow of its former self, it was no longer even called Jerusalem. After the second Jewish revolt in 135 Hadrian had refounded the city as 'Aelia Capitolina', a pagan name which clearly spelt the end of Jewish aspirations for Jerusalem. Moreover, despite these pagan connotations Christians clearly accepted with everyone else that this was now the correct name for what had been the Jerusalem of the Bible. Jerusalem effectively no longer existed.[9] The new Hadrianic town was less than half the size of the Jerusalem before AD 70[10] and its roads were laid out according to the standard plan of a normal Roman camp. A single Roman legion was left to ensure that there was no repeat of the two Jewish revolts and its garrison was naturally located on the highest point in the town. The second highest point lay a little to the north and was conveniently close

[6] The results of the exciting archaeological work done recently at the site (including underwater exploration) have not yet been published in extended form; for some preliminary discussions, see Raban (1985), 165–204. Otherwise, for the archaeology and history of Caesarea, founded by Herod on the site of Strato's Tower, see esp. Levine (1975b), Stevenson (1928), 1–17 and bibliography cited in Vogel (1971), 23 ff.

[7] Barnes (1981), 104; cf. Harnack (1908), i, 106–14. Levine (1975a), 113–34 outlines the 'power and prestige' of this Church which resulted not least from the influence of Origen.

[8] For the civil and religious nature of third century Palestine, see Levine (1975a), 46–60 and De Lange (1976), 1–2, 10–12.

[9] Although Eusebius referred to the contemporary city as 'Jerusalem' on several occasions (see, e.g., *Hist. Eccl.*, 5.12, 22; 6.8, 11, 27 etc) he clearly accepted that its true name was now 'Aelia': 'the Roman city changed its name and *is* called [προσαγορεύεται] Aelia' (*Hist. Eccl.*, 4.6.4; cf. *idem*, 2.12.3; 7.5.1; 7.20). In his *Onom.* he clearly assumed (though this was never explained) that 'Jerusalem' was only to be used in anachronistic contexts which were expressly biblical, or which referred to AD 70 and the importance of the city to Jews; when speaking of the city in contemporary Palestine, its correct name was 'Aelia'. Thus in his entry for Cariathiarim (114.23–7), for example, Eusebius used 'Jerusalem' when referring to the relevant biblical episode, but 'Aelia' (twice) when locating it in contemporary Palestine. For a complete list of Eusebius' eighteen uses of 'Jerusalem' in this work, compared with his thirty-eight of 'Aelia', see the register in GCS, iii.1, 193–4, 197; to these can be added the reference on p. 42.10.

[10] For the geography of Aelia see Tsafrir (1978), 543–51.

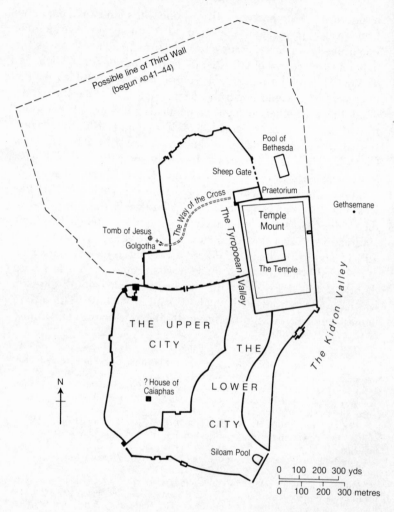

Fig. 2. Plan of Jerusalem in the time of Jesus

to the central crossroads of the town. Here Hadrian had naturally built a forum (market-place) for the town and a temple. The dedication of the temple to Venus, the goddess of sexual love, was a clear pagan statement by Hadrian, designed to show to the Jews that their 'holy city of Jerusalem' was now a thing of the past, never to be revived.

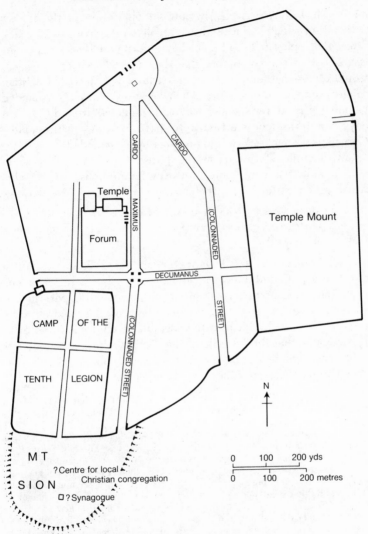

Fig. 3. Plan of Aelia Capitolina

It was, needless to say, unfortunate that this temple happened to be built over what was almost definitely the site of Christ's tomb. Thus Christians too could take offence at Hadrian's action and later generations would be quick to impute all sorts of uncharacteristic motives to this famous emperor. Hadrian's prime motive, however, was clearly outright opposition to the Jewish nationalism which had caused two revolts in the space of 70 years. Yet that opposition had a further unfortunate consequence for the Christian church. Before that date the Church in Jerusalem would almost certainly have been exclusively a Jewish–Christian congregation; for the pressure of living in Jerusalem and surrounded by non-Christian Jews, which had made it difficult from the earliest days for Jerusalem Christians to have dealings with Gentile Christians elsewhere,[11] would presumably have made the presence of any Gentile Christians in the Jerusalem Church a cause of embarassment and division. However, Hadrian issued an edict which exiled all Jews from the city:

> It is forbidden for all circumcized persons to enter or stay within the territory of Aelia Capitolina; any person contravening this prohibition shall be put to death.[12]

The effect of this on the Jews was, as intended, enormous. Yet it also had a profound affect on the Christian Church in Jerusalem, even though Christians had probably played little part in Bar Chochba's revolt. Since all the members of this Church were themselves Jews by birth, it too was effectively forced into exile. It is possible that the Jerusalem Church had voluntarily 'gone into exile' once before during the first Jewish revolt;[13] but this time they had no choice and there would be no return.

[11] As evidenced, for example, in the great council at Jerusalem (Acts 15.1–29), the treatment of Paul in Jerusalem (Acts 21.17–26) and the dispute between Paul and Peter (Gal. 2.11–21).

[12] As reconstructed by Avi-Yonah (1976), 50 f., following the wording of Tertullian (*Adv. Jud.*, 13), Justin Martyr (*DT*, 16; *Apol.*, 1.77) and Eusebius (*Hist. Eccl.*, 4.6.3), as well as the modern arguments of Harris (1926). Avi-Yonah suggests that in the 'anarchical third century' this edict, 'even though never finally annulled' came to be 'evaded in practice' (163 f.). Hence several rabbis seem to have visited Aelia and R. Meir seems actually to have settled there for a while with some pupils (79); cf. *JN*, 450 and Safrai (1973). Eusebius' insistence in *Hist. Eccl.*, 4 that the Jews were still excluded from the city may therefore reflect mere wishful thinking rather than strict actuality—a desire that the statute should be reinforced. This indeed seems then to have taken place under Constantine, though the Jews were then allowed to visit it once a year (a matter already mentioned in 333: see *BP*, 591.5) and to settle somewhat nearer to the city (Jews were living in Bethlehem in Jerome's day: see *Ep.* 84). Eusebius refers to the Jews' exclusion from the city three times after 325: *Theoph.*, 4.20, *Comm. in Is.* [6.11–13], 43.16–19, *Comm. in Ps.* [58.7], 541c. This naturally aided the establishment of a distinctively Christian Jerusalem after 325: cf. Linder (1985). For the probable area of this exclusion zone in the second century, see map at fig. 1, following Avi-Yonah, (1976), 17.

[13] On this 'Pella tradition', see Eus., *Hist. Eccl.*, 3.5.3, and Pritz (1988), 122–7.

The new town of Aelia thus needed to be populated by Gentile colonists from other parts of the empire, and any Church in Aelia would have consisted simply of those among the colonists who happened to be Christians. As a result the Jerusalem Church before 135 and the Aelia Church after 135 were effectively two quite separate bodies.[14] Traditions concerning the location of major Gospel sites would presumably have survived this exchange of population (and conceivably some more minor traditions such as the throne of James and the names of the former bishops?),[15] and some sense of historic identity might have inspired Christians living in Jerusalem. Their own roots, however, really lay elsewhere and any continuity with the Jerusalem Church of the apostolic age had effectively been broken.

Moreover, if even in the apostles' lifetime the Jerusalem Church had been unable to maintain a position of undisputed ecclesiastical primacy,[16] there was no way in which the small Church in Aelia Capitolina, a minor garrison town, could claim any special position. The enterprising leadership of bishops Narcissus and Alexander around AD 200 increased the prestige of this Church, but in general the story of 'Christianity in Jerusalem makes depressing reading'.[17] How could it be that 'in Jerusalem, of all places in the world, Christianity could be so small and weak?'[18] Yet weak it was. The centre of Christianity in Palestine was therefore not in Jerusalem, but in Caesarea, and it was the bishop of Caesarea who was the metropolitan bishop of Palestine.[19]

[14] As suggested by Eusebius' description of the foundation of Aelia (*Hist. Eccl.*, 4.6.4) and the way in which he breaks up the episcopal lists (see next fn.) which no doubt the Jerusalem Church had made available to him in a continuous form.

[15] However, these could easily have been first promoted some time later. For the throne of James see Eus., *Hist. Eccl.*, 7.19, and for the episcopal lists see ibid., 4.5.3–5; 5.12.1–2. The throne could indeed have been 'discovered' even later, perhaps around the time in the third century when the desire to increase the status of the Jerusalem Church led to the exaggeration of the numbers of bishops on these lists: see Turner (1900).

[16] The tensions can be sensed in Paul's encounters with the Jerusalem Church, as recounted in Acts 15 and Gal. 2. The success of the Gentile mission took matters far beyond the control of the Jerusalem leaders. If there was in practice any one centre for the early Church, that centre seems to have been Antioch (see, e.g., Acts 11.26, 13.1–3).

[17] Wilkinson (1978), 176.

[18] Ibid. For an outline history of the Jerusalem Church in the first three centuries, see, e.g., Telfer (1955a), 54–63.

[19] Caesarea was made the 'metropolis' of the province by Septimius Severus in 201: see Kardman (1959), 139 and Levine (1975a), 115.

Such in outline was the Palestine in which the most famous bishop of Caesarea, Eusebius, was born around 260. It was little different from any other province of the Graeco-Roman Empire; if anything, it was something of a 'poor relation'. Thus Eusebius himself could say quite realistically and honestly that Palestine 'in no way excels the rest [of the earth]'.[20]

First, Palestine bore the scars of its past. To Christian eyes perhaps it even manifested the judgement of God: the fall of Jerusalem, the ravaging of the land, and even the weak state of their own Christian Church as it struggled to gain a foothold might all have been taken as signs that God had rejected not only his former people, but somehow even their land. 'I saw the land', said Pionius, a Christian who visited Palestine in the third century, 'which to this day bears witness to the wrath of God'.[21]

Palestine's theological importance was therefore quite clearly a thing of the past. Certainly the great expansion of the worldwide Church suggested that God's purposes had moved elsewhere. Caesarea might be of some importance in local Christian terms, but of much greater importance were the two Mediterranean cities of Alexandria and Antioch which lay to the south and north of Caesarea. From the available evidence it seems that it was the bishoprics of these two cities, along with that of Rome, which were assuming focal positions within the Church. Palestine was therefore by no means integral to the Church's life. The centre of gravity had clearly shifted away from Jerusalem and away from Palestine.

Secondly, Palestine had less religious attachment than at any time in its lengthy history, before or since. In the third century the Jews were no longer stressing their attachment to Jerusalem, nor were Christians yet really discovering the potential of this 'Holy Land'. The number of Jews in the north was considerable but two crushed revolts had taught them a bitter lesson. Their attachment to Jerusalem and the land was largely kept to themselves, and indeed even spiritualized. There was certainly no opportunity for it to be given any practical or politicial expression. The actual attitudes of the Jews towards Jerusalem at this time are very difficult to determine. Several rabbinical sayings, probably intended to prevent Jewish emigration from Palestine, have been

---

[20] *Dem. Ev.*, 3.2.10 (*FPG*, i, 105).
[21] *Mart. Pionii*, 4.18 in Knopf, R., and Kruger, G. (1929). *Ausgewählte Märtyrerakten* (Tubingen), 47.33–4.

preserved concerning the sanctity of the land itself,[22] but there is little mention of Jerusalem. Does the silence of the Jewish sources reflect desire tactfully suppressed or, instead, desire tacitly abandoned? The events during the reign of the Emperor Julian (361–3), when the Jews were encouraged to rebuild the Temple, certainly show how old passions could be reawakened; a century later the temporal Jerusalem evidently still had a great religious appeal. Yet it is hard to know the extent of that appeal back in the third century. Eusebius, of course, as shall be seen, made his own constructions of Jewish attitudes towards Jerusalem, emphasizing their enduring devotion to the physical city, against which he could so easily contrast the more 'spiritual' approach of Christians; but we cannot be certain how much of this stereotype was true and how much was a useful apologetic fiction. For reasons either of necessity or conviction Jerusalem was not to have the importance for the Jews in this era that it had had previously.

Meanwhile for Christians the land of Palestine as a whole was still something of an unopened treasure. In the three hundred years after the time of Christ, Eusebius, himself our principal source, names only four Christians who visited the homeland of Jesus because of its historic associations.[23] Some time around 170 Melito of Sardis had come on a study visit to Palestine seeking to determine the extent of the Old Testament canon:

When I came to the east and reached the place where these things were preached and done and learnt accurately the books of the Old Testament, I set down the facts.[24]

As a result, Melito's later reference in his *Paschal Homily* to Christ being crucified 'in the *middle* of Jerusalem', not outside the city wall, probably reflects his knowledge of contemporary Aelia and

---

[22] See, e.g., Avi-Yonah (1976), 26–7, who quotes from b *Ketubot* 110b–111a and M *Kelim*, 1.6.

[23] Cf. Windisch (1925), 145 ff.; for a general discussion of pilgrimage before Constantine, see Kotting (1950), Wilkinson (1978), 33 f. and (1981), 10–13, 311 f. For a more theological presentation, which assesses the attitudes of the early Church to the places of Christ, see W. D. Davies (1974); see also Cardman (1984), 49 ff..

[24] Recorded in Eus., *Hist. Eccl.*, 4.26.14. The context of this letter from Melito to Onesimus is entirely that of an enquiry into the extent of the Old Testament canon; 'these things' therefore refers not narrowly to the places of Christ but more widely to the entire biblical narrative, especially the Law and the Prophets: see Wilkinson (1981), 311.

of the fact that the site of Golgotha was now known to be buried beneath the centre of the Roman town.[25]

Then, in the 230s Origen arrived in Caesarea. Expelled from the Church in Alexandria, he was welcomed by the bishops in Palestine who had earlier ordained him as a presbyter in the Church in Caesarea;[26] there he founded a Christian school, which in years to come would be an important influence on Eusebius. In trying to establish the reasons why Origen settled in Caesarea, it is tempting to suggest that he may have been influenced by the city's proximity to so many biblical sites; for he certainly visited such sites on occasion.[27] Yet in the first instance Caesarea must simply have been the nearest haven of safety, a place where he had already been made welcome in times past by Church leaders.[28] If he had any higher motivation, it is more likely that he was attracted by the proximity, not of the biblical sites, but of the strong Jewish schools of learning, in both Caesarea and Tiberias.[29] For from these schools he would be able to learn yet more about the Hebrew of the Old Testament; yet at the same time he would be able in opposition to these schools to establish the rival strength and viability of Christian exegesis, which did not need especially to prove itself in the land of Jesus but did in the land of the Jews.

A third visitor to Palestine was a man named Alexander. Although shortly after his arrival he found himself consecrated as bishop of Jerusalem, he had originally come to Palestine, says Eusebius, with the express purpose of seeking out 'the places' and 'to pray' (εὐχῆς καὶ τῶν τόπων ἱστορίας ἕνεκεν).[30] Here for the first time the germinal ideas of pilgrimage, the conjunction of places and prayer, can be plainly sensed. However, another visitor from Cappadocia, Firmilian, was more attracted by the teaching of Origen and seems to have returned several times to Origen's now

[25] *Paschal Homily*, 71; see Harvey (1966), 403.

[26] See Eus. *Hist. Eccl.*, 6.23.4.

[27] In discussing the identification of 'Bethany beyond the Jordan' (John 1.28) he explained that he had himself visited that area 'in search of the traces' (ἐπὶ ἱστορίαν τῶν ἰχνῶν) of Jesus and his disciples (*Comm. in Jo.* [1.28], 6.40, 150.3–20); compare also his reference to the Bethlehem cave in *C. Cels.*, 1.51. Hunt (1982), 92–3 cites a few further places which Origen may have visited; Goodman (1983), 15 is more sceptical.

[28] See Eus. *Hist. Eccl.*, 6.19.16. It was also the nearest place to Alexandria which was at all similar in ambience to that great city: see Trigg (1983), 133.

[29] De Lange (1976), 28.

[30] *Hist. Eccl.*, 6.11.2.

famous school in Caesarea.[31] Yet on one of these occasions he too must have gone up to witness the worship of the Church in Jerusalem, for he would later compare the liturgical practice of the Jerusalem Church favourably with that of Rome.[32]

No doubt there were many others. For example, as already noted, Pionius, a contemporary of Origen, used his eye-witness experience of the 'Holy Land' in his defence of the faith prior to his martyrdom in Smyrna. 'The volume of devout tourism must have been much greater than these isolated examples suggest.'[33] Since Christians were unable to visit Golgotha, covered as it was by Hadrian's temple and forum, Eusebius himself records how instead they sought out both Bethlehem[34] and the Mount of Olives,[35] how they prayed in Gethsemane,[36] and perhaps even travelled to the Jordan to be baptized.[37] Much of this interest, however, to which Eusebius refers was probably quite local in origin. The apologetic concerns of his *Proof of the Gospel* probably encouraged him to paint a more international perspective for the attraction of Bethlehem and the Mount of Olives than may truly have been the case.[38] His wording in the *Onomasticon* concerning Gethsemane and the Jordan certainly suggests something on a much smaller scale.

Plainly there was a growing interest in the Gospel sites, but Palestine was not yet really a major focus of pilgrimage in any sense. Local Christians no doubt kept some local traditions alive but in general the interests of the worldwide Church lay elsewhere. Justin Martyr, himself a native of Neapolis in Palestine,[39] together with Tertullian and Irenaeus, would express some apocalyptic notions that Judaea/Palestine would be the location of Christ's

[31] Ibid., 6.27.

[32] According to Cyprian, *Ep.* 75.6. Jerome, of course, sees his visits as inspired expressly 'for the sake of the holy places' ('sub occasione sanctorum locorum') in *de Vir. Illust.*, 54.

[33] Chadwick (1959), 7.

[34] *Dem. Ev.*, 1.1.2, 3.2.47, 7.2.1–17 (*FPG*, i, 3, 112, ii, 78–9).

[35] Ibid., 6.18.23 (*FPG*, ii, 29).

[36] *Onom.*, 74.16–18.

[37] Ibid., 58.19.

[38] See 6.1 below.

[39] In his pre-Christian days he therefore learnt of the supposed site of Sodom and Gomorrah (*Apol.*, 1.53) and of Jesus' birth being celebrated in a cave (*DT*, 78); but there is no indication that he returned there once he became a Christian. He gives us a 'useful view of contemporary Palestine, but from outside': Goodman (1983), 14.

second coming, but those same authors showed little interest theologically in the scenes of Christ's first coming. Almost from the beginning Christianity had come to see itself as a 'diaspora' movement, removed from the geography of the 'Holy Land'. Its theology and its identity were little indebted in practice to Palestine. It was thus quite possible for Eusebius' physical home to be Palestine, but his spiritual 'home' to be the Church now spread throughout the world.

Thirdly, Palestine was deprived of the symbol of Jerusalem. For two hundred years the 'Holy Land' was without its crowning religious jewel, the mystique of Jerusalem; for two hundred years paganism had been seeking to abolish the religious attraction which Jews had felt towards the 'holy city' of Jerusalem. As yet, therefore, Christians had neither the occasion nor the desire to appropriate that mystique and to make Jerusalem a 'holy city' of their own.

Caesarea now came to the fore in its stead. Yet it symbolized something quite different from Jerusalem. To Jewish minds the sudden rise to power of Caesarea, almost simultaneously with the fall of Jerusalem, was not a coincidence. 'Jerusalem and Caesarea are rivals'.[40] 'Before Jerusalem was destroyed no other town was held in any esteem; but after Jerusalem was destroyed Caesarea became a metropolis.'[41] The two cities, they sensed, had stood for two different realms, one religious, the other political; one 'ideological', the other 'material'.[42] Jerusalem had owed its status to the numinous, Caesarea only to the bald realities of commerce and power in the Graeco-Roman world. With the decline of Jerusalem, Palestine lost its religious heart and much of its religious character. Palestine in the third century with Caesarea as its capital was quite a different place from Judaea in the first century centred on Jerusalem. Although Eusebius was born not sixty miles from the Jerusalem of the Gospels, he lived in a quite different milieu and in a Palestine without the religious focus of Jerusalem.

Third-century Palestine was of little importance. Economically it was poor; and its religious significance had been eclipsed. Ecclesiastically it counted for little; theologically it counted for less. It would therefore only be natural for Eusebius to assume that in theological terms Jerusalem and Palestine no longer had

---

[40] Babylonian Talmud, *Meg.* 6a, quoted in De Lange (1976), 10–11.
[41] *Lam. Rabba* 1.5.31.
[42] The terminology of Avi-Yonah (1957) in its English abstract.

any special significance or distinctive function. The age-long function of Palestine as a religious centre was at its lowest ebb.

2. PALESTINE AND THE CHURCH AFTER 325

With the arrival of a Christian emperor in the East in 324/5, however, the situation would change dramatically. Naturally the Church throughout the empire was affected by this dramatic event; but no single province was to be affected quite as much as Palestine. It was not simply that the Church in Palestine, which in many ways had borne the brunt of the persecution in the early years of the fourth century,[43] would now be free from the threat of such persecution; nor that the emperor himself would begin to foster the reinstatement of Palestine to the centre of the Christian mind (by encouraging pilgrimage to the 'holy sites' and by using the 'holy city' of Jerusalem as a symbolic focus of his new Christian empire).[44] Palestine of its own accord began to act as a natural, but unwitting, focus for those changes that Constantine's accession brought to the worldwide Church. Palestine was thus affected not only by the understandable new interest in this historic land but also by the new, more general, concerns of the worldwide Church.

A few examples may be suggested in order to illustrate this point. If Christians experienced an understandable sense of triumph at having a Christian emperor on the throne, what better place to express that triumph than in Jerusalem, the former city both of the Jews and recently of pagans, both of whom were now defeated by this seemingly superior religion? What better place to celebrate the paradoxical victory of the Crucified One than in the Jerusalem that rejected him?

Then again, if the new and exciting demands of a Christian empire caused the Church to seek out its historic roots, to test out its new identity with the yardstick of its original identity, what was more natural than to look once again to Palestine, the place of the Church's origin, in order to receive, as it were, a new mandate which was both authentic and original? If the eschatological hope of the persecuted minority gave way to a sharper historical sense,

---

[43] As recounted in Eus., *Mart. Pal.*
[44] As argued especially by Telfer in his description of Constantine's 'Holy Land Plan' (1955b).

a new desire to find and locate God in this world rather than in the next, what was more natural than to increase veneration for 'holy sites' and relics, things which could mediate God to the believer not from above, but from below? Above all, if Christians now desired to affirm 'this world', if they sensed that they were now at home in the world and not merely called out 'from the world', what better way to celebrate it than to focus on the locality of the Incarnation, that event which more than any other might legitimize such an affirmation of this world?

A Christian Palestine, or at least a Christian Jerusalem, thus fitted the mood of the moment perfectly. In religious terms Palestine had temporarily been left as a vacuum, its potential untapped. Together the new Christian emperor and the recently victorious Christian Church could fill that vacuum and use the land as a powerful symbol of the new era and its distinctively Christian identity. Once again the religious potential of Palestine would be tapped for a useful purpose. Or was it, one might ask, more truly an 'exploitation' which would only cause the Palestinian population more heartache in the future?

So much was sudden and new in the years after 325. In a sense Christian identity was in need of redefinition, now that the persecuted Church had come to power. In these circumstances the land of Palestine could serve several useful purposes. It could be used as a place to rediscover authentic Christian identity; yet it could also be used to express the new Christian identity of the victorious Church. The unity of Palestine might then ensure that this new identity was continuous with, and not contradictory to, that original identity.

Such at least might be the theory. However, there have been Christian historians ever since who have felt that in reality the new identity of the fourth-century Church may have drowned out the cries of the original; that the original was swamped by the new; that, for example, the 'holy sites' developed at that time bear little relation to that which they seek to commemorate. Yet in any age, how is that original and authentic Christian identity embodied in contemporary practice? It is too easy to pull down, never so easy to build.

Palestine thus changed considerably and dramatically in a very short space of time. It was no longer a backwater, but a historic and inspirational source; no longer marginal but central, the object of endless attention. That attention came from every quarter, most notably from the emperor and his family. Constantine himself, though frustrated in his own keen wishes to visit the land of Christ before his death,[45] sanctioned the destruction of the temple of Venus and the building of a vast imperial basilica to mark the site of Christ's passion.[46] Then in 326/7 his mother, Helena, was despatched on her celebrated pilgrimage, with the result that work was begun on at least two more imperial churches, at Bethlehem and on the Mount of Olives.[47] Moreover, a further Constantinian church was built at Mamre, the site of Abraham's encounter with the three 'angels', seemingly the result of a visit made to Palestine by Constantine's mother-in-law, Eutropia.[48]

Groves, caves and pagan shrines thus gave way to magnificent basilicas. Within a matter of years the new euphoric climate must have brought countless visitors to the land, including one in 333 all the way from Bordeaux, whose 'travelogue' remains a fascinating window into the early years of the emerging 'Holy Land'. Any traditional identifications of Gospel sites, whether true or false, were evidently now in high demand. One can only surmise that the number of guides, who were required to point out Gospel sites to pilgrims, must have risen dramatically with little time for them to be centrally trained!

The pilgrim's appetite, once awakened, was seemingly insatiable. Liturgical celebrations in Jerusalem became more and more complex (not to say exhausting), while holy sites proliferated. Within two generations, by the time the nun Egeria came from Spain and Jerome's friend Paula made her great tour of the 'holy places', the list of sites was endless. By that period the sites of other major episodes in the Gospel story had been securely identified (the Ascension on the Mount of Olives, the Transfiguration on Mt. Tabor, Pentecost on Mt. Sion, the feeding of the five thousand at Tabgha); so too had some more minor places in the Gospels (ranging from Cana in Galilee to the sycamore tree of Zacchaeus in Jericho), together with several Old Testament

[45] As can be learnt from Eus., *V. Const.*, 2.72.2; 4.62.2.

[46] Ibid., 3.25 ff. This Eusebian description of events in Palestine after 325 can be accepted as a generally reliable account (though with one major exception: see below 4.5). For a brief reconstruction of these events, see below 8.5.

[47] Ibid., 3.41–5.

[48] Ibid., 3.53.

sites. In many of these places churches had been built by the end of the century.[49]

Not all visitors, however, returned home. Many decided to stay. The Mount of Olives in particular became a favourite spot for monastic settlements,[50] while Jerome established his famous rival centre at Bethlehem. Gradually the nearby Judaean wilderness also began to exert its appeal to the monastic spirit and within a century numerous *lavra* had been established. The Holy Spirit could be thought to have caused the desert to blossom and brought a renewal to the city, not seen since Pentecost.[51]

In this way Jerusalem and Palestine might begin to be truly 'Christian', not just in name. Yet it was far from enough. Galilee remained solidly Jewish; Count Joseph made his celebrated request of Constantine that he might be allowed to build Christian churches in the area,[52] but such attempts at establishing a Christian presence in the region frequented by Christ in his ministry seem to have met with little real success. Meanwhile the rest of the province was still largely pagan. One town, which according to Eusebius had previously been 'given to superstition', 'embraced the saving religion' soon after 325 and as a result was elevated by the emperor to the status of a city and renamed 'Constantia'. Yet this was very much the exception.[53]

Jerusalem itself will have continued to have a strong pagan element.[54] Christians might optimistically claim that 'this Jerusalem worships [Christ]',[55] saturating the streets with elaborate liturgical celebrations for the influx of Christian visitors, but there is nothing to suggest that the resident population was more Christian than elsewhere. In the years just before 325 Eusebius had spoken quite frequently (when chiding the Jews) of Jerusalem being 'inhabited by idolaters'.[56] Yet the situation seems to have changed little after

[49] On the development of pilgrimage during the fourth century, as recorded in the writings of the Bordeaux Pilgrim, Egeria, and Jerome, see Wilkinson (1978) and (1981); also Hunt (1982) and Kelly (1975), 176–24.

[50] See Hunt (1982), 167 ff.

[51] See Chitty (1966) and the forthcoming work by Y. Hirschfeld.

[52] Recounted in Epiph., *Haer.*, 30.11 (PG, xli, 426).

[53] *V. Const.*, 4.38; this was probably the small town of Maïuma, not Gaza (as suggested in NPNF, i, 550).

[54] In keeping with this the provincial administration continued to refer to the city as 'Aelia' for quite some considerable time: see Hunt (1982), 149.

[55] As does Cyril in *Catech.*, 13.7.

[56] *Dem. Ev.*, 7.1.79, 91 (*FPG*, ii, 63, 65); 8.3.10–12 (ii, 141); cf. also Just., *DT*, 16, and Origen, *Comm. in lib. Jes.*, 17.1, 401.

325. For later in the century both Jerome and Gregory of Nyssa could depict it as the 'sin city' of their day, in no way different from any other city in the world. It was, they claimed, a 'crowded city with the whole variety of people you normally find in such centres—prostitutes, actors, and clowns'.[57] It was full of 'evil, adultery, stealing and idolatry'; indeed in no other city were people 'so ready to kill each other'.[58] All this was, of course, in stark contrast to the growing Christian belief in Jerusalem as the 'holy city', both for what it had been and for what it now was. The myth thus needed to be maintained in the face of unobliging reality. A 'holy city' was one thing, a true renewal of Christian commitment within the city quite another.

Then there were the problems that resulted from the way in which Jerusalem and Palestine acted as a focus for the wider Christian Church. Not all was peaceful and harmonious. Theological debate in the fourth century was normally a heated affair and Palestine would not be able to remain coolly detached. Its focal and symbolic importance brought it into the centre of these debates. Palestine's bishops, especially the bishop of Jerusalem, naturally wished to become involved in matters of universal Christian significance, whilst Palestine itself might act (as it does today) as a useful sanctuary for all sorts of Christians with questionable ideas who hoped that this historic land would somehow authenticate their views. Thus Palestine found itself, for example, inexorably involved with the Arian controversy from the outset, playing host to a most volcanic council at Tyre in 335, and seeing its leading bishops (of Caesarea and Jerusalem) invariably at odds on the issue. Then, at the end of the century, Cyril's successor, John, by his very position as bishop of Jerusalem would find himself needing to pronounce on the theological issues of his day (such as the past orthodoxy of Origen or the present orthodoxy of a visitor like Pelagius) only to meet with vehement opposition from Jerome in Bethlehem.[59] In some of these episodes one senses that the bishops of Jerusalem may have been deliberately wishing to make vocal and important contributions to the contemporary debates in order to increase the status of their bishopric. That was undoubtedly the case in the middle of the next century when Bishop Juvenal

[57] Jerome, *Ep.* 58.4.
[58] Greg. Nys., *Ep.* 2 (PG, xlvi, 1012d).
[59] Jerome, *Ep.* 137; see Hunt (1982), 210.

succeeded in securing Jerusalem's position as the fifth patriarchate in the Church, but only through a doctrinal volte-face which was little to his credit.[60] Nevertheless, if Jerusalem and Palestine were to take a central position in the life of the Church, it was inevitable that they should become deeply embroiled in all the controversies which beset the Church in that period.

Imperial and ecclesiastical attention thus brought Palestine many changes, but also many problems. It also gave Jerusalem an indeterminate but real power. This power might be wielded politically, through its bishops gaining increased episcopal prestige, or more personally, by encouraging Christian visitors to take home relics or other momentos and keen memories of the Jerusalem Church's liturgical hospitality. In these and other ways Jerusalem might prove itself worthy of its central and focal function, gaining a power which, as with all power, would bring its attendant problems.

Meanwhile Eusebius' native Caesarea was progressively eclipsed.[61] It was, needless to say, a great irony that the one man who in the long term stood to lose most from the elevation of Palestine within the Christian world was its metropolitan bishop, the learned Eusebius. Yet this was effectively the case. For Christian interest in Palestine naturally led to an increased interest in Jerusalem, not in Caesarea; as a result, the role of the Caesarean bishop as metropolitan was inevitably threatened by the rising prestige of the Church in Jerusalem and its bishop. In these circumstances, with his own ecclesiastical position under threat, it would not be surprising if Eusebius' attitude towards the new developments in Palestine was somewhat ambivalent. For the great changes which affected Palestine after 325, for good and for ill, affected Eusebius personally; potentially his own position as metropolitan bishop was in jeopardy.

Palestine therefore experienced a momentous change during the

---

[60] See Turner (1900), 551–3 and Honigmann (1950). Yet it marks the end of a remarkable chapter in the Church's history, as the forgotten town of Aelia re-emerged as the 'holy city' of Jerusalem, a major patriarchate within Christendom.

[61] This tension between the sees of Caesarea and Jerusalem will be a major theme in our overall presentation. Its existence was noted by Honigmann (1950), 215, Chadwick (1960), 174, fn. 10 and Heyer (1984), 30–34; yet it has been brought to the fore chiefly through the articles of Rubin (1982a and 1984), which begin an unfinished series on the subject of this episcopal tension throughout the fourth century.

fourth century. At its beginning Christians were being severely persecuted in Caesarea by a pagan official who seemingly had never even heard of a city called Jerusalem.[62] Yet by its end Egeria might have been enthusing for many years in her native Spain about the great liturgical celebrations of Jerusalem; the annual calendar of the whole Church would have been affected in different ways by the historical emphasis of the Church in Jerusalem, [63] and fragments of the 'wood of the cross' would have been spread throughout the world for many years.[64] Meanwhile Jerome was ensconced in one of the many Palestinian monasteries, publishing the great benefits to the believer of a visit to the Holy Land,[65] proclaiming that Jerusalem contained a 'host of marvels'[66] and was indeed a 'holy city'.[67] The effect on Palestine of Christianity's triumphant arrival was thus spectacular. Not much less significant, it would seem, was the effect of Palestine on the worldwide Church.

It was then an era of great change, both within Palestine and within the empire as a whole. Fortunately the Church would be blessed with many great theologians who would be able to deliberate upon the deep issues of the day. Among these theologians it was Eusebius of Caesarea and Cyril of Jerusalem who addressed themselves especially to the Palestinian issue in its earliest stages.

Eusebius was born around 260, Cyril around 320. They were thus a full two generations apart; when Constantine came to power in the East in 324/5, Eusebius was approximately sixty-five while Cyril was no more than five years old. Nevertheless, since Cyril began his public career at such a young age and Eusebius was active into his eighties, their most important pronouncements on our theme were separated by little more than decade. These two men would, more than any others, determine the nature of Christian Palestine and thereby affect in many ways the subsequent life of the whole Church.

---

[62] Firmilianus, governor of Caesarea, in the year 309, as recounted in *Mart. Pal.*, 11.9; discussed below in ch. 11 at fn. 6.

[63] According to Dix's famous theory (1945), it was the development of liturgical celebrations at the very Gospel sites that fostered a new historical perspective on the liturgy, replacing its former eschatological focus.

[64] See below 4.5 and 10.3(*d*).

[65] See, for example, his preface to *Chronicles* (PL, xxix, 401a) and *Ep.* 46.9.

[66] *Apol.*, 3.22.

[67] *Ep.* 46.7.

Eusebius spent the last fourteen years of his life assessing the phenomenon of a Christian empire and propounding his more Arian theology, but he also assessed and influenced the new developments within Palestine. Then, a decade after Eusebius' death, the young Cyril delivered his *Catechetical Lectures*, teaching the annual candidates for baptism in Jerusalem not just about their faith, but also about the unique privilege they alone enjoyed of residing in Jerusalem. If he was not already bishop of Jerusalem his elevation was swift. It was a position he held for over thirty-five years until his death in 386. During that time the liturgical celebration in Jerusalem rose to the heights attested by Egeria, an achievement which almost certainly reflects the leadership and organizational genius of bishop Cyril.

It is therefore our task to examine the statements of these two bishops which relate to the issues of Palestine, and especially to note the many differences between them previously unnoticed. With the hindrance of hindsight it has been easy for observers of fourth-century Palestine to presume that what Cyril said Eusebius would also have said; to believe that Christian Jerusalem and Christian 'holy places' emerged fully-fledged from Eusebius' mind in the year 325; and to assume that the development of these phenomena in subsequent years was but an outworking of ideas latent from the beginning, not an evolution and a progression from something which was originally different.

The evidence, however, suggests otherwise. Eusebius' ideas were not identical with Cyril's; his original plans were altered by Cyril, his intentions on some occasions deliberately flouted. Eusebius had objectives of his own and a distinctive theology of the role of 'holy places' and of the physical Jerusalem which until now has not been sufficiently noted, nor indeed heeded.

3. EUSEBIUS' LIFE

Eusebius' life was a long one, which only became more eventful as the years went by.[68] Had he died at the age of sixty, a few

[68] For detailed biographies of Eusebius (with a discussion of his writings), see Lightfoot (1880), Wallace-Hadrill (1960), and Barnes (1981). For a chronological listing of all his theological works, see the Appendix, where all questions concerning the dating of his works are discussed together. It will be noted that in almost every instance it is the chronology of Barnes which has been followed.

years after his consecration as metropolitan bishop of Caesarea in 313, he would have been remembered as a great scholar who had seldom left his native Caesarea.[69] For Caesarea held Pamphilus' famous library, and it was Eusebius' chosen life-work to bring to the Church's attention the intellectual riches which were contained there and to collate its information, information which could not similarly be collated anywhere else in the Christian world.

In that library, for example, he had the necessary sources for his first major work, the *Chronicle*, which harmonized the events and dates of all the various ancient histories with those revealed in the Bible. In this important work secular history was effectively gridded onto the matrix of biblical history and chronology; 'biblical, Roman and Christian realities' were neatly 'brought together'.[70] Moreover, the library had accumulated the necessary sources for his history of Christianity since the days of the New Testament. Since no one before him had apparently attempted such a major undertaking, Eusebius' *Ecclesiastical History* remains to this day a primary source for our understanding of the history of the early Church. It also provided all he would need for his apologetic works, defending Christianity against both pagans and Jews. In his *Preparation for the Gospel* he quoted and refuted numerous pagan philosophers, while in the *Proof of the Gospel* he explained and defended the difference between Judaism and Christianity, especially showing how Christ's coming was the true fulfilment of Old Testament prophecies.

However, these apologetic works, produced in his fifties (c.312–22) marked a quite distinct second phase in Eusebius' career and interests, which no doubt had been prompted in part by the painful experience of the extended years of persecution in Caesarea from 303 to 311.[71] Later there would be yet another new phase in his career as he entered the troubled waters of philosophical theology. Yet it has been observed that 'Eusebius was not by nature a

[69] The only place outside Palestine which Eusebius is known to have visited before the council of Nicaea in 325 is Egypt, which he visited during the painful years of the persecution (perhaps even being imprisoned there): see *Hist. Eccl.*, 8.9; cf. Epiph., *Haer.*, 68.8.

[70] Groh (1983), 29.

[71] Eusebius wrote two different accounts of these local persecutions: the long recension of the *Martyrs of Palestine* probably appeared in 311, while the shorter version was written to be incorporated in his second, updated version of the *Ecclesiastical History* around 313: see Barnes (1981), 278.

philosopher or theologian' and indeed that he only 'turned to apologetics only under the pressure of circumstances'.[72] For it was scripture and history which together were his first love.

This primary concern is seen in the *Chronicle* and the *Ecclesiastical History*, his first two major works, both of which were published, it seems, by the time he was forty. It is seen also in two much smaller works which he also produced in that early period. The *Prophetic Eclogues* formed a brief collection of Old Testament texts relating to Christ. The *Onomasticon*, on the other hand, was a biblical gazetteer, gridding the places mentioned in scripture onto the contemporary map of Palestine.[73]

Naturally the latter is an invaluable source to this day not just for biblical and archaeological students but also for those examining Eusebius' whole attitude towards pilgrimage and 'holy places'.[74] Yet again our hindsight may tempt us to distort his original intention. For the *Onomasticon*, as recent studies have shown, was really 'a plank in Eusebius' early historical and apologetical platform and not a pioneering work in Christian pilgrimage'.[75] Nevertheless it clearly showed his keen awareness of living in the very land of the Bible and gave him a natural authority on topographical matters which would serve him in good stead for the rest of his life.

Even at this point in our enquiry, it will be valuable to highlight an interesting tension which can be observed in these earlier works of Eusebius, and which for our purposes would prove its significance towards the end of his life. On the one hand, in the basic outline and thrust of his theology, Eusebius stood firmly within the great 'spiritualizing' tradition which Origen had brought to Caesarea from Alexandria.[76] The focus of this school of thought, in which Eusebius grew up and to which he was so 'profoundly indebted',[77]

[72] Ibid., 94, 104.

[73] For its early date, see the Appendix; on its originality, see Barnes (1981), 106-9. For a thorough and detailed analysis, see Thomsen (1903). The *Onomasticon* was evidently accompanied by three other (non-extant) works concerning Jerusalem and the twelve tribes (see *Onom.*, 2.7-9); one of these may have been a map (as suggested by Avi-Yonah (1954), 30).

[74] Hence it will be discussed more fully below in 2.2.

[75] Groh (1983), 29.

[76] On Origen's theology, see most recently Crouzel (1985) and Trigg (1983); on Origen's influence more generally in Caesarea, see Barnes (1981), 81 ff. and De Lange (1976).

[77] Barnes, 100. Eusebius' personal admiration for Origen (who had sadly died before Eusebius was born) is seen throughout *Hist. Eccl.*, 6, and by his assistance

was almost exclusively upon the invisible *Logos* who called man away from mere physical concerns to a spiritual, and seemingly very cerebral, worship. Origen had made it quite clear, for example, that the purpose of the Incarnation was not to draw attention to the physical realm, but had been a temporary phase designed to reveal the exalted and eternal *Logos*. To concentrate one's devotion on the Incarnate Christ was the mark of a 'simpler' Christian; instead, the true 'gnostic, the man of real spiritual advancement and insight, strains upward to the *Logos*'.[78]

On the other hand, Eusebius' own personal interest lay in a rather different area, in the realm of history, the study of the affairs of men in this world. As a result, while the theological tradition which he inherited would have encouraged him to focus on the spiritual, his own personal abilities and aptitude led him to focus on the historical. As has been recently observed, Eusebius could thus indeed be an 'admirer of Origen, sharing his *Logos* theology, but not his disdain for history';[79] Eusebius thus began to immerse himself in 'biblical ways of historical thinking to a degree which Origen would have found alien and unspiritual'.[80]

These twin commitments were by no means contradictory or irreconcilable; yet they were at the least a cause for potential tension. With regard to 'holy places', for example, they would mean that his interest in them was almost totally that of a historian; the focus of his spirituality would not be on them (or through them) but only on the eternal *Logos*. Then again, with regard to the question of Jerusalem, they would similarly cause him to be fascinated by the tumultuous history of this nearby city, even down to the present day, but it would have no spiritual significance for him; his spiritual attention would be focused exclusively on the heavenly Jerusalem.

Inheriting this strong spiritualizing tradition from Origen, Eusebius thus had the awkward task of endorsing in the homeland

to Pamphilus in the composition of a (now non-extant) *Apology* on Origen's behalf (see *Hist. Eccl.*, 6.23.4).

[78] Origen, *Comm. in Jo.* [1.1], 2.3, 56.29–57.7, *idem*, 1.7, 13.3–10; see Kelly (1977), 157.

[79] Frend (1984), 477.

[80] Barnes (1981), 94–105, esp. 97 (an extended analysis of the way in which Eusebius' 'historical interests' affected his theological relationship with Origen). See also Levine (1975a) who concludes that 'Eusebius was totally different . . . in scholarly emphasis'.

of Christ a spirituality that had developed in Alexandria without reference to Palestine. It would not therefore be surprising if throughout his life Eusebius would find himself nearer in his heart to the theology of Alexandria than to the sacred geography of Jerusalem.

However, Eusebius did not die at the age of sixty; he lived on almost to his eightieth year. The last twenty years of his life witnessed some of the greatest changes and reversals ever to be experienced within the Church in such a short space of time. The great scholar from the library in Caesarea would be thrust, by circumstances and no doubt by his own desire, onto the centre of the world stage, first as metropolitan bishop of Palestine, secondly as theological proponent of the Arian cause, and thirdly as political evaluator of Constantine. Three great areas of responsibility suddenly became his.

Eusebius may well indeed have been prepared for the eventual triumph of the Church and of its theology.[81] Yet he was certainly not prepared for all the political ramifications of that triumph. Who could be? The new tasks and responsibilities thrust on the Church after its victory through Constantine, however much desired or expected, must have taken all Church leaders a little by surprise; opposition spokesmen seldom realize the burden of governmental responsibility until it becomes theirs. All these three areas of responsibility thus required a major amount of rethinking, a task which Eusebius did not try to avoid. Indeed the elderly scholar, excited by the uncharted possibilities, and aware of the vital and deep issues which were at stake, suddenly found a quite remarkable new lease of life.

Eusebius' activity and literary output during these last years of his life are quite phenomenal. After finding himself on the losing side in the Arian debate at Nicaea,[82] he became one of the principal leaders of the disaffected party, seeking to reassert the cause of Arius, even if in a slightly modified form. The extreme wing of the Nicene camp became the object of his unceasing opposition. Marcellus of Ancyra, whose views seemed to Eusebius to come close to Sabellianism,[83] was rebutted both on paper (in the *Ecclesiastical Theology* and his work *Against Marcellus*) and in

---

[81] This is one of the central conclusions of Barnes (1981).
[82] On this, see further below 4.1.
[83] *Theol. Eccl.*, 1.1 ff.; 1.20.6 ff.

effective action: Marcellus was successfully deposed from his see.[84] The same fate had earlier befallen Eustathius of Antioch, again largely as a result of Eusebius' untiring efforts.[85]

Similarly, Athanasius, the great champion of 'orthodoxy', who was deposed from his see no less than five times, found Eusebius to be one of his most vociferous opponents. For it was Eusebius who, as the presiding bishop over the council at Tyre in September 335, ensured Athanasius' first exile from his see. It was also Eusebius who then, after attending the dedication of the Holy Sepulchre in Jerusalem, hastened with five other bishops to Constantinople in order to confirm the emperor's approval of this excommunication. Athanasius had fled from the council and it was rightly surmised that he must have made his way to Constantine. Eusebius arrived on 6 November to discover that Athanasius had succeeded in persuading the emperor to overturn the rulings of the council. Within twenty-four hours, however, Athanasius was on his way to Trier, exiled by the emperor. Once again the energy and determination of Eusebius must largely have been responsible. Yet at the time of this exhausting episode Eusebius was nearly eighty, Athanasius no more than thirty-five![86]

That journey to Constantinople had another fortunate result. Eusebius was thus able to deliver an oration to Constantine (*On Christ's Sepulchre*) on the significance of the recently dedicated church of the Holy Sepulchre.[87] The emperor stood throughout Eusebius' delivery;[88] indeed the oration was so successful that Eusebius was asked to prepare a panegyric (*In Praise of Constantine*) to be delivered the following July in Constantinople as

[84] His theology was denounced by the bishops assembled at Tyre under Eusebius in 335, though his deposition was not ratified until the emperor's council in Constantinople in 336; see Barnes (1981), 241.

[85] Eustathius was deposed from his see after a council held in Antioch in 327. Again it was Eusebius who presided; see Barnes, 227 f.

[86] Barnes (1981), 236–40; cf. Drake (1986).

[87] Following the arguments of Drake (1976), supported by, e.g., Cameron (1983), 75 ff., this has come down to us as chapters 11–18 of the work formerly known to us as *de laudibus Constantini* (see Appendix). Hereafter these chapters will be referred to as *On Christ's Sepulchre* [*Sep. Chr.*]. It must be admitted that it remains unclear whether the summons to deliver this speech before the emperor concerning the Holy Sepulchre preceded Eusebius' travelling to Constantinople (as Stevenson (1928), 125) or was made only after his arrival on this other business (as Drake (1986), 5, and Barnes (1981), 239 f.). Eusebius' wording in *V. Const.*, 4.33 seems to favour the latter position.

[88] *V. Const.*, 4.33.

part of the celebrations for the thirtieth anniversary of Constantine's rule.[89] It may well be that it was also at this time that Eusebius was able to gain Constantine's permission to write his biography. For Eusebius certainly seems to have used his stay in Constantinople to do some of the necessary research for this work before returning to Caesarea, where he completed the *Life of Constantine* some time after the emperor's death in 337 and before his own in 339.[90]

The political involvement of Eusebius with Constantine in the last decade of his life has naturally been the subject of endless scholarly study. So too, though to a lesser extent, the very active part played by Eusebius in the Arian controversy.[91] These cannot be our concerns here since it is the third issue, that relating to Palestine, which has been insufficiently studied and requires our detailed analysis. Yet it can be sensed how these three issues may well have interrelated with one another, as indeed would only be natural for three major issues simultaneously on the agenda of a single person.

For example, it may well be that it was the shock of finding himself in danger of being excommunicated for his Arian sympathies at Nicaea which then prompted all this activity; and that his involvement in the Palestinian issue and with Constantine was part of his desire to reinstate himself and to re-establish his doubted credentials.

More importantly, it may well be that in each of these three different areas Eusebius' methods were quite similar. For in all of them Eusebius had ideas and convictions which were not totally shared by the emperor. Constantine may understandably have been confused by the intricacies of the Arian controversy, desiring peace at whatever theological cost, but he must surely have been aware that Eusebius was one of those who had only agreed to his

---

[89] Ibid., 4.46. It is widely agreed that this speech survives in the first ten chapters of the *de laudibus Constantini* (again see Appendix); these chapters will be referred to as *In Praise of Constantine* [*L. Const.*].

[90] Drake (1988) suggests quite plausibly that Eusebius may have stayed in Constantinople from November 335 to July 336, rather than returning to Caesarea. The 'round trip' would have taken around three months in total, and Eusebius was not young! However, Eusebius' wording in *V. Const.*, 4.33, 46, may suggest that he *did* travel to Constantinople twice (as presumed by Barnes (1981, 253). Even if this were so, however, Eusebius would still presumably have had sufficient time to do some necessary research.

[91] For extensive bibliography on both these issues see Barnes (1981) and Drake (1976); cf. also Winkelmann (1962).

Nicene proposals with great difficulty. Plainly, Eusebius had to be very subtle as he sought to influence the emperor's way of thinking, for there had been, not long before, a marked discrepancy between them.

So too on the political issue. Eusebius has often been portrayed as a naive supporter of all that Constantine stood for, a puppet pulled by strings from the imperial hand. Recently, however, it has been strongly argued that this was far from being the case. Eusebius was not so close to the emperor as he himself would have wished us to believe;[92] nor did he always agree with Constantine's imperial and ecclesiastical policy. Rather he used those few opportunities that he did have of speaking in the presence of the emperor in order to colour Constantine's thought with his own.[93] Eusebius was thus using such proximity to Constantine, not simply to have greater influence over others, but to have a greater influence over Constantine himself. He was glad of a Christian emperor, but he was not totally enamoured of all that he did. The relation between Constantine and Eusebius is a complex one and it may never be clear which of the two finally influenced the other more; but it now seems clear that Eusebius at least tried.

Such a picture, which is inherently so much more probable, bears an important relation to our discussion of the Palestinian question. For here too it must now be conceded that there could perhaps have been a discrepancy between the views of Constantine and Eusebius. Perhaps after all Eusebius did not really endorse every aspect of Constantine's so-called 'Holy Land plan';[94] perhaps the emperor's theological understanding of the Incarnation was always slightly at odds with his own; so too the emperor's rather materialistic notions concerning 'holy places' and his evident fascination with relics.[95] If so, the emperor's keen interest in Palestine might not have been something to which Eusebius would wish to give his unqualified approval.

No doubt Eusebius was delighted with Constantine's interest in the province which was under his own episcopal jurisdiction, and

[92] See Barnes (1981), 265 ff. (and fn. 66).
[93] This discrepancy between Eusebius' own thinking and that of Constantine has been brought to light especially in Drake (1976), who shows how skilful and subtle Eusebius was in achieving his purposes.
[94] The phrase coined by Telfer (1955b).
[95] See further below in 4.3(b).

sought to be as involved as possible in the exciting new developments. Yet that did not mean necessarily that every imperial whim was to be heeded or praised without demur. In particular, Eusebius may have had some concern over Constantine's concept of a Christian Jerusalem acting as a spiritual focus for the new empire,[96] a concept which introduced something quite novel into the Christian system and also had the unfortunate local consequence of elevating the status of the see of Jerusalem to his own personal loss. Constantine's thinking would thus need chanelling.

The life story of Eusebius comes to an end two years after the death of Constantine. He died in 339, an old man whose last fifteen years had been incredibly active, perhaps the most productive span of his long and fruitful life. For in those last years he had also completed three other major works. Two were exegetical, the large commentaries on Isaiah and the Psalms, the third was a mixture of theology and apologetics, the *Theophany*. The last, which appeared soon after Nicaea, popularized some of the longer arguments in the *Proof of the Gospel* and itself became the basis for the speech in which Eusebius sought to explain to Constantine the theological significance of the Holy Sepulchre.

All three of these works, written in the light of an increasingly Christian Palestine, contain interesting testimony, hitherto largely unnoticed, of Eusebius' attitude to Jerusalem and the places of Christ. They reveal how the essential convictions of the Caesarean scholar had not substantially changed: Jerusalem was a fascinating place, but it no longer had any special theological significance; biblical locations had an importance because of their historical associations but they were to be understood within a context which preserved the essentially spiritual nature of Christianity. That remained Eusebius' top priority.

His attitudes, it must be admitted, had been formed in the very different climate of the late third century. In the intervening years so much had changed in such a short space of time, and the questions being asked were in so many ways so different, that it would not be surprising if on occasion Eusebius found it difficult to adapt to the very new circumstances of the Constantinian era. If his theology had taken shape in the third century, it would not so easily accommodate the new perspectives of the fourth. As a

---

[96] As suggested by Telfer (1955b).

result it may be reckoned by some that Eusebius' attitudes to Palestine, as revealed in the following pages, were old-fashioned or insufficient, unable to become an effective policy for Christian attitudes to 'holy places' and Jerusalem, either in the fourth century or today. Of this, however, we can be sure: Eusebius was beginning to see what the issues were and in his first responses to them he saw no good reason to modify his position substantially. Eusebius wrestled with the new challenges, but retained his essential and original convictions.

4. CYRIL'S LIFE

Within a decade of Eusebius' death, Cyril became bishop of Jerusalem. Cyril too was destined for a colourful career and from the very beginning of his long episcopate he would be taking the Christian understanding of Jerusalem and 'holy places' several stages beyond anything which Eusebius had ever intended. Again, paradoxically, despite the widespread acknowledgement of Cyril's part in the development of pilgrimage, Cyril's attitude to Jerusalem and the 'holy places' seems to have been somewhat overlooked. Others have concentrated on the questions of Cyril's orthodoxy,[97] or his involvement in the wider concerns of the Church and empire;[98] our task will be to concentrate on these more local issues.

Cyril was a child of the new age, who had never known an empire without a Christian on the throne; he had a pastoral warmth and liturgical concern which our available sources suggest was lacking in Eusebius. Cyril had a lively intelligence, but his was not an especially scholarly mind, not especially learned in history, apologetics or philosophy; his theology was of a more practical nature. Those were days, however, when a philosophical theology was a chief requirement of any aspiring bishop and Cyril inevitably found himself buffeted by the great and heated arguments of the day. Indeed, because of his opposition to the

[97] See, e.g., Lebon (1924), Stephenson (1955), Wolfson (1957), Quasten, iii (1960), 369–77, and *WCJ*, i, 34–60.
[98] Telfer (1955a), 19–30.

more Arian theology prevalent in his day, he was exiled from Jerusalem twice, for a total of nearly twenty years.[99]

It is unclear exactly when or where he was born.[100] The fact that he was appointed to the see of Jerusalem by Eusebius' successor in Caesarea, Acacius, might at first sight indicate that he was a native of Caesarea.[101] However, for at least two reasons, this would be slightly paradoxical.

First, the reason for his appointment by Acacius was his supposed doctrinal affinity to Acacius' own Arian views. In this way the Nicene stance of Jerusalem, first espoused by Macarius and then by Maximus, could be terminated and Maximus' attempt to decide his own Nicene successor by nominating Heraclius was brought to nought. Yet, as is shown by his consistent terminology in the *Catechetical Lectures* and by his own theological opposition to Acacius within a matter of years, Cyril was clearly orthodox and 'conservative' in his theology. Jerome later cast doubt on Cyril's motives, painting him as a theological turncoat who had shifted his stance to suit his own ends but who had deep down remained an Arian throughout his life,[102] but it is more likely and more charitable to suppose, as his *Lectures* indicate, that Cyril always held to a theology which was orthodox in its content and meaning but that (and here he *did* differ from the two previous Nicene bishops of Jerusalem) he was wary of using the Nicene term *homoousios* which was not found in the ancient credal formularies of the East.[103] Evidently therefore Cyril did not share Acacius' theology at all. It seems instead that Acacius did not know the true theological colours of his nominee as well as he should have done. As a result, one wonders if it was right to presume that Cyril really was a native of Acacius' Caesarea.

Secondly, Cyril's supposed Caesarean origin seems questionable for a quite different reason. Once he was installed in Jerusalem,

---

[99]   From 355 (banished by Acacius) till the reign of Julian (363) and from 367 (under Valens) till 378 (under Gratian). On this intriguing later history, see, e.g., Telfer (1955a), 20–30, *WCJ*, i, 21–34.

[100]   On the little known of Cyril's early years, see Telfer (1955a), 19 f.

[101]   See, e.g., Quasten, iii (1960), 309.

[102]   As Jerome suggested in his translation of Eusebius' *Chronicle*, written *c*.380 (PL, xxvii, 501 f.).

[103]   This case is well argued in *WCJ*, i, 22 and Telfer (1955a), 24. In both assessments it is argued that Cyril 'did not sacrifice doctrinal loyalties to obtain the bishopric'.

Cyril quickly accepted, endorsed, and indeed promoted all the notions then current in the Jerusalem Church to the effect that Jerusalem deserved a primacy over Caesarea in the ecclesiastical realm. Again this is apparent from his whole attitude towards Jerusalem as expressed in his *Lectures*. Yet it is also seen quite clearly in his own immediate antagonism towards his recent sponsor, Acacius of Caesarea. For, exploiting the ecclesiastical tension between Jerusalem and Caesarea which had existed in Eusebius' day, Cyril declared polemically that his own see of Jerusalem was an 'apostolic see' which should therefore not have to submit to the metropolitan see of Caesarea.[104] Cyril's political opportunism is not necessarily defensible, but it would be easier to understand him being so forthright in Jerusalem's defence if he was a native of Jerusalem, not Caesarea, especially if his appointment by Acacius, as just suggested, is no firm guarantee of his birth in Caesarea.[105] For the Jerusalem Church there could hardly have been a better choice. This was a young man destined himself to go far and capable of taking Jerusalem a long way too.

Apart from one surviving homily, *On the Paralytic*, and his famous *Letter to Constantius* (on the occasion of a luminous cross appearing in the Jerusalem sky during May 351), our knowledge of Cyril's thought comes from two chief sources, one direct, the other more indirect. His own *Catechetical Lectures*, delivered in either 348 or 350,[106] give us a direct insight into his thought and theology at an early stage in his career. The pilgrimage narrative of Egeria, however, which describes her visit to Jerusalem and the Holy Land in 384, provides us with an indirect source, though a very reliable one, which complements Cyril's own words; for Egeria effectively outlines for us the liturgical practice which Cyril had instigated in Jerusalem by the end of his life.[107]

---

[104] Soz., *Hist. Eccl.*, 4.25.2; Sozomen wrote in the next century and his terminology may be anachronistic but the intention of Cyril's claim was evidently to bid for a certain primacy over Caesarea (see also Theodt., *Hist. Eccl.*, 2.26).

[105] Moreover, if he was a stranger to Jerusalem, it is difficult to see why or how he could have delivered the *Catechetical Lectures* while still a presbyter, as is often supposed (see Appendix).

[106] In the following it has been simplest to assume throughout a date of 348. The precise date cannot be fixed and is of little consequence. For the arguments either way, as well as for a discussion of the probable inauthenticity of the *Mystagogic Lectures* often attributed to Cyril, see Appendix.

[107] This use of Egeria's narrative as a witness to the activity of bishop Cyril is in line with the picture (even if there overstated) developed by Dix (1945), 329

These two complementary sources can thus give us a more rounded picture of Cyril than perhaps any other bishop of his time, including the earlier Eusebius. For with this two-fold perspective we can see how theory was translated into action, how theological reasoning found its liturgical expression, and how ideas implicit at the start of his episcopate worked themselves out into practice by its end. They also give us a detailed picture of Christian Jerusalem and Christian 'holy places' in the middle of the fourth century.

Eusebius and Cyril thus lived in an interesting land at an important time. Their attitudes, however, towards the new developments in Church life which surrounded them will be seen to have been by no means identical. Two local questions especially confronted them, the question of Jerusalem the 'holy city' and of the 'holy places' of Christ. How did they respond to these two important contemporary issues?

and 349 ff. Cf. also Cross (1951), p. xxviii, and Telfer (1955a), 30 who sees Egeria's account as the 'most impressive monument to Cyril's genius'.

2

EUSEBIUS AND CYRIL
ON JERUSALEM
AND THE PLACES OF CHRIST

What then were the attitudes of Eusebius and Cyril to the local issues: the question of Jerusalem and of 'holy places'?[1] These seemingly domestic affairs would in their own way almost be as important for the future of the Church as the imperial activity and the great theological debates which were the major feature of the same century. The latter might affect the Church's systems of thought and its status in the world, but the former would touch a nerve more raw and more central, the Church's very life and faith.

During this chapter we will attempt to distinguish the two principal aspects of the Palestinian question: First, what was to be the Christian attitude towards the city of Jerusalem? Secondly, what was to be the Christian attitude towards the individual places associated with the life of Christ?

Although many of the most important sites mentioned in the Gospels are in or near Jerusalem, these two areas of study are notionally quite distinct. One concerns individual places whose significance is dependent solely on the Incarnation, the other concerns a city, an entity over and above such individual places, which had a theological status and significance before the coming of Christ. The most casual observer, even from outside the Church, might immediately sense how a Christian might come to different conclusions on these two questions; for was not the coming of Jesus, the event to which the individual places owe their sole

---

[1] In this chapter an overview is given of the issues to be discussed more fully in the remainder of the book. Our authors' attitudes towards Jerusalem (here only briefly summarized) are set out fully in chapters ten and eleven respectively; their attitudes to 'holy places' (outlined here in slightly more detail) will pervade most of the discussion of individual sites in chapters 5 to 9, but will also be dealt with in some detail in chapters 3 and 4.

significance, also the very moment at which the continuing significance of the city was denied? If, he might argue, the place of Christ's crucifixion outside the city wall was to be deemed a 'holy place' by later Christians, surely the same claim of holiness could not be made for the city that rejected Christ? In accord with the writer of the Epistle to the Hebrews (13.12 f.), Christians must presumably chose either to be part of the city or 'go forth to him' outside the city. They could not have both; they could not affirm both the city and the sepulchre. From such a perspective the holy places of Christ seem to be incompatible with a holy Jerusalem; one cannot have both holy city and holy sites.

The matter, of course, is by no means so simple—a straight affirmation of one and denial of the other. For those Christians who have affirmed the holiness of individual sites have normally proceeded to ascribe that holiness to the present city of Jerusalem which witnessed these great events of salvation. On the other hand, those Christians who have denied the holiness of Jerusalem have often been those who further deny the holiness of individual sites; Jesus and all that he did is important but not so the place where those events occurred. Affirmation has thus tended to lead to affirmation, denial to denial.

As a result the distinction between the two questions has often been ignored, with people assuming that a verdict on one entailed the same verdict on the other. In the following it will be seen that the two matters do naturally tend to interrelate, but also that the preservation of this distinction is important, not least because Eusebius himself seems to have noticed it and felt it to be crucial.

The conclusions of Cyril, eager as he was to promote the cause of Jerusalem, will come as no surprise. Jerusalem was no ordinary city. It was a holy city, clearly chosen by God to be the scene and even the instrument of his activity, both in times past and in the present day. It had a unique theological status for all time, which (he hoped) was to be reflected in an increased recognition of its ecclesiastical status. For it had an evident pre-eminence not only in the Holy Land, but in the world at large; not only in an individual pilgrim's life of faith, but also in the institutional life of the corporate Church. In no way therefore was the city's treatment of Jesus to be seen as the grounds for its judgement and for the end of its status in God's sight. God's judgement on that evil episode had fallen squarely on the Jews and their Temple, not upon the city itself which was still as precious to God as it had been in the days of the Old Testament. It was therefore not only a place with significant historical associations; it was a city that continued to enjoy a significant *divine* association. It had a significant past; but it also had a special God-given status in the present, perhaps also even a strategic potential for the future. In any case, there could be nothing wrong in Christians describing it as a 'holy city', whatever they might more precisely mean by that term.

Cyril's attitude towards the places of Christ was not surprisingly just as positive and clear-cut. These were not simply places that had enjoyed a temporary contact with Jesus, or which believers associated historically with the events of the New Testament; rather, they had gained an inherent quality of holiness through that divine association at the time of the Incarnation. Throughout his lectures Cyril described them as 'holy' places,[2] sometimes even as 'all-holy' ($\pi\alpha\nu\alpha\gamma\iota\delta$) or 'blessed' ($\mu\alpha\kappa\alpha\rho\iota\sigma$).[3] Thus again they possessed something more than a merely significant past. For those with faith they had a certain spiritual potency or even 'sacramental' significance, as places which God might use to convey a special sense of his presence.[4]

Jerusalem (and indeed the whole of Palestine) was therefore filled with numerous such 'holy places', each of which was more than a visual aid to the Gospel. They were inanimate but nevertheless real witnesses, which confirmed the truth of the Gospel.[5] As places which sometimes revealed Christ's power[6] or 'all but showed Christ to the eyes of the faithful',[7] they also had the power to 'shame', to 'reprove', and to 'confute' any who were tempted to disbelieve the message of Christ.[8]

However, these 'holy places' did not just confirm facts and inspire faith. They themselves were an appropriate medium for

[2] *Catech.*, 5.10, 10.19, 13.38-9.
[3] Ibid., 1.1, 13.22 [all-holy]; 4.10, 10.19 [blessed].
[4] For analyses of such thinking, which note this 'sacramental concentration' or 'imagination' in the fourth century, see, e.g., W. D. Davies (1974), 367 and Cardman (1979), 19.
[5] Hence Cyril's three extended lists of such physical witnesses in *Catech.*, 10.19, 13.38-9 and 14.22-3.
[6] For example, Caiaphas' ruined house and the 'rent rocks' (ibid., 13.38).
[7] As the Mount of Olives (ibid., 14.23).
[8] Ibid., 4.10, 12.32, 13.4, and 13.38.

faith, places where the divine had touched the human and the physical, places where through the physical means of touch, of sight and liturgical action human beings could now in return come close to the divine. As Thomas had once had the unique opportunity to touch the Risen Christ, so pilgrims now had a unique opportunity to 'see and touch' the physical places and objects that had once themselves been in contact with Christ. In this way Christians in Jerusalem could experience a privileged proximity to Christ that was not shared by others. 'Others merely hear', said Cyril to his catechumens, 'but we see and touch.'[9] Indeed 'it was for our sake that [Thomas] touched so carefully; for what you, who were not present, would have sought, he who was present did seek'.[10]

Sadly, as Cyril here admits, Christ himself was no longer physically present; but fortunately for Cyril's catechumens and for all pilgrims those places in which Christ had once been *did* survive. The boundaries of time, which separated the first century from the fourth, could here begin to collapse;[11] so too even the boundary between the human and the divine. Speaking of the descent of the Holy Spirit at Pentecost Cyril hinted that this might still be a cause of special blessing for Christians in Jerusalem: 'for we speak not of the blessings of others, but of those granted amongst us ($\pi\alpha\rho$' $\dot{\eta}\mu\hat{\iota}\nu$)'.[12] Thus because of the many 'holy places' in Jerusalem and because of God's gracious activity there in the past, those with faith might expect in Cyril's own day to receive the blessing of God's special presence. It was good to be a Christian in such a special locality. These were places where God had come near; these were places in which his special presence might still be found.

Cyril evidently knew how to promote the cause of pilgrimage and how to awaken the unspoken needs of pilgrims; but he also possessed the pastoral sensitivity to meet those needs, as well as the skill of novel biblical interpretation which might justify his awakening of those needs. Yet at the root of all his thinking there was a simple, but deep conviction: these Gospel sites were in a true sense 'holy'.

[9] *Catech.*, 13.22.
[10] Ibid., 13.29.
[11] Cf. Strange and Meyers (1981), 171: the pilgrim seeks 'to collapse the boundaries of time between now and then, a feat somehow facilitated in the places where the sacred deeds were done.'
[12] *Catech.*, 17.13.

What then of Eusebius? Would he have agreed with this developed understanding of the role of Jerusalem and 'holy places'? Customarily the answer has been 'yes'. Cyril and Eusebius have been 'tarred with the same brush', in such a way that Cyril's words have been taken as evidence of Eusebius' thought as well. Just as with Eusebius' relation to Constantine, so too his relation to Cyril: Eusebius is often presumed to have agreed with both in almost every detail, and to have been particularly enthusiastic about both Constantine and the Christian 'Holy Land'.

Yet the evidence suggests, as indeed one might have expected, that his views were independent from theirs and were also more cautious. If in that century of rapid change his opinions were soon overtaken by others, that should not deter us from attempting to hear them today. Perhaps today, when we lack the headlong enthusiasm of Cyril but have a sobre awareness of the modern Middle East, they will make more sense in their own right. Great changes, in our own day as in Eusebius', are seldom accompanied by unanimous voices of approval; voices of qualm, such as Eusebius', are a necessary sign of a commitment to the value of the past.

What, though, if Eusebius had been the bishop of Jerusalem in Cyril's day? Surely, some might argue, he would have said exactly what Cyril did? This might have been the case; but such suggestions do no help us to understand the authentic Eusebius. He was not the bishop of Jerusalem, did not live in the middle of the fourth century, and above all was not Cyril. Instead he was born a full two generations before Cyril, he lived most of his life before the Peace of the Church, in an age when pilgrimage was the luxury of the few, not the habit of the many, in the days when to assert the value of visiting holy sites would have entailed denying that privilege to almost all, and moreover, he was the metropolitan bishop of Caesarea.

Nor can it be argued that his views contained the latent ideas and the implicit potential that it was later Cyril's good fortune to make public and viable on Eusebius' behalf. Eusebius' ideas would never have developed into Cyril's. Cyril could no doubt on occasion use Eusebius' ideas in defence of his own, and he might claim that he was developing them to their logical conclusion; but it was not strictly so (as Cyril himself may have known all too well). Eusebius' theology had some essential ingredients deep within it which would never allow his perhaps mild approval of Jerusalem or holy sites to develop further into that wholesale promotion soon practised by Cyril. Eusebius' thinking went so far and no further—not because of limitation but essential conviction, not because of puritanical small-mindedness but commitment to the very centre of his theological system. If it was to be taken further, with or without Eusebius' blessing and approval, a new man with a fresh mind was needed. That man was Cyril. What then, in outline, were those Eusebian attitudes to Jerusalem and 'holy places' that were so different from Cyril's, and what were the theological reasons that explain those essential differences?

1. EUSEBIUS ON JERUSALEM

Eusebius' attitude to Jerusalem was quite clear. Whatever theological status Jerusalem had had in the Old Testament was now lost forever. God had surely in some way committed himself to that city as part of his revelation of himself under the old covenant; but that commitment had now been decisively withdrawn. Naturally, as a result of the events in both the Old and New Testaments, Jerusalem had a distinctive history and had played a unique role in the drama of salvation; it was therefore significant to all students of scripture for its past *historical* associations, but it now lacked *theological* significance.

To summarize it: man might have an interest in Jerusalem because of its past, but God, despite or even because of that past, no longer had any special interest in contemporary Jerusalem. It was no longer a 'holy city' and no longer special in God's sight.

The events of the New Testament, far from affirming the holiness of Jerusalem, only revealed its unholiness, its capacity to reject its Messiah. Moreover, the dramatic and decisive events of AD 70 confirmed that the city had received a divine judgement, a judgement which, even if especially focused on the Jews and their Temple, yet also included the city as a whole. In contrast to Judaism, therefore, there was no place in Christianity for a devotion to Jerusalem or a belief in its inherent holiness; Christians were not at liberty to affirm what God had negated. Nor should Christians suppose that Jerusalem would play a special part in God's future purposes, especially at the time of the Second Coming. The New

Testament instead encouraged Christians to focus their spiritual attention on the heavenly Jerusalem (Gal. 4.26; Heb. 12.22), for this heavenly city now fulfilled all that the earthly city of Jerusalem had been intended to signify (including all the Old Testament pictures of Jerusalem and 'Sion' as the place of God's special presence and blessing; for examples, see Psalms 46 and 48). The Old Testament could only be read in the light of the New. Eusebius might naturally be very interested in the history of Jerusalem, but that was quite different from being committed to Jerusalem as a theological symbol.

Such (briefly) would be Eusebius' developed understanding of the city in the years before 325. Our task will be to establish just how much his views were altered by Constantine and the possibility of a new, distinctively Christian, Jerusalem. Could Eusebius find a place within such a system for the unprecedented Christian interest in temporal Jerusalem? Indeed what would Eusebius do with this theological system? Would he abandon it, retain it, or modify it?

On this issue as on the other issue of the 'holy places', Eusebius was, by dint of his lifetime's study and reflection, better prepared than Cyril for the task of assessing these major questions. Yet that preparation could also (paradoxically) prove to be a limitation, so thoroughly had Eusebius developed a theological system in the light of the New Testament which denied any special status to Jerusalem. In that sense therefore he was quite *unpre-pared* for the sudden flood of Christian interest in Jerusalem which developed in the Church towards the end of his life. Cyril would have the chance to start with a clean slate.

2. EUSEBIUS ON THE PLACES OF CHRIST

How about the places of Christ? Surely these at least could be deemed 'holy places' in virtue of their integral involvement in the life of Jesus? Eusebius' attitudes on this second matter are less clear. In principle the New Testament presented a faith which had little concern for such 'holy places' and which emphasized the possibility and importance of worship 'in spirit and in truth' (John 4.24) since the coming of Christ. Clearly too there were no more places like the Old Testament Temple which had been 'holy' in the sense of being special in God's sight, a special place for his presence and for his encounter with his people; such ideas, ascribing an inherent or ontological divine status of holiness to particular places, had been fulfilled and outmoded in Christ. Yet it was perhaps still permissible to talk of 'holy places' in a weaker sense, as a useful means of expressing the historical and religious significance of particular places. There was thus perhaps more room for flexibility on this issue than that of Jerusalem.

Eusebius' initial approach, however, still seems to have been markedly more negative than Cyril's. The force of his apologetics, the focus of his spirituality, and his theological approach to the Incarnation all encouraged him to adopt a Christianity which set little store by physical phenomena; 'holy places' might not be contradictory to his understanding of the Christian faith, but they were certainly not central.

Once again the events of 325 will have brought such matters to the surface. On this issue, compared with the question of Jerusalem, Eusebius had more room for manoeuvre and for legitimate development, and one senses that he took advantage of this during his final years to modify his earlier position and to begin to incorporate 'holy places' into his theological system. Yet it seems clear that ultimately he would still have understood or accepted 'holy places' in quite a different sense from Cyril.

His was instinctively a more historical and less devotional approach. His innate historical inclination and his love of scripture naturally led him at an early stage in his career to locate as many as possible of the biblical locations in his native Palestine. Hence his biblical gazetteer, the *Onomasticon*, which he completed during his thirties. Here scriptural history was matched with contemporary geography, the past with the present. Most of the work, however, concerned the many place-names of the Old Testament; the New Testament sites associated with the life of Jesus in no way received any special treatment or distinction. Indeed, when discussing Bethlehem, for example, he managed to omit any reference to the New Testament at all![13] He was not therefore writing as a 'proto-pilgrim'. Later pilgrims may indeed have used the *Onomasticon* as a guide to help them in their travels,[14] but Eusebius

---

[13] *Onom.*, 42.10–14.
[14] See Wilkinson (1978), 15.

himself originally intended the book to be simply an 'aid to exegesis'.[15] The distinctively Christian nature of the work is therefore to be found, not in any personal piety, but in its close adherence to scripture.[16]

Eusebius' attitude to Gospel places at this stage seems to have been founded on his two-fold commitment to scripture and history, and in that order of priority. Scripture was the prime object of his study, for it was the prime means whereby man could meet God; it might be an ancient historical book, but it was also the living Word from God: God would bring the truth from the past to be the relevance of the present. As a result, any notion that the places of Christ could have a function similar to scripture would have been quite alien to Eusebius' thinking. God had not ordained 'holy places' to be a meeting-point between God and man; that was the unique role of scripture. 'Holy places' were not responsible for making the truth of the past to be meaningful in the present; that was the *Logos* working in the individual's soul. As a result, the places of Christ might be mentioned in the text of scripture but they had no right to complement the function of scripture. Eusebius therefore only came to the places of Christ because of his prior commitment to scripture, not because of his commitment to them in their own right.

Secondly, he came to the places of Christ because of his commitment to history. His Christian commitment to scripture ensured that he came to them as a believer, not as a pagan; his commitment to history ensured that he came to them as a historian, not as a pilgrim. His was the approach of a Christian historian whose faith is fixed on Christ and dependent on the Gospel events, but whose faith is not in any sense dependent on the places of those events. Thus, as with Jerusalem, if the places of Christ had any present importance, it was simply because of their historical association; they could not have any real theological significance or spiritual function in the here and now.

Such was Eusebius' instinctive approach. Yet surely, it may be asked, would not fourth-century developments—the great events of 325, the erection of shrine-basilicas, the discovery of the tomb of Christ—lead Eusebius to modify his thinking? It was one thing

---

[15] Barnes (1981), 110.
[16] Cf. Groh (1983), 29.

to retain a negative attitude towards Jerusalem the city, for that was a matter on which the Bible seemed to speak with a clearer voice; but what was to be gained from maintaining a similar negative attitude towards the individual places of Christ? The New Testament, a product of its time, simply had not envisaged the possibility of Christian devotion to the places of Jesus; such devotion would surely not really affect any theological system or principle to which Eusebius had committed himself?

No doubt Eusebius sensed the force of these arguments. However, the matter was not quite so simple; for, despite what has just been said, there *were* still some important theological principles within Eusebius' thought that would act as a major check on his endorsement of this new movement towards 'holy places'.

As will be argued shortly,[17] 'holy places' would introduce something quite foreign into the Christianity espoused by Eusebius, which in its essential nature (and in contrast to Judaism) was characteristically a *spiritual* religion paying scant regard to the more physical aspects of the world. Moreover, it will be seen how it was not simply his apologetics and his spirituality which militated against an immediate endorsement of 'holy places'. Such a theology in any age must inevitably be related to an understanding of the significance and purpose of the Incarnation. Yet Eusebius, without denying the truth of the Incarnation as such, failed to make it very central to his theology, seeing its more physical and worldly aspects as subsequently being eclipsed by an emphasis on the spiritual and heavenly *Logos*.

This then explains why after 325, despite his many references to Gospel locations in such works as the Isaiah and Psalms commentaries, the *Theophany* and most noticeably his speech *On Christ's Sepulchre*, he only ever refers to 'holy places' as such in perhaps his final work, the *Life of Constantine*, where he refers to Christ's tomb as 'sacred' and 'most holy', and speaks of Palestine as this 'venerable land'.[18] These references, however, must be seen as more exceptional than normative within Eusebius' thought, as late additions to his vast theological corpus. Moreover, in the light of all his previous theology, it is more than probable that he was using this sacral language with quite a different purpose, and

---

[17] Below 3.2.
[18] *V. Const.*, 3.25, 28, 42.

attaching quite a different meaning, from that later espoused by
Cyril. It has been too easy for scholars to assume from these few
references in Eusebius that such sacral language was the norm
rather than the exception and that Eusebius' understanding of
'holy places' was identical with that of Cyril and later pilgrims. A
few preliminary comments at this stage, however, may help us to
see what Eusebius may have meant by the word 'holy' in this
context and why he was prepared in his final years to come round
at last to this qualified acceptance of 'holy places'.

A concept like a 'holy place' has indeed a wide spectrum of
meanings the limits of which are not easily defined. Yet it is
possible perhaps to distinguish on the one hand approaches that
are primarily historical and associative in emphasis from those on
the other that are more spiritual and ontological. The latter is the
approach of pilgrim devotion, the belief that such 'holy' places and
objects have an inherent or ontological quality or status, a quality
or status which moreover is conferred on them not just by human
commemoration but even by divine will. This divine status may
be variously explained: some might emphasize the will of God the
Father in having chosen that place to achieve his eternal purposes
in the past, others the contact which that place once had with God
the Son in the person of Jesus Christ, yet others the blessing of
God the Holy Spirit in giving a sense of God's presence to those
who pray at them. In some sense, however explained, those who
advocate this latter approach assert that the place is truly 'holy'
from a divine perspective. The former, however, is the approach
of the Christian historian who denies this inherent quality but
nevertheless can talk of a place as 'holy' because of its *historical
association*, its involvement in 'sacred history'. The *event* that
occurred in any one place may have been of marked religious
significance, but the *place itself* in the present has no enduring
theological status whatsoever.

As a modern illustration of this distinction at its most extreme
one might consider how Jerusalem at the end of the last century
hosted Western Christian archaeologists and also countless Orthodox pilgrims from the Eastern Churches (especially from Russia).
Both groups might have spoken of 'holy places' but evidently their
understanding of the term would have been widely divergent.[19]

[19] Compare the writings of scholars such as Conder, Wilson and others involved
in the publication of the *Palestine Exploration Quarterly* with the account of the
Russian pilgrimage to Jerusalem in Graham (1913).

Meanwhile many might find themselves more naturally some-where in the middle, wishing to assert that such places have a spiritual significance over and above that of mere historical association, yet not wishing to go so far as to assert any inherent specialness to these places in God's sight. Where on this spectrum were Eusebius and Cyril?

One senses from his frequent references to 'holy places', his emphasis on their value as witnesses and even as manifestations of Christ's truth, his development of the liturgy for pilgrims, and from his whole devotional approach, that Cyril had a stronger and more ontological approach to 'holy places'. It was naturally in his own interests to stress the importance of what Jerusalem, uniquely, could offer to people, and the importance of such 'holy places' would be greatly helped if they were presented within this more ontological framework.

By contrast, Eusebius' lifelong interest in history and indeed his historical context when writing the *Life of Constantine* immediately suggests that he was probably talking of 'holy places' within a more historical framework. On this understanding Eusebius' references to Christ's tomb as 'holy' would not yet be a statement about these places in the present, so much as a confession about the unique event which had occurred there in the past. The tomb discovered under the temple of Venus was the place where God had revealed not just the Resurrection of Christ but the immortality of believers; the Resurrection was the 'prototype of that immortality with God that is our common hope'.[20] As such, the Resurrection for Eusebius was the most 'holy' event of all and the place by association could indeed be termed 'holy'.

However, Eusebius' colourful narrative in the *Life of Constantine*, as he relates the exciting uncovering of the tomb, might indicate that he would willingly have gone one stage further. He suggests that the very act of discovering the tomb, so long buried in darkness but now miraculously brought back to light, was in its own way a picture (εἰκών) of the Resurrection.

Then indeed did this most holy cave present a faithful similitude of his return to life, in that, after lying buried in darkness, it again emerged to light.[21]

---

[20] *Sep. Chr.*, 15.9 (*DPC*, 118).
[21] *V. Const.*, 3.28 (NPNF, i, 527–8).

This attractive idea only properly relates to the unique event of the tomb's discovery in 325/6; it was only at the moment of its coming to light that it really reflected the Resurrection. However, it suggests that Eusebius would have been happy to admit that the tomb itself had a continuing contemporary function of helping people in their faith. It was indeed 'holy' by association, but it also had a present function, as a visual prompt to faith.

This may well underly Eusebius' next comment in this same sentence. The cave 'afforded to all a clear and visible proof, . . . a testimony to the Resurrection of the Saviour clearer than any voice could give'. In fact 'proof' is a slightly misleading translation of ἱστορία which does not strictly include the notion of 'proof' at all. ἱστορία refers instead to an investigative enquiry or to the 'knowledge obtained' from such an enquiry.[22] Thus Eusebius was saying that the existence of the tomb now allowed people to make their own enquiry into the Resurrection. In other words, though the tomb might not offer *proof* of the Resurrection, nevertheless, if a person was inclined to doubt, it did offer supportive evidence. Meanwhile for those who already accepted the truth of the Resurrection, the tomb functioned slightly differently, offering *corroborative* evidence; it acted as a 'testimony' to that which was already believed.

However, even with this advance from the notion of association to that of 'evidence' Eusebius has clearly not moved very far. His basic approach is clearly still that of a historian. A 'holy place' for him is not a place imbued with intrinsic holiness, nor a place where God is in any sense to be deemed nearer than elsewhere. It is simply a place associated with a past event that can aid any visitors in their understanding of the truth. Thus Wilkinson could say correctly:

Eusebius . . . was not himself a pilgrim. To him [holy places] are holy first and foremost because they are visible witnesses to the truth of the biblical narrative. . . . The revealing of the monument is wonderful, but rather because it witnesses to the faith than because it stimulates devotion.[23]

'Holy places' for Eusebius thus had more to do with the vindication

---

[22] *Lex*, 842.
[23] Wilkinson (1981), 19 f.; cf. revd opinion p. 312.

of past biblical history than with divine encounters through prayer in the present.

There may, however, be yet a further reason why Eusebius' statements in the *Life of Constantine* should not be taken as a straightforward endorsement of the sanctification of places. Eusebius' understanding of 'holy places' was not only different from Cyril's; it was also at variance with those of the emperor himself.[24] In the famous letter which Constantine wrote to Bishop Macarius of Jerusalem in connection with the Holy Sepulchre and which is so central to Eusebius' account here in the *Life*, Constantine describes Calvary as a 'sacred spot which has been accounted holy from the beginning in God's judgement, but which now appears holier still'.[25] In other words Constantine was already ascribing a full theological status to that location, an inherent and eternal holiness 'in God's judgement'. This high doctrine of holy places, which is evidenced on other occasions in Constantine's life, was plainly far beyond anything that Eusebius could himself have accepted.

If so, Eusebius was presented with an awkward problem. Obviously he needed to include this letter in Constantine's official biography, but it included certain aspects of Constantine's piety, including this understanding of 'holy places', of which Eusebius himself would not have wholeheartedly approved. His way of solving the dilemma was to place the letter in a context that effectively diluted Constantine's meaning. By introducing some references of his own to 'holy places' (both before and after the letter) Eusebius was able to give this concept a meaning that was more acceptable and in accord with his own theology. It was his means of glossing Constantine's words, of toning down the emperor's false implications.[26] If this is true, then there is all the more reason for interpreting these few references in Eusebius to 'holy places' with a certain degree of caution.

The picture is thus more complicated than is commonly supposed. No longer can it be painted in a monochrome fashion, on the assumption that all opinions were identical. On the contrary, the possibility needs to be entertained that Eusebius and Cyril (and

---

[24] On Constantine's attitude to holy places, see below 4.3(*b*).

[25] *V. Const.*, 3.30.4 (NPNF, i, 528).

[26] I am grateful to Professor Drake for his suggestions and guidance on this point.

indeed Constantine) were attaching quite different meanings to 'holy places'. Indeed it is possible that Cyril may have taken as the starting-point of his positive attitude towards 'holy places' what in Eusebius had really been only a temporary concession to the idea.

Eusebius' understanding certainly seems to have been quite far removed from that of the average pilgrim; his thinking was based on such concepts as evidence and truth, but the devotion of those pilgrims for whom Cyril had to cater would be centred on mystery and faith. Eusebius' understanding was the formulation of an academic historian; Cyril's, though couched superficially in similar words, would need to be that of a pilgrim pastor.

Moreover, these differences would almost certainly have been appreciated at the time. Cyril would inevitably have known of the approach favoured earlier by Eusebius: despite the possibility that the *Life of Constantine* may have been published posthumously,[27] Eusebius had publicized his thinking in several other works and especially in his speeches both in Jerusalem and Constantinople in 335. Conversely, Eusebius evidently knew of the emperor's strong attachment to holy places and was also most probably quite aware of the more devotional approach which was already being developed in Jerusalem. Although Cyril was responsible for much of this development, he was building on a local tradition, with which Eusebius would have been fully acquainted.[28]

In these circumstances, noting the possible differences between Eusebius and Cyril concerning both 'holy places' and the 'holy city', a more detailed analysis is clearly required of the theologies of both bishops before we can proceed to examine their comments on individual Gospel sites and on the city of Jerusalem. Only within this wider framework will we be able to do justice to their more specific comments. Since 325 was such a pivotal date, it will be valuable first (as far as it is possible) to examine Eusebius' theology before that date; then, secondly, to see if there is any observable

---

[27] See Appendix.
[28] Telfer (1955a), 54–63, commenting on Cyril's exposition of doctrine, asserts that Cyril was expressing the opinions which the Jerusalem Church had held long before Nicaea.

development in his theology after that date; and then, finally, to see how this compares with the theology of Cyril. In both areas of our study—'holy places' and the 'holy city'—we can expect there to emerge a consistent note of contrast.

3

EUSEBIUS' THEOLOGY BEFORE 325

In an attempt to summarise the thought of any author who has produced an extensive number of publications over a period spanning forty years or more, there will always be the temptation to concentrate on his final works; for these supposedly represent the final synthesis of the author's thought. Hence an analysis of these will spare the enquirer the lengthy and laborious task of combing back through the many previous publications. This has been the natural temptation for students of Eusebius; but it has been unfortunate. For the result of any such attempted short cut, which views everything from the too advantageous position of hindsight, can be a monochrome and simplistic picture that misses the internal dynamics of an author's thought, which can thus be severely distorted.[1]

This is especially the case with Eusebius, and for at least two reasons. First, in his lifetime there occurred the major events of AD 325 which upturned so much of the Church's life. It ushered in a time of true celebration but it was also necessarily a time of great uncertainty, and Eusebius in particular would have some major rethinking to do. It is therefore natural and proper to ask what was the shape of his theology before that date. For we would expect it by that date to have gained a recognizable character and an established set of priorities, which would then affect his approach to the great new issues raised after 325.

The issues of Jerusalem and of the 'holy places' were not, of course, entirely new in 325; after all, these historic places had always been there for Eusebius and others to contemplate. What was new was the unforeseen possibility of Christians now exerting a control over those sites and their significance, and the sudden forceful attraction which that possibility produced in Christian

---

[1] The value of this more comprehensive approach is amply attested in the important work of Barnes (1981).

believers. The speed of this change can be discerned in the fact
that almost all of Eusebius' explicit statements on this question
date from the period after 325. It must not, however, be assumed
that Eusebius had therefore not considered these issues previously.
Thus it is our task to discern what Eusebius' opinions would have
been during that earlier period, even though these were seldom
expressed explicitly at the time. This will best be achieved by
noting those factors, both personal and theological, which would
have coloured and influenced the essential shape of his thinking
before 325.

Secondly, it will only be through a careful assessment of Eusebius'
earlier theology that we will be able to perceive and understand
the distinctive meaning of the modifications that he made to his
theological system in his final years. We need to know the earlier
Eusebius in order to comprehend what really underlay his later
statements. To use an analogy, two composers may support the
same tune with quite different harmonies. It is those underlying
harmonies in Eusebius' thought that Cyril himself may have
misheard or chosen to ignore; it is those underlying harmonies that
modern scholars too have, until recently, failed to discern or to
distinguish from Cyril's. It is our task to discover the distinctive
Eusebian 'harmony'. It is therefore doubly important for us to look
at Eusebius' earlier thought, not just his final formulations, and to
see those factors which throughout his life would colour his attitude
to Jerusalem and to 'holy places'. Again the question of Jerusalem
will be taken first.

1. THE QUESTION OF JERUSALEM

(a) Ecclesiastical politics

Eusebius' attitude towards Jerusalem before 325 was principally
affected by two factors: first, his ecclesiastical role as bishop of
Caesarea and metropolitan over the whole province of Palestine,
and, secondly, his apologetic task of establishing the identity and
defending the truth of the Christian Gospel over against Judaism.

On the former count, Eusebius seems to have had a natural
interest and concern for all Palestinian issues but would scarcely
countenance the rise of a prestigious and distinctive Church in

Jerusalem which could challenge and threaten his own position as metropolitan. On the latter count, in the course of his contrast of Judaism with Christianity (especially in the *Proof of the Gospel*), Eusebius naturally considered the role of Jerusalem in scripture, inevitably concluding that any interest in the physical Jerusalem was the characteristic hallmark of Judaism. By contrast, he would claim, Christians had grown out of such thinking and saw that Jerusalem no longer had any theological significance. Eusebius thus had two major reasons for assessing Jerusalem in a negative light: the one theological and academic, the other personal and political.

Interestingly the full force of these reasons may only have come home to Eusebius in the decade before 325 when he was already in his fifties. His ecclesiastical concerns would have been heightened after his elevation to the bishopric of Caesarea in 313, while his apologetic work, the *Proof of the Gospel*, in which he began to emphasize the irrelevance of Jerusalem for Christians, was the fruit of his labours in the last few years before 325. His previous interest in Jerusalem as a historian was thus now eclipsed by ecclesiastical and apologetic needs which pulled him in the opposite direction. As a result, it cannot be claimed that in 325 his negative attitude towards Jerusalem was a youthful thought now very much in a state of decline. On the contrary, it had just reached a new height. The paradox of the year 325 was that it found Eusebius, who was to become such an important figure in Constantinian Palestine, firmly on the wrong foot when it came to the question of Jerusalem. Jerusalem's consequent elevation within Christianity, both ecclesiastically and theologically, ran quite counter to all that Eusebius had so recently been propounding.

Naturally, such thinking would then require some modification; yet it would never lose its instinctively negative strand. For, despite the Church's natural tendency to triumphalism after 325, Eusebius himself was still concerned as a Christian apologist both to maintain a contrast with Judaism concerning Jerusalem, and to preserve Christianity's essential identity as the religion which focused on spiritual entities, not physical ones. Thus the apologetic argument against Christian devotion to Jerusalem hardly weakened, whilst the ecclesiastical one only became stronger.

This ecclesiastical tension between Caesarea and Jerusalem, as already noted, would be a key factor in the Palestinian Church throughout this period. It was occasioned by the natural aspirations of those in the Jerusalem Church who wished to regain something of the status that in the intervening years had been lost to Caesarea. The events of 325 naturally played very strongly into the hands of the Jerusalem Church to the detriment of Caesarea; Christians the world over gained a new interest in this city and its historic Church. The result in ecclesiastical terms was that Jerusalem gradually eclipsed Caesarea in importance, rising from relative obscurity under the jurisdiction of Caesarea at the beginning of the fourth century to a position as one of the five patriarchates within Christendom by the middle of the fifth.

Such a shift in ecclesiastical status would not occur without some natural friction between these two sees. It would therefore be strange indeed if Eusebius had remained unaware or unaffected by such an explosive issue, or if his attitude to Jerusalem was not markedly influenced by it. Although his negative attitude towards Jerusalem was no doubt founded upon sincere theological convictions,[2] it would be naïve to suggest that it was not coloured as well by these more personal considerations.

The climate between the two sees in the important decade before 325 may best be sensed by noting the words of the famous seventh canon of Nicaea which expressly dealt with this ecclesiastical tension in Palestine. The Peace of the Church paradoxically only brought to light the internal divisions within the Church; thus the bishops gathered at Nicaea not only had to resolve the Arian question but also such political squabbles as this between Caesarea and Jerusalem. The canon to which they agreed was worded as follows:

Since a custom and ancient tradition has held good that the bishop of Aelia should be honoured, let him have his proper honour, saving to the metropolitan the honour peculiar to it.[3]

Not surprisingly such a compromise was more a statement of the problem than a solution! It revealed clearly that Jerusalem's bishop, Macarius, was taking full advantage of his good standing as one of the few Palestinian bishops to have condemned Arius' teaching from the very beginning,[4] and that he had raised the question of

---

[2] See below 3.2 (*b*).

[3] Council of Nicaea, canon 7; see *NE*, p. 360.

[4] As recounted in Soz., *Hist. Eccl.*, 1.15 (PG, lxvii, 904–8); see also Chadwick (1960), 173.

his own episcopal status in the hope that the Nicene bishops would recognize the prestige of his Church. Indeed it was timely for another reason, for Eusebius had arrived at Nicaea under a threat of excommunication for his Arian sympathies.[5] Now was the ideal moment for the Jerusalem Church through Bishop Macarius to make a major attack on the supposed supremacy of Caesarea. The result, though difficult for us to determine with complete confidence, was evidently much in Macarius' favour, even if his see was still referred to by its pagan name 'Aelia' and not as 'Jerusalem'.

The very occurrence of this canon reveals two important factors. First, from the outset the Jerusalem Church would evidently be seeking to use the new circumstances of a Christian empire to increase its own ecclesiastical status. Secondly, this dispute with Caesarea was clearly *already* a 'bone of contention'. 'It is plain that the campaign for the aggrandisement of the Jerusalem Church was already proceeding.'[6] The relationship was already sour.[7] Indeed the issue may have been 'outgrowing its local and provincial context and turning into an imperial and ecumenical problem'.[8]

If this was true, then it is reasonable to suppose that this tension was already coming to the fore when Eusebius first became the metropolitan bishop in 313. Before that time, it seems, the relationship between the two sees had been more amicable. For Eusebius himself in his *Ecclesiastical History* had shown evident interest in the history of the Church in Jerusalem[9] and had referred to the helpful collaboration between the bishops of Caesarea and Jerusalem which existed throughout much of the third century; the bishop of Caesarea evidently retained a position of pre-eminence but it was not unnatural in those days for the bishop of Jerusalem to act in conjunction with him and even on occasion for Eusebius to refer to the bishop of Jerusalem before the bishop of Caesarea.[10] At this stage no tension can be sensed; as yet no fear felt for the future.[11]

---

[5] For further discussion see below 4.1.

[6] Stevenson (1928), 135.

[7] As seen by Stanley (1883), 157 ff., Lightfoot (1880), 314 and Rubin (1982a), unlike *WCJ*, i, 20.

[8] Rubin (1982a), 95–6.

[9] Hence his references to the local episcopal lists (*Hist. Eccl.*, 4.5.3–5, 5.12.1–2) and to the throne of James (*idem*, 7.19).

[10] Levine (1975a), 115, lists the ten passages in *Hist. Eccl.* which speak of both bishoprics (see also the register in GCS, ii.3, 141–2). Nevertheless, he concludes, Caesarea is listed before Jerusalem 'in the more significant contexts'.

[11] As concluded in *WCJ*, i, 13–21.

Something, however, went wrong. It is no coincidence that after those positive references to the Jerusalem Church in the *Ecclesiastical History* (published in 303) and after mentioning some martyrs from the Jerusalem Church in the *Martyrs of Palestine* (published in 311) Eusebius only refers to the contemporary Jerusalem Church on just one further occasion, and that at the very end of his life in the *Life of Constantine* (when he had no reasonable alternative but to include Constantine's letter to Bishop Macarius concerning the Holy Sepulchre).[12] Twenty-five years is a long time to remain silent.

It is quite possible then that the campaign of the Jerusalem Church began to assume worrying proportions at just that time when Eusebius became metropolitan (313). This was the time when the persecution was over but the final Peace of the Church had not reached the East. Jerusalem already began to see its opportunities.

Meanwhile the hierarchy of the Caesarean Church would perceive things very differently. Perhaps they too could see that the coming of a Christian emperor would play into the hands of the Jerusalem Church. It was all very galling, especially since it was the Caesarean Church who, because of their location in the provincial metropolis, had taken the major brunt of the persecution.[13] It is conceivable, therefore, that Eusebius came under the influence of a 'hawk' party in Caesarea. Indeed he might have been indebted to their support for his successful elevation to the bishopric; they would gain the most eminent of bishops on the clear understanding that for his part Eusebius would use his prestige to combat the rise of Jerusalem.

However, even if this last suggestion is no more than a surmise, it seems almost certain that, after his consecration, Eusebius saw the potential problem for himself; for it would have taken little imagination to recognize that Macarius was probably being motivated by reasons not purely theological when in 318 he so quickly took the opposite side to Eusebius on the question of Arius' orthodoxy. The battle lines were being drawn. Little could Eusebius know then that bishops from all over the empire would soon be adjudicating in that battle.

---

[12] *V. Const.*, 3.29.
[13] As seen clearly in Eus., *Mart. Pal.*

Such experiences would do little to endear him to Jerusalem, whether in thought or practice. As a result, Eusebius' attitude towards Jerusalem before 325 would have been decidedly negative. In such circumstances he might wish to emphasize the role of the *whole* of Palestine in the Bible but it is unlikely that he would be promoting the importance and significance of Jerusalem alone.

(b) Eusebius' apologetics

In his more negative approach to Jerusalem, however, Eusebius was far from being a mere petty politician, anxious merely to defend his ecclesiastical position. For the second major factor which influenced his thinking was strictly theological.

One of the defining characteristics of Christianity for Eusebius was precisely that, unlike Judaism, it gave no theological significance to Jerusalem. This was precisely what Eusebius had been stressing throughout his apologetic works against the Jews in the years before 325. Thus, if it was galling for Eusebius as metropolitan to see the elevation of Jerusalem in ecclesiastical terms, it was also embarrassing for him as an apologist to recognize the possible elevation of Jerusalem in theological terms. He had portrayed the Jews still mourning for the loss of their holy city in the war of AD 70; Christians by contrast were to see that event as expressing God's final judgement on the Jews and their rebellious city. It would smack of considerable inconsistency if Christians now (even in a modified way and on slightly different grounds) began to express their own interest in the city and to attribute to it some special status in God's sight.

This apologetic definition of Christianity in contrast to Judaism as an essentially spiritual and non-territorial religion was naturally allied closely to his own Caesarean brand of spirituality, which set little store by the physical realm, and which emphasized the spiritual nature of the Christian faith. Plainly this would affect his attitude to temporal matters other than Jerusalem, such as 'holy places' and any idea of Palestine as a 'holy land'; for the Judaism from which he sought to distinguish Christianity was a religion that not only gave theological significance to the city of Jerusalem, but also gave special significance both to particular places (most notably the Temple) and to the land as a whole. Eusebius would thus seek to mimimize the validity of the Jewish notion of a 'promised land'. He would also emphasize biblical passages such as John 4.21-3 ('neither on this mountain nor in Jerusalem will you worship the Father; . . . true worshippers will worship the Father in spirit and in truth') which directly countered any Jewish attachment either to 'holy places' or to Jerusalem.

This is made quite clear by a representative and foundational section right at the beginning of Eusebius' *Proof of the Gospel* in which he gave an overview of the essential differences between Christianity and its parent religion, Judaism. Judaism was caricatured as being totally place-bound. Only the inhabitants of Judaea could fulfil certain commands within Judaism:[14] young mothers, for example, needed to travel to Jerusalem for sacrifices.[15] However, in the light of Jesus' teaching in John 4,[16] such restrictions of country ($\chi\omega\rho\alpha\varsigma$), race or locality ($\tau\acute{o}\pi ov$) fortunately did not apply to members of the new Christian community.[17] Since the coming of Christ, God no longer needed to be worshipped in specific places ($\dot{\alpha}\phi\omega\rho\iota\sigma\mu\acute{\epsilon}\nu o\iota\varsigma$ $\tau\acute{o}\pi o\iota\varsigma$), nor indeed in 'Jerusalem, which is in Palestine'; rather, each person could worship him 'from his own place'.[18] Moreover this had been foretold long before by the prophets.[19] There was therefore now no need to 'run' to Jerusalem.[20]

Then, as he concludes his argument, Eusebius paraphrases the Gospel teachings of Jesus in such a way as to throw light on these specific apologetic issues. In contrast to the Law of Moses, worship of God no longer needed to be in one 'corner of the earth' ($\dot{\epsilon}\nu$ $\gamma\omega\nu\acute{\iota}\alpha$ $\gamma\eta\varsigma$);[21] nor was the kingdom of God related any longer to a land 'flowing with milk and honey' but simply to the heavenly kingdom of Christ.[22] Interest in Jerusalem, Palestine or particular

[14] *Dem. Ev.*, 1.2.16 and 1.3 (*FPG*, i, 11-22); cf. *Praep. Ev.*, 8.1.2.

[15] *Dem. Ev.*, 1.3.40, 1.7.4 (*FPG*, i, 19, 44). The Jews' three required visits to Jerusalem each year are also contrasted with Christ's coming in *Comm. in Ps.* [70.16], 784a.

[16] Quoted by Eus. in *Dem. Ev.*, 1.6.40 (*FPG*, i, 35).

[17] Ibid., 1.5.1 (*FPG*, i, 25).

[18] Ibid., 1.6.40 (*FPG*, i, 35); *idem*, 2.3.38 (i, 74).

[19] Namely in Zeph. 2.11 (*Dem. Ev.*, 1.6.42, 2.3.38), Mal. 1.11 (*idem*, 1.6.43) and Isa. 19.19-22 (*idem*, 1.6.45). The last of these verses was a favourite Eusebian text for justifying the breaking down of Palestinian limitations on true worship (see e.g., *Comm. in Is.* [19] 124.4 ff.; *Dem. Ev.*, 2.3.33 f., 6.20, 8.5.3-6).

[20] *Dem. Ev.*, 1.6.57 (*FPG*, i, 39).

[21] Ibid., 1.6.65 (i, 41).

[22] Ibid., 1.6.73 (i, 42).

'holy places' was thus a characteristic of Judaism; Christianity, by contrast, defined itself as the religion which was not dependent on any of these.

Thus, though as a native of Palestine and as a Christian historian Eusebius had a natural love for Palestine and its historic sites (including Jerusalem), as a Christian apologist he was convinced that all such were theologically redundant. It was no doubt paradoxical for a Palestinian to deny the intrinsic value of his own homeland, but Eusebius clearly did so. Moreover his evident historical and ecclesiastical commitment to Palestine ensures that we cannot accuse him of disinterest or ignorance. Instead his theology must be taken seriously as that of a man who had grappled with the issues at first hand and who had concluded that the priority of the spiritual was an essential and non-negotiable attribute of the Christian theology to which he subscribed.

Since Jerusalem and the 'holy places' are our prime concern, it will be valuable at this stage to concentrate briefly on the third issue, the attitude of Eusebius the apologist to the wider issue of Palestine. Had it ever truly been the 'promised land'? Did the events of the New Testament make it in some sense significant in the present? Would it have a future role in God's purposes?

This will naturally be of interest in its own right and will help to set our future discussion within a wider context. Yet it will also bring to light three important factors within Eusebius' thinking: first, his capacity to dismiss much of the Old Testament as of merely temporary significance; secondly, his worldwide perspective and universal emphasis; thirdly, his general avoidance of eschatological issues. Each of these three factors would then influence his understanding of Jerusalem as well.

It will become plain that Eusebius gave to Palestine little significance. First, Palestine was not (and perhaps never had been) the 'promised land'. Secondly, it could not, simply because of its integral involvement in the events of the Old and New Testaments, claim a position of 'central' importance in the world; it was, of course, the historical 'source' of the Gospel but it was now but a 'corner' of the worldwide Church. Thirdly, Palestine would play no special role in the events of the Second Coming. Palestine might therefore have many historical associations for Eusebius as the land of the Bible[23] and the ancient home of the Jews,[24] but it completely lacked any theological significance whatsoever.

(1) What of Palestine as the 'promised land' of the Old Testament? Surely this land in which Eusebius lived had once genuinely had a special status in God's purposes? Surprisingly Eusebius rarely offers a Christian assessment of this important local issue; when he does, however, his answer is ambivalent. Sometimes he affirms the land's past status in God's economy of salvation; at other times he comes close to suggesting that it was all a false notion invented by the Jews.[25]

Eusebius sometimes uses 'the promised land' ($\dot{\eta}$ $\gamma \hat{\eta}$ $\tau \hat{\eta}s$ $\dot{\epsilon}\pi \alpha \gamma \gamma \epsilon \lambda \dot{\iota} \alpha s$) simply as an alternative name for the ancient historical land of the Bible.[26] Only on three occasions, however, does he pause to examine the theological meaning of this concept in any way.[27] One of these, as already noted,[28] occurs in the opening book of the *Proof of the Gospel*, in a context which is especially derogatory to the Law of Moses. Christ does not just fulfill the Mosaic Law; he almost negates its former validity. The Mosaic dispensation is seen as a temporary parenthesis, a concession to the hardness of the Jewish heart, indeed almost a 'false track'. This device of the 'Mosaic parenthesis' seems to have been a hermeneutical argument that was especially the brainchild of Eusebius and one that he certainly used frequently as a means of contrasting Christianity with Judaism.[29] Many Old Testament ideas could then be dubbed not only temporary but 'Jewish' and false, never sanctioned by

[23] Witness again his production of the *Onomasticon* and his anachronistic use of 'Palestine' when referring to the land in the Old Testament period: see, e.g., *Chron.*, §2, 383c; *Dem. Ev.*, 5.19.5 (*FPG*, i, 263); *Comm. in Ps.* [79], synopsis on 829a.

[24] See, e.g., *Comm. in Is.* [13.17], 99.33–4, and *idem* [30.19], 198.2.

[25] For a modern Christian assessment of this theme, see esp. Brueggemann (1977). C. J. H. Wright (1983), 88–103, develops the interesting idea that for Christians the genuine theological role of the land in the Old Testament has now been fulfilled in the New Testament concept of 'fellowship'.

[26] For example in *Chron.*, §1, 16.19, 160a; *Comm. in Ps.* [77.54], 932b; *Comm. in Is.* [11.15], 90.25.

[27] Origen, by contrast, had used it frequently; indeed it was the basis for his whole interpretation in *Comm. in lib. Jes.*, 286–463. Perhaps this very frequency in Origen explains why Eusebius felt no need to repeat or develop such ideas.

[28] *Dem. Ev.*, 1.6.73 (*FPG*, i, 42).

[29] On the originality of this Eusebian motif, see Avi-Yonah (1976), 151, who notes that Eusebius, when wishing to refer to the religion of the Old Testament in a positive way, always spoke of 'the Hebrews', not of the 'the Jews'.

God. The 'promised land' could be one such notion, the 'holy city' of Jerusalem another. With regard to the promised land this meant that, on one further occasion, Eusebius almost suggested that Moses' promise of a 'land flowing with milk and honey' was deliberately designed to prevent the Jews from seeing the secret of the 'kingdom of heaven'.[30] As will be seen, the same would be true of such concepts as the 'city of God' when applied to Jerusalem.[31] Rather than explaining the complex truth that these places had once had a genuine theological status which they had lost since the coming of Christ, it was simpler for Eusebius to deny that former status altogether. On such occasions Palestine had, he claimed, never truly been the promised land.

However, at other times, such concepts could be viewed positively, as true statements of God's genuine involvement with these geographical entities. Thus, two books later in the *Proof of the Gospel*, Eusebius refers to this concept again, but this time in a context in which Moses is being depicted positively as a prefigurement of Christ. The contrast still remains: Moses' promise of a 'holy land' (ἀγία γῆ) contrasts to Jesus' promise of a 'much greater land, truly holy and beloved of God, not located in Judaea' (πολὺ κρείττονα γῆν, ἀληθῶς ἀγίαν καὶ θεοφιλῆ οὐχὶ τὴν ἐπὶ τῆς Ἰουδαίας).[32] Nevertheless, the generally positive context suggests that Eusebius may here have been endorsing the legitimate 'holy' status of the land in Old Testament times. He was clearly convinced that the coming of Jesus had ended all such notions, that Christianity no longer had such a 'holy land', but he was aware that this might have been a true description of Palestine *before* Christ.

There are, however, some further indications that Eusebius would have tended by and large to deny Palestine this past status. This is seen by his frequent hermeneutical assumption that the biblical writers were themselves consciously using such concepts as 'promised land' and 'Judah' in a spiritual and non-physical sense. If Eusebius was to deny the special status of these entities in the past, he would need to make this further presumption that the biblical writers themselves also denied such a status and that they had used the terms only in a spiritual sense. Thus, for example, when the psalmist said, 'In Judah God is known', LXX Ps. 75.2

[30] *Theol. Eccl.*, 2.20.
[31] See esp. below 11.2–3.
[32] *Dem. Ev.*, 3.2.10 (*FPG*, i, 105).

[76.1], Eusebuis claims he was using 'Judah' in an abstract sense; it referred to any place where God was known, now identified by Eusebius with the Christian Church.[33] In this Eusebius was more adamant than Origen. For Origen this particular verse from the Psalms did indeed suggest that God's glory was once genuinely confined to just 'one corner of the earth'.[34] Eusebius now denied this; the psalmist had not been referring to territorial Judaea at all.

His insistence upon the 'spiritual' reference of such Old Testament concepts would then naturally result in his tendency to deny any genuine theological significance either to the 'promised land' or Jerusalem. Such entities would always have only a doubtful value in Eusebius' system.

Moreover, the sorry state of Palestine in Eusebius' day, bearing the scars of AD 70 and 135, might only confirm God's judgement on all such 'Jewish' notions. It was a province which 'in no way excels the rest [of the earth]'.[35] Thus in his apologetics Eusebius did not confine his attacks merely to 'Judaea', the former Jewish region, but expressly spoke of the theological irrelevance of 'Palestine'.[36] Despite its role in biblical history, there was nothing, whether in present appearance or in past scriptural theology, to mark out Palestine as different from anywhere else.

(2) Eusebius denied any notion that Palestine, as a result of its being the scene of biblical history and the Incarnation, was in any sense now *central* to the world in its history or geography. For him the whole thrust of the Bible was one of latent universalism and as a result his own theological focus was ever fixed on that universal dimension. It was impossible that God's purposes could be constricted. The Christian God was clearly concerned not just with Palestine but with the whole of his world. The 'promised land' thus gave way theologically to the worldwide community of the Church; so too Palestine was not the 'centre' of the world but just an insignificant 'corner' (γωνία).

Eusebius' frequent use of this word γωνία will usefully illustrate

---

[33] *Comm. in Ps.* [75.2], 876b. Elsewhere 'Judah' was defined with little clarity as the place near to the 'heavenly Jerusalem': see *Comm. in Is.* [26.1], 166.9.

[34] *Comm. in Is.*, 4.2, 259.13.

[35] *Dem. Ev.*, 3.2.10 (*FPG*, i, 105); cf. also Celsus' denigration of Palestine according to Origen, *C. Cels.*, 5.50.

[36] For examples, *Dem. Ev.*, 1.3.1–3 (*FPG*, i, 11–12), *Comm. in Is.* [49.14–16], 314.11, and *Comm. in Ps.* [75.24], 877d.

how much he belittled Palestine in theological terms. This dis-
paraging description of Palestine had been used by Celsus to
ridicule God's particular interest in the Jews of Palestine in just
'one corner of the world'.[37] Origen, by contrast, had accepted quite
readily the paradox that God had particularly revealed Himself in
Judaea, that 'one corner of the world', and admitted to Celsus that
Christ's 'sojourn' had also been 'in a corner'. However, he argued
that both these shocking particularities had been replaced by
equally remarkable universals, the 'churches of the faithful' and
the 'worldwide spread of the Gospel'.[38] Christ's healing power
was therefore known not 'just in one corner' (ἐν μίᾳ γωνίᾳ) but
'everywhere' (πανταχοῦ).[39]

Eusebius adopted the positive, universal aspect of this motif with
great vigour. Thus the Church had become established 'not in a
corner but everywhere under the sun'.[40] Christ had founded his
own nation 'not in some obscure corner of the earth' (οὐκ ἐν γωνίᾳ
ποι γῆς λεληθώς)[41] and his dominion now extended not just over
'some thin corner of the world but everywhere' (βραχείας τινὸς
γωνίας . . . ἀπανταχοῦ τῆς γῆς).[42] God had sent his illumination to
help people not in 'one corner but in the whole world'.[43] As a
result man's worship was also not to be restricted to 'one particular
corner of the world'.[44] Meanwhile Eusebius could parody the
particularistic notions of the Jews by saying that their God and
their concerns were all tied to just such a corner, indeed one
particular 'corner' of Palestine.[45]

In all these ways Eusebius was reiterating a basic conviction. In
theological terms Palestine was but a 'corner' of the world,
essentially insignificant to the worldwide purposes of the Christian
God. God had broken free from any such physical restrictions in
Palestine and it was not for Christians to revert once more to a
particularistic interest in that 'corner' of the world. Eusebius may
have been a Palestinian by birth but in his theology he belonged
to the universal Church spread throughout the world.

37 According to Origen, *C. Cels.*, 6.78; cf. 4.23, 36.
38 *Comm. in Is.*, 4.2, 259.16; *C. Cels.*, 6.78.
39 *C.Cels.*, 4.4.
40 *Hist. Eccl.*, 10.4.19; cf. ibid., 1.4.
41 *Theoph.*, 3.9, repeated in *Sep. Chr.*, 16.9.
42 *Comm. In Is.* [11.10], 85.18–19; cf. too *Comm. in Ps.* [72.8], 804b.
43 *Praep. Ev.*, 2.5.2; 6.6.71.
44 *Theoph.*, 4.23; also in *Dem. Ev.*, 1.6.65 (*FPG*, i, 41).
45 In, e.g., *Comm in Is.* [11.9], 85.7.

Eusebius would not therefore have been prepared to elevate the theological importance of Palestine on the grounds that this had been the scene of the Incarnation. Only on one occasion before 325 did he comment expressly on the fact that his Palestine, the Palestine of the recent martyrs, was ironically the land where the 'Saviour of all men arose like a thirst-quenching spring'.[46] Yet that did not give Palestine any special importance in the present. The whole purpose of the Incarnation had been to break down such place-bound notions and to establish the universal nature of the Church. This essential conviction, that the Incarnation should be seen to have had universal, not local, significance, can be seen in three brief examples.

First, the psalmist on one occasion spoke of God 'working salvation in the midst of the earth' (Ps. 74.12). Whatever the author's original meaning, Cyril would be quick to see this as a reference to Christ's work of salvation on the Cross and therefore as an endorsement that Golgotha and Jerusalem were truly in the very 'centre of the world'.[47] Eusebius, however, in his exegesis of this same psalm, whilst accepting the reference to Christ, was not tempted to see this as an endorsement of Palestine's centrality; on the contrary it referred instead to the universal spread of Christ's salvation throughout 'the whole earth'.[48] The Incarnation did not make Palestine central to the world nor in any sense special to God.

Then again in his commentary on LXX Ps. 84 [85], despite the Christological interpretation which he was advocating, he was in no way tempted to see the clause 'our land will yield its increase' (v. 12) as a reference to impoverished third-century Palestine. Almost pointedly he states instead that his interpretation related to the whole 'inhabited world of mankind' (λέγω τῇ τῶν ἀνθρώπων οἰκουμένῃ).[49]

Thirdly, and more importantly, this universal purpose of the Incarnation for Eusebius is seen in the way in which Eusebius seems to see the apostles' proclamation of the Gospel as an integral second part of the single Christ-event. On occasions indeed it is hard to draw a neat line between a Eusebian reference to the

---

[46] *Mart. Pal.*, 1.1.8 (L) in Lawlor and Oulton (1928), i, 331.
[47] *Catech.*, 13.28.
[48] *Comm. in Ps.* [73.12], 862a–c.
[49] *Comm. in Ps.* [84.10–12], 1021d–1025c.

'Incarnation' (ἐνανθρώπησις) and the 'preaching of the Father's
love to all nations'.[50] Eusebius seemed almost to be wanting to
forget that Christ himself in his incarnate ministry had been limited
to one place. He therefore saw the evangelistic outreach of the
apostles essentially as the work of Christ himself, for this universal
result was the sole purpose of the Incarnation's necessary particularity.[51] Thus he repeatedly emphasized the apostolic exodus
to the 'ends of the earth',[52] sometimes noting how this universal
thrust of the Gospel coincided with the destruction of that Jerusalem
which had once been its source.[53]

With this emphasis upon the universal consequences of the
Incarnation, the only prestige (if prestige it was) which Palestine
could claim was that it had indeed been the historical *source* of
that Gospel which had since spread across the whole world. This
concept of Palestine as the source of the Gospel (which can perhaps
be sensed already in that reference to Christ's appearing there as
a 'thirst-quenching spring') would become Eusebius' chief means
of expressing the historical significance of Palestine after 325.[54] It
neatly satisfied all of Eusebius' requirements. First, the concept of
Palestine as the source of the Gospel did not give to Palestine any
theological significance in the present, only a historical significance
drawn from the past. Secondly, it inherently preserved Eusebius'
emphasis on the universal and the worldwide spread of the Gospel;
it looked behind the present day to the Palestine of the apostolic
era but then beyond to the world of the universal Church. Thirdly
and finally, what historical significance it did give to Palestine was
'evangelical', not 'incarnational'; in other words it was not the
Incarnation which was suddenly being used to give Palestine a
new status but simply the spread of the Gospel from that land.

[50] As in, e.g., *Dem. Ev.*, 8.pref.11 (*FPG*, ii, 98).

[51] Most probably this explains his belief in the almost instantaneous spread of
Christ's fame: the disciples 'ran over the whole earth' (*Dem. Ev.*, 3.1.4) and filled
it with the Gospel 'as if in a single day' (ὥσπερ ὑπὸ μίαν ἡμέραν) in *Comm. in Is.*
[66.7–9], 403.6–7; as a result even Tiberius was supposed to have heard of Christ
before his own death in AD 37 (*Hist. Eccl.*, 2.2). Note too the stark contrast which
he draws between the 'great commission' (Matt. 28.19), which was heard by only
a few men in one 'corner of the earth', and its almost immediate results seen the
world over (*Dem. Ev.*, 3.7.14, repeated in *Theoph.*, 5.46).

[52] See, e.g., *Comm. in Ps.* [66.8], 677c; *Comm. in Is.* [42.10], 272.17 ff.; *Proph.
Eclg.*, 2.10.

[53] *Proph. Eclg.*, 4.1 (in fulfilment of Isa. 2.3).

[54] See both *L. Const.*, 9.15 and *Sep. Chr.*, 11.2, discussed more fully below in
4.3(*a*) and esp. 10.3(*b*).

Palestine therefore did not have any special significance in the present; the fact that this had been the scene of the Incarnation was of no lasting account. Palestine in the era of the universal Church was therefore just a 'corner' which three centuries before had happened to be the source and the starting-point of the Gospel's proclamation to the world.

(3) If Eusebius minimized the theological significance of Palestine as the promised land in the Old Testament and, with his emphasis on the universal, completely denied its having any special or 'central' significance in the present on the grounds of the Incarnation, what about its role in the future? Did he envisage that Palestine would still play a significant part in God's future purposes, and especially in relation to the Second Coming of Christ?

Millenialists such as Tertullian, Justin Martyr and Irenaeus in the second century seem to have suggested that Christ's Second Coming would be integrally related to Palestine, the scene of his first coming, and that the city of Jerusalem might be rebuilt for the thousand year reign of the saints.[55] Admittedly they spoke in very pictorial terms, but Tertullian made explicit his more physical interpretation of the millenium by commenting on a strange event associated with a recent campaign of the Emperor Severus to the East: for it was reported that 'in Judaea for forty days there was a city suspended from the sky at the break of morning'.[56] In this way these writers could preserve the Palestinian origin of the Gospel, yet in a context which still emphasized the dynamic focus of the new Christian Church; Christians looked forward to Christ's return, not backward with nostalgia to the time of the Incarnation.

In the third century, however, probably as a result of the Church's response to the Montanist heresy with its bizarre collection of charismatic and eschatological ideas,[57] such perspectives seem by and large to have disappeared from the mainstream of the Church's life, to be replaced in the following century by a more retrospective focus on the Incarnation.

Eusebius' theology reflects this transition exactly. For while he does not as yet emphasize the Incarnation, he now plays down

[55] Tert., *Adv. Marc.*, 3.25; Just., *DT*, 80–81; Iren., *Haer.*, 5.32–6.
[56] Tert., loc. cit.
[57] As outlined by Eusebius himself in *Hist. Eccl.*, 5.3.14, 16, 18, and also *Theoph.*, 4.35; cf. also Cyril, *Catech.*, 16.8.

any emphasis on eschatology.[58] Thus it is hard to find any passage in his writings before 325 which really raises the issue of the Second Coming at all. Our one piece of information must be taken from the years after 325 when Eusebius needed to expound Jesus' Apocalyptic Discourse as part of his survey of Jesus' prophecies in the fourth book of the *Theophany*.

Here at least he was obliged to subscribe to a traditional Christian belief in the reality of Christ's return. In his exposition, however, he was at pains to emphasize that this Second Coming would in no way be related to Palestine. Jesus himself had indicated that this would not be a local event, but an event witnessed by all people simultaneously. Was this not the point of the Lord's picture of 'lightening which goes from the east to the west' (Matt. 24.27)? As a result Eusebius could conclude categorically: 'Our Saviour taught that his glorious Second Coming should not again be, as it was at the first, in some one place, so that it might be visible in some corner of the earth'.[59]

Cyril, by contrast, would see the Temple ruins in Jerusalem as the focal point for that activity of the anti-Christ which would precede Christ's return;[60] for him Jerusalem and Palestine continued to be central in God's purposes and would remain so until the end of the age. Eusebius, however, strove to get away from all such physical notions. Palestine and Jerusalem had no special role to play in God's future plans.

From this analysis of his attitudes towards Palestine three important aspects of Eusebius' thinking have thus been brought to light. Eusebius came to minimize the theological significance of Palestine in the past, present and future for three reasons: his frequently dismissive attitude to the Old Testament, his consistently universal emphasis, and his downplay of eschatology.

The same would then be true of Jerusalem. For all these three principles would apply equally to the question of Jerusalem. Thus, with Eusebius' dislike of eschatology, it is impossible to detect in his writings any hint that Jerusalem might again play a significant role in God's future purposes. Secondly, those divine purposes

[58] As noted by, e.g., Pollard (1970), 297. This disinclination towards eschatology may partially explain why Eusebius was so hesitant concerning the canonicity of the book of Revelation (*Hist. Eccl.*, 3.25.4).

[59] *Theoph.*, 4.35 (*LET*, 280).

[60] *Catech.*, 15.15.

were now universal in extent and were no longer bound in any
way to Jerusalem. Finally, if so much of the Old Testament was
to be dismissed as a 'Mosaic parenthesis', Jerusalem too would be
seen as but of temporary significance. Eusebius asserted that
Judaism, if it was conducted strictly according to the Law of Moses,
was dependent totally upon Jerusalem; but Christ, he argued, had
come to end this dependency and to destroy the religious importance
of Jerusalem.

Thus Eusebius could say in a typical passage near the start of
the *Proof of the Gospel*:

Although Moses himself foresaw by the Holy Spirit that, when the new
covenant was revived by Christ and preached to all nations, his own
legislation would become superfluous, he rightly confined its influence to
one place, so that if they were ever deprived of it, and shut out from
their national freedom, it might not be possible for them to carry out the
ordinances of his law in a foreign country, and as of necessity they would
have to receive the new covenant announced by Christ. Moses had
foretold this very thing, and in due course Christ sojourned in this life,
and the teaching of the new covenant was borne to all nations, and at
once the Romans besieged Jerusalem, and destroyed it and the Temple
there. At once the whole of the Mosaic law was abolished, with all that
remained of the old covenant.[61]

In the light of such statements which are so characteristic of
Eusebius in the *Proof of the Gospel*,[62] it would indeed be hard
(though not strictly impossible) to suggest that Jerusalem was the
one aspect of the old covenant which survived into the era of the
new covenant and to believe that something of its significance in
God's sight had been preserved. No, the coming of Christ spelt
the end of Jerusalem's significance; this was then only confirmed
for Eusebius by the crushing events of AD 70. As a result, all that
Jerusalem had signified in the Old Testament writings was to be
deemed a purely temporary phenomenon, which was now eclipsed
by the 'teaching of the new covenant' 'borne to all nations'.

Eusebius proceeds to question the whole notion that Jerusalem
had been legitimately a 'holy city'.[63] The Law of Moses certainly
gave a special place to the Temple and indeed Jesus himself
affirmed that this Temple had been the object of God's special

---

[61] *Dem. Ev.*, 1.6.38–9 (*FPG*, i, 34–5).
[62] Cf. ibid., 1.3.41, 1.6.43, 1.7.6, 2.3.38 (i, 19, 36, 44, 74 respectively).
[63] See esp. ibid., 8.2.9–16 (ii, 118–19), discussed in detail below in 11.2.

oversight and protection,[64] but perhaps all notions that the temporal city of Jerusalem was in some sense special to God were but fond inventions of the Jews; for if there was a true 'holy city', this was clearly now the 'heavenly Jerusalem'.[65] In any case, Ezekiel had prophesied the departure of God's presence from the Temple, a clear sign of God's abandonment of the city.[66] Jerusalem was therefore now a redundant phenomenon. Indeed certain passages in Zechariah could be interpreted symbolically to show how the Church (represented by the Mount of Olives) had replaced Judaism (represented by Jerusalem).[67]

Such, briefly, were some of Eusebius' statements in the *Proof of the Gospel*. They were strong statements, penned less than a decade before 325, in which Eusebius seemingly dismissed the significance of Jerusalem in its entirety. Naturally it is possible to argue that these negative attitudes towards Jerusalem were simply the result of their apologetic context. Surely, some might say, these were stock points of defence which Eusebius was repeating with little understanding of contemporary Judaism and with little personal conviction? Or perhaps he was only attacking some *Jewish* attitudes to Jerusalem, not Jerusalem in its own right? Yet the evidence seems to suggest that Eusebius was convinced by his own apologetic; that he was loathe to draw this convenient distinction between Jewish Jerusalem and Jerusalem *per se*. Eusebius had committed himself to presenting a form of Christianity that was no longer concerned with, or bound to, Jerusalem in any way. Christianity, for Eusebius, needed to retain its distinctiveness from Judaism: 'precisely because they owed so much to Judaism, [Christians] regarded . . . the parallels between the two religions with caution. Any undue emphasis on . . . the similarities threatened to blur the distinctions'.[68]

It would not then be easy for Eusebius, in the years after 325, to start propounding a Christianity that reintroduced the notion of Jerusalem's special significance. Yes, some neat distinctions could be drawn (for example, between a Jewish and a Christian Jerusalem, or perhaps between its theological and historical

---

[64] Ibid., 8.2.111–20 (ii, 136–7).
[65] Ibid., 4.12.4 (i, 186), 10.8.64 (ii, 227).
[66] Ibid., 6.18.22 (ii, 29).
[67] Ibid., 6.18.20–6 (ii, 29–31).
[68] Wilkinson (1979), 347; cf. below 10.1.

significance), that might allow later modifications and refinements in Eusebius' thought. Yet, by and large, Eusebius seems to have preserved to the end this negative attitude towards Jerusalem *per se*.

With his life's experience of living as a theologian and historian in the land, Eusebius was strategically placed to assess Palestine and Jerusalem theologically when they suddenly appeared on the Christian 'map'. But his theology was not one which could give a primary place to such physical entities and, as the bishop of Caesarea, he was in a very vulnerable position. On two accounts therefore (one theological, the other ecclesiastical) Eusebius was caught in an awkward tension. In such circumstances his approach to Jerusalem would inevitably be one of great caution.

2. THE QUESTION OF 'HOLY PLACES'

Eusebius had given quite a considerable amount of thought before 325 to the question of the theological role of Jerusalem. Was the same true of 'holy places'? If we insist on looking only for *explicit* statements on this subject, then the answer will almost certainly be negative. However, it will be appreciated by now that such insistence on this difficult subject is quite inappropriate. Instead, so long as we proceed with great care, it should be possible to make an assessment of Eusebius' attitude to 'holy places' before 325. Yet the issue of 'holy places' is indeed the more nebulous of the two. The precise meaning and function of 'holy places' within any one theological system is very difficult to define, and the range of such possible meanings and functions quite extensive; the question also touches on several other important aspects of theology and spirituality.

Our task of establishing Eusebius' attitudes to 'holy places' is made more complex by the fact that with hindsight we are asking Eusebius an anachronistic question. Within a hundred years the cult of 'holy places' and relics developed dramatically; 'holy places' became an important aid to faith in Christ, a valuable means of experiencing a new sense of proximity to God. All this would no doubt have been far beyond anything Eusebius could have foreseen. Yet we now seem to be asking how Eusebius would have assessed this unforeseen development.

However, this is not entirely an unfair question to ask of Eusebius, since he has often been portrayed as the conscious and glad initiator of later developments. If it is our task to counter this retrospective assumption, we will be forced of necessity to be equally retrospective ourselves. If we wish to show that his theology would have been opposed to, or at least unprepared for, such a full-scale development, then we must be open to the possibility at least that we may need to extract certain principles from Eusebius' theology which bear on the question of 'holy places' *in a way which Eusebius himself might not have appreciated*. Nevertheless, having admitted this possibility, it should not be supposed that Eusebius was quite unaware of these issues or totally unable to see their importance and the likely direction in which things would develop. The great changes after 325 would have alerted even the most insensitive to the fact that major changes in Christian life and practice were on their way. In such circumstances, even if Eusebius never formulated a definitive answer to the questions that we are now asking of him, he would naturally have begun to draw on certain aspects of his established theology which were related in a new way to the questions being posed after 325.

In the remainder of this chapter we shall examine three areas of Eusebius' earlier theology that would at least colour his initial response to the new theological climate. Only in the next chapter will we ask whether Eusebius would have allowed these earlier formulations to dictate his final response or whether he would have begun to revise them in the light of the developing situation. The relevant three areas on which we will concentrate are respectively Eusebius' apologetics, his spirituality, and his theology of the Incarnation. Each of these was an area of Eusebius' thinking that was well formulated before 325; each too in its own way had the potential to exert a real and negative influence on Eusebius' subsequent approach to 'holy places'.

First, however, it is well to remind ourselves again that, even if the development of 'holy places' after 325 brought some new questions to the surface, those places had been in existence ever since New Testament times and Eusebius had written about them in several places, perhaps having visited them himself on many occasions. This led, as noted above, to a few references to Gospel sites in the *Proof of the Gospel* and especially in the *Onomasticon*. Eusebius had thus spent a lifetime in a privileged proximity to these sites and must inevitably have resolved, even if this was not articulated, his opinions about their significance. It was suggested earlier that his deliberations were directed by scriptural and historical concerns. It is now time to show how these three further aspects of his thought would only have consolidated his historical approach to 'holy places' at this early stage.

(a) Eusebius' apologetics

First, Eusebius' attitudes towards 'holy places', as to Jerusalem, would have been coloured by his concerns as a Christian apologist. With the question of Jerusalem the issue had been quitè sharply focused and the 'opponents' quite clearly defined, namely the Jews. The issue of 'holy places', however, was more diffuse and the 'opponents' from whom Eusebius sought to distinguish Christian truth included not just the Jews but pagans as well. Almost all ancient religion, whether Hebraic or other, employed a category of the 'sacred' which it customarily applied to certain places or objects. In Judaism, with its stance against idolatry and the memory of prophetic attacks against the corruptions of local 'high places', this sanctity of particular places had eventually been refined until the Jerusalem Temple became its sole legitimate expression. In paganism the sacred impinged on the physical world in a more widespread fashion, worship being associated with many sacred shrines and focused on a wide variety of cultic objects. The great pilgrim centres (such as Delphi and Didyma) and the multiplicity of religious statues and votive objects were but a tiny part of a physical world which was suffused by the sacred. Was Christianity to be any different?

Eusebius the apologist would naturally want to say that it was. His whole purpose in the *Preparation for the Gospel* and the *Proof of the Gospel* was to cut out for Christianity a distinctive character between paganism on the one hand and Judaism on the other. Christianity was truly a third way. It might embrace the best and most noble aspects of paganism and Judaism (especially the latter) but it was quite distinct from, and in many matters directly opposed to, both. The question of the sacred was one of those areas in which it was clearly to be opposed and quite distinct.

Eusebius' opposition to the ways of Judaism on this point is expressed clearly in the first book of the *Proof of the Gospel*, not least in that section (already discussed) in which he also denied the importance of Jerusalem and Palestine. Eusebius was here taking Jesus' words, as recounted in John 4.21–4 ('neither in this mountain nor in Jerusalem shall you worship; . . . true worshipppers will worship in spirit and in truth'), as a dominical judgement on the Temple and on all such 'holy places' that in some sense acted as a restriction on true spiritual worship. Eusebius intimated that particular places were no longer of special interest to 'God the Father' and of no real benefit to the 'worshipper'. God no longer desired or commanded worship which was bound to specified places (ἀφωρισμένοις τόποις);[69] he simply wanted worship that was 'in spirit and in truth'. Indeed Jesus' teaching could be paraphrased as follows:

> The Law of Moses required all who desired to be holy to speed from all directions to one definite place; but I, giving freedom to all, teach men not to look for God in a corner of the earth, nor in mountains, nor in temples made with hands, but that each should worship and adore him at home.[70]

In so saying Eusebius was presumably not denying the functional advantage of Christian worship occurring in certain, fixed locations; but he was denying the necessity of such connections to particular places for true worship. He was emphasizing that Christianity taught as one of its essential ingredients that God was equally available in Christ to worshippers, regardless of their location. God's criteria for manifesting his presence or for encountering men and women were thus entirely personal. Since the coming of Christ the question was not *where* worshippers were but only *who* they were.

Advocates of a high doctrine of Christian 'holy places' would clearly not wish to counter this dominical statement. Nevertheless they often seem to suggest that these locations have some special religious significance, perhaps even a special divine presence. Eusebius was opposed to any such notions. If the Christian God was formerly tied to a specific location (Jerusalem and the Temple), he was so no longer; it was possible to encounter him anywhere in the world, and any emphasis on particular places by Christians might be seen as a potential denial of this important truth.

[69] *Dem. Ev.*, 1.6.40 (*FPG*, i, 35).
[70] Ibid., 1.6.65 (i, 40–41).

Even if such advocates could reply that 'holy places' did not automatically deny this important truth, Eusebius' apologetical concerns and his desire for consistency would mean nevertheless that he would be concerned that Christianity should be *seen* to be different. This would inevitably mean that Eusebius the apologist would be far more cautious than others in introducing any practice which might be misunderstood by outsiders. Other Christians might convince themselves that 'holy places' did not really deny the universal possibilities of Christian worship, but Eusebius would be less happy with such neat internal distinctions which might appear to outsiders as 'special pleadings' and which threatened to blur the more important *external* distinction between Christianity and Judaism. Christianity needed, at least according to Eusebius in the years before 325, to be visibly different.[71]

The same, of course, was true (and perhaps even more so) of the distinctions that Eusebius wished to preserve between Christianity and *paganism*. Modern scholars, rightly or wrongly, may interpret much of the development of Christian life and practice in the fourth century (both in our field and in others) as the result of Christianity's encounter, and even compromise, with the popular paganism of the empire. Eusebius would clearly have been opposed to any such compromise. Later fourth-century theologians sincerely endorsed the new attitudes to Christian worship and the new use of the physical realm in the life of faith by appealing to the truth of the Incarnation and by developing a more sacramental approach to the physical. Eusebius, however, might well have seen such attempts as but an illegitimate baptism of natural, pagan religion. Even if such a picture of Eusebius and later fourth century theologians is oversimplified, or even incorrect, it remains true that by the end of the century the distinctions in practice between Christianity and paganism had been blurred, distinctions which Eusebius attempted in his early fourth-century writings to keep quite plain.

Seen against this background it is quite clear that so-called 'holy places' would seem to Eusebius to be very much on the pagan side of the divide. The same would be true of any attempt to imbue any particular *object* in the physical realm with some divine

[71] Cf. again the comment of Wilkinson, quoted above.

association.[72] Thus it was that Eusebius frequently parodied the pagan tendency to 'deify' the physical. Even Plato had known that 'there is nothing venerable nor suited to the divine nature in gold or ivory and things manufactured out of lifeless material'.[73] Yet pagan man, as Eusebius lists in the *Theophany*, had continued to deify and term 'divine' all sorts of physical entities: the sun and moon, the fruits of the earth, his personal passions, other mortals, animals, man-made idols, and even the evil spirits who 'lurk in carved images and hide in shadowy recesses'.[74] Pagan man was therefore quite mistaken to believe that a god might be contained in an image (εἰκών), as it were in a 'holy place' (ἱερῷ χωρίῳ).[75] No, the Holy Spirit did not come to those who enclosed the divine in 'lifeless matter and dusky caves' (ἐν ἀψύχῳ ὕλῃ καὶ σκοτίοις μυχοῖς), but only to those 'souls purified and prepared with rational and clear minds' (ψυχαῖς κεκαθαρμέναις καὶ νῷ ογικῷ παρεσκευασμέναις).[76] The contrast with Eusebius' Christianity was clear: unlike paganism, Christian worship was personal, moral and rational, and in no way to be associated with such objects and places.

Again, such arguments were no doubt part of the apologist's customary armour, as he sought to maximize the supposed differences between Christianity and all other religions; no doubt too later advocates of Christian 'holy places' would still feel able to make the same charges against paganism. Nevertheless, it would prove hard for Eusebius openly to countenance the development of 'holy places' and the promulgation of relics in the wake of such forthright comments.

Some Christians might claim that their use of 'holy places' and

[72] It would of course be valuable to know at this point how exactly Eusebius viewed the Eucharist; for here might be the authentic Christian version of such attempts to relate the divine realm to the physical. Unfortunately, however, in Eusebius' day it was customary to guard the Lord's Table by not referring to the Eucharist in written works, which could be read by those not yet baptized into the Church (the so-called 'discipline of the secret', mentioned in Origen, *Comm. in Lev.*, 9.10, 438; *Comm. in lib. Jes.*, 4.1, 307–309, and Cyril, *Catech.*, 5.12, 6.29, 16.26, and *Procat.*, 12: see Baus (1965), 284–5). This resulted in Eusebius referring to the Eucharist only rarely. His two allusions to it in *Dem. Ev.*, 1.10.39 (*FPG*, i, 62) and 8.1.79–81 (ii, 114–15), in which he speaks of the eucharistic bread as a 'symbol' or 'image of Christ's body', indeed suggest that Eusebius' emphasis was on a merely '*spiritual* identification' (as argued by Kelly (1977), 441).

[73] *Praep. Ev.*, 3.8.2; cf. 5.36.

[74] *Theoph.*, 2.4–13, repeated in *Sep. Chr.*, 13.1–5 (*DPC*, 111).

[75] *Praep. Ev.*, 5.15.2.

[76] *Dem. Ev.*, 5.pref.29 (*FPG*, i, 228–9).

relics was essentially different from their Jewish and pagan counterparts, simply because they were 'Christian'; attempts would be made to endorse Eusebius' remarks and claim that he was only attacking the Jewish or pagan nature of these practices, the religion that was false, not the religious practice itself. It would be more correct, however, to take Eusebius' clear statements at their face value and to conclude that he was opposed to these religious practices in their own right. Attachment to relics and devotion to Jerusalem or other particular places in the belief that they were somehow special to God, was essentially alien to the very spirit of his Christianity and could not simply be 'Christianized'. There was no legitimate Christian equivalent to such practices. Christianity, as Eusebius defined it in his apologetic works was a religion from which all of these were essentially excluded.

This was Eusebius' apologetic stance in the years shortly before 325. Again it would be a question after that date of how much Eusebius would be able to accommodate of the new developments in a way which was consistent with this earlier, more rigorous approach. Would he be prepared to make some qualifications? Would he discover some of these internal distinctions which could calm his own conscience as the more external distinctions between Christianity and the other religions began somewhat to be corroded?

(b) Eusebius' spirituality

Eusebius' qualms about 'holy places', however, were not based solely on such apologetic arguments. A second factor which would influence his thinking and which reflected even more closely the very essence of his own thought, was his own spirituality. In a sense Eusebius' apologetics and his spirituality are hard to separate; for what he was defending in his apologetics was the Christian spirituality to which he himself subscribed. Thus from his apologetics we have learnt many things that were also characteristic of his own spirituality. Christianity was not, for example, a matter of physical place but a matter of the heart; God was a person who could be known by all people and whose concerns were universal in scope and not tied to particular places; Christian worship was to be essentially 'spiritual', a pure response of the mind in obedience to God's revelation of himself in the *Logos*.

Such statements, if considered only from the perspective of

apologetics, might appear simply to be matters of convention; viewed however from the perspective of spirituality, they come to us instead as expressions of conviction. Our point is simply then that Eusebius' apologetic statements can truly be taken as indicative of his own spirituality. As a result, it is reasonable to suppose that, as matters of personal conviction, they would have a formative influence on any future revision of his position. However, there is more to Eusebius' spirituality than has emerged in our brief overview of his apologetics. Above all, it needs to be reiterated that Eusebius' spirituality was heavily influenced by Origen; and therefore he laid perhaps an excessive emphasis on the *spiritual* nature of Christianity.

It is hard in a brief span to give a satisfactory picture of a complete way of life and thought, but the following must serve as a summary. First, Christian spirituality within this Origenian school was very much focused upon the revelatory function of the invisible *Logos*, not so much upon the redemptive activity of the incarnate Christ. This meant first that Christian worship was primarily obedience of the mind to this revelation; it would be quite a cerebral affair. Secondly, the elevation and glorification of the *Logos* after his temporary visitation to this earth set an essential stamp on Christian attitudes to the physical realm. Advancement in the Christian way came to be conceived in a quasi-Platonic fashion as being a progessive elevation away from physical concerns to a contemplation of the *Logos*. Thirdly, this in turn affected the Origenian attitude towards scripture, which thus came to be interpreted in a highly spiritualized way, with its historical and physical events being reinterpreted as pictures of the internal spiritual life.[77]

Armed with such convictions, an Origenian like Eusebius would naturally find little place in his spirituality for 'holy places'; for such places tend to emphasize once more the particular, not the universal, the physical and historical rather than the spiritual, the importance of places rather than people.[78] Major readjustment to

[77] On Origen's theology in general, see again Crouzel (1985) and Trigg (1983); also Kelly (1977), 154-8.

[78] For a modern critique of devotion to 'holy places' and to Jerusalem, which emphasizes this priority of the personal, see, Neville, (1971), 104-6: 'Jerusalem was not a place but a community'; 'the mature Christian [has] little interest in holy places but an eagerness to go to Church'. 'The cultivation of holy places [is] a kind of religiosity which shuns the demand of personal encounter.'

his essential convictions was necessary before Eusebius could accommodate such places into his spirituality; and even then he would clearly never ascribe to them the same significance that they would have for later Christians, who would not be emphasizing so strongly the spiritual realm at the expense of the physical.

Eusebius' exegetical works throughout his life, both before and after 325, consistently reflect this spiritualizing approach. Indeed this emphasis is so characteristic as to become almost monotonous. A good example, which reveals very clearly Eusebius' priorities, is his oft-repeated explanation of the exegetical meaning of 'Sion'. He goes to great and repetitive lengths to stress on almost every occasion that there are several true interpretations of this biblical name (which, of course, have nothing to do with any hill in Jerusalem!). The four levels of meaning that he extracts are as follows: the heavenly Jerusalem, the universal Church, the individual soul, and the evangelical Word.[79] These interpretations were not especially original, but Eusebius' repeated emphasis and insistence on this matter indicates that here lay some of the central items in his own spirituality and theological system. These four levels of meaning encapsulated Eusebius' set of priorities and embodied his picture of the essence of the Christian life. Christianity was a religion in which individual souls received the Word ($\lambda\acute{o}\gamma o\varsigma$) of the Gospel drawn from scripture and obeyed the revelation of the *Logos*; they were thereby incorporated into a universal and worldwide community of people whose sights were set on heaven, not on this world. Christianity was a personal, rational, universal and spiritual affair.

Eusebius' conviction on this matter was buttressed by, perhaps even founded upon, his own distinctive understanding of two pivotal eras of biblical history. First, he derived the maximum possible breadth of meaning from the Fall of Jerusalem in AD 70. This had been an act of God, which to Eusebius revealed several vitally important points: not just God's judgement upon the Jews, nor just the end of Jerusalem's theological significance, but also a definitive statement from God that Christianity was not to become once again a religion bound by externals, tied to physical 'realia', and limited in location. Thus, despite his own historical interests, the sight of the ruined Temple sixty miles away in Aelia only

---

[79] For references, see below 9.3 at fn. 61 ff.

confirmed Eusebius in the theological conviction that the physical was no longer of any real value in the new covenant.

The other major confirmation that God intended Christianity to be a spiritual religion was to be found at the other end of the biblical narrative—in the pure faith of the Hebrew patriarchs. For many this might seem a strange place to turn; but for Eusebius this provided a powerful biblical support for his theology and gave a distinctive coherence to his system. Christianity, so Eusebius could claim, was essentially a rediscovery of that pure, joyful, and unaffected worship which once upon a time had been known to Abraham, Isaac and Jacob. This experience of unmediated proximity to God had unfortunately been brought to an end by Moses because of the hardness of Jewish hearts; but now the *Logos* had come to reinstitute this pristine and unsullied form of worship. Moreover, through the universal Church this direct and immediate access to God could now be experienced the world over. Thus

the religion of those blessed and godly men, who did not worship in any one place exclusively, neither by symbols nor types, but as our Lord and Saviour requires 'in spirit and in truth', by our Saviour's appearance became the possession of all the nations.[80]

This was a neat picture which, as has been noted, was Eusebius' own unique way of interpreting the biblical narrative. It served several purposes. Naturally it showed that Christianity, despite its apparent novelty, was the most ancient religion of all; the rug was effectively pulled out from under Jewish feet as Eusebius appropriated for the Church their most hallowed patriarchs of the faith. For our purposes, however, its chief value is that it explains the essential difference between Judaism and Christianity and lends support to Eusebius' definition of the new faith: Christianity unlike Judaism was essentially a spiritual religion, a personal response to God's revelation of himself, an encounter with God which was in no way bound by physical or other external phenomena. In both his apologetics and his spirituality Eusebius had thus committed himself to the essential irrelevance of all such physical phenomena.

Finally, we may note how this perhaps excessively 'spiritual'

[80] *Dem. Ev.*, 1.6.42 (*FPG*, i, 35). Jesus calls us to 'live according to the ideals of those of Abraham's day and men more ancient of pre-Mosaic date': see ibid., 1.6.64 (i, 40).

emphasis might well be seen by later Christians, including ourselves, as belonging to that earlier period through which Eusebius lived, an outlook which even in the fourth century might well have seemed conservative or even reactionary. His was simply the theological perspective of the third century not of the fourth, somewhat out of touch with the groundswell of Christian belief and practice. For the mood of the times would soon be changing. The Church of the fourth century would soon be preferring to re-establish its historical roots in the physical world, rather than maintain this emphasis on the 'spiritual'. Conceivably Eusebius' own historical interests marked the beginnings of that wider desire in the Church, but he himself was able to hold the two emphases in tension and to retain his commitment to the priority of the spiritual over the physical.[81] Others in later years might have neither the theological capacity nor the convinced motivation to retain that priority.

Christian identity may therefore have been changing in a way that left both Eusebius' apologetics and his spirituality rather 'high and dry'. In the new climate that would soon sweep across the Church, Christians began instead to reincorporate the physical dimension into the life of the Church. In so doing they might naturally appeal to one particular Christian doctrine that could be taken as the divine legitimation for a healthy interest in, and use of, the physical realm, and that would necessarily be involved in any development of a doctrine of 'holy places'. That doctrine was, of course, none other than that of the Incarnation. Consequently we must turn finally to a study of Eusebius' theological understanding of the Incarnation.

(c) *Eusebius' theology of the Incarnation*

The Origenian school of theology to which Eusebius was so committed had tended to focus on the exaltation of the *Logos* and to see this as the legitimation for their tendency to emphasize the

---

[81] A good example of this is Eusebius' lengthy speech at the dedication of the new Church at Tyre (*Hist. Eccl.*, 10.4.2–72). This naturally called him to evaluate theologically the significance of physical buildings. He is happy to describe the altar as the 'holy of holies' but in a spiritual sense, linking it to the 'soul of the common priest of all'. Yet the whole sermon reveals his priority of preaching and teaching about the heavenly city of God, about the spiritual Temple of 1 Pet. 2.5, and about Jesus the true high priest (see esp. *Hist. Eccl.*, 10.4.65, 68, 70).

spiritual realm to the cost of the physical. Later Christians would find that a different emphasis, focused on the Incarnation, was ideal for redressing the balance. The fourth century was a time when the Church, now more settled 'in the world', began to reaffirm the proper value of the temporal. Not surprisingly this would lead to a greater appreciation of the Incarnation in the Church's life and thought. If the Cross and the exaltation of Christ were always open to the danger of being interpreted in such a way as to cast a negative light upon the world, the Incarnation of Christ was the biblical principle *par excellence* that could effectively reverse that trend. The Incarnation, its potency now uncovered, could help the Church in a new and positive approach to the world at large and to its own place within it.

Further, the Incarnation could allow a new attitude to physical *matter*, the very stuff of the world. It could be used to affirm not just the goodness of this world-order, of creation and of humanity at a general level; it might also be used to inculcate a new approach to material objects and places, a new expectation that physical reality might in some way be important in the meeting between God and man. For in the Incarnation God had not only been entering this human world; he had also been using physical matter, and with no apparent disdain, in order to reveal his purposes and his presence among men and women. Surely therefore, it might be argued, Christians (of all people) could have a positive attitude towards the physical? Indeed could they not even see it as a means through which God might still wish to meet mankind?

Moreover, could not the Incarnation be used by Christians with some validity and without fear of inconsistency, to establish a distinctively Christian approach to Palestine, Jerusalem and the 'holy places', which was quite different from any former Jewish or pagan attitude? Eusebius might be concerned about the need for the Church to be distinctive in its religious practice from Judaism and paganism, but surely the Incarnation meant that a Christian approach to these physical entities could be founded on quite a different principle? In particular, was not speaking of 'holy places' only a respectful and natural way of affirming one's Christian faith in the Incarnation, that great divine event that had occurred in these few privileged places? For the Incarnation was, after all, a true legitimation of the physical realm and, of course, quite unique to Christianity.

Before looking at Eusebius' understanding of the Incarnation to see if he would have been prepared to employ the doctrine of the Incarnation in this way, it would be well to note that the New Testament writers do not themselves seem to have used the Incarnation for this purpose. If they believed that 'God was in Christ' (2 Cor. 5.19), that God in the person of his Son had been entering his world (cf. John 3.16 f.), that the eternal Word of God had 'become flesh and dwelt among us' (ibid. 1.14), this did not lead in their minds to theological investment in the places visited by Jesus; rather the Incarnation was the seal of God's identification with, and affirmation of, humanity as a whole.[82] Evidently the fact that God had 'become man' showed that physical matter was not inherently evil. The purpose of the Incarnation, however, was not that we might focus on such physical concerns, but rather that we might 'seek the things that are above, where Christ is'; 'set your minds', Paul counselled, 'on things that are above, not in things that are on the earth' (Col. 3.1 f.). The coming of Christ into the world seems therefore within the New Testament to have led to an increased love for the world that 'God so loved . . .' (John 3.16), and for the humanity whom Christ came to redeem, but not to any elevated understanding of the role of the physical within the life of faith. For our purposes it could be stated summarily that for the New Testament writers the Incarnation affirmed people, but not place; God was indeed identifying himself with humanity, but not with physical matter as such.[83]

The affirming significance of the Incarnation can thus, broadly speaking, be appreciated on two levels: the general, which concerns the 'world', humanity and humanness; and the more particular,

[82] See among other references, Gal. 4.4 f., Rom. 8.3 f.; Heb. 2.14–18, 4.15; 1 John 1.1–4.

[83] A full assessment of New Testament attitudes and principles which bear on this theme of 'holy places' would require a separate study. As yet the fullest treatment of this subject, though approached primarily with a concern for the wider question of the 'land', is W. D. Davies (1974), in which it is argued that the New Testament (with its overriding emphasis on the person of Jesus) rejected, spiritualized and indeed 'christified' holy space (see esp. 366–8); cf. also Cardman (1984), 49–51. Much of the debate would revolve around an interpretation of John's Gospel, which can be seen by some as an explicit encouragement of a more sacramental approach to the physical, e.g., R. Brown (1966) and Cullmann (1953), but by others as a sustained attack on all 'holy places' including the Temple (Davies, op. cit.) and an emphatic exposition of the exclusive role of the Holy Spirit as the one who alone now since the departure of Christ mediates to us the presence of Christ, cf. Dunn (1975), 350–357.

which concerns the physical and material constituents of the world. If the New Testament authors began to understand the Incarnation at the more general level, Cyril believed the Incarnation to have significant consequences at *both* levels, and that it was quite legitimate to apply the doctrine of the Incarnation in ways beyond that which had been developed by the New Testament writers.[84] Consequently Cyril had a strong sense not only of Christ incarnate as God's identification with humanity, but also a firm belief, as have many others since, that the Incarnation was the legitimation of a sacramental attitude towards matter, and especially towards those physical places and objects associated with the very scenes of Christ's incarnate life. The Incarnation for Cyril affirmed *both* people and place.

But what about Eusebius? Did he evaluate the purpose and significance of the Incarnation in the same way? Did he deduce from the incarnate life of Christ these two different forms of affirmation? Apparently not. His was a much weaker theological emphasis on the Incarnation, and as a result he appears not to have explored in any depth its possible corollaries. Concerning the question of Christ's incarnate identification with humanity, it has been correctly observed that, following the 'tendency of Alexandria', Eusebius did not especially stress Christ's 'humanity and sympathy with mankind'.[85] If this more general application of the Incarnation was indeed not very developed in his thinking, one wonders if the other, more particular application would be very prominent in his thought. Would Eusebius have been able or willing to use the doctrine of the Incarnation in such a way as to endorse a theology of 'holy places'? Moreover, would he see this use of the Incarnation as a legitimate *Christian* development? Eusebius the apologist had given little prominence to physical entities. Would Eusebius the theologian have the means and the desire to reintroduce them?[86]

Our answer to this question will only come as a surprise to those who have portrayed Eusebius as the great proponent of incarnational 'holy places'. But to those who (from our previous discussion) have sensed the quite different contours of Eusebius'

[84] See below 10.2.

[85] Foakes-Jackson (1933), 34.

[86] This section has a strictly limited purpose; strictly it is not Eusebius' 'theology' (with its tendency towards Arianism) that is under discussion, but rather his understanding of the Incarnation within the 'economy' of salvation.

thought, it will be no surprise at all to learn that the Incarnation did not itself play an especially important part in Eusebius' theology.

Eusebius' Origenian emphasis on the spiritual revelation of the *Logos* meant that he saw the Incarnation as but the most important of several such 'theophanies' (to Abraham, Jacob, Moses, and Joshua) that the *Logos* had bestowed on mankind; thus the Incarnation was not unique and certainly not to be made the single focal point of theology or devotion. Moreover, the purpose of this temporary phase in the activity of the eternal *Logos* was, as indicated, almost entirely a matter of revelation. The *Logos* took flesh, not so much in order to effect the work of redemption, as to reveal the spiritual truth about himself and God. Nor had he entered into our world in order to encourage us to seek God through the physical realm; on the contrary, this was but a temporary and passing act which was designed to reveal the normally invisible *Logos* and to lift our attention instead away from this world to the spiritual realm.

The Incarnation was not therefore a doctrinal category that Eusebius would be happy to itemize and make the central foundation of any theological system. It was but one aspect of the much more important doctrine of spiritual revelation. As a result, to Eusebius' way of thinking the Incarnation was quite different in its purpose from that which most advocates of 'holy places' would wish to ascribe to it; moreover, the Incarnation was not the unique and central doctrine that others would soon be claiming. In other words, both the purpose and the status of the Incarnation were quite diminished in Eusebius' theology. It will therefore be valuable to look briefly at both these aspects in turn in order that we may evaluate how little Eusebius would have been prepared to use the Incarnation to defend and foster the development of 'holy places' after 325.

The *Theophany* has rightly been called the 'distilled essence' of Eusebius' thought.[87] Thus, even though it was published shortly after 325,[88] it is fair to believe that, at least in its general outline, it is also a reliable reflection of Eusebius' thinking before that date. In this work, as its name suggests, Eusebius explains the work of

[87] Barnes (1981), 186.
[88] Hence it can also be used on certain more specific matters to show Eusebius' thinking in the first years *after* that pivotal date; see below 4.2.

the *Logos* using the model of 'theophany' or 'divine manifestation'. The Incarnation is thus from the outset considered against the backdrop of revelation.

The importance of that will be seen presently. First, however, we must note that on only one occasion during the first three books, which present his essential argument, does he intimate that one of the 'many causes' for this great act of 'divine manifestation' might have been the *human need* to perceive the divine through the medium of the physical realm.

How could the divine and intangible, the immaterial and invisible Being manifest himself to those who sought God in creatures and below the earth, who were unable and unwilling to contemplate the Creator and Maker of all things, than through a human shape and appearance? And certainly it was for those who prefer the perception of visible objects, who look for gods in statues and in carvings of inanimate images, who imagine the divine exists in matter and in flesh, . . . that the *Logos* of God also revealed himself in this way. So for this reason he himself prepared an all-holy temple, a physical instrument . . . preferable by far to all inanimate carvings. For a repesentation made out of inanimate matter . . . might be a suitable dwelling for demons. But the divine image . . . was the dwelling of the divine *Logos*, the holy temple of a holy God.[89]

Clearly then the Incarnation was designed amongst other things to help man to meet with an invisible God. God became knowable and visible in *human* terms. However, Eusebius is quick to point out that this was not the same as a divine revelation through mere physical matter: the *Logos* took a '*human* shape and appearance'. Moreover, the whole thrust of his argument is that this human need for sensing the divine in physical terms, imagining that the 'divine exists in matter', was a grave error of fallen man which the theophany of the *Logos* was expressly designed to bring to an end. The result of this manifestation was that men and women should be made ready

to draw near to the heavenly city which is above and to hasten to their fellow-citizens there; . . . also to know their Father who is in heaven and the excellency of their kind, which is of the essence that is intellectual and rational, teaching them that they should no more err.[90]

[89] *Theoph.*, 3.39, given here in the translation of the identical passage (*Sep. Chr.*, 14.1–3) found in *DPC*, 115.

[90] *Theoph.*, 3.39 (*LET*, 180).

This divine manifestation in a human instrument was therefore intended to put an end to all such erroneous devotion to the physical realm, not to be a new mandate for its continuance. The Incarnation was not to be taken as a divine affirmation of this need, but rather as a temporary condescension designed expressly to lift man from this fallen state. The 'all-holy temple' that had been the 'dwelling of the divine *Logos*' could alone be truly called 'holy'.

The theophany of the *Logos* was thus to Eusebius a temporary and exceptional event. Christians were not to seek in some way to prolong its benefits by using it as an endorsement of a continued sacramental approach to the physical. God's use of the physical realm to reveal himself in such a direct way had been quite exceptional and not the norm. The theophany of the *Logos* might indeed show that physical matter was not inherently evil, but it did not show that matter would always thereafter be a potential medium for divine revelation. If this explanation is correct, then this solitary passage (in which Eusebius assessed the purpose of the Incarnation more from the angle of human need) conforms well to Eusebius' theology as found elsewhere. For in general he seems to have disparaged such human desires for the physical.

The best example of this dismissive attitude is Eusebius' celebrated letter to to the emperor's sister, Constantia. When, a few years after 325, she requested Eusebius as bishop of the province of Palestine to provide her with an 'icon' of Christ, his response was quite heated and 'vitriolic'.[91] He refused her request, not because it was a practical impossibility, but because it was theologically and spiritually perverse. Constantia's devotional focus, he stated, was not to be on the incarnate Christ, during that time when he had assumed the 'form of a servant' (cf. Phil. 2.7), nor indeed on 'graven images'; rather she was to be fixing her attention on that divine and spiritual essence of the heavenly *Logos* which was only once revealed on earth—at the moment of the Transfiguration.[92] The Incarnation was exceptional; it was the heavenly Christ, the spiritual *Logos*, who was to be the constant object of a Christian's devotion.

Therefore, to Eusebius the purpose of the Incarnation was not

[91] Murray (1977), 335.
[92] *Ep. Const.*, 1545b-c; on the question of its authenticity, see Appendix.

to sacramentalize the physical but rather to inaugurate the renewed possibility of universal and spiritual worship through a manifestation of spiritual truth and of the divine *Logos*. Nor was it an endorsement of Jerusalem or Palestine; God's purpose, as already noted, had been precisely to break away from such particularity to the universal. Jerusalem was no longer important and Palestine had been but a necessary 'source'. If these had been God's purposes in the Incarnation, Christians had no right now to use that event for their own, rather different purposes. The Incarnation did not, and could not, affirm particular physical places.

It was therefore no coincidence that Eusebius' favourite word for describing the coming of Christ was not 'incarnation' (ἐνανθρώπησις) but 'theophany' (θεοφάνεια). This concept occurs far more frequently than does 'incarnation',[93] and in particular it was the very theme and title of this central work, the *Theophany*, which effectively summarized his entire theology.[94] Moreover, it seems from lexicographical studies that this concept was distinctively Eusebian, not used to any great extent by any other major theologian before or since.[95]

The chief reason for this preference for the 'theophany'-model should by now be quite clear: 'theophany', or 'divine manifestation', was a concept that, unlike our 'incarnation', emphasized God's activity of self-revelation. For if the Incarnation emphasizes the full residence of the divine person in a single human person,[96] 'theophany' speaks instead of a divine manifestation or revelation. The former term highlights a unique moment in human history when the divine and human/physical realms were somehow

---

[93] This would be confirmed if there were space for a detailed analysis of Eusebius' terminology for the 'Incarnation'. Our reading of his corpus indicates that ἐνανθρώπησις is used very rarely, whilst ἐπιφάνεια and θεοφάνεια and metaphors of illumination (such as ἐπιλάμψας) abound on almost every page. Naturally παρουσία is common but so too is ἐπιδημία, which emphasizes its merely temporary and passing nature. For a brief analysis of the terminology of Origen, which confirms this overall preference in the Caesarean school for a model of 'revelation', see Harl (1958), 205–9.

[94] Barnes (1981), 186.

[95] See *PGL*, 641 f.

[96] Though, of course, even between the Latin-derived 'incarnation' and the Greek ἐνανθρώπησις there is an important difference of perspective. The Latin word, no doubt reflecting the more particularized and physical mentality of the West, focuses on God being 'enfleshed', being involved with physical matter; the Greek mind, more fond of abstractions, focuses by contrast on God being 'en-personed', or being identified with humanity.

intertwined. The latter, however, focuses more on the purpose of that event, the manifestation of God; it leaves the precise means of that manifestation unspecified. The focus of the former is on the physical and human; the focus of the latter on the divine. Eusebius' distinctive fondness for this term had many advantages, but above all it reflected his conviction that the purpose of the Incarnation was primarily, almost exclusively, for the revelation of the spiritual realm. Eusebius was not strictly a theologian of the Incarnation at all; he was a theologian of theophany.

But surely the Incarnation might have had some other function than this mere revelation of the spiritual realm? In particular was it not also a necessary and effective part of redemption and of the history of *salvation*? Obviously Eusebius would never have denied this completely, but recently scholars have noted how this Eusebian emphasis on revelation almost totally eclipsed other aspects of the Incarnation, including these purposes of redemption and salvation. Thus one scholar has asserted that within Eusebius' system 'the *Logos* had the modest role of proclaiming His own existence and the oneness of God'.[97] Christ did not come so much to save mankind as to reveal to mankind spiritual truth. God's purpose in the Incarnation was the revelation of himself, not so much the salvation of humanity.

For Cyril, the salvific dimension was of central importance,[98] but for Eusebius it was more marginal. Man's greatest need was for illumination, not so much for salvation. Thus, as another scholar has observed, 'the saving purpose of the Incarnation had a very minor place in Eusebius' theology'.[99] The Incarnation thus became more expressive than effective. 'Christ's light has arisen', Eusebius would say in a typical passage in the *Theophany*, 'and has given illumination from the East even to the West by the bright rays of his doctrine'.[100] The historic event of the Incarnation was thus

---

[97] G. H. Williams (1951a), 12. The present section owes much to this two-part article in which he develops the observations made first by Opitz (1935) and Berkhof (1939) concerning Eusebius' emphasis on cosmology to the detriment of soteriology.

[98] See below 4.4.

[99] Pollard (1970), 169.

[100] *Theoph.*, 3.34 (*LET*, 172).

neatly eclipsed through this emphasis on revelation and illumination; it began to lose both its status as a separate theological
category and even its salvific purpose.[101]

As a result it could be concluded that the Incarnation was 'almost
totally evaporated' in Eusebius' theology by its 'assimilation to a
theory of general revelation'.[102] Eusebius' emphasis on revelation
so minimized the importance of salvation that it began to undermine
the very category of the Incarnation itself. For Eusebius, therefore,
the Incarnation did not have a central and unique function in
its own right. It was part, though naturally the greatest part, of
a wider phenomenon—the revelation of God to mankind. Precisely
because the purpose of the Incarnation was primarily revelation,
it could not be given a unique status within Eusebius' theology.

Thus we can appreciate that the spiritual and universal thrusts
already observed in Eusebius' thought were not in opposition to
his theology of the Incarnation; rather they were the paradoxical
result of that theology. Eusebius had processed the coming of
Christ theologically in such a way that these emphases on the
spiritual and universal, rather than on the physical and the
particular, were endorsed and legitimized. These emphases then
in their turn naturally prejudged the significance of the particular
and physical nature of the Incarnation. Any notion that the
Incarnation could be used to endorse the value for faith of particular
physical places or objects would have run counter to Eusebius'
whole understanding of its purpose. Eusebius emphasis on revelation and his use of the 'theophany'-model thus took attention
away both from the physical aspects of the Incarnation and also
from its importance in salvation. Its purpose was the revelation of
the spiritual. Yet it had one further corollary, already hinted at,
which will bear on our enquiry into 'holy places'.

Incarnational 'holy places' depend for their compelling power
on the unfathomable paradox that God once became man, that a
particular Palestinian place or locality 'witnessed' none other than
the Son of God. Yet it is the paradoxical nature of the Incarnation
that Eusebius deliberately attempts to play down. For God had
always been revealing himself to mankind, both before and since

---

[101] Compare the assessment of Daniélou (1963), 145, following Sirinelli (1961):
'le Verbe a essentiellement une fonction cosmologique. . . . Son rôle historique est
au contraire très réduit'.

[102] Pollard (1970), 128.

the Incarnation; 'theophany' was not a once-off event but God's continual activity towards men and women through the *Logos*. In particular there had been earlier theophanies of the *Logos* to various Hebrew sages, such as Abraham, Jacob, Moses, and Joshua. 'The Word of God . . . appeared to human eyes, to the pious men of Abraham's day, made in the form and likeness of man (ἐν ἀνθρώπου μορφῇ καὶ σχήματι)'.[103] Thus the appearance of the *Logos* in the first century was strictly a 'return': 'he appeared in human form long before to those with Abraham . . . and was predicted to appear *again* among men by human birth'.[104]

Although Eusebius was by no means the first Christian exegete to make this suggestion that the *Logos* had visited the earth before,[105] he gave it a quite special prominence in his theology. For it not only undergirded his arguments for the authentic antiquity of the Christian religion but also conveniently removed the sudden, 'irruptive and paradoxical aspects'[106] of an otherwise unique Incarnation. No doubt with the noble intention of making it more intelligible, Eusebius apparently wished to downplay the dramatic surprise of this event: the Incarnation was not to be thought of as a strange, surprising event, but rather as the climax of a continuing process of God's revelation to mankind. Thus its uniqueness was dissolved in the general, its suddenness in the eternal. It did not mark a new phase in God's dealings with humanity; it was but a clarification of the old.[107]

Eusebius thus sought to minimize the paradoxical particularity of the Incarnation. Yet this was precisely the source of the magnetic power of 'holy places' that drew the pilgrim's wonder and devotion. Paradox, colour and drama suffuse Cyril's thinking.[108] Eusebius' theophany-theology, however, led in quite the opposite direction;

---

[103] *Dem. Ev.*, 6.pref.1 (*FPG*, ii, 1); cf. also *Proph. Eclg.*, 1.3; *Hist. Eccl.*, 1.2.6–16; *Dem. Ev.*, 5.9–15, 19 (*FPG*, i, 252–63).

[104] *Dem. Ev.*, 5.pref.2 (*FPG*, i, 221, italics mine).

[105] It is seen especially in the work of Justin Martyr, well analysed by Trakatellis (1976).

[106] Williams (1951a), 18.

[107] Eusebius undermined the uniqueness of the Incarnation so effectively that he even came close to denying its necessity. 'There was no real need for an Incarnation, for all that Jesus Christ makes known was already known to the Patriarchs and Prophets'. 'It was little more than an appendix to the paedagogic work of the *Logos* throughout history' and 'only a passing phase in God's . . . providential care for men' (Pollard (1970), 294, 128).

[108] See below, e.g., 4.4–5.

it did not endorse the specialness of 'holy places', but, if anything, undermined them.

It may be noted in passing that Eusebius' dislike of the paradoxical and dramatic extends naturally to the Cross and Resurrection, a fact that inevitably coloured his subsequent understanding of the Holy Sepulchre. The Resurrection (for Eusebius) was not a dramatic or surprising event, but rather the revelation of our natural immortality, 'the prototype of that immortality and life with God that is our common hope'.[109] Although Eusebius could use atonement language of the Cross,[110] and sometimes saw it as a victorious struggle with demons,[111] he saw it chiefly as but a necessary prerequisite for the revelation of the Resurrection:[112] just as asbestos could only be proved in the fire, so too the immortality of the *Logos* could only be proved to us through a period of death.[113] The drama of the Resurrection was undercut by an emphasis on its inevitability and by seeing it as a picture of man's natural immortality. In Eusebius, therefore, the Resurrection eclipses the Cross in importance. Yet both the Resurrection and the Incarnation are eclipsed by Eusebius' yet greater emphasis on revelation or 'theophany'.

Our brief examination of Eusebius' attitudes towards the Incarnation, its purpose and consequences, has thus revealed some interesting factors. First, it has shown that Eusebius, unlike Cyril and later Christians, would not have been prepared to use the Incarnation as an endorsement of a more sacramental approach to the physical; God's whole purpose in the Incarnation was to lift man from such concerns to an understanding of the spiritual realm and the divine *Logos*. Secondly, it has revealed just how little the Incarnation meant to Eusebius as a separate theological category or doctrine; because of his prime concern with revelation, Eusebius was willing neither to give to the Incarnation a central place in his theology nor to acknowledge its necessary and effective role in salvation.

Our conclusions therefore endorse those made by other investigators into Eusebius' theology: Eusebius had 'little interest in

---

109 *Sep. Chr.*, 15.9 (*DPC*, 118); cf. the identical passage in *Theoph.*, 3.79.
110 Ibid., 3.59 (= *Sep. Chr.*, 15.11–12).
111 *Theoph.*, 3.55–7, omitted from *Sep. Chr.*.
112 *Theoph.*, 3.57–8, 60.
113 *Theoph.*, 3.60 (= *Sep. Chr.*, 15.6).

the Incarnation and none whatsoever in the Redemption'.[114] Indeed he 'robbed Bethlehem and Calvary of their primacy' and 'was unable to make either the Incarnation or the Crucifixion central in his theology'.[115] These may be attractive overstatements but they are nevertheless fair assessments of the kernel of Eusebius' theology. They are also, needless to say, surprising descriptions of the supposed proponent of incarnational 'holy places'.

Eusebius thus did not have ready to hand a strong doctrine of 'Incarnation' with which to justify Christian 'holy places' or indeed a 'Christian Jerusalem'. Instead, Eusebius' theophany-model of revelation diffused the significance of the Incarnation and emphasized precisely those spiritual and universal elements that were seen earlier to be so central to all his apologetics and spirituality. How well would Eusebius fare in 325 when for the first time Jerusalem and the places of Christ come to the fore within Christian thinking? His earlier theology was plainly not of the kind that could automatically encourage the development of 'holy places' and a Christian Jerusalem. On the contrary, his apologetics, his spirituality, and his theology all seem to have led in quite the opposite direction. Eusebius' theological system was impressive, but he was in for something of a shock.

---

[114] Pollard (1970), 295.
[115] Williams (1951a), 17.

4

THE AFTERMATH OF 325

Few dates are as pivotal as historians like to convey. However, the year of 324/5, which witnessed Constantine's victory over Licinius at Adrianople (September 324) and the Council of Nicaea (June/July 325) must on any reckoning be considered one of the major dates in world history. The East was given a 'Nova Roma', a Byzantium of a thousand years; the Eastern Church was given its first Christian emperor and its bishops experienced the first of seven oecumenical councils. The effect on Palestine, as already noted, was particularly dramatic. The land became a focus of Christian interest and the former pagan city in its midst became instead Christian Jerusalem, the scene of some elaborate churches and host to imperial visitors, churchmen and pilgrims. However prevalent Christian pilgrimage and interest in Jerusalem had been previously, and however surreptitiously there had been a desire for better things, these events must surely have been for all alike 'beyond all expectation'.[1]

Eusebius may indeed have been prophesying the eventual triumph of Christianity since before 300[2] and have been 'one of those rare writers who was to see the hopes of a lifetime fulfilled'.[3] His triumphalistic theology may indeed have prepared him for the phenomenon of a Christian emperor, such that he could assess the Constantinian event in terms quite consistent with his pre-Constantinian theology. But was he quite so well prepared, we might ask, for other aspects of this new era? In particular, if in his theology before 325 he had developed a largely negative attitude towards the significance of both Jerusalem and 'holy places', how well would he be able to accommodate the new interest in them which would emerge so strongly in the Christian world after 325?

---

[1] Eusebius' own words on the discovery of Christ's tomb in V. Const., 3.28.
[2] The central thesis of Barnes (1981).
[3] Frend (1971), 39.

1. EUSEBIUS' RESPONSE TO 325

The year 325 began for Eusebius in a most alarming way. Constantine's adviser, Hosius of Cordoba, in collaboration with other bishops meeting in Antioch in January 325, provisionally excommunicated Eusebius for his Arian sympathies.[4] This was to be ratified, they hoped, at the forthcoming great council of bishops in the presence of the emperor scheduled to take place in Ancyra in June. Since Ancyra was the see of Bishop Marcellus, the bishop whose views were so directly opposed to his, Eusebius could have had little doubt as to the likely result. At the very moment of the Constantinian triumph, at the very first oecumenical council of the Church and in the presence of so many fellow-bishops, Eusebius was likely to to suffer the appalling indignity of being excommunicated.

Fortunately, for reasons of convenience for the emperor, the venue was soon changed to Nicaea, an alteration that would be slightly to Eusebius' advantage. Nevertheless, Eusebius will have gone to that council very much 'under a cloud', 'with the stigma of condemnation upon him',[5] and presumably with much anxiety.

As it turned out, he emerged reinstated, but not unscathed.[6] Somehow he found himself able to sign in agreement with the Nicene formulations; as a result, his disgrace was formally revoked. Yet this act of signing evidently involved heart-searching[7] and, in the eyes of many, a 'sacrifice both of himself and of his friends'.[8] It was at the very least an 'outstanding volte-face'.[9] The whole affair, with its humiliation and awkwardness, can only have caused a personal scar quite deep and left his public reputation at its lowest ebb.

The opportunist activity of the bishop of Aelia/Jerusalem, Macarius, only deepened the wound. For, as already noted, this enterprising bishop took advantage of Eusebius' temporary censure to gain the ear of the emperor both for the removal of the Venus Temple and for an imperial recognition of his rightful honour as

---

[4] On this episode, see Chadwick (1960), 173–4.

[5] Stevenson (1929), 96.

[6] For a detailed discussion of Eusebius' action in this embarrassing episode, see Schwartz (1913), 136–40, Kelly (1972), 220–26 and Barnes (1981), ch. xii.

[7] As seen especially in his letter to his congregation in Caesarea (according to Soc., *Hist. Eccl.*, 1.8).

[8] Stevenson (1929), 103.

[9] Chadwick (1960), 173.

bishop of Christianity's founding city. In matters Arian and Palestinian Eusebius was thus caught firmly on the wrong foot. He was evidently not so well prepared after all.

It is hard for us to imagine how exactly Eusebius would have felt in the light of these painful events. Here was a man who as a writer 'towered above his opponents' and indeed above all his contemporaries, yet who as bishop before the eyes of the whole Church had 'ironically faced censure and the threat of oblivion';[10] a man who for a few months had had ample reason for fearing that all his historical, apologetic and theological experience would count for nothing and that his vast learning would be judged of no value or importance.

Of this, however, we can be certain: the whole episode would have had at least the following two effects. As Eusebius began the task of recovery, he would be propelled, first, into a spate of new activity. His prolific literary output in the final fourteen years of his life has already been noted; so too the forceful and leading role that he played in ecclesiastical politics. But perhaps only now can we appreciate the motivation for all this activity: Eusebius' reputation was at stake and he had much ground to recover. Secondly, and of particular relevance to our own enquiry, his thinking would naturally be propelled in a more conservative direction. A man whose great learning had temporarily been denigrated would not rebuild his reputation by abandoning or jettisoning the past. On the contrary, he would try to defend that past experience in order to show its great merits, and to demonstrate its vital contemporary relevance. Even without this humiliating episode at Nicaea, we would have fully expected this elderly Church historian to be conservative in his theological approach to the new era. After all, he was not young. 'It would be little short of a miracle that a man of sixty-five, justly regarded as the most learned man of his age, should have abandoned all the convictions and, one may add, the prejudices of a lifetime.'[11] He would be eager to demonstrate not only the consistency of his own thought but also the continuity of practice within the Church. This conservative tendency, however, would only have been

---

[10] Frend (1984), 479.

[11] Foakes-Jackson (1933), 133; on Eusebius' conservatism in other theological matters, see, e.g., Swete (1912), 194 and especially Pollard (1970), 170: 'Eusebius takes refuge in archaism'.

strengthened as Eusebius began to salvage his theological reputation after Nicaea.

Moreover, his unequalled knowledge of earlier Church history and his awareness of Christian identity in the pre-Constantinian era would also naturally have led him in a theologically conservative direction; for he would inevitably have tried to ensure that any new identity for the Christian Church, forged amidst all the euphoria of the new era, was not glaringly inconsistent with its past. His whole purpose in compiling the *Ecclesiastical History* seems therefore to derive from his desire for continuity and consistency in the Church. 'Standing between two epochs, in the Church as well as in world history, he responded by attempting to organise and preserve what had been, and to eternalise important aspects of the previous period of history which might otherwise be lost.'[12]

Naturally the situation after 325 in the worldwide Church and in Palestine in particular was redolent of new possibilities; but Eusebius would be applying himself diligently to the perennial task of any conservative theologian: applying old truths to new situations. He would not, on the one hand, be inventing new ideas that lacked any real precedent in the thinking of the Church. His great knowledge of the past (which he would be anxious not to pass unnoticed) would give him the opportunity to think wisely but also the responsibility to act consistently; not surprisingly, therefore, it has been observed that his 'vast learning' caused him often to be 'restrained in his enthusiasm' for anything that was especially novel.[13] Nor, on the other hand, would he be forging a new theology which could be construed as a novel departure from his own established thinking. Visible inconsistency at any time is something to be avoided; it would certainly be avoided at all costs by the elderly Church historian in the wake of Nicaea.

The relevance of this to our enquiry concerning Eusebius' attitude towards Jerusalem and the 'holy places' should be apparent. Influenced by his spirituality, his apologetics, his theology, and his ecclesiastical position, Eusebius' thinking on these questions in the years before 325 has been shown to be largely negative. Many today might argue, perhaps correctly, that this negative stance only

---

[12] Levine (1975a), 127.
[13] Foakes-Jackson (1933), 43.

reveals how little prepared he was for the sudden events of 325. However, some might legitimately expect a radically different picture after 325: Eusebius responding to the new situation and gradually abandoning his earlier negative thinking. Our discussion above now suggests that this is most unlikely to have been the case.

Eusebius' frequent apologetic statements, for example, defining the nature of Christian identity, could not easily be dismissed as confessed pretence or ignorance. His theophany-theology could not easily be replaced by a new emphasis on the Incarnation. His spiritualizing tendency could not easily give way to an elevation of the physical. For Eusebius' theological system pre-325 was a coherent whole of which he might justly be proud. It is never an easy thing to change course in mid-stream; for Eusebius such a change would have been not only extremely difficult but also an admission of defeat.

Customarily it has been assumed that Eusebius' attitude to Constantine provides ample evidence of just such a change of direction. Does not Eusebius' eulogistic praise of Constantine show his naïve love of the novel, his easy abandonment of his former thinking? However, the recent studies by Barnes and Drake only confirm what becomes apparent from a less casual reading of the evidence: namely that Eusebius was able, on the one hand, to accept Constantine into his theological system without too much difficulty precisely because that system had for a long time been presuming the eventual triumph of Christianity;[14] and on the other hand, to resist a naïve endorsement of Constantine's views by careful wording and strategic silences, steering the Constantinian regime in ways more acceptable to his own theology.[15] Eusebius, therefore, was evidently not someone who would easily surrender his lifelong convictions; on the contrary, he fought hard to preserve them.

He was wrestling not only with the Constantinian question; there were also the Arian and Palestinian questions. It is quite reasonable to expect that Eusebius would respond in a similar fashion to all three. This in fact proves to be the case. In each he showed his natural tenacity to the essentials of his earlier position.

[14] Barnes (1981).
[15] Drake (1976), *passim*; see further below 4.3(*b*).

The new situations might indeed naturally demand a re-assessment of his thinking; that re-assessment, however, even if it allowed for certain modifications and encouraged certain clarifications (which need to be noted), only reinforced his earlier essential convictions. As a result, Eusebius' attitudes to Jerusalem and the places of Christ after 325 can be expected to be little different from those which he held before that important date.

On each of these three issues Eusebius betrays a similar method of dealing with divergent opinions, most notably by using carefully chosen words and being strategic in his omissions. The linguistic subtlety which Eusebius employed when he delivered his tri- cennalian speeches before Constantine has been brought to light by Drake only recently; but it has long been noted how Eusebius was similarly careful in the *Life of Constantine*, preserving, for example, a tactful silence concerning his own involvement in the Arian controversy.[16] As a result, one scholar has gone so far as to conclude that students of Eusebius 'must consider what Eusebius omits as carefully as what he includes'.[17] Silences in Eusebius are thus common and frequently significant. Eusebius was perhaps a sensitive man and his convictions, though strong, may therefore be expected to be seen in more subtle ways. It will be our task to detect his subtlety of method but, yet more importantly, to discern those strong convictions that were its cause.

2. PALESTINE SOON AFTER 325: THE *THEOPHANY*

How then did Eusebius respond to the new questions raised in Palestine as a result of 325? What were his initial reactions on the subjects of Jerusalem and the 'holy places'? Was he indeed aware of these questions and concerned in some way to answer them? Any doubts concerning Eusebius' awareness or concern are immediately

[16] Little idea is given in the *V. Const.* of the real purpose of the Council at Nicaea, and nowhere in that work does Eusebius mention Athanasius. The council was 'not a pleasant subject; hence Eusebius laid low and said nothing' (Stevenson (1929), 106; see also Barnes (1981), 269–70, who had previously noted (p. 149) Eusebius' silence concerning his own imprisonment in AD 312 and his omission of people he disliked from his revised *Hist. Eccl.* (p. 193).

[17] Thus Levine (1975a), 134, on the far more neutral subject of Caesarea and its Christian community. For a less charitable assessment of Eusebius' 'notorious distortions and falsehoods', see, e.g., Cameron (1983), 85–6.

dispelled upon examination of the *Theophany*. This important book which was evidently composed not long after the discovery of Christ's tomb,[18] seems to have been prompted by Eusebius' painful experience at Nicaea. For in its first three books Eusebius effectively popularized the central tenets of his theology, revealing in the process his great wealth of accumulated wisdom. Moreover, it also brought to the reading public's attention Eusebius' emphasis on 'theophany', revealing how, within the context of this theophany-model, his suspected theology was, he claimed, quite orthodox. Eusebius' past learning was not to be dismissed, nor the soundness of his theology to be disputed.

For our purposes, however, it will be the fourth book of the *Theophany* that will be most intriguing. For here Eusebius set out his latest thinking on matters Palestinian, speaking in his capacities as an apologist, theologian and local metropolitan bishop. Eusebius was evidently well aware of the issues, and actively concerned.

In this book Eusebius chose to analyse afresh all the prophecies of Jesus in order to show their fulfilment both in Palestine and in the world. This choice of subject matter was hardly coincidental; it enabled him to make some important preliminary points concerning the Palestinian question. First, it inevitably focused the reader's attention on the *whole* of Palestine, the historic scene of the Gospels. Yet it did so in such a way as to preserve Eusebius' characteristic emphasis on the importance of the spoken words of Jesus and also on the fulfilment of his prophecies at a universal level in the worldwide Church; thus if people were looking for some kind of 'hard' proof in the physical realm with which to bolster their faith in Christ, Eusebius offered them not particular places in Palestine but Jesus' prophecies fulfilled in the world. Furthermore, the prophetic words of Christ in the first century were also for Eusebius the natural starting point for any Christian assessment of the city of Jerusalem in the fourth; this was the biblical material that was of central importance in any quest to establish the precise theological status of Jerusalem in the present.

Evidently these local questions, on the role of Jerusalem in the purposes of God and the role of physical places in the life of faith, were very much on his mind. Moreover, Eusebius could not avoid

[18] Referred to in *Theoph.*, 3.61 (*LET*, 199).

referring to the local, ecclesiastical tension between the sees of
Jerusalem and Caesarea. As a result, one clearly senses that the
whole book is breathing the atmosphere of those first years after
the Peace of the Church and the Council of Nicaea.

(a) Jerusalem

With the arrival of Constantine, Christians gained many new
privileges but also important responsibilities. The opportunity to
'possess' Jerusalem was both: it was certainly a privilege, full of
exciting potential, but it was also an awesome responsibility. They
needed to deal with it, if possible, in a way that was not only
politically expedient but also theologically correct, in keeping with
the essence of their faith. A theologian, such as Eusebius, would
thus be concerned to discern what aspects of imperial policy the
Christian faith could endorse. The imperial will was powerful, but
the divine will was more important. How then were Christians to
deal with this important item in accordance with God's will? Was
the city still under judgement? At the other extreme, Could
Christians reintroduce the concept of a 'holy city'? And what, more
practically, was to be done with the Temple?

These were all vital questions after 325. It is, therefore no
coincidence that in his first work to be published after that date
Eusebius chose to examine in detail the prophetic words of Jesus
on the subject.[19] What had the Lord himself prophesied for the
Jerusalem of the future? This was the vital question that Christians
with their new responsibilities and powers in Jerusalem urgently
needed to have answered.

This concern of Eusebius' contemporaries—to be guided in their
action through a correct understanding of Jesus' words—comes
over quite clearly in the pages of the *Theophany*. One of Jesus'
most memorable statements, for example, had concerned the
Temple: 'not one stone', he claimed, would be 'left one upon
another' (Luke 19.44).[20] The Temple platform, however, still
survived. Evidently some Christians were therefore asking if this
meant that this prophecy of Jesus was still awaiting its fulfilment.
Eusebius attempted to deal with this contemporary enquiry by

[19] *Theoph.*, 4.18–22, discussed fully below in 11.5.
[20] Discussed in *Theoph.*, 4.18 (*LET*, 247–8).

Eusebius attempted to deal with this contemporary enquiry by affirming that this prophecy only referred to that portion of the Temple to which the disciples had actually pointed, not to the whole of it. However, if it *did* refer to the whole Temple, then Eusebius assured his readers that the prophecy was now in process of being fulfilled: natural decay, empowered by the Word of God, was seeing to that. Either way, however, it may be noted that Eusebius was clearly anxious to dissuade Christians from lending the Almighty a helping hand in the demolition process!

In the light of these pressing contemporary questions Eusebius thus discussed these and other dominical prophecies which related to the Temple and Jerusalem in quite some detail. Eusebius became convinced that Christians needed to make a sharp distinction between the Temple and the city. Jesus' words, at least according to Eusebius' understanding, suggested that God's eternal judgement rested solely on the Temple and not upon the city; the Temple was to be left completely desolate ('your house is forsaken and desolate', Matt. 23.38) but the city could legitimately be inhabited by Gentiles ('Jerusalem will be trodden down by the Gentiles', Luke 21.24).

As a result, Eusebius' message to the Jews was clear and uncompromising; their expulsion from the city of Jerusalem was a divine punishment which they were to endure indefinitely.[21] Christians, on the other hand, armed with such divine assurances, were supposed to have no qualms about inhabiting the city, so long as they ensured the continued desolation of the Temple. Nevertheless, since Jesus still condemned both the Temple *and* the city, Eusebius believed that there was no way in which Christians could now begin to reintroduce the idea that 'Jerusalem' had some special theological significance. As if to make this quite clear, Eusebius then referred to the city by its pagan name, 'Aelia'—a perjorative term which neatly denied the surviving city any Christian theological significance it might have as 'Jerusalem'.[22]

Eusebius followed this a few chapters later with an extended discussion of John 4.21-4, a passage so vital for Christians assessing the role of Jerusalem (and indeed of the 'holy places'). Jesus had prophesied the destruction of the Temple and Mt. Gerizim but

---

[16] Little idea is given in the V. *Const.* of the real purpose of the Council at Nicaea, and nowhere in that work does Eusebius mention Athanasius. The council was 'not a pleasant subject; hence Eusebius laid low and said nothing' (Stevenson

no more on any mount, nor in any distinct corner of the earth, but throughout the whole creation should 'true worshippers' worship.[23]

It has already been noted how Eusebius used this concept of the 'corner' to parody any ascription of religious significance to Jerusalem or Palestine. In this passage, however, he did not imply that such thinking was limited only to the Jews; he clearly saw that Jesus' words had a wider application. Was he perhaps suggesting that Christians were now themselves in danger of making just such a retrogressive step? In the light of Jesus' clear statements (and indeed of the whole spiritual nature of Christian worship) Jerusalem could not be made special again.

This neutral position on Jerusalem's significance, which cleared the city of judgement but which denied any more positive affirmation, was naturally influenced by his own ecclesiastical position as bishop of Caesarea and by that awkward interchange with Bishop Macarius at the recent council of Nicaea. This Caesarean ecclesiastical perspective becomes plain on several occasions in the fourth book of the *Theophany*.

For example, when discussing Jesus' words to the woman at Shechem, Eusebius described Neapolis (the Roman city subsequently founded near Shechem) from his position in Caesarea as 'our neighbouring city'.[24] The author wished his readers to know that he spoke from Caesarea, not Jerusalem, and to sense the proximity and importance of Caesarea.

On another, earlier, occasion Eusebius' ecclesiastical concerns as metropolitan were more explicit. The episode of Peter's first calling gave Eusebius the perfect excuse to list those Churches which this mere fisherman had subsequently founded. Caesarea heads this list, followed by Rome, Antioch and Alexandria.[25] This was not, we may presume, a forlorn attempt on the part of Eusebius to give the contemporary Caesarean Church a status equal to these three future patriarchates. In the light of the recent seventh canon of Nicaea it was, however, a robust declaration of Caesarea's scriptural claim to apostolic status.

This tension between Caesarea and Jerusalem can perhaps be sensed in two further ways. First, it most probably provided an extra

[23] Theoph., 4.23 (*LET*, 258).
[24] Ibid., 4.23 ('der uns benachbarten Stadt' in the German translation in GCS, iii.2, 200.12).
[25] Ibid., 4.7.

personal motivation for that reference in Eusebius to Jerusalem as 'Aelia'.[26] Secondly, it may well explain his failure to mention the Jerusalem Church as a contemporary phenomenon. He had needed to talk of James, the Lord's brother,[27] and of the early community in Jerusalem as the prime example of the coexistence of Jewish and Gentile believers;[28] but he never indicated that an important Church was still present in the city, a Church which claimed continuous episcopal succession from the time of James. In the earlier *Ecclesiastical History* the Jerusalem Church had frequently been in his thoughts[29] and its episcopal lists constantly interwoven with those of Rome, Antioch and Alexandria.[30] Significantly, however, Caesarea now took Jerusalem's place.

There were thus personal and ecclesiastical considerations, not totally concealed, that influenced Eusebius' attitude towards Jerusalem and which may have coloured his interpretation of Jesus' words. Eusebius naturally had every reason for not wishing to emphasize Jerusalem.

He also had good reason for promoting instead a wider emphasis on Palestine as a whole. If this more comprehensive perspective was also part of his purpose in writing book four of the *Theophany*, then again his choice of subject matter was amply suited. Jerusalem was the subject of only some of the dominical sayings used; the rest were located elsewhere, in Galilee and in such places as Capernaum[31] and Bethany.[32] Eusebius could thereby convey this wider perspective and the historical value of the whole of Palestine. It was not that Palestine could claim any special theological status as a result of Christ's former presence, for it was in this same book that Eusebius would refer to the area of Christ's first coming as but a 'corner' of the world.[33] Yet it clearly was a of great *historical* significance. It would thus be no surprise if in the future Eusebius were to deny that Jerusalem was a 'holy city', while promoting the whole of Palestine as the historic source of the Gospel message.

An examination of the *Theophany* thus helps us to detect

---

26 Ibid., 4.20, discussed more fully below in 11.5.
27 Ibid., 4.17.
28 Ibid., 4.24.
29 See, e.g., *Hist. Eccl.*, 4.5.3–5; 5.12.1–2; 7.19.
30 See, e.g., ibid., 5.2.2; 5.23.3; 7.14; 7.32.29.
31 *Theoph.*, 4.7 (*LET*, 221).
32 Ibid., 4.10 (228).
33 Ibid., 4.35 (280).

Eusebius' attitudes to Jerusalem (and Palestine) soon after 325. Although his attitudes required further clarification in the years before his death, the essential outline of his thought is quite clear: for scriptural, ecclesiastical and other reasons, Jerusalem was not to be given any new theological status. Eusebius found himself in a new situation with new responsibilities, but his thinking remained manifestly constant.

(b) 'Holy places'

Eusebius' approach in the *Theophany* to 'holy places' as such is a little more difficult to determine. Naturally it is highly significant that the first three books of this work, as indeed its title suggests, were devoted to a presentation of Christ's coming in terms of the theophany-model. At the end of his life he would rework these three books for his speech *On Christ's Sepulchre*, and we shall note shortly in our discussion of that speech how his emphasis on 'theophany' rather than 'incarnation' would militate against any strong understanding of 'holy places'.[34]

However, the last part of the *Theophany*, with its more historical emphasis on the Christ of the Gospels, provides us with some clues of a different kind. Some are positive, suggesting a new appreciation in Eusebius of the value of such places for Christians; others are more negative, calling into question such an appreciation.

On the positive side can be noted Eusebius' one reference to what could be seen in his own day of a Gospel site in contemporary Palestine. Not surprisingly its subject is the recently discovered tomb of Christ:

> it is marvellous to see even this rock, standing out erect and alone in a level land, and having only one cavern in it; lest, had there been many, the miracle of Him who overcame death should be obscured.[35]

Eusebius clearly had a sense of wonder as he looked on this important tomb. Yet what moved him most was not its preservation, nor indeed its unique and tangible involvement in the foundational event of the Christian faith, but the fact that it was not surrounded by other tombs and in itself consisted of only one 'cave', a fact

---

[34] See below 4.3(*b*).
[35] *Theoph.*, 3.61 (*LET*, 199); see further below 8.4.

that somehow for Eusebius neatly portrayed the uniqueness of the Resurrection!

Perhaps of greater significance for noting a more positive approach in Eusebius to 'holy places', is his failure in the *Theophany* to attack the use of 'specific places' (ἀφωρισμένοις τόποις) for worship in that discussion of John 4.21-4.[36] Before 325, in the admittedly longer treatment of these verses in the *Proof of the Gospel*, the use of such 'specific places' had been expressly deemed incompatible with Christian 'spiritual worship'.[37] We wondered in our previous discussion of this passage (p. 73) how far Eusebius would have wished to press this point; in particular, was he in danger of decrying the use even of particular church buildings? After some further thought, and writing in a less apologetic context, Eusebius seems to have become aware of this inconsistency. For now Jesus' words are related more expressly to worship in Jerusalem; Jesus was setting his followers free only from *that* particular restriction on the location of worship.

Perhaps then this was a slight concession, an acknowledgement that, even if Jerusalem could not be special to Christians, then at least particular *sites* could be, whether they be historic sites connected with the life of Jesus or simply Christian church buildings. If this is so, it marks the start of a tendency, seen more clearly in Eusebius' later writings, whereby he would come to accept in some form the concept of a 'holy place' but not that of a 'holy city'.

On the negative side, however, it is clear from his several references to other Gospel sites in book four of the *Theophany* that Eusebius at this stage still stopped short of thinking of these sites as 'holy places'. He refers to Bethany, to Capernaum and to Galilee but with no apparent interest in the contemporary existence of these places.[38] His own interests at this juncture were still exegetical and historical. Particular places were but the backdrop for the biblical events; their significance was merely that of historical association, nothing more.

If contemporaries had suggested that these places could act as a visible witness to the truth of the biblical narrative, Eusebius would not have denied it but would have replied that the fulfilment of Jesus' prophecies in the vibrant life of the now worldwide

[36] Ibid., 4.23 (257-8).
[37] *Dem. Ev.*, 1.6.40 (*FPG*, i, 41).
[38] *Theoph.*, 4.10 (*LET*, 229), 4.7 (221).

Church was a far more visible and powerful witness. Throughout this fourth book Eusebius consistently emphasizes the universal Church and stresses that the spread of the Gospel to the ends of the world is the most visible fulfilment and vindication of Jesus' words.

By doing this Eusebius not only exposed that universal thrust which was so characteristic of his theology, but also subtly corrected the desires of would-be pilgrims, those who had to content themselves with pilgrimage instead of an encounter with Jesus. He begins this book with a sustained attack on such wistful thinking. Yes, Eusebius admits, those 'men who happened to exist at that time' (in the days of Jesus) were able to see 'those great acts' and the 'evident powers of God' which Eusebius' generation could not. However, by way of compensation, there were things that 'are now visible to our own eyes' which had been spoken by Jesus 'in only the hearing of our predecessors'.[39] Eusebius' generation had the advantage of hindsight. Such advantages might be dismissed by the pilgrim, who sought more concrete witnesses, but for Eusebius the academic theologian they were vitally important.

Eusebius thus continued to set his sights on the spiritual and universal aspects of the faith; meanwhile he caricatured human religious interest in the physical (especially pagan interest in 'temples, images, and holy places') as a ridiculous enterprise, comparable to seeking for the sun 'in mud and muck'.[40] The pilgrim might desire to see the places of Jesus 'in the flesh'; Eusebius pointed instead to the prophecies of Jesus in their fulfilment. The words and deeds of Christ were more important than their original locations. Once again, even though the times were changing, Eusebius remained remarkably consistent.

3. THE FINAL EUSEBIUS

The celebrations which marked Constantine's thirtieth year as emperor in 335/6 found Eusebius in a quite different position from that which he he had known ten years earlier, when Constantine was celebrating his twentieth year. In 325 Eusebius had only just

[39] Ibid., 4.1 (210).
[40] Ibid., 2.52 (in the translation of the identical *Sep. Chr.*, 13.6 in *DPC*, 112).

been exonerated and spared excommunication; in 335/6 by any account he played a leading role in the celebrations.

It was during that year that Eusebius delivered before Constantine his two speeches *On Christ's Sepulchre* and *In Praise of Constantine*; he probably also started work on the emperor's *Life*. What do we learn from these works (and from his last two commentaries, on Isaiah and the Psalms) of Eusebius' final attitudes to Jerusalem and the 'holy places'?

(a) Jerusalem

His attitude towards Jerusalem changed little. Eusebius never gave to 'Jerusalem' as a city any special status, whether in imperial, ecclesiastical or theological terms. Eusebius did not use it as a political symbol of the new empire; he did not comment on it being the birthplace of the Church. Jerusalem, for Christians as opposed to Jews, was not a 'mother city' ecclesiologically or theologically. Eusebius emphatically denied that Jerusalem was a 'holy city'. Thus, when St Matthew used this phrase in his Passion narrative, he could not possibly have been referring to the physical Jerusalem on earth; the 'holy city' was 'clearly the holy city of God, the heavenly one' (τὴν ἁγίαν πόλιν του θεοῦ δηλαδὴ τὴν ἐπουράνιον).[41]

Though Eusebius' restrained, indeed negative, approach to Jerusalem was based on sincere theological convictions, the tense relations between Caesarea and Jerusalem would also naturally have influenced his thought. This tension most probably explains his continued silence concerning the Church in Jerusalem. Only once (when he needed to include Constantine's important letter to Bishop Macarius after the discovery of Christ's tomb) does he break a silence that had already lasted twenty-five years.[42] Thus we hear nothing of the prestigious history of the Jerusalem Church and nothing more about that intriguing throne of St James; nor does he mention Mt. Sion, the traditional place for commemorating Pentecost, since this was also the traditional centre of the Jerusalem

[41] Matt. 27.53 in *Comm. in Ps.* [87.11–13], 1064b; discussed fully below in 11.2.
[42] *V. Const.*, 3.29–32; cf. above 3.1(a). Moreover, Rubin (1982a), 87–91, suggests that Eusebius deliberately placed his account of the 'Mamre-affair' (*V. Const.*, 3.51–3) *after* this letter in order to cast Bishop Macarius once more in a bad light: see further below 8.5.

Church. Relations between Caesarea and Jerusalem were evidently no better. As a result, Eusebius' attitudes to Jerusalem were unlikely to be much more positive that they had been at any time in the past.

This ecclesiastical tension would also mean that he would be seeking to promote a broader perspective and to emphasize the historical significance of Palestine as a whole, rather than of Jerusalem. Eusebius stressed that it was this 'venerable *land*' which had been the object of Helena's journey.[43]

Yet more pointedly, Eusebius changed his mind over the historical 'source' of the Gospel. Around 315 he had been happy to expound Zechariah 14.8 ('on that day living waters shall flow out from Jerusalem') to show how Jerusalem was the 'source' of the saving message;[44] twenty years later he used this imagery again but stressed that the whole of Palestine, not just Jerusalem, was the 'source of the life-giving stream to all'.[45] Jerusalem could not now claim that it had some greater significance than had Palestine as a whole: both were but the historical setting for the biblical events.

Eusebius' estimate of Jerusalem had thus by no means increased. If anything indeed, it had lost ground in the face of that new sense of pride which Eusebius felt towards the whole of his province. Palestine, not Jerusalem, was the source of Christ's Gospel and the focus of Eusebius' pride.

(b) 'Holy places'

On the question of 'holy places', however, it is possible to detect an observable, even if small, development in Eusebius' thinking. He was evidently increasingly enthusiastic, as was only natural, about the discovery of Christ's tomb and the building of several new churches in Palestine; so much so that by the end of his long life he would find himself just beginning to refer to some of these places as 'holy'. Yet it will be appreciated in the following that his understanding of this term was still quite different from that of either Constantine or Cyril.

Eusebius may have been cool in his attitude towards Jerusalem

[43] *V. Const.*, 3.42.1 (NPNF, i, 530; italics mine).
[44] *Dem. Ev.*, 6.18.50, 10.7.7 (*FPG*, ii, 36, 215).
[45] *L. Const.*, 9.15; *Sep. Chr.*, 11.2. This point was first noted by Rubin (1982a), 95; cf. also Groh (1983), 28.

as a whole; but this did not mean that he felt constrained to be similarly cool towards the church of the Holy Sepulchre. This clear distinction in his thought between the part and the whole, the individual 'holy place' and the 'holy city' is epitomized neatly in his commentary on LXX Ps. 87 [88]. It was here that he had given one of his clearest pronouncements, denying that the physical Jerusalem was a 'holy city'. Yet just a few sentences earlier he had expressly commented on the wonderful buildings now being erected around Christ's tomb; for these contemporary 'wonders' were, according to Eusebius, God's answer to the despairing question of the psalmist (speaking prophetically for Christ), 'shall thy wonders . . . be declared in the grave?'[46] The contemporary city of Jerusalem might not be 'holy' but the church of the Holy Sepulchre within it was none the less a legitimate object of 'wonder'.

This distinction between the whole city and the particular church needs especially to be borne in mind when interpreting Eusebius' fanciful reference in the *Life of Constantine* to the 'new Jerusalem'.[47] Whatever is to be made of this uncharacteristic suggestion,[48] its location between Constantine's letter giving instructions for the building of the Holy Sepulchre and Eusebius' own description of that basilica clearly indicates that Eusebius was referring only to this church, not to the wider city. Once again the focus of Eusebius' warm affirmation and approval was this single location, not the city as a whole.

For our purposes perhaps the most important passage in Eusebius is his enthusiastic description a few chapters earlier in the *Life of Constantine* of the exciting first discovery of the tomb; for it is here that Eusebius speaks for the first and only time of a Christian 'holy place'. The excavations suddenly brought to light the 'venerable and hallowed monument' of Christ's Resurrection, that

---

[46] *Comm. in Ps.* [87.11–13], 1064a.

[47] *V. Const.*, 3.33.

[48] To earlier commentators this was an 'extraordinary, nay, almost ludicrous application of Scripture' (see NPNF, i, 529, fn. 1). However the force of this charge is lessened if Eusebius was referring only to the church; his meaning must therefore have been more subtle. Furthermore, since he did not accept fully the canonicity of Revelation (see *Hist. Eccl.*, 3.25.4), he must have been referring to the less eschatological passages of Isa. 60 ff.. Eusebius was evidently quite tentative in offering this suggestion (hence his use of τάχα που) and was probably attempting to use this building simply as a symbol of the universal reign of Christ on earth, now being realised under Constantine's rule.

'most holy cave' (τὸ σεμνὸν καὶ πανάγιον μαρτύριον . . . τὸ ἅγιον τῶν ἁγίων ἄντρον).[49] In the drama of this emotional event, Eusebius struggled to find adequate words and was forced into new pastures. Twenty years earlier, when describing another new church (the church at Tyre), Eusebius had used the Old Testament motif of the 'holy of holies' in a highly symbolic manner;[50] now he meant something more. This was a 'holy place' of a quite different kind. In the light of his earlier theology his understanding of what was meant by this term may have been set about with certain qualifications; nevertheless, the aged Eusebius had clearly concluded that, even if Christians could not refer to Jerusalem as a 'holy city', they could legitimately refer in some sense to the places of Christ as 'holy places'. There was indeed something different, even if hard to explain, about 'worship at the place whereon his feet have stood'.[51]

Meanwhile this interest of Eusebius in such particular places extended to the churches built over the 'mystic caves' at Bethlehem and on the Mount of Olives.[52] These formed in his mind an effective 'Triad'.[53] Bethlehem and the Mount of Olives had been the two places of Christian interest in Palestine that Eusebius had especially highlighted in the years before the coming of Constantine.[54] Now, however, the underground nature of that former devotion could be crowned with imperial vindication; the pre-Constantinian past could be brought consistently but gloriously into the present. As a result, the Triad consumed almost all of Eusebius' attention in his final years.[55] It reflected his own theological and historical perspectives, and promoted both to the visiting pilgrims and to the empire at large.

In the face of these sudden events there was therefore both continuity and change. Aware of the intentions of the Jerusalem Church and the necessary distinction between Christianity and Judaism, Eusebius did not give a special status to Jerusalem; he

[49] *V. Const.*, 3.28 (NPNF, i, 527); cf. also *idem*, 3.25.
[50] *Hist. Eccl.*, 10.4.68.
[51] Eusebius' quotation of LXX Ps. 132.7 when describing Helena's pilgrimage to Palestine in *V. Const.*, 3.42.2 (NPNF, i, 530); see further below in 6.1.
[52] *V. Const.*, 3.41.
[53] *L. Const.*, 9.17.
[54] *Dem. Ev.*, 1.1.2, 3.2.47, 7.2.1–17 (*FPG* i, 3, 112; ii, 78–9) for Bethlehem; *idem*, 6.18.4–26 (ii, 29) for the Mount of Olives.
[55] See *L. Const.*, 9.15–17 and *V. Const.*, 3.41–3.

sought instead to deflect the focus of Christian interest onto this triad of sites and thereby onto Palestine as a whole. However, these individual sites, the location of major Gospel events, could rightly be called 'holy' in a Christian sense. His earlier theology may not have fully prepared him for such an admission; but in the face of the great and exciting changes after 325, this was a hard thing to deny completely. The door was gradually being opened to a theology of pilgrimage.

However, as has already been suggested, these references to the 'holy cave', which are quite exceptional within Eusebius' theological writings, need to be understood against the backdrop of his earlier theology; they also need to be compared with the stronger notions of 'holy places' that were being espoused by the emperor himself, as evidenced in the *Life of Constantine*. As a result, it becomes clear that, if anything, it was really the emperor, and not Eusebius, who was the person with a convinced devotion to 'holy places'.

In the imperial letters that Eusebius quotes, Constantine emphasizes his conviction that the area to be covered by the church of the Holy Sepulchre had really been 'holy from the beginning' (ἅγιον ἐξ ἀρχῆς) but was now 'holier still' (ἁγιώτερον) as a result of the recent discoveries.[56] Then again, he stresses that the site of Abraham's meeting with the *Logos* at Mamre had an 'ancient holiness' (ἀρχαίαν ἁγιότητα); it was for this reason that Christians now needed to defend and preserve the 'holiness of the site' (τὴν ἁγιότητα τοῦ τόπου).[57] Elsewhere in the *Life of Constantine* we learn that the emperor took with him on his campaigns what some have termed a 'mobile church',[58] and from later historians we gather that he placed the 'wood of the cross' in his bridle and helmet.[59] Plainly, as others have noted, it was really Constantine, and not Eusebius, who 'could not escape from the idea of a holy place'.[60] It was Constantine who was 'mystical about the holy places'.[61]

In the light of this, it can be seen that Eusebius' references to

---

[56] According to *V. Const.*, 3.30.
[57] Ibid., 3.53.
[58] Ibid., 4.56.
[59] Soc., *Hist. Eccl.*, 1.17; cf. Soz., *Hist. Eccl.*, 2.1.
[60] A phrase of Professor J. G. Davies.
[61] Chadwick (1960), 174, following Telfer (1955b).

'holy places' were less frequent and also less forceful than Constantine's. Moreover, he not only talked of 'holy places' less than the emperor, he would also have meant something slightly different when he did so. He still approached the 'holy cave' with the detachment of an academic historian, emphasizing its 'witness to the truth of the biblical narrative', not its capacity to 'stimulate devotion'.[62] Thus for Eusebius a 'holy cave' seems to have been but a form of description; for Constantine a 'holy place' implied a form of devotion. In Eusebius' understanding these places had more to do with the vindication of past biblical history and prophecy than with prayer in the present. It is therefore not impossible that Eusebius used the term 'holy place' on this one occasion expressly to counterbalance Constantine's rather different understanding which had perforce to be included in the emperor's biography. To do so would at least ensure that his own, more historical approach, could be heard.

This difference in the meaning and significance of 'holy places' was no doubt partly the result of the literary contexts for which Eusebius was writing, and partly of his more academic and less devotional approach. Others have noted how it is impossible in Eusebius 'to feel the warmth of a religious heart',[63] and that his mind 'seems to have been scholarly rather than devout'.[64] As a result he would instinctively have been attracted to more grandiose schemes. The 'holy place' in Eusebius' understanding sent a message to the world (of Christ's truth and the triumph of the universal Church) more than to the individual believer. His thinking operated on a different plane.

Another, more important reason for Eusebius' comparative 'detachment' would have been his long-established theological method, and in particular his emphasis on the *Logos* and on 'theophany'. His system did not encourage the believer to relate to Christ's person humanly and empathetically; faith was portrayed more as a cerebral response of obedience to the revelation of the *Logos*.[65] Eusebius thus might have come to accept in some form the phenomenon of 'holy places' but so long as he approached them within this particular theological framework they would never

---

[62] From the comment of Wilkinson (1981), 19–20, quoted fully above in 2.2.
[63] Gressmann (1903), 34.
[64] Foakes-Jackson (1933), 34.
[65] See below 4.5.

have the same personal meaning and warm significance as they
would for Cyril and later Christians.

This *Logos*-theology, with its corresponding emphasis on 'theophany', had of course been at the very centre of the first three
books of the *Theophany*. Yet such was the importance of that
theology for Eusebius that he chose to reuse the material of those
books on one of the most important occasions towards the end of
his life, an occasion of unique interest for our enquiry. As presiding
bishop over the many who had recently convened at Tyre, Eusebius
was one of several people to give speeches at the dedication of
the Holy Sepulchre in 335. The aging metropolitan had the
unsurpassed privilege of being able to expound in the very place
of the Resurrection his distinctive and definitive view of the
Christ-event. This was the culmination of a lifetime, a chance to
offer in prestigious company and in a unique building his 'final
opinions'.[66] What did he take for his theme? It is very indicative
of the man, both of his convictions and perhaps also of his
limitations, that what he chose to make known was his distinctive
theophany-model, the very heart of his theological system. Thus
his speech *On Christ's Sepulchre* (which he repeated two months
later before Constantine) is a condensed version of the first three
books of the *Theophany*.

This speech has only recently been identified as that given at
the dedication of the Holy Sepulchre.[67] As a result, the great
significance that this speech has for our evaluation of Eusebius'
attitudes to 'holy places' has not yet been noted. A close reading
of it thus enables us in a new way to complement the evidence of
the *Life of Constantine* when considering Eusebius' thought on
this subject. The result is a more rounded and interesting picture
which confirms our contention here that Eusebius would have
understood 'holy places' in a distinctive and less physical sense
because of his long-established theological system.

Eusebius used the theophany-model during his addresses in the
Holy Sepulchre and in front of Constantine in order to ensure that
this 'holy place' (which was never referred to as such in the

[66] Barnes (1981), 187.
[67] By Drake (1976); see Appendix. For Drake this identification was valuable
only for the light which it threw on the Constantinian question.

speech)[68] was set within its proper context and understood from a correct perspective. By using this model of 'theophany', he was able above all to to preserve his overriding rational and 'spiritual' emphasis and to play down any more 'sacramental' approach to the physical. By emphasizing 'theophany' Eusebius was able to portray the Christ-event as a revelation of God's essentially spiritual nature and to draw attention away from the human Christ and the physical places where he had lived. Thus even when a few years later, in the *Life of Constantine*, Eusebius refers to the tomb of Christ as 'holy' because of its association with an important event of the past, it would clearly not hold any more 'sacramental' significance in his faith.

At first sight it seems odd that Eusebius should have chosen in this speech to play down the importance of physical places; he was, after all, speaking in none other than the Holy Sepulchre! Yet, on further reflection, one can appreciate that for this particular speaker it was absolutely natural. Confronted with widespread fascination with the particular and physical, Eusebius responded confidently with his favoured universal *Logos*-theology, developed in the Caesarean school. Rather than allowing this new church and this auspicious event to displace his earlier theology, he brought that theology into its very centre.

The theophany-model manifested its great value, as far as Eusebius was concerned, in a second slightly different way when he used this speech in November before Constantine. Eusebius needed to relate the significance of the Holy Sepulchre to an emperor who had sadly been absent from these celebrations in Jerusalem.[69]

Again this was a historic moment as the metropolitan of Palestine, hot-foot from Jerusalem, praised Constantine for his personal devotion to the 'Holy Land' and described the fruition of his building projects. However, it was also a slightly delicate moment. For Constantine was a frustrated pilgrim who had been unable personally to experience the fruit of his own devotion.[70]

[68] Indeed he gives in *Sep. Chr.*, 16.3 (a 'bridge-passage' not paralleled in the *Theophany*) a new, clear, statement of where alone holiness resided in the physical realm: 'the all-holy body of Christ' (τὸ πανάγιον τοῦ Χριστοῦ σῶμα).

[69] It is often mistakenly assumed that Constantine was present at this dedication in Jerusalem; see most recently Frend (1984), 527.

[70] He had wanted to make a visit soon after his victory at Adrianople (*V. Const.*, 2.72.2) but had been 'debarred by the dissensions of his ecclesiastics from entering

Once again the theophany-model proved its worth. For not only could it offset Constantine's own interest in physical particulars (which to Eusebius may well have seemed rather excessive); it could also comfort the emperor by showing that his frustration was not really necessary. A theology that emphasized the 'incarnation' (ἐνανθρώπησις) might have concentrated too much on first-century Palestine; Eusebius' emphasis on 'theophany' (θεοφάνεια), however, saw the Christ-event as but one of the many manifestations of the *Logos* which could occur at any time and in any place. Most importantly, therefore, Eusebius could assert that Constantine in his palace in Constantinople was not debarred from receiving a personal theophany himself; indeed he suggested that this had already occurred many times.

> You yourself, my emperor, could tell us if you wished of the countless manifestations [μυρίας θεοφανείας] of your Saviour and his countless personal visits during sleep.[71]

Constantine's frustration in being unable to visit the scenes of the principal theophany of the *Logos* could thus be borne more easily if he realised the blessings of the theophanies that he had himself experienced far away from Palestine. His inability to travel to visit the East did not deny the completeness of his Christian experience. The emperor's development of the 'Holy Land' was admirable, perhaps beneficial, but a visit was by no means essential.[72] Thus he was not to let his rather physical and particular devotion to 'holy places' cause him further upset. A thankful consideration of the spiritual *Logos*, who had been revealed to him already on so many occasions, would dispel all such feelings and, in any case, was more authentically 'Christian'.

The theophany-model was thus the ideal solution. It affirmed the significance of the first-century event in Palestine but ultimately transcended that event by setting it in a much wider context which was universally applicable. There was affirmation, but also a definite strand of negation. Eusebius' reuse of his earlier *Theophany*

---

the Holy Land in person' (Telfer (1955b), 699). Later he hoped to be baptized in the Jordan, but this did not prove possible before his death (ibid., 4.62.2).

[71] *Sep. Chr.*, 18.1 (*DPC*, 126–7); Yarnold (1983), 27, neatly calls these 'Constantine's hot-line to heaven'.

[72] For this similar tension between value and non-necessity, compare Jerome's famous *Ep.* 108 with *Ep.* 58.

was therefore quite natural but also most strategic.[73] It was a natural expression of his life's theology; but it was also skilfully used to make a purposeful impression on the opinions of the leaders of both Church and state. His 'distilled essence' from the past was carefully 'refined' to be programmatic for the future.

Speaking in the supposed centres both of the Christian and the imperial worlds, Eusebius was not overawed or swayed from his convictions. On the contrary he retained those convictions and asserted his own set of priorities. His personal theological conservatism was freshly reapplied. 'Holy places' and a theology of the Incarnation that stressed the spiritual value of the material were in the ascendant, but Eusebius was making his opinions quite clear as to how Christians were rightly to respond to these new developments. Hence it is indeed true that 'for all his apparent moderation, the bishop of Caesarea more and more emerges as a man of intense conviction. He had a mission of his own, a goal as clear as Constantine's. He was a determined man—more determined, perhaps, than yet we know'.[74]

4. CYRIL AND THE 'HOLY PLACES'

Cyril too had a mission in life. Within ten years of Eusebius' death this enterprising young man would be bishop of the Church in the 'historic centre of the Christian world',[75] and one of his principal aims would be the promotion of Jerusalem and its 'holy places'. Naturally there were many personal and ecclesiastical factors that encouraged him to develop a stonger commitment to these places than Eusebius; a high doctrine of the importance of Jerusalem and the places of the incarnate Christ would work wonders for the prestige of the Jerusalem Church and its bishop. But it was not all a matter of ecclesiastical politics or personal ambition. There were also genuine theological differences between Cyril and Eusebius which contributed to their divergent approaches to these questions, especially so on the question of 'holy places'.

First, however, it is only fair to note the obvious contrast between

---

[73] Barnes (1981), 188 highlights the same combination of the natural and strategic in Eusebius' use of the *Theophany* to influence Constantine's theology.

[74] Drake (1976), 79.

[75] Cross (1951), p. xxxiv.

the two personalities and their respective situations. Eusebius had been an academic, at home in the Caesarean library; Cyril's location in Jerusalem required of him gifts that were more practical and pastoral. Thus, despite his inevitable involvement in the turbulent theological debates of his age, Cyril was a 'pastor and essentially practical, not given to speculation or dogma'.[76] Eusebius, when visiting Jerusalem for the dedication of the Holy Sepulchre, waxed lyrical on the theophany of the *Logos*; Cyril in the same building would be pointing to Golgotha and the tomb, using them to portray the original Gospel events and to evoke faith in his hearers. Eusebius' was a cerebral approach, designed to illuminate the minds of learned prelates and Church dignitaries; Cyril's a practical and personal approach, intended to warm the hearts of those who were soon to be baptized.[77] No doubt each of them might have spoken differently if they had been in each other's situation, but how differently we cannot now determine. For indeed their immediate situations, the contexts in which they spoke, affected what they said and, more deeply, the formation of their theologies.

It is therefore our task to look at Cyril's theology and to note some of the important characteristics that would in turn influence his approach to the places of Christ. Cyril was 'gifted with imagination', and had an 'earnest sympathy with the religion of unlearned people'; yet this was 'combined with a real if not profound theological understanding of doctrine' which enabled him to bring 'ancient conceptions into living contact with new needs'.[78] What was his theology? What were those 'ancient conceptions', and how did he apply them?

The three important theological convictions which become readily apparent reading Cyril's *Catechetical Lectures* and which immediately mark a contrast with the theology of Eusebius are as follows: his greater understanding of the *person* of Christ and the *person* of the Holy Spirit; his fuller acceptance of the Incarnation

[76] Ibid., p. xxxii.

[77] On this more personal aspect of Cyril, see the comprehensive study of Paulin (1959). In his useful depiction of Cyril's character, he draws attention to Cyril's love of nature (p. 20), his humility and concern for the poor (pp. 30–32), and his overriding desire for internal truth and honesty (p. 39). Bindley (1917) called attention as well to Cyril's 'full and minute knowledge of Scripture' (p. 599) and his 'splendid breadth' (p. 607).

[78] Dix (1945), 352.

as a central tenet of the faith; and his stronger affirmation of the primacy of salvation. In other words, Cyril's theology was more personal, incarnational, and soteriological.

Of the three, the first is perhaps the most likely to have been influenced by his immediate context which, as he prepared his candidates for baptism, was inevitably more personal. However, Eusebius would have had plenty of opportunity in his lifetime, had he so wished, to emphasize the person of Christ and the person of the Holy Spirit; instead he propounded consistently his more impersonal theology of the *Logos*.

For Cyril the person of Christ and the person of the Holy Spirit were not abstract entities, objects to be contemplated in the mind, but real persons to be encountered in the heart. Cyril's purpose, it has been suggested, was none other than to 'form Christ in men'; this central goal was something that gave to his thinking a 'unity, which was based upon the Person of Christ'.[79] His catechumens were thus encouraged to meet Christ personally.

Cyril's emphasis on the person of Christ was closely linked to his easy acceptance of Christ's humanity. Eusebius, with his emphasis upon the *Logos*, had found it difficult to incorporate this fully into his system. This can be seen especially in his speech *On Christ's Sepulchre* and the *Theophany*; Christ on earth was really but an instrument assumed by the *Logos* to reveal his truth, a necessary divine mouthpiece or vehicle. To Eusebius the *Logos* had assumed human flesh. To Cyril the Word had become Man:

Let us adore him as God, but believe that he became Man also. . . . For Jesus the King . . . girded himself with the linen towel of humanity and cared for that which was sick.[80]

The incarnate Christ in Galilee and Jerusalem had indeed taken on 'this passible nature of ours' and truly shared the same 'feelings of the flesh'.[81] He was truly human, a real person.

Coupled with this, Cyril had a parallel conviction that the Holy Spirit too was both ontologically and experientially a person. Cyril 'affirmed repeatedly the distinct personality of the Spirit and

---

[79] Paulin (1959), 237–41.

[80] *Catech.*, 12.1 (*WCJ*, i, 227).

[81] Ibid., 4.9 (i, 123–4); cf. also Lecture 10 on the 'Lord, Jesus Christ' (esp. 19–20).

[drew] attention to the directly personal action attributed to him'.[82] Thus he concluded his lecture concerning the Holy Spirit by commending to his audience the 'personal, sanctifying and efficacious power of the Holy Spirit'.[83] He also thereby indicated, it seems, that he had 'no shadow of hesitation'[84] concerning the deity of the Holy Spirit. For the Holy Spirit was above creation, omniscient, and eternal;[85] and he was to be 'ranked in honour of dignity with Father and Son'.[86]

This was especially remarkable, as Lebon pointed out, not just in the light of the contemporary trinitarian debates but also when compared with Eusebius who, at least according to some, 'had clearly made the Holy Spirit a creature'.[87] Eusebius' understanding of the Holy Spirit was, at the least, a diminished one. This has been sensed especially in an important passage in his *Ecclesiastical Theology*,[88] in which Eusebius is deemed to have shown that he had 'no place' for the Holy Spirit in his theology,[89] and to have revealed his 'subordinationism in its most outspoken boldness'.[90] Cyril, by contrast, even if admittedly not explicit on his theology of the Trinity, was quite clear about the divine person and work of the Holy Spirit. On this, it has been suggested, 'no writer of the fourth century has spoken more fully or convincingly'.[91]

Cyril's theology, influenced no doubt by his pastoral context, was thus essentially personal. He sought to convey to his audience the reality of Christ's person, both human and divine, and also the work and person of the Holy Spirit.

Secondly, this regained focus on Christ's person was closely related by Cyril to his more settled acceptance of the Incarnation. Both Eusebius and Cyril believed in the same paradox, that God had somehow truly been 'in Christ'. Eusebius, however, had a tendency to see the Incarnation as a temporary expedient in an overall plan of divine revelation, an exceptional act designed to

[82] Quasten, iii (1960), 372.
[83] *Catech.*, 17.34 (*WCJ*, ii, 117). See also ibid., 17.9, 11, 28 and 33.
[84] Dix (1945), 353.
[85] *Catech.*, 16.23, 25; 17.5.
[86] Ibid., 4.16 (*WCJ*, i, 127).
[87] Lebon (1924), 383.
[88] Especially *Theol. Eccl.*, 3.4–6.
[89] Ricken (1967), 358, following Berkhof (1939), 87.
[90] Swete (1912), 197. Stevenson (1929), 89–90, similarly concludes his discussion of this and other passages by stating that Eusebius 'degrades the Holy Spirit'.
[91] Swete (1912), 210.

point away from itself to the spiritual realm above.[92] For Cyril, by contrast, the Incarnation was not just a necessary revelation to our human perception, but rather a chosen act of divine identification with our humanity. It was a divine endorsement of the physical realm, not a supposed encouragement to our attempts to transcend that realm. Thus the incarnate Christ purposefully took upon him our physical and 'passible nature'.[93]

The perfect teacher of children became himself a child among children, that he might instruct the unwise. The bread of heaven came down to earth to feed the hungry.[94]

The Incarnation was therefore for Cyril more normative than exceptional within God's purpose and had a function in and of itself; it could legitimately be focused upon by the Christian and given a central place in his devotion, precisely because of its central place within the purposes of God. Eusebius had rebuked Constantia for her interest in the incarnate phase of the *Logos*; but Cyril would understand and fully endorse the desire of his audience to have been with Thomas in the Upper Room.[95] It was quite legitimate to focus on the episode of the Incarnation, for the Incarnation was a permanent expression of God's disposition and will towards men and women.

Finally, undergirding this emphasis on the person of Christ, but especially the Incarnation, lay Cyril's commitment to the primacy of salvation. If, as Eusebius tended to suggest, revelation and illumination were the prime needs of man, then the incarnate Christ might indeed be portrayed as little more than a vessel of God's words.[96] If, however, as Cyril stressed, man's need was more serious, if he stood in need of salvation, Christ needed to have been a person, a representative man and fully identified with our humanity.

Cyril thus placed the Incarnation firmly within a soteriological

[92] Although for Eusebius the theophany of the *Logos* in the first century was *not* exceptional in the sense that there had been other similar theophanies in the past (above 3.2(*c*)), all these manifestations of the *Logos* in the human realm *were* exceptional, and inherently temporary, inasmuch as their purpose was to point away from themselves to the eternal and spiritual *Logos*.

[93] See *Catech.*, 4.9 again.

[94] Ibid., 12.1 (*WCJ*, i, 227–8).

[95] Ibid., 13.39.

[96] See below in 4.5.

framework. Salvation was the central issue, the most important thing of which one needed to be certain: 'if the Incarnation was a fantasy, salvation is also a fantasy';[97] 'if Christ is God, but did not assume manhood, then we are strangers to salvation'.[98]

This soteriological interest manifests itself supremely in his consistent emphasis on the Cross as the moment of salvation from sin.[99] Thus he could stress in a similar vein that 'if [Christ] was crucified in fancy only, salvation is a fancy only'.[100] The Cross and not the Incarnation, therefore, was the salvific work *par excellence*; but the Incarnation too (as a necessary means to that end, and perhaps partially as an end in itself) had a similarly salvific function. Cyril's purpose therefore was to outline this salvation to his catechumens, a salvation dependent upon such reliable persons as Christ and the Holy Spirit and upon such great events as the Cross and Incarnation. These were the 'ancient conceptions' that Cyril attempted to bring into 'living contact' with the needs of his audience.[101]

This sketch highlights three contrasts in theology between Cyril and Eusebius. These theological differences would naturally effect, and perhaps already reflected, different approaches to those sites visited by the incarnate Christ. Theology coloured the places and the places coloured theology. Plainly 'holy places' would fit much more easily into Cyril's theological system than into Eusebius'. Cyril's theology gave a central importance to the Incarnation as a historical event: the sites in question were the locations of the incarnate life. Cyril saw the Incarnation as a divine affirmation of the physical: these were the physical vestiges of that event. Cyril knew the need of people to meet with the person of Christ and to live the life of faith: these were places in which they could come close to Him. For Eusebius, however, the Incarnation had not had that kind of centrality, nor had it been used as an endorsement of the physical; Christian faith had also perhaps been more a response to the revelation of the *Logos* than an encounter with the Living

[97] Ibid., 4.9 (*WCJ*, i, 123).

[98] Ibid., 12.1 (i, 227).

[99] Outlined with full references below in 8.2.

[100] *Catech.*, 13.37 (*WCJ*, ii, 29). Cf. ibid., 13.4: 'for the Cross was no illusion; otherwise our redemption also is an illusion'.

[101] Dix (1945), 352. For a far more detailed discussion of Cyril's theology, which suggests that in his doctrine Cyril was drawing upon the ancient tradition of the Jerusalem Church, see Telfer (1955a), 54–63.

Christ. As a result the places of Christ could never be imbued by Eusebius with the warm, colourful and personal significance that would characterize all of Cyril's thinking.

5. THE CONTRAST OBSERVED

The theological perspectives of Cyril and Eusebius were evidently quite different in many ways. It should not then be any surprise if this resulted in their having quite different understandings of 'holy places'. The contrast between the two bishops can be neatly focused for us in conclusion by a re-examination of Eusebius' strategic speech *On Christ's Sepulchre*, where we may not only note Eusebius' *Logos*-theology once again, but also observe the way in which he had made some significant alterations to his earlier presentation of this material in the *Theophany*. Fundamental differences between Eusebius and Cyril will emerge in matters both theological and practical. Furthermore, Eusebius delivered this oration *On Christ's Sepulchre* in the very building in which within less than fifteen years Cyril would be delivering his *Catechetical Lectures*. Despite the admitted difference in their audiences, the two men are here at their closest—at least in time and location, if not in theology.

The speech *On Christ's Sepulchre* was not only the refined essence of Eusebius' thought, it was also a classic, succinct exposition of *Logos*-theology. This model permeates the speech and provides its abiding theme. The model had three seemingly necessary theological corollaries, each of which ran directly counter to the three emphases just noted in Cyril.

First, Eusebius' *Logos*-theology, as presented in this important speech, addressed itself more to the problem of God's self-revelation than to the problem of man's salvation. It sought to answer the question, 'how could the divine and intangible, immortal, and invisible Being manifest Himself?'[102] The divine response was to 'use a corporeal instrument' ($\theta\nu\eta\tau\grave{o}\nu$ $\mathring{o}\rho\gamma\alpha\nu o\nu$)[103] 'because this was agreeable to [men] who prefer the perception of visible objects'.[104] Man's problem, therefore, was not his sin but his perceptions,

---

[102] *Sep. Chr.*, 14.1 (*DPC*, 115).
[103] Ibid., and *idem*, 14.2 (loc. cit.).
[104] Ibid.

while God's 'problem', according to Eusebius, was how to meet that human need. Eusebius, unlike Cyril, tended to emphasize revelation rather than salvation.[105]

Secondly, the essence of this *Logos*-theology was to give priority not to the Son of God in his Incarnation but to the *Logos* of God in his eternal pre-existence. The Incarnation as an event was subsumed under this all-pervasive emphasis on the incorporeal and spiritual *Logos*. Thus Eusebius never comes to rest theologically on the Incarnation but is always pressing on to higher things; the Incarnation was to be seen as essentially exceptional and temporary. 'He entered into communion with all mortals, not in the manner customary to him— since he is incorporeal and pervades invisibly the entire cosmos—but in a newer form, far different from his custom'.[106] Cyril's theological appreciation of the Incarnation, which focused on the Incarnation in its own right, was simply not shared by Eusebius.

Thirdly, and integrally related to this, the *Logos* too did not identify himself with mankind in any permanent way. Eusebius never uses in this work ἐνανθρώπησις, a word which might indicate such a full identification with humanity; instead he uses throughout his concept of θεοφάνεια and speaks of the *Logos* using the 'instrument of a mortal body with the intention of saving humanity through the *resemblance*'.[107] The *Logos* assumed a mortal instrument, but did he really become a man? Was he truly, we might be tempted to ask, one of us? As a result, Eusebius' Christ fails to come across as a convincing person. The *Logos* was merely using this 'mortal instrument' in the same way as of old Orpheus had used his lyre.[108] This instrument was but a necessary and convenient vehicle for the performance of miracles and the pronouncement of divine truth:

he allowed eyes of flesh to behold certain amazing sights; . . . for ears of flesh He intoned instructions through a tongue also of flesh.[109]

In Eusebius' theology there was hardly a *person* of Christ to which the believer could personally respond. When compared with Cyril's, Eusebius' system, seems quite impersonal.

105 Cf. Pollard (1970), 168–70, and above 3.2(c).
106 *Sep. Chr.*, 13.16 (*DPC*, 114–15).
107 Ibid., 13.16 (115, italics mine).
108 Ibid., 14.5.
109 Ibid., 14.6 (*DPC*, 116).

All these aspects of Eusebius' *Logos*-theology (its emphasis on revelation, its upward focus away from the Incarnation and from a genuine identification of God in man, and its failure to portray adequately the person of Christ) can be recognized in the one sentence with which Eusebius concluded his own chapter on the incarnate phase of the *Logos*:

So He completed a whole life in this way, simultaneously showing the empathy of his physical instrument with us, while giving glimpses of the divine *Logos*, working marvels and miracles like a God, uttering . . . prophecies . . . and by His very acts revealing the *Logos* of God (who is not visible to the many) through extraordinary deeds . . . and especially through his divine instructions that led souls upward to prepare for the celestial kingdom.[110]

The contrast with Cyril's theology, with its emphasis on the Incarnation, the person of Christ and salvation, is indeed marked. 'Holy places' could scarcely mean the same to them both.

Eusebius' speech *On Christ's Sepulchre* is, however, instructive for a second reason. Almost all of it had appeared once before in the *Theophany*; yet Eusebius made certain small, intriguing changes. 'Not the least puzzling feature of [this speech] is the nature of the minor verbal alterations it makes in the text of the earlier works it cites, omitting and adding words, phrases and sentences whose omission or inclusion does not appear to warrant a deliberate alteration'.[111] Many of these alterations remain unexplained; but several of them can now be seen to reflect the quite new situation in which Eusebius found himself in 335. He was naturally influenced by the venue of the Holy Sepulchre, by the audience of assembled bishops, but also, it appears, by a local event (that had occurred in the intervening ten years) of which he evidently disapproved.

One example of this alteration of the earlier work can be seen in the long sentence just quoted, where 'the celestial kingdom' (ὑπερουράνιον τόπον) replaces a reference to the 'heavenly city'.[112] What could be the reason for such a seemingly insignificant alteration?

---

[110] *Sep. Chr.*, 14.12 (*DPC*, 116–17).

[111] Wallace-Hadrill (1960), 55, who, however, favoured the priority of *Sep. Chr.*, over *Theoph.*. These alterations are collected in detail by Gressmann (1903).

[112] *Sep. Chr.*, 14.12, compared with *Theoph.*, 3.39.

All becomes clear as soon as we remember that the Jerusalem Church was probably already asserting what Cyril would later make explicit: namely that Jerusalem was indeed a 'holy city' and that St Matthew's reference (27.53) to the 'holy city' was a straightforward reference to the physical Jerusalem on earth.[113] Eusebius, however, as we have learnt, continued to favour an interpretation using the 'heavenly city'.[114] But now Eusebius found himself speaking in that very city! It was only tactful therefore to avoid any allusion to this difference of opinion. The concept of the 'city', earthly or heavenly, holy or otherwise, was best omitted altogether.

His location near the recently discovered tomb of Christ also had its natural affect. The speech now gave slightly more emphasis to the Resurrection, and slightly less to theophany. This led to the alteration of a few phrases. For example, the phrase 'proof of the revelation of God' was exchanged for 'proof of the divine life after death'.[115] Yet it also led to major structural alterations. In the *Theophany* Eusebius had listed the great changes that had occurred in the world as a result of this theophany in the first century; he did this before returning to discuss briefly the Resurrection, its reasons and its results.[116] In its later, adapted form this list of 'after-effects' was placed *after* the discussion about the Resurrection, in such a way that the Resurrection, rather than the theophany as a whole, was portrayed as the great cause of all these world changes.[117] The Resurrection was thus, under this new arrangement, portrayed as the single cause of the great changes experienced subsequently throughout the world.

Nevertheless, 'theophany' quite unmistakeably remains the predominant theme. At the end of the list he concludes that all these changes in the world simply prove 'that the true Son of God has been seen on earth'.[118] The argument's theme throughout has thus really been 'theophany', not Resurrection. Eusebius' attempted remodelling only serves to reveal his continuing preference for the

[113] See more fully below 10.2.
[114] *Comm. in Ps.* [87.7], 1064b.
[115] *Sep. Chr.*, 16.9, compared with the earlier *Theoph.*, 3.7. Another example occurs in *Sep. Chr.*, 15.7: 'stronger than death' replaced the earlier 'strong in the yoke of righteousness' (*Theoph.*, 3.60).
[116] *Theoph.*, 3.2–38, preceding ibid., 3.39–61.
[117] *Sep. Chr.*, 16–17, now following ibid., 15.
[118] Ibid., 17.15 (*DPC*, 126), an adaptation of *Theoph.*, 3.38.

theophany-concept. The Holy Sepulchre made him 'change his tune' slightly, but not the underlying harmony.

Despite the proximity of Christ's tomb, Eusebius thus did not allow his theophany-model to be eclipsed by the Resurrection. Nor, however, was there any increased emphasis on Christ's death, even though the cross of Calvary would, it was believed, have stood not many yards away. On the contrary, Eusebius seems instead to have shied away from the subject. There had not been many references even in the *Theophany* to Christ's death but Eusebius for some reason now excised two of these from his later speech. One was only a passing reference to Christ's crucifixion and human burial;[119] the other, however, was a most significant discussion of Jesus' burial and the unique nature of his tomb.[120] Why was this?

In part it could be a reflection of Eusebius' overall theology which tended to emphasize Christ's Resurrection and not his death. Thus the tomb was now to be seen almost exclusively in this positive light as the place where the *Logos* 'proved that the eternal life promised by him was stronger than any form of death'.[121] But could there have been a yet more pointed local reason?

The evidence suggests that there was. For it is probably no coincidence that, in omitting these two passages, Eusebius succeeded in excising no less than four references to the cross of Christ.[122] As a result, although he necessarily had to refer to Jesus' death,[123] he never once actually referred to the cross. Why this conscious excision of any reference to the cross?

Cyril's lectures just over a decade later would present a very different picture. It was not simply that he disagreed with Eusebius on those three central aspects of theology, nor that he depicted Jerusalem as a 'holy city', nor that he emphasized consistently that the cross was the 'glory of the Catholic Church'.[124] Even more importantly Cyril spoke on no less than five occasions of a well-known recent discovery—the discovery of the supposedly

---

[119] *Theoph.*, 3.42–4.
[120] Ibid., 3.61, quoted fully below in 8.4; cf. above fn. 35.
[121] *Sep. Chr.*, 15.6 (*DPC*, 118).
[122] τὸ τοῦ σταυροῦ τροπαῖον in *Theoph.*, 3.42, 61; ἐπὶ τοῦ ξύλου and ἀνασταυρόμενον in ibid., 3.61.
[123] Especially in *Sep. Chr.*, 15.
[124] *Catech.*, 13.1 (*WCJ*, ii, 4).

original wood of Jesus' cross.[125] Could Eusebius' omission of all references to the cross in this important speech *On Christ's Sepulchre* be a reflection of his adverse reaction to this recent discovery by the Jerusalem Church?

It has long been a matter of scholarly debate as to whether this famous relic, whatever its dubious claims to authenticity, could really have been discovered at this early date. In subsequent centuries various legends expanded the story in many directions and would associate the discovery with the visit of Helena, the emperor's mother.[126] In the light of these subsequent exaggerations and noting that there is indeed little evidence to confirm any direct involvement of Helena, many scholars have seen fit to dismiss the whole episode as a later phenomenon, the 'invention' either being dated to the 340s[127] or, if Cyril's clear references to it are somehow deemed inauthentic, to much later in the century.[128]

One of the chief arguments in defence of such a position is precisely this oft-noted silence of Eusebius on the subject. How, it is asked, could a man, endowed with such theological authority and placed in such an ideal situation as a contemporary historian and as the local metropolitan, have kept quiet about such an event?[129] Thus it has been claimed that Eusebius 'could not have failed to exploit the appearance of the sacred wood as an unsolicited affirmation of God's favour'. His silence on the matter was therefore 'impressively convincing' evidence that the 'true cross' had not yet been discovered during Eusebius' lifetime.[130]

Now, however, there is an increasing scholarly consensus that this relic may after all have indeed been discovered in those first years after 325.[131] For not only is it hard to deny the authenticity of Cyril's unambiguous statements;[132] it also seems inherently likely that such a 'discovery' would be made (or, at least, would be *claimed* to have been made) in the years of excavation that

[125] Ibid., 4.10, 10.19, 13.4, 13.39, and *Ep. Const.*, 3.

[126] See Hunt (1982), 40–42 for discussion of the references in Ambrose and Jerome; on the legend's development in the next centuries, see, e.g., Drake (1980).

[127] See most recently Hunt (1982), 38.

[128] See, for example, the attacks on Cyril in Bindley (1917), 603–4.

[129] Drake (1985), 2–3, lists the normal range of such questions well .

[130] Hunt, loc. cit.

[131] See esp. Rubin (1982a), 82–7, and Drake (1985); this is accepted by e.g., Barnes (1981), 248, and Cardman (1979), 22, fn. 39; cf. also Wilkinson (1981), 240.

[132] Rubin (1982 a), Appendix 3, cites the strong arguments in favour of accepting their authenticity.

preceded the construction of the church of the Holy Sepulchre. Once the basilica was built there was clearly less opportunity for unearthing such important finds. Thus, even if it was a few years before the Jerusalem Church began to publicize this story, they would naturally cite those first years after 325 as the time of its original discovery.

Moreover, a puzzling phrase in Constantine's letter to Macarius is now reckoned by some scholars to be in fact a veiled reference to this very relic.[133] The emperor spoke of the discovery of τὸ γνώρισμα τοῦ πάθους ('the sign of his passion') and of the site in general 'evincing itself daily' through such 'fresh wonders' and bringing to light clear assurances 'of the Saviour's passion'.[134] Eusebius did not explain Constantine's meaning, hoping no doubt that his readers would assume that the emperor had been speaking of the 'cave of the Resurrection', which Eusebius had just been describing. However, such references to Christ's 'passion' are strange if Constantine really was referring to the cave. Could he not, it has been suggested, have been referring instead to the discovery of the 'wood of the cross', a 'fresh wonder' coming shortly after the initial excitement of uncovering the tomb?

Finally, the argument based on Eusebius' silence has increasingly been weakened as scholars have noticed Eusebius' other strategic silences on several matters that were not to his liking. Eusebius' silence might indeed mean nothing one way or the other, but scholars observed that it often reflected his conscious unease. Thus, for example, Drake noticed that no reference was made to 'the cross' in his speech *In Praise of Constantine*; Eusebius' ambiguous language might encourage those who wished to do so to hear an allusion to the 'wood of the cross', but Eusebius himself betrayed no such personal commitment.[135]

It was becoming more and more apparent that in all probablity the 'wood of the cross' had indeed been discovered during Eusebius' lifetime, that he knew about it, but that for some reason he chose to avoid ever making a public reference to it. These four conscious excisions of the 'cross' in his definitive speech *On Christ's Sepulchre* now complete the picture. His failure to refer to this subject in

---

[133] Rubin (1982a), 83, and Drake (1985), 8; the latter notes that Cardinal Newman made this identification as long ago as 1875!

[134] *V. Const.*, 3.30 (NPNF, i, 528).

[135] Drake (1985), 15–20, commenting upon *L. Const.*, 9.15–17.

any of his three 'Constantinian' works was clearly no coincidence. There were evidently some important reasons for Eusebius' silence. What were they?

With the understanding gained from our analysis of the characteristic essentials of Eusebius' thought, it is possible to speculate four possible factors that might have disposed Eusebius to be somewhat opposed to the promotion of this relic. Each might on its own have proved sufficient for some reticence on Eusebius' part; combined, however, they make it only too clear why his response was one of total silence.

First, as a historian, Eusebius might well have had some natural doubts over the possible authenticity of such an object. Eusebius was a man to whom historical truth and authenticity were important and who would not easily be swayed by attractive, but too simplistic, assumptions.

Secondly, as a theologian Eusebius tended, when called upon, to emphasize the Resurrection more than Christ's death, unlike Cyril. This was not uncommon but, as a result, the 'wood of the cross' would inevitably be a less attractive focus within Eusebius' theology than the tomb of the Resurrection.

Moreover, as a theologian, Eusebius had continuously emphasized the spiritual nature of Christianity and the need for a progression away from more physical considerations in Christian worship. The cult of physical relics, which the discovery of the 'true cross' (consciously or otherwise) heralded and encouraged in the fourth-century Church, would hardly have been attractive to a man steeped in the spirituality of the Origenian school.

Finally, as the metropolitan of Palestine, naturally concerned about the growing aspirations of the Jerusalem Church, Eusebius would no doubt have been quite concerned, to say the least, about the way in which the bishop of Jerusalem could use this exciting dicovery to further his own ends. The prestige of the local Church in Jerusalem could scarcely fail to be increased as parts of this relic were swiftly and generously distributed around the world!

For all these reasons the discovery of the 'wood of the cross' was unlikely to have been warmly welcomed by Eusebius. As bishop of Caesarea and diligent historian, as theologian of theophany and apologist of the spiritual, Eusebius would have had little room for such a relic. Thus he had every reason for playing down its importance and doubting its authenticity. Cyril, however, would

have every reason for coming to the opposite conclusion: his
theology and spirituality were quite different from Eusebius',
while his position in Jerusalem and his 'parochial pride'[136] would
also quite naturally prove to be a great influence upon his
assumptions.[137] Eusebius and Cyril would thus come to adopt
positions diametrically opposed to each other. In the first century
the Cross had truly been a work of reconciliation (Eph. 2.13–14);
but the rediscovery of the wood of the cross in the fourth became
immediately a focus for division.

This major difference between Eusebius and Cyril on the 'wood
of the cross', which has come to light in our analysis of their
different presentations of the Gospel in the same church but fifteen
years apart, naturally acts as a useful focus for the whole of our
enquiry into those differences that are to be observed between
these two bishops on matters Palestinian. Here their disagreement
is at its sharpest. But where else did they disagree? How would
these two Christians, with their clear differences in theology and
spirituality, in their approach to history and in local Church politics,
assess their native Palestine? In particular, how would they evaluate
Jerusalem and how would they respond to the particular places
visited by the incarnate Christ? Suddenly it becomes almost obvious
that their responses to both these questions will inevitably contain
some important differences.

It is now time to consider their references to the Gospel sites
and to Jerusalem, and to seek out the precise extent of their
disagreement. Our quest therefore takes us to each of those Gospel
sites in turn and then finally to the city of Jerusalem.

---

[136] Dix (1945), 352.

[137] See below 8.1 for a further analysis of these opposite responses to the 'true
cross' in Eusebius and Cyril.

II

THE PLACES OF CHRIST

5

GALILEE

The open spaces of Galilee are an attractive place to begin. Perhaps in every age there have been Christian visitors to the 'Holy Land' who have found Galilee to be a restful contrast to the claustrophobia and intensity of Jerusalem. Here there is more space to consider the meaning of that 'one solitary life' that has proved so momentous in the history of the world. Although more modern and romantic notions concerning the tranquillity and 'Sabbath rest' of Galilee bear little relation to the bustling reality and turbulent history of this area throughout the ages, it remains true that there has always been a perceptible contrast between Galilee and Jerusalem, if only the difference between a major city and the country, between the centre and the more peripheral. Jesus himself exploited this contrast between Jerusalem and Galilee for his purposes; his ministry was structured almost rhythmically, by seasons of detachment in preparation for the times of painful involvement with that strategic city. It is hardly surprising therefore if his followers, in visiting his homeland, have sensed and valued this same contrast.

Yet it is not only visitors or residents who can benefit from an environment some distance from Jerusalem; it will greatly assist us too, as students of this land and its meaning. It was suggested above that for Christians the questions of Jerusalem and of 'holy places' are notionally quite separate; yet in practice the two issues often become inexorably intertwined, for the simple reason that so many of the 'holy places' are located in or very near to Jerusalem. It is therefore appropriate, before we turn our attention to Bethlehem (perhaps, some might suggest, the more logical place to start), to the Mount of Olives, the Holy Sepulchre and Mt. Sion, to concentrate on Galilee. Here the question of Jerusalem can largely be laid aside. The 'holy places' of Christ can be approached in their own right, without constant reference to the phenomenon of Jerusalem.

Likewise, Eusebius had the opportunity to reflect on the places of Christ in Galilee little disturbed by the question of Jerusalem or the aspirations of the Jerusalem Church. Even if as a result there are fewer references in Cyril with which we may compare Eusebius' comments, we have here the rare opportunity of concentrating upon his attitude to 'holy places' *per se*. It is an opportunity not to be missed; for this will prove increasingly difficult in future chapters as the question of Jerusalem colours his thinking more and more. Galilee, itself the starting-point of Jesus' ministry, is therefore a very good place for us to start.

Yet in our study of Eusebius' references to those places associated with the life of Jesus, both in Galilee and in Jerusalem, we will inevitably be interested in questions other than just this one concerning Eusebius' theological and spiritual approach to such places. In particular, since Eusebius is such an important witness to the tradition of the early Church regarding the authenticity of these sites, it will always be necessary ourselves to be considering the question of authenticity and to be evaluating Eusebius' own conclusions on such matters.[1] We will need to know not simply how Eusebius evaluated the significance of such places theologically but what he tells us about them historically. Thus his historical testimony will need to be considered as thoroughly as his theo-logical reflection; and often, since Eusebius' historical and theo-logical interests were intertwined, these twin aspects will prove inseparable.

Finally, the region prompts one further question: what was Eusebius' attitude to Galilee as a whole? Did he emphasize the unique role of this region in the Gospel story? Did he understand Galilee to have any distinctive significance, whether in the past or in the present? This wider question will be considered first, providing a natural context within which then to discuss Eusebius' historical and theological approach to individual places in the region.

1. GALILEE AS A WHOLE

Although Galilee is attractive to the Christian visitor because of its contrast to Jerusalem, yet clearly the true source of its appeal

[1] Nevertheless, space prevents any full-scale discussion of authenticity, which would require a detailed assessment of the New Testament sources and of archaeology: for a comprehensive study, see, e.g., Kopp (1963). Our discussion of Eusebius' writings will play a useful part, but only a part, in that debate.

lies much deeper. Those who emphasize the humanity of Jesus find in it the ordinariness and the earthy reality of that human life, while those who emphasize the reality of the Incarnation are moved by the extraordinary love of God in dwelling in this one area for so long. Jerusalem may speak of the Resurrection or the Redemption; but Galilee can speak of Christ's humanity and of the Incarnation.

As a result it is hardly a surprise that by the end of the fourth century numerous 'holy places' had been identified and many churches built to accommodate the steady stream of pilgrims. Egeria[2] and then Jerome[3] both describe possible routes and the sites that one might expect to have been shown at that time; these include Nazareth, Mt. Tabor, Cana, Capernaum and the place of the feeding of the five thousand. Galilee, with its many incarnational 'holy places' was evidently on the Christian map.

How though did Eusebius view this area back at the beginning of the fourth century? Here, not fifty miles from the city where Eusebius spent all his life, was the region in which Christ had spent the major part of *his* life. If he so wished Eusebius could have visited it on several occasions.[4] This was the one place in the world which had witnessed the humanity and the Incarnation of Christ for so long. Was Eusebius moved by such thoughts as much as later pilgrims?

From our previous discussion it seems plain that such thoughts would probably have occurred to Eusebius only rarely, or at least with little force. For his *Logos*-theology was not one that easily

---

[2] Extracts of this now lost (Galilee) section of Egeria's work can be found in the later work of Peter the Deacon: see Wilkinson (1981), 193–203.

[3] *Ep.* 46.12 and 108.13.

[4] Eusebius' continuous close proximity makes it almost certain that he personally knew the area of Galilee from several visits. Although *Onom.* is clearly dependent upon other written sources (see Thomsen (1902) and (1906)) and upon the testimony of other travellers (cf. e.g., those who informed him of the now deserted Babylon: see *Comm. in Is.* [13.19], 100.5), Eusebius' own experience must lie behind much of the work. Moreover, we know that he visited Jerusalem frequently, and had been to both Caesarea Philippi, where he saw the supposed statue of the woman healed by Christ (*Comm. in Luc.* [8.43 ff.], 524c–544a); *Hist. Eccl.*, 7.18), and the mountains of Lebanon (*Chron.*, §1, 16.12). Foakes-Jackson (1933), 39, thus concludes that Eusebius must have known the area well from personal experience. Nevertheless, the fact that Barnes (1981), 108 ff. and Goodman (1983), 15, could come to the opposite conclusion only reveals the paucity of the evidence and the comparatively little interest that Eusebius betrays in such 'holy places', however much he may have visited them.

dwelt on the humanity of Christ, and his emphasis on 'theophany' took attention away from the paradoxes of the Incarnation and the particularity of place. When Eusebius considered the Incarnation, he always viewed it in quite general terms as a temporary divine association with man's life and mortality,[5] without especially concentrating on the particularity of the place where it had occurred; meanwhile, when he considered Jesus' humanity, his emphasis on revelation tended to result in a Jesus who was little more than a mouthpiece for the revelation of God's truth.[6] Neither the humanity of Jesus nor the truth of the Incarnation were denied, but neither were they very central to Eusebius' thought. Within such a framework, Galilee, the place where God was most truly man, could never assume such a great significance.

As a result, Eusebius' references to the ministry of Jesus in Galilee are quite rare. His emphasis on the revelation of the Word made him see this primarily as a time of 'teaching and preaching',[7] and only secondarily as the occasion for Christ's miracles.[8] In book four of the *Theophany*, his most extended discussion of the Gospel narratives, his focus, as has been seen, was almost solely on the prophetic words of Jesus, thus leaving little room for either Jesus' miracles or Jesus' real humanity. Not surprisingly the one event from Jesus' ministry on which Eusebius did concentrate was the Transfiguration, where according to Eusebius' own understanding, the true nature of the *Logos* was disclosed and Christ's humanity was 'utterly transformed and absorbed by the divinity'.[9] In his otherwise scant treatment of Jesus' ministry he seems to have focused chiefly on Jesus' walking on the water and the feeding of the five thousand.[10]

These last two miracles were similarly emphasized by Cyril, but precisely because they highlighted the conjunction of the human and the divine within Christ's Person:

[5] As suggested in the following characteristic phrases: τὸν σὺν ἀνθρώποις βίον: *Comm. in Luc.* [19.12], 589b; καθομιλῶν τῷ τῶν ἀνθρώπων γένει: *Theol. Eccl.*, 1.13; ἐν τῷ καθ' ἡμᾶς βίῳ *Dem. Ev.*, 9.12.5 (*FPG*, ii, 177); ἐπιδημῶν τῷ θνητῷ βίῳ *Comm. in Is.* [42.2.-3], 269.9; θνητοῖς ὁμιλίαν (*L. Const.*, 4.2).

[6] See above in 4.2(*b*) and 4.5.

[7] *Hist. Eccl.*, 1.10.2; *Comm. in Is.* [29.1], 186.16, and [19.23], 136.23.

[8] *Dem. Ev.*, 8.2.108 (*FPG*, ii, 135), *Theol. Eccl.*, 1.13.

[9] Gero (1981), 466. For full discussion on the Transfiguration in Eusebius, see below 5.2(*b*).

[10] These are given as the climax of Christ's miracles when listed in *Dem. Ev.*, 3.4.21–6 (repeated in *Theoph.*, 3.40).

As man he truly ate as we do—for he had feelings of the flesh with us [ὁμοιοπαθές]—but as God he fed the five thousand from five loaves. He died truly as man, but raised him who was four days dead, as God. He truly slept in the ship as man, and walked upon the waters as God.[11]

Cyril here reveals a developed sense, quite lacking in Eusebius, both of the Incarnation and of the humanity of Christ, which, in turn, coloured his understanding of the Galilean ministry of Jesus.

Accordingly his descriptions of Gospel events in Galilee are characterized by a personal and imaginative warmth. A good example is his description of Peter's walking on the water.

Peter was a man like ourselves, composed of flesh and blood, and living on like foods. But when Jesus said, 'Come', believing, he walked on the waters. Now as long as he believed, he had firm footing on the water, but when he doubted, then he began to sink; for as his faith gradually gave way, his body also was drawn down along with it. Realizing his predicament, Jesus, who cures our soul's sicknesses, said, 'O thou of little faith, why dost thou doubt?' Then, strengthened by him who grasped his right hand and led by the hand of the Master, he walked upon the waters as before. For the Gospel . . . does not say, swimming to the boat, Peter got into it, but it gives us to understand that, after retracing the distance he had traversed in going to Jesus, he re-entered the boat. [12]

Although again the different contexts of Cyril and Eusebius explain much, their approaches to the ministry of Christ reveal their essential differences: one's spirituality was warm and personal, the other's too 'spiritualized', theological and abstract to be warm.

Thus it is that, as others have noted, there are indeed 'few notices of Galilee in Eusebius'.[13] Eusebius does not seem to have been especially moved by the fact that this was the very region that God the Son had visited in his Incarnation, that this was the place which had witnessed the humanity of Jesus. His spirituality was not one to be touched by the proximity of Galilee.

Nevertheless there is possibly some evidence, though not much, to indicate that Eusebius may have come to show an increased interest in Galilee after 325; once again, however, as in the

---

11 *Catech.*, 4.9 (WCJ, i, 123).

12 *Catech.*, 5.7 (WCJ, i, 135). Both these colourful descriptions contrast with Eusebius' less imaginative discussion in *Dem. Ev.*, 9.12. For some more human touches in Eusebius, however, see his description of the woman with the haemorrhage, ibid., 3.4.23 (FPG, i, 124) and of the haul of fish (*Theoph.*, 4.6).

13 Elliott-Binns (1956), 74.

Onomasticon, this was simply a historical and exegetical interest in the place which had seen the fulfilment of certain Old Testament prophecies with the coming of Jesus. The evidence for this renewed focus on the historical Galilee comes through a comparison of two different expositions by Eusebius of Isaiah 9.1–2 and its quotation by Matthew (4.15–16): 'the land of Zebulun and the land of Naphtali, towards the sea, across the Jordan, Galilee of the Gentiles—the people who sat in darkness have seen a great light'. One of these expositions was written before 325 (in the *Proof of the Gospel*) and tends to spiritualize this reference, paying little heed to the physical Galilee; the other was written after 325 (in the *Commentary on Isaiah*) and focuses much more on the real place, Galilee, which had acted as the fulfilment of this Old Testament prophecy in the days of Jesus. This difference can be partly explained by the different overall contexts of the respective works, the former being apologetic, the latter more strictly exegetical. Yet it could also reflect the new confidence of Christians in Palestine after 325 and Eusebius' own determination to emphasize the involvement of the *whole* of Palestine in biblical history.

Before 325 Eusebius' attention had been focused on the Isaianic phrase 'Galilee of the Gentiles', to such an extent indeed that 'Galilee' almost came to be synonymous with the 'Gentile Church':

The prophecy [Isa. 9.1–6] promised that there would be a great light in Galilee. Now why did [Christ] pass most of his life in Galilee of the Gentiles? Surely that he might make a beginning of the calling of the Gentiles, for he called his disciples from thence . . .

The prophecy says that they will rejoice before Him, 'as men rejoice in harvest'. . . By this he meant the gathering in of the Gentiles . . .

For 'unto us a child is born'. Who are meant by 'us', but we who have believed in him, and all Galilee of the Gentiles, in whom the great light has sprung up? [14]

The role of the physical and historical Galilee was thus quite secondary to its symbolic or 'spiritualized' significance.

After 325, however, in the *Commentary on Isaiah*, Eusebius does not especially discuss Isaiah's phrase, 'Galilee of the Gentiles', and makes nothing of the future Gentile Church. His concerns instead are geographical and historical. Having discussed the place

[14] *Dem. Ev.*, 9.8.6–16 (*FPG*, ii, 170–71). This 'personal' interpretation is seen just as clearly in ibid., 7.1.152 (ii, 77).

of Zebulun and Naphtali in Joshua's division of the land amongst the twelve tribes, he notes how in recent centuries this area had been inhabited by 'Greeks'. Then he argues that Isaiah's phrase 'by the sea' (παράλιον) is a perfect description of Galilee, since by this phrase the prophet was referring to

all the land around lake Gennesaret, which the Gospels term a 'sea'. . . . Moreover, Capernaum, Bethsaida, and Chorazin and the other villages referred to in the Gospels are now even to this day pointed out around the lake of Tiberias. This Galilee in which the Christ of God passed most of his life also stretches 'beyond the Jordan'. [15]

Eusebius was evidently thinking more imaginatively and in greater detail about Jesus' ministry as an actual event in a physical Galilee, and was anxious to show how Isaiah's ancient prophecy had accurately foretold the very place where Jesus would start to preach the Gospel: part of Galilee was indeed 'beyond the Jordan' and as a whole it was indeed 'by the sea', since Lake Gennesaret (or more correctly now, Lake Tiberias) could also be referred to as a 'sea'. Thus, if Eusebius had previously seen Isaiah's text fulfilled in the spread of the Gospel to the Gentile Church in the world, he now saw it also fulfilled more narrowly in Christ's historical presence around the lake of Tiberias.

There was thus a new focus on the territory of Galilee, as opposed to an emphasis on its people or its symbolic meaning. Yet, as the rest of his discussion makes clear, the reason for this was primarily exegetical and historical; there was no hint of a pilgrim's interest in the area through a contemplation of the mystery of the Incarnation. For Eusebius did not speak of the 'Incarnation' as such but once again of the 'Saviour's *theophany*',[16] and was clearly thinking of this event in quite general terms as a meeting with humankind in general (ἀνθρώποις) rather than with particular individuals.[17] Eusebius was not therefore exploring at this point the paradox of the Incarnation having occurred so extensively in this one place. His focus as ever was upon the text of scripture and the fulfilment of its words in history.

This discussion in the commentary contains two further points of note. First, Eusebius comments that Galilee was the place where

---

[15] *Comm. in Is.* [9.1], 62.20–33.
[16] Ibid. [9.2], 63.6.
[17] Ibid. [9.1], 62.16.

Jesus had spent most of his life (τὰς πλείστας διατριβὰς). This was reasonable enough and indeed Eusebius had said the same of Galilee in the earlier passage quoted from the *Proof of the Gospel*. Yet in several other passages in the *Proof* he had also, for some reason, given the same accolade to Mt. Sion in Jerusalem.[18] No doubt Eusebius' intention had been to suggest that *when he was in Jerusalem* Mt. Sion was the place that Jesus had frequented most; but he had not actually said this. After 325, in the Isaiah commentary, the confusion disappears. When expounding Isaiah 2.3 ('for out of Mt. Sion shall go forth the law'), Eusebius makes no mention of Mt. Sion but, almost pointedly, stresses that Judaea, Jerusalem *and Galilee* had all been the scenes of Christ's life.[19] Then, when expounding Isaiah 9.1-2 (see quote above) he stresses once again that Galilee was where Christ had spent τὰς πλείστας διατριβὰς. It was an obvious point, but in the years after 325 it fitted in very nicely with Eusebius' intention to stress the whole of Palestine, and not just Jerusalem, as the historical source of the Gospel.

Secondly, a few lines later, Eusebius remarked with a note of realism that, despite the 'great light' of Jesus' theophany, many of Jesus' contemporaries had continued 'in their unbelief'.[20] The region had not automatically become 'Christian'. Again this was an obvious point. Yet it may also conceivably have been intended to convey a more contemporary consolation. There may have been a handful of Jewish-Christians living in a few of its villages (probably including Capernaum and Nazareth),[21] but otherwise the Galilee region was very much a Jewish stronghold. After the expulsion of the Jews from Jerusalem in 135, Galilee had become the 'main bastion of Judaism in the Holy Land',[22] the new focus of rabbinic Judaism and the new seat of the Sanhedrin. This state of affairs, as far as the Jews were concerned did indeed mark a 'singular revolution'; for Galilee, now the 'sanctuary of [their] race' had by

---

[18] *Dem. Ev.*, 1.4.8, 6.13.4, 9.14.6 (FPG, i, 24; ii, 13, 181 respectively). He also spoke once of Christ's οἰκείας διατριβὰς on the Mount of Olives: ibid., 8.4.25 (ii, 146).

[19] *Comm. in Is.* [2.1-4], 15.25-26.

[20] Ibid. [9.2], 63.24.

[21] See below 5.2(*c*).

[22] Avi-Yonah (1976), 18.

many Jews been previously 'condemned as profane and heretical'.[23] However, this flowering of Jewish life in Galilee proved to be one of the most fruitful eras in Jewish history.

As far as Christians were concerned, however, it must have seemed quite ironic: truly a 'prophet was not without honour except in his own country'. Indeed it could have been the cause of some pain and embarrassment. For Eusebius had always been quick to highlight how the Jews had been expelled from Jerusalem, their mother-city;[24] yet, as a result of that expulsion, they had only migrated northwards, so that Christians themselves were now effectively expelled from Galilee, the homeland of their Lord.

This ironic and painful state of affairs may well then explain Eusebius' comparative reticence on all matters Galilean. Christianity's weakness in Palestine was nowhere more apparent than in Galilee, the scene of Christ's ministry; and Eusebius was not one who readily emphasized Christianity's weaknesses! His very spiritualized interpretation in the *Proof of the Gospel* (in which, as we have noted, Galilee was seen merely as a symbol of the Gentile Church) may thus have been coloured by this more local and political factor.

However, confident after 325, Christians could attempt to rectify this difficult situation. Count Joseph made his celebrated request of Constantine to sponsor his church-building programme in the region[25] and several other sanctuaries, as we have noted, were soon to be established for Christian pilgrims as a statement of Christian presence.[26]

Seen in this light, Eusebius' brief but definite refocusing upon the physical Galilee in his *Commentary on Isaiah* takes on a new significance. Previously it would scarcely have helped Eusebius' apologetic arguments for the truth and victory of Christianity over Judaism if he had revealed a Christian interest in Galilee; a reference to the physical Galilee only highlighted the weakness of the Church in that historic region. Now, however, with the coming of Constantine, he perhaps hoped that such a reference would not

[23] Smith (1931), 277; cf. Elliott-Binns (1956), 74. Tiberias itself, the centre of this renaissance in Jewish life and scholarship, had been particularly condemned for the paganism of its foundation in honour of Tiberis.

[24] See above ch. 1, fn. 12.

[25] See Epiph., *Haer.*, 30.11 (PL, xli, 426a). The kernel of this story is accepted as historical by Avi-Yonah (1976), 167-9, Barnes (1981), 252, and Rubin (1982b).

[26] Hence the testimony of Egeria and Jerome: see above at fn. 2 and 3.

have that unfortunate affect; indeed it might awaken a Christian desire for better things, but that desire now had a greater chance of becoming reality.

If this reading of the commentary is correct, then there was a slight shift in Eusebius' thinking afer 325. He was more eager than before to emphasize the role of the Galilean territory in Gospel history. For after that date he himself was in any case increasingly concerned to stress the significance of the whole of Palestine, whilst Christians in general were in a stronger position (despite the Jewish majority in the area) to highlight the natural historical associations which Galilee had within their faith.

Yet this new interest, at least in Eusebius, did not derive from a fascination with the paradoxes of the Incarnation and with the humanity of Jesus such as would fuel the hearts of later pilgrims. His interest was based instead, as one might have expected, on his lifelong commitment to scripture and to history. It was the past historical and scriptural significance of Galilee (inasmuch as it both confirmed the prophecies of the Old Testament and was itself the scene of Christ's ministry in the New) which attracted his attention; it did not have a special place in either his spirituality or his theology. Moreover, his understanding of the Incarnation and his emphasis on theophany would not allow Galilee a special status over and above the rest of Palestine; Eusebius simply wished to stress that it was the *whole* of Palestine which had been the scene of God's revelation to mankind throughout history.

2. INDIVIDUAL SITES

It is time at last to concentrate on some of the major sites associated with Jesus' Galilean ministry and to comment on Eusebius' references to them. Again, though we are interested to know what these sites meant more personally to Eusebius' spirituality, normally that will remain unclear. Instead Eusebius' more historical interests will often come to the fore and, since we too in our day share those historical interests and are presented with the same perennial questions of authenticity, it will not be unreasonable to allow these other issues to begin to feature more prominently in our analysis.

(a) Cana: the first draught

It is fitting to begin with Cana. For 'Cana of Galilee', according to St John, was where Jesus had performed the first of his signs, the changing of water into wine (John 2.11). Moreover, Eusebius appears to have given to this event a special theological significance. The same Isaianic prophecy concerning 'Galilee of the Gentiles', which he had expounded in both the *Proof of the Gospel* and the *Commentary on Isaiah*, begins (in the LXX version, Isaiah 8.23 [9.1]) with a strange summons: 'drink this first!' (τοῦτο πρῶτον πίε). Eusebius presumed that this was an invitation made especially to the Gentiles to drink from the cup of salvation, and was quick therefore to see Jesus' action at Cana as an enacted symbol of this Gospel 'draught'. Hence in both these expositions he uses the miracle at Cana as a means of encapsulating almost the entire significance of Galilee according to this prophecy. The light of the Gospel had shone in 'Galilee of the Gentiles' and the wine of the Gospel had first been drunk in 'Cana of Galilee'.[27]

However, the importance of Cana for Eusebius might have been sensed much earlier, in the *Onomasticon*. For although Eusebius sometimes gave less coverage to New Testament sites in this gazetteer than we might have expected (especialy if their 'entry' was dependent on an earlier Old Testament reference),[28] he gave Cana a surprisingly full description:

Here our Lord and God, Jesus Christ, changed the water into [the nature of] wine. Nathaniel came from there and it is located in 'Galilee of the Gentiles'. [29]

First, it should be noted that Eusebius' reference to Christ as 'our Lord and God' (ὁ κύριος ἡμῶν καὶ θεὸς) is the most exalted in the whole of the *Onomasticon*.[30] Then too it can be sensed that

[27] *Dem. Ev.*, 9.8 (*FPG*, ii, 170-71); *Comm. in. Is.* [9.1-2], 62.1-63.30. Eusebius was probably following Origen's exposition of this passage in his (now non-extant) ninth book of *Comm. in Jo.*

[28] The Old Testament verse in this case is Josh. 19.28. For such examples of surprising brevity in *Onom.*, see 104.25-31 (Jericho), 172.12-13 (Chenereth), and esp. 42.10-14 (Bethlehem).

[29] *Onom.*, 116.4-8.

[30] The nearest equivalent occurs in the Jericho passage (*Onom.*, 104.25-31), where the exalted description of Christ is used to magnify by contrast the disobedience of the inhabitants, which Eusebius believed led to the town's destruction. Eusebius normally uses the simple ὁ Χριστὸς which (except in 175.24) Jerome consistently translates as 'dominus' or 'salvator' (see ibid., 43.19-20, 75.20, 139.26).

Eusebius was already (at this quite early date) interpreting the Cana miracle in the light of Isaiah 9.1; for why else would he locate Cana in 'Galilee of the Gentiles'? Cana was thus already for Eusebius the place where Christ not only revealed his divinity but also intimated the future Gospel invitation to the Gentiles.

Thus the miracle at Cana was indeed an event of special significance for Eusebius. May we then presume that the same was true of the place where this event had occurred? Apparently not. For the evidence suggests that Eusebius had no real idea where Cana was! The event may thus have been vitally important; but evidently the place itself was of no importance whatsoever.

It is commonly agreed that St John's constant description of Cana as 'of Galilee' had been a means of distinguishing this Cana from another town of the same name,[31] perhaps even indeed the Cana of Joshua 19.28. Yet what John had so carefully distinguished, Eusebius in the *Onomasticon* now joined together; for he used the Old Testament reference and its place-reference ('near Sidon') as his sole means of identifying the New Testament site! This effectively covered his ignorance, but it also resulted in his location of Cana many miles to the north-west of the lake. It was indeed an unlikely identification, evidently based not on any contemporary knowledge but only upon the coincidence of the name.

By Jerome's day, however, a Cana would have been confidently identified in southern Galilee,[32] conveniently located not far from both Nazareth and Mt. Tabor.[33] For pilgrims such an important event naturally required an observable and particular site.

The same necessity, however, did not pertain for Eusebius, the historian and exegete; he neither needed, nor perhaps even desired, such a neat identification. Indeed it is probably no coincidence that this one place, which he emphasized so repeatedly, was one of the few places named in the Gospels that could no longer be

[31] Strange and Meyers (1981), 161; Mackowski (1979), 279; unlike Freyne (1980), 369.

[32] *Ep.* 46.12, 108.13. In his translation of *Onom.* Jerome was clearly more confident than Eusebius had been of Cana's contemporary existence; characteristically, however, he followed Eusebius' framework, even in its *known* error.

[33] This proximity to Nazareth and Mt. Tabor indeed suggests that the Byzantine site for Cana was modern Kefr Kenna, not Khirbet Qana (Wilkinson (1977), 153; unlike Dalman (1935), 101–6). The historical authenticity of this site is defended by Bagatti (1965) but attacked by Mackowski (1979); for its archaeology, see, e.g., Loffreda (1969).

identified. For as a result he was set free to emphasize the *theology* of Cana, not its setting. The lesson of Cana for us is clear: Eusebius evidently fixed his attention upon the theological and symbolic significance of Gospel events, not upon their particular contemporary location.

(b) Mt. Tabor: scene of the Transfiguration?

There was, however, another event, not so closely connected to the phenomenon of 'Galilee' as such, that was even more important in Eusebius' understanding of Christ's earthly life. This too was at a quite uncertain location; even the evangelists do not offer a place-name. This important event of uncertain location was, of course, the Transfiguration.

Origen had given a special prominence to the Transfiguration as the paradigm of Christian spirituality: it was an encouragement for the soul to transcend the physical realm in its contemplation of the *Logos*.[34] Eusebius too emphasized this event, though perhaps having a tendency to see it in more historical terms as a unique revelation of Christ's eternal nature.[35] Where then did Eusebius locate this important event?

Just over ten miles to the south-west of Tiberias and the lake, not far from both Nazareth and pilgrims' Cana, is the beautiful Mt. Tabor, an almost hemispherical hill rising up amidst the extensive plains of the Jezreel valley. Many have sensed that it has by its very nature the 'aura of a sacred mountain'.[36] Thus, when Christians sought to locate the Transfiguration, that unique act of divine disclosure, Mt. Tabor was easily the most obvious candidate. As a result Cyril stated categorically and without hesitation that Christ's Transfiguration had occurred 'on Mt. Tabor'.[37] However, although he referred to Mt. Tabor no less than

---

[34] See esp. *Comm. in Matt.* [17.1-3], 12.35–13.2, 150–185, and Fr. 357 and 365, 152.30–153.15 and 156.1–73; *Comm in Luc.*, 20, 121; *Hom. in Jer.*, 17.2, 133; *Comm. in Gen.*, 1.7, 10; *Cant.* 3, 205. See a discussion in Harl (1958), 249–53.

[35] As suggested in Gero (1981), 470, fn. 2.

[36] Murphy-O'Connor (1988), 301.

[37] *Catech.*, 12.16; followed by Jerome in *Ep.* 46.12 and 108.13. Mt. Tabor's capacity to attract Gospel events can be seen in subsequent centuries. Jerome speaks of some 'simpler brethren' who made this the scene of the Sermon on the Mount (*Comm. in Matt.* [5.1], PL, xxvi, 34), while Theodosius in the sixth century asserted that his Lord here 'appeared to the disciples after the Resurrection': see Wilkinson (1977), 165.

thirteen times in the *Onomasticon*,[38] and frequently discussed the Transfiguration as an event,[39] Eusebius only once ever linked the Transfiguration with Mt. Tabor explicitly; and even then he did so in quite a tentatitve fashion. This occurred when he expounded LXX Ps. 88.13 [89.12]: 'Mt. Tabor and Hermon joyously praise your name'. Eusebius suggested that the naming of both mountains, 'Tabor and Hermon', might perhaps be a prophecy of Christ's 'marvellous transfigurations' (παραδόξους μεταμορφώσεις) on these two mountains and his 'frequent visits' (τὰς πλείους διατριβάς) to them.[40]

It is indeed a confusing comment, hardly designed to help his readers or ourselves to identify the one mountain of the one Transfiguration. Commentators have rightly concluded that Eusebius clearly had 'no idea which of these two mountains was the scene of the Transfiguration'.[41] Thus his identification is quite uncertain and indeed only forced upon him, one must presume, by the exegetical necessity of proposing a distinctively Christian interpretation that would somehow reveal the common factor linking the two mountains mentioned in the psalm.

Writing in the very last years of his life, Eusebius thus seems on the one hand to have acknowledged the existence of the Mt.

Eusebius, however, had never suggested a location for either the Sermon on the Mount or this post-Resurrection appearance in Galilee. For the latter he merely noted the advantage of Galilee's spaciousness (*QMS*, 10 (1004b)). Although he frequently discussed the great commission of Matt. 28.18-20, he never quoted Matt. 28.16 with its specific reference to the 'mountain which Jesus had told them', neither in *Theoph.* 4.8 (when imaginatively recreating a picture of the apostles' weakness on receiving this commission), nor in his more historical reconstruction in *QMS*, 11 (1006).

[38] For references other than its own separate entry (*Onom.*, 98.23-5), see the register in *GCS*, iii.1.

[39] Especially in *Comm. in Luc.* [9.28], 549a-d, where Eusebius drew a sustained parallel between the Transfiguration and the consummation (συντέλεια); see also *QS*, 14 (928c); *Dem. Ev.*, 3.2.19-20 (*FPG*, i, 107); *Ep. Const.*, 1545b-c; *Comm. in Is.* [17.6], 116.10-14; *Theol. Eccl.*, 1.9.4 and 3.10. In these passages the location is only intimated through either the quotation of the Gospels or the unspecified use of the phrase 'on the mountain' (ἐπὶ τοῦ ὄρους).

[40] *Comm. in Ps.* [88.13], 1092d. Eusebius may here be following Origen, whose Psalms commentary has not survived.

[41] Kopp (1963), 246. Eusebius is 'perplexe' (Abel, i (1933), 353), an opinion shared by Murphy-O'Connor (1988), 301-2, and Wilkinson (1977), 173. He began with the tentative 'I believe' (οἶμαί γε), then blurred the issue by speaking of plural 'transfigurations' and finally concluded by asking his readers to formulate their own solution!

Tabor-tradition;[42] on the other hand, he seems still to have been convinced that Mt. Hermon, forty miles to the north-east of the lake, had an equal, if not greater, chance of having been the actual location of this event.

Within little more than a decade, however, such honest Christian uncertainty would come to an end. Cyril, in a passing reference to the Transfiguration, which required no identification, succinctly stated his settled opinion: the Transfiguration had definitely occured 'on Mt. Tabor'.[43] Once again the contrast can be sensed between our two bishops. It will therefore be most instructive to ask what it was that made Eusebius uncertain and then to note what it was, by contrast, that caused Cyril to be so assured.

There are several possible reasons for Eusebius' lack of conviction about the identification of Mt. Tabor as the scene of the Transfiguration. First, as a keen student of the scriptures he will no doubt have examined the Gospel text quite closely in order to evaluate the competing claims of Mt. Tabor and Mt. Hermon; such a study, we suggest, would probably have inclined him slightly in favour of Mt. Hermon. Then, as an experienced local historian, he would have known something of the history of Mt. Tabor; this seems only to have confirmed his opinion that Mt. Tabor could not have witnessed the Transfiguration at that time. Finally, as a theologian, we shall note briefly once more that Eusebius would not have seen the need to come down decisively in favour of any one location. Thus, if his exegetical and historical enquiries caused him to be uncertain, his theology would convince him that such uncertainty was indeed quite acceptable.

Eusebius naturally accepted the witness of scripture, including that of the evangelists, as statements of historical and geographical fact. Although in theological terms the Transfiguration perhaps

---

[42] The pre-existence of this tradition, though not assured, is more than probable. In the second century *Gospel of the Hebrews* Jesus is carried to 'great Mt. Tabor' (quoted by Origen in *Comm. in Jo.*, 2.12, 67, and *Hom. in Jer.*, 15.4, 128.26–29: see Hennecke, i (1963), 54). Although this in itself probably refers to Christ's temptations (Kopp (1963), 245; Abel, i (1933), 354; Bagatti (1971), 24; unlike Barnabé (1901), 50–54), it reveals an undercurrent of Christian interest in this mountain that could well have led to the identification of Mt. Tabor as the scene of the Transfiguration by the time of Origen. In Origen's many references to the Transfiguration he admittedly never suggested a location for this event, but he may, like Eusebius, have used Ps. 89.12 as a verse which neatly summarized the two most likely possibilities.

[43] *Catech.*, 12.16.

encourages a concentration on the invisible realm, and despite the fact that the evangelists had not specified its location, it remained for Eusebius a truly historical event, firmly located in time and place.[44]

While Eusebius studied the Gospels with this question of location in his mind, he would have noted that, though the evangelists did not name that location precisely, nevertheless Matthew·and Mark concurred that Jesus had taken his disciples to a 'high mountain' (ὄρος ὑψηλὸν) just six days after Peter's confession in the area of Caesarea Philippi,[45] an important city at the foot of Mt. Hermon. Eusebius' study of the Gospels thus might have suggested to him, as to many others since, that this private disclosure may also have occurred in this remote part of the country, perhaps indeed on some part of the Hermon 'massif' (though conceivably lower down in some part of the modern 'Golan Heights').[46]

For Eusebius had noted Jesus' frequent desire for privacy in less populated parts and may have concluded that the Lord especially frequented these more remote mountainous areas to the north-east of the lake.[47] Moreover, in his own usage of τὸ ὄρος ('the

---

[44] There is no indication, for example, that Eusebius would have interpreted the Gospel references to the 'high mountain' as intentionally pure allegory: Eusebius does indeed draw a contrast with Moses on Sinai (*Dem. Ev.*, 3.2.19–20 (*FPG*, i, 107); cf. Origen, *Comm. in Ex.*, 3.2, 165 and 12.3, 265; and *Comm. in Num.*, 7.2–4, 40–44) but this did not negate the testimony of the Gospels as history.

[45] Matt. 17.1 (= Mark 9.2) and Matt. 16.13 (= Mark 8.27). Luke 9.28 speaks only of 'the mountain' (τὸ ὄρος); cf. also 'the holy mountain' (τῷ ἁγίῳ ὄρει) in 2 Pet. 1.18.

[46] For a summary of modern suggestions that endorse this general vicinity see Kopp (1963), 243; also Maraval (1982). The authenticity of the traditional site on Mt. Tabor was defended by Barnabé (1901).

[47] See *QS*, 14 (928c) and *Dem. Ev.*, 3.6.6 (*FPG*, i, 145–6); the former leads directly into a discussion of the Transfiguration. Many visitors today draw the same conclusion, that the deserted hills on the north-east side of the lake could well have been an area frequented by Jesus for prayer. If this was Eusebius' assumption, then he would also have probably located the feeding of the five thousand on the eastern side of the lake. By Egeria's day (Wilkinson (1981), 196–200) this was commemorated, again conveniently, at Tabgha on the western shore near Capernaum: see Jerome, *Ep.* 46.12, 108.13. Tabgha was also the place where the story of John 21 was commemorated, an episode only discussed once by Eusebius in his entire corpus: in *QMS*, 10, 1006. For Cyril, however, the 'fish' and 'hot coals' of this story were important witnesses to Christ (*Catech.*, 14.23). The pioneer of Tabgha, the most important new development in fourth century Galilee, is therefore more likely to have been Cyril than Eusebius. For the archaeology of the site, see Loffreda (1975); and for discussion of these miracle sites, see Kopp (1963), 204–30.

mountain')[48] he showed an awareness that the evangelists need not necessarily have been thinking of a large, independent 'mountain' that our own English word tends to suggest. Thus the Gospel writers might well have been referring to this mountainous area, now known as the Golan Heights.[49] Strictly therefore, Eusebius may have concluded, Mt. Hermon itself was no more necessary than Mt. Tabor; anywhere in the whole area that culminates in Hermon might have been the authentic site.

As a result, Eusebius would probably not have seen the distinct and separate nature of Mt. Tabor as a necessary endorsement of the Gospel text; this was simply not the kind of 'mountain' to which they had been referring. Indeed Mt. Tabor's location sixty miles away from Caesarea Philippi and on precisely the opposite side of the lake only militated further against its claims to authenticity. All in all, the text of scripture seemed instead to favour a location in the mountainous region near Caesarea Philippi and below Mt. Hermon.

Eusebius' scepticism concerning Mt. Tabor would have been strengthened by his unique knowledge of local history. Unlike many of his Christian contemporaries, Eusebius would have known something of Mt. Tabor's military and demographic history. In particular, Josephus had recorded how he himself had needed to build a surrounding wall in order to defend Mt. Tabor in the Jewish Revolt of AD 67;[50] moreover, he had elsewhere implied that before that date there had been a village on its summit.[51] Was

---

[48] E.g., Gergesa and Gadara (*Onom.*, 74.11–15). On the awkward issue of Gergesa, Gadara and Gerasa, the three different names in the Gospels for the location of 'Legion' (Matt. 8.28; Mark 5.1; Luke 8.26), see Eus., *Onom.* (loc. cit.; 64.1–4) and Origen, *Comm. in Jo.* [1.28], 6.41, 150.3–20. Lagrange (1896) saw Origen's confident assertion of a contemporary Gergesa as a fabrication, followed blindly (p. 522) by Eusebius, 'le plus fervent de ses admirateurs' (p. 502). A closer comparison between the precise wording of Origen and Eusebius, however, reveals, we suggest, Eusebius' independence and his own research (thus Dalman (1935), 178; unlike Lagrange 515), though also perhaps his lesser confidence in dismissing other possibilities (see *Onom.*, 64.3–4; Gadara, like Gergesa, is conveniently located by Eusebius 'on the mountain' (ἐν τῷ ὄρει): *Onom.*, 74.11–14). His apparently indirect identification of Gergesa with a contemporary village (noted by Abel (1927), 119) does not necessarily deny its contemporary existence. Gergesa's validity was accepted by Dalman, op. cit., 178 but attacked by Romanoff (1937), p. vii and Murphy-O'Connor (1988), 263.

[49] As argued in modern times by Dalman (1935), 155.

[50] *BJ*, 2.20.6.

[51] Ibid., 4.1.8 and *Vita*, 37, discussed in Kopp (1963), 244.

this really, Eusebius may have asked, a likely site for the Transfiguration, Jesus' intimate and personal disclosure to his disciples?

Plainly, given the unclear nature of the Gospel evidence and the varied nature of contemporary history and geography, an assured identification was quite impossible. On the other hand, what biblical and historical evidence there was favoured Mt. Hermon rather more than Mt. Tabor. This did not, of course, prevent other Christians from advocating Mt. Tabor and Eusebius acknowledged this, as we have seen, when it aided his exegesis of LXX Ps. 88.13 [89.12].[52] However, in his otherwise total silence about this tradition, he clearly manifests a historian's scepticism and a scholar's ambivalence.

This silence is only the more remarkable in the light of Eusebius' twin interest in both Mt. Tabor itself and the event of the Transfiguration. He talked of both frequently, but only once ever linked them together. However, this dual interest in both Mt. Tabor and the Transfiguration highlights for us a possible tension within Eusebius, at once both historical geographer and theologian of the *Logos*. The Transfiguration, as recorded in the Gospels and as understood by Eusebius, with its rebuke of Peter's desire to 'capture' this spiritual revelation in physical structures[53] and with its revelation of Christ as the eternal *Logos*, was the one Gospel event that might militate most strongly against subsequent Christian interest in physical location.[54] Surely this of all Gospel events beckoned the believer to forsake the physical realm and instead to contemplate the eternal. Its precise physical location was strictly irrelevant.

Eusebius himself drew this very lesson from the Transfiguration in his *Letter to Constantia*.[55] Interest in Christ incarnate, he asserted, should be superseded by devotion to Christ's invisible, but eternal, nature that was revealed on that one occasion in the Transfiguration; the physical realm was but a temporary necessity

---

[52] *Comm. in Ps.* [88.13], 1092d.

[53] See Matt. 17.4 (= Mark 9.5, Luke 9.33).

[54] Cf. Wilkinson (1977), 173; visitors today frequently comment on the irony of the three chapels, built in apparent fulfilment of Peter's desire, against dominical command.

[55] *Ep. Const.*, 1545b–c.

in the revelation of the spiritual.[56] Since Eusebius' general approach to the Christ-event, which reckons the Incarnation as more exceptional than normative, coloured his attitude to 'holy places' in general,[57] surely would it not especially influence his attitude to the scene of the Transfiguration?

Thus, though an interest in the historical geography of the New Testament was by no means inconsistent with such a spiritualizing theology, Eusebius would on this issue have had an extra theological reason for being content with the impossibility of precise identification. The Transfiguration was very important, but that importance did not necessitate a selected site: this of all events did not require place. Once again Eusebius reveals his colours. As an exegete and historian he was content without certainty; as a theologian that certainty was unnecessary.

Cyril's response was entirely different. For him certainty as to the location of the Transfiguration was quite possible and indeed quite necessary. His own sense of the appropriate and even of the aesthetic would give him every reason for believing the growing tradition that favoured Mt. Tabor; tradition and common sense made it quite possible to fix the location of the Transfiguration with certainty. Then again, it will be seen how Cyril, as a pilgrim–pastor, knew the need for pilgrims to have a fixed place at which to commemorate this event, the need for this to conform if possible to their expectations, and the need for such places, again if possible, to be conveniently located. The identification of the site was a practical necessity.

But such a sense of necessity was no doubt prompted by Cyril's theology. Eusebius' attitude to the Transfiguration and the Incarnation in general would, we have suggested, have caused him to disparage the need for any fixed identification; the Transfiguration was intended by God to lure us away from such physical concerns. Cyril, however, emphasized the importance of the Incarnation in its own right and saw the Transfiguration as a great event in Christ's incarnate life. To Eusebius the Incarnation was a temporary and exceptional phenomenon; it was the revelation of the spiritual *Logos*, revealed at the Transfiguration, that was to be considered normative. To Cyril the Incarnation had an inherent

---

[56] Did Eusebius see Constantia as really a latter-day St Peter in her desire for the tangible, visible and constant?

[57] See above 3.2(*c*) and 4.4.

status and lasting value, and the Transfiguration only contributed yet more to its wonder. For Eusebius, therefore, the 'dynamic' of the Transfiguration was very much 'from earth to heaven', while for Cyril it was probably the reverse: heaven, he might sense, had been revealed on earth and such a great event clearly required an appropriate and matching location. This is not, of course, to say that Cyril would have invented a site *ex nihilo*. What it does mean, however, is that with his more incarnational theology he would have had extra incentive for accepting wholeheartedly any existing tradition; and acceptance would be easier when the place suggested was as plausible and as attractive as Mt. Tabor.

It has already been suggested that such a tradition, identifying Mt. Tabor as the scene of the Transfiguration, was in existence in Cyril's day, and indeed had probably been established for quite some time.[58] Thus, when he declared his own confident belief in the authenticity of Mt. Tabor in his *Lectures*, Cyril was probably not advocating anything radically new. On the contrary, he may indeed have felt that his case was the stronger for resting on such a long-standing tradition. Seen in this light, his acceptance of Mt. Tabor may perhaps be less remarkable than Eusebius' continuing scepticism. Nevertheless, we would do well still to ask what were some of those reasons for the growth of this tradition and what it was in that tradition which attracted Cyril but left Eusebius unmoved. Why was Cyril so convinced that the Transfiguration had occurred on Mt. Tabor?

Mt. Tabor had certain irresistible attractions. Its abrupt stance is without parallel in the rest of Palestine. Unlike the Hermon range it is solitary. Moreover, its summit is accessible and quite suitable for church-building; since Christians easily assumed (though it was not strictly necessary) that the Transfiguration could only have occurred on the very top of a mountain, Mt. Tabor, unlike Mt. Hermon, offerred them an ideal and exact place at which to commemorate the Transfiguration *in situ*.

Then again, Tabor's (previously noted) numinous quality meets perfectly the retrospective needs of pilgrims. Although they desire the presence of Christ, his absence is more easily accepted if the location is appropriate, if it conforms to their expectations, and if

---

[58] This tradition can only have developed after the desertion of the village and in ignorance of Josephus.

it is conducive to prayer. Mt. Tabor is all of these. It would be hard therefore to find a place that is more appropriate, religiously, practically or aesthetically, than Mt. Tabor. Such may be our thoughts today; such too may have been the reasons for the inception of the tradition. But would Cyril himself have been influenced by such factors? Such questions cannot be answered at this distance in time with total confidence, yet a brief comparison of Eusebius and Cyril (taking in Jerome) seems to confirm that Cyril, unlike Eusebius, would have been quite open to such considerations.

With regard to Eusebius we take but one example: his very bald account of Palestine in the *Onomasticon*. This work is so void of colourful and pictorial comments that Jerome, when translating it, naturally felt compelled to add a few comments of his own, based on his own experience of Palestine. Thus the Jordan, he notes, reaches the Dead Sea only after much meandering ('post multos circuitos').[59] More intersting still, Jerome describes Mt. Tabor as a 'sublime mountain, remarkably rounded' ('mira rotunditate sublimis').[60] Elsewhere he similarly remarks on this mountain's unique qualities,[61] but Eusebius never did. Evidently Jerome responded warmly to these geographical stimuli. Eusebius did not.

Admittedly Cyril also failed to comment on Mt. Tabor's attractions. Yet his one reference to it was only a passing one[62] and elsewhere in his *Lectures* he would reveal quite clearly his imaginative and colourful mind. For example, he commented on the beauty of the recent spring flowers,[63] the majesty of the moon and sun,[64] the variety of trees in their seasons[65] and the violence of a recent storm.[66] Such a pastor evidently knew his people's need to find God in creation. Such a man, we may presume, would also have known their warm response to Mt. Tabor.

Cyril was thus more than likely to have been attracted to the

---

[59] *Onom.*, 105.17–18.

[60] *Onom.*, 99.23; a comment caused by his 'admiration religieuse' for this mountain, according to Abel, i (1933), 353.

[61] Noticeably in *Comm. in Hos.*, 1.5.1 (CCSL, lxxvi, 51): 'rotundus atque sublimis, et ex omni parte finitur aequaliter'.

[62] *Catech.*, 12.16.

[63] Ibid., 14.10.

[64] Ibid., 18.6–9; 14.22.

[65] Ibid., 18.6.

[66] Ibid., 6.4.

identification of Mt. Tabor as the scene of the Transfiguration on the grounds that this mountain was religiously and aesthetically appropriate. Moreover, it is clear that as a liturgist too he saw the great importance of what is appropriate and fitting: Egeria was constantly struck by how the worship in Jerusalem was always 'appropriate' to the particular place.[67] If therefore, as all this evidence suggests, Cyril was indeed concerned to find the place which was most appropriate for the commemoration of the Transfiguration, it can be little surprise that he came down so decisively in favour of Mt. Tabor.

However, it must be noted that there may have been a further, decidedly practical, motive for his decision: Mt. Tabor's convenient position. Eusebius had noted Mt. Tabor's proximity to Nazareth;[68] but this would scarcely have been a consideration in his strictly academic pursuit of finding the correct site for this Gospel event. Practical convenience for Christian visiting was not a factor at all.

For Cyril, a generation later, it was. Eusebius might reckon that Mt. Hermon had the greater claim to authenticity, but Cyril knew well that only the most enthusiastic pilgrims would venture so far out of their way. Mt. Tabor, however, much further south and located neatly between Nazareth and Lake Galilee, was eminently suitable. With the rising demands of pilgrims, only the most stringent academic could have settled for the uncertainties of distant Hermon. It made perfect sense for Cyril to decide instead in favour of Mt. Tabor.[69]

The question of Mt. Tabor thus focuses for us some of the essential differences between Eusebius and Cyril. In particular it shows the difference between the academic and the pilgrim–pastor. Eusebius could discuss the academic arguments; Cyril did not have that luxury. Liturgy demands place, and pilgrims often desire even more—a precise identification. Cyril needed to make a clear-cut decision. As a result, whereas Eusebius might have been unhappy with any claim to assured authenticity that could not survive historical scrutiny, Cyril needed to pay attention to factors other

---

[67] See *Egeria*, 25.5 (cf. also 31.1, 32.1, 35.4, 36.3).

[68] *Onom.*, 138.24–140.2.

[69] Christian confidence in Mt. Tabor's selection could perhaps have been cemented by the factor of Jewish predominance in Galilee. Dabeira, for example, was a large Jewish town located at the very foot of the mount (*Onom.*, 78.5–7). Was a Christian Mt. Tabor therefore a 'display of force' or, conversely, a more timid appropriation of a defensible unit?

than strict historical accuracy. Contemporary criteria, such as the practical and the appropriate, especially when endorsed by an established tradition, were sufficient to carry the day.

Finally, our discussion can be seen to have highlighted something that has proved to be a perennial problem in the 'Holy Land' ever since the days of Cyril. It is not just at Mt. Tabor that the claims of strict historical authenticity run counter to the requirements of pilgrims.[70] Although a pilgrim is indeed concerned with the exact location, another 'appropriate' place, more conducive to prayer, may be of greater value. Cyril, understood the mind of the pilgrim; Eusebius' mind was that of a historian.

(c) *Nazareth and Capernaum: occupied villages*

Capernaum and Nazareth introduce us to a completely new range of problems, because these villages, explicitly named in the Gospels as the places respectively of Christ's childhood[71] and ministry,[72] had been continuously inhabited since the time of Christ. It was perhaps ironic to Christians that the inhabitants were almost all non-Christian Jews,[73] but this continuous inhabitation at least had the advantage for Nazareth and Capernaum (unlike Cana and Mt. Tabor) of removing the initial problems of identification. There was no possible doubt that these were truly the Nazareth and Capernaum of the Gospels.[74] Moreover, according to the canons of archaeological enquiry, the continuous inhabitation of these villages would also enhance the probable authenticity of any Christian sites within them. Such continuous inhabitation would probably have encouraged a continuous and reliable tradition, while any animosity between the Christian few and the Jewish

---

[70] The obvious modern example is the Garden Tomb. Our analysis of Eusebius' evidence seems to confirm the probable authenticity of the Holy Sepulchre, yet the natural appeal of this quiet garden cannot be denied and should not be disparaged. Its custodians can rightly claim that theology is more important than geography, that the truth of the Resurrection is ultimately more important than its supposed location. Even if, therefore, the Resurrection did not occur in this garden, it is still an appropriate place for the truth of the Resurrection to be proclaimed.

[71] Matt. 2.23; Luke 2.51, 4.16.

[72] Matt. 4.13b; Mark 1.21; Luke 4.31; John 2.12.

[73] This was especially the case at Nazareth: see Dalman (1935), 68; Kopp (1963), 54–5; Wilkinson (1977), 165.

[74] For the modern debate over, and eventual acceptance of, Tel Hum as the site of ancient Capernaum, see Kopp (1963), 171–9.

majority would only have strengthened the Christians' determination to preserve that tradition.[75] Indeed recent archaeology
has revealed in Capernaum a house used for Christian worship
before Constantine, believed then (or later) to have been that of
St Peter,[76] and in Nazareth a grotto showing signs of third century
veneration as the home of Mary.[77]

However, Eusebius reveals no awareness of these important and
intimate sites from Christ's life. If the archaeologists are right,
Eusebius would definitely have known of their existence and would
probably have visited them himself. Again, as with the 'true cross',
we are faced with the task of evaluating Eusebius' silence. Does
his silence here indicate that our presuppositions (in this case the
converging conclusions of several archaeologists) are wrong and
need revision. Or can Eusebius' silence be satisfactorily explained,

---

[75] However, according to Epiphanius—*Haer.*, 30.11 (*PL*, xli, 426a), writing in
374—when Count Joseph (fifty years previously) had sought Constantine's permission to build churches in Galilee no Christians were allowed by the Jews to
live in Nazareth, Capernaum, Sepphoris or Tiberias. However, this, a monochrome
picture of Jewish hostility is contradicted not only by the evidence of the
archaeologists, in favour of some Jewish-Christian presence, but also by ancient
literary sources: Eusebius himself speaks of the Lord's relatives continuing to live
in Nazareth (following the testimony of Julius Africanus, in *Hist. Eccl.*, 1.7.14) and
there is evidence that one Conon from Nazareth suffered in the Decian Persecution
(*AnBoll*, xviii, 180: see Kopp (1963), 54). Rabbinic sources too (e.g., *Midrash
Koheleth*, vii, 20 ff.: 14.2; 109.4) imply a Christian presence in second-century
Capernaum and perhaps into the fourth century (Murphy-O'Connor (1988), 188;
unlike Dalman (1935), 150 and Orfali (1922), 2–3). Epiphanius may thus conceivably
have been referring only to Gentile Christians (as suggested by Bagatti (1969), 17);
more probably, however, he was simply overstating the case. Despite Kopp (loc.
cit.), Goodman (1983), and Pritz (1988), who argue that the Christian congregations
had totally disappeared by the fourth century, it seems best in the following to
suppose that they continued to exist into our period, even if small in number, as
argued by Tsafrir (1975b). Epiphanius' evidence would nevertheless confirm that
the Jewish stronghold in Galilee could at times make it difficult for Christians living
in the region.

[76] An ordinary house was apparently set aside for worship from an early date.
This became the centre first of a *domus ecclesia* in the fourth century, probably
seen by Egeria (see Wilkinson (1981), 194), and then in the next century of an
octagonal church (see especially Strange and Shanks (1982), following Corbo (1969)
and (1975)). For some criticisms of Corbo's conclusions, see Foerster (1971) and
even Strange (1977). A little further to the north is the Capernaum synagogue; the
nature and date of this (and its predecessors) continues to be a matter of much
debate and little certainty: see, e.g., Corbo, *et al.* (1970), Loffreda (1972), Strange
and Shanks (1983).

[77] Bagatti (1969), esp. 172–3; this grotto may be the 'cave' seen by Egeria
(Wilkinson (1981), 193). Bagatti's arguments for an adjacent Jewish-Christian
synagogue are not so convincing (see Strange and Meyers (1981), 56–7, 106–7).

either as a sign of some characteristic disinterest or as a sign of some conscious disapproval?

Our portrait of him so far would predispose us to endorse the conclusions of the archaeologists, and to suggest that Eusebius' silence should in no way be taken as a contradiction of the archaeological evidence, but rather as a sign of some disinterest or disapproval.

It therefore comes as no surprise to learn that Bagatti, one of the archaeologists responsible for excavation at Nazareth, has concluded, for example, that Eusebius' silence concerning Nazareth reflects his disapproval of the local Jewish-Christian sects who were probably responsible for the preservation of these Christian sites.[78] Such silence due to disapproval would match exactly his response to the the discovery of the 'true cross'.

It will be noticed, however, in what follows that, while this disapproval of Jewish-Christians may have contributed to his silence concerning these local sites, there were no doubt other factors as well. Most probably his silence was chiefly a sign of his comparative disinterest in such places and of his greater concern with the text of scripture, its proper exegesis, and the vindication of its prophecies. Conceivably too he was influenced by the strong Jewish presence in Galilee, in the light of which any interest in Christian sites was faintly embarassing (revealing the strange weakness of Christianity in its place of origin) and perhaps even slightly foolish (since it is never wise to publicize one's hopes when in a vulnerable position). Certainty on this matter will therefore elude us. Eusebius' silence was most probably a natural one, in keeping with his more exegetical concerns; yet it remains possible that his silence was also somewhat more strategic and deliberate.

Eusebius refers to Capernaum explicitly on just three occasions, in the *Onomasticon*, the *Theophany*, and the *Commentary on Isaiah*.

Capernaum, beside Lake Gennesaret. It is a village still to this day in 'Galilee of the Gentiles', in the territory of Zebulun and Naphtali. [79]

---

[78] Bagatti (1969), 18–20. However, the possibility of Gentile Christian presence and ownership, especially in Capernaum, cannot be ignored. The archaeological argument for the existence of these pre-Constantinian sites is stronger than the Franciscans' deduction that the Christians concerned must necessarily have been *Jewish*-Christians.

[79] *Onom.*, 120.2–4.

Simon went forth from Capernaum, which is a village of Galilee, and became known throughout the whole creation even to the regions of the west. [80]

Capernaum, Bethsaida and Chorazin and the other villages recorded in the Gospels are still to this day to be seen beside the Lake of Tiberias. [81]

Meanwhile, his references to contemporary Nazareth are even fewer. There is naturally an entry in the *Onomasticon*:

Nazareth, from which Christ gained his name the 'Nazarene', and from which we who are now called 'Christians' long ago gained the name 'Nazarenes'. [The village] is still to this day in Galilee . . . near Mt. Tabor. [82]

Apart from this there are just two other passages of any length that discuss the Gospel events associated with Nazareth. One is an exposition of Matthew 2.23 ('he shall be called a Nazarene'),[83] the other a discussion of Jesus' reading from the scroll of Isaiah, as recounted in Luke 4.16-22.[84] On neither of these occasions, however, did Eusebius suggest the continuance of a village of that name in his local Palestine.

On all these occasions Eusebius seems instead to have been principally concerned with the exposition of scripture, trying to highlight the truth of its prophecies. Such an apologetic purpose was only to be expected in the *Proof of the Gospel*; yet seemingly it spread over as well into the *Theophany*, his commentaries, and even into the *Onomasticon*!

Thus it was, for example, that he seldom dwelt upon the significance of the Annunciation at Nazareth. Cyril, with his more incarnational theology, might refer to this event on several occasions, asserting that the Archangel Gabriel and the Virgin *theotokos* were important witnesses to Christ;[85] but Eusebius scarcely discussed this event, except to affirm its historical nature.[86]

---

[80] *Theoph.*, 4.7 (*LET*, 221).

[81] *Comm. in Is.* [9.1–3], 62.30–32.

[82] *Onom.*, 138.24–140.2.

[83] *Dem. Ev.*, 7.2.46–53 (*FPG*, ii, 84–6).

[84] *Comm. in Is.* [61.1–3], 378.30–379.30. There were, of course, not a few occasions when 'Nazareth' was referred to briefly in passing.

[85] *Catech.*, 10.19; see also 10.10, 12.31, and 17.6.

[86] For his reconciliation of Luke's Nazareth with Matthew's Bethlehem, see *QS*, 16, 933–5. The Annunciation does not really feature in the Lukan commentary and it is never linked directly to Nazareth. Origen, by contrast, in *Comm. in Jo.* [1.50], Fr. 27, 504.20, would see Nazareth straightforwardly as the 'city of the virgin' (ἡ πόλις τῆς παρθένου).

Instead, apart from one reference to Jesus' childhood in Nazareth,[87] he focused exclusively on Jesus' visit to the synagogue (Luke 4.16 ff.); for this was an explicit fulfilment of Isaiah 61.1–3.[88]

Some words from Isaiah's prophecy similarly coloured his attitude towards Capernaum. Obviously the fulfilment of Isaiah 9.1 was the cause of his reference to Capernaum in the commentary. More interestingly, however, in his entry for Capernaum in the *Onomasticon* he would not comment on this as the place of Christ's ministry or miracles;[89] indeed Christ is not mentioned at all. Instead the village is simply described as being in 'Galilee of the Gentiles'. Once again the fulfilment of prophecy is in his mind, almost to the exclusion of all other considerations; the pilgrim's interest in this as the chief place of Christ's incarnate ministry was scarcely shared by Eusebius.

The same disinterest in Capernaum as the former scene of Christ's ministry can be noted throughout his writings. Cyril might refer without hesitation to Capernaum in the briefest of allusions to the healing of the paralytic,[90] but Eusebius would not refer to it at all in any of his discussions of Christ's ministry; unlike Origen,[91] he would never state in so many words that Capernaum was the chief scene of that ministry.

Capernaum was thus not a 'holy place' in any sense; there was no amazement in Eusebius that *this* had been the home of the incarnate Christ. His reference to Capernaum in the *Theophany* only proves the point. Capernaum is mentioned not because of Christ's ministry there, but only because of Peter's residence there! If in his other references Eusebius' concerns were exegetical, on this one occasion they were more historical. At no time, however, were his interests a reflection of an incarnational or prayerful spirituality.

---

[87] *Comm. in Ps.* [87.16], 1065a; note how he never described Nazareth as the 'nurse of the Lord', as later did Jerome in *Ep.* 108.13.

[88] See *Comm in Luc.* [4.18], 533a–b; *Dem. Ev.*, 3.1.1 and 9.10; *Comm. in Is.* [61.1–3], 378.30–379.30; *Comm. in Ps.* [52.7], 461c–d. In these passages he habitually sees this episode at the synagogue as marking the effective beginning of Jesus' ministry, after the descent of the Holy Spirit but before his preaching to the 'poor in spirit' (Matt. 5.2). It is interesting to note that he never discusses the Pinnacle incident (Luke 4.29–30) nor the theme of Christ's rejection in his 'home-country' (Luke 4.24).

[89] *Onom.*, 120.2–4; unlike Jerome in *Ep.* 108.13.

[90] *Catech.*, 5.8.

[91] In his extended discussion of Jesus' movement to Capernaum in *Comm. in Jo.* [2.12], 170.1–183.6.

Eusebius' predominant concern for the fulfilment of prophecy is seen finally, and most clearly, in his entry for Nazareth in the *Onomasticon*. St Matthew had asserted that Christ's residence there fulfilled an Old Testament prophecy: 'he shall be called a Nazarene' (Matt. 2.23). The fact that such a prophecy could not readily be found in the Old Testament posed a well-known exegetical problem, which Eusebius himself would tackle with typical confidence in the *Proof of the Gospel*.[92] It was this problematic fulfilment of prophecy that was clearly in his mind as he compiled the *Onomasticon*; for the whole entry focuses on the name 'Nazarene' as applied to Christ (and later to the first Christians). No other Gospel events are mentioned.

Eusebius' approach therefore to both Capernaum and Nazareth was almost totally dependent on his interest in prophecy. The events of Christ's life were not emphasized in their own right and no attention was given to any surviving sites. Most probably this reflected Eusebius' over-riding interest in exegetical matters and his comparative disinterest in the 'pilgrimage potential' of Gospel locations; the text was more important than the place. Yet it is not impossible that this rather exclusive concentration on prophecy with regard to Capernaum and Nazareth might have been encouraged by another factor: his desire to avoid referring to Christian sites within villages that were preserved (most probably) by Jewish-Christians, and located in the middle of Jewish communities largely opposed to the message of Christ. There were thus two local situations that Eusebius might have wished to obscure.

The non-Christian nature of Galilee might well have been an influential factor; this state of affairs must have been slightly embarassing, indeed painful.[93] Anything that might draw attention to the contemporary situation in Galilee was therefore best avoided. Jewish predominance there revealed Christianity's weakness. It was safer instead to concentrate on the fulfilment of prophecy, which for Eusebius was a vindication of the truth of Christ.

However, the affect on Eusebius of the presence of Jewish-*Christians* in these villages is less clear. Bagatti portrays Eusebius

---

[92] *Dem. Ev.*, 7.2.46–53 (*FPG*, ii, 84–6); for a similar argument concerning Jesus as the 'Christ' and the 'high priest', see *Hist. Eccl.*, 1.3 *passim*.

[93] Kopp (1963), 58, even suggests that Christians such as Origen converted this pain into a theological anathema upon the places that had rejected Christ.

as fiercely opposed to all Jewish-Christians,[94] and suggests that Eusebius' comment in the *Onomasticon* concerning the former use of 'Nazarenes' as a name for Christians reflects his disagreement with the 'Nazarene' sect, one of the major Jewish-Christian groupings.[95] Eusebius, he claims, wished to 'show the distinction between the ancient Nazarenes and those of his own day who inhabited this village'.[96] On this reading Eusebius would have been deliberately trying to show that orthodox Gentile Christians were the true Nazarenes, and was disassociating himself from this Jewish-Christian group, members of which may have lived in the village of the same name.

Bagatti's suggestion is quite plausible. But so much of this debate is conjecture founded on insufficient evidence. It would indeed come as little surprise if it could be proved that Eusebius' silence concerning the Christian sites in Nazareth and Capernaum was caused by his disapproval of the Jewish-Christians who looked after them. But in the absence of further evidence it seems safest to suggest that Eusebius' silence is chiefly a reflection of the high priority that he gave to the exegesis of scripture and of his comparative disinterest in the places of contemporary Galilee. 'Holy places' as such seem to have been far from his mind. Such pilgrimage interest was perhaps a luxury only for a later age; for Eusebius it was certainly an untried avenue.

(d) Bethsaida: unfulfilled prophecy

The identification of Bethsaida was similarly no problem for Eusebius.[97] Eusebius knew only too well that the Bethsaida of the Gospels had been refounded by Philip as Bethsaida-Julias just a few years before the start of Jesus' ministry.[98] Situated by the Jordan as that river entered the lake from the north, it had soon

---

[94] Bagatti (1969), 18–20, based on passages such as *Hist. Eccl.*, 3.27.1–6 (analysed in Pritz (1988), 15–20).

[95] The group was attacked by Epiphanius for their observation of the Law, but not for any heterodoxy: see *Haer.*, 29.7.2 ff. (PL, xli, 401b–405a).

[96] Bagatti (1969), 20.

[97] For the modern problem of the identification of this Bethsaida-Julias, at once both 'city' and 'village' (Luke 9.10, John 1.44; cf. Mark 8.23), both in Galilee and Gaulonitis (John 12.21; cf. Josephus, *BJ*, 2.9.1; 3.3.1), see Dalman (1935), 161–4, Baldi (1960), and Kopp (1963), 180–86.

[98] *Chron.*, §2, 533c; following Josephus, *AJ*, 18.2.1, and *BJ*, 2.9.1.

become a flourishing and important town, second only to Tiberias.[99]

Despite that, it has been observed by scholars that, once again, Eusebius draws little or no attention to this contemporary town in the *Onomasticon*: 'Bethsaida is located in Galilee on Lake Gennesaret.'[100] His reference is instead anachronistic in style: he uses the more ancient name for the lake, 'Lake Gennesaret', and omits the town's more contemporary name of 'Julias'. Only the present tense of the verb ($\kappa\epsilon\hat{\iota}\tau\alpha\iota$) suggests its continued existence. In a second, passing reference to Bethsaida twenty years later in the *Proof of the Gospel*, even this suggestion would be removed: 'Bethsaida *was* ($\hat{\eta}\nu$) in Galilee'.[101] The impression conveyed was that Bethsaida was a thing of the past. Yet in his day it was a flourishing town of almost comparable standing to Tiberias. Did Eusebius have any particular reason for not referring to this contemporary town?

A possible explanation for Eusebius' reticence comes to light when it is considered that his ordering of place-names in the *Onomasticon* was not strictly alphabetical. The entries for each letter instead were listed in the order of the Bible, being 'arranged book by book; and within each [biblical] book, in the order of their occurrence'.[102] Thus, for example, when he came to the Gospels, Eusebius scanned the text of Matthew first, before supplementing his results from texts in the other Gospels.[103] However, this selection process had an unfortunate result. The first reference to Bethsaida in Matthew reads as follows: 'woe to you, Bethsaida!' (Matt. 11.21). In the other Gospels this dominical curse either does not occur at all (Mark and John) or is preceded by a harmless place-reference (Luke 9.10 precedes the curses in 10.13). With priority given to Matthew, however, Eusebius' own method brought him face to face with an awkward reality: Christ had cursed Bethsaida, yet to all appearances the town had only gone from strength to strength. Jesus' prophecy had seemingly failed.

That Eusebius would have wished otherwise is obvious. Another statement, later in the *Onomasticon* makes this quite clear.

[99] As suggested by both Ptolemy, *Geographia*, 5.5.3 and Pliny, *Nat. Hist.*, 5.71.
[100] *Onom.*, 58.11–12. Baldi (1960), 128 speaks of Eusebius' 'laconica notizia'.
[101] *Dem. Ev.*, 9.8.7 (*FPG*, ii, 170).
[102] Barnes (1981), 107.
[103] This is seen most clearly with letters '*B*', '*E*' and '*N*'.

Although Jesus had not prophesied the actual *destruction* of Bethsaida and Chorazin (as opposed to Capernaum: Matt. 11.20–24, = Luke 10.13–15), Eusebius was more than pleased to note the deserted and destroyed state of Chorazin: 'Chorazin, which Christ cursed according to the evangelists; it is now deserted.'[104] Bethsaida, however, still stood and, worse still, so did Capernaum, which supposedly should have been 'brought down to Hades' (Matt. 11.23). Christ's words, therefore, had so far proved true in only one out of three instances. As yet this was a prophecy that definitely could *not* be used as confirmation of the truth of Christ!

Eusebius' reference to Capernaum (discussed above) can now be seen in a new light. First, it can now be observed that this was the only other time in the *Onomasticon* when Eusebius referred to 'Lake Gennesaret', the lake's more ancient name; as with Bethsaida, Eusebius concentrated, conveniently, on the Capernaum of the first century. Secondly, he chose to see Capernaum solely in the light of Isaiah 9.1; for, unlike Jesus' words of cursing, this prophecy, he believed, had truly been fulfilled.

Thus it was that, when expounding this same verse in the *Commentary on Isaiah*, Eusebius was quite prepared to list these three towns (even though they were supposedly cursed) as evidence that Galilee was by the sea, even noting their present visibility: 'Capernaum, Bethsaida and Chorazin and the other villages recorded in the Gospels are still to this day to be seen beside the lake of Tiberias.'[105] This was Eusebius' third and final reference to Bethsaida. In this context Bethsaida's existence could be used to corroborate Christian truth. In the context of Jesus' cursing, however, its existence posed a real threat to that truth. Eusebius' attempts to draw attention away from contemporary Bethsaida in the *Onomasticon* and in the *Proof of the Gospel* made perfect sense.

[104] *Onom.*, 174.23–5. Note Jerome's even stronger addition: 'propter incredulitatem miserabiliter deplorat et plangit' (175.24–6). There is, however, some archaeological evidence to suggest that the synagogue was still standing after Eusebius' death: see Goodman (1983), 15. It must therefore be allowed that Eusebius and Jerome misidentified the site.

[105] *Comm. in Is.* [9.1–2], 62.30–32. Note that if Chorazin was truly 'deserted' (ἔρημος), as claimed in *Onom.*, 174.23–5, then the phrase 'still seen to this day' (εἰς ἔτι νῦν δείκνυνται) cannot be taken, here or elsewhere, as indicative of continued inhabitation.

Eusebius' natural desire only to publicize that evidence from contemporary Palestine which confirmed Christianity's truth can, of course, be seen on many occasions. The destroyed Temple, for example, in Jerusalem had been used by Eusebius for just such a purpose in almost every chapter of the *Proof of the Gospel!* Yet there was also New Testament Jericho: though it had been privileged to receive the 'personal presence' (τὴν ἰδίαν παρουσίαν) of Christ, it had soon been destroyed because of the 'unbelief of its inhabitants' (διὰ τὴν τῶν ἐνοικούντων ἀπιστίαν). There was also Mt. Gerizim, which had been 'defiled . . . and rendered abominable' a hundred years after Jesus' prophetic words about the end of worship 'on this mountain or in Jerusalem' (John 4.19–24).[106] However, the disappearance of neighbouring Sychar, the village that had received Christ so warmly in John's account (John 4.39–42), was not quite so comforting.[107] This was one part of Palestine that, unlike these other places, did not yet vindicate the truth of Christ.

Yet perhaps the most disconcerting factor in contemporary Palestine was this prospering of Bethsaida-Julias. Striking confirmation of our argument that Eusebius was concerned for this particular reason comes from the *Theophany*. Book four is a comprehensive analysis of all Jesus' divinely-inspired prophecies. Yet this particular dominical curse is omitted. The reason for the omission clearly seems to be that the survival of Capernaum and the prosperity of Bethsaida apparently denied the truth of Christ's words. Silence was thus the safest policy. Much as he would have liked to, Eusebius could not say of these three villages what a much later Christian could: namely, that their 'well-nigh complete obliteration . . . is remarkable in this, that they were the three towns which our Lord condemned to humiliation'.[108] So far, after three hundred years, only one of the three had disappeared.

[106] *Onom.*, 104.7–9. *Theoph.*, 4.23; the Gospel text once again had not spoken of destruction, but Eusebius interpreted it as if it had.

[107] This may explain Eusebius' ambiguities over the issue of its contemporary existence (*Onom.*, 164.1–4; cf. ibid., 150.1–7: see Abel, ii (1938), 472–3). It may also explain his use of LXX Ps. 59.7, in *Comm. in Ps.*, 563b, to condone the paganism of nearby Neapolis. For other references in Eusebius to Shechem, see *Onom.*, 158.1–3; *Praep. Ev.*, 9.22, and *Theoph.*, 4.23; for discussion of relevant primary texts, see Avi-Yonah (1954), 45–7.

[108] Smith (1931), 297.

(e) The lake itself: history versus theology

Finally, what about the lake itself? Naturally, in contrast to individual sites, this could scarcely become a 'holy place' as such. Yet it had a natural beauty of its own; well might Jewish rabbis of that period conclude that 'the Lord created the seven seas, but the sea of Gennesaret is his delight'.[109] Did Eusebius feel anything similar? For Christians the lake, with its many Gospel associations, obviously had an extra appeal. Would Eusebius have agreed?

Once again Eusebius seems to be disinterested in the contemporary existence of Gospel locations. He was not a proto-pilgrim, wondering at the mystery of Christ's unique involvement in Galilee. Nor was he eager to describe the appearance of Galilee and its lake to absent bible students; Josephus, Pliny, and Origen had all (though to quite different extents) commented on the physical nature of the area, but Eusebius never did so.[110] Eusebius thus did not approach the lake as a geographer or as a pilgrim. His concerns instead, as by now we might expect, seem to have been entirely historical and exegetical.

These twin intersts of Eusebius may be recognized in an analysis of the various names that he used at different times to describe this small stretch of water. Over the previous few centuries people had referred to it by several different names, which Eusebius as a historian evidently knew and frequently used. Yet at other times he had an exegetical need to refer to it slightly differently.

After the founding of Tiberias[111] the lake's earlier name, Gennesaret, had begun to fall into disuse;[112] it became known instead as the 'lake of Tiberias'.[113] Eusebius evidently knew of this transition. For in the *Onomasticon* he consistently uses the

---

[109] Ibid., 286.

[110] See Josephus, *BJ*, 3.10.7; Pliny, *Nat. Hist.*, 5.71; Origen, *Comm. in Luc.*, Fr. 3, 233.8–9.

[111] In AD 18: see Avi-Yonah (1950–51), 167.

[112] Josephus explicitly states that this was the name still given to the lake by local people in his own day, because of its proximity to the important Plain of Gennesaret (*BJ*, 3.10.1–7). The new connection with Tiberias naturally only received approval quite slowly amongst the indigenous people, and Josephus himself consistently preferred this original name (*AJ*, 13.5.7, 18.2.1; *BJ*, 2.20.6, 3.10.1–7–8) to the new 'Lake of Tiberias' (used in only *BJ*, 3.3.5, 4.8.2).

[113] 'Lake Gennesaret, now called Lake Tiberias' (Origen, *Comm. in Luc.*, Fr. 3, 233.8–9); see Dalman (1935), 121.

contemporary 'lake of Tiberias',[114] except on those two occasions when, as already noted, he had good reason for a conscious archaism. Since Bethsaida and Capernaum continued to exist, even though they had been cursed by Jesus, Eusebius had described them as on 'Lake Gennesaret' in a deliberate attempt to focus his readers on the first century and not on contemporary realities.[115] These two references, however, act thereby as the exceptions that prove the rule. For they show that Eusebius the historian indeed knew both the present and the past names of the lake but that he only used the latter when it suited his particular purpose.[116] At other times he was quite happy to use the present name, 'Lake Tiberias', even if this did not match exactly with the usage of the New Testament.

But what happened when Eusebius left the strictly historical realm for the world of exegesis and theology? In these contexts Eusebius had good reasons for following more closely the distinctive terminology of the New Testament. For the Gospel writers had referred to the lake rather differently. In fact it was only St Luke who had referred to the lake as 'Gennesaret' (Luke 5.1); indeed, even more surprisingly, only St Luke had referred to it as a 'lake' (λίμνη: 5.2, 8.22–33). All the other evangelists had instead called it a 'sea' (θάλασσα),[117] Matthew and Mark calling it the 'sea of Galilee'[118] and John the 'sea of Tiberias'.[119] There was nothing especially inconsistent here, since the original Aramaic *yam* would naturally have included both 'lake' and 'sea';[120] but the New Testament preference for 'sea' proved its value when Eusebius found himself writing in exegetical and theological contexts.

[114] Galilee (*Onom.*, 72.20); Gergesa (*idem*, 74.11); Saron (*idem*, 162.4) and Aulon (*idem*, 16.1–2). Thus, despite Thomsen's assessment in (1902), 152–3, he was not merely imitating the outdated usage of Josephus; he was evidently more than happy to use the contemporary name. Later, however, both Jerome (in his altered translation of the entry on Galilee: *Onom.*, 73.21) and his friends Paula and Eustochium (in Jer., *Ep.* 46.12) prefer 'Gennesaret'. This might have been either the wistful archaism of Christian pilgrimage, or else perhaps an attempt to give the lake a Christian context, not dependent on the now Jewish Tiberias.

[115] *Onom.*, 58.11–12; 120.2–4.

[116] This also explains, as noted, the only other use of 'Lake Gennesaret' in *Comm. in Is.* [9.12], 62.27.

[117] Examples include Matt. 4.15, 8.24 ff., 13.1–47, 14.24 ff., 15.29, 17.27, and Markan parallels; cf. John 6 *passim*, 21.7.

[118] Matt. 4.18, 15.29; Mark 1.16, 7.31.

[119] John 6.1, cf. 21.2.

[120] See Dalman (1935), 121.

Origen had already drawn attention to this discrepancy between the evangelists' usage and the current name, 'Lake Tiberias'; in the light of Genesis 1.10 ('and the waters he called "seas" '), however, he suggested that any system of water might legitimately be called a 'sea'.[121] Eusebius too noted this difference in terminology, suggesting three possible alternative names for the lake within a couple of sentences: 'Lake Gennesaret, which the Gospel refers to as a 'sea'. . . . Capernaum, Bethsaida, and Chorazin . . . are still to be seen today around the lake of Tiberias.'[122] Unlike Origen, however, he did not feel that it was necessary to justify this Gospel usage; he merely quoted Matthew 4.18 without comment. However, one senses that he acknowledged that 'lake' ($\lambda i\mu\nu\eta$) was strictly more correct and a more helpful description of this small stretch of water.

The precise reason for this Gospel usage remains unclear. However, as a result of his frequent discussions (here and elsewhere) of the prophecy in Isaiah (9.1) concerning 'Galilee of the Gentiles' and its quotation by St Matthew (4.15–16), Eusebius may have surmised that St Matthew's terminology was itself influenced by Isaiah's; for in the version of the Old Testament that St Matthew seems to have followed Isaiah's prophecy included a reference to the 'way of the sea' ($\delta\delta\delta\nu$ $\theta\alpha\lambda\alpha\sigma\sigma\eta$s).[123] Surely, Eusebius might have supposed, it was this Isaian prophecy that caused St Matthew, desiring to show the fulfilment of prophecy, to talk of the '*sea* of Galilee'. In any case, Eusebius, as we have noticed clearly, shared his conviction that this one Old Testament prophecy provided a vitally important context within which to understand Jesus' ministry.

Yet, like St Matthew, he had further theological and exegetical reasons for preferring to talk of the 'sea' ($\theta\alpha\lambda\alpha\sigma\sigma\alpha$). As St Matthew's use of Isaiah showed, $\theta\alpha\lambda\alpha\sigma\sigma\alpha$ could be linked much more easily than could $\lambda i\mu\nu\eta$ to the prophetic or typological passages of the Old Testament. Then again, it could also be used as a starting-point for more metaphorical interpretations relating to the 'sea of life'.

---

121 Origen, loc. cit.; cf. *Comm. in Jo.* [1.28], 6.41, 150.15–20, where interestingly he uses $\theta\alpha\lambda\alpha\sigma\sigma\alpha$ in discussing the Gospels, but $\lambda i\mu\nu\eta$ when thinking of the contemporary lake.

122 *Comm. in Is.* [9.1], 62.27–32.

123 See Matt., 4.15, a verse quoted by Eusebius but placed without comment alongside his own slightly different LXX reading of $\tau\dot{\eta}\nu$ $\pi\alpha\rho\dot{\alpha}\lambda\iota\nu$ in both *Dem. Ev.*, 9.8, and *Comm. in Is.*, [9.1], 62.10, 26.

In all such contexts we find that Eusebius used θάλασσα without exception.

For example, Jesus' walking on the water fulfilled Job 9.8: 'he alone trampled on the waves of the sea';[124] his calming of the storm fulfilled LXX Ps. 76.17 [77.16 ff.]: 'the waters were afraid ... thy way was through the sea'.[125] Both events, moreover, were foreshadowed by Moses' parting of the Red Sea.[126] The name, 'sea of Galilee', was thus far more useful than 'Lake Gennesaret' for exegesis.

Moreover, θάλασσα had a further advantage in that it encouraged more metaphorical associations. For example, Origen had earlier developed the imagery of the disciples' fishing for souls lost in the 'sea of this world'.[127] So too (though less colourfully and dramatically) Eusebius depicted the 'fishers of men' sailing on the 'sea of human life'[128] and going out to work in the 'sea of mankind'.[129] Thus he could state straightforwardly that Galilee was situated 'on the sea'.[130] In all these ways θάλασσα proved itself to be so much more fruitful in exegesis and theology. The niceties of historical claims and of contemporary usage were evidently not to interfere.

This theological preference for 'sea' was naturally not limited to Eusebius, nor indeed to Christians. The Jewish rabbis similarly used θάλασσα when comparing the lake to the 'Red Sea' in the Mosaic story[131] and Cyril too found it useful for his exegesis. Indeed he went somewhat further than Eusebius: he used not only Job 9.8, and Ps. 77.16–19,[132] but also Ps. 114.3 ('the sea looked and fled');[133] furthermore, he developed an interesting contrast with Jonah.[134] Not surprisingly therefore Cyril never used λίμνη; his terminology, like Eusebius', was coloured by his theology.

Yet one can still appreciate a contrast between Eusebius and Cyril. They might both share a theological preference for θάλασσα over λίμνη, but their reasons would not fully coincide. Eusebius'

---

[124] *Proph. Eclg.*, 3.7 and *Dem. Ev.*, 9.12.
[125] *Comm. in Ps.* [76.17], 896c–d.
[126] *Dem. Ev.*, 3.2.15–17 (*FPG*, i, 106).
[127] *Hom. in Jer.*, 17.1, 131–3.
[128] *Comm. in Is.* [42.10], 272.25 ff.; cf. also *Comm. in Ps.* [76.20], 900c.
[129] *Theoph.*, 4.6.
[130] Ibid., 4.7 (*LET*, 220).
[131] For example, in *j.Sanh* 25d (quoted in Herford (1903), 112–3).
[132] *Catech.*, 11.23, 13.9; cf. *Hom. Para.*, 8.
[133] *Catech.*, 12.25.
[134] *Catech.*, 14.17–18; perhaps implied also in 14.23.

theology here consisted solely of prophetic and metaphorical exegesis; Cyril's included the needs of the faithful. As a result Cyril had an extra reason for using θάλασσα: Christ's association with the sea of Tiberias, he claimed, now made every 'sea' in the world a potential 'witness' to the reality of Christ.[135] Thus if Eusebius had seen the universal relevance of the sea of Tiberias in terms of the abstract 'sea of mankind', Cyril now saw it in the existence of all physical seas.

Ironically therefore, Cyril in some ways endorsed the patterns of Eusebius' thinking but, in his novel additions, introduced something quite alien to Eusebius' thought. The external shape of Eusebius' thought was appropriated but its internal and more abstract nature abandoned. Eusebius the historian had referred to the lake as 'Lake Tiberias'; Eusebius the theologian, for exegetical and typological reasons, had referred to it as a 'sea'. Cyril the pilgrim-pastor similarly referred to it as a 'sea'. Yet his motives for so doing were not simply exegetical; they were also devotional.

The widespread nature of Galilee has allowed us to observe some of the important contours of Eusebius' mind and especially to sense his quite disinterested approach. His thinking operated at a general level, so that few individual places were given special importance or precise detail, and he approached the places of Galilee with a mind deeply shaped by theological presuppositions. Theology dictated to 'place' and not vice versa. His theology emphasized especially the universal nature of the Gentile Church, concentrated little on the Incarnation as such, and made little room for the humanity of Christ; its focus instead was on the Word of God, both as the eternal *Logos* (revealed at the Transfiguration) and in its written form as scripture. The vindication of scripture's prophecies was therefore of paramount importance. Sometimes this may conveniently have obscured less attractive local issues, but sometimes even the solidity of this argument could be threatened by apparent instances of Jesus' words still unfulfilled. Nevertheless Eusebius' emphasis on the Word left little room for the places of Christ in themselves to be meaningful.

Eusebius is seen thus to be primarily a Christian exegete, not so much (in this instance) a Christian historian. Nevertheless, that

135 Ibid., 10.19; cf. also 14.23.

historical interest was strong enough to prevent him accepting the over-confident identifications that were welcomed by subsequent pilgrims. He was far more of a historian than a pilgrim, but ultimately more of an exegete than a historian. This double layer of history and exegesis thus effectively dulls any murmurings from the heart of Eusebius the pilgrim. If he was ever warmed by being himself in the very places of Christ, his own more rational characteristics soon had their chilling effect.

6

BETHLEHEM AND THE TRIAD

1. BETHLEHEM

The nativity of Christ takes us back to the outskirts of Jerusalem. Galilee has an attraction and importance of its own, but the most central events of salvation history all occurred within a few miles of Jerusalem. In later years this proved most convenient for Christian pilgrims. Yet it also means for us that the remainder of our enquiry will be focused in or near Jerusalem; the question of Jerusalem, comparatively neglected in our study of Galilee, will thus once again appear as a vital factor in any assessment of the individual places of Christ.

Five miles to the south of Jerusalem, beyond an intervening hill, lies the tiny village of Bethlehem, the 'house of bread', the ancient home of David,[1] and, most famously, the birthplace of Christ. By Eusebius' day the precise location of Christ's birth had been established by Christian tradition for some time. This historic event was believed to have occurred in some caves on the western side of the village.[2] Admittedly St Matthew and St Luke had not referred in their nativity narratives to any such 'cave'. Already by the second century, however, it seems to have been an accepted tradition that Christ had indeed been born 'in a cave',[3] and by Origen's day visitors were evidently being shown one particular 'cave', as well as the supposed 'manger' of the Gospel story.[4] Of all the sites in the 'Holy Land' this cave has the longest attested

---

[1] For the value of this etymological connection to 'bread', see, e.g., Origen, *Com. in Lam.*, 104, 272, *Comm in Luc.*, 66, 252, and *Comm. in Matt.*, Fr. 25, 26; also Eusebius once in *Dem. Ev.*, 7.2.44 (*FPG*, ii, 84).

[2] For excavations and some conclusions concerning first-century Bethlehem, see Bagatti (1952), and (1968), and Benoit (1975).

[3] See both Just., *DT*, 78 and the *Proto-Evangelium of James*, 18; both works probably date to around AD 150 (see Hennecke, i (1963), 372).

[4] See Origen, *C. Cels.*, 1.51.

tradition and perhaps, therefore, the strongest claim to authenticity.[5]

However, there is some evidence that during the years of the mid-third century this cave may have been surrounded by a pagan grove or *temenos*. If so, this unfortunate circumstance is certainly not mentioned by Eusebius, whose attitude to Bethlehem and the cave seems to have been highly positive throughout his life. It is true that in the *Onomasticon* his entries for Bethlehem and Ephrathah barely mention the birth of Christ;[6] but this is probably because the purpose of the work is to highlight instead the Old Testament associations of such biblical places. In the *Proof of the Gospel*, by contrast, he speaks quite confidently of this cave and of its widespread interest for Christians.

Now all agree that Jesus Christ was born in Bethlehem, and the cave is shown there by the inhabitants to those who come from abroad to see it.[7]

To this day the inhabitants of the place, who have received the tradition from their fathers, confirm the truth of the story by showing to those who visit Bethlehem because of its history [ἱστορίας χάριν] the cave in which the Virgin bore and laid her infant.[8]

Then, within fifteen years of Eusebius' writing the *Proof of the Gospel*, this cave became the site of one of the three Constantinian basilicas in the Jerusalem area; the emperor's mother, Helena, was apparently present at the commencement of the project.[9] Thus the cave that had been concealed for so long was now brought into the open to receive the attention of royalty.[10]

---

[5] However, among those who accept the basic historicity of the biblical account at this point there are many today who would question this subsequent tradition; perhaps, they suggest, this cave was originally just a convenient landmark, or perhaps its identification as the birthplace of Christ was influenced by certain folk traditions? Nevertheless, whatever our own conclusions on this matter, it is clear from the following account that Eusebius, gifted with a historical and critical mind, clearly found it quite easy to accept the authenticity of this cave.

[6] *Onom.*, 42.10–14, 82.10–14.

[7] *Dem. Ev.*, 3.2.47 (*FPG*, i, 112).

[8] Ibid., 7.2.14 (ii, 79).

[9] *V. Const.*, 3.41–2; for the truth and fiction of her visit (and for its dating to c. 327), see Hunt (1982), 29–37.

[10] It is possible that the Constantinian church took the roof off the cave to allow viewing from above: see Crowfoot (1941), 27, though this is disputed by Ovadiah (rev. edn., 1982), 128. For the archaeology of this building, see Harvey (1935b), Hamilton (1947), Kopp (1963), 14 ff., and Wilkinson (1981), 46–8.

Several quite different questions immediately present themselves for our attention. How convinced was Eusebius of the authenticity of this cave? Why, unlike Origen and Cyril, does he seem never to have referred to the 'manger'? What was his attitude towards the phenomenon of pre-Constantinian pilgrimage? Did he link Bethlehem expressly with the Incarnation? What was Eusebius' approach to the pagan grove (if indeed it existed in his day)? Finally, if (as argued below) Eusebius had some responsibility for the development of this Constantinian 'Triad' of churches, how did he view the relation of Bethlehem to Jerusalem? Once again Cyril's opinions provide a valuable contrast. Although his written corpus is so much smaller than Eusebius', it is noteworthy, for example, that he never referred to this cave but only to the manger. Then again, both he and Eusebius began to expound certain biblical verses in novel ways to refer to contemporary Bethlehem, but remarkably they never used the same verse for this purpose. Finally, Cyril linked Bethlehem much more closely than Eusebius to the concept of the Incarnation and made it a more integral part of the 'greater Jerusalem area'. Some of these differences may be insignificant, but others reflect a deeper divergence of approach, perhaps one even of conscious opposition. As we examine briefly some of the questions that concern Bethlehem and then the Triad, we will gain the impression of two men looking at the same issues from quite different positions. In their selection, their terminology, their scriptural interpretation, their theology and their sense of contemporary Palestine, they were almost consistently at variance.

In the absence of a Gospel reference to this 'cave', those Christians in any age who have a prior commitment to the scriptural text may have certain qualms concerning its authenticity. Does it conform with the biblical narrative, or does it contradict it in some way? For Origen, two generations before Eusebius, there seems to have been little doubt on this score: there was nothing about the cave that contradicted the evangelists' testimony. Indeed the cave's existence endorsed and confirmed the truth of Scripture: 'In accordance with (ἀκολούθως) the story in the Gospel concerning his birth there is now shown in Bethlehem the cave where he was born and the manger in the cave.'[11]

---

[11] *C. Cels.*, 1.51.

Quite conceivably Origen would have known that dwelling-places in the Palestine of Jesus' time were frequently built out forwards from such natural shelters.[12] There was therefore every possibility that this cave had really been the backroom of the 'inn' (Luke 2.7).[13]

Did Eusebius share Origen's conviction about the authenticity of this cave? The overwhelming probability is that indeed he did. Once such an identification had been accepted by a scholar of Origen's standing it was unlikely to be later discredited. Moreover, in the light of the importance that Eusebius later attached to this cave within the Triad, it would be surprising to discover that he still had misgivings and qualms. As a result, the above quotations from the *Proof of the Gospel* should be taken as an indication that Eusebius followed Origen in accepting the existence of this cave as strong corroboration of the Gospel witness. Eusebius the historian seems to have happily accepted the cumulative evidence of a tradition, which had become established very early in the Church's life.

However, there is just one piece of evidence that might militate against such a conclusion. This comes to light by comparing the slightly different ways in which Origen and then Eusebius attempt to harmonize the nativity narratives of Matthew and Luke.[14] Origen was clearly not worried by the absence of any reference to this cave in scripture and was happy to introduce it into his

[12] As even today in, for example, the village of Silwan to the south of Jerusalem.

[13] Justin Martyr, *DT*, 78, seems to be working on some such understanding in his discussion of the 'house' of Matt. 2.11. Clearly he found no contradiction between Matthew's 'house' and Luke's 'inn', though Origen (*Comm. in Matt.* [2.1–21], Fr. 23, 25) and Epiph. (*Haer.*, 51.9.6) in later centuries drew a contrast between this 'cave' and the 'house' later visited by the Magi. At that earlier period Justin naturally had a more flexible approach to the canonical Gospels, which is seen in his 'free' harmonization of Luke and Matthew. His use of Isa. 33.16 as a prophecy of the nativity cave was also rather strange and would not enter into the mainstream of established prophetic testimonies; thus it was not followed by any later writers, including Eusebius in *Comm. in Is.* [33.16], 217.14–21. For more on Justin and Bethlehem, see Kopp (1963), 8–10.

[14] Origen, *Comm. in Matt.* [2.1–21], Fr. 23, 25, compared with Eus., *QS*, 16, 933–5. Both believe that the Magi visited Christ a full two years after Jesus' birth, when the 'holy family' had returned to Bethlehem from Nazareth. Eusebius adds the explanation that thay may have thus returned not just once, but 'on several occasions' in order to 'remember the miracle' of Christ's birth (936a). The Syriac version of *QS*, 16 (reproduced with Latin translation in PG, xxii, 975–9) adds certain elements to Eusebius' account, all of which clearly betray interests other than Eusebius' own.

reconstruction of the first Christmas: Christ was 'born in a cave' and was 'worshipped in the manger'.[15] Eusebius, however, did not do so; noting the exact words of the text, he kept rigidly within the scriptural terminology. The cave is not mentioned.

If Eusebius had qualms concerning the authenticity of this cave, such an omission would be readily explicable: he was choosing to accept the testimony of scripture and not an extra-canonical tradition of dubious authenticity. Yet in the light of his other enthusiastic references to this cave, this cannot be the correct explanation. It is more likely that the omission simply reflects the consistent priority that he gave to the exegesis of scripture and his comparative disinterest in the physical places of Palestine. In other words, the cave was not necessarily inauthentic but, within Eusebius' current context, it was simply unimportant. When his concerns were historical or apologetical, the cave was indeed of value; when his concerns were exegetical, it was not.

Consequently he only spoke of the cave in contemporary terms and never sought, unlike Origen, to integrate it into his presentation of scripture. Strangely, however, exactly the reverse was the case with regard to the 'manger'. This was naturally for Eusebius an integral part of the canonical nativity;[16] yet, unlike Origen who had claimed that the manger could be seen by any visitors to Bethlehem,[17] Eusebius never once referred to any surviving manger. That is: when thinking about the first century Eusebius mentioned the manger but not the cave; when thinking in more contemporary terms, however, he spoke of the cave and not the manger. His 'scriptural' silence about the cave has been seen not necessarily to be a denial of its authenticity. But could his *contemporary* silence about the manger reflect some such doubts?

Eusebius' silence concerning the manger goes further than a mere failure to refer to any manger existing in his own day. Origen, in his enthusiasm for the nativity manger, interpreted Isaiah 1.3 ('the ox knows his master, the donkey his owner's manger') as a direct prophecy of Christ's birth.[18] However, Eusebius did not

---

[15] Origen, loc. cit.

[16] Luke 2.7, used by Eusebius only in quotation: *QS*, 16, 936a–b; *Dem. Ev.*, 7.2.6 (*FPG*, ii, 78).

[17] *C. Cels.*, 1.51.

[18] *Comm in Luc.*, 13 fin., 82; this was followed naturally, with additions, by Jerome when translating this work in Bethlehem (for text, see Origen, loc. cit.) and again in *Ep.* 108.2–7 and his *Nativity Homily* (CCSL, lxxviii, 524).

follow the great Origen at this point. Any reference to the nativity manger is noticeably absent from his exposition of this verse in the Isaiah commentary.[19] The same is true in the *Proof of the Gospel*, the only other book in which he quotes this verse in full.[20] Evidently the nativity manger was not of any great importance to him.

This lack of interest in the manger contrasts not just with Origen, but also with Cyril and Jerome. Even within the limited length of his lectures, Cyril referred to the manger no less than three times. Once was to draw a contrast between the Christ once 'laid in the manger' and the Christ who would return in glory at the Second Coming.[21] On the other two occasions he cited the continued existence of the manger in Bethlehem as a compelling witness to the truth of Christ, both as an aid to faith and as a challenge to disbelief: 'The virgin mother of God is his witness; the blessed place of the manger is his witness.' 'If the heretics deny the truth, . . . the place of the manger, which received the Lord, will put them to shame.'[22] Similarly Jerome, at the end of the century, though upset that the former manger of clay had been replaced by one of silver, evidently gave this manger where the 'infant Lord was laid' a central place within his devotion.[23] He delighted to paint an emotive picture of the infant Christ and, like Origen, was pleased to notice in the wording of Isaiah 1.3 a prophecy of this unique manger.[24] Such comparisons with other authors only reveal the extent of Eusebius' silence. The exact nature of the manger on view at Bethlehem in his day can only be a matter for speculation. Yet it is quite possible that Eusebius felt it was evidently inauthentic and that he was therefore not prepared to waste his attention upon it. For Eusebius the historian the issue of authenticity was a real one and in this case the item concerned seems to have failed the test.

Yet it may be that the historian's disinclination to highlight this manger was endorsed by other factors more theological and personal. For within Eusebius' theological system the infant Christ of the nativity manger would not have been an exceptional object

---

[19] *Comm. in Is.* [1.2–4], 5.11–12.
[20] *Dem. Ev.*, 2.3.50 (*FPG*, i, 77).
[21] *Catech.*, 15.1.
[22] *Catech.*, 10.19, 12.32.
[23] Jerome, *Ep.* 108.10, and 147.4,
[24] *Nativity Homily* (CCSL, lxxviii, 524).

of devotion. Indeed the consistent object of Eusebius' worship, as already noted, was the spiritual *Logos* of God; it was not so readily the 'little Lord' in the manger. Again, on a more personal level, Eusebius' temperament was not one to be much moved by the more 'human' touches in the nativity story. Thus, for example, Eusebius drew little or no attention to the 'pastoral' context of the nativity, never talking of the shepherds and their visit to the infant Christ. Once again this would be in stark contrast both to Origen[25] and later to Jerome;[26] and once again it would contrast with Cyril who saw the shepherds, like the manger, as important witnesses to Christ.[27]

Eusebius' total omission of both the shepherds and the manger seems therefore to reflect several aspects of his character. As a historian, as a theologian, and on grounds of personality, Eusebius had good reasons for focusing his attention elsewhere. Increasingly this would lead in turn to an emphasis on the cave. For this he seems to have accepted as most probably authentic; it could be taken as corroborative evidence for the truth of the historical event, the birth of Christ. Other aspects of the nativity story, however, which, even if he deemed them equally historical, might now only have a more sentimental function, he was keen to lay aside.

Eusebius' approach to Bethlehem was thus comparatively cool and detached. He clearly did not share with Cyril and Jerome their warm devotion to the place as the scene of the nativity of the incarnate Christ. Cyril might seek to integrate the phenomenon of this contemporary 'holy place' into the faith-life of the Christian believer, but Eusebius assessed Bethlehem with a marked degree of detachment, never intimating what he or others might have felt when present in this supposedly august location.

It is therefore no accident that Eusebius' only reference to the possible attractions of this cave for the Christian visitor comes in the strictly apologetic context of the *Proof of the Gospel*, in which he attempted to show the Christian fulfilment of Old Testament prophecy. Christ's birth in Bethlehem was, of course, in Eusebius' understanding, a fulfilment of Micah 5.1–5 (the passage that gives

---

[25] See *Comm. in Matt.* [2.1–21], Fr. 23, 25; *Comm. in Luc.* [2.8–12], 12, 72 ff., [2.33–4], 16, 95.
[26] See again *Ep.* 108.10, and 147.4. Jerome even felt the need to add a reference to the shepherds in his translation of Eusebius' *Onomasticon* (see *Onom.*, 43.23).
[27] See *Catech.*, 10.19 and 12.32.

rise to most of his references to Bethlehem in the *Proof*); but
another fulfilment, he claimed, was the widespread interest in
Bethlehem among Christians all over the world, deriving from
their faith in him who once was born there. For this Old Testament
passage had also foretold, as had others, the universal effects of
the Messiah's coming: 'he shall be great to the ends of the earth'
(Mic. 5.4). Eusebius thus needed to focus his readers' attention not
only on the nativity itself but also on its widespread consequences:

> It seems now time . . . to draw from the prophetic writings for the proof
> of the Gospel. They said that Christ . . . would one day dwell among
> men, and would become for all the nations of the world, both Greek and
> barbarian, a teacher of true knowledge of God. . . . They foretold the
> wondrous fashion of his birth from a virgin, and—strangest of all—they
> did not omit to name Bethlehem the place of his birth, which is so famous
> that men hasten from the ends of the earth to see it . . .[28]

Naturally this passage has been taken by many as confirmation
that the practice of pilgrimage was extremely common in the
pre-Constantinian era. However, although it certainly contradicts
any simplistic notion that Christians had no interest whatsoever in
the Gospel sites before 325 (and the arrival of Helena!), we would
do well to remember Eusebius' apologetic context. Given the
emphasis throughout the *Proof of the Gospel* on the universality
of Christianity, Eusebius the apologist would have had every reason
for painting a somewhat exaggerated picture of Bethlehem's
universal appeal. This is not to deny that Christians visiting the
land (whether expressly 'on pilgrimage' or for some quite different
reason) may have travelled from many different places; it is simply
to suggest that 'pilgrimage' before 325 is likely by and large to
have been a far more local phenomenon than this one, apologetic,
reference might suggest.

Moreover, that universal emphasis, seen here and throughout
the *Proof of the Gospel* (with its attacks on Jewish interest in
particular places for worship),[29] ensures that Bethlehem is not
given any great importance by Eusebius. The 'universal' appeal of
Bethlehem had itself only come about through the prior expansion

[28] *Dem. Ev.*, 1.1.2 (*FPG*, i, 2–3); cf. the two passages quoted above at fn. 7–8
and also the more general discussion of Mic. 5.2–3 in ibid., 2.3.150–51 (*FPG*, i, 96)
and 6.13.22–3 (ii, 17).
[29] See above 3.2(*a*).

of the Gospel 'to the ends of the earth'. Only within such a universal context might Eusebius begin to draw attention with any consistency to a specific place in Palestine that was of importance to Christians.

Naturally these were ideas that in time might have developed further in such a way as to sanction Christian 'holy places'. Yet at this stage such developments lay in the future. Eusebius adhered to the primary importance of the universal aspect of Christianity, an emphasis that coloured his thinking for the rest of his life. Despite some adjustments in later life, Eusebius always found it easiest to accept the concept of 'holy places' when it was set in such a universal context. Thus Bethlehem became part of the triad of sites that summarized the Christian Gospel and proclaimed to the 'ends of the earth' the Messiah who was born in Palestine but who now through the Church could be known throughout the world.

It is also to be noted that Eusebius approached Bethlehem, both here in the *Proof of the Gospel* and in his later works, without a great emphasis on the Incarnation. Cyril spoke of Christ 'descending from heaven to Bethlehem'[30] and saw Bethlehem as the place of the virgin 'mother of God' ($\theta\epsilon o\tau\acute{o}\kappa o\varsigma$).[31] This was where the great mystery of the Incarnation was first enacted; this was where the divine entered the human world.

With that much Eusebius would not have disagreed, but his emphasis remained quite different. He never linked Bethlehem to the truth of the 'Incarnation' as such, but instead saw it chiefly as just the place of Christ's 'birth'.[32] When viewed more theologically, Bethlehem would be for Eusebius the place of Christ's 'appearance' ($\dot{\epsilon}\pi\iota\phi\acute{a}\nu\epsilon\iota a$)[33] or, more latterly, the first scene of his 'theophany' ($\pi\rho\acute{\omega}\tau\eta\varsigma$ $\theta\epsilon o\phi\alpha\nu\epsilon\acute{\iota}a\varsigma$).[34] Naturally this reflected Eusebius' theophany-theology. But, in its turn, it influenced his approach to Bethlehem. A more incarnational theology would have encouraged a

---

[30] *Catech.*, 14.23.

[31] Ibid., 10.19.

[32] See *Onom.*, 42.10–14, *Proph. Eclg.*, 3.19, and all the references quoted above from *Dem. Ev.*

[33] *Hist. Eccl.*, 1.5.1; *Dem. Ev.*, 8.pref.13 (*FPG*, ii, 99).

[34] *L. Const.*, 9.17 and *V. Const.*, 3.41.1. This connection with 'theophany' had begun in *Theoph.*, 3.25; for some reason, in the reworking of this passage in *Sep. Chr.*, 17.7, he used $\gamma\acute{\epsilon}\nu\epsilon\sigma\iota\varsigma$, but then, in these two final works, he now returned firmly to $\theta\epsilon o\phi\acute{a}\nu\epsilon\iota a$.

more sacramental and awestruck approach to the place. Working with his model of theophany, however, Eusebius focused instead on the spiritual more than on the physical reality. As a result, Bethlehem itself, though not unimportant, could never mean as much to Eusebius as it might to others.

The above analysis of Eusebius' attitude to Bethlehem reveals once again the characteristic contours of his thought. He valued Bethlehem more as an apologist than as a potential pilgrim. Moreover, he approached it with a keen historical sense, which encouraged him in contemporary terms to concentrate on the cave as confirmation of the Gospel history and to eschew the more emotive and personal aspects of any supposed 'manger'.

In the years after 325 such thoughts would develop naturally into the Triad of 'caves'. However, before we turn to examine that development, there are two further points to be discussed, which emerge from a surprising quarter: the interpretation of verses two to seven of Ps. 132.

> [Dàvid] made a vow to the Mighty One of Jacob:
> I will not enter my house or get into my bed . . .
> until I find a place for the Lord, a dwelling place for the Mighty One of Jacob.
> Lo, we heard of it in Ephrathah,
> we found it in the fields of Jaar [LXX: in the fields of the wood]:
> 'Let us go to his dwelling-place; let us worship at his footstool [LXX: the place where his feet stood].'

Whatever the origins of this psalm, it would seem at first sight to be referring quite clearly to the Jerusalem Temple. Christian exegetes in the early Church, however, thought otherwise. Origen, with his spiritualizing tendency, saw it as a picture of the Christian creating a spiritual home for his Lord.[35] Then two generations later, Eusebius, with his more historical perspective, pioneered an interpretation of it as a prophecy of Christ's birth in Bethlehem. Since 'Ephrathah' (v. 6) seemed to be an alternative name for Bethlehem,[36] Eusebius supposed that David was attempting to know the 'place' (v. 5) where the future Christ would be born. Eusebius was evidently enthusiastic about this innovative piece of

---

[35] *Comm in Luc.* [12.35], Fr. 195, 310; compare too his comment quoted by Jerome in *Ep.* 119.9–10: 'haud dubium quin in anima tua.'
[36] See Mic. 5.2.

exegesis; for he alluded to it on at least three different occasions in the *Proof of the Gospel*.[37] Moreover, both Cyril and Jerome in different ways, would adopt it as well.[38] It is in comparing their comments on these few verses (especially vv. 6–7) that some intriguing points emerge.

Most of our attention will be focused on verse 6 which in the Septuagint (unlike most modern versions) spoke of the 'fields of the wood'. Despite the overall reference to Bethlehem which he was pursuing, Eusebius never made any explicit identification of this 'wood' with any such wood in Bethlehem. Cyril, however, did. He understood this to be a reference to the wooded area around the cave which had only recently been cleared for the construction there of Constantine's basilica: 'not many years ago the place was wooded'.[39] Why did Eusebius fail to make this identification, a fulfilment of prophecy that seems to have fitted in so well with his concentration on Bethlehem.

Some words of Jerome later in the century may provide us with an answer. For he asserts that in the years before 325 the cave of the nativity was 'overshadowed by a grove (*lucus*) of Thamuz'; moreover, 'in the cave where the infant Messiah once cried, the paramour of Venus was bewailed'.[40] If Jerome was correct, then Eusebius' silence concerning such a wooded grove in his exposition of Ps. 132 would be immediately explicable. So too would be his rather strange references to Bethlehem in the *Onomasticon*, where Christ's birth is mentioned in passing under the entry for Ephrathah but omitted altogether under that for Bethlehem.[41] Perhaps, despite his more confident references in the later *Proof of the Gospel*, contemporary Bethlehem was not all that a Christian might have desired. Things changed for the better only with the arrival of Constantine, when the pagan grove was removed. As a result Cyril was in a position to refer with confidence to its previous existence. In his day the site testified to Christian victory; in Eusebius' day, however, it did not.

[37] *Dem. Ev.*, 4.16.23–29, 7.2.28–45, 9.7.18–20 (*FPG*, i, 208–9, ii, 81–4, 168 respectively); cf. also ibid., 3.2.45 and 6.12.7 ff. (*FPG*, i, 111, ii, 12). It is not found in Pseudo-Eusebius, *Comm. in Ps.* [131], PG, xxiv, 25–8.

[38] For Cyril, see *Catech.*, 12.20, 12.23, and perhaps 10.15. For Jerome, see *Comm. in Ps.* [131] and *Ep.* 108.10.

[39] *Catech.*, 12.20.

[40] *Ep.* 58.3, as translated in Murphy-O'Connor (1988), 166.

[41] A silence noted without explanation by Groh (1983), 28.

Such a reconstruction, which accepts the testimony of Jerome as reliable, would fit in well with our general understanding of Eusebius' methods and his tendency to remain silent on potentially awkward subjects. However, Jerome's testimony might be questioned on several accounts. For example, would a full-grown wood really have been located so close to a continuously inhabited village?[42] Importantly, given Jerome's intention in this letter to portray the essential unholiness of Palestine and also his rivalry with the Jerusalem Church of his day,[43] one wonders too if his story of pagan worship flourishing before 325 over both the Holy Sepulchre and the nativity cave is not perhaps a little too neat to be true. It places Bethlehem and Jerusalem very much on an even-footing and implies that both sites were the object of conscious pagan opposition.[44] Then again, if Jerome were indeed correct, one might question why Eusebius never referred to the clearance of this pagan abomination in 325, which would have been comparable (though on a smaller scale) to the destruction of the temple of Venus that Eusebius described at length,[45] and why Justin Martyr and Origen had referred so confidently to the cave in their own day (as did Eusebius in the *Proof of the Gospel*) when in fact its surroundings were the occasion for quite some

[42] A question raised by Murphy-O'Connor during a personal conversation, in which he shifted from his written opinion (1988), 166.

[43] For this rivalry between Jerusalem and Bethlehem in Jerome's day, see Kelly (1975), 195–209, and esp. Hunt (1982), 192–3: 'the dissension between Jerusalem and Bethlehem was pervasive'. This rivalry might also explain the way in which Jerome in his *Nativity Homily* (CCSL, lxxviii, 528) belittles the value of the local Jerusalem tradition, when compared with that of the worldwide Catholic Church, and the way he uses 'Aelia' anachronistically throughout the *Onom.*
Jerome's exposition of Ps. 85.11 ('truth has spring forth from the earth') might be another example of this local tension. For, in contrast to Cyril, who had applied this verse to Christ's burial 'in the earth', in the Holy Sepulchre (14.10), Jerome applied it to Bethlehem: in *Ep.* 58.3 to Bethlehem as a whole, and in *Ep.* 147.4 to its famous 'cave'. Characteristically Eusebius in *Comm. in Ps.* [84.12], 1021d–1025c, had instead applied this verse universally to the 'world of mankind'; cf. Origen, *Comm. in lib. Jes.*, 17.1, 400, *Cant.*, 1 fin., 113.

[44] This was an easy retrospective assumption for Christians to make. It was also easy to assume that what was true of the Holy Sepulchre was also true of the nativity cave. Paulinus of Nola, the recipient of Jerome's letter, in *Ep.* 31 would seem to have inferred this motive of conscious malice from Jerome's statements, and it has commonly been inferred in modern times: e.g., by Jeremias (1926), 153; Telfer (1955b), 697–8; Parrot (1957), 52; Testa (1964), 113; Hollis and Brownrigg (1969), 77; Murphy-O'Connor (1988), 166, and more cautiously by Kopp (1963), 11–13.

[45] See *V. Const.*, 3.26–7.

embarrassment.[46] Jerome's statement might therefore be not so much an honest revelation of what earlier Christians could not admit, but rather the result of colourful retrospective imagination.

It is impossible to decide conclusively between these alternatives. Yet, on balance, it is probably correct to follow the scholarly consensus which accepts the general outline of Jerome's account (if not its every detail). Jerome's portrait may be over-simplified, but there is no reason to doubt the underlying tradition that the 'wood' (noted by Cyril, but omitted by Eusebius) had indeed had pagan associations before Constantine. In such circumstances Eusebius would not have wished to ignore completely the importance of Bethlehem to Christians, but neither would he have drawn excessive attention to it; for to do so would have highlighted the weakness of Christianity just as much as it supposedly confirmed its truth.

It is perhaps therefore no accident that Eusebius' positive references to Bethlehem all occur in the *Proof of the Gospel*, a work designed to show the supremacy of Christianity over Judaism. For the Jews were not even allowed to visit Bethlehem, because of its proximity to Jerusalem from which they were debarred. Thus even if Bethlehem was not all that Christians might have desired, *they* at least were not prevented from visiting it. All the same, it was only tactful, whether here or elsewhere, for Eusebius to avoid referring to the existence of this 'wood'. As a result, it was left to Cyril, developing Eusebius' exegesis of Ps. 132, to introduce this, a fulfilment of prophecy which *now* vindicated the cause of Christ.

Thereby Cyril developed Eusebius' exegesis further than Eusebius had done himself. Yet in their exposition of the following verse from LXX Ps. 131.7 (132.7)—'let us worship in the place where his feet stood'—the reverse was the case. Eusebius in his final years suggested an attractive new interpretation of this verse, relating it to the pilgrimage of Helena and her worship in the places where Christ had 'stood' (especially at Bethlehem and on the Mount of Olives).[47] Strangely, however, Cyril never made use

[46] Wilkinson (1977), 151, finds these earlier references 'hard to square' with Jerome's evidence.

[47] *V. Const.*, 3.42. Eusebius had earlier quoted this verse but without comment in *Dem. Ev.*, 7.2.37 (*FPG*, ii, 83). Other Christians saw this verse as referring to the feet of Christ's apostles in the worldwide Church (thus Clement of Alexandria, *Paed.*, 2.8.62.1) or in Judaea (as Victorinus, *Comm. in. Apoc.* [1.15a], CSEL, lvi, 26.6) or to the divine presence in Mary's womb (pseudo-Origen in Pitra, iii (1876–91), 300).

of this verse, a verse which could have been so useful in justifying his understanding of pilgrimage.[48] Eusebius had here endorsed and understood the motivation of pilgrimage more clearly perhaps than anywhere else in his writings; but for some reason Cyril never followed suit.

Thus, though both authors began to see Ps. 132 as specifically related to Bethlehem, they seem to have concentrated on quite different verses. Was this mere coincidence? Or was Cyril consciously developing his thought along different lines from those of Eusebius? Such a difference might seem extremely small; yet if it was at all conscious, it only reveals how deep the differences between Caesarea and Jerusalem could go. The interpretation of Ps. 132 has thus highlighted some interesting, though perhaps quite minor, differences between Eusebius and Cyril; Cyril accepted the general application of this psalm to Bethlehem, but his more specific applications never precisely matched those of Eusebius.

Our analysis has also brought to light some of the changes brought about in 325, in the light of which both Eusebius and Cyril could look afresh at the scriptures and discover novel fulfilments of the ancient text. It is therefore time to look more closely at these changes, noting how Bethlehem became incorporated into a triad of Christian sites and how the nativity cave, which had meant much to Eusebius the historian and apologist, now gained a new value to Eusebius the imperial theologian.[49]

2. THE TRIAD

Although Constantine's first concern in Palestine was naturally the uncovering of the tomb of Christ, within only a matter of years his building programme had been extended to include the two other sites that, before the tomb's uncovering, had been perforce the two major focuses of Christian interest before 325. The caves at Bethlehem and on the Mount of Olives, long associated with

---

[48] Jerome, *Ep.* 108.10, followed Eusebius, though he naturally related the verse more exclusively to Bethlehem! Meanwhile Paulinus of Nola (*Ep.* 31.4) related the same verse to Christ's footprints on the Mount of Olives: see Desjardins (1972). For this verse's popularity in the fourth century, see Cardman (1979), fn. 23.

[49] In so doing we shall naturally begin to discuss the 'caves' on the Mount of Olives and in the Holy Sepulchre, a discussion which will provide a useful framework for our more detailed analysis of these in chapters 7 and 8.

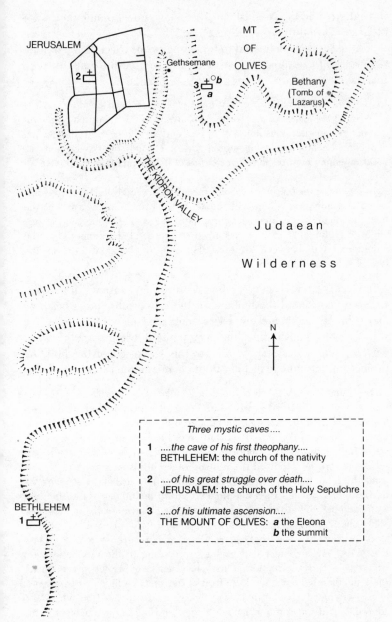

JERUSALEM

MT
OF
OLIVES

Gethsemane

Bethany
(Tomb of
Lazarus)

THE KIDRON VALLEY

Judaean

Wilderness

N

BETHLEHEM

Three mystic caves....

1 ....*the cave of his first theophany....*
BETHLEHEM: the church of the nativity

2 ....*of his great struggle over death....*
JERUSALEM: the church of the Holy Sepulchre

3 ....*of his ultimate ascension....*
THE MOUNT OF OLIVES: *a* the Eleona
b the summit

Fig. 4. The Triad

the nativity and the Ascension respectively, now became the centre of large Constantinian basilicas.

When Eusebius delivered to the emperor his tricennalian oration (*In Praise of Constantine*), he naturally credited the emperor with this development.

In the Palestinian nation, in the heart of the Hebrew kingdom, on the very site of the evidence of salvation, he outfitted with many and abundant distinctions an enormous house of prayer and temple sacred to the Saving Sign, and he honoured a memorial full of eternal significance and the great Saviour's own trophies over death with ornaments beyond description.

In the same region, he recovered three sites revered for three mystical caves and enhanced them with opulent structures. On the cave of the first theophany he conferred appropriate marks of honour; at the one where the ultimate Ascension occurred he consecrated a memorial on the mountain ridge; between these, at the scene of the great struggle, the sign of salvation and victory.[50]

A few years later, however, when writing Constantine's biography, Eusebius associated the building of these two subsequent basilicas more directly with the emperor's mother, Helena. The initiative still lay with Constantine but in practice it was his mother who was the real agent responsible for this extension of the building projects in Palestine to include Bethlehem and the Mount of Olives.

In the same country he discovered other places, venerable as being the localities of two sacred caves; and these also he adorned with lavish magnificence. In the one case, he rendered due honour to that which had been the scene of the first manifestation of the Saviour's divine presence, when he submitted to be born in mortal flesh; while in the case of the second cavern he hallowed the remembrance of his Ascension to heaven from the mountain top. And while he thus nobly testified his reverence for these places, he at the same time eternized the memory of his mother, who had been the instrument of conferring so noble a benefit on mankind.

For she . . . had hastened with youthful alacrity to survey this venerable land. As soon then as she had rendered due reverence to the ground which the Saviour's feet had trodden, according to the prophetic word which says, 'Let us worship at the place whereon his feet have stood', she immediately bequeathed the fruit of her piety to future generations.

For without delay she dedicated two churches to the God whom she adored, one at the grotto which had been the scene of the Saviour's birth;

[50] *L. Const.*, 9.16–17 (*DPC*, 101).

the other on the mount of his Ascension. For he who was 'God with us' had submitted to be born even in a cave of the earth, and the place of his nativity was called Bethlehem by the Hebrews. Accordingly the pious empress honoured with rare memorial the scene of her travail who bore this heavenly child, and beautified the cave with all possible splendour. The emperor himself soon after testified his reverence for the spot by princely offerings, and added to his mother's magnificence by costly presents of silver and gold, and embroidered hangings. . . .

Thus did Helena Augusta, the pious mother of a pious emperor, erect over the two mystic caverns these two noble and beautiful monuments of devotion . . .[51]

According to Eusebius in this later passage it was Helena who in her visit soon after 325 (whether under imperial instruction or acting within a granted independence) actually gave the command for the work to proceed at Bethlehem and on the Mount of Olives. Thus, though all three basilicas are rightly associated with Constantine, two of them must also be associated directly with this elderly lady.

The result of this imperial action was a 'Triad' of caves which both Eusebius himself and more modern writers have seen as a fitting summary of Christian belief. In both these passages Eusebius emphasized that the 'first theophany' ($\pi\rho\omega\tau\eta$ $\theta\epsilon o\phi\acute{a}\nu\epsilon\iota a$) of the *Logos* at Bethlehem had been followed by his 'great struggle' ($\dot{a}\gamma\acute{\omega}\nu$) over death in the Holy Sepulchre, and then finally by his 'ultimate ascension' ($\dot{v}\sigma\tau\acute{a}\tau\eta$ $\dot{a}\nu a\lambda\acute{\eta}\psi\iota s$) on the Mount of Olives. The Christ-event, its beginning, middle and end, was now neatly encapsulated in this Constantinian arrangement, which could communicate the essence of the Gospel from Palestine to the empire. There was thus produced a 'mystical and monumental trinity, designed to commemorate the very starting-point of Christianity'.[52]

How did Eusebius respond to this Constantinian development? Very positively indeed; indeed, it will be suggested in what follows that this Triad was in some sense peculiarly the brainchild of

[51] *V. Const.*, 3.41–3 (NPNF, i, 530–31).

[52] A comment of De Vogue in the middle of the last century, quoted in Vincent (1957), 49. Vincent himself spoke of 'the great monumental trilogy of Constantine': (1957), 70; cf. also *JN*, 360. Wilkinson (1978), 177, notes how this 'expressed straightforwardly the essentials of the Christian faith'; for his useful comparison of this Triad to the tripartite baptismal and credal formulae of that time see his discussion in (1977), 35.

Eusebius. Obviously Constantine and Helena were the official instigators of the project, but Eusebius was most probably their chief adviser, the real source of the initiative. This suggestion that Eusebius was especially responsible for the extension of Constantine's interest in Palestine (after the initial work at the Holy Sepulchre) is based on several factors that, when combined, constitute quite a compelling argument. In the first case, this is only what we would expect. Even if we judge that Bishop Macarius of Jerusalem played the more important role in the initial work on the Holy Sepulchre, it is hard to imagine that Metropolitan Eusebius would have failed to play a strategic part in subsequent developments. He had a reputation to defend after Nicaea, and much local expertise to offer. This initial assumption is substantiated by Eusebius' enthusiastic description of Helena's involvement in this enterprise and the great lengths to which he was evidently prepared to go in his attempt to bring these three otherwise quite diverse sites into a cohesive Triad.

The evidence suggests that the matter of the triad of caves was very close to Eusebius' heart, indeed that he himself was largely responsible for its development. As a result, it certainly cannot be claimed that Eusebius had no interest in the places of Christ. Nevertheless, such interest would be directed in such a way as to promote his own distinctive attitudes towards both Jerusalem and 'holy places'.

(a) The Triad of Eusebius

The first indication that Eusebius may have been integrally involved himself with the development of the Triad is the very colour and enthusiasm with which Eusebius describes in the *Life of Constantine* Helena's visit to the Holy Land and her founding of the churches at Bethlehem and on the Mount of Olives. His account is full of 'profuse praise'.[53] Not only did he pioneer his new interpretation of Ps. 132.7 in order to describe the empress' pious devotion as a pilgrim. He also drew an artful comparison between Helena, as the mother of the emperor, and Mary, as the mother of Jesus. For in his description of Helena's action at Bethlehem Eusebius deliberately brought these two important women into

[53] Rubin (1982a), 86.

close juxtaposition. 'The most pious empress honoured the scene of her travail who bore this heavenly child' (βασιλὶς ἡ θεοσεβεστάτη τῆς θεοτόκου τὴν κύησιν κατεκόσμει). Moreover, just as Constantine the emperor (or 'king') venerated the heavenly king, so too his mother, the 'pious mother of a pious king' (θεοφιλοῦς βασιλέως θεοφιλὴς μήτηρ) honoured the birth of that heavenly king from the womb of the 'mother of God' (θεοτόκος). Such fertile ideas may indeed only have occurred to Eusebius at the time of writing. But it is not impossible that they were present in his mind at the very time of Helena's visit; indeed he may have used them to encourage her to perform this most fitting task.[54]

However, the clearest indication that Eusebius was himself largely responsible for the development of the Triad is the way in which he alone sought to bring these three places together into one coherent system. No one apart from Eusebius would ever suggest that Christ's tomb was a 'cave'. No one apart from Eusebius would ever try to make the cave on the Mount of Olives, previously associated with Jesus' teaching of the apocalyptic discourse, to be seen so exclusively as the 'cave of the Ascension'. Indeed no one apart from Eusebius would consistently describe these 'caves' using the less common word ἄντρον rather than σπήλαιον. In each of these three ways Eusebius' terminology was quite unique, clearly reflecting his desire to establish a distinct and unified Triad, a triad of caves that summarized the three most important events within the Christian creed. Cyril and others, by contrast, simply ignored these special qualifications of Eusebius; the three sites were obviously not unimportant, but there was no need to describe them in such exclusive and often misleading terms. Only Eusebius attempted to see these three diverse sites as a single unit. As a result, it seems quite justifiable to suggest that Eusebius was the instigator of this whole concept, that his was the originating genius behind the idea.

The first piece of terminology that was unique to Eusebius was the suggestion that Christ's tomb was really a 'cave'. According to the Gospels, Christ's tomb seems not to have been a natural cave, but rather to have been cut out from the living rock by human

---

[54] It is hard at this point not to be reminded of the famous treatment of the Helena legend by Evelyn Waugh (1950), which builds intriguingly on precisely on this range of ideas.

190   *The places of Christ*

hands.[55] If this was truly what the Constantinian excavators found, it is strange that Eusebius should describe it as a 'cave'. Yet he did so consistently, not only in his Constantinian works,[56] but also in the earlier *Theophany*.[57] Many, both ancient and modern, have found this terminology of Eusebius decidedly odd,[58] and none have sought to imitate it. Yet the reasons for it now become clear. For only in this way could he begin to talk of a triad of *caves*. It may indeed seem a strange use of language but that strain is the measure of his desire to promote a cohesive and unified 'Triad'.

Secondly, it was thoroughly odd to attempt to associate the Ascension, of all events, with a cave. Yet Eusebius clearly tried to do so. No doubt the cave not far from the summit of the Mount of Olives had in pre-Constantinian days been a useful place for Christians to gather in prayer and to commemorate *all* that Jesus had done on the Mount (including the delivery of the apocalyptic discourse and the Ascension). Yet it seems clear that the Ascension itself had long been associated instead with the *summit*; the *cave* was associated primarily with Jesus' teaching. Later developments in the fourth century, as well as Eusebius' own testimony before 325, seem to confirm this distinction between the cave of teaching and the summit of the Ascension. Yet after 325 Eusebius evidently tried for a while to dissolve this distinction and to link this cave primarily, perhaps exclusively, with the Ascension.[59] The reason for this artificial presentation is once again quite clear: Eusebius' desire to portray a *triad* of sites, all caves, and all involved with the central events of the creed. Yet the result was this strange 'cave of the Ascension'.

The conscious ambiguities that seem to emerge within Eusebius' descriptions of the Mount of Olives are thus perhaps the best single piece of evidence for the personal importance that Eusebius attached to this Triad. As with the rock-cut tomb, Eusebius' schema did not truly fit. To Eusebius the theologian, however, the overall

[55] See, e.g., Matt. 27.60; Mark 15.46; Luke 23.53; John 19.41. Modern archaeologists suggest that the actual place of burial was of the 'archesolium' type: see esp. Wilkinson (1972).

[56] In *L. Const.*, 9.17, and *V. Const.*, 3.25–33.

[57] *Theoph.*, 3.61.

[58] See, for example, the delightfully critical comment in NPNF, i, 531, fn. 1.

[59] See *L. Const.*, 9.17; *V. Const.*, 3.41.1, 43.3. This whole position will be defended below in 7.1.

theological pattern that emerged was more important than precise practical details. He needed a triad of 'caves'.

Eusebius' third means of drawing these three diverse sites together into a cohesive unity was a to develop a distinctive terminology after 325, by no longer referring to these caves as σπήλαια (the more common word for 'cave') but instead as ἄντρα.[60]

The difference between these two terms in meaning seems to have been very slight[61] and it is hard to determine exactly why Eusebius preferred the latter term. ἄντρον may perhaps have been the more comprehensive word for referring both to the natural caves of Bethlehem and Olivet and to the artificial 'cave' cut by Joseph of Arimathaea;[62] alternatively it may have been the word with the more religious and numinous associations (similar to our English 'grotto').[63] Yet most probably the chief attraction of this term was simply that ἄντρον was the less common and therefore the more distinctive term. By using it Eusebius could thus emphasize the unparalleled value of these caves and set them apart as an important unit which had its own theological distinctiveness. Yet it was a usage which again was quite unique to Eusebius, shared

---

[60] Before 325, in the *Proof of the Gospel*, Eusebius had been happy to use σπήλαιον, in *Dem. Ev.*, 3.2.47 (*FPG*, i, 112) and 6.18.23 (ii, 30); only once did he use ἄντρον—ibid., 7.2.14 (ii, 79)—and this is a reading disputed by Bagatti (1964), 46. After that date, however, he only ever uses σπήλαιον once: *Comm. in Is.* [51.1-2], 321.10-11. From *Theoph.*, 3.61 onwards (where both terms are used), he consistently uses ἄντρον instead: see *L. Const.*, 9.17, *V. Const.*, 3.25-33, 41.1, 43.3.

[61] ἄντρον was the more poetic word, occurring frequently in Homer (*Lex*, 167); σπήλαιον was more neutral and had been used by e.g., Plato in his *Republic* (ibid., 1627).

[62] A suggestion of Murphy-O'Connor: see, however, *Comm. in Is.* [51.1-2], 321.10-11.

[63] This religious association, however, would naturally have been a pagan one, as the *Life of Constantine* clearly reveals. For in that work both Eusebius himself (in *V. Const.*, 3.57.4) and Constantine (according to idem., 2.50) use ἄντρον in conjunction with the word μυχός, a term consistently used elsewhere by Eusebius in a perjorative context (see e.g., *Dem. Ev.*, 5.pref.29 (*FPG*, i, 229), *Theoph.*, 4.6, *Sep. Chr.*, 13.4 (= *Theoph.*, 2.11), *V. Cosnt.*, 3.26.3, and 54.6). Eusebius clearly did not feel the need to use a word less tarnished with pagan associations. However, it remains possible that Eusebius' usage was really a reflection of Constantine's personal preference (dependent on the Latin *antrum*?) and not something to which he was so entirely committed himself.

by neither his predecessors[64] nor his successors.[65] Eusebius clearly had reasons of his own.

He thus went to great lengths to produce this interpretation of these three sites, which treated them as a cohesive Triad. It is therefore not unreasonable, we suggest, to deduce that Eusebius was also integrally involved in the initial development of these sites back in the first years after 325, and to conclude that he was both the practical initiator and the later theological interpreter. Strictly, of course, it can never be ruled out that Eusebius might have developed this theological framework in response to a *fait accompli* instigated on the initiatives of others (in Constantinople or Jerusalem). Yet the prominence that he gives to the Triad strongly suggests that, in practice and in thought, it was peculiarly Eusebius' own creation.

If this is correct, then it is natural for us to go one stage further in our enquiry, seeking to discern the possible reasons for Eusebius' emphasis on the Triad, and for his widening of the Christian focus from the Holy Sepulchre to all three of these sites.

Our understanding of Eusebius thus far might indicate certain possible reasons immediately. First, as a historian, and with his experience of pre-Constantinian Palestine, Eusebius would have been quick to see that the two most important sites for Christians *before* 325 should receive due attention after the natural excitement caused by the rediscovery of Christ's tomb. Despite the presence of the temple of Venus, which covered the tomb of Christ before 325, there must surely have been an *implicit* Triad in earlier Christian thinking, focusing on Bethlehem, the Mount of Olives and Calvary; for 'one could hardly hear the Gospel in Jerusalem without desiring to know where Calvary was'.[66] Strong in his desire for continuity with the past, Eusebius would then naturally have tried to give such thinking public recognition.

Again, as the metropolitan bishop who had temporarily been placed at an embarrassing disadvantage compared with Bishop Macarius of Jerusalem, Eusebius would have been anxious to

---

[64] σπήλαιον is used of the Bethlehem cave by both Justin Martyr in *DT*, 78, and Origen in *C. Cels.*, 1.51.

[65] Note, for example, the use of σπήλαιον by Epiph. (*Haer.*, 51.9.6) and Soz. (*Hist. Eccl.*, 2.2), both of whom knew Jerusalem from personal experience. For a solitary exception to this rule (which was caused in any case by explicit dependence on Eusebius), see Soc. *Hist. Eccl.*, 1.17.

[66] Conant (1956), 14.

become involved as quickly as possible in the new Palestinian developments. If, as will be argued below, it was Macarius who had taken the credit for initiating under Constantine the building project over the Holy Sepulchre, Eusebius needed to ensure that he, and not Macarius, was chiefly responsible for encouraging the second stage in Constantine's plans. The Triad, undergirded by clever theology, could thus become Eusebius' distinctive contribution within the Constantinian developments in Palestine.

A further advantage of the Triad for the metropolitan was that it slightly reduced the exclusive concentration of Christian attention on the city of Jerusalem. The inclusion of Bethlehem, five miles away to the south, encouraged a broader perspective, in keeping with Eusebius' own increasing emphasis on the *whole* of Palestine. Meanwhile, the tight cohesiveness of the Triad discouraged the inclusion of any other places, most notably Mt. Sion (the scene of Pentecost), which might be used by the Jerusalem Church to bolster its own prestige. With this blend of inclusiveness and exclusiveness the Triad would thus be attractive to anyone desiring to play down the uniqueness of the *city* of Jerusalem. It was an effective reminder that some of the major events in Christian history had occurred *outside* Jerusalem.

However, Eusebius' promotion of the Triad would have been inspired by more than these historical, personal and ecclesiastical factors: it would have appealed to him as an apologist and theologian. As an apologist, keen to proclaim the universal truth of the Christian Gospel, Eusebius would have seen this triad of sites as the ideal means of proclaiming to all the world the three basic elements of the Christian creed on which the new Constantinian empire was supposedly to be built. In this way the Triad indeed had an 'international role',[67] proclaiming to the world the victory of the Christian message from the very place where that message had first been proclaimed. Thereby each of these three important sites could be seen by Eusebius very much within a universal context, comporting with the universal emphasis of his theology.

Moreover, it is as a theologian that Eusebius may have had yet one more reason for emphasizing the Triad in the particular way that he did. His strenuous attempt to see all these three major

[67] Wilkinson (1977), 35.

sites as essentially similar (all caves, indeed ἄντρα) may have reflected not simply his own desire for symmetry and consistency, but also his belief in a purposeful God who similarly worked according to a consistent and recognizable pattern. If so, then the unifying mind of Eusebius was in this instance really only uncovering the prior unified activity of God himself. In His major acts amongst men, Eusebius might suggest, God had evidently chosen to select three very similar locations; there was a divine pattern in the history of salvation. The advantage of Eusebius' fixed (and occasionally rather 'forced') terminology was thus that it introduced the possibility that God himself had consciously foreordained these three sites to accomplish his will. The Triad therefore became more than a human summary of the Gospel; it reflected instead a prior unity and a consistent purpose within the eternal will of God.

For all these reasons, some substantial though some merely suggestive, the Triad appears more and more to be the result of Eusebius' own thinking and activity. His enthusiasm in describing the Triad, his quite distinctive terminology, and the general way in which the Triad fitted his own purposes, all combine to suggest that Eusebius was its chief proponent. Although he had not previously linked these places of the Christ-event, he now bound them tightly together and infused them with a deep sense of God's eternal purposes. Such a triad of caves reflected his character, as both theologian and historian, and suited his particular purposes as a politician and apologist within Palestine and beyond. The Triad of Gospel sites was thus most probably also the Triad of Eusebius.

(b) Cyril's response

How then did Cyril respond to Eusebius' brainchild? Would the new bishop of Jerusalem approve of the legacy left by the former metropolitan? Would the picture of Christian Palestine, which Eusebius sought to present to the emperor, be acceptable back home in Jerusalem? Naturally, in asking this it becomes apparent once more that Cyril was speaking in a very different context. Eusebius may, for example, have understood the Triad from quite an international perspective, seeing it as a means of proclaiming Christian truth to the empire, but Cyril's concerns were far more immediate and local; he was dealing with present Christians, not absent admirers. Nevertheless, a close reading of his lectures reveals in what ways the future bishop of Jerusalem might view this phenomenon of the Triad quite differently. He never referred to any of these three 'caves' as such and never hinted that he thought of the Triad as a special unit of some kind. The 'triad of caves' seems thus to have been of very little importance to him — indeed perhaps something with which he totally disagreed. In the following it will be suggested that there were at least three aspects of Eusebius' Triad to which Cyril might well have taken exception: the emphasis on caves, the effective exclusion of other places, and the failure to link the Triad in any way to the city of Jerusalem. As a result the 'triad of caves', the high point of Eusebius' contribution to the 'Holy Land', was effectively eclipsed within little more than a decade.

First, and quite remarkably, Cyril never referred to any of these 'caves'. In later years Egeria wrote frequently of the 'cave where the Lord taught' on the Mount of Olives[68] and Jerome, the proud resident of Bethlehem, waxed lyrical about the 'cave of the nativity'.[69] Cyril, however, never referred to these 'caves' at all. Instead he associated the nativity with the manger,[70] and the Ascension with the summit of the Mount of Olives.[71] Meanwhile the tomb of Christ was not to be understood as a 'cave' at all.

Some of Cyril's silences, when compared with Eusebius', may be deemed accidental or insignificant; but his failure to refer to any of these three sites as a 'cave' (whether ἄντρον or σπήλαιον) requires some explanation. And the impression we begin to receive is that Cyril wished to discard the whole concept of the Triad altogether. Partly no doubt this was brought about by Cyril noting the evident incongruities within Eusebius' system. No one apart from him would ever think of Christ's tomb as a 'cave'; nor would anyone apart from him ever try to link the Ascension so closely to a cave. Both notions, when wrenched from Eusebius' context, were quite incongruous, if not faintly absurd. Thus Eusebius' grandiose theory had to be rejected because it failed to make sense at a more popular level.

A second reason, however, for Cyril's disinterest in the 'caves'

---

[68] *Egeria*, e.g., 33.1-2, 39.3; cf. 35.2-3.
[69] *Ep.* 58.3, 108.2-7, and 147.4.
[70] *Catech.*, 10.19, 12.32.
[71] The case for this is argued below in 7.1.

and indeed in the Triad as a whole may have been his reaction to
Eusebius' exclusivism. Eusebius' Triad was simple, cohesive and
neat but it also thereby had an air of finality. The three distinctive
and exclusive ἄντρα had been elevated in significance. Cyril,
however, would be wanting to introduce several other sites of
importance. Eusebius' framework was far too restricting. Our
analysis in later chapters will show that there were at least three
other sites that Cyril saw as of importance: the actual summit of
the Ascension, the rock of Golgotha, and the 'upper room' on Mt.
Sion. The local Jerusalem liturgy would, of course, then introduce
several other, more minor, sites, such as the Lazarium at Bethany.[72]
Yet all of these were effectively excluded by Eusebius in his narrow
concentration upon the three caves; was that in fact part of
Eusebius' deliberate intention? For Eusebius the Triad might
indeed have acted as a summary of the basic Gospel, but for Cyril
it seemed in many ways actually to be hampering the exposition
of the whole truth of Christ. The Triad might have been a useful
first statement of Christian presence in Palestine, but Cyril pressed
for more. He was not going to be fettered.

There may have been yet another, third, reason for Cyril's
disavowal of Eusebius' Triad. Eusebius never linked the Triad in
any way to the city of Jerusalem; indeed he may have seen it as
a means of beginning to shift the focus of Christian interest away
from Jerusalem onto the whole of Palestine. Cyril, by contrast,
viewing the matter from the perspective of Jerusalem, would wish
to see all these sites as part of Jerusalem's heritage, as integral
parts of the Jerusalem area.

Eusebius' failure to link the Triad with Jerusalem can be seen
in both of his extended descriptions of the Triad (quoted above).
In neither passage is Jerusalem named as such. In his tricennalian
speech, Eusebius located the caves by referring to the 'Palestinian
nation' and the 'heart of the Hebrew kingdom'; the caves were
then simply described as being 'in the same region' (τρεῖς ἐν
τῇδε χώρᾳ).[73] This circumlocution might indeed reflect Eusebius'
panegyrical context and ornamental style, but it conveniently meant
that Jerusalem was never mentioned by name and was given a
status dependent solely on its Old Testament past; it was not a

---

[72] See *Egeria*, 29.3–6.
[73] *L. Const.*, 9.16–17.

Christian Jerusalem as such. Later in the *Life of Constantine* Eusebius used similar language, though in that case it is Bethlehem that is identified from a Hebraic perspective.[74] In both works any centrality acknowledged by Eusebius was given, not to the city of Jerusalem, but to the Holy Sepulchre itself, which housed the 'middle' one of the three caves.[75]

However, the close proximity of both the Mount of Olives and Bethlehem to Jerusalem was of great significance to Cyril. Indeed they were not so much 'close to' Jerusalem as 'part' of it. Thus, whereas Eusebius might have been tempted to see the Mount of Olives in opposition to the city of Jerusalem,[76] Cyril emphasized its close relation.[77] The place of the Ascension on the Mount of Olives was 'clearly visible' from the city.[78] Bethlehem too, even though five miles away, was clearly an integral part of Jerusalem as far as Cyril was concerned; for he talked of Christ's 'descent' in the Incarnation as occurring 'here' ($\dot{\epsilon}\nu\tau\alpha\hat{v}\theta\alpha$) in Jerusalem.[79] In Cyril's system the two outer members of this Triad were integral to an explicitly *Christian* Jerusalem. As a result, he quite frequently linked the sites together and indeed on one occasion referred to all three major sites within the space of a few sentences.

For he descended from heaven to Bethlehem, but from Mount Olivet he ascended to heaven; he began in Bethlehem his struggles for men, but on Olivet he was crowned for them. You have many witnesses, therefore; you have this place of the Resurrection; you have to the east the place of the Ascension.[80]

Yet the way in which he linked these sites together owed nothing to Eusebius' Triad. He did not refer to any 'caves' (only to different 'places'), and certainly did not imply that these three sites should be seen differently from other less important sites.

Eusebius' presentation had been artificial, exclusive, and focused away from Jerusalem. On all these grounds Cyril found Eusebius' framework an impossible one within which to work. He was both a pastor, concerned for the needs of ordinary pilgrims, and a

---

[74] *V. Const.*, 3.43.
[75] $\mu\dot{\epsilon}\sigma\sigma$ in *L. Const.*, 9.17.
[76] *Dem. Ev.*, 6.18.4–26 (*FPG*, ii, 26–31).
[77] Again this is examined in 7.2.
[78] *Catech.*, 12.1; cf. 14.23.
[79] Ibid., 16.4.
[80] Ibid., 14.23.

bishop, concerned to see the expanding importance of Jerusalem. For all Eusebius' attempts to present a simple, coherent system, his Triad had still been a rather complex phenomenon with several puzzling features; Cyril needed something more straightforward. The Triad was also rather limiting; Cyril needed to be moving on.

Eusebius and Cyril thus had some differing views both of Bethlehem itself and also of the Triad. These were great places with great significance but that significance was itself a matter for some dispute. This in turn affected Eusebius and Cyril in their interpretation of scripture, in their description of the sites, and in the way they related these sites to Jerusalem. On some issues Cyril's thinking may indeed have been but a continuation of Eusebius' own; but on others it seems clear that his approach was consciously different.

7

THE MOUNT OF OLIVES

The cave of his first theophany . . . , the cave of his ultimate Ascension, . . . and between these the cave of his great struggle and victory over death.[1]

Eusebius evidently sensed the climactic nature of Christ's death and Resurrection. As a result in this description of the Triad he gave his final focus to the church of the Holy Sepulchre, even though according to the Gospels the Ascension was the true *finale*. Eusebius' order will be ours too. Thus we leave Bethlehem, not just yet for the church of the Holy Sepulchre, but for the Mount of Olives, the hill to the east of Jerusalem that has such a commanding view and evokes such a wealth of memories.

Although so close to the Temple mount, the Mount of Olives, with its own greater height and the intervening chasm of the Kidron Valley below, can seem quite distant from the city; a person on its slopes can look down over the sprawling buildings below and with some objectivity and detachment contemplate the phenomenon of Jerusalem. At the same time, however, the proximity of the mount means that it has been integrally involved in the life and history of the city; visitors may seek here to 'come apart' *from* the city, yet in a true sense they still remain a part *of* the city.

For Christians, however, the mount is clearly more than just a vantage-point. On its far side they are reminded of Bethany, the 'home' of Jesus,[2] on its near side of Gethsemane, Jesus' last

---

[1] *L. Const.* 9.17 (*DPC*, 101).

[2] Space forbids a full discussion of Bethany. Eusebius' two explicit references to Bethany occur in *Onom.*, 58.15–17, and *Theoph.*, 4.10. The former passage provides probable evidence for an already identified 'tomb of Lazarus'; the reading 'τάφος' (adopted, e.g., by Storme (1969), 22) seems to be endorsed by the evidence of the the Bordeaux Pilgrim, who refers to the 'crypt where the Lord was laid' (*BP*, 596.2). In the latter passage Eusebius' subsequent discussion of the universal spread of the Gospel (following Mark 14.9) makes him see Bethany itself as of little importance. In his references to the Gospel events there, Eusebius did not respond to Bethany as the home of Mary and Martha, nor indeed as the 'home' of Jesus, even though this had been common in Origen (see e.g., *Comm. in Gen.* [1.7], 9;

haven;[3] near its summit, in the vicinity of a natural cave, they remember both Jesus' apocalyptic teaching and his final departure. Thus, although it was integrally involved with the dark drama of the impending crucifixion, the mount has also been remembered in Christian tradition as the scene of heavenly revelation. As both a vantage-point and as the venue of the climactic events of the incarnate life of Christ Olivet has both positive and negative associations. It stands opposed to Jerusalem but is also an integral part of the city; it stands for the Passion of Christ but also for his final victory.

This double-edged quality has been a great attraction to Christians down the centuries. It was only natural, before the Christian possession of the formerly Jewish and then pagan city, that the Mount of Olives (more so perhaps than Bethlehem) should become a chief focus for Christian interest in Palestine. Christians visited it 'from all over the world' in order to 'learn about the city being taken and devastated' and to 'worship [there] opposite to the city'.[4] In the years after 325 its attraction would only increase yet

---

Cant., 2, 121; *Comm. in Jo.* [11.2], Fr. 78, 545; *idem* [1.28], 6.40, 149; *Comm. in Matt.* [26.26], 561; *idem*, Fr. 526, 215). Instead Eusebius focused almost exclusively on the raising of Lazarus. Origen may have developed some interesting parallels between the tomb of Lazarus and the tomb of Jesus himself, but Eusebius was less imaginative. He mentioned the event when listing Jesus' miracles—*Dem. Ev.*, 3.4.25 (*FPG*, i, 125)—and those occasions when Jesus 'shouted'—*Comm. in Ps.* [68.4], 730c; his most colourful reference was a brief comment on the contrast between Christ's dereliction on the cross and the way God so clearly heard Jesus' prayer on this earlier occasion—*Dem. Ev.*, 10.8.43–4 (*FPG*, ii, 222); for other passing references, see *Proph. Eclg.*, 4.24 and *Comm in Is.* [49.9], 312.11. Cyril, by contrast, developed a dramatic sense of this miracle and its relevance for the believer: it revealed Christ's divine nature, his power over death, his capacity to raise us too and the efficacy of faith (see *Catech.*, 4.9, 18.16, 13.1, and 5.9 respectively); he would also see Bethany as an integral part of Jerusalem (see below 10.3(*c*)). For recent excavations in Bethany, see Saller (1957) and a general discussion in Storme (1969).

Eusebius' meagre reference to Bethphage in *Onom.*, 58.13–14 may reveal an ignorance of the location of the contemporary village. Since the archaeological evidence in Saller and Testa (1961) suggests that this village was continuously occupied, it has been suggested recently by Murphy-O'Connor that in Eusebius' day the area was called by a different name.

[3] Eusebius' references to Gethsemane are discussed separately at the end of this chapter.

[4] *Dem. Ev.*, 6.18.23 (*FPG*, ii, 29). As with his comments concerning Bethlehem elsewhere in the same work, it would be wise to allow Eusebius at least some scope for exaggeration due to his apologetic context.

further, such that it became a veritable Christian colony, bespeckled with monasteries and other foundations.[5]

The complexities of a comprehensive account of the Mount of Olives in Christian tradition are therefore immense,[6] and our attention will necessarily be restricted quite narrowly to just two questions, which themselves reflect the two-fold significance of the mount. First, the mount was an important Gospel site; how then did Eusebius view that cave near its summit which had been used to commemorate both the apocalyptic discourse and the Ascension? Secondly, the mount was a vantage-point, from which to evaluate the city of Jerusalem, and a place that in many ways acted as a contrast to the city; how then did Eusebius relate it to the city of Jerusalem?

It is particularly interesting to note that Eusebius, writing in the *Proof of the Gospel* not many years before 325, had paradoxically developed quite a strong sense of the contrast between the Mount of Olives and Jerusalem. He uses aspects of this inherent opposition to explain Christ's use of the mount for his Ascension as an act of judgement upon the city. After 325 this stance of opposition to Jerusalem would need some modification; for inevitably, as seen in Cyril and later Egeria, the mount would come to be seen as an integral part of Jerusalem. But just how much in reality did the Caesarean Eusebius begin to accept this, the natural view of those in Jerusalem? In his final years he did develop a new contrast, this time between the Church of the Holy Sepulchre and the Jewish Temple. However, would his attitude to Jerusalem not perhaps still retain some of the aspects of opposition that he had propounded so strongly before 325? For example, does his failure to relate the Triad to Jerusalem reflect a continuingly negative approach to the city?

It should also be noted that in his development of the Triad and in his description of Helena's activity Eusebius drew much attention to the cave on this mount, but that he associated it chiefly with the Ascension. By the time of Egeria, by contrast, this cave would

---

[5] See Hunt (1982), 167 ff. and Chitty (1966), 48–51; the latter also notes the attraction of the mount because of its 'two-fold view of the city and the wilderness— time and eternity' (p. 48).

[6] For a thorough analysis of the mount's significance for both Jews and Christians, see Limor (1978); her advice on this chapter has been most helpful. See also a discussion of biblical references in Curtis (1957).

be exclusively known as the place of Christ's teaching;[7] in her day
the Ascension was commemorated instead at a separate site on
the summit about fifty yards away to the north.[8] Indeed within a
few years of Egeria's visit, a third Western lady, called Poemenia,
built the so-called 'Imbomon' to demarcate this 'place of the
Ascension'.[9] Would Eusebius have been surprised by such a
development, considering it to be a denial of the way he had linked
the Ascension with the cave? Or was he already aware that the
Ascension was popularly supposed to have occurred on the summit?
Moreover, can we detect from the few references to the Ascension
in his *Lectures* what Cyril's attitude was towards this cave near
the beginning of his episcopate? Does his failure to mention the
cave, despite his emphasis on the Ascension, suggest that already
he and his audience associated the Ascension, not with the cave,
but with the summit? While answering these questions interesting
contrasts will once again be observed between Eusebius and Cyril.

1. THE CAVE AND THE ASCENSION

Almost at the highest point of the mount lies this important cave.
Even though the Gospels make no reference to any such cave, its
convenient location (adjacent to the most natural route from
Jerusalem to Bethany)[10] at some perhaps very early date in
Christian history made it an obvious place for Christian commemoration of various events in the life of Jesus. Some time shortly
before 325 Eusebius referred to the 'cave that is shown there' in

---

[7] See, e.g., *Egeria*, 33.1–2; 39.3; cf. 35.2–3.

[8] *Egeria*, 43.5; cf. also 31.2, 35.4, and 39.3. Strict logic, of course, did not require
a summit for the Ascension; but this natural assumption will be seen to have been
made by both Eusebius and Cyril; cf. the similar reasoning over the Transfiguration
on Mt. Tabor.

[9] This conclusion, that the Imbomon was built only after Egeria's visit, was
established by Devos (1968). Egeria never mentions a building there, but Jerome
does so in AD 392 in his commentary on Zeph. 1.15–16 (CCSL, lxxvi a, 673); see
also Wilkinson (1981), 51. On Poemenia, see Hunt (1982), 161–3; for the recent
excavations at the Imbomon, see Corbo (1965), pt ii.

Grabar (1946), 288, and Kopp (1963), 414, believe some 'footprints' of Christ
were shown on the summit during the Constantinian period or even earlier.
However, the complete literary silence on this matter before Paulinus of Nola—in
Ep. 31.4 (PL, lxi, 328)—suggests that these appeared only *after* the building of the
Imbomon: see Desjardins (1972).

[10] Dalman (1935), 265.

an extended reference to the Mount of Olives in the *Proof of the Gospel*,[11] and then again at the very end of his life in both of his references to the Triad.[12] Soon after 325 (through the mediation of Helena and probably Eusebius) Constantine incorporated this cave under the apse of his third Jerusalem basilica, commonly known as the 'Eleona'.[13]

The precise reasons why Christians used this cave (and those at Bethlehem, and Tabgha in Galilee) in the centuries before Constantine must remain uncertain. Was the chief merit of a cave simply that it provided Christians with a discreet place in which to congregate for prayer? Alternatively, Christians may have valued its permanence, which ensured a consistency and continuity of Christian commemoration, and evoked a confidence that this of all places must have been present at the time of Christ. It thus provided not just practical shelter but historical and theological fixity as well. If so, then this cave too was perhaps primarily one of commemoration, not of identification: it was a convenient place to remember the Lord's several actions upon the Mount of Olives, but was not necessarily the *locus ipsissimus* for any of them.

This distinction between commemoration and identification, it will be suggested, was one that Eusebius the historian would recognize and employ for his own theological purposes. However, for the more ordinary Christian visitor, in those days as in ours, such a distinction might become a cause of confusion and could be lost altogether. The place where pilgrims commemorated a gospel event could so easily become the very place where that event was believed to have actually occurred in history.

In this instance, despite the absence of a 'cave' in the canonical Gospels, the intimacy of the cave encouraged its identification with the scene of one particular event in the Gospels: namely the apocalyptic discourse during which Jesus taught some of his disciples 'secret mysteries' about the fall of Jerusalem and the end of the age (Matt. 24.3 and parallels). Eusebius himself, writing in the *Life of Constantine*, seems to have accepted this particular identification as a 'true account' ($\lambda\acute{o}\gamma os$ $\dot{a}\lambda\eta\theta\grave{\eta}s$),[14] which may

---

[11] *Dem. Ev.*, 6.18.23, quoted below at fn. 22 ff.

[12] In *L. Const.*, 9.17, and *V. Const.*, 3.41–3, both quoted below at fn. 37 ff.

[13] For the archaeological excavations of the cave and the Eleona, see *JN*, 337–74; Ovadiah (1970), 71–82; cf. also Wilkinson (1981), 49–50.

[14] *V. Const.*, 3.43.3.

suggest that it had been established for some considerable time. Although he does not normally refer to this cave when discussing the discourse,[15] he may well have accepted this tradition. Certainly it seems to explain, for example, the way in which he clearly distinguished Jesus' memorable comment on the future destruction of the Temple ('not one stone will be left upon another': Matt. 24.2) from the discourse proper, which begins in the following verse. For the former he believed would have occurred, not on the mount itself, but when Jesus was walking 'around the Temple' ($\dot{\alpha}\mu\phi\iota$ $\tau\grave{o}$ $\dot{\iota}\epsilon\rho\acute{o}\nu$).[16] As a result, the subsequent discourse could perfectly well have been given in a place such as this cave, from which the Temple itself could not be seen. Eusebius' distinction (based indeed on a suggestion within the Gospels themselves) thus neatly removed one of the possible objections to the identification of this cave with the scene of this discourse: namely that it would have prevented Jesus' disciples from being able actually to see the Temple for themselves at the moment when Jesus was speaking. When asked squarely, Eusebius would thus most probably have revealed his conviction that this was the cave where Christ had taught his disciples the secrets of the future. It was the cave of Jesus' teaching.

However, in the same passage in the *Life of Constantine* and especially in his speech *In Praise of Constantine*, Eusebius tried to give another impression. Evidently the cave was chiefly to be connected, not so much with this teaching, but with the Ascension. Moreover, in the restricted context of his speech before Constantine, no mention was made of Jesus' teaching at all.[17]

Eusebius' references in these two works to the cave and to the Ascension have been described as 'notoriously unclear',[18] and have been interpreted in two quite different ways. Grabar saw in this Eusebian narrative evidence for two different buildings founded by Helena (one on the summit, the other over the cave).[19] On the other hand, Vincent, wanting to contradict this, drew on the same evidence to show how the Ascension was located for Eusebius

---

[15] E.g., in *Theoph.*, 4.35; cf. also *Comm in Luc.* [21.25 ff.], 596-604.
[16] *Theoph.*, 4.18 (*LET*, 247).
[17] *V. Const.*, 3.41-43, *L. Const.*, 9.17, quoted in full below at fn. 37 ff.
[18] Hunt (1982), 161.
[19] Grabar (1946), i, 284 ff. FR

immediately beside the cave.[20] Where then did Eusebius locate
the Ascension, on the summit of the Mount of Olives or by this
cave (the cave of teaching)?

His peculiar theological and political purposes in presenting a
cohesive Triad, as outlined above, can now help to explain this
confusion. Although Eusebius did not explicitly suggest a location
for the Ascension in his other writings,[21] it is our point that
Eusebius *did* locate the Ascension on the summit, but that he
needed to sacrifice this belief temporarily in order to establish his
tidy 'triad of caves'. The cave of Jesus' teaching thus needed, for
the sake of the Triad, to be seen instead as the cave of the
Ascension. The resultant confusion was in a sense deliberate.

As we shall see, Eusebius knew what he was doing. He was
careful, for example, never to talk explicitly of the 'cave of the
Ascension', which would have sounded absurd. Secondly, in the
less restricted context of the *Life of Constantine*, he reintroduced
the function of the cave as the scene of Jesus' teaching and subtly
suggested that the summit was really the more likely place for the
Ascension. Writing the *Life of Constantine* thus gave Eusebius the
opportunity to complement and correct his earlier over-neat
presentation in the *Praise of Constantine*—a presentation forced
upon him no doubt by the presence of Constantine and the
occasion of the tricennalian celebrations. If Cyril saw matters more
straightforwardly, linking the cave to the teaching but the summit
to the Ascension, he was not then necessarily contradicting
Eusebius' own private opinion. Hence the differences in this issue
between Cyril and Eusebius may not be so radical as on other
occasions: one was primarily a pastor, the other had the constraints
of court politics as well.

(a) The cave before 325

Eusebius' first and most extended discussion of the Mount of Olives
occurs in the *Proof of the Gospel* when he expounds Zechariah

[20] Vincent (1957), 53; this is followed by Wilkinson (1981), 49, and Hunt (1982),
162: 'there was *no* separate tradition attaching to the actual summit'. Kopp (1963),
412, also follows this, suggesting that interest in the summit only began after the
unnatural enclosure of the Ascension place by the Eleona buildings.
[21] The Ascension is discussed but without location in, e.g., *Theoph.*, 3.44 (excised
from the later *Sep. Chr.*), *Comm. in Ps.* [67.33], 720a, [90.12], 1161d. In these
latter two passages Eusebius' comparison of the Ascension with, respectively, the

14.4: 'on that day his feet shall stand on the Mount of Olives which lies before Jerusalem to the east'. It is here that he refers to the way Christians love to visit the Mount of Olives. Eusebius had already offered a characteristic 'spiritual' interpretation of how this prophecy had been fulfilled. Now he suggested two more 'literal' interpretations. First, this Old Testament prophecy could perhaps be being fulfilled in the way

believers in Christ congregate from all parts of the world, not as of old time because of the glory of Jerusalem, nor that they may worship in the ancient Temple at Jerusalem, but they rest there that they may learn both about the city being taken and devastated as the prophets foretold, and that they may worship at the Mount of Olives opposite to the city.[22]

More importantly, however, this was the place where Christ's own feet had stood; this was where 'the glory of the Lord' had 'migrated when it left the former city'.

There stood in truth according to the common and received account the feet of our Lord and Saviour, Himself the Word of God, through that tabernacle of humanity he had borne up the Mount of Olives to the cave that is shown there; there he prayed and delivered to his disciples on the summit of the Mount of Olives the mysteries of his end, and thence he made his Ascension into heaven, as Luke tells us in the Acts of the Apostles . . .[23]

This reference to the cave shows, of course, that Eusebius' interest in this site did not begin in 325; indeed it might suggest that the cave had been of importance to Christians for quite some time. This earlier history of the cave, however, is quite hard to reconstruct. Both Justin Martyr and Origen, who had lived in Palestine, had commented on the cave at Bethlehem[24] but not so this second cave; although they referred in quite imaginative ways to the Mount of Olives in general, neither of them revealed anything of the mount's contemporary appearance.[25] The only

crucifixion and the pinnacle temptation could have been endorsed neatly in geographical terms.

[22] *Dem. Ev.*, 6.18.23 (*FPG*, ii, 29).

[23] Ibid. (*FPG*, ii, 29–30).

[24] Just., *DT*, 78; Origen, *C. Cels.*, 1.51.

[25] Justin located Christ's agony and betrayal 'on the Mount of Olives', not in Gethsemane (*DT*, 99, 103.1). Origen interpreted the 'Mount of Olives' (τὸ ὄρος τῶν ἐλαιῶν) to mean the 'mount of pity' (ἔλεος); thus it was appropriate for Jesus here to foretell his disciples' desertion (*Comm. in Matt.* [26.26–30], CS 86, 200 ff.).

reference to the cave before Eusebius comes instead from a surprising source. In the apocryphal *Acts of John*, which dates from the third century,[26] the apostle John supposedly flees during the crucifixion to the Mount of Olives only to be met 'in the middle of the cave by his Lord'.[27] Evidently this cave was well known at that date, perhaps already associated by more 'orthodox' Christians with the life of Jesus; clearly too, however, it had an attractive function in apocryphal Christian thinking.

No other apocryphal work refers to this cave. However, there are at least six apocryphal writings that refer to the Mount of Olives as a whole, an interesting factor that needs to be noted in our analysis of the years before the coming of Constantine.[28] In each of these apocryphal works the mount is used as the *locus* for a special encounter with Christ or some revelation of his truth, especially in the period after his Resurrection. However, with the exception of the *Acts of John*, none reveals any knowledge of the contemporary mount, and one may reasonably presume that most of the authors involved had never seen the real Mount of Olives. They will most probably have referred to this mount, not because they had personally visited it, but because it was the 'biblical mountain *par excellence*',[29] associated canonically with revelation both of the future and of the heavenly realm; it could therefore be used by absentee writers as a natural authenticating touch for extra-canonical material. The result was inevitably that it attracted to its slopes 'several floating traditions'.[30]

This apocryphal use of the mount in general, but especially the reference in the *Acts of John* to the cave, now alerts us to a factor that may have affected the experience of Christian visitors in the

---

In ibid., [24.3], CS 32, 57, when discussing the apocalyptic discourse, he emphasized the secrecy of this disclosure but did not mention any 'cave'.

[26] See Hennecke, ii (1965), 214–5.

[27] *Acts of John*, 97. M. R. James—according to Lawlor and Oulton (1928), ii, 97—describes this work as the 'best popular expression of the Docetic view of our Lord's Passion'.

[28] In the chronological order outlined in the two-volume collected edition by Hennecke (1963–5) these are:- *Apocalypse of Peter* (ii, 668); *Apocalypse of Paul* (ii, 757, 795–6); a Manichaean fragment (i, 353); *The Wisdom of Jesus Christ* (i, 246–8); *Pistis Sophia* (i, 253–6); *Acts of John*; *Gospel of Bartholomew* (i, 492 ff.). There has been little discussion of their use of the Mount of Olives: for a partial evaluation, see Bagatti (1964), 42.

[29] Abel, in *JN*, 377.

[30] Ibid.

centuries before Constantine to an extent that cannot now be determined. For, even if the above apocryphal sources only mentioned the mount because of its frequent appearance in canonical scripture, would not such references to the mount eventually have affected the *local* traditions about it? The mutual influence of non-canonical traditions and the places they involve must be recognized.

The paucity of evidence prevents any firm conclusion. Nor can we know with any certainty how Eusebius would have responded to any such non-canonical traditions. Did their existence affect his attitude to the mount? Eusebius certainly knew of the existence of many of these apocryphal works, including the *Acts of John* which he was swift to dismiss as 'heretical'.[31] As a historian of literature Eusebius would have had a good knowledge of these non-canonical traditions in their literary form. Moreover, as a historian of Palestine he would have been well placed to learn of any such traditions in their 'living' form, as they were passed on by the local Jerusalem community.

Inasmuch as it can be determined, Eusebius' response was probably not one of outright opposition but of partial and gentle appropriation. For example, his mystic language later in the *Life of Constantine*, when he spoke of Christ 'initiating his disciples into the secret mysteries',[32] and his apparent belief (expressed in the *Proof of the Gospel*) that Christ taught his disciples in this cave *after* the Resurrection immediately prior to his Ascension,[33] could each reflect piecemeal acceptance of some elements of apocryphal thinking.[34] Yet, at the same time, his confident use of the cave in this passage shows his own more 'orthodox' approval.

Despite some of these heterodox associations, therefore, Eusebius

[31] See *Hist. Eccl.*, 3.25.6. Concerning the *Apocalypse of Peter* he was less certain (*idem*, 3.25.4); cf. *idem*, 3.3.2, and 6.14.1.

[32] *V. Const.*, 3.43.3, discussed briefly in Wilkinson (1977), 166, and Yarnold (1983).

[33] *Dem. Ev.*, 6.18.23 (*FPG*, ii, 30).

[34] Except for the *Acts of John*, probably all the above apocryphal works purport to describe episodes *after* the Resurrection (see M. R. James (1953), 54, for discussion of the *Apocalypse of Peter*). The *Pistis Sophia* extends this period to twelve years. Strangely Eusebius himself, attempting to match the prophecies of Daniel with the period of Christ's first coming, suggested an 'equality' between the pre- and post-Resurrection phases of Jesus' ministry (*Dem. Ev.*, 8.2.109)—though this may indeed have been an equality of importance, not of duration (see *FPG*, ii, 135, fn. 2).

seems to have accepted the authenticity of this special cave. This was well before 325. His desire to promote a neat triad of caves after that date would then have encouraged a whole-hearted acceptance of this identification, yet that acceptance and approval was clearly based on other, prior considerations. As far as Eusebius was concerned this cave was correctly associated with Christ's teaching.

A closer examination of this text from the *Proof of the Gospel* reveals some further interesting points. Eusebius had just quoted Ezekiel, 11.22-3: 'then the cherubim lifted up their wings . . . and the glory of the Lord went up from the midst of the city and stood upon the mountain which is on the east side of the city'. Influenced by these verses, Eusebius clearly wanted to interpret the Ascension as the moment *par excellence* when Jesus fulfilled the prophecy in Zechariah, 14.4: 'his feet shall stand on the Mount of Olives'. This was the climax of all of Jesus' other activity on the mount. As a result Eusebius summarized all that activity in one long sentence which culminated in his description of the Ascension. In so doing, however, he neatly took attention away from a potential weakness: the Ascension was hardly the best event to illustrate the Lord's feet *standing* upon the Mount of Olives! This was neatly obscured by the length of Eusebius' sentence. Yet at the same time the climactic thrust of this sentence only confirms that for Eusebius the Ascension, the final moment in the incarnate life of Christ, was truly the precise instant of this verse's fulfilment.

Yet there was a second anomaly that he needed to obscure: any suggestion that Jesus' Ascension had actually occurred *in* the cave. He achieved this in two ways. First, he used the phrase '*near* the cave' ($\pi\rho\grave{o}s$ $\tau\hat{\omega}$ $\sigma\pi\eta\lambda\alpha\acute{\iota}\omega$); thus, strictly speaking, not even Jesus' praying[35] and teaching had occurred *inside* the cave. Secondly, after this reference to the 'cave', he inserts an otherwise repetitious place-reference: 'on the summit of the Mount of Olives'. Consequently, later mention of Jesus' Ascension 'thence' ($\grave{\epsilon}\nu\tau\epsilon\hat{\upsilon}\theta\epsilon\nu$) clearly refers back to the 'summit' ($\grave{\alpha}\kappa\rho\omega\rho\epsilon\acute{\iota}\alpha$), not to the 'cave' ($\sigma\pi\acute{\eta}\lambda\alpha\iota o\nu$). Evidently, therefore, Eusebius did not locate Christ's Ascension by reference to the cave after all; rather, he associated it with the 'summit'.

[35] Eusebius seems to have concluded (from, e.g., Luke 22.39) that Jesus often prayed on the Mount of Olives, and indeed in this very cave. This is indicated later in *V. Const.*, 3.43.3, when he speaks of the Saviour 'spending time' ($\delta\iota\alpha\tau\rho\iota\beta\grave{\alpha}s$

Three conclusions can now be drawn from our discussion of this passage, each of which will prove most relevant for our understanding of Eusebius' position after 325. First, Eusebius was evidently fond of this cave; despite some of its apocryphal associations and some resultant clumsiness in his exegesis, he gives it quite some prominence in his description of Jesus on the mount. Secondly, he was nevertheless chiefly interested in the Ascension, not in Jesus' teaching or praying; thus the location of these *within* the cave was sacrificed in order to suit his greater emphasis on the Ascension. Finally, the feature which best located the scene of the Ascension was not the cave but the summit. Eusebius thus emphasized both the cave and the Ascension but, according to his understanding, the Ascension was not necessarily supposed to have occurred very close to the cave, which instead was to be chiefly remembered as the place of Jesus' teaching.

(b) The cave after 325

This dual emphasis in the *Proof of the Gospel* on both the cave and the Ascension, despite his clear capacity to distinguish them, led naturally to his incorporation of the cave into the Constantinian Triad after 325.[36] Giving his first description of the triad of caves when speaking before Constantine, Eusebius calmly omitted any reference to Christ's teaching: 'On the cave of the first theophany he conferred appropriate marks of honour; at the one where the ultimate Ascension occurred he consecrated a memorial on the mountain ridge.'[37] Once again this aspect was sacrificed to fit his current framework: if formerly that had been an exegesis of prophecy, now it was politics.

However, in so doing Eusebius was now heading towards precisely the same anomaly that he had sought to avoid in the *Proof of the Gospel*: the third Constantinian basilica was apparently being built over the strangely-named 'cave of the Ascension'. In

---

ἑλομένῳ) on this mount. By implication Helena's 'house of prayer' (προσευκτήριον) over this cave was thus especially appropriate.

[36] Though argued for separately, Eusebius' personal involvement with the Triad (as outlined in 6.2(a)) and his conscious ambiguities (discussed here) strictly belong close together as 'cause and effect'; Eusebius' subtlety here endorses the case for Eusebius' personal commitment to the Triad, while that commitment explains his conscious ambiguity here.

[37] *L. Const.*, 9.17 (*DPC*, 101).

fact for the purposes of his Triad Eusebius needed this to be true; each of the three major events of salvation had to be connected with such a 'cave' (ἄντρον). Yet, at the same time, given the incongruity of such a 'cave of the Ascension', he needed to avoid ever ultimately identifying them.

He did so in two ways. First, his Greek never actually contains the oxymoron. The 'cave of the Ascension' never appears as such; ἄντρον is conveniently only mentioned in the first half of the sentence with reference to Bethlehem. Secondly, with this cave on the Mount of Olives (unlike those at Bethlehem and in the Holy Sepulchre), he talks of Constantine 'hallowing the memory' of the Ascension (μνήμην σεμνύνων).[38] The wording is significant. For if, as we have suggested, Christians before Constantine had, for aesthetic reasons, traditionally located the Ascension on the summit but for practical purposes commemorated it in the cave a little lower down the hill, then Eusebius may simply have been implying that this cave was not after all the precise location of the Ascension, but rather the place of its traditional commemoration. This was where Christians had remembered the Ascension and Constantine's church hallowed the tradition. If so, then Eusebius was acknowledging the important distinction to be made between the precise event and this traditional commemoration, a distinction which could neatly diffuse the anomaly of the 'cave of the Ascension'.

Eusebius repeats some of these phrases verbatim in his second and final description of the Triad in the *Life of Constantine*. Moreover, when he adds to this material he continues to use these two same devices to prevent the misunderstanding of precise identification:

In the same country he discovered other places, venerable as being the localities of two sacred caves. . . . In the one case, he rendered due honour to that which had been the scene of the first manifestation of the Saviour's divine presence, . . . while in the case of the second cavern he hallowed the remembrance of his ascension to heaven from the mountain top.

For without delay [Helena] dedicated two churches to the God whom she adored, one at the grotto which had been the scene of the Saviour's

---

[38] Drake's translation of this phrase by 'he consecrated a memorial' (*DPC*, 101) is more concrete and physical than Eusebius' original; 'hallowing the memory' (the translation of this same phrase in *V. Const.*, 3.41 in *NPNF*, i, 530) is more accurate.

birth; the other on the mount of his Ascension. . . . And farther, the mother of the emperor raised a stately structure on the Mount of Olives also, in memory of his ascent to heaven who is the Saviour of mankind, erecting a sacred church and temple on the very summit of the mount, and building there a house of prayer to the Saviour who passed his time in that place. And indeed authentic history informs us that in this very cave the Saviour imparted his secret revelations to his disciples. And here also the emperor testified his reverence for the king of kings, by diverse and costly offerings.

Thus did Helena Augusta, the pious mother of a pious emperor, erect over the two mystic caverns these two noble and beautiful monuments of devotion . . . [39]

Once again Eusebius never expressly refers to the 'cave of the Ascension'; the church built over the 'grotto which had been the scene of the Saviour's birth' was balanced by a church built 'on the mount of his Ascension'. Then again the theme of commemoration ($\mu\nu\dot{\eta}\mu\eta$) is alluded to in his statement that the church on the Mount of Olives was built 'in memory ($\mu\nu\dot{\eta}\mu\eta\nu$) of his ascent to heaven'. Eusebius' methods for defending his Triad were much the same.

However, he now took advantage of his less restricted context to reintroduce the themes from the *Proof of the Gospel*, concerning Christ's teaching and his praying.[40] In this way he could correct any imbalance that had been necessary in his speech before Constantine. Nevertheless, he did so only towards the end of his account; the primary emphasis of the Triad still needed to remain on the Ascension. Furthermore, Eusebius also acknowledges more clearly than in the *Proof of the Gospel* that Christians past and present tended to associate the Ascension with the actual *summit* of the mount. For he notes carefully that Helena's church was built 'near to the summit ($\dot{\alpha}\kappa\rho\omega\rho\epsilon\dot{\iota}\alpha$), indeed close to the peak ($\kappa\sigma\rho\nu\phi\dot{\eta}$) of the whole mountain'. This extended reference only has any significance if Eusebius knew that his readers would be expecting a reference to the summit as the place of the Ascension. Indeed Eusebius' emphatic language suggests that the author himself shared with his readers this natural assumption. The idea

---

[39] *V. Const.*, 3.41–3, following the translation in NPNF, i, 530–31, in which, however, the phrase describing the peak ($\kappa\sigma\rho\nu\phi\dot{\eta}$) is for some reason omitted.

[40] A reference to Christ's praying on the mount is most probably implied by his speaking of Helena's 'house of prayer'.

that the Ascension must have occurred on the summit of the Mount of Olives may indeed have been based only on a retrospective sense of the appropriate; but Eusebius and other Christians (both previous and contemporary) accepted it as fact.

The above extended analysis thus shows how the truth lies between the two extremes that we noted had been adopted by Grabar and Vincent. Contrary to Grabar, Eusebius is only talking about *one* church; but, contrary to Vincent, he is clearly aware of the summit and of the '*bifocal*' nature of Christian tradition on the mount. In both the *Proof of the Gospel* and the *Life of Constantine* Eusebius showed a keen interest in both the cave and the Ascension; nevertheless he distinguished quite strictly between them when fixing their location. He was himself quite clear about that distinction but, again, had his own particular reasons for being consciously ambiguous. In particular, concerning the Ascension, he was able to use to good effect the discrepancy between the place of aesthetic identification and the place of pragmatic commemoration. This discrepancy suited his own purposes perfectly and allowed the development of his cohesive theological Triad. In that context the Ascension had of necessity to be associated directly with the cave. Eusebius succeeded in bringing the cave and the Ascension into sufficient contact for his Triad of credal sites to hang together as a unity; yet, at the same time, he ensured that they were also kept sufficiently apart.

(c) Cyril's response

Such conscious ambiguity was unlikely to be continued for long by those without the particular purposes of Eusebius. A neat theological, or even political, motif in Eusebius' mind did not necessarily mean much, nor indeed make much sense, to the pilgrim 'on the ground'. The notorious error of the Bordeaux Pilgrim, for example, who confused the Ascension with the Transfiguration, could well reflect the misunderstandings which Eusebius' academic 'schema' caused within a matter of years:

On the Mount of Olives, where the Lord taught the apostles before his Passion, a basilica has been built by command of Constantine. Then not far away is the hillock [*monticulus*] where the Lord went up [*ascendit*] to pray and there appeared Moses and Elijah, when he took Peter and John apart with him.[41]

Evidently the pilgrim had learnt that both sites (the cave and the summit) were important. Yet he could see that a church was being built only over one of them.[42] If he was then told that the church somehow commemorated the Ascension, the relevance of the summit would suddenly have become unclear. The result was that he came to associate the summit instead with the Transfiguration.[43] The Bordeaux Pilgrim may thus have been one of many for whom any glaring discrepancy between the place of the commemoration of the Ascension and its supposed authentic location was puzzling.

This situation was unlikely to last for long. The new generation of Christians wanted clarity and indeed had no need for such restrictions. Pre-Constantinian commemorations might of necessity have been imposed on certain convenient locations, but in the new era they had the chance to multiply. Thus if a Gospel site could now be confidently identified, Christians would soon be commemorating it in that very location. The summit of the Mount of Olives, long identified as the scene of the Ascension, soon became the place where it was commemorated.

The use of the summit for Christian worship was well established by the time of Egeria's visit in the 380s, and within a few years the Jerusalem Church received (from Poemenia) the benefaction required for the erection of an appropriate building (the

[41] *BP*, 595.4–596.1, as translated in Wilkinson (1981), 160. This confusion is mentioned but without any suggested explanation by Milik (1960), 557, fn. 5; Donner (1979), 60, fn. 9; *JN*, 381; Hamilton (1952), 87 and Wilkinson, op. cit., 160 and 49.

[42] However confused this account appears the Pilgrim's evidence neatly contradicts both Grabar's argument for there being two churches built at this time and also Vincent's denial of any two-fold commemoration at all.

[43] This assumes that the the Bordeaux Pilgrim himself made the mistake (cf. Vincent (1957), 55, fn. 2). However, it could have been the pilgrim's guide who spoke of the Transfiguration. If so, Kopp (1963), 411–13, suggests that the Jerusalem Church may already have begun to commemorate the Transfiguration there; but his evidence comes from the seventh-century Georgian Canons and is contradicted by Cyril's clear identification of Mt. Tabor in *Catech.*, 12.16. Perhaps instead the guide had been following a tradition similar to that found in the *Apocalypse of Peter* 1 and 15 (in Hennecke, ii (1965), 664) in which an event similar to the canonical Transfiguration preceded the final Ascension; the pilgrim then recorded the less well-known half of the story. If so, this would again be evidence, though less direct, for the way the Ascension was connected with the summit, not with the cave.

'Imbomon'). This occurred at the very end of Cyril's life. Our task is to note briefly Cyril's own attitude to this problem in his much earlier *Catechetical Lectures* of 348. Where did he locate the Ascension and what did he make of the cave?

It would certainly suit our purposes best if Eusebius' position were as dismissive of the summit as Vincent suggests and if, on the other hand, Cyril's evidence were much clearer; it would be convenient to demonstrate how Eusebius identified the Ascension exclusively with the cave, while Cyril by contrast identified it clearly with the summit. The evidence available, however, does not permit such a tidy conclusion. Cyril's references are not very specific, and Eusebius' position, as noted, was far more subtle.

Nevertheless, it is more than likely that Cyril located the Ascension on the summit of the Mount of Olives. Constantine's new Eleona church naturally came to have an important place within the Jerusalem liturgy;[44] yet in all probability Cyril did not associate this building directly with the Ascension. Eusebius himself had given sufficient evidence of the importance of the summit and Egeria reveals the established belief of the Jerusalem Church by the end of Cyril's episcopate: the hillock, and not the area around the cave, was the place 'from which the Lord ascended into heaven'.[45] As a pastor involved with ordinary people, Cyril would have had little time for the intricacies of the Eusebian Triad. He had no political need to defend it, indeed the ambiguities surrounding the 'cave of the Ascension' would prompt him to abandon this rather limiting interpretation. Hence even by 348 Cyril most probably located the Ascension specifically on the summit.

This assumption seems to be corroborated upon examination of Cyril's seven brief references to the Mount of Olives.[46] In all but two of these Cyril was referring to the Ascension; yet in not one

---

[44] Indeed, Cyril's predecessor, Bishop Maximus, had been buried close to it, a pattern which may have been followed for subsequent bishops (including Cyril?): see Milik (1960), 555. This church was used during Passion Week to commemorate both the apocalyptic discourse (on the Tuesday: see *Egeria*, 33) and the Johannine discourse (John, 14–17, on the Thursday: see *Egeria*, 35.1–3). Moreover, the newly baptized met there daily during the Easter octave for further instruction (*Egeria*, 39.3). However, Egeria's narrative in most of these instances reveals how an equal, if not greater, place was given within liturgical activity to the hillock or summit.

[45] Repeated by Egeria no less than four times: for references, see above fn. 8.

[46] *Catech.*, 2.12, 4.13–14, 10.19, 12.10–11, 13.38, 14.23, 25.

of them does he ever refer either to the cave or to the Eleona
church.[47] His attention seems to have been elsewhere.

The nearest possible reference to the Eleona appears when he
lists various witnesses to the Resurrection:

Yonder stands even to this day Mount Olivet, all but showing even now
to the eyes of the faithful him who ascended, and the heavenly gate of
the Ascension.

You have many witnesses, therefore; you have this place of the
Resurrection [τῆς ἀναστάσεως τὸν τόπον]; you have to the east the place
of his Ascension [τῆς ἀναβάσεως τὸν τόπον] . . .[48]

Are we to presume from this statement that for Cyril the 'place
of the Resurrection' and the 'place of the Ascension' were strictly
parallel, both being marked by churches? Although this is possible,
there is actually nothing in Cyril's wording to suggest that such a
conclusion is necessary. Indeed his talk of Olivet continuing 'to
this day' (μέχρι σήμερον) to reveal the ascended Christ might, if
anything, suggest that the particular place of the Ascension had
remained unchanged since the time of Christ. Then again, his
picturesque imagery here of the 'heavenly gate',[49] and his frequent
references to the 'clouds',[50] and to Christ being 'crowned',[51] all
suggest that Cyril was probably thinking of the crest of the mount
which was still 'open to the elements'.

Some possible confirmation of Cyril's association of the Ascension
with the summit of the Mount of Olives, not with the Eleona,
comes surprisingly from his discussion of Palm Sunday. Eusebius,
as we have seen, had interpreted Zechariah 14.4 ('in that day his
feet shall stand on the Mount of Olives') as a reference to the
Ascension.[52] Interestingly, however, Cyril saw it instead as a
prophecy of Jesus' activity on Palm Sunday: 'But it might happen
that he should sit upon a foal; give us rather a sign where the
king who enters will stand. "That day his feet shall rest upon the
Mount of Olives . . ."'.[53] Nevertheless, both Eusebius and Cyril

[47] Nor indeed does he refer to the cave when discussing the apocalyptic discourse
in *Catech.*, 15.
[48] Ibid., 14.23 (*WCJ*, ii, 47–8).
[49] Cf. ibid., 10.19.
[50] Ibid., 4.13, 10.19, 14.25.
[51] Ibid., 14.23.
[52] *Dem. Ev.*, 6.18.23 (*FPG*, ii, 30).
[53] *Catech.*, 12.10–11 (*WCJ*, i, 233).

seem to have associated this verse particularly with the *summit* of the mount. Cyril told his catechumens that the place prophesied by Zechariah was 'clearly visible' to anyone 'standing inside the city',[54] and in the Jerusalem liturgy the Palm Sunday procession began from the summit, not from the Eleona.[55] The summit, after all, would have been the best place from which Jesus could view the city. Moreover, Cyril might presume it to have been the most suitable place for Jesus' Ascension and return to heaven.

He does not specify his meaning further. Yet his very imprecision suggests in its own way, especially when coupled with his silence over the cave, that he was not thinking of the now clearly marked Eleona. The 'place of the Ascension', the place where it had actually occurred, was identified but as yet not built upon. If so, Cyril would not in this instance be contradicting Eusebius. Both of them tended to associate the Ascension with the summit, not with the cave. Instead Cyril was endorsing what Eusebius had privately acknowledged but had publicly suppressed. As a result, we can assert that the eventual building of the Imbomon on the summit of the Mount of Olives was by no means a contradiction of Eusebius' historical belief: it would merely have upset his tidy theological Triad. However, Cyril placed himself under no such limitations. The Eusebian Triad was a 'straitjacket' that Jerusalem's bishop had no reason to wear.

2. THE MOUNT OF OLIVES IN RELATION TO JERUSALEM

The Mount of Olives, was not, however just the location for these special events in the life of Christ. Its unique geographical position, close to but separate from the city, made it also a unique vantage-point from which to assess Jerusalem. For some people the mount might seem to function as a centre of opposition, standing over against the city both in geographical and theological terms, a place of contrast from which to judge the city. For others, however, the perspective might be quite different; no such antagonism was really to be sensed and indeed the mount could be seen as a glorious extension of the city's heritage. Thus on its

---

[54] Ibid.
[55] *Egeria*, 31.1–2.

slopes there could meet both the lovers and opponents of Jerusalem. Cyril loved Jerusalem, but Eusebius in the days before the possibility of a Christian Jerusalem, when attachment to Jerusalem in his apologetics was a mark of Judaism and not of Christianity, fell more easily into the camp of the opponents.

Eusebius' opposition to Jerusalem can be judged from that same passage in the *Proof of the Gospel* which has already been discussed.[56] Ten years later, however, with the arrival of Constantine, Eusebius' whole outlook would suddenly need a major reassessment. Yet his own long-established attitude of opposition to Jerusalem would make it hard for him ever to endorse the city as wholeheartedly as Cyril.

By its very nature the Mount of Olives, as we have suggested, can be taken as a 'touchstone' of this evaluation of Jerusalem. For divergent attitudes towards Jerusalem will inevitably lead to divergent attitudes towards the Mount of Olives. Someone opposed to Jerusalem will tend to see the Mount of Olives as itself opposed to the city and separate from it. By contrast, someone strongly in favour of Jerusalem will tend to see the Mount of Olives as but an extension of the city, an integral part of it. It is our task now to note how Eusebius and Cyril would come to view the Mount of Olives quite differently as a result of their divergent attitudes towards Jerusalem.

Cyril's positive attitude towards Jerusalem predisposed him to reckon the Mount of Olives as an integral part of an 'expanded' Jerusalem, and he minimized any sense of opposition between the mount and the city. This in turn coloured his attitude to Gospel events located on the mount. Any elements of opposition to Jerusalem discernible in Jesus' use of the mount (such as the triumphal entry, the apocalyptic discourse or the Ascension) would be minimized or excluded; instead these events would be interpreted in such a way as to affirm Jerusalem.

Eusebius' perspective was quite different. Because of his more negative attitude towards Jerusalem, at least in the years before 325, he tended to see the Mount of Olives as standing opposed or 'opposite' to the city. As a result, 'Jerusalem' was to him a much smaller entity, a small city lying below the mount to the west. More importantly, this opposition to Jerusalem caused him to sense

---

[56] *Dem. Ev.*, 6.18.4–26 (*FPG*, ii, 26–31).

a strand of opposition to Jerusalem even within the Gospels. Jesus' apparent love of that mount could be interpreted as indicative of his comparable distaste for the city. Thus, for example, Eusebius understood Jesus' triumphal entry from the mount as redounding not to Jerusalem's glory but to its shame. Moreover, Jesus' choice of Bethany, not Jerusalem, for his temporary home would be seen as underlining this opposition; and the fact that the apocalyptic discourse occurred on the mount would be seen as no coincidence. Finally, Jesus' selection of the mount for his Ascension was taken by Eusebius as revealing the Lord's disregard for the city below which had crucified him; just as the *shekinah* glory had deserted the Temple in Ezekiel's vision, so too the Lord left the city of Jerusalem for his Ascension.

In this way the very same Gospel events on the Mount of Olives could be imbued with quite different meanings and significance; it all depended on the interpreter's assessment of Jerusalem. As a result, our study of the Mount of Olives will show how the differences between Eusebius and Cyril on the question of Jerusalem affected their attitudes towards individual places associated with the life of Jesus. The 'holy city' question affected the 'holy place' question; the shadow of 'Jerusalem' would fall inevitably upon the Mount of Olives.

(a) Cyril and the Mount of Olives

Eusebius' more negative approach may best be brought to light through acquainting ourselves first with the approach later developed by Cyril. Cyril's positive attitude to Jerusalem gave him good reason, not only for asserting the great value of the Mount of Olives, but also for seeing it as an integral part of Jerusalem.

Strictly, of course, the 'city' as such remained the walled area to the west.[57] Yet the proximity of the mount and its importance for Christian memory made it an integral part of that wider phenomenon, the 'Christian Jerusalem'. If Cyril could speak of Christ's birth in Bethlehem occurring 'here in Jerusalem',[58] the same would be true of Christ's Ascension from the Mount of

[57] See, e.g., *Egeria*, 25.6, 25.11–12, 29.4, and 37.3; though she too could use the wider meaning: Constantine's three buildings were the 'Jerusalem holy places' (25.10).

[58] *Catech.*, 16.4.

Olives. Thus Cyril stressed to his catechumens time and again that they had in their own immediate vicinity many witnesses, which included not just the Holy Sepulchre but the 'place of the Ascension' as well.[59] The mount was not distant; it was an integral part of Cyril's Jerusalem.

Nor indeed did he think of the mount lying 'opposite' or opposed to the city. That important prophetic verse, Zechariah 14.4, speaks of the mount being 'opposite' (κατέναντι) to Jerusalem. Eusebius had used this verse to highlight the sense of opposition.[60] Cyril, however, tactfully avoids commenting on this word when expounding the verse.[61] Instead he regularly described the mount simply as 'to the east'.[62]

Then again, if the Mount of Olives was an important part of Jerusalem's heritage, so too were the Gospel events that had occurred there. This was especially true of the Ascension itself, the chief Christian remembrance on the mount. Cyril thus emphasized that the Ascension was not the last event in the New Testament story, nor a final dismissive judgement upon Jerusalem; instead the disciples had returned immediately to take their place within the city in order to receive the 'blessing' of Pentecost on Mt. Sion.[63] If the apostles temporarily left Jerusalem, they soon resumed their place in its centre.

His approach to other Gospel events on the Mount of Olives was similarly influenced by his high regard for Jerusalem. Negatively, this could explain, for example, why neither the apocalyptic discourse,[64] nor the cursing of the fig-tree[65] (both of which depict Jerusalem adversely), were ever located explicitly by Cyril on the mount. Similarly, Cyril may have drawn a distinction between the 'Mount of Olives' and 'Gethsemane', a distinction which enabled the mount to be seen in a more positive light: 'Gethsemane bears witness, where the betrayal took place; not yet do I speak of the Mount of Olives, where they who were with him that night were

---

[59] Ibid., 14.23.
[60] *Dem. Ev.*, 6.18.23 (*FPG*, ii, 29).
[61] *Catech.*, 12.11.
[62] Ibid., 4.14, 14.23, and 14.25.
[63] Ibid., 14.23; cf. 17.13.
[64] Ibid., 15.4 ff. Naturally in his discussion here of the apocalyptic discourse he focuses chiefly on the theme of the Second Coming and then on God's judgement of the Temple, not on any divine judgement of the city itself.
[65] Ibid., 13.38 fin.

praying.'[66] The evil betrayal in Gethsemane had occured down in the valley; the mount itself could be seen more positively as the place of prayer. All such potentially negative aspects, which depicted the Mount of Olives and Jerusalem in a less than flattering light, were given only scanty attention.

However, by far the best example of Cyril's positive attitude to Gospel events associated with the Mount of Olives is his discussion of Jesus' triumphal entry into Jerusalem from the mount.

Alone of kings, Jesus sat upon a foal untried in the yoke, entering Jerusalem with acclaims as a king. . . . Give us a sign where the king who enters will stand. Give us a sign not far from the city, that it may not be unknown to us; give us a sign nearby and clearly visible, that being in the city we may behold the place. Again the prophet answers, saying, 'That day his feet shall stand upon the Mount of Olives, which is opposite Jerusalem to the east'. Is it possible for anyone standing within the city not to behold the place?[67]

Evidently he did not see the triumphal entry as a poignant event that highlighted Jerusalem's rejection of her true king. The subsequent cleansing of the Temple is not mentioned and instead he concentrates on those shortlived moments when Christ entered the city amidst popular acclamation.

Cyril's approach here contrasts markedly with his Christian predecessors in Palestine. Origen had seen the triumphal entry as a judgement upon the earthly Jerusalem; any positive meaning in the event was derived solely from it as a picture of Christ entering the heavenly Sion.[68] Similarly, Eusebius had focused on the heavenly realm, interpreting this Gospel event as an exhibition of the contrast between Christ's humble first coming and his glorious Second Coming.[69] His attention, like Origen's, was fixed away from the physical Jerusalem; any positive meaning for these authors was only found by concentrating on the heavenly realm.

Cyril, however, saw this event as speaking very positively about the physical Jerusalem. The reason, of course, is not hard to find. Cyril was speaking in a city that could now claim, at least with some justification, to be accepting the kingship of Christ: 'that

[66] *Catech.*, 13.38 (*WCJ*, ii, 29).
[67] Ibid., 12.10–11 (*WCJ*, i, 233).
[68] *Comm. in Matt.* [21.1–5], 16.15, 523.
[69] *Dem. Ev.*, 9.17.6 (*FPG*, ii, 186); cf. also ibid., 6.8. Eusebius seems not to refer to the triumphal entry in any other work.

Jerusalem crucified Christ, but that which now is worships him'.[70]
Even more poignantly, a re-enactment of the 'Palm Sunday
procession' would soon be, if it was not already, a natural development within the Jerusalem liturgy.[71] In this liturgical act the
contemporary, physical Jerusalem, not the heavenly one, received
Christ as her true king. It would be very hard indeed in this
context of celebration either to emphasize the fickle treatment of
Jesus by Jerusalem's inhabitants or to appreciate that Jesus' action
had in part been a form of judgement upon the city. Although
strictly a distinction could be drawn between the judgement on
the Jewish Jerusalem of Jesus' day and the glorification of the
Christian Jerusalem symbolized by this procession, this liturgical
action naturally influenced the pilgrims' subsequent understanding
of the Gospels. The triumphal entry was inevitably seen as
redounding to the glory of Jerusalem; it was a natural part of the
great heritage of the fourth-century city.

Cyril's environment in fourth-century Jerusalem thus encouraged
him to excise any negative elements within the first-century story.
His positive attitude to contemporary Jerusalem extended to the
Mount of Olives. Thus the Mount of Olives for Cyril was by no
means a place which spoke of Jerusalem's judgement. It was rather
a glorious 'outpost' of the city, and the Gospel events located there
were to be reinterpreted in this positive light.

(b) Eusebius before 325

Cyril's attitudes contrast starkly with Eusebius' original views,
expressed just ten years before the coming of Constantine in the
Proof of the Gospel. It was not just that Eusebius saw the triumphal
entry in terms of the heavenly Jerusalem; for, influenced by his
negative attitude to Jerusalem, he had also developed in quite

[70] *Catech.*, 13.7 (*WCJ*, ii, 9).

[71] *Egeria*, 31.1–4. Cyril's positive evaluation of the triumphal entry is seen also
in his use of the 'palm tree' as a 'witness' in *Catech.*, 10.19: he thereby lent implicit
support to the assumption of the Bordeaux Pilgrim fifteen years earlier that this
was truly the original, dating from the time of Christ (594.7–595.2). Not surprisingly
Eusebius never mentions this feature of contemporary Jerusalem: knowing the
ravages of the city during AD 70 Eusebius was unlikely to endorse, as a historian,
any such naïve identification and, as a theologian, any such abuse of the
'witness'-concept. If the fate of the 'true cross' is a fair example (*Egeria*, 37.2) the
popularity of this tree among pilgrims may have ensured its rapid demise! It is not
mentioned by Egeria (e.g., in 31.3) or later pilgrims.

explicit terms a strong sense of opposition between Jerusalem and the Mount of Olives. The most relevant passage in Eusebius' writings is again his exegesis of Zechariah 14.4 ('his feet shall stand on the Mount of Olives'), which was the primary text for Eusebius' discussion of the Olivet cave.[72]

The following paragraphs surround the passage quoted earlier about the cave and Christian visitors to Jerusalem, and offers us Eusebius' more spiritualized interpretation of these verses:

This Mount of Olives is said to be over against [κατέναντι] Jerusalem, because it was established by God after the fall of Jerusalem, instead of the old earthly Jerusalem and its worship. For since scripture said above with reference to Jerusalem, 'the city shall be taken . . .', it could not say that the feet of the Lord stand upon Jerusalem. How could that be, once it were destroyed? But it says that they will stand with them that depart from it to the mount opposite [ἄντικρυς] the city called the Mount of Olives. And this too the prophet Ezekiel foretells: 'And the cherubim lifted their wings, and the wheels beside them, and the glory of the God of Israel was on them above them, and he stood on the mount which was opposite [ἀπέναντι] to the city' [Ezk. 11.22–3].

The Mount of Olives is therefore literally 'opposite' to Jerusalem and 'to the east' of it, but also the Church of God, . . . raised up in place of Jerusalem that is fallen never to rise again [μὴ ἐγερθείσης], and thought worthy of the feet of the Lord, is figuratively not only 'opposite' to Jerusalem, but also 'east' of it as well, receiving the rays of the divine light . . .[73]

In contrast to Cyril who later used this verse when discussing the triumphal entry, Eusebius considered it to have been fulfilled supremely in the Ascension. Thus one applied it to the moment when Christ began his entrance into Jerusalem, the other to that

[72] *Dem. Ev.*, 6.18.4–26 (*FPG*, ii, 26–31). Prior to Eusebius this particular verse had only been used (in our extant sources) by Tertullian, who related it to Christ's visit each evening to the mount (cf. Luke 21.37) in the days before his crucifixion (*Adv. Marc.*, 4.39.19). Origen indeed spoke loosely of the Mount of Olives 'de quo prophetat et Zecharias' (*Comm. in Matt.* [26.26–30], CS 86, 200) and saw other verses in Zech. 14 (esp. v.6) fulfilled in the Passion narrative (*idem* [27.45], Fr. 554, 227) but never expounded this particular verse. Eusebius himself also used the chapter in a wider sense as a prophecy of the Passion (*Dem. Ev.*, 10.7.3–6) or of Christ's life as a whole (*idem*, 2.3.160–61 (*FPG*, i, 97), and even here in 6.18.6). This passage was, however, by far his most extended analysis. Since no commmentary by Origen on Zechariah has survived, Eusebius' discussion here is for us an interpretation without precedent.

[73] *Dem. Ev.*, 6.18.20–22, 26 (*FPG*, ii, 29–31).

moment when he made his final departure—his entrance, as it were, into the heavenly Jerusalem. Underlying this contrast between Eusebius and Cyril lurked the same powerful motive: their differing attitudes towards Jerusalem.

The beginning of the 'Palm Sunday procession' was, naturally, an important moment in the liturgy. Cyril therefore used this verse to highlight that poignant moment in the Gospel narrative when Jesus began his glorious entrance into Jerusalem.[74] Eusebius, however, used its precise language instead to emphasize the moment of Christ's final rejection of the city, that moment when in a sense Jesus had 'wiped the dust' of Jerusalem 'off his feet' (cf. Matt. 10.14). Cyril applied this verse to a moment in the Gospels that affirmed the physical Jerusalem; Eusebius applied it to a moment of judgement.

Moreover, both authors evidently set great store by being able to use this prophecy; it was of some importance to them. Each one's desire to interpret Zechariah in this way forced them into positions that did not square very well with other aspects of the Gospel narrative. For example, the Gospels suggest that Jesus mounted a colt from the region of Bethany on the far side of the mount (Matt. 21.7 and parallels); however, in order to show Jesus' fulfilment of this prophecy, Cyril needed Jesus' feet to be standing firmly on the summit of the mount![75] Then again the Gospels clearly mention Jesus using the mount more frequently before the Passion than after the Resurrection; yet Eusebius, with his desire to see this verse only fulfilled *after* the Resurrection at the moment of the Ascension, was forced to imply that Jesus' praying and teaching on the mount also occurred at this later stage.[76] At any

[74] *Catech.*, 12.10–11.

[75] Naturally this exegesis is inextricably linked with the developing liturgical practice of the Jerusalem Church: the fourth-century procession evidently began only at the Imbomon, not back at Bethany. No doubt there were very practical reasons for this, since Egeria (31.4) notes that the 'older women and men' found even this distance tiring after the previous day's celebrations at the Lazarium in Bethany (*Egeria*, 29.3–6). Theology might on occasion colour liturgical practice, but the influence could equally (and perhaps more frequently) work as here in the reverse direction.

[76] Wilkinson (1981), 49, alone has noted correctly that Eusebius is here implying some *post*-Resurrection teaching. However, he fails to recognize the particular prophetic and theological context which has forced Eusebius into this temporary necessity. Eusebius' language later in *V. Const.*, 3.43.3, is too vague to determine what teaching he had in mind; but the unambiguous evidence of the the the Bordeaux Pilgrim (595.5) favours a reference to the apocalyptic discourse that occurred *before* the Passion.

time, both Cyril and Eusebius strove hard to understand the way prophecy had been fulfilled in Christ's life. Here, however, they were forced by their theology of Jerusalem, into positions which were not only quite at variance with each other's but also in themselves seemingly contrary to scripture.

Secondly, it now needs to be observed that this fulfilment of Zechariah in the Ascension was not for Eusebius the most important fulfilment. If length of treatment is a reliable indication, then it is clear that the chief fulfilment of Zechariah's words was to be found simply in the very existence of the Church, of which the Mount of Olives was supposedly a symbol. For this is the point that Eusebius is eager to stress throughout the rest of the passage in the *Proof of the Gospel* (6.18). Zechariah's emphasis on the Mount of Olives as opposed to Jerusalem signified the future emergence of the Church in opposition to Judaism. This 'spiritualized' interpretation was entirely in keeping with Eusebius' more 'spiritual' approach to the places of Christ and to scripture. Yet it also caused Eusebius to emphasize very strongly this contrast between Jerusalem and the Mount of Olives.

Furthermore, one of the central themes of this passage is the Mount of Olives' *opposition* to Jerusalem. Zechariah 14.4, the verse which he was expounding, used the word κατέναντι, and Ezekiel 11.27 (which he quoted during the course of his exposition), used ἀπέναντι. Eusebius himself then emphasized this theme of opposition and contrast by using the yet more forceful ἄντικρυς ('over against') and also (in part of this passage not quoted above) by substituting κατέναντι ('opposite') for Luke's more neutral ἐγγύς ('near') when quoting Acts 1.12: 'the disciples returned from the Mount of Olives which is *opposite* to Jerusalem'.[77] As the Mount of Olives was opposite to Jerusalem, so the Church, he claimed, was opposed to Judaism. Eusebius had thus not only highlighted this opposition in geographical terms but proceeded to imbue it with a very strong theological significance.

The result was a seemingly unqualified opposition in Eusebius to Jerusalem. However, a perspicacious reader (or perhaps Eusebius himself in his final years) might point out that in Eusebius' own context the physical Jerusalem was really synonymous with

---

[77] *Dem. Ev.*, 6.18.25 (*FPG*, ii, 30); later in *idem.*, 8.4.25 (ii, 146–7) he uses the yet more forceful κατναντικρύς.

Judaism: it was not Jerusalem *per se* that had been divinely judged
but only Jewish Jerusalem. Alternatively a Christian observer might
distinguish between the Temple and the city, seeing only the
former as destroyed in divine judgement of the Jews.

These were the distinctions with which Eusebius wrestled in his
final years and which Cyril of Jerusalem seems to adopt without
hesitation. At this stage, however, Eusebius does not yet seem to
have made them, even though he was writing less than a decade
before the Constantinian triumph and the development of the
Christian 'Holy Land'. In both his literal and more 'spiritual'
expositions here of Zechariah 14.4, he used language which quite
clearly implied that Jerusalem as a whole entity no longer had (nor
could have) any theological status within God's purposes. In
accordance with prophecy the earthly Jerusalem had lost both its
Temple and its 'glory', and the whole city was now termed the
'former city' ($\tau\grave{\eta}\nu$ $\pi\rho\sigma\tau\acute{\epsilon}\rho\alpha\nu$ $\pi\acute{o}\lambda\iota\nu$).[78] Indeed it was a relic of the
theological past that had fallen 'never to rise again'.[79]

That these negative corollaries were indeed intended by Eusebius
to refer to the earthly Jerusalem in Palestine is clearly endorsed
by the fact that they are intertwined with his more 'physical' or
literal interpretation, in which he speaks of Jesus' Ascension and
of Christian visitors overlooking the ruins of Jerusalem. This shows
that territorial Jerusalem (rather than just Judaism as an abstraction)
was clearly in his mind. He implies that Christian visitors upon
seeing the destroyed Jerusalem have no special desire for its
restoration. On the contrary, its ruin speaks loudly of God's
judgement and Christians must respond obediently to such major
lessons from sacred history.

Finally, Eusebius endorses this judgement of Jerusalem in
physical terms by then imbuing even the Gospel narrative with
the theme of opposition. According to Eusebius, the Lord himself
seems to have selected the mount for his Ascension precisely in
order to enact this negative judgement upon the city below, the
city that had so recently crucified him. For Eusebius, this final
departure from the city of Jerusalem fulfilled Ezekiel's picture of
the cherubim deserting the Temple: the 'glory of the Lord migrated
to the Mount of Olives when it left the former city'.[80] This

---

[78] *Dem. Ev.*, 6.18.23 (*FPG*, ii, 29), quoted above at fn. 23.
[79] Ibid., 6.18.26 (ii, 30).
[80] Ibid., 6.18.23 (ii, 29).

opposition to, and judgement on, Jerusalem was also, he implies, something that was sensed by the writer of Acts: the 'disciples returned from the Mount of Olives which is opposite to Jerusalem'.[81] In this way Eusebius' interpretation suddenly gained dominical authority. He could suggest that his own opposition to Jerusalem had the full backing of the evangelists and even of the Lord himself. Thus the location of the Ascension on the Mount of Olives was, he asserted, no coincidence. The Mount of Olives stood opposed to the city, and Jesus' use of the mount was deliberately designed to express his judgement upon it.

(c) Eusebius after 325

The situation after 325 would not, however, allow Eusebius to persist with such opinions without modification. If this passage in the *Proof of the Gospel* revealed to his contemporaries his need for such a radical reassessment, it reveals to us how little he was prepared for the great changes of 325. It might be argued that in this passage Eusebius had only been employing stock apologetic themes without much personal commitment, that he was not himself therefore tied to such a strong opposition to Jerusalem. However, the apparent novelty of his exegesis and the colourful tone of his language suggests instead that Eusebius was betraying something of his real self. At this stage his own theology had little, indeed no, place for the physical Jerusalem. Just how far would Eusebius be prepared to change this stance towards Jerusalem after 325? The fuller analysis in our final chapter will reveal his wrestling with this issue and some of his eventual resolutions. He did make some modifications, but not many. For our present purpose we need only note briefly how such modifications might have affected his understanding of the Mount of Olives.

The uncovering of the tomb of Christ shortly after 325 had many repercussions. One of these was that, because the Holy Sepulchre was located within the city of Jerusalem on a hill rising slightly higher than the Temple mount to its east, Eusebius had the opportunity after 325 to develop his opposition motif in a new way. No longer did he need to stress that the Mount of Olives, symbolizing the Church, stood opposed to the city of Jerusalem.

---

[81] Ibid.

Now in the *Life of Constantine* he could suggest that the Holy Sepulchre, symbolizing the 'New Jerusalem' and certainly the Church, stood opposed (ἄντικρυς) to the hill of the Jewish Temple:

the New Jerusalem was built over against [ἀντιπρόσωπος] the one so celebrated of old which . . . had experienced that last extremity of desolation.[82]

Geography could once again embody a picture of theological truth: Christianity had conquered Judaism.

Yet the geographical location was different. Formerly, in the *Proof of the Gospel*, Eusebius had looked over the city and Temple from the east, but now in the *Life of Constantine* he looked over the Temple mount from within the city and from the west. In geographical terms Eusebius' about-turn was therefore almost exactly 180 degrees. In strictly theological terms, however, it will be understood from our final chapter that his opinions had not changed nearly so much. His opposition was now more clearly focused on the Temple, but he retained an essentially negative approach to the city of Jerusalem as well.

Yet the interesting result for our present purposes was that Eusebius could begin to see the Mount of Olives in a new light. No longer did it need to be seen as inherently opposed to the city of Jerusalem. Thus in those three passages (already discussed in relation to the triad of caves)[83] in which he refers to the Mount of Olives after 325, there was now no suggestion of this geographical opposition, nor of the Ascension being in part an act of judgement on the city. The shadow over Jerusalem was beginning to lift. On the other hand, as noted already, these passages with their descriptions of the Triad never include a positive assessment of Jerusalem, nor do they suggest the way in which these outlying caves relate to Jerusalem. Eusebius may indeed have lost some of the negative strands within his thinking, but this was not the occasion for publishing his current reassessment.

Having studied the thoughts of both Eusebius and Cyril towards the Mount of Olives, it will be appreciated that the differences between the two bishops were not as great on this issue as they were perhaps elsewhere. Both on this question of the relationship

---

[82] *V. Const.*, 3.33 (NPNF, i, 529).
[83] *L. Const.*, 9.17; *V. Const.*, 3.41.1, and 3.43.3.

between the mount and the city and also on the question of the cave and the Ascension, Eusebius' final views were not so far from those which were to be voiced by Cyril a decade later.

However, that proximity of opinions was slightly different in each case. With regard to the question of the cave and the summit, Eusebius' opinion was constant throughout his lifetime: the Ascension was always connected in his mind with the mountain-top, but after 325 he had particular reasons for suppressing this and for linking the Ascension instead with the cave. Thus Eusebius in his final years was close to Cyril but his subtlety made him seem more distant. In his assessment of the mount's relation to Jerusalem, however, Eusebius' opinion seems to have changed after 325; at least any earlier suggestions of outright opposition seem now to have disappeared. In his final years Eusebius was again quite close to Cyril but perhaps not so ready to admit it. His development of the Triad therefore acted as a convenient half-way response to both these questions. It left the precise status of Jerusalem unspecified while focusing single-mindedly upon the traditional cave located on the mount. Cyril, however, naturally broke through beyond this. He attempted to increase the number of Christian sites and to expand both the content and concept of Christian Jerusalem.

3. GETHSEMANE

Our discussion of the Mount of Olives has prepared us well for our final analysis of the two most important sites in the Christian Holy Land, which lie below the mount to the west: the church of the Holy Sepulchre and the city of Jerusalem itself. However, on our way down from its peak we must pass, as did Jesus, as did Egeria, and as have pilgrims ever since, a place called Gethsemane. Here the painful paradoxes of the Incarnation found their most dramatic expression, a pain that must cause us to pause. On the top of the mount Christians might remember with joy the clamour of the triumphal entry or the consummating victory of the Ascension; but at its foot, separating them from the city and from the scene of the Resurrection, lay a valley filled with the 'shadow of death' (Ps. 23.4).

Already in the third century Origen in his perceptive manner had noted the appropriate nature, indeed the divine necessity, of Jesus' betrayal near the Kidron brook down in the valley;[84] and soon Eusebius would be noting in his *Onomasticon* how faithful Christians 'loved to pray' in the Gethsemane where their Lord had prayed.[85] For here they could sense a closeness to Christ's divinity as they prayed in the place of his most raw humanity.

How did Eusebius and Cyril approach this place associated both with Jesus' prayer (or 'agony') and his betrayal? This two-fold commemoration within Gethsemane (the two events, after all, had occurred only a 'stone's throw apart': Luke 22.41) seems to have led to some confusion in Christian thought both in the fourth century and in our own day. Yet it can also reveal quite usefully to us some of the differences between Eusebius and Cyril. By Cyril's day Gethsemane would be associated more narrowly with the betrayal; Jesus' agony would be remembered further up the Mount of Olives. Eusebius, however, associated Gethsemane with both Jesus' betrayal *and* his agony. Nevertheless, in this greater emphasis on Jesus' prayer Eusebius characteristically revealed little personal response to this moment of agony.

Gethsemane is understood from the Gospels[86] to have been the name for a 'garden' at the foot of the Mount of Olives near the 'brook Kidron'. The precise appearance of this area in the fourth century is quite uncertain. There was a cave in the vicinity[87] but the only natural phenomenon mentioned explicitly in our literary sources was a 'rock', which the the Bordeaux Pilgrim associated expressly with Judas' betrayal of Jesus.[88] However, in the *Onomasticon* Eusebius makes no comment about any such rock; indeed his attention seems to be located elsewhere, on the place where Jesus prayed: 'Gethsemane, the place where Christ prayed before the Passion. It lies close to ($\pi\rho\delta s$) the Mount of Olives and

---

[84] Just as at the time of the Transfiguration, it was appropriate for Jesus before his arrest to have been praying 'super montem' (*Comm. in Matt.* [26.36–9], CS 90, 205); it was fitting too for his arrest to have occured in the valley (*Comm. in Jo.* [8.20], 19.10; cf. also *Comm. in Matt.* [26.26–30], CS 86, 199.29).

[85] *Onom.*, 74.16–18.

[86] Matt. 26.36; Mark 14.32; cf. Luke 22.39, and John 18.1.

[87] Later associated strangely with the Last Supper: see Wilkinson (1977), 158. Contrary to the assertion of Meistermann (1920), 50–51, this was clearly not the same 'cave' as that referred to by Eusebius in *Dem. Ev.*, 6.18, and mentioned in the *Acts of John*.

[88] *BP*, 594.7; yet he does not relate this rock to 'Gethsemane' as such.

the faithful now love to pray there.'⁸⁹ Conceivably Eusebius may again have questioned the presumed authenticity of this rock. More probably he may simply have located the betrayal further down into the Kidron valley, because in the *Onomasticon* it is the Kidron valley which he describes as the 'place where Christ was betrayed'.⁹⁰ Thus his entry here for Gethsemane probably focuses elsewere and certainly on Christ's agony rather than on his betrayal. Eusebius made two other explicit references to Gethsemane, though very much in passing.⁹¹ In both of these, unlike the entry in the *Onomasticon*, Eusebius' attention was focused more on the betrayal. Thus in his day the identification was evidently quite fluid, 'Gethsemane' being the accepted name for the place of both the agony and the betrayal.

Cyril and Egeria, however, began to associate 'Gethsemane' exclusively with the betrayal; Christ's agony was located elsewhere. For Cyril Christ's agony had occurred instead simply on the 'Mount of Olives': 'Gethsemane bears witness, where the betrayal took place; not yet do I speak of the Mount of Olives, where they who were with him that night were praying.'⁹² For Egeria it seemingly had occurred quite some way further up the hill;⁹³ in her day the place of Christ's agony was marked by a 'graceful church' ('elegans ecclesia')⁹⁴ but 'Gethsemane' was the name for a quite separate area, not yet built upon, where she remembered Christ's betrayal.⁹⁵

Egeria's evidence seems to be contradicted, however, by that of Jerome in his translation of Eusebius' *Onomasticon*; for after. repeating Eusebius' identification of Gethsemane with the 'place where the Saviour prayed before the passion', he claimed that a church had now been built over this site 'at the foot of the Mount of Olives' ('ad radices montis Oliveti').⁹⁶ According to Egeria,

⁸⁹ *Onom.*, 74.16–18.
⁹⁰ Ibid., 174.26–27.
⁹¹ *Dem. Ev.*, 10.3.12 (*FPG*, ii, 204) and *Comm. in Is.*[28.1], 179.10.
⁹² *Catech.*, 13.38 (*WCJ*, ii, 29).
⁹³ *Egeria*, 36.1–3. We should not seek to minimize the evident distance that there was, according to Egeria's words here, between the place of Jesus' agony and that of his arrest. For it is between these two places that she comments on the 'very big hill' which they needed to come down: see Renoux, i (1969), 136–42, for a discussion of the Maundy Thursday texts and liturgy which endorse the likelihood of this distance.
⁹⁴ Ibid., 36.1.
⁹⁵ Ibid., 36.2–3.
⁹⁶ *Onom.*, 75.18–19.

however, this church of the agony was certainly not 'at the foot' of the hill but quite some way up the hillside.

It is quite uncertain how this discrepancy can be resolved. Conceivably Egeria has become confused in her memory of the Maundy Thursday procession. Alternatively, and perhaps more probably, the Jerusalem Church may have celebrated the betrayal at the *very* bottom of the valley, far lower down than it is today, such that this 'church' (though higher up) could still legitimately be described as being 'at the foot' of the Mount of Olives.[97]

Alternatively, it is possible that Jerome, whose testimony is not always as reliable as one might have expected from one resident in Palestine,[98] has given us a confusing description in his *Onomasticon*. If by Jerome's day the flexible terminology of Eusebius had been lost ('Gethsemane' now being associated exclusively with the betrayal and not at all with Christ's agony), then Eusebius' outdated identification of Gethsemane with the place of Christ's agony would have caused a slight problem. Jerome's compromise solution may have been to refer indeed to the church now built over the site of Christ's agony (even though this was now no longer known as 'Gethsemane'), but also to locate this 'at the foot' of the mount (a description more in keeping with the 'Gethsemane' of his own day). If so, then this church may in fact have been further up the hill than his description suggests, an outcome that would agree with the testimony of Egeria.[99]

The problems of authenticity and identification will remain. Yet we can note that our modern uncertainty is largely a reflection of this fourth-century confusion as to whether 'Gethsemane' was to be associated with Christ's agony or with his betrayal. Cyril clearly associated it more narrowly than Eusebius with the betrayal alone. This in turn had other interesting results. For example, it meant that when he was interpreting as prophecies the verses of certain

[97] Such arguments would endorse the case of those who try to identify the present church of All Nations with this 'elegans ecclesia' of Egeria and thereby perhaps even with the very place of Christ's agony: see Meistermann (1920), and Storme (1969); cf. also Murphy-O'Connor (1988), 106.

[98] Jerome's 'limited knowledge of topography' is commented upon by Murphy-O'Connor (1988), 263, and Wilkinson (1974).

[99] This alternative solution would then probably militate against the identification of Egeria's church with the present church of All Nations: see Milik (1960), 555-6, and Wilkinson (1981), 53 (though not as revised on p. 391). For more recent excavations at Gethsemane, see Corbo (1965), pt I.

psalms, which Eusebius had earlier applied more broadly to include Christ's agony, Cyril applied them exclusively to the the betrayal alone.[100] It also meant that Gethsemane could be used by Cyril to emphasize the treachery of Judas, an emphasis that may deliberately have been designed to instil a deeper antagonism amongst Christians towards the Jews.[101]

Eusebius' alternative emphasis on Christ's praying, however, never seems to have caused him to respond in his own spirituality to this most human moment in the story of Christ. Like Origen before him, Eusebius on several occasions discussed some of the theological problems raised by this episode of Christ's praying to the Father.[102] Origen had, however, gone further than Eusebius in noting how this incident reflected the true humanity of Jesus' soul,[103] and Jesus' natural desire to pray on his own.[104] By contrast, Eusebius' treatment of Jesus' agony, especially in the *Proof of the Gospel*[105] and in his *Commentary on the Psalms*,[106] was rather clinical: Jesus, unlike many martyrs, simply succeeded in fighting off the 'spirit of fear'.[107] Moreover, in the former passage he had just referred to the contemporary Holy Sepulchre[108] but he did not likewise comment on the site of Gethsemane. The place of Christ's agony did not especially move him.

The surviving sources do not permit a clear picture. However, despite his reference in the *Onomasticon*, which does convey the

[100] See especially *Catech.*, 13.9–11 for his use of Ps. 55.21 and Ps. 109.2–3; cf. Eusebius in *Dem. Ev.*, 10.2–3, and *Comm. in Ps.* [54.7–22], 480c–488d.

[101] This could in part explain the extraordinary and heightened emotion that the pilgrims with Egeria manifested at this moment of the betrayal; their groaning could be heard in the city (*Egeria*, 36.3). Eusebius, however, was no less hostile towards the Jews. Indeed, though Cyril interpreted LXX Ps. 58.7 [59.6] ('they prowled about the city') as a prophecy of the treachery of Judas and the city leaders, Eusebius in *Comm. in Ps.* [58.7], 541c, understood this 'prowling' to be fulfilled in the contemporary Jews who (since Hadrian's decree) could encircle the area of Jerusalem but never set foot within it.

[102] Especially the problem of Christ's 'unanswered' prayer: see Eus., *Comm. in Is.* [28.1], 179 and [49.8], 311.25 ff., *Comm. in Ps.* [87.16–19], 1068a–69a; cf. Origen, *Comm. in Jo.*, 32.23, 466, *Mart.*, 29, 25–6, *Comm. in Matt.* [26.37–44], Fr. 530, 217, *C. Cels.*, 2.25. Eusebius also commented on the unlikelihood of the evangelists' inventing such a revealing story (*Dem. Ev.*, 3.5.100: *FPG*, i, 141).

[103] *Hom. in Jer.*, 15, 27; *de Princ.*, 2.6.2.

[104] *Comm. in Matt.* [26.36–47], CS 89–99, 204–217.

[105] *Dem. Ev.*, 10.2–3. (*FPG*, ii, 199 ff.).

[106] *Comm. in Ps.* [87.16–19], 1068a–69a.

[107] *Dem. Ev.*, 10.2.13 (*FPG*, ii, 201).

[108] *Comm. in Ps.* [87.7], 1064a.

value Christians found in praying there, Eusebius himself comes across as a man little moved by the place. The events commemorated there neatly fulfilled some prophecies but they were equally well the source of certain problems. For Cyril, however, the contemporary place had an important story to tell; it was a powerful 'witness' that revealed Christ to the eyes of those with faith and 'all but showed Judas still, to those who understand'.[109] Cyril could respond to the place in its powerful simplicity; Eusebius had a mind more attracted to complexity and was apparently little affected by this place which revealed so poignantly the depths of Christ's Passion. Eusebius would have paused with us on our way down the hillside, but he would soon have been wanting to be on his way up into the city. There lay the 'cave' of Christ's Resurrection, the 'witness' to our own immortality.

---

[109] *Catech.*, 10.19 (*WCJ*, i, 209).

8

THE CHURCH OF THE
HOLY SEPULCHRE

We too must make our way up from the Kidron valley into the city of Jerusalem. Two particular places, quite different from one another, await our attention: one of these used to be 'outside the city wall' on the far, western side, but now lies very much in the heart of the 'old city'; the other was very much an integral part of Jerusalem in Jesus' day but now lies just outside the wall of the 'old city' to the south. Since in the fourth century this second location, Mt. Sion, was chiefly associated with the coming of the Spirit at Pentecost, our attention must focus first on the other site, the church of the Holy Sepulchre, which commemorates the Death and Resurrection of Christ. This is the 'place of Christ' *par excellence*; it may be the last in our enquiry but it is certainly not the least. Indeed, as we enter the church of the Holy Sepulchre, we sense that this is truly our beginning. Here Christians of all persuasions, and in every age from the fourth century until now, have come to acknowledge their common origin in the Death and Resurrection of Christ. It was the first object of Christian attention in 325 and it retains that primacy to this day.

That primacy can, however, have a negative corollary. The presence today of so many Christian denominations, each with its own segment within the building and each with its keenly defended rights, epitomises for many the disunity of the Church and (paradoxically, in the very place of mankind's redemption) the fallenness of man.[1] However, the tensions of disunity derive directly from the primacy which is ascribed to this church. Denominational representation there is felt to be vital precisely

---

[1] Others, however, find that this aspect only increases their attraction to the building. Simply because 'it is the most human church on earth . . . it is also the most divine': see Perowne (1976), 70.

because the church is so important. This precious location represents for all Christians an ideal, and it is notoriously in the quest for an imagined ideal that even those most close dispute most fiercely.

This aspect of the building's significance, its primacy and yet its potential for conflict, came to the fore from the moment its foundation-stone was laid. Eusebius and Cyril both acknowledged this primacy but they wished to express it differently: they had divergent ideals.

That they both acknowledged in some sense the primacy of this historic basilica is quite clear. Eusebius may have emphasized the importance of the Triad as a whole but the 'cave' of the Saviour's victory over death lay theologically and geographically in its centre;[2] indeed on one occasion he tentatively suggested that this church was the 'new Jerusalem' prophesied of old.[3] Meanwhile Cyril, who at other times might wish to emphasize the importance of Mt. Sion or of the city of Jerusalem in its own right, nevertheless stressed his belief that the rock of Golgotha within this basilica was the 'very centre of the world'.[4] Yet, as shall be seen, both men recognized and promoted that primacy in a host of quite different ways. Eusebius, for example, never refers to that vast rock of Golgotha at all and concentrated instead simply on the tomb. Cyril, by contrast, would never endorse Eusebius' use of the term 'new Jerusalem' and, while naturally giving to the tomb itself a great importance, concentrated again and again on Golgotha. Then again, with his greater theological emphasis on Christ's Cross and Death, Cyril understood the tomb not so much as a witness to the Resurrection (as it was for Eusebius) but simply as the place of Christ's burial. For Cyril the chief witness to the Resurrection was the survival of the 'stone' that had been 'rolled away'. Eusebius, however, would most probably have had doubts about the authenticity of such a 'stone'. The same would be true, yet more so, of the supposed 'wood of the cross'; this evidently meant so much to Cyril, but Eusebius, careful historian and concerned metropolitan that he was, would never refer to it at all. The focus of the building for him was not the Cross or Golgotha but the tomb of the Resurrection. Cyril, however, stressed the 'bifocal' nature of the basilica, at once the scene of both the Cross and the Resurrection.

[2] See *L. Const.*, 9.17 (quoted at the head of ch. 7).
[3] *V. Const.*, 3.33.
[4] *Catech.*, 13.28.

Thus, for example, unlike Eusebius, he emphasized the 'rock' ($\pi\acute{\epsilon}\tau\rho\alpha$) of the tomb; this established a neat link with the 'rock' of Golgotha and could be used by Cyril to draw together these two different focuses of the building. This emphasis on natural 'rock' visible within the basilica led him to observe an apparent fissure in that Golgotha rock, which he suggested was evidence of the 'rending of the rocks' mentioned in St Matthew's Passion narrative (27.51). Eusebius, however, had always interpreted this dramatic episode in a strictly spiritual sense.

Such in outline were some of their differences, some minor, some more important. From the outset, therefore, the building in its details could reflect divergent theological approaches. Cyril and Eusebius will be seen to have been quite at variance in their emphases, in their terminology, and in their use of certain scriptures. Above all, they disagreed over the central significance and message of the basilica; for Cyril the church spoke equally about Christ's Death and about his Resurrection, but for Eusebius the church spoke almost exclusively of the Resurrection. Interestingly in our own day a somewhat similar difference in emphasis can still be recognized: the Western Church, emphasizing Calvary and Christ's Death, refers to this building as 'the church of the Holy Sepulchre', whilst the Eastern Church speaks instead of the 'church of the Resurrection'. Thus, had they lived today, Cyril would evidently have been happy with the former name, but Eusebius would definitely have preferred the latter. (In the following, for the sake of simplicity, 'the church of the Holy Sepulchre' is always used: but it should be remembered throughout that this is a later term and almost certainly one of which Eusebius himself would not have especially approved.)

These differences between Eusebius and Cyril are, of course, all the more intriguing precisely because they were both so integrally involved with the very beginnings of this historic church. Unlike ourselves, they were not mere visitors, responding to a building constructed many years before. Both had the opportunity of speaking in this august location within the first fifteen years of its use. This was where Cyril taught his catechumens; this was where the bishops had listened to Eusebius' speech *On Christ's Sepulchre* during the dedication services in September 335.[5] Again, Eusebius

[5] Cf. above 4.3 on the significance of the *Sep. Chr.* being identified with the dedication speech in the Holy Sepulchre. This means that Cyril and Eusebius are here at their closest in time; the differences observed below are therefore all the more striking.

spoke about this church in more imperial contexts: in his speech *In Praise of Constantine* and especially in the *Life of Constantine*.[6] As a result, they were both in a position to establish and to dictate for others the theological meaning that this building should have for the future. Indeed, at this very early stage, their opinion could affect not only the building's theological meaning but even its very shape and architectural structure.

These two men, therefore, had the daunting responsibility of laying both the physical and the theological foundations for this focal building in Christendom. They were very active participants. Cyril, of course, would not have been involved in the very first planning, but as the representative of the Jerusalem Church he would naturally be defending that Church's earlier activity and attempting to continue its tradition. As a result these different approaches to the Holy Sepulchre were not simply different responses to a *fait accompli*. They might instead reflect their own past activity or their active hopes for the future. Moreover it is not impossible that the difference in these approaches would have been recognized at the time by those involved. Yet, even if this were not the case, it will still be instructive for us to be presented with what was indeed a very real contrast.

Much of our discussion will be centred around Eusebius' account of the Holy Sepulchre in the *Life of Constantine*, which may be summarized as follows.

The pious emperor addressed himself to another work truly worthy of record, in the province of Palestine. He judged it incumbent on him to render the blessed locality of our Saviour's Resurrection an object of attraction and veneration to all. He issued immediate instructions therefore for the erection in that spot of a house of prayer . . .

Certain 'impious men' had attempted to 'consign to oblivion that divine monument of immortality . . . from which the angel had rolled away the stone [λίθος] for those who still had stony hearts' and 'stony-hearted unbelief'. They had covered the entire spot with much earth 'brought from a distance' and with paved stone, erecting a 'gloomy shrine of lifeless idols to the impure spirit whom they call Venus' over the 'sacred cave'. Yet they could not conquer him who conquered death. Constantine, opposing this malice

6 *L. Const.*, 9.25–17; *V. Const.*, 3.25–40.

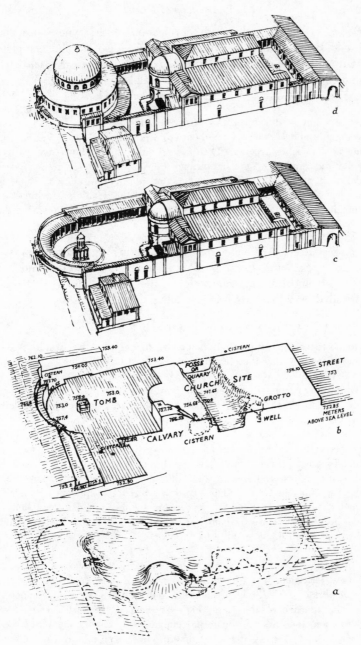

Fig. 5. The site of the Holy Sepulchre (after Conant)

(κακία), ordered a thorough purification of the whole site and the destruction of the temple, zealously ensuring the complete transference of its 'stone and timber' (τὴν ἐν λίθοις καὶ χύλοις ὕλην) and even of the polluted soil to a 'far place'.

Then, once down to bedrock, there appeared

immediately and contrary to all expectation (παρ' ἐλπίδα πᾶσαν) the venerable and hallowed monument (τὸ σεμνὸν καὶ πανάγιον μαρτύριον) of our Saviour's Resurrection. Then indeed did this most holy cave present a faithful similitude of his return to life, in that, after lying buried in darkness, it again emerged to light, and afforded to all who came to witness the sight, a clear and visible proof of the wonders of which that spot had once been the scene, a testimony to the Resurrection of the Saviour clearer than any voice could give.

Constantine then commanded the building of a house of prayer near the Saviour's tomb, sending instructions to the governors of the East and the following letter to the 'bishop who at that time presided over the church in Jerusalem':

'VICTOR CONSTANTIUS, MAXIMUS AUGUSTUS, to Macarius:

No power of language seems adequate to describe the wondrous circumstance, . . . that the monument of his most holy passion (τὸ γνώρισμα τοῦ ἁγιωτάτου ἐκείνου πάθους), so long buried beneath the ground, . . . should now reappear. . . . For this cause it is ever my first, and indeed my only object, that, as the authority of the truth is evincing itself daily by fresh wonders, so our souls may become more zealous . . . for the honour of the divine law. I desire, therefore, especially, that you should be persuaded of that which I suppose is evident to all beside, namely, that I have no greater care than how I may best adorn with a splendid structure that sacred spot, a spot which has been accounted holy from the beginning in God's judgement, but which now appears holier still, since it has brought to light a clear assurance of our Saviour's Passion. It will be well therefore for your sagacity to make such arrangements and provision of all things needful for the work . . .'

Accordingly, on the very spot which witnessed the Saviour's sufferings, a new Jerusalem was constructed, over against (ἀντιπρόσωπος) the one so celebrated of old, which, since the foul stain of guilt brought upon it by the murder of the Lord, had experienced the last extremity of desolation, the effect of divine judgement on its impious people. It was opposite this [ἄντικρυς] that the emperor now began to rear a monument to the Saviour's victory over death. And it may be that this was that second and new Jerusalem spoken of in the predictions of the prophets . . .

First of all then he adorned the sacred cave itself, as the chief part of the whole work, and the hallowed monument at which the angel radiant with light had once declared to all that regeneration which was manifested in the Saviour's person. This monument therefore, first of all, as the chief part of the whole, the emperor's magnificence beautified with rare columns . . .

The next object of his attention was a space of ground of great extent, and open to the pure air of heaven. . . . Then, at the side opposite the cave, which was the eastern side, the church itself was erected. . . . Besides this there were two porticos on each side . . . Their gates, placed exactly east, were intended to receive the multitudes who entered the church. Opposite these gates the crowning part of the whole was the *hemisphairion*, which rose to the very summit of the church. . . . In the next place he enclosed the atrium . . .

This temple, then, the emperor erected as a conspicuous monument of the Saviour's Resurrection and embellished it throughout on an imperial scale of magnificence.[7]

1. THE AUTHENTICITY OF THE TOMB AND THE PLAN OF THE BASILICA

A building of such importance has naturally attracted not only ancient pilgrims but also modern scholars. Our analysis of Eusebius and Cyril will therefore be of extra interest inasmuch as it can throw some light on the two major questions that such scholars have been asking throughout the last century: namely is the site authentic and what was the exact nature of the Constantinian buildings?

With regard to the former question, that of authenticity, Eusebius comes across as a man not easily given to simple credulity. Rather, with his historical mind, he is revealed as one for whom authenticity was a real issue; he seems to have had real doubts about the 'wood of the cross' and also of the 'stone' rolled away from the mouth of the tomb. The same cannot readily be said for Cyril. Thus, when Eusebius accepts the authenticity of the tomb, we would do well to accept this as the testimony of a reasonably reliable historian. There is, of course, no final way of proving that

---

[7] *V. Const.*, 3.25–40, based on the translation in NPNF, i, 526–30. For some criticisms of this translation and some analysis of Eusebius' meaning, see above 2.2 and 4.3(*b*).

this was truly the tomb of Christ and Eusebius certainly was far from infallible; yet his testimony cannot be sweepingly dismissed as the product of mere credulity. On the other hand, on those occasions when Eusebius was being influenced more by matters of theology or politics, his evidence becomes a little more suspect. He clearly had theological and political concerns that coloured his description of the basilica. Naturally this must be taken into consideration by those scholars more concerned with the second question, the problem of establishing the layout of the new basilica, because Eusebius' description in the *Life of Constantine* remains our principal source. As a historian Eusebius' evidence is 'clear and plausible', but his narrative could yet become 'clouded by the interjection of theological interpretation'.[8]

The following discussion may thus enable us the better to evaluate Eusebius as a source. Comparison with Cyril will indeed reveal Eusebius' essential reliability as a historian, but also his distinctive emphases and qualms, which would colour all his descriptions of this basilica. Before noting these it will be best to concentrate first on the former, more historical question, that of the site's authenticity.

Not surprisingly the debate over the authenticity of such an important place has often been quite heated. Nevertheless, the general authenticity of the site (if not of the precise tomb) now seems to be increasingly accepted. This has been disputed for several reasons,[9] including the great silence of Christians on the subject before 325. Yet their silence on such an important matter, especially when they could so easily visit the 'caves' at Bethlehem and the Mount of Olives, would surely seem to suggest not a lack of interest but a known inaccessibility. Moreover, the one exception

[8] Drake (1985), 5.

[9] Not least because of the uncertain line of Jerusalem's 'second wall'; for a summary of arguments on this and bibliography, see Hamrick (1977), 18–23. Harvey (1966), 403, argues that the presence of the nearby *kokim* tombs indicates that this area was indeed outside the walls in Jesus' day. He also adduces the interesting evidence of Melito who visited Palestine in the second century (Eus. *Hist. Eccl.*, 4.26.13–14) and who spoke of the crucifixion having occurred 'in the *middle* of Jerusalem' (*Paschal Homily*, 71); this could well reflect his awareness that the course of the city walls had been changed. Cyril too (14.9) seems to have been quite aware of the movements of the wall since the first century: see Drake (1985), 4, and Coüasnon (1974), 11, *contra* Parrot (1957), 56–7. Nevertheless, the case for the 'Garden Tomb' remains intriguing: see Mcbirnie (1975).

to this otherwise pervasive silence, Eusebius' entry for Golgotha
in the *Onomasticon* (written in the 290s), makes it quite clear that
Christians at that time preserved a tradition of the general locality:
'Golgotha: the 'place of the skull', where Christ was crucified. This
is pointed out in Aelia to the north of Mt. Sion.'[10] Thus in all
probability Christians knew only too well that both Calvary and
the tomb of Christ were covered by the area of the temple of
Venus and the forum. Indeed only the existence of a strong tradition
could possibly have caused them to opt for this inconvenient and
unlikely site, buried under the forum and in the middle of the city.
'The Jerusalem tradition had established a site so difficult to admit,
that it must have taken all the weight of an extremely strongly
rooted tradition to make such an improbablity acceptable.'[11]
The authenticity of the general site seems therefore reasonably
assured.[12]

However, the same assurance is not necessarily justified concerning the actual tomb itself. The drama and excitement experienced when the excavations brought to light 'contrary to all
expectation'[13] a tomb not demolished by Hadrian's workmen would
so easily have prompted a swift and assured assumption that this
was the tomb of Christ, which may or may not have been correct.

There was, we may presume, a natural pressure on Christians
to find results and to justify their request to demolish the pagan
temple; this was a quite risky request to make of Constantine.[14]
Eusebius' words may therefore reflect not only excitement but also
a sense of great relief: Christians had something tangible to show
in defence of their haughty action. Given this pressure on Christians
to justify themselves, and the rarity of such archaeological excavations in the ancient world, it was only natural that the discovery

[10] *Onom.*, 74.19–21. The vagueness of this reference is exactly what we would
expect if such an important site was so painfully buried under a pagan temple;
since Eusebius was wont to taunt the Jews on their exclusion from Jerusalem, he
would naturally not draw attention to his own Christian exclusion from Golgotha.

[11] Coüasnon (1974), 11; cf. Parrot, (1957), 54.

[12] It is accepted by Jeremias (1926), 7–22, Conant (1956), 15, Parrot (1957), 49
ff, Coüasnon (1974), 8–11, Wilkinson (1977), 174, Hunt (1982), 2–3, and Drake
(1985), 4; it is not accepted by Rubin (1982a), 101 and fn. 21, nor naturally by
Mcbirnie (1975).

[13] *V. Const.*, 3.28.

[14] Drake (1984). Telfer (1955b), 698, suggests Christians may have made an
earlier unsuccessful appeal for the site's clearance to Constantine's predecessor,
Licinius.

was immediately was accepted without hesitation as the tomb of Christ. Nevertheless, it was far from an unreasonable assumption and Eusebius seems to have endorsed it fully and confidently. There is no suggestion in his writings of any doubt whatsoever that this was truly the tomb of Christ.

This conviction of the tomb's authenticity may well have been strengthened, consciously or unconsciously, by his assumption that Hadrian, building this temple over the site of Christ's tomb, had been deliberately acting to spite Christians.[15] In fact, Hadrian's selection of that site may have been for quite other reasons;[16] yet Christians, perhaps from the very beginning, naturally interpreted his building programme as an act of conscious malice. As a result Eusebius would be able to assume that the tomb of Christ had been well known in second-century Jerusalem.[17] Thus the temple of Venus, although in itself an evil phenomenon, only served to preserve the historical site, thereby increasing the likelihood of the tomb's authenticity.[18]

However, the same historian, contemplating the very same facts, might come to quite the opposite conclusion concerning any supposed 'wood of the cross'. After the dramatic discovery of the tomb local Christians might naturally desire yet further 'miracles';

[15] This assumption of malice is seen clearly in V. Const., 3.26-7, though Eusebius tactfully avoids naming Constantine's prestigious forbear, Hadrian; the perpetrators were instead some anonymous 'impious men' (δυσσεβεῖς τινες).

[16] As suggested by Coüasnon (1974), 11-12, and Wilkinson (1978), 178. In Hadrian's new city the Roman Legion was placed on the highest hill; the next highest hill, which unfortunately happened to be the area of Golgotha, was chosen for the civic centre (the forum and the temple).

[17] Naturally Christians ever since Eusebius (and influenced by his account) have seen Hadrian's action in similar terms, thereby confirming for them the existence of an active Christian tradition back in the second century (see e.g., Parrot (1957), 52). On the other hand those seeking to discredit the Holy Sepulchre might tend to see Hadrian's activity as accidental. However, it is more than possible to avoid these extremes, affirming the authenticity of the general locality but not necessarily attributing to Hadrian a conscious malice.

[18] It was this very paradox, whereby conscious evil worked to Christian advantage, which then inspired Eusebius' theological presentation of the events of both 135 and 325 in V. Const., 3.26 ff. If the site had previously revealed the temporary triumph of evil and the apparent weakness of the Christian God, that had now been reversed; the Christian God in the era of Constantine now revealed his power, his foresight and his capacity to turn even evil into good. Thus the fourth-century recovery of the tomb could indeed be a 'similitude' (εἰκών) of Jesus' Resurrection in the first century (see idem, 3.28); for the Resurrection had similarly been a divine act, temporarily delayed, which then revealed God's victory and his ability to bring the greatest good out of the greatest evil.

the excitement would be infectious, giving them eyes to see yet further corroborations of God's hand upon them. For Eusebius, however, one 'miracle' may have been quite sufficient.[19] Providentially, the building of Hadrian's temple had preserved the tomb still intact, but little else from the time of Christ, he might argue, could reasonably be expected to have survived. Indeed the 'stone and timber'[20] used by Hadrian's builders, both in their construction of the temple and in creating a necessary fill for its foundation, would make it quite impossible to identify with any certainty the 'wood of the cross' (or even the 'stone' that had lain at the mouth of the tomb).[21] Moreover, was there any good reason for supposing that the cross would have been left on that site after the crucifixion?

Such apparently modern scepticism could well have lurked in Eusebius' mind. The same Hadrianic temple which confirmed the probable authenticity of the tomb surely militated against the authenticity of any other relics. Eusebius' doubts about the 'true cross' would then only have been strengthened by those other factors,[22] which gave him a prior disinclination to accept any such 'true cross'. It appears that Eusebius would have been tempted to disapprove of such a piece of wood in his several capacities, as a historian, as a theologian, and as the metropolitan bishop of Palestine.

For Cyril and the Jerusalem Church, however, all their prior assumptions would lead them in the opposite direction: nothing could be more attractive than the *lignum crucis*. A conscious fraud and known fabrication is not to be supposed. Nevertheless, it can only be said that Christians in Jerusalem did have every incentive for accepting, though sincerely, an over-hasty identification. 'The excited mood of the fourth-century excavators virtually guaranteed that any suitable beams unearthed by them would be identified with the true cross'.[23] They would also have good reason for trying to overlook the violent vicissitudes that the area had undergone since the time of Christ; for these might raise questions

[19] 'His refusal to accept the popular stories of miracles is quite notable': Foakes-Jackson (1933), 140.
[20] *V. Const.*, 3.27.
[21] This need for more precise identification became the fuel of many subsequent legends; these are discussed in e.g., Rubin (1982a), 87.
[22] Cf. above 4.5.
[23] Drake (1985), 21.

about the possible authenticity of the 'true cross' which they did not especially wish to hear. Cyril would thus never mention the Hadrianic temple. Nor in his lectures would he highlight the dramatic recent discovery of the 'true cross', since this too might raise questions of authenticity.[24] Instead it had already been distributed 'to the ends of the earth'.[25] Its universal popularity quenched any voices of doubt.

The reason for this silence both about the Hadrianic temple and about the moment of the wood's discovery, was that Cyril wished instead to emphasize the continuity that linked this contemporary phenomenon directly with the very days of Christ. This emphasis on continuity, manifested especially in his frequent use of the phrase, 'to this day' ($\mu\acute{\epsilon}\chi\rho\iota$ $\sigma\acute{\eta}\mu\epsilon\rho o\nu$),[26] appears throughout Cyril's work and reflects his careful response to the need of the faithful for a sense of unbroken and unmediated contact with Christ; yet it was also a means of bypassing certain historical questions of authenticity and true identification. In contrast to Eusebius, who as a historian applied himself to what had happened in the intervening three hundred years, Cyril as a pastor preferred, where possible, to ignore it. If for Eusebius the intervening history confirmed the authenticity of the tomb, it equally raised for him questions over the authenticity of other items such as the 'true cross'. Cyril, however, could conveniently ignore that intervening history, thus permitting straightforward and precise identifications that met the pilgrim's need. The pilgrim needed to live at the end of a reliable continuum; the historian unhappily needed to acknowledge the vicissitudes in between.

Eusebius thus emerges as a person for whom historical exactitude was important wherever possible. His assumptions and his testimony may not always have been correct, but if ever he was in error we can be sure that credulity was not the cause. Cyril, by contrast, emerges as a man less interested in history, more in meaning. With the increasing demands of pilgrims and the rising hopes of the Jerusalem Church, he was also in a situation that very much encouraged the confident identification of Gospel places

---

[24] He naturally mentions its discovery under Constantine when writing to Constantine's son (*Ep. Const.*, 3), but with little of the colour and drama so characteristic of later stories.

[25] For references, see below fn. 76 ff.

[26] *Catech.*, 10.19, 13.39, and 14.22.

and relics when such confidence might strictly be unfounded. It therefore seems fair to suggest that in their quest for establishing authenticity today modern scholars should be disposed to accept the testimony of Eusebius far more than that of Cyril. With regard to the church of the Holy Sepulchre they should note how Eusebius would share their doubts concerning the 'wood of the cross' and thus be encouraged to accept his contrasting confidence in the authenticity of the tomb.

Other modern scholars, however, have been concerned to establish the exact nature and plan of the Constantinian basilica. They therefore need to know how to evaluate Eusebius' unique description of the building in the *Life of Constantine*.[27] Our detailed comparison of Eusebius and Cyril in their references to Golgotha and the tomb will reveal how both bishops were influenced by their different situations and their different theologies. The result, among other things, is that modern scholars would do well to be quite careful in their acceptance of Eusebius' description. His attitude towards the tomb may indeed deserve our respect, but his approach to the buildings may demand caution, because, strangely, the same man who was genuinely concerned with historical truth was evidently prepared on occasions to portray that truth in potentially distorting ways.

This ambivalent evaluation of Eusebius has been forced upon us, in the first instance, by the discoveries of recent archaeological excavations under the present church of the Holy Sepulchre. These reveal that Eusebius' account is over-simplified and indeed slightly distorted. In that account Eusebius makes the tomb the sole and central focus of the building and, as we shall discover, never mentions Golgotha. Thus earlier scholars (such as Vincent and Abel), solely dependent as they were on Eusebius' words, reconstructed a plan of the basilica which was similarly neat and symmetrical, focused directly on the tomb.[28] Now, however, recent archaeology has established a far more complex picture.[29] Contrary

---

[27] *V. Const.*, 3.34–40.

[28] See fig. 6, the work of Vincent and Abel: *JN*, 154–206. This is followed by e.g., Conant (1956), 19, Ward-Perkins (1954), 83; cf. similarly Telfer (1955a), 44.

[29] See fig. 7, from Coüasnon (1974). The most comprehensive recent analysis, which endorses Coüasnon's argument is in Corbo (1981); Wilkinson (1977), 174–8 provides a useful summary, as does Ovadiah in (rev. edn. 1982), 134–8.

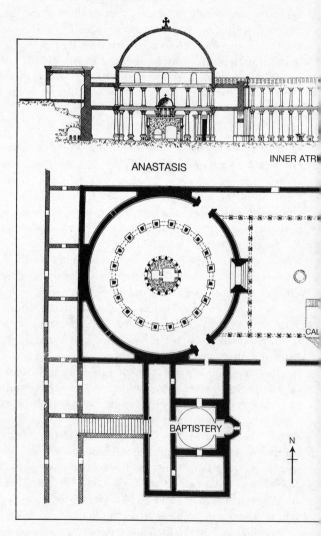

Fig. 6. Plan of the church of the Holy Sepulchre (after Vincent and Abe

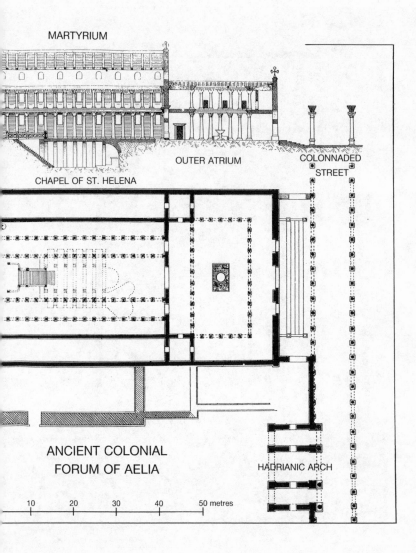

MARTYRIUM

OUTER ATRIUM

COLONNADED STREET

CHAPEL OF ST. HELENA

ANCIENT COLONIAL
FORUM OF AELIA

HADRIANIC ARCH

10   20   30   40   50 metres

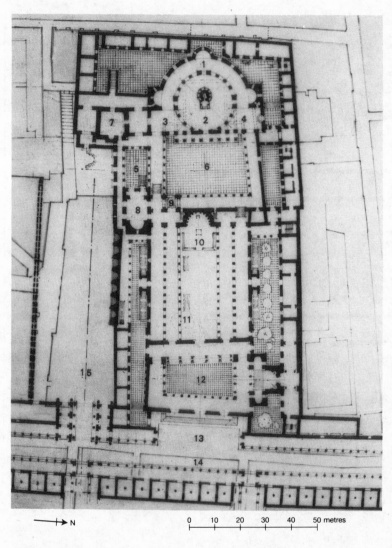

Fig. 7. Plan of the church of the Holy Sepulchre (after Coüasnon).

to the impression received from Eusebius' account,[30] the building did not focus quite so thoroughly upon the tomb. Instead the main basilica to the east of the tomb (known in time as the *Martyrium*) had a focus of its own in an apse (known as the *hemisphairion*); moreover, the basilica's location and shape seems to have been largely determined by the immense and awkward rock of Golgotha which caused the whole building to be 'completely offset to the south'.[31] Eusebius described this *hemisphairion*[32] but in so unclear a way that hardly distinguished it from the tomb;[33] meanwhile the massive rock of Golgotha he would somehow succeed in ignoring altogether.

Moreover, the archaeological evidence confirms that the rotunda which was constructed over the tomb was not part of the original structure; for there are archaeological remains that suggest that the tomb was originally surrounded by a courtyard open to the sky and that the rotunda was an afterthought.[34] However, even if its delayed construction was merely the result of the inevitable time-delay in building such a phenomenon,[35] at the time when Eusebius delivered his speech *On Christ's Sepulchre* in 335 and when he described the building in the *Life of Constantine* this rotunda was certainly not complete. This is important because once again such archaeological evidence seems to conflict with Eusebius' literary evidence. Eusebius, emphasizing the tomb, gives little purpose to the *Martyrium* basilica in its own right; it is something of an appendage. Yet this delayed building of the rotunda now suggests that the *Martyrium* was very much a self-contained unit; *this* was the structure that was completed and ready for dedication in 335.[36] Eusebius' description has therefore

[30] And indeed contrary to the impression received by visitors ever since as a result of the artful bias of successive structures which have all given the impression that the buildings focused directly on the tomb.

[31] Coüasnon (1974), 41; followed by Drake (1985), 7.

[32] *V. Const.*, 3.38.

[33] As argued by Rubin (1982a), 80 and Drake (1985), 9–10; cf. Crowfoot (1941), 16, Wistrand (1952), 13–14 and Telfer (1955a), 50–51. Davies (1957), 53 believes that this *hemisphairion* 'enshrined the very place of the 'invention' of the cross', a suggestion that would amply explain Eusebius' reticence on the subject.

[34] See esp. Wistrand (1952); then followed by Conant (1956), 47, who suggests that Constantine gave the orders for the rotunda just before his death; see also Wilkinson (1981), 40 ff., Hunt (1982), 11, and Rubin (1982a), 81.

[35] As suggested by Coüasnon (1974), 15.

[36] This point is made by Rubin (1982a), 86.

proved quite misleading. Previously his account had of necessity been unchallenged. Now, however, the archaeological evidence has at last given scholars the grounds upon which to question it.

However, such questioning has recently been continued by scholars with interests other than archaeology: Drake, in his investigation of Eusebius' relationship with Constantine, and Rubin, in his enquiries into the local Palestinian tension between Caesarea and Jerusalem, have both begun to notice major oddities in Eusebius' whole account. Eusebius clearly held convictions, they argue, that were shared by neither Constantine nor the Jerusalem Church.[37] The following comparison of Eusebius and Cyril will endorse and develop their conclusions, revealing some of the ecclesiastical and imperial factors that coloured Eusebius' attitude to the Holy Sepulchre. Yet the oddities in Eusebius' account need also to be explained theologically; for his noted omission of any reference to Golgotha (perhaps the most stiking oddity of all) was based on a prior *theological* commitment to the Resurrection.

2. GOLGOTHA

The pagan temple of Venus was eagerly demolished. Then began the anxious task of clearing away its deep foundations and excavating further in the hope of discovering the tomb of Christ. Eusebius describes movingly that moment when the tomb came to light. Yet, contrary to the impression received from Eusebius, this was not the only important discovery. When the task of digging was complete, the excavators were presented with the sight of a knoll of natural rock standing a full five metres above the level of the adjacent bed-rock;[38] well could Cyril describe this solitary outcrop of rock as 'conspicuous in its elevation' and 'rising on high' ($\dot{\upsilon}\pi\epsilon\rho\alpha\nu\epsilon\sigma\tau\eta\kappa\dot{\omega}s$ and $\dot{\upsilon}\pi\epsilon\rho\alpha\nu\epsilon\sigma\tau\dot{\omega}s$).[39] Most probably in the centuries before Christ this whole area had been quarried for stone; this section of the rock, however, was flawed and thus had been left

---

[37] In the two important articles already cited: Rubin (1982a) and Drake (1985). To both of these scholars I am immensely grateful for their kind reading of this chapter in its draft stages. Unfortunately the important work of Kretschmar (1988), in which he advances further reasons for Eusebius' silence concerning Golgotha, came to my attention too late for examination here.

[38] As shown in Corbo (1981), table 3.

[39] *Catech.*, 10.19, and 13.39.

untouched.[40] It was not therefore unreasonable for Christians in the fourth century, on discovering this unexpected phenomenon, to identify this with Golgotha. It may have been hard for them to imagine what exactly this outcrop of rock would have looked like in Jesus' day and to know where exactly Jesus would have been crucified in relation to it, but nevertheless they might well conclude that it was the 'place of the skull', the place where Jesus and many others had been crucified in those distant days.

It was an exciting discovery, but also a rather awkward one which would make the plan of the whole site a little more complex. What were the Constantinian architects to do with it? Modern archaeology has confirmed that they must have decided to 'cut away the superfluous rocks that formed its slopes', thus making its appearance even more abrupt and impressive.[41] They also included it within the open courtyard which lay in front of the tomb, thus enabling visitors to see from a distance both Golgotha and the tomb at the same time.[42] Evidently the 'obvious architectural purpose' of all this was simply to 'emphasize this second essential feature of the site'.[43]

It would be hard for any visitor not to notice this rock of Golgotha, and hard for anyone describing the new buildings around the Holy Sepulchre to overlook it in an account. Yet this is precisely what Eusebius does! In his lengthy description of the building complex in the *Life of Constantine*[44] and in his other references to the site[45] he somehow succeeded in never mentioning this rock and in never using the word 'Golgotha' of this rock (or of the basilica as a whole). How could Eusebius possibly have missed such an important and singular phenomenon?[46] What was the cause of this 'glaring *lacuna*' in Eusebius' account?[47]

[40] As suggested in Conant (1956), 14.

[41] E. T. Richmond in his introduction to Harvey (1935a), p. vi; followed by Crowfoot (1941), 19; unlike Conant (1956), 21-2.

[42] It remains uncertain, however, how exactly Golgotha related to the *Martyrium* basilica: see Wilkinson (1981), 43; cf. also Rubin (1982a), fn. 43.

[43] Richmond: Harvey (1935a), p. vi.

[44] *V. Const.*, 3.25-40.

[45] *L. Const.*, 9.16, *Sep. Chr.*, 11-18, and *Comm in Ps.* [87.7], 1064a.

[46] Jeremias (1926), 159, fn. 4 noted Eusebius' silence but implausibly suggested that Golgotha must have formed a later part of the building. No explanation is offered in Wilkinson (1979), 351. Crowfoot (1941), 17, believes Eusebius was simply not interested, whilst Conant (1956), 5, suggests that Golgotha was 'still rather plain'.

[47] Yarnold (1983), 108.

On no issue could the differences of Eusebius and Cyril be more apparent. For Cyril referred in his lectures to this rock of Golgotha on no less than ten separate occasions.[48] Obviously this is partially to be explained by the fact that Cyril delivered some, if not all, of his lectures actually within sight of this rock.[49] Nevertheless, his frequent references to Golgotha also reflect his whole theological approach to the the church of the Holy Sepulchre. For even if this rock was not physically in the centre of the building complex, there was a sense in which 'Golgotha' had an unquestioned theological centrality in his understanding. This is seen, for example, in the way his lecture on the Resurrection does not refer to the tomb nearly as frequently as his preceding lecture on the crucifixion does to Golgotha.[50] More importantly, he was happy to use the term 'Golgotha' not simply as a name for this outcrop of rock[51] but also as a fitting name for the whole building complex.[52] In other words, Cyril was more than happy for the dark shadows of the Cross to colour his whole approach to the building.

Yet there was also a sense in which he wished the shadow of the cross to cover not just this building but the whole world. For Cyril understood LXX Ps. 73.12 [74.12]—'you work salvation in the midst of the earth'—to be a reference specifically to Golgotha, the place where (even more than the tomb of the Resurrection) God had supremely 'worked salvation'. The result was that this rock of Golgotha, which Eusebius had never mentioned, was for Cyril 'the very centre of the world'.[53]

A comparison of their differing interpretations of this verse from the Psalms reveals how far apart Eusebius and Cyril were in their thinking. Interestingly, Origen had applied this particular verse primarily to Jesus' burial in the 'heart of the earth', an understanding which, had it been followed by Eusebius, would have focused attention on Christ's tomb.[54] Eusebius however interpreted

---

[48] *Catech.*, 1.1, 4.14, 5.10, 10.19, 13.4, 13.26, 13.22, 13.23, 13.28, and 13.32.

[49] Hence the consistent reference to '*this* Golgotha' in the above references.

[50] *Catech.*, 14; cf. *idem*, 13.

[51] Ibid., 13.23; cf. 10.19 and 13.39.

[52] Ibid., 16.4; it remains unclear whether he is talking here about the *Martyrium* alone or the *Martyrium* and the *Anastasis*.

[53] Ibid., 13.28.

[54] *Comm. in Ps.* [73.12], PG, xii, 1532b. The commentary reproduced in Pitra, iii (1883), 99 is taken as inauthentic (see BibPat, iii, 27, 174). For other passing references to this verse, see Cypr., *Testimonia ad Quirinium*, 2.29 (CCSL, iii, 70) and pseudo-Irenaeus, *Fragmanta varia* (TU, 36.3 (1913), 189.279).

the verse quite differently. The psalmist had been prophesying the eventual abandonment of the place restrictions of Old Testament religion: no longer would salvation be known only 'in one corner' (ἐν μίᾳ γωνίᾳ) but rather in the 'midst of the earth', throughout the whole 'inhabited world' (οἰκουμένη).[55] Moreover, the moment when this dramatic universalization would occur was not the crucifixion but rather when God raised 'Christ the Saviour for all'.[56] If, as is probable, Eusebius wrote this commentary after 325,[57] his emphasis both on the Resurrection and on the universal nature of Christianity are all the more striking. For, as was seen in our study of his speech *On Christ's Sepulchre* these would be the very same two categories on which he would base his theological understanding of the new church of the Holy Sepulchre. Cyril, however, speaking in that building fifteen years later, reversed the whole process: he emphasized the Cross, not the Resurrection, and would focus on one particular place, the rock of Golgotha.

Thus, despite its obvious importance within the Gospels, Eusebius, like Origen,[58] rarely, if ever, referred explicitly to 'Golgotha'. Indeed, apart from one place in the commentary on the Psalms (when he quoted the Gospel's phrase, 'they led him to a place called Golgotha' without comment),[59] Eusebius seems only really to have focused on Golgotha as a location on one occasion, namely his entry for Golgotha in the *Onomasticon*.[60] No doubt in the years before 325 this silence concerning Golgotha was partially caused

---

[55] *Comm. in Ps.* [73.12], 862b.

[56] Ibid.

[57] As suggested by the reference to the Holy Sepulchre in ibid. [87.7], 1064a.

[58] In his six references to Matt. 27.53, for example, Origen only mentions Golgotha twice: see *Comm. in Matt.* [27.53], CS 126, 264, and idem, Fr. 551, 255-6.

The suggestion in the latter that the 'place of the skull' was so called because of Adam's burial there may well betray its inauthenticity (as suggested in BibPat, iii, 22, 279). For it is more probable that this Adam legend, popular later with both Epiphanius (*Haer.*, 4.6.5) and Jerome (*Ep.*, 46.3), originated later (in the mid-fourth century?); Cyril makes no such suggestion, either in *Catech.*, 13.23 or in his references to Adam (*idem*, 13.2, 13.9, 13.32), nor does Eusebius (in *Onom.*, 74.19-21). Constantine's description of the site as 'holy from the beginning' (Eus., *V. Const.*, 3.30) would then refer, not to such a legend, but to God's eternal will in purposing the crucifixion. For other primary sources which later associate Adam with Golgotha, see Baldi (1955), 784; for some discussion, see Wistrand (1952), 32 ff., Wilkinson (1977), 177, and Vilnay (1973), 212-13.

[59] *Comm. in Ps.* [54.7-12], 480c-d.

[60] *Onom.*, 74. 19-21. This is despite several references to the crucifixion in, e.g., *Dem. Ev.*, 10, *Pasch.*, and *QMS*.

by a practical consideration, the obliteration of the site by the temple of Venus. Yet that reason was removed after 325. Why did his silence continue?

The principal answer seems to lie in the area of theology. The Cross of Christ simply was not a vital part of his theology. Naturally it was not unimportant but his theology, as we have noted, tended to focus instead on 'theophany' and then, if necessary, on the Resurrection; the result was that he indeed 'robbed Bethlehem and Calvary of their significance'.[61] Moreover, the crucifixion was not in Eusebius' understanding efficacious for salvation; he could never have described it, as did Cyril, as the precise moment when salvation was 'worked'.[62] Rather it was but a necessary prerequisite for the revelation of the Resurrection; just as a scorchproof material has to be tested in the fire, so too Jesus' body had to be temporarily abandoned to death in order to prove its immortality.[63]

Eusebius' thinking, therefore, clearly focused more on revelation than on soteriology. Theologically this meant that the Cross tended to lose its distinctive role. More practically, however, it meant that Eusebius would never give to the rock of Golgotha a central place in his understanding of the Holy Sepulchre. As a result, he concentrated on the tomb and failed to refer to Golgotha in any of his references to the church. Theology clearly coloured place.

Theology similarly affected Cyril, though in the opposite direction. For his frequent references to Golgotha flowed out naturally from his prior theological commitment to the Cross. The Cross seems to have been the apex of his system.[64] The Resurrection and the Incarnation were not to be denied,[65] but once confessed they formed but the necessary context for this, the moment of salvation. Thus Cyril clearly 'placed more emphasis on Christ's Death than on his Resurrection'.[66] For the Cross, he claimed, was the foundation of faith,[67] the ground of salvation,[68] the end of sin,[69] a

[61] Williams (1951a), 17; see our fuller discussion of Eusebius' theology and his attitudes to the crucifixion above in 3.2(c) and 4.5.
[62] *Catech.*, 13.28.
[63] *Sep. Chr.*, 15.6–9; see Drake (1976), 118.
[64] As seen clearly in *Catech.*, 13 (on the Cross).
[65] See ibid., 13.4 and 4.9 respectively.
[66] Yarnold (1983), fn. 29, on the basis of *Catech.*, 13 and 14.
[67] *Catech.*, 13.38.
[68] Ibid., 13.37; cf. 13.2–4.
[69] Ibid., 13.19.

source of illumination and redemption[70] and of life,[71] the 'crown' of Christ,[72] the glory of the Catholic Church[73] and the sign of Christ's Second Coming in the future.[74]

Two conflicting theologies thus met in the same building. In their differences towards Golgotha (and indeed, as shall be seen, to the whole of the Holy Sepulchre) Eusebius and Cyril were revealing first and foremost a difference in theology. Cyril's soteriological interest and his emphasis on the Cross took him and his hearers irresistibly to Golgotha, the place where God had acted in history to save mankind. Eusebius' revelatory interest led him, if anywhere, to the empty tomb, where he could emphasize the spiritual nature of the *Logos* and the desire of the *Logos* now to reveal himself to people throughout the world. Cyril's devotion to the Death of Christ would then, as shall be seen, lead him to see even the tomb in part as also the place of burial; for Eusebius it would be the place of the Resurrection and the scene of the revelation of immortality. This omission of any reference in Eusebius to Golgotha, 'though surprising', is therefore indeed quite 'consistent with Eusebius' theology'.[75] The drama of Christ's Death did not occupy a central place in his theology. As a result Golgotha could never have any centrality in Eusebius' understanding of the Holy Sepulchre. For Cyril, by contrast, the Cross was at the centre

[70] Ibid., 13.1.

[71] Ibid., 13.20: 'life ever comes from wood'. This was a bald statement showing how the 'wood of the cross' influenced Cyril's thinking. In the light of its discovery Cyril naturally had an extra incentive for referring to Christ's crucifixion on the 'wood' (ξύλον), a usage in keeping with 1 Pet. 2.24: see, e.g., 17.10. Eusebius by contrast hardly used ξύλον at all: for a rare example, see *Comm. in Is.* [56.3], 349.1. It was also to Cyril's advantage to develop typological parallels to this 'wood' from the Old Testament. For example, Jer. 11.19, used by Cyril in 13.19, had from the time of Justin Martyr (*DT*, 72.2) been a text commonly used in this way; thus see Eusebius himself in the early *Proph. Eclg.*, 3.33. Cyril's use in *Hom. para.*, 11, of some obscure references to 'wood' in Cant., 3.9–10, however, was probably his own invention. Then again Cyril would also enjoy developing a parallel between the tree in the Garden of Eden and this 'wood of the cross': see *Catech.*, 13.19. For a partial list of patristic references to the cross in the Old Testament, see Armstrong (1979).

[72] *Catech.*, 13.22.

[73] Ibid., 13.1.

[74] Ibid., 15.22. After such words it was hardly surprising that, when people saw the cross-shaped *parhelion* in the Jerusalem sky just three years later, they ran to Golgotha believing in Christ's imminent return (*Ep. Const.*, 4).

[75] Yarnold (1983), 108.

of his theology and Golgotha was at the 'centre' of the Holy Sepulchre.

However, theology and contemporary history are ever hard to disentangle. These opposing theologies were indeed inherent within the two men. Cyril's cross-centred theology was an essential part of his character, just as Eusebius' theophany-model was an essential part of his. But these inherent differences could well have been exacerbated by recent events. Did these opposing attitudes towards Golgotha reflect some earlier practical disagreement between the bishops of Caesarea and Jerusalem? For this marked divergence in their descriptions might indeed suggest that the Jerusalem Church and its bishop, Macarius, from the outset had emphasized the rock of Golgotha, while Eusebius had been working instead for primacy to be given to the tomb. If so, the subsequent wording both of Eusebius and Cyril may be not just an expression of theological disagreement, but an endorsement of an earlier, more practical differrence of opinion between the two sees.

The practical issue over which Caesarea and Jerusalem disagreed, however, may have been something yet more pointed than this mere matter of emphasis. For it has been suggested above that very soon after 325 some wood found in those excavations had been identified as none other than the 'true cross'. If so, Eusebius and Cyril in their attitudes to Golgotha could well have been influenced by their attitude to this relic. Cyril's positive attitude to Golgotha and his theological emphasis on the Cross would then have been integrally connected with his warm approval of the *lignum crucis*. The reverse would have been true for Eusebius. Admittedly his less cross-centred theology was already established before 325, but his failure to refer to Golgotha after that date could well have been caused in part by his disapproval of this relic.

The reasons for his disapproval have already been surmised. As a historian he might first have questioned its authenticity and have feared the development of a misplaced devotion. However, as metropolitan bishop, he might then have been suspicious of the intentions of the Jerusalem Church: were they strictly honourable? If this wood could be a potent force within the life of faith, it could also no doubt be a powerful force within the world of ecclesiastical politics.

By contrast, Cyril inevitably saw the *lignum crucis* as a prime witness to Christ,[76] with a capacity even of rebuking and convicting those without faith.[77] But one senses that Cyril was also well aware of this relic's ecclesiastical usefulness. For if Golgotha and therefore Jerusalem were now, as Cyril claimed, the very 'centre of the world',[78] there could be no more effective way of communicating the message of that centrality to the waiting world than through the speedy distribution of portions of this powerful relic. The *lignum crucis* could convey not just a proximity to Christ's person but also a message about Jerusalem's importance. Not surprisingly, therefore, when Cyril spoke of this relic, he consistently emphasized how it had already 'filled almost the whole world'.[79] This rapid and widespread distribution was no doubt a sincere act of sharing generosity but it simultaneously conveyed a telling message: Jerusalem was back on the 'Christian map', indeed at its very centre. Such implications for the future status of the see of Jerusalem would not have passed unnoticed by Eusebius in Caesarea.

Eusebius' theological prejudices would thus only have been confirmed by the uneasy reality of contemporary circumstances. It would hardly be a matter for surprise if Eusebius, who in any case was less inclined theologically to emphasize the Cross, now as a result of this ecclesiastical use of the *lignum crucis* avoided any reference to Golgotha altogether. Thus both in his practical description of the church of the Holy Sepulchre (in the *Life of Constantine*) and in his more theological presentation (in his speech *On Christ's Sepulchre*), he omitted any reference either to Golgotha or to the Cross. This latter speech was a reworking of the first three books of the *Theophany*; the few references to the Cross in those books were now all carefully excised.[80]

---

[76] *Catech.*, 10.19 and 13.39.

[77] Ibid., 13.34 and 13.39. The great popularity of this relic (which brought the faithful into almost direct contact with the body of Jesus in his moment of agony) and its veneration in Passion week are described by Egeria: someone, she explains, even bit off a piece of it! (*Egeria*, 37.2).

[78] *Catech.*, 13.28.

[79] Ibid., 4.10, 10.19, 13.4, 13.39, and *Ep. Const.* 3. The close link between the cross and Golgotha in these references may indeed imply that for Cyril and other pilgrims it was the *lignum crucis* that endorsed the authentic identification of Golgotha and even of the tomb, and not the other way round; this relic proved to them that these were truly the places of Christ (see Rubin, (1982a), 82). For Eusebius, however, as for ourselves, it was really the tomb and Golgotha that had the stronger claim to authenticity.

[80] As argued above in 4.5.

Metropolitan Eusebius thus stood to lose quite personally from the way the *lignum crucis* was being used by the Jerusalem Church. Yet it is probable that he will also have had some more objective reasons for emphasizing the Resurrection and the tomb at the expense of Golgotha and the Cross. Given his theology and spirituality he may well have been attempting to wean both Constantine and the world at large away from a theology centred on Golgotha and from a spirituality and piety based on the relic of the cross. Sadly, however, both the emperor[81] and the world were not to be dissuaded. Eusebius was privileged to be closely involved both with the emperor and with the Holy Sepulchre, but that proximity did not necessarily ensure the endorsement of his ideas.

Recently it has been correctly observed that Eusebius was 'far from being the originator of the plan of the buildings' over the Holy Sepulchre,[82] because the prominence of Golgotha within the scheme was clearly not according to Eusebius' own preference, nor of course was the discovery of the *lignum crucis*. Now, however, it can be further observed that he was also far from able to dictate at a later stage the 'correct' meaning and significance of this building to the wider Church. He may have tried in his writings to concentrate exclusively on the tomb and to avoid any reference to Golgotha or the Cross, but Cyril, in touch with the need of contemporary Christians for a God of dramatic salvation and for a faith that could be felt in the physical world, swept such esoteric exclusivism away. The church of the Holy Sepulchre, of course, was a celebration of the Resurrection, but it was also a celebration of the Cross.

3. GOLGOTHA AND THE TOMB: CYRIL'S METHODS OF CONNECTION

Unlike Eusebius, therefore, Cyril saw the church of the Holy Sepulchre as having two important focuses not just one. Eusebius'

[81] For Constantine's intriguing devotion to the cross, see above 4.3 at fn. 59. Constantine's theology, influenced perhaps by more Western thought forms, may always have focused more on Christ's Death: see, for example, his description of the 'feast day of the Passion' as 'brighter than the light of the sun' in *Oratio Constantini*, 1.1 (according to Eus., GCS, i, 154.2–5). This encouragement from the emperor would naturally only have increased the intensity of the issue within Palestine.

[82] Yarnold (1983), 108.

emphasis on the tomb alone was indeed simple and straightforward but, according to Cyril, it had a major drawback: it was quite false. However, even if Cyril's 'bifocal' approach was more correct and preserved an important theological balance, it gave rise to a certain difficulty: how could these two ingredients, the rock of Golgotha and the tomb of Christ, be brought together into a coherent system? Apart from emphasizing the Gospel story of the Cross having been followed by the Resurrection, were there any ways in which such seemingly diverse objects could be linked so as to reveal their underlying theological unity? Cyril believed that there were. Before we concentrate exclusively on the tomb, it will therefore be good to examine the connections that Cyril drew between Golgotha and the tomb.

He discovered two ways of making the connection. First, he could draw attention to the fact that both Golgotha and the tomb had originally been located in the same garden; secondly, he could point out that both were objects made out of rock. These were obvious and, at first sight, not especially important points to be making. Clearly they might appeal to a man like Cyril who was more interested than Eusebius in the things of nature, but did they have a particular function of their own? The way Cyril developed these two points suggests that there was. For this emphasis on the 'garden' and the 'rock' not only brought to light the fulfilment in Christ of certain scriptures, but also, and more importantly, linked Golgotha and the tomb together in such a way as to reinforce the essential unity of this unique building.

Cyril's emphasis on the 'garden' arose from a single, rather ambiguous verse in John's Gospel: 'in the place were he was crucified, there was a garden' (19.41). It is unclear from this verse whether John was asserting that Golgotha was actually itself in that garden or whether it was simply adjacent to the garden in which lay the tomb. Cyril, seemingly the first Christian theologian to address himself to this particular problem,[83] came down decisively in favour of the former option: Golgotha had indeed been itself located in the garden. Indeed he slightly misquoted John in order to make his point: ' "for it was a garden where he

---

[83] Eusebius never discussed this verse at all, not even in his discussion of the Passion/Resurrection narratives in *QMS*; the only previous quotations of it, which were made without any further comment, occur in Tert., *de Carne Christi*, 5.1, and Origen, *C. Cels.*, 2.69, *Comm. in Matt.* [27.60], CS 143, 296.

was crucified". Though now richly adorned with kingly gifts, it was formerly a garden.'[84]

There were, however, some further, more exegetical, advantages of this interpretation. Just as the location of Christ's tomb of burial in a garden might be seen by Cyril as the fulfilment of certain Old Testament prophecies,[85] so too, if Golgotha was now assumed to have been in that garden as well, a neat typological parallel could be established between the garden of Eden (where sin first entered the world) and the garden of Golgotha (where the sin of the world was finally redeemed). Thus the cross of salvation and the original tree of temptation had both been located in a garden: 'In Paradise was the fall and in a garden our salvation. From the tree came sin, and until the Tree sin lasted.'[86] Cyril's system was indeed neat—geographically, exegetically and theologically.

Cyril therefore had no hesitation in stating plainly that Christ was 'crucified in a garden'.[87] To our modern ears, with our inappropriate understanding of the term 'garden', Cyril's statement may sound more odd than it would have done to his audience. Indeed he may have been quite correct.[88] Yet the point under consideration is that he was driven to this conclusion by the need

[84] *Catech.*, 14.5. Again we can note the way in which Cyril here paints a picture of continuity that obscures the radical changes of the intervening years. It may indeed, as he claims, have been a garden before (πρότερον) the coming of royal munificence—but that was 300 years before! Cyril's simple statement might suggest something much more recent. He then went on to say that 'tokens and traces of this garden still remain'. It is difficult to imagine what these may have been, especially again when one considers the fact that a pagan temple had been on the site for two hundred years. Was he referring to root systems of some kind or perhaps to the 'cisterns' that the Bordeaux Pilgrim remembered (594.3–4) and which would become an integral part of later legends of the 'invention' of the cross? Alternatively was he simply implying that the open space of the *atrium* was intended to represent a garden? For some discussion of this difficult point, see Wistrand (1952), 28, fn. 2.

[85] See, for example, *Catech.*, 13.22, 14.5, and *Hom. para.*, 11, for his novel use of three verses from the Song of Songs (Cant. 4.12, 5.1a, 6.11a) for this purpose, verses which previous writers had unanimously applied to the Church: see Cypr., *Ep.* 74.1 and Origen, *Schol. in Cant.* [4.12], PG, xvii, 272d–73a.

[86] *Catech.*, 13.19 (*WCJ*, ii, 16). Had he been Eusebius, who linked salvation more to the Resurrection, he would have been happy to see the sin of the garden of Eden overturned in the 'garden tomb' of the Resurrection; with his emphasis on the Cross, however, Cyril needed Golgotha, not the tomb, to be in a garden.

[87] Ibid., 13.8.

[88] In the first century this derelict quarry around Golgotha may well have been developed into a public grove of trees; yet this would not have made it impossible for Golgotha and a place of execution still to have been located in its midst.

for unity, both in his exegesis of scripture and in his presentation of the contemporary church buildings. For exegetical and typological reasons it was neat to speak of the garden of Eden and the garden of Golgotha; for more practical reasons, which highlighted the unity of the Holy Sepulchre, it was neat to talk of the garden of Golgotha and the garden tomb. In this way God's eternal purposes in salvation could be seen to be a unity; in this way too the Constantinian building with its bifocal significance could be seen as a single and coherent unit.

Cyril's second method of drawing together the tomb and Golgotha into a coherent system was to emphasize the fact that both of these were objects 'made of rock' ($\pi\acute{\epsilon}\tau\rho\alpha$).[89]

In the now uncovered rock of Golgotha there was a geological fault which Cyril saw as an important vindication of the divine nature of Christ.[90] Evidently he was assuming that this crack had occurred at the time of Christ's Passion, an assumption derived from that episode in Matthew's Gospel (27.51 ff.) when the 'rocks were split' at the time of Jesus' death.[91] Cyril clearly felt that this episode was quite important; he referred to it on three other occasions as well.[92] In the first of these, however, he had clearly attempted to connect this dramatic occurrence, not with Christ's death on the rock of Golgotha, but with his burial 'in the rock' of the tomb: 'He was truly laid as man in a tomb of rock, but the rocks were rent for fear of him.'[93] The two events, the death and the burial, though strictly separate both in time and space, were thus linked closely together; the rock of Golgotha had been cracked at the time when Christ was laid in the nearby rock-cut tomb. In this very simple way, however, Cyril was able once again to connect these physical entities in a theological unity.

However, Cyril's love for this passage and his firm belief that the rock of Golgotha now bore the marks of this dramatic episode was not shared by Eusebius. As shall be discovered in our final

---

[89] This emphasis on Christ's tomb being of rock is seen in *Catech.*, 13.38, 13.35, and 14.22. It also enabled him to develop some interesting parallels between Christ's burial 'in the rock' and that both of Jonah (*idem*, 14.20) and of his own baptismal candidates 'in water' (*idem*, 3.12); it also suggested a further case of fulfilled prophecy, again from the Song of Songs (Cant. 2.14 in *Catech.*, 14.9).

[90] Ibid., 13.39.

[91] For an alternative, modern explanation, see above fn. 40.

[92] Ibid., 4.12, 13.34, 18.16.

[93] Ibid., 4.12.

chapters, this was a passage that Eusebius consistently interpreted in a purely spiritual manner, understanding it to be a picture of the saints entering the heavenly Jerusalem as a result of Christ's Resurrection.[94]

This was no doubt partly because St Matthew's text here included a reference to the 'holy city' which Eusebius would instinctively want to apply to the heavenly Jerusalem, not the physical Jerusalem in Palestine.[95] Yet Eusebius may have had other reasons for denying that this episode had truly occurred in the physical realm. First, its dramatic and sensational elements that so attracted Cyril might only have had the opposite effect on Eusebius; such interest in the dramatic and physical was quite alien to Eusebius' thought.[96] Then, after 325, this verse could also be used by Christians in Jerusalem to draw attention both to the rock of Golgotha (the importance of which Eusebius was trying to minimize) and more particularly to the geological fault within it (which Eusebius may have recknoned to be nothing but a natural flaw). Noting its dramatic and physical nature, its reference to Jerusalem as a 'holy city', and its fulfilment in the split rock of Golgotha, Eusebius would thus have had every reason for insisting on his spiritual interpretation of this verse. For precisely these same reasons Cyril would not.

It comes, therefore, as no surprise that, after commenting on the 'rock' (πέτρα) of the tomb in the *Theophany*,[97] Eusebius never referred to it again. In his account in the *Life of Constantine* he succeeded in omitting any reference to it,[98] because to have mentioned the πέτρα would only have encouraged the reader to recall that more massive πέτρα within the building which Eusebius,

[94] See esp. *Comm. in Ps.* [87.7], 1064b. Does Cyril's use (in *Catech.*, 13.34) of a verse from this same LXX Ps. 87 [88], when referring to the 'rocks being rent' (Matt. 27.51 ff.), reflect his awareness that Eusebius had also linked these two passages of scripture together in this commentary on the psalm? Eusebius used them to stress his spiritual interpretation; Cyril now answered with his more physical interpretation. Eusebius himself in *Dem. Ev.*, 6.18.41 (*FPG*, ii, 34) had temporarily needed a more physical interpretation of this episode to show the fulfilment of Zech. 14.5; in doing so, however, he ensured that he did not include a reference to the 'holy city' and sought to associate the 'earth shaking' only with the Temple mount, not with Golgotha.

[95] See further below 10.2 and 11.2.

[96] Cf. above 3.2(b)-(c).

[97] *Theoph.*; 3.61; cf. also *Comm. in Is.* [51.1-2], 321.10-11, where it is introduced only through the quotation of Isa. 51.1.

[98] See *V. Const.*, 3.25-40.

for this and for many other reasons, was so anxious to avoid. Eusebius did not wish the bifocal significance of the building to be grasped; he did not wish the tomb in any way to be linked with Golgotha. Cyril's thinking, by contrast, was clearly centred upon 'two highly decorated *rocks* both connected with the Passion, Calvary and the Tomb'.[99] For this reason he emphasized the episode of the 'rocks being rent', which he could use (along with his emphasis on the 'garden') to make this vital connection between Golgotha and the tomb that was so vital to his system. What Cyril joined together, however, Eusebius quietly rent asunder.

4. THE TOMB

At last we approach the most important part of this unique building, the tomb itself.[100] For many visitors this is indeed the chief focus of the building, though for Eusebius it was its sole focus. Once again it will be our task to discover how Eusebius and Cyril approached the tomb of their Lord in their quite different ways. True, there were indeed things (both major and minor) which they held in common: both were convinced of its authenticity and of its quite unique importance; both tended to refer to it as a μνῆμα, even though the evangelists' most frequent word for this 'tomb' had been μνημεῖον.[101] But there were also some important differences.

[99] Yarnold (1983), 108 (italics mine).

[100] For the probable appearance and architecture of the tomb in Eusebius' day, see Wilkinson (1972), and (1981), 242–52.

[101] The evangelists had used three different words (τάφος, μνημεῖον and μνῆμα), though with an evident preference for μνημεῖον. τάφος occurs in only Matt. 27.61–6, and μνῆμα in only Luke 23.53, 24.1 and Acts 2.29; but μνημεῖον is used by Mark (15.46, 16.2–8), Luke (23.55, 24.2–24), and John (19.41–2, 20.1–11). This preference must have been sensed by Eusebius in his discussion of these texts in *Dem. Ev.*, 10.8.17–22 (*FPG*, ii, 218–19), where μνημεῖον occurs seven times, τάφος but once and μνῆμα not at all. However, in *QMS* his own preference for μνῆμα begins to make itself apparent: he uses μνῆμα 34 times, μνημεῖον 19 times and τάφος only five times. Thereafter, apart from a passing reference in *Comm. in Is.* [51.1–2], 321.10–11, μνημεῖον does not occur again in any work after 325. Cyril similarly shows this preference. He only uses μνημεῖον when quoting Matt. 27.52 in *Catech.*, 18.16 and 14.16, and again when needing a touch of variety in *idem*, 13.39. Otherwise he invariably uses μνῆμα: see *idem*, 4.11, 10.19, 13.35, 13.39, 14.9, and 14.22. The reason for this preference in both Eusebius and Cyril for μνῆμα is not clear. Drake has suggested that, since Constantine had scorned pagan τάφους and θήκας in *Oratio Constantini*, 4.3 (according to Eus., *GCS*, i, 158.3), Eusebius may conceivably have been anxious to assure him that this tomb was of quite a different order.

Eusebius referred to the tomb as a 'cave' (ἄντρον), a term integrally related to his 'Triad' of caves which, as already noted, Cyril would later repudiate. To Eusebius the tomb was testimony almost solely to the Resurrection; Cyril, however, linked the tomb far more to Christ's death and burial. This explains in part his emphasis on the 'rock' (πέτρα) on which Christ was laid in burial, but also his emphasis on the 'stone' (λίθος) rolled away on the first Easter morning: if the tomb pointed to the reality of Christ's death, it was the entrance stone that pointed more directly to the reality of his Resurrection. Eusebius never mentioned this stone, perhaps through doubts over its authenticity. Although both saw the tomb as a witness (μαρτύριον), whether to Christ's burial or his Resurrection, by Cyril's day μαρτύριον was becoming almost the definitive title for the basilica to the east of the tomb. Moreover, their descriptions of recent work on the tomb, while complementing one another in factual detail, may betray conflicting opinions as to what really should have been done with the tomb in those early years after its discovery. Unique and prized objects arouse conflicting desires and intentions; the following reveals that the tomb of Christ was no exception.

A tomb is a tomb. It was not unreasonable for Cyril to emphasize that this, like all others, was truly a place of burial and real death. Yet, of course, this tomb was believed to be different from all others in that it had witnessed the Resurrection of the One who overcame death; it was *this* which Eusebius sought to emphasize. Cyril, however, despite his belief in the Resurrection (indeed perhaps because of it) felt it was still important to emphasize the reality of Christ's death and burial. 'He was truly laid as man in the tomb';[102] his body was laid 'on the rock';[103] the rock-tomb witnessed to Christ by being the place which 'received him in death'.[104] Jonah's 'burial' in the whale for three days was a type of Christ's burial for three days 'in the rock-cut tomb'.[105] In all these ways Cyril revealed his concern that his catechumens should be sure that Christ had truly died, and that they should see the tomb as the chief witness to this. As a result, he mentioned the

---

[102] *Catech.* 4.11 (*WCJ*, i, 124).
[103] Ibid., 13.8.
[104] Ibid., 14.22.
[105] Ibid., 14.20.

tomb more frequently in contexts which related to his death than in contexts which related to his Resurrection.[106] Indeed he never speaks of the 'tomb of the Resurrection'.

One reason for this may indeed have been Cyril's catechetical context; since baptism is a baptism into Christ's death, Cyril could draw a neat parallel between his catechumens' forthcoming burial in water and Christ's burial 'in the rock'.[107] Yet it also reflected his theology which concentrated more than Eusebius' on Christ's death, and which took greater delight in the physical and human aspects of the Gospel story.

Conversely, Eusebius in his Constantinian works speaks primarily, indeed almost exclusively, of the 'tomb of the Resurrection' (ἀνάστασις) or of 'immortality' (ἀθανασία).[108] Earlier, in a brief reference in the Isaian commentary[109] and at greater length in the *Theophany* he had indeed viewed the tomb from the perspective of Christ's death and burial.

This corpse too, of which death had now taken possession, was now borne by men; and, being worthy of the usual care, was afterwards consigned to burial. The grave itself was a cave which had recently been hewn out; a cave that had now been cut out in a rock, and which had experienced the reception of no other body. For it was necessary that it, which was itself a wonder, should have the care of that corpse only. . . . The corpse was therefore laid there . . . and a great stone held the entrance of the cave.[110]

However, this intriguing passage was strategically omitted by Eusebius when he reworked these chapters for his speech *On Christ's Sepulchre*. In that speech he did not refer to Christ's burial at all, and Christ's death was very much surrounded by the context of the Resurrection.[111] In the *Life of Constantine* Christ's burial is not mentioned at all. The burial—Resurrection motif only appears as a picture of the way the tomb had itself been submerged before at last coming to light; it was not applied to Christ himself.

---

[106] Hence, for example, in his summary of the Creed in ibid., 4.10–12, the tomb is mentioned in connection with the cross and burial but not in connection with the Resurrection. Hence too his frequent references in his lecture 13 on the crucifixion, compared to lecture 14 on the Resurrection.

[107] Ibid., 3.12, quoting Rom. 6.4.

[108] See, e.g., *Sep. Chr.*, 11.6, 18.3; *V. Const.*, 3.25, 26 and esp. 28.

[109] *Comm. in Is.* [51.1–2], 321.10–11.

[110] *Theoph.*, 3.61 (*LET*, 199).

[111] See esp. *Sep. Chr.* 15 *passim*.

Evidently for Eusebius the tomb was the place, not of Christ's burial, but of the Resurrection and of immortality.[112]

In his final years, perhaps influenced by the need to offset any morbidity within Constantine himself, perhaps influenced by the theological practice of the Jerusalem Church, Eusebius aimed to link the tomb with the Resurrection alone: it was not so much the 'Holy Sepulchre' as the 'cave of the Resurrection'. His increasing use of the word ἄντρον ('cave') to describe Christ's tomb fits in very well with this increased emphasis on the Resurrection and immortality. To be sure, it fitted in as well with his desire to develop a cohesive triad of caves;[113] yet it also had further advantages. Most importantly, despite being an inappropriate word to describe a man-made tomb it was without any overtones of death. The 'cave of the Resurrection' sounded more positive and less paradoxical than the 'tomb of the Resurrection'. Thus only twice in his final works did Eusebius speak of Christ's 'tomb' (μνῆμα), and in both cases it was qualified by a more positive description. In one he spoke also of the 'saving cave' (σωτήριον ἄντρον);[114] in the other he balanced μνῆμα with the description τὸ μαρτύριον τῆς ἀθανάτου ζωῆς ('the witness to eternal life'), since μαρτύριον, though a word increasingly linked with death, still retained the more positive notion of 'witness'.[115] On every other

112 See, e.g., *V. Const.*, 3.25, 26, 28.

113 See above 6.2(*a*).

114 *V. Const.*, 3.26.

115 *Sep. Chr.* 18.3. A full analysis of Eusebius' usage of μαρτύριον might yield interesting results; for some discussion of this, which concurs with the following outline, see Rubin (1982a), 82 and fn. 17–19. As suggested above, from perhaps as early as the dedication service (see the heading of the synodical letter, according to Athanasius, *de Synodis*, 21 ff.), this became a distinctive name for the basilica, in contrast to the tomb which later received the name *Anastasis* (see *Egeria, passim*). Eusebius himself, however, preferred to use this as the name, not for the basilica, but rather for the tomb itself. At the climax of his discovery narrative, it was the 'all-holy μαρτύριον of the Saviour's Resurrection' which came to light (*V. Const.*, 3.25). This identification of μαρτύριον with the tomb is seen similarly in *Comm. in Ps.* [87.7], 1064a, and *Sep. Chr.*, 11.2 and 11.6. Constantine himself, however, may have preferred μαρτύριον to be used as the name of his basilica (the *Martyrium*): hence the wording of the dedication letter and Eusebius' usage before Constantine in *L. Const.*, 9.16. The precise reference of μαρτύριον in *V. Const.*, 3.33 remains unclear, but by the time he completed ibid., 4, Eusebius himself may have conceded to this imperial preference, because whereas previously the Constantinian buildings had been 'around' (ἀμφὶ/περὶ) τὸ μαρτύριον and τὸ μνῆμα (above references in Psalms commentary and *Sep. Chr.*,) now the μαρτύριον itself was ἀμφὶ τὸ μνῆμα (*V. Const.*, 4.47, cf. also 4.40 and 4.45). This would again suggest that Eusebius' own preferences were not always heeded. If, as Rubin speculates—(1982a), 82—the use of μαρτύριον

occasion in his Constantinian works Eusebius used either ἄντρον or μαρτύριον to describe the tomb. It was a useful way of reinforcing his positive emphasis on the tomb, which was not so much a tomb of death but rather a cave which witnessed to the Resurrection.

If ἄντρον was free of more morbid overtones, it had the further advantage that it took attention away from the physical consituents of the tomb. Cyril predictably emphasized the 'stone' and especially the 'rock' of the tomb. Eusebius' chosen word (ἄντρον), however, not only avoided any parallels being made with Golgotha but also emphasized the cave's interior space where the Resurrection had occurred. The angel had said, 'He is risen, he is not here' (Mark 16.6); in the same way Eusebius' concept of the ἄντρον could lift Christian interest beyond that physical presence to a contemplation of the past event and the now spiritual *Logos*. It was not the rock of the cave which was of first importance, but its emptiness. The single message, therefore, that Eusebius wished this church to convey was the truth of the Resurrection, the possibility of our own immortality: the victory of the *Logos* over death was a 'prototype of that immortality and life with God which is our common hope'.[116] Moreover, the focus of this within the Constantinian church was a 'cave'; yes, indeed it had been a tomb but it now had a quite different significance, pointing us to the victory of the now exalted *Logos*.

It may well now be asked if Cyril would not have fully agreed with this focus on the tomb as the place of the Resurrection; he may never have used the notion of a 'cave', he may have associated the tomb more than Eusebius with Christ's burial, but surely that did not deny that the tomb also remained a chief pointer to the Resurrection? In many ways this must indeed be true. Yet from the wording of Cyril's lectures one senses that he was attempting introduce quite a different 'witness' which would have the task of focusing his catechumens' attention on the Resurrection.

by Constantine was integrally connected with the discovery of the cross, Eusebius' reasons for this distinct usage would again be apparent.

Cyril's exposition in *Catech.*, 14.16 of Zeph. 3.8a (LXX), which interpreted this verse as referring to the *Martyrium* and the *Anastasis* of this Constantinian church, was thus quite novel and contrary to Eusebius' preferred usage. For earlier references to this verse, see Cypr., *Testimonia ad Quirinium*, 3.106, *de Bono Patientiae*, 21; also Origen, *C. Cels.*, 8.72, *Cant.*, 2, 116.15. Eusebius himself had indeed related it more historically to the Resurrection, but also in *Dem. Ev.*, 2.2.9 (*FPG*, i, 69) to the Second Coming and the calling of the Gentiles.

[116] *Sep. Chr.*, 15.9 (*DPC*, 118).

This new witness was the 'stone' that had been 'rolled away'. By promoting this as a more conclusive testimony to the Resurrection, the tomb could be set free to testify to Christ's burial. This can be sensed by the way Cyril introduces this stone in two of his three 'lists of witnesses': 'The wood of the cross is a witness . . . ; Golgotha . . . is a witness; the holy tomb is a witness and the stone still lying there.'[117] 'The rock of the tomb which received . . . and this stone, which was rolled away at that time and lies here to this day, witness to the Resurrection.'[118] In Cyril's scheme of things the *lignum crucis* and Golgotha pointed to the cross, the tomb to Christ's burial, and this stone to the reality of Christ's Resurrection. To our modern minds the 'wood of the cross' and the 'stone' were perhaps the least convincing of all, but for Cyril their inclusion was important. In particular, the inclusion of the λίθος meant that there was something that pointed exclusively to the Resurrection. The tomb, of course, did so as well, but that could now be allowed to speak more strongly of Christ's burial.[119]

Had Eusebius known of this supposed 'stone' of the Resurrection he would almost certainly have been as sceptical on this issue as he was about the 'wood of the cross'. There is nothing in the *Life of Constantine* to suggest that this particular item mentioned by the evangelists had survived into the fourth century. Instead he spoke in pictorial terms of the 'stone of unbelief', which the angels needed to remove from the women on the first Easter day.[120] Moreover, he commented on the great amount of 'stones and timber' that had been strewn about the site and needed to be removed by Constantine's excavators.[121] In so saying, as suggested above, Eusebius may have been gently suggesting that the filling of the Hadrianic foundations provided plenty of opportunities for naive and false identification. At the very least the violence that occurred on the site in both 135 and 325 militated against Cyril's rather quaint and idyllic picture of this stone sitting nonchalantly

---

[117] *Catech.*, 10.19 (*WCJ*, i, 209).

[118] Ibid., 14.22 (ii, 46–7). He also refers to it in *idem*, 13.35, where he develops a novel interpretation of Lam. 3.53 to endorse his point. This verse was not discussed by either Origen or Eusebius, but was normally taken as a simple reference to Jeremiah's stoning (see, e.g., Hipp., *Antichrist*, 31).

[119] Rubin (1982a), Appendix II, notes the new importance that Cyril attaches to the λίθος, but sees it only in terms of his need for further authentication.

[120] *V. Const.*, 3.26.

[121] Ibid., 3.27.

in position from the day of the Resurrection 'to this day'.[122]
Nevertheless, even if Eusebius had accepted its authenticity, it is
clear that he would never have allowed the stone to become a
chief witness to the Resurrection, thereby leaving the tomb to
commemorate the burial; for the witness to the Resurrection,
according to Eusebius, was clearly to be none other than the
ἄντρον itself.

All these were questions of theology and emphasis, of authenticity
and terminology. Finally, however, we may ask a different type of
question. How did Eusebius and Cyril respond to the actual work
done on the tomb? It must indeed have been exhilarating for
Christians in the fourth century to discover the tomb of Christ.
Yet it was also an awesome responsibility. What was the best and
most fitting way of preserving it for future generations? One can
suppose that there was quite some debate between Constantine's
builders and various local Christians, including the bishops of
Caesarea and Jerusalem. But were they unanimous? We will never
know.

Yet two remarks made by Cyril could tentatively be taken as an
indication that not all the recent work had gone to his own
satisfaction. On one occasion he asked a string of questions about
the nature of the tomb designed to show his hearers the clear
answer provided by a verse in Isaiah (51.1): ' Was his tomb made
with hands? Does it rise above the ground, like the tombs of kings?
Was the sepulchre made of stones joined together? And what is
laid upon it? "Look upon the solid rock which you have hewn" '.[123]
In his commentary on Isaiah Eusebius had suggested that this
'rock' might refer to Christ's tomb; but he had not developed it
any further.[124] Cyril now interpreted it as a compelling prophetic
testimony to this tomb. Yet in asking these questions he highlighted
a dramatic difference between Christ's tomb in the first century
and its appearance now in the fourth. In the first century the
answer to all of Cyril's taunting questions would have been
negative; no, Jesus' tomb was to be cut out of 'solid rock'. In
particular, it did not 'rise above the ground, like that of kings';
instead it was embedded in a cliff-face. But now in Cyril's day, it
did: Christ's tomb had been cut free from its surrounding rock

---

[122] *Catech.*, 10.19 and 14.22.
[123] *Catech.*, 13.35 (*WCJ*, ii, 28).
[124] *Comm. in Is.* [51.1–2], 321.10–11.

and left as a single free-standing structure.[125] Indeed it had become
a royal tomb 'rising above the ground'. In this way Jesus, who had
been buried in humility and ignominy, was now given a royal
burial and proclaimed publicly as the true 'king of kings'.[126]

It seems unlikely that Cyril was suggesting that it would have
been better to leave the tomb entirely in its natural state. Such
thoughts of preserving the original appearance, though common
today, would not readily have occurred to Christians in the fourth
century.[127] It would have seemed only right to give the site with
a new appearance, reflecting the great value of this tomb to
retrospective Christian belief. Yet Cyril's comments might betray
just an element of misgiving, a slight suggestion that the regal
nature of the tomb in his day bore too little resesmblance to the
original.

A second comment of Cyril's concerning the present appearance
of the tomb might confirm this impression. Again he was trying to
show how the tomb fulfilled an Old Testament statement, this time
a verse in the Song of Songs (2.14) referring to a 'cleft of rock'.[128]

For he calls a 'cleft of rock' the hollow place originally in front of the
sepulchre; this had been hewn out of the rock itself, a practice customary
in front of sepulchres. It is not visible now, it is true, because the outer
hollowed-out rock [προσκέπασμα] was hewn away to make room for the
present adornment. Before royal magnificence embellished the monument,
there was a hollow place beore the sepulchre.[129]

Cyril seems to have visited the tomb himself at a much earlier
date,[130] when there had been an 'outer hollowed-out rock'
(προσκέπασμα) in front of the tomb. This he claimed was the 'cleft
in the rock' prophesied long before in the Old Testament. Yet now

[125] This decision may have been inspired in part by the tombs in the Kidron
valley: see Wilkinson (1981), 243.
[126] Compare Conant (1956), 17, on the way Jesus' ignominious burial could thus
be forgotten.
[127] Ibid.: 'There was no thought of preserving the natural . . . tomb in [its]
original condition, which would have been done today as a matter of course'.
[128] Eusebius had never discussed this verse and when Origen had done so he
had seen it as a picture of the spiritual life, an invitation for the Bride–Church to
seek her Lord. The 'cover of rock' spoke of secrecy while the 'outer wall' was a
call to leave the 'temporal' and to strive for the 'eternal': see *Cant.*, 3, 228–35.
[129] *Catech.*, 14.9 (*WCJ*, ii, 37).
[130] As inferred by, e.g., Gifford in NPNF, vii, pp. i and xli, who quotes Besant:
'though a boy at the time, [Cyril] must have watched, step by step, the progress
of the great basilica'.

it was no more. 'Royal magnificence' had generously removed it for all time; Cyril's artful discovery of a prophetic text had already become redundant.

One senses that Cyril was slightly aggrieved. This removal of the προσκέπασμα was indeed a 'drastic action'[131] and the Jerusalem Church might well have disagreed with the plans of Constantine to decorate the tomb according to his own regal taste. Quite possibly the desires of the Church and the will of the emperor had here been somewhat at variance. Although Constantine shared their love for the 'wood of the cross'[132] and therefore for Golgotha and the *Martyrium* church,[133] the emperor's designs on the tomb may not have been so agreeable. Did the Jerusalem Church wish to preserve more of the tomb's original appearance, and especially to keep this natural προσκέπασμα over its entrance?

At this point we may note, by contrast, how Eusebius had enthused in the *Theophany* about the uncomplicated and simple appearance of the tomb:

The grave itself was a cave which had recently been hewn out, a cave that had now been cut out in a rock, and which had experienced the reception of no other body. For it was necessary that it, which was itself a wonder, should have the care of that corpse only. For it is astonishing to see even this rock, standing out erect and alone in a level land, and having only one cavern within it; lest, had there been many, the miracle of him who overcame death should have been obscured.[134]

At the time of writing, soon after 325, the work on the site was certainly well under way: the surrounding rock had been removed, leaving the tomb as a free-standing structure in a 'level land'. However, Eusebius evidently wanted to praise not only its solitary

---

[131] Telfer (1955a), 45, fn. 1.

[132] *V. Const.*, 3.30.

[133] Note Cyril's praise of Constantine in *Catech.*, 14.22.

[134] *Theoph.*, 3.61. Eusebius considers it appropriate that Jesus' tomb had not been used before; yet he does not comment explicitly on it being a 'new' one. This aspect of the Gospel story was only used by Eusebius when quoting Matt. 27.60 in *Comm. in Is.* [51.1–2], 321.10–11; otherwise both he and Cyril never drew attention to it. Origen, however, in one of his rare references to the tomb, had based an important theological point on the newness of this tomb: its undefiled nature ensured that Jesus could sanctify the new sacrament of Baptism in water (*Comm. in Matt.* [27.59–60], CS 143, 296.21 ff.; cf. *C. Cels.*, 2.69). Once the tomb was discovered Eusebius and Cyril may not have continued this thinking through a natural desire to emphasize, not its newness, but its historical antiquity.

situation[135] but also its internal unity: 'it had only one cavern [ἄντρον] within it'. Thereby in every aspect, within and without, it proclaimed the uniqueness of Christ in his victory in the Resurrection. If, however, just at the time of writing the σπήλαιον currently contained more than just this one ἄντρον, Eusebius was making his desires quite clear: for the sake of theological neatness this προσκέπασμα should now be removed. Alternatively, if this had already been done, Eusebius was clearly pleased; his theological and personal opinions had evidently won the day.[136]

Seen in this light Cyril's statements and tone may well suggest that Eusebius, having his relationship with the emperor restored, may in this instance have achieved his personal goal: the tomb was decorated in accordance with Eusebius' own wishes. If this were indeed the case, Cyril's 'royal magnificence', could then be construed as a polite way of describing the meddling of the Caesarean metropolitan. In other instances, and especially concerning Golgotha and the *lignum crucis*, the Jerusalem Church had their way; hence Cyril's frequent references to both, and Eusebius' corresponding silence. With the tomb of Christ, however, it was Eusebius' turn. With his own greater interest in the Resurrection, Eusebius seems to have decided to concentrate on the tomb and had apparently been able gradually to dictate its eventual appearance.[137]

Even if this last argument is more suggestive than substantial, Eusebius' own emphasis on the tomb has now been clearly seen. His enthusiasm here in the *Theophany* for this recently discovered treasure spilt over into all his final works. The tomb was evidently very close to his heart. Indeed his descriptions may reflect something very personal: Eusebius was aware that he was one of the few men in history who had had the august privilege of deciding how the tomb of his Lord was to be preserved for the

[135] Again, the nearby *kokim* tombs, some of which are still visible today, slightly confound Eusebius' neat theological presentation.

[136] Wilkinson (1981), 168, is uncertain whether this description in *Theoph.* was written before or after the decoration. However, Barnes' dating of *Theoph.* to the first few years 'after 324' (see Appendix), and the picture of Palestine portrayed in that work (see above 4.2(a)–(b)), could suggest, as we have hinted, that it was written *in medias res*, when the external clearance of the area had begun but the precise internal decoration of the tomb was as yet still a matter for discussion.

[137] The later rotunda was conceivably part of this 'second round' of Eusebian planning, which intentionally supplemented those suggestions that had been made initially by the Jerusalem Church.

future. Although in his theology he still tried to emphasize the importance of the universal aspect of Christianity, here was a particular site of unrivalled significance for which Eusebius himself had been responsible: the tomb of Christ was, in a real sense, also the ἄντρον of Eusebius.

5. A NARRATIVE SUMMARY

By way of conclusion, it may be valuable briefly to posit an outline of the historical events relating to the church of the Holy Sepulchre which formed the backdrop for the thinking of both Eusebius and Cyril. Many of the differences observed above reflect genuine theological divergence between the two bishops; a few may be matters of mere accident and therefore quite insignificant. Yet some of them, including those dependent on theological assumptions, may also have been coloured to a greater or lesser extent by contemporary circumstances, such as the evident tension between the sees of Caesarea and Jerusalem and the aspirations of the emperor and his family. Neither Cyril nor Eusebius lived in a historical vacuum. What then actually happened in that first generation after Nicaea? Can we discern some more practical reasons for the differences noted above between Eusebius and Cyril in their approach to the Holy Sepulchre?[138]

Nine months after Constantine's victory over Licinius at Adrianople in September 324 the bishops of both Caesarea and Jerusalem found themselves at the Council of Nicaea. Eusebius came to that council with much anxiety, Macarius with much hope. For in the intervening months, as has been noted, Eusebius had been provisionally excommunicated for his Arian sympathies. This gave Macarius, an opponent of Arius from the outset, every hope that the assembled bishops would recognize the anomaly of his position as suffragan to the bishop of Caesarea and that they would acknowledge the prestige of his historic see, Jerusalem. Yet it would also have strengthened his resolve to make a most important request of Constantine and would have encouraged his expectation that, if the request were granted, he would play a major role in

---

[138] I am particularly indebted to Professor. Drake and Professor Rubin for their help in constructing the following historical outline which draws together and develops their previously published suggestions.

its implementation. Eusebius' embarrassing position gave Macarius the ideal opportunity to ask the emperor in person for his permission to destroy the temple of Venus in the quest for the tomb of Christ.[139]

Constantine could well have known in advance of this painful state of affairs in Jerusalem. For he had recently been contemplating a visit to the East, a visit that conceivably was inspired in part by a desire to see the Palestine of the Gospels for himself.[140] It has also been suggested recently that in the nine months between Adrianople and Nicaea Constantine's own mother-in-law, Eutropia, had visited Palestine and returned with a sorry account concerning both the pagan temple that covered Christ's tomb and the pagan worship that was still being conducted at Mamre, the place where the *Logos* had revealed himself to Abraham.[141] If this were the case, Constantine might indeed have had time to develop a considered 'holy land plan'.[142]

Nevertheless the emperor needed direct consultation with the local bishop to ensure that such drastic action was indeed truly necessary. The destruction of a Hadrianic temple was not to be entertained too swiftly: just how sure were the Christians of their tradition?[143] However, in keeping with the desires of both parties, consultation resulted in Constantine granting the bishop's request: initial instructions and relevant personnel were probably despatched with Macarius back to Jerusalem.[144]

The distinct role in all this of Macarius, rather than of Eusebius, can be detected in the way Constantine soon writes a letter addressed to Macarius alone.[145] From this letter we learn that the

[139] As suggested by, e.g., Coüasnon (1974), 12.

[140] *V. Const.*, 2.72.2; see Telfer (1955b), 699.

[141] See Rubin (1982a), 88–91, who bases his argument on Eus., *V. Const.*, 3.51-3. From this Rubin develops an attractive hypothesis to the effect that this episode concerning Mamre was the occasion for some conflict between Eusebius and Macarius. However, the early dating of Eutropia's visit (before Nicaea), on which his argument depends, has yet to gain scholarly acceptance. Nevertheless the theophany at Mamre was clearly of some importance within Eusebius' theology: see, e.g., *Chron.*, §2, 355a; *Onom.*, 6.8-16, 76.1-3, 124.5-7; *Proph. Eclg.*, 1.3; *Hist. Eccl.*, 1.2.6-8; *Dem. Ev.*, 5.9. Hence it is probable that he was indeed instrumental in encouraging Constantine to build a church on the site. The Bordeaux Pilgrim saw the church in 333 (*BP*, 599.5-6), but the precise date remains uncertain.

[142] Cf. Telfer (1955b).

[143] See Drake (1984).

[144] See, e.g., Gray (1969), 199.

[145] *V. Const.*, 3.30–32; see Rubin (1982a), 87.

demolition and excavation had not been a waste of time. Not only had they brought to light Christ's tomb but also, despite all the complexities of the site's clearance, something of special interest to Constantine. The site was continuously bringing forth 'fresh wonders', but this time what had been discovered was none other than the 'sign' or 'monument . . . of his most holy passion' (τὸ γνώρισμα τοῦ ἁγιωτάτου ἐκείνου πάθους), most probably the very wood of Christ's cross.[146]

Macarius was swift to inform the emperor, who in turn replied with due elation and repeated his earlier instructions only with more enthusiasm. Eusebius needed to include this letter in the *Life* for the clear evidence that it provided of Constantine's personal piety and devotion.[147] Yet it also unfortunately revealed some truths which Eusebius would otherwise have preferred to remain concealed: Macarius' prior personal involvement with the emperor, the supposed discovery of the 'true cross' and Constantine's personal intention to commemorate *this* within his basilica.[148] In the first round of events, Bishop Macarius had clearly gained the upper hand.

Eusebius was not, however, to be discounted for long: he soon turned the timely arrival of an important personage to his own advantage. Palestine was blessed by the visit of the emperor's mother, Helena.[149] Her interest in sites other than the Holy Sepulchre gave Eusebius the ideal opportunity to brand the 'Holy Land' with his own theology and especially to promote his distinctive triad of caves. The development of the Triad thus neatly satisfied the aspirations of Helena as benefactor but also of Eusebius as the metropolitan.

With regard to the church of the Holy Sepulchre itself, however, Eusebius now began his corrective emphasis on the tomb. Although

---

[146] *V. Const.*, 3.30; for this identification of this phrase with the *lignum crucis*, see above 4.5.

[147] Rubin (1982a), 88, 91.

[148] Cf. Drake (1985), 8–11. On Constantine's own devotion to the cross, see above 4.3(*b*).

[149] *V. Const.*, 3.41–3. Despite the many later legends Helena herself does not seem to have been involved with the discovery of the 'true cross': see Drake (1985), 1, Yarnold (1983), 106, and Wilkinson (1981), 240; *contra* Rubin, (1982a), 87. We can note how Cyril himself never mentions her in connection with this discovery, not even in *Ep. Const.* Moreover, Eusebius' praise of Helena indicates his strong approval of her visit (see above 6.2(*a*)), something which we would not expect had she been involved with this discovery of which Eusebius so much disapproved.

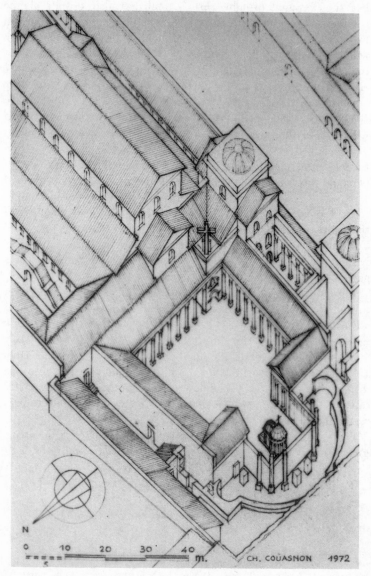

Fig. 8. The church of the Holy Sepulchre before the construction of the Rotunda (after Coüasnon)

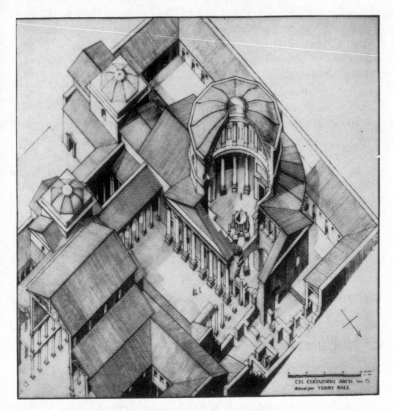

Fig. 9. The church of the Holy Sepulchre after the construction of the Rotunda (after Coüasnon)

Constantine himself and the Jerusalem Church were emphasizing Golgotha and the 'wood of the cross', to Eusebius the discovery of the latter was an 'unpleasant fact to be suppressed'; thus 'any reference to the cross was carefully avoided as indeed was any reference to Golgotha'.[150] Therefore in his alternative approach Eusebius naturally focused instead on the tomb. He would be seeking to ensure that this particular part of the complex would bear his distinctive hallmark within the church, just as much as would the Triad within Palestine. Most probably therefore Eusebius sought to play a strategic role in any decisions relating to the tomb. How this tomb in a natural cliff-face should be converted into a distinct shrine and how exactly it should be adorned were both important questions; the answers may have emerged only over a period and after much consultation. However, it could well have been Eusebius as metropolitan who made the final decision to cut it free from the living rock and to reduce the tomb down to a single and cohesive ἄντρον. Perhaps also at a later stage it was Eusebius who suggested that the cave be brought inside under the roof of a large rotunda—even though this would only be completed after his own death.

By September 335 (and perhaps long before) Eusebius had clearly reassumed his position of leadership and influence, for he presided over the the bishops assembled at Tyre, who then proceeded to Jerusalem for the dedication of the Holy Sepulchre during that same month. That auspicious occasion gave him an unrivalled opportunity to assert his own understanding of this church and to set it firmly within a theology close to his heart; thus he emphasized the theophany of the *Logos* and the Resurrection but played down any discussion of Christ's death, tactfully avoiding any reference to the 'cross'. Around this time he may have written his more physical description of the building, which survives in the *Life of Constantine*,[151] but which he most probably used in part when speaking before Constantine a few months later.[152] Here again his own emphasis was clearly on the tomb—though the clever reader can detect that the building did not exactly embody the priorities which Eusebius tried to assert.[153] In this he also

[150] Rubin (1982a), 92.
[151] *V. Const.*, 3.25–40.
[152] See Appendix.
[153] In particular, see just above for Constantine's letter to Macarius in *V. Const.*, 3.30; see both Rubin (1982a), and Drake (1984).

asserted that Constantine had conceived of the whole idea as a result of divine inspiration,[154] and emphasized the speed with which his orders were obeyed:[155] no room was given for readers to suspect the possible initiative of Macarius. This was to be Eusebius' final statement on the matter and was included in the the *Life of Constantine*.

Eusebius had clearly been influential in many practical decisions. Yet he also wished to play a leading theological role, guiding people in their understanding of the Holy Sepulchre and overcoming the bad affects of those decisions that had not gone in his favour. Thus his own written works, which we have been studying, are coloured strongly by his own recent experiences, as he sought to impress upon his readers a more 'correct' view of the building's role and significance. Contrary to what the Church in Jerusalem was saying and even the views of Constantine, it was not Golgotha nor the 'wood of the cross' which was of central importance, but only the tomb. Moreover, this in its turn was to be understood not so much as the place of Christ's burial, but instead as the scene of the Resurrection, and as the particular place where the universal presence of Christ had been unleashed into the world and our own immortality assured. Thus the buildings that surrounded it might indeed be associated tentatively with the 'New Jerusalem',[156] because they symbolized the kingdom of Christ now established in the world and in the Constantinian Empire. Here was where it had all begun.

The church of the Holy Sepulchre might indeed be the place that commemorated the beginning of the Christian Gospel, yet if it was to be hoped that that same building might therefore act as a perennial focus for unity within the Church, it was a forlorn hope. In the course of time differences of interpretation and insight, important and often valuable, would be bound to occur. Our study has shown that they began at the very beginning.

[154] *V. Const.*, 3.25.
[155] For example, ibid., 3.29.1.
[156] Ibid., 3.33.

9

MOUNT SION

According to the Acts of the Apostles (2.1–4), just seven weeks after the death of Jesus his disciples were gathered together in a house in Jerusalem, when they were filled with the new power of the Holy Spirit. The Resurrection of Christ at Easter was followed by the descent of the Spirit at Pentecost. And so we leave the church of the Holy Sepulchre and proceed finally to Mt. Sion, the place that since the time of Cyril (and probably long before) has been identified as the scene of this mysterious event. In so doing we begin to move in our enquiry from places associated solely with the incarnate life of Christ. As it happens, it has often been supposed that the Last Supper must have occurred in this area, so too Jesus' trial before Caiaphas and perhaps even the post-Resurrection appearances described in John 20; for this was a densely populated area in Jesus' day, the so-called 'upper city' within Jerusalem. It is therefore a place still to be associated in many ways with the life of Christ and with the Gospels. Yet it is more than that. It is a place associated with the work of the Holy Spirit and with the life of the Church. Moreover, since 'Sion' was a favoured biblical synonym for 'Jerusalem', our discussion of Eusebius' attitude to Mt. Sion will inevitably begin to raise our second major question, the question of Jerusalem. Therefore this examination of the role and meaning of Mt. Sion will act as a useful means of transition, because it was simultaneously an 'ecclesiastical' location, associated with the Church (and especially with the local Jerusalem Church), and also a 'Jerusalem' location, affecting the Christian understanding of the city.

At this point attention must be drawn to the perennial confusion concerning the identity of this 'Mt. Sion'. 'Sion' in Old Testament times is now known to have been the name for the Ophel ridge that runs southwards from the Temple area; it was this much lower hill that was David's citadel and the original 'Jerusalem'.

However, the city gradually expanded, first to include the large area designated for the Temple and then over the centuries to include the large and much higher western ridge across the Tyropoean valley. Thus by Jesus' day David's Mt. Sion was termed the 'lower city' in comparison with the more wealthy 'upper city' in which was located, for example, Herod's great palace. From the vantage-point of this 'upper city' David's original city can seem so small and insignificant. It is therefore hardly surprising that around the first century people in Jerusalem, forgetting that for David the proximity of a sure water-supply (in the Gihon spring) was a more important factor than mere altitude, came to presume that David must have chosen this great hill of the 'upper city' to be his 'Sion'. Mt. Sion thus came to be identified incorrectly with the western hill. (See fig. 10.)[1]

Moreover, when in 135 Hadrian's new city of Aelia Capitolina was founded further to the north, excluding both the original 'Sion' (on the Ophel ridge) and much of the more recent 'Mt. Sion' (the 'upper city'), it was natural that that part of the western hill which was now outside the walls and which could no longer be termed the 'upper city' came to be identified more consciously and narrowly as 'Mt. Sion'. Strictly 'Sion' might indeed still be an applicable name for *all* the western ridge, some of which was still within the city walls (on which was located the camp of the Roman Tenth Legion and also Golgotha),[2] but it was more common to use 'Mt. Sion' as a distinctive name for that part which was now left isolated and deserted to the south.[3] Although towards the end of his life Eusebius began to apply some biblical references to 'Sion' to the Temple area (or more generally to 'Jerusalem' was a whole), along with Cyril and all his contemporaries he had no idea that the 'Mt. Sion' of the fourth century was not the same as that of the Old Testament. It is the contrasting attitudes of Eusebius and Cyril to

[1] For the dating of this mistaken identification to the Second Temple Period, see Tsafrir, (1978). Although Christians may have had motives for continuing this false identification (as suggested for different reasons in *GP*, i, 374, *JN*, 448–50, Wilson (1902), 983, and Wilkinson (1977), 171), this is unlikely to have been its original cause.

[2] See, e.g., Eus., *Comm. in Is.* [2.1–4], 16.28–9; on this Roman camp, see Tsafrir (1978), 543 ff..

[3] See figure 10. Contrary to Wilkinson (1981), 183, fn. 5, Tsafrir (1978), 543 believes there would not have been any walls around Aelia till the departure of the Tenth Legion around AD 300 and certainly none around Mt. Sion.

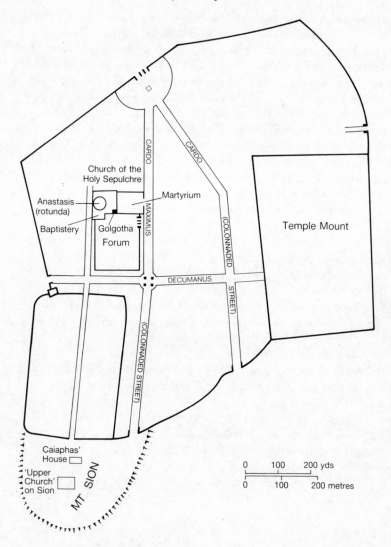

Fig. 10. Plan of Constantinian Jerusalem

this 'false' Mt. Sion, a largely uninhabited area given over to vegetation and farming but also littered with ruins, with which we are here concerned.

Once again it will become clear through comparing his references

to Mt. Sion with those of Cyril (and indeed of the Bordeaux
Pilgrim) that Eusebius was remarkably silent concerning this
important area associated with such a variety of New Testament
events. Apart from three passing references in the *Proof of the
Gospel*, where he suggests that Jerusalem and the adjacent Mt.
Sion should be seen as the places 'where our Lord and Saviour for
the most part lived and taught,[4] Eusebius appears to have been
mostly concerned to indicate instead the great desolation of the
area (in fulfilment of certain Old Testament prophecies, such as
Mic. 3.12, and Isa. 1.8). Moreover, he never describes the
contemporary appearance of this desolate Mt. Sion, and his
reference in the *Onomasticon* merely states that Mt. Sion is a 'hill
in Jerusalem'.[5] He never specifies which, if any, of the New
Testament events he believes had occurred on Mt. Sion, and after
325 he seems never to have referred to this hill at all.

Thus, were we reliant on Eusebius' words alone, we would have
no idea of what buildings and ruins were to be seen on this Mt.
Sion before 325; for that we are indebted to the Bordeaux Pilgrim.
Nor indeed would we have any idea of the extra significance that
this Mt. Sion had for many Christians who believed it to be, among
other things, the location of the descent of the Spirit at Pentecost;
for that we are indebted to Cyril. These younger contemporaries
of Eusebius reveal in just a few references more knowledge and
greater interest in Mt. Sion than does Eusebius in his entire corpus:
why?

1. THE STATE AND SIGNIFICANCE OF MT. SION

The testimony of the Bordeaux Pilgrim is indeed helpful, though
it is not without its difficulties.

Climbing Sion from there you can see the place where once the house of
Caiaphas used to stand, and the column at which they fell on Christ and
scourged him still remains there. Inside Sion, within the wall, you can
see where David had his palace. Seven synagogues were there, but only
one is left—the rest have been 'ploughed and sown', as was said by the
prophet Isaiah.[6]

---

[4] *Dem. Ev.*, 1.4.8 (*FPG*, i, 24); cf. *idem*, 6.13.4, 9.14.6 (ii, 13, 181).
[5] *Onom.*, 162.12.
[6] *BP*, 591.7–93.1: trans. Wilkinson (1981), 157–8.

Clearly this now largely desolate site had for some time been of interest to Christian visitors. The ruined house of Caiaphas is also mentioned by Cyril as a compelling witness to Christ, though he does not refer to any such column of flagellation.[7]

More problematic is the pilgrim's reference to the one remaining synagogue and his failure to refer to any church on Mt. Sion. For some years later Epiphanius asserted that back in the days of Hadrian (in the second century) there had not only been these seven synagogues but also a 'little church of God'.[8] Moreover, Cyril is soon referring confidently to the descent of the Spirit at Pentecost 'here in Jerusalem, in the upper church of the apostles'.[9] As we shall discover, there is evidence that in the years after 333 this 'upper church' may have been built by Cyril's predecessor, Maximus. There is also strong evidence that suggests that a building of some sort, associated with the Pentecost event, had been in existence for quite some time.

If so, we must presume that the short acount of the Bordeaux Pilgrim is slightly mistaken, or at least simply misleading. Conceivably the one remaining synagogue mentioned by the pilgrim was indeed the 'little church of God' mentioned by Epiphanius. Although it would indeed be strange for Christians to be using for worship a building which could be described as a 'synagogue', this is not totally impossible, and Epiphanius' preference in referring to it as a 'church' would be readily intelligible.[10] Alternatively the Bordeaux Pilgrim may simply have mistaken the Christians' church for a synagogue when it was no such thing at all.[11] Or again he may simply have forgotten to include this church in his narrative.[12] Ultimately it is impossible to decide; for 'our knowledge is too patchy to permit a definite conclusion.'[13]

---

[7] *Catech.*, 13.38; discussed in Wilkinson (1981), 157, fn. 9, and Kopp (1963), 352-7.

[8] *Mens.*, 14 (PG, xliii, 261).

[9] *Catech.*, 16.4.

[10] This is the position taken by Pinkerfeld (1960), Bagatti (1971), 118, and now Wilkinson (1981), 322, modifying his earlier belief that there had been no church at all (158, fn. 2).

[11] The Bordeaux Pilgrim and his guide were not above making major mistakes: see above 7.1(*c*).

[12] This omission, though indeed 'odd' (Bagatti, (1971), 117) would not be entirely uncharacteristic. His interrupted train of thought, when referring in this passage to the palace of David (see Kopp (1963), 354) might indeed be responsible for this.

[13] Ibid., 324

The evidence for the existence of a Christian building of some kind on Mt. Sion before 325, however, comes not just from this statement of Cyril in 348 concerning the 'upper church'. It also comes from the strong sense derived from our ancient sources that in the centuries before Constantine Mt. Sion had been the traditional centre of the Jerusalem Church. Mt. Sion was, many scholars conclude, the home of the small Christian congregation living in Aelia.[14] If so, there must have been some kind of church on Mt. Sion.

When Hadrian had refounded the city as a pagan foundation, it may not have been especially easy for the small Christian community to meet together within the city.[15] Moreover, the new forum prevented their use of the area around Golgotha. For their focal point they might therefore naturally have chosen instead the place where they believed their Church had come into being at Pentecost. Quite probably this had been used for Christian worship in the years before 135; yet it now had the advantage of being located outside pagan Aelia while still being on the celebrated Mt. Sion of the biblical period.

This assumption that Mt. Sion was the pre-Constantinian home of the Jerusalem church is based largely on the fact that Mt. Sion was clearly associated in the fourth century not simply with Pentecost but also with the 'throne' of St James. 'As evident proof of its continuity with Christian origins this church would display an episcopal throne said to be that of James, the Lord's brother and first bishop of Jerusalem.'[16] Eusebius himself had mentioned the way in which this interesting item was lovingly preserved by the Jerusalem Church,[17] but he never mentioned where it was kept, nor where the Jerusalem Christians met for worship.[18] Later in the fourth century, however, it becomes clear that the throne was being kept in this church on Mt. Sion: 'in the church called

[14] This has been accepted by Wilkinson (1981), 158, fn. 2, Hunt (1982), 2, Telfer (1955a), 56, and Kopp (1963), 324, fn. 8; it is also implicitly asssumed by Testa (1972), 69–71 and Bagatti (1971), 116–22. Tsafrir therefore suggests that Sion might have been a fringe suburb for minority groups.
[15] Hunt (1982), 19 indeed sees the Jerusalem Church as '*confined* to its place of worship on Mt. Sion outside the walls of Aelia' (italics mine).
[16] Ibid., 2.
[17] *Hist. Eccl.*, 7.19, 7.32.19.
[18] Contrary to the automatic assumption of Telfer (1955a), 56.

'Holy Sion' is the throne of James'.[19] Here too, on 25 December each year, there was a liturgical celebration to commemorate St James;[20] this was a 'great commemoration for Sion, which contained the throne of the first bishop, James the Just' and would have been a feast 'second only to Pentecost' in importance for this Church.[21] Mt. Sion was therefore clearly important to local Christians for two reasons: it was believed to be not only the scene of Pentecost but also the ancient and traditional home of the Jerusalem Church.

If this is accepted, then it becomes overwhelmingly probable that there was indeed a 'church' of some kind on Mt. Sion before the time of Constantine. Unfortunately in his short description the Bordeaux Pilgrim failed to mention this. Moreover, in the light of the centrality of Mt. Sion in the tradition of the Jerusalem Church, its identification as the site of Pentecost and the appearances in John 20 becomes even more intelligible; for, even if incorrect, the Jerusalem Church would have had every reason for locating these great New Testament events on the site of their church. In this way the local Church, which in many ways was quite weak, could bolster its identity; they might be a small and struggling church, but this was where the apostles had once been and where the Holy Spirit had given birth to the Church. The Jerusalem Church therefore had some quite personal motives for asserting the assured identification of Mt. Sion as the scene of Pentecost. For the same reason it would also be assumed that this had been the scene of the post-Resurrection appearances described in John 20.19–31. Egeria believed that the church on Mt. Sion marked the 'very place' where the Lord had earlier appeared to the disciples and to Thomas.[22] This may indeed have been an ancient tradition going back well before Constantine; on the other hand, since Cyril himself does not mention it in his two (admittedly very brief) references to 'doubting Thomas',[23] the tradition may only have become established in the years after 348.[24]

---

[19] This is the testimony of Peter the Deacon, but Wilkinson (1981), 183, fn. 1 sees no reason to date the details of this statement later than Egeria's time.

[20] *AL*, 71.

[21] Wilkinson (1981), 275; cf. Renoux (1969), 73.

[22] *Egeria*, 39.5; cf. 40.2.

[23] *Catech.*, 13.39, 14.22.

[24] It is therefore quite surprising that the third Jerusalem event 'indoors', the Last Supper, was not located here by tradition until the fifth century: see *AL*, 39, compared with *Egeria*, 35.2. The identity of these two 'upper rooms' (for the Last Supper and for Pentecost) was assumed around AD 370 by an absentee Christian in

Finally, if the church on Mt. Sion was the home church or 'cathedral' of the local Jerusalem Church, it becomes quite clear why the bishops of Jerusalem sought steadily to increase the importance of this church on Mt. Sion throughout the fourth century. Eusebius' neat Triad ensured that Mt. Sion was excluded from the sites selected for imperial munificence, but Macarius' successor, Maximus (335-49), made it his first priority to start on the renovation of the existing building.[25] However, without imperial resources, this building was perhaps quite small; hence Cyril's successor, Bishop John, expanded it.[26] Then at the beginning of the next century, this same bishop ensured that this church, because it had been the 'first church', was the place where the recently discovered relics of St Stephen were now kept.[27] Meanwhile throughout this period this church was playing an increasingly important part in the Jerusalem liturgy, second only to the church of the Holy Sepulchre.[28]

Mt. Sion might have been a largely uninhabited area at the beginning of the fourth century, but it was clearly an important place for Christians. There were some interesting ruins there (one identified as the house of Caiaphas) and a synagogue (if not identical with the 'church'). Far more importantly there was a Christian church there, small but historic and important. For it was not only the home of the Jerusalem Church, the place where the throne of James was preserved, but also the place where Christians had long commemorated the coming of the Spirit at Pentecost and perhaps too the appearances of the Risen Christ to his first disciples. Eusebius, however, hardly ever mentions it at all. Why?

the *Didaskaleia of Addai*: see Baldi (1955), 478, and *JN*, 453. Origen had correctly placed the Last Supper in the 'upper city': *Comm. in Matt.* [26. 26–30], CS 86, 199.29. Contrary to Bagatti (1964), 38, this need not reflect a precise and fixed tradition; nevertheless Origen's reconstructive imagination does indeed contrast with Eusebius, who never located this important event at all: see, e.g., *Pasch.*, 9.

[25] For discussion of the building work of Maximus, see Wilkinson (1977), 171, *JN*, 450, and Kopp (1963), 325. Epiphanius (*Mens.*, 14) refers to 'Bishop Maximona' (a Syriac variant) in connection with Mt. Sion. It is possible that, when Cyril referred to the 'upper church' in *Catech.*, 16.4, this new building was not yet completed.

[26] See Wilkinson (1977), 171, for this interpretation of *GL*, 565.

[27] *Ep. Luciani*, 6–8 (PL, xli, 813–15).

[28] Hence the special services there mentioned by Egeria (27.5-7, 29.1-2, 39.5, 41, 43.8).

2. EUSEBIUS' SILENCE CONCERNING MT. SION

Eusebius was silent on several issues concerning Mt. Sion. As has been noted, he never mentioned the survival of this synagogue nor the ruins of the house of Caiaphas; nor did he ever locate those Resurrection appearances or Pentecost on Mt. Sion. The silence concerning the synagogue might be truly insignificant; yet, as we shall see, it could have been influenced by his apologetic stance against Judaism. His failure to mention the house of Caiaphas might be similarly unimportant; yet it could also be the result of his historical scepticism about the ruins. Historical scepticism and scholarly ambivalence are probably responsible as well for his failure to identify the location of the Resurrection appearances. However, his silence concerning Pentecost betrays something more; historical scepticism contributed to his silence, but there was also a more personal and ecclesiastical reason—a fear of the Jerusalem Church. Taken individually Eusebius' silences might be deemed accidental or insignificant; taken together, however, even if they reveal the variety of Eusebius' reasons, they suggest something more conscious.

If the 'synagogue' mentioned by the Bordeaux Pilgrim was really the local church for Jerusalem Christians, then Eusebius' failure to refer to any 'synagogue' as such is readily explicable. If, on the other hand, this was a synagogue now being used by Jews (or even Jewish-Christians), as some modern scholars have suggested, Eusebius' silence will have been for quite a different reason. For he himself claimed that Jews were no longer able to visit Jerusalem; from the time of Hadrian they had not been allowed to set eye on the city 'even from a distance'.[29] This ban on Jews visiting Jerusalem would automatically have included any Jewish-Christians as well; hence Eusebius' emphasis on the now totally Gentile Church of Aelia.[30] Yet there is good reason for believing that some time in the third century enforcement of this statute became lax: the reality did not conform to Eusebius' desire. As a result, the existence of resident Jews (or Jewish-Christians) was something that Eusebius would have preferred to ignore: any synagogue in Jerusalem, whether disused or not, threatened to blur his

---

[29] *Hist. Eccl.*, 4.6.3.
[30] Ibid., 4.6.4.

over-simplified picture and was therefore not mentioned. For this synagogue tradition could be used, as it is by scholars today,[31] to contradict his own presentation of a total exclusion of Jews from the city. Thus instead Eusebius claimed that Jewish synagogues had been established 'in every city apart from Jerusalem and Mt. Sion'.[32] If there was indeed such a synagogue on Mt. Sion as the Bordeaux Pilgrim suggests, it is not surprising that Eusebius failed to mention it.

The Bordeaux Pilgrim was also shown the ruined house of Caiaphas the High Priest, which Cyril also mentions in his lectures.[33] Eusebius, however, never refers to the survival of these ruins and indeed never explicitly locates Caiaphas' house on Mt. Sion. In his four explicit references to Jesus' trial before Caiaphas he never once offers even a general geographical setting. When he narrates the story of Jesus' last hours before the crucifixion in both the *Paschal Homily* and the *Proof of the Gospel* he adds no geographical touches to his account.[34] Nor does he suggest any location for Peter's three-fold denial of Christ.[35] The only hint of his thinking in geographical terms comes in his exposition of LXX Ps. 54.10 [55.9-10]—'I see violence and strife in the city; day and night they go around it on its walls'—when he sees the 'violence in the city' as a prophetic reference to Jesus' trial at Caiaphas' house, and the the crucifixion at Golgotha as showing the Jews' evil 'around the walls'.[36] However, again there is no reference to the area of Mt. Sion and no suggestion of what might be seen in contemporary Jerusalem. In all of these passages the house of Caiaphas is mentioned through his exposition of the scriptural text but no link is made between the text and geography.

Nevertheless there is one possible hint that Eusebius did indeed believe the High Priest to have lived on Mt. Sion. Paradoxically it occurs in an exposition of LXX Ps. 49.2 [50.2]—'out of Sion, the perfection of beauty, God shines forth'—in which he makes no explicit reference to Caiaphas' house. For in the course of

---

[31] See, e.g., *JN*, 450, and Safrai (1973). For a defence of the continued presence of Jewish-Christians, see the works of the Franciscans (esp. Bagatti and Testa) who see Eusebius' silence as quite deliberate.

[32] *Dem. Ev.*, 6.13.5 (*FPG*, ii, 13).

[33] *BP*, 592.4; Cyril, *Catech.*, 13.38.

[34] *Pasch.*, 10; *Dem. Ev.*, 10.7.6 (*FPG*, ii, 214), expounding Zech. 14.5-9.

[35] *Comm. in Ps.* [87.8], 1060d; cf. *idem* [68.9], 737c.

[36] Ibid. [54.10], 480c–d.

interpreting 'out of Sion' as a reference to Christ's glorious and public Second Coming, he notes how this will contrast with Christ's first appearance when he kept silence when 'being judged by men'.[37] Despite his overriding desire to give only a spiritual meaning to 'Sion' he seems accidentally and subconsciously to have concentrated on one of the most important events to have occurred on the physical Mt. Sion during Christ's life.

This passage may therefore suggest that Eusebius knew full well these local Jerusalem traditions; yet it also shows how in general he sought to exclude them from his theological writings. As a theologian he seems to have been little interested in geography and, especially with 'Sion', keen to emphasize spiritual realities rather than physical ones. Yet it is not unreasonable to suggest that he may also have been sceptical as a historian of any such precise identifications. The violent upheavals of both AD 70 and 135 would surely have removed most identifiable traces of first-century Jerusalem.[38] Moreover, he would scarcely accept the survival of a column in one of the ruins as a means of identifying the place of Jesus' trial; the column of flagellation might be important for later pilgrims in its emotive appeal,[39] but there was no hint of such an item in the Gospels and it could hardly itself claim an undisputed authenticity.

By contrast Cyril had no doubts about the authenticity of this site and believed its ruins had a telling message to convey. It was more than just a 'witness' to Christ: it revealed the spiritual power that Christ now wielded but which he had not used at the time of his Passion: 'the house of Caiaphas will convince you, which by its present desolation manifests the power of him who once was judged in it.'[40] That is, the visible and continued ruins proclaimed a striking reversal: the passive judged 'man' had proved to be an effective spiritual Lord, capable of powerful judgement. In highlighting the contrast between Christ's silence and humility before Caiaphas and his spiritual power and majesty, Cyril's point was not dissimilar from that which Eusebius had been making in his commentary on LXX Ps. 49; the difference is that Cyril takes

[37] Ibid. [49.2], repr. in Devreesse (1924), 79.
[38] Cf. Kopp (1963), 357.
[39] *BP*, 592.4; *Egeria*, 37.1.
[40] *Catech.*, 13.38.

advantage of the physical place to make his point in colourful geographical terms, whereas Eusebius decidedly does not.

Eusebius' third silence with regard to Mt. Sion concerns the two-fold Resurrection appearance described in John 20.19–31. Of all events or places on Mt. Sion presently under discussion this is the one about which we can be least certain as to whether Eusebius knew of this local association with Mt. Sion. For the assumption that the Risen Christ appeared to his disciples on Mt. Sion and indeed in the same place as Pentecost a few weeks later does not appear in our sources before Egeria.[41] Since, as already noted, Cyril does not locate Jesus' appearance to Thomas, this identification may only have gained acceptance during the middle years of that century, as the new church on Mt. Sion began itself to gain in importance. Eusebius' failure to suggest a location would then be quite unexceptional. However, it remains possible that this tradition was already in existence in Jerusalem; Eusebius' non-committal approach would then reflect once again his historical scepticism and scholarly ambivalence.

Eusebius discussed this passage from John's Gospel at some length in his *Gospel Questions and Solutions* (addressed to Marinus),[42] where he sought to reconstruct the Easter events in such a way as to answer possible inconsistencies within the Gospel accounts. Here, if anywhere, one might expect Eusebius to suggest a location for this event since the whole context of his analysis is historical and geographical. Yet his reconstruction only serves to reveal his scholarly uncertainty. Why, he was asked, did Peter and John risk a visit to the tomb if they were indeed racked by 'fear of the Jews (John 20.19)?[43] Eusebius suggests two alternative solutions. Perhaps the place where they were staying during those days was outside the city; this would at least mean that their running to the tomb did not involve their being observed in the city streets. Alternatively they may simply have had more courage than the others in leaving 'the house'.[44] Eusebius does not decide between these two options. Clearly at this stage he had not fixed

[41] *Egeria* 39.5; cf. *idem*, 40.2.

[42] See esp. *QMS*, 1–11, 983–1006.

[43] Elsewhere Eusebius himself suggests that because of this fear the disciples were effectively 'incarcerated' from immediately after Jesus' arrest: see *Comm. in Ps.* [68.20], 748d.

[44] Ibid. 988a–b.

in his own mind on any one definitive location, nor indeed on any one particular quarter of the city. If there was a tradition emerging that assumed that the house where the disciples were staying was on Mt. Sion, Eusebius was clearly not convinced—the Gospels were themselves far from specific, and after so many years final historical certainty was strictly impossible.

Finally, and most importantly, there is the question of Eusebius' attitude to the identification of Mt. Sion as the scene of Pentecost. Cyril had no doubts that the 'upper church' marked the site of this event.[45] What did Eusebius think?

First, it is interesting to note that, in his thinking about the Holy Spirit, Eusebius often showed a preference for the less dramatic picture of Jesus breathing his Holy Spirit on the disciples during this same post-Resurrection disclosure as described in John 20. Thus he normally quoted verses from John's Gospel rather than Acts 2 if ever he wished to illustrate the straightforward fulfilment of Old Testament references to the Spirit.[46] For this reason, and also because theologically he did not give a special prominence to the role of the Holy Spirit,[47] he did not speak of the Pentecost event, as described in Acts 2, as often as one might expect. Yet that did not shelve the problem of deciding a location for the coming of the Spirit; for the Jerusalem Church would soon be locating the events of both John 20 and Acts 2 in one and the same place.

Nevertheless there were indeed occasions when Eusebius saw some advantage in referring to the dramatic story in Acts. For the foreign multitude which witnessed the event according to Luke could be seen as a prophetic fulfilment of the psalmist's phrase, 'envoys from Egypt',[48] as a demonstration that the first believers included many Jews[49] or even as an 'apostolic choir' similar to the great episcopal gathering at Nicaea.[50] There were also two occasions when he referred to the Church's annual festival of Pentecost. This festival was seen as a reminder of the future rest

---

[45] *Catech.*, 16.4.
[46] For examples: *Comm. in Is.* [32.15], 211.6–18, *idem* [59.21], 368.12; *Dem. Ev.*, 3.7.23, 4.16.31 (*FPG*, i, 160, 210); *Theoph.*; 5.49; for an exceptional use of Acts, see *Comm. in Is.* [59.19], 367.28.
[47] See above 4.4–5.
[48] *Comm. in Ps.* [67.31–3], 718b–c.
[49] *Comm. in Is.* [11.1], 87.8 ff.
[50] *V. Const.*, 3.7–8.

which Christians would enjoy in the heavenly kingdom[51] and then as a fitting day for Constantine to have entered into eternal fellowship with God; for it was an 'august and holy festival' which celebrated both the 'Ascension of our common Saviour and the descent of the Holy Spirit among men' ($\epsilon i \varsigma$ $\dot{a} \nu \theta \rho \dot{\omega} \pi o \nu \varsigma$).[52] In these references to Pentecost there is nothing beyond the bare information given in Acts and no suggestion of any location in contemporary Jerusalem for this auspicious event. There was certainly no hint that the relevant place might be none other than the place where Jerusalem Christians were wont to meet, the place where they preserved the throne of St James.

Both before and after 325 Eusebius remained resolutely silent. Interestingly his reference above in the *Life of Constantine*, which equated the 'Ascension of our common Saviour' with the 'descent of the Holy Spirit' made quite clear that in many ways these two events were of equal importance; in geographical terms Mt. Sion was strictly equal to the Mount of Olives. Yet in his final years the focus of Eusebius' attention (as that of Helena and Constantine) had been almost exclusively on the Triad, a focus that effectively excluded the merits of Mt. Sion from consideration. Why did Eusebius give so little attention Mt. Sion? Why did he never locate the scene of Pentecost? Before 325 in the *Proof of the Gospel* he had had given ample coverage to Bethlehem and the Mount of Olives, but why did he only commemorate Mt. Sion for its desolation?

As with the discovery of the 'true cross', the confident and joyful certainty of Cyril and Egeria in identifying the location of Pentecost contrasts with, and reveals, Eusebius' silence; and similarly it must be asked if this identification, as that discovery, was known to Eusebius. Was it made before, during or after his lifetime? If only after his death, his silence would again be quite unexceptional, a reflection of genuine ignorance. Yet such ignorance seems highly improbable; for it would then be quite remarkable that within a decade Cyril could be stating so calmly as a matter of fact (indeed almost as an 'aside') that the Holy Spirit had 'descended . . . in

---

[51] In the more liturgical context of *Pasch.*, 4–5.

[52] *V. Const.*, 4.64 (NPNF, i, 557). For this seeming identification of Ascension and Pentecost in the Church's calendar, see also *Egeria*, 43.5; for the debate over the 'fortieth day after Easter' in Egeria's narrative, see J. G. Davies (1954), Devos (1968), and Wilkinson (1981), 77–8.

the upper church on Mt. Sion'.[53] On the other hand, if, as is more probable, this identification was indeed already established by local Christians (whether before or during Eusebius' lifetime), then it is Eusebius' silence that becomes the remarkable factor; this would reflect either some genuine historical scepticism or, worse, qualms about the motivations of the local Jerusalem Church. Both of these reasons would match exactly what we have come to recognize as Eusebius' characteristic concerns.

First, Eusebius may have been genuinely sceptical of such an assured identification. He knew from his own visiting and from Josephus' narrative just how sweeping had been the destruction of AD 70. That was only augmented by Hadrian's suppression of the second Jewish revolt in 135 and his foundation of the new Aelia Capitolina. By only referring to Mt. Sion as a ruined and quarried area[54] Eusebius could well have been desiring not simply to exhibit fulfilled prophecies but also to dash pious Christian hopes of naive identification by showing the vicissitudes that the area had undergone since New Testament times. Unlike at Bethlehem or on the Mount of Olives, here on Mt. Sion there was no immobile 'cave' to ensure a semblance of physical continuity. Thus only with difficulty could the correct site have been preserved or subsequently identified. It was therefore unlikely that any church on the site could be the original 'house' mentioned in Acts 2.2.[55]

However, Eusebius might well have had a second, somewhat different reason for his failure to identify the scene of Pentecost. Was he also alarmed by the intentions of the local Jerusalem Christians? Their use of an ancient church was harmless enough, as was the preservation of James' throne—something he was happy to note, at least in his earliest writings.[56] However, in their confident exact identification of their church with the scene of Pentecost they could have been making a more subtle, ecclesiastical point. Pentecost might then be seen more clearly as the first beginning, not only of the worldwide Church, but also of the local Jerusalem Church; the identification of their traditional church

[53] *Catech.*, 14.6.
[54] See, e.g., *Dem. Ev.*, 6.13.15–17, 8.3.1–15 (*FPG*, ii, 15–16, 140–1).
[55] Interestingly Hamilton (1952), 87–90, as a modern historian, detects this scepticism of Eusebius concerning Mt. Sion and contrasts this with his conviction of the authenticity of the Holy Sepulchre.
[56] *Hist. Eccl.*, 7.19; 7.32.19.

centre with the scene of Pentecost would in this way enable
Christians in Jerusalem with greater justice to claim that their
church was the 'mother' of all the churches.[57] In the light of the
known tension between the sees of Jerusalem and Caesarea in this
period and the increasing prestige afforded to the Jerusalem
Church, the existence of such ecclesiastical motivations seems
highly probable. Moreover, their presence explains perfectly the
different responses of the Jerusalem Church and Eusebius respectively towards Mt. Sion and its ancient church.

On the one hand, there was the positive attitude of the Jerusalem
Church. As we have seen, successive bishops, both in word
and deed, were evidently keen to emphasize and increase the
importance of this church. Meanwhile Egeria observed the special
way in which the local presbyters 'concerned themselves with the
reading' of this particular passage from Acts 2.[58] Over and above
their glad commemoration of the coming of the Spirit (which had
universal significance for all visiting pilgrims), there was clearly a
more domestic cause for celebration for the local Church. On the
other hand, there was the negative attitude of Eusebius the
metropolitan. In referring to the coming of the Spirit, as already
noted, he not only preferred the Johannine version and revealed
no interest in its precise location, but, when using the Acts
narrative, he did so almost always in such a way as to show how
this first gathering was very 'international' and also very Jewish—
the precise opposite of the small group of *Gentile* believers who
now constituted the Jerusalem Church. If anything, the true
inheritor of the Pentecost event was the worldwide Church whose
bishops had recently gathered at Nicaea; that was what truly
reflected (as an εἰκών of the 'apostolic choir') the continuation of
God's original purposes.[59] The Spirit had descended not on a
restricted group of apostles in Jerusalem, but universally 'among
mankind' (εἰς ἀνθρώπους).[60] Eusebius clearly wished to draw his
readers' attention away from the original Pentecost event and
certainly to deny any prestige which the local Jerusalem Church
might seek to claim for itself as a result of that event.

[57] As indeed the Jerusalem Church was called in the canons of Constantinople in
382 (according to Theodt., *Hist. Eccl.*, 5.9.17).
[58] *Egeria*, 43.3 in Wilkinson (1981), 141.
[59] *V. Const.*, 3.7–8.
[60] Ibid., 4.64.

It should therefore be no surprise to learn that, apart from his several comments concerning its desolation and his unhelpful brief comment in the *Onomasticon*, Eusebius succeeded in pursuing a policy of almost total silence concerning Mt. Sion. He never referred to any of its buildings; he never expressly suggested that this was the location of any particular Gospel event; above all he avoided making any connection between Mt. Sion and Pentecost and excluded it neatly from his Triad of important sites. The vocal testimony of the Jerusalem Church was thus confronted by the silent response of Eusebius. The probable use of Mt. Sion by the local Church before 325 ensures that, in this instance, Eusebius' silences cannot be dismissed as an accident of his date in history. Already, and perhaps for a long time, Mt. Sion had been a place of central significance for Jerusalem Christians. Eusebius must surely have known of this; yet he refused to acknowledge it.

3. THE REFERENCE OF BIBLICAL 'SION'

Eusebius might thus be able to avoid relating contemporary Mt. Sion to various events within the New Testament; after all, this physical Mt. Sion in Jerusalem was never referred to explicitly in the Gospels or in Acts. There were, however, frequent references to 'Sion' in the Old Testament which Eusebius could not similarly avoid; indeed discussions of the true reference of this 'Sion' recur in all his writings with repetitive regularity. On almost every occasion he stressed that 'Sion' was to be interpreted spiritually in one or more of at least four different ways: it could refer to the 'heavenly Sion',[61] or to the Church of God on earth,[62] to the individual soul,[63] or (especially in his later *Commentary on Isaiah*) to the 'evangelical word' ($\epsilon\dot{\upsilon}\alpha\gamma\gamma\epsilon\lambda\iota\kappa\grave{o}\varsigma$ $\lambda\acute{o}\gamma o\varsigma$) and its preaching ($\kappa\acute{\eta}\rho\upsilon\gamma\mu\alpha$) on which the Church of God is built.[64] However, there

---

[61] *Dem. Ev.*, 6.24.5 (*FPG*, ii, 45–6); *Proph. Eclg.*, 2.2, 3.24; *Comm. in Is.* [19.24, 24.23, 35.10], 137.6, 161.5–10, 230.22, respectively; *Comm. in Ps.* [73.2], 856c.

[62] *Dem. Ev.*, 6.24.6; *Proph. Eclg.*, 3.24, 4.30; *Comm. in Is.* [1.25–6, 52.8, 66.7–13], 12.21–2, 331.26, 402.34–404.15 respectively. This second interpretation of 'Sion' is coupled with the first interpretation (the 'heavenly Sion') in *Dem. Ev.*, 5.26.2, *Comm. in Ps.* [64.2], 625c, [75.3], 880c–d, and *Comm. in Is.* [49.11], 312.32 ff.

[63] *Dem. Ev.*, 6.24.7; *Proph. Eclg.*, 3.24. Christ himself is the true 'mountain' in *idem*, 4.1; cf. *Comm. in Is.* [40.9], 252.17–21.

[64] See *Comm. in Is.* [11.9, 12.4–6, 22.1], 85.5, 93.26, 144.6 respectively.

were three separate verses in the Old Testament that lent
themselves instead to a more physical interpretation and which
therefore caused Eusebius temporarily to abandon this overriding
emphasis on the spiritual reference of 'Sion'. It is in looking briefly
at Eusebius' interpretation of these three verses and his general
understanding of biblical 'Sion' that once again we shall see his
increasing avoidance of the hill called 'Mt. Sion' in his own day.
For even the term 'Sion' as used in the Bible was clearly a matter
of some fluidity, admitting of various interpretations; sometimes it
seems to refer very specifically to a 'Mt. Sion', at other times it is
seemingly used instead as a synonym for the Temple mount, whilst
on yet other occasions it is apparently just another way of referring
to 'Jerusalem' as a whole.[65] The evidence below suggests that
Eusebius came increasingly to favour an identification of biblical
'Sion' with the Temple mount, not with the so-called 'Mt. Sion' of
his own day.[66]

The three relevant verses from the Old Testament were as
follows: 'Sion shall be ploughed as a field, Jerusalem shall become
a heap of ruins and the mountain of the house a wooded height.'
(Mic. 3.12). 'The daughter of Sion is left like a shelter in a vineyard,
like a hut in a field of melons . . . (Isa. 1.8).' 'The law will go out
from Sion, the word of the Lord from Jerusalem.' (Isa. 2.3c). Of
these it will be seen that only the first caused Eusebius to refer
unmistakeably to 'Mt. Sion', the south-western hill associated by
Cyril with Pentecost and described by the Bordeaux Pilgrim. On
the contrary, in his later writings (especially the Psalms and Isaiah
commentaries) an observable shift can be noted in Eusebius away
from this Mt. Sion. When interpreting biblical 'Sion' in a physical
sense, Eusebius's attention becomes fixed instead upon the Temple
and (on one occasion) upon the area of the Holy Sepulchre.

[65] For a useful summary of biblical usage, see Wilson (1902), 983.

[66] In all this discussion the modern reader, knowing that Eusebius' 'Mt. Sion' was
not the 'Sion' of the Old Testament, is apt to become confused. Apart from observing
that with this modern knowledge Eusebius would have been in a better position to
understand why the Temple mount (a continuation northwards of the Ophel ridge)
was called 'Sion' by the Old Testament writers, it is best temporarily to banish this
extra complication from our minds; for there will be no need to mention the true
'Sion' of David in the following pages. To save confusion, 'Mt. Sion' will always be
used, as throughout the chapter, to refer to the south-western hill outside the walls
of Aelia/Jerusalem in Eusebius' day and outside the walls of the 'old city' today;
'Sion' will be reserved for biblical contexts. This may serve to highlight Eusebius'
increasing disassociation of biblical 'Sion' from contemporary 'Mt. Sion'.

It may be simplest if this later understanding of 'Sion' is highlighted first. In his *Commentary on the Psalms* 'Sion' is either a straightforward synonym for Jerusalem[67] or else identified quite explicitly with the Temple mount. Sion, he explains, was the 'royal mountain, on which the Temple was built and the house of God's dwelling';[68] a few psalms later he states unequivocally that the altar of the Temple was 'on Mt. Sion'.[69] 'Sion' clearly was taken to include the Temple mount, indeed to be especially identified with it. As a result, when in his commentary on this same psalm he speaks of ancient Jerusalem having been built 'on Mt. Sion', his reference must include the Temple mount, even though clearly it could also include contemporary Mt. Sion. Mt. Sion could not be excluded altogether from biblical 'Sion' but Eusebius could ensure that the chief focus of the word was the Temple mount.

This attempt to focus the meaning of 'Sion' away from contemporary Mt. Sion is seen even more clearly in his *Commentary on Isaiah*. On a couple of occasions 'Sion' was used as a synonym for Jerusalem[70] and on one occasion, as shall be seen, it was understood as a reference even to the place of Christ's death and Resurrection.[71] At all other times, however, 'Sion' is clearly identified with the Temple mount: it is the high mountain 'on which the Temple of God was built'[72] and the place where God was worshipped (τῷ ἔν αὐτῷ τιμωμένῳ θεῷ).[73] This is seen most clearly and significantly when he came to expound the important text of Isaiah 1.8 because this verse, which he himself in the *Proof of the Gospel* had seen as referring to Mt. Sion (as would Cyril later), he now clearly sought to apply solely to the Temple mount; it was expressly and only the 'Temple in Jerusalem' which had become 'like a shelter in the middle of all', 'like a hut in a field of melons'.[74] No indication was given that this verse could also be taken as a reference to his contemporary Mt. Sion. Indeed, in order to avoid any such assumption on the part of his readers, he actually avoided referring to 'Sion' in his own exegesis and

67 For examples: *Comm. in Ps.* [64.2], 624–8, and [75.3], 880a–81a.
68 Ibid. [73.2], 856c.
69 Ibid. [77.68], 938d.
70 See, e.g., *Comm. in Is.* [1.21], 10.22, [14.32], 107.19.
71 Ibid. [2.1–4], 16.28–9.
72 Ibid. [22.1], 144.4.
73 Ibid. [9.11–13], 69.28–35.
74 Ibid. [1.7–9], 7.9–12.

exposition. For the 'Sion' of this verse did not refer to Mt. Sion but to the Temple mount.

This exclusive focus on the Temple when interpreting Isaiah 1.8 marks a notable shift from Eusebius' own earlier position in the *Proof of the Gospel*. In that work his thinking was less clear-cut. To be sure, he was clearly thinking of the Temple mount but the wider reference which included Mt. Sion seems still at this stage to have been in his mind.

For the daughter of Sion (by whom was meant the worship celebrated on Mt. Sion) from the time of the coming of our Saviour has been left as a tent in a vineyard, as a hut in a garden of cucumbers, or as anything that is more desolate than these. . . . Yea, and the beauteous Temple of their mother-city was laid low, being cast down by alien peoples . . ., and Jerusalem became truly a besieged city.[75]

At first sight his definition of 'daughter of Sion' as '*worship celebrated on Mt. Sion*' might appear to be a clear reference to the Temple mount.[76] Yet his reference to the destruction of the Temple a few lines later gives the impression that this is a new item not previously mentioned. If so, the previous reference to 'Sion' may have been less specific, perhaps even a reference to contemporary Mt. Sion. At any rate, Eusebius' interpretation at this earlier date was less concise and less well-focused than it would be in the Isaiah commentary. In that later work the possibility of any supposed reference to contemporary Mt. Sion would be definitely excluded.

This focus on the Temple mount when interpreting this one verse would also be in marked contrast to the interpretation offered by Cyril a few years later:

Isaiah saw Sion as a hut. The city was still standing, beautified with public squares and clothed in honour; yet he says, 'Sion shall be ploughed like a field' (Mic. 3.12), foretelling what has been fulfilled in our day. Observe the exactness of the prophecy; for he said, 'Daughter Sion [*sic*] shall be left like a hut in a vineyard, like a shed in a melon patch' (Isa. 1.8). Now the place is full of melon patches.[77]

Since Eusebius had himself to interpret Micah 3.12 (with its reference to 'ploughing') as a prophecy relating to contemporary

---

[75] *Dem. Ev.*, 2.3.53 (*FPG*, i, 77–8).
[76] As interpreted in *JN*, 450, fn. 2.
[77] *Catech.*, 16.18; Cyril mistakenly attributes Mic. 3.12 to the prophet Isaiah.

Mt. Sion and since Cyril speaks of the destroyed 'city and squares', it is clear that this passage should be taken as a reference not to the Temple mount but to Mt. Sion. Other sources confirm that this Mt. Sion was being ploughed throughout the fourth century, and thus Christians continued to mention it as a precise instance of fulfilled prophecy.[78] Cyril thus sees Isaiah 1.8 as endorsing this prophecy concerning Mt. Sion. Yet Eusebius had applied this verse from Isaiah instead to the Temple mount. The two bishops were speaking of a completely different hill!

Moreover, Eusebius had understood the prophet's imagery of the 'hut in a cucumber field' simply as a *metaphor* for desolation. Cyril, however, now claimed instead that this was a prophecy that had been fulfilled literally on Mt. Sion: 'the place is full of melon patches'. In so doing, Cyril reveals that, despite the renovation of the 'upper church', large areas of Mt. Sion remained abandoned and desolate in 348. Thus, had Eusebius wished to apply this verse to Mt. Sion when writing his commentary twenty years earlier, he could easily have done so. The fact that there was this shift in Eusebius' focus after 325 towards the Temple mount must therefore be construed not as a change of affairs in Jerusalem but as a change of heart in Eusebius. For some reason Eusebius was avoiding any reference to Mt. Sion, the same Mt. Sion that meant so much to the Jerusalem church.

Yet Eusebius had not always avoided this Mt. Sion. As we have already begun to observe, in his *Proof of the Gospel* Eusebius was far more willing to refer to Mt. Sion than he was after 325 in the *Commentary on Isaiah*. An examination of his exegesis of the other two verses (Mic. 3.12, and Isa. 2.3) that encouraged such a literal reference will endorse this picture. Micah 3.12 he clearly saw as a prophecy concerning the narrow Mt. Sion outside the city wall to the south, but after 325 Eusebius only used this verse again in a spiritual sense.[79] Meanwhile Isaiah 2.3, which in the *Proof of the Gospel* he had also applied to Mt. Sion, in the Isaiah commentary he now applied instead to the place of Christ's death and Resurrection, somewhat further to the north and now well inside the city.

It was indeed hard in Eusebius' day to apply the 'Sion' of Micah

[78] See *BP*, 592.7, Optatus, *de Schismate Donatistorum*, 3.2 (PL, xi, 994–5) and Jerome, *Comm. in Ps.* [86.2], PL, xxvi, 1080c–d.

[79] *Comm. in Is.* [24.17–20], 159.3.

3.12 to anything other than Mt. Sion. For not only did the triplicate nature of the verse encourage a temporary distinction between 'Sion', 'Jerusalem' and the 'mountain of the house', but the reference to Sion 'being ploughed' seemed so obviously to refer to contemporary Mt. Sion, which, as other authors in that century assure us, was indeed being ploughed at that time. Thus Eusebius emphasized how 'Mt. Sion was burned and left utterly desolate' while by contrast the 'Mount of the house of God became as a grove of the wood'.[80] In support of this he noted his own eye-witness experience of 'Sion so famous, ploughed with yokes of oxen by the Romans'.[81] This reference to contemporary Mt. Sion is confirmed by Eusebius' statement two books later in the *Proof of the Gospel* to the effect that he had already shown, when interpreting this verse, the prophesied destruction of things revered by the Jews such as the 'mountains [ὄρη] called Sion' and the different buildings thereon dedicated to God.[82] Since Micah 3.12 had spoken of the 'mountain of the house', the Temple mount was naturally in Eusebius' mind; yet the unique plural, 'mountains', revealing that 'Sion' could refer to more than one hill, shows that he had been thinking not only of the Temple but also of a second hill, namely Mt. Sion. Thus, when in this later passage he again offers his own eye-witness experience as support for the fulfilment of Micah 3.12, it is clearly Mt. Sion, and not the Temple, which he has seen ploughed by Roman oxen and 'sown with seed'.[83] The use of Mt. Sion for farming is, as already noted, well attested in the fourth century, being mentioned not just by Cyril, but also by the Bordeaux Pilgrim, Jerome and Optatus. By contrast, none of these writers ever hinted that the Temple area had also been used for agriculture, and Eusebius would presumably have been far more explicit if he were making such an amazing assertion. It is therefore best to understand these two separate discussions in the *Proof of the Gospel* as references to contemporary Mt. Sion that were caused by the very structure of Micah 3.12.[84]

---

[80] *Dem. Ev.*, 6.13.15 (*FPG*, ii, 15).

[81] Ibid., 6.13.17 (ii, 15).

[82] Ibid., 8.3.6 (ii, 140, in which, however, the plural of the original is ignored).

[83] Ibid., 8.3.10 (ii, 141).

[84] Ferrar (*FPG*, ii, 15, fn. 1) saw this statement of Eusebius as a claim that 'part of the Temple area was under cultivation'. If this were true, then it would only highlight all the more the way Eusebius, unlike Cyril and others, concentrates on the Temple mount. Yet the evidence suggests that this reading is mistaken.

That Eusebius was quite prepared in the *Proof of the Gospel* to draw some attention to Mt. Sion is, however, seen perhaps most clearly in his interpretation of the third verse quoted above: Isaiah 2.3. These other references to Mt. Sion in this work had simply focused on its desolation; but here there was a hint of something more positive. The law which according to this prophecy 'went forth from Sion' and 'from Jerusalem' was clearly the 'word of the Gospel' (εὐαγγελικὸς λόγος),

for it is plain that it was in Jerusalem and Mt. Sion adjacent thereto [τοῦ ταύτῃ προσπαρακειμένου Σιὼν ὄρους], where our Lord and Saviour for the most part lived and taught, that the law of the new covenant began . . .[85]

Eusebius was evidently speaking here of the Mt. Sion of his own day, for his description of it as 'adjacent to Jerusalem' (though strictly anachronistic as a description of the Jerusalem of Jesus' day, when Mt. Sion was such an integral part of the city) was a perfect description of this hill now left stranded outside the city walls to the south. What he now indicates (though almost in passing) is that this, along with all Jerusalem to some extent, was the place where Jesus had spent so much of his time (τὰς πλείστας διατριβάς . . . πεποίητο). Mt. Sion, as the 'upper city' of Jesus' day, had a special claim to fame: it was one of the places most visited by Jesus.

This was quite a significant accolade for this now largely deserted hill and Eusebius repeated it twice more later in the *Proof of the Gospel*.[86] Yet in so saying Eusebius almost certainly betrays the fact that he was fully aware of the various local traditions that associated Jesus' activity in Jerusalem with this quarter of the city. Elsewhere in his writings, as we have seen, all such explicit suggestions of Mt. Sion's associations with New Testament events are avoided. Here, however, there is a definite hint that Eusebius was inclined to accept the validity of these associations, at least inasmuch as they suited his own purposes. Indeed it is just conceivable that in here affirming Mt. Sion's association with *Jesus* Eusebius was attempting to play down the association of Mt. Sion with the descent of the *Holy Spirit*,

Nevertheless the fact that Eusebius can be misunderstood in this way acts as a rebuke towards those who take his words too straightforwardly as referring to Mt. Sion, without noting that such a reference is very much the exception in Eusebius.

[85] *Dem. Ev.*, 1.4.8 (*FPG*, i, 24). For other quotations of Isa. 2.3 in Eusebius before 325, see *Proph. Eclg.*, 4.1, *Dem. Ev.*, 6.13.19, 6.18.50, 9.13.15; in none of these does he refer to the physical Mt. Sion.

[86] Ibid., 6.13.4, 9.14.6 (ii, 13, 181).

the event naturally of most significance for the Jerusalem Church. Whether or not this is the case, the most important factor for us to note is that this accolade was never affirmed by Eusebius after 325. It was an accolade briefly given and then swiftly withdrawn.

Eusebius' exposition of this verse in his commentary on Isaiah is especially interesting from this point of view. Mt. Sion's accolade has disappeared. Instead, in keeping with his statement later in the commentary (that of course Galilee was most truly the place where Jesus spent the majority of his time),[87] he emphasizes that Isaiah's reference at the beginning of this second chapter to 'Judah and Jerusalem' shows that this prophecy should not be understood in too narrow a sense: Christ's ministry, he reminds us, included not just Jerusalem but 'Judaea and Galilee' as well.[88] This broader perspective which emphasized Galilee at the expense of Mt. Sion, can now be seen to match exactly Eusebius' particular concerns as the metropolitan of Palestine after 325. The Jerusalem Church might be wishing to emphasize Mt. Sion but the bishop of Caesarea would continue to emphasize the whole of Palestine.

Yet there is a second, perhaps even more intriguing development in Eusebius' thinking which may be observed in this section of his commentary on Isaiah. He may have been seeking to emphasize the whole of Palestine, but when he needed to consider the meaning of 'Sion' in a more restricted sense (in relation to Jerusalem), he tried to redefine its meaning. Once again his purpose was to take attention away from the the narrow Mt. Sion of his own day. For though in general he was advocating a spiritual understanding of 'Sion' as the heavenly Jerusalem, he now suggests that it could refer to that 'earthly Sion in which occurred the Saviour's death and Resurrection'.[89]

This was a completely new interpretation, inspired almost certainly by the recent uncovering of Christ's tomb. As with 'Sion' on all previous occasions, its precise meaning in this instance cannot be pinned down in such a way as to exclude the possibility of a reference to Jerusalem as a whole. Yet Eusebius was clearly seeking to show that Christ's death and Resurrection had occurred on Mt. Sion in some more restricted sense. The church of the Holy Sepulchre was located due north of 'Mt. Sion' on some high ground which

---

[87] *Comm. in Is.* [9.1], 62.16–17.
[88] Ibid. [2.1–4], 15.25–6. Cf. above 5.1.
[89] Ibid. [2.1–4], 16.28–9.

could legitimately be seen as an extension of the same hill. As a result Eusebius was now able to offer a new understanding of 'Mt. Sion' that despite its novelty, was yet quite feasible. In the *Onomasticon*, when using 'Sion' in its original, more restricted, sense he had described Golgotha as 'to the north of Mt. Sion';[90] now, however, there was a sense in which Golgotha *was* Mt. Sion!

Suddenly the whole meaning of Mt. Sion had changed. No longer was Eusebius confining the term to refer to the southern end of that hill to the south of the Aelia / Jerusalem walls. Instead the newly discovered Holy Sepulchre, along the same ridge to the north but well within the city, had become the chief focus of Mt. Sion. Christ's death and Resurrection, not merely his teaching and life (διατριβάς καὶ διδασκαλείας)[91] were now clearly the most significant fulfilment of this Isaian prophecy; for this was the true source-point of the Gospel, the place where it had truly begun. Once again it is possible that this emphasis on the church of the Holy Sepulchre as the true moment when the Gospel began its spread across the world was a conscious correction of ideas prevalent in the Jerusalem Church, which emphasized that the spread of the Gospel had only begun with the descent of the Spirit at Pentecost. On such a reckoning Mt. Sion could easily be seen as the true fulfilment of this prophecy and indeed a place worthy of some centrality in Christian devotion. Eusebius denied this.

Be that as it may, it cannot be denied that Eusebius' thinking, here as elsewhere, shows a marked development after 325 and a definite move away from any emphasis on Mt. Sion in its normal, restricted sense. Indeed Mt. Sion as such disappears from Eusebius' map and from his writings after that date. Normally, when obliged to interpret a biblical reference to 'Sion' in a physical sense, he now chose to apply it to the Temple; here on this one occasion he applied it to the opposite hill on which stood the church of the Holy Sepulchre. Either way, the result was the same: the narrow, contemporary Mt. Sion was conveniently forgotten.

Not surprisingly the Jerusalem Church saw its task in quite a different light. Since Mt. Sion had been the 'centre' for Christians in Jerusalem in the difficult days before the coming of Constantine, it now played an integral part in their identity. As a result they naturally pressed for it to be given greater recognition and asserted (as they had for some time) that this important site had been integrally involved with New Testament events; indeed their church was to be identified with the location of Pentecost (perhaps too with the scene of Jesus' appearances to the apostles after the Resurrection)—an identification that naturally would not be without its consequences in the world of ecclesiastical politics.

Eusebius' response was one of historical scepticism blended with ecclesiastical concern. Any earlier interest in this Mt. Sion and in the historic Church of Jerusalem (its history and its preserved throne of St James) gave way to a policy of seemingly quite conscious silence. Both in his biblical exegesis and in his practical activity Eusebius' attention was increasingly focused elsewhere, on the desolation of the Jewish Temple or on the glories of the Christian Triad, itself focused on the church of the Holy Sepulchre.

Eusebius' attitude to Mt. Sion matches exactly those attitudes that have been uncovered in our study of the other places associated with the Incarnation. Eusebius was evidently a man who allowed his approach to these 'holy places' to be tempered by ecclesiastical and, especially, historical concerns. The Eusebius who as metropolitan was cool towards the Jerusalem Church's promotion of Mt. Sion was equally cool towards its promotion of the 'wood of the cross'. The Eusebius who as a historian was sceptical of the confident identification of the location of Pentecost had similar qualms concerning Mt. Tabor as the scene of the Transfiguration, the manger of the nativity, and even the rock of Golgotha. Inevitably this meant that even those sites which he *did* accept as probably authentic he yet assessed very much from a historical perspective. It would be hard for him in such circumstances to cultivate the warm devotional response of Cyril.

Yet there were also more *theological* factors that coloured his approach to these 'holy places'. For example, as a result of his theological emphasis on scripture, on the Bible as the written word of God and the need for its proper exegesis, his attention would often be focused on the question of prophecy and how such places fulfilled prophecies made either in the Old Testament or by Jesus himself. Then again, as a result of his theological emphasis on theophany, on Christ as the *Logos* of God and the need for our contemplation of his essentially spiritual nature, there was little emphasis on the Incarnation, little wonder at the mystery of how such physical places had been involved in this great event, and little idea of their great potential to help ordinary people in the life of faith. For these reasons too 'holy places', even if just occasionally named as such, could never have the same warm significance, the same religious potential, as they would have for Cyril and later pilgrims.

It will easily be recognized, as we turn to consider the other major question in the Palestine of their day, how these same factors again caused Eusebius to think quite differently from Cyril. History, ecclesiastical politics, and theology had all been influential factors in colouring Eusebius' attitude to 'holy places'. The same would be true of his attitude to Jerusalem as a 'holy city', only on this second issue the order of these influencing factors would be reversed.

III

THE CITY OF JERUSALEM

10

CYRIL'S ATTITUDE TO JERUSALEM

The church of the Holy Sepulchre and the church on Mt. Sion may together commemorate the inauguration of the Christian Gospel and of the worldwide Church, but they are also at the heart of a particular city. Ever since the time of David until our own, Jerusalem has exercised a unique function and held a special place within the affection and thought of faithful people, whether Jewish, Christian or Muslim. So far our study has deliberately focused on specific places. It is now time to address ourselves to the more major question that confronts every sensitive visitor to Jerusalem, and which has been constantly lurking not far from our attention in previous chapters: how are we to understand and evaluate the city of Jerusalem?

From our concern with individual 'holy places' we must turn to the question of the 'holy city', a question which our own contemporary events ensure cannot be of merely academic interest. The seemingly irreconcilable tension between Jewish and Muslim thought on the religious and political importance of Jerusalem only highlights the need for a sensitive, clear-sighted Christian approach which attempts to be abreast both of the current situation and of the varieties of Christian perspectives evidenced over the last two thousand years. Eusebius and Cyril bear ample witness to that variety. With regard to Jerusalem they stand almost, but not quite, at opposite ends of the spectrum, the one being largely negative and dismissive of Jerusalem's continuing significance, the other being overwhelmingly positive.

Eusebius, as will be demonstrated in our final chapter, exhibits the more negative approach, the predominant view of the Christian Church throughout the preceding three centuries. The Christians of this early period, naturally influenced by their initial separation from Judaism and then their continuing weakness in terms of imperial power, had come to see the physical Jerusalem as both theologically and practically irrelevant. Their need for a theology distinctive from the Jews caused them, first, to emphasize Jesus' opposition to Jerusalem, his rejection by its inhabitants and the evident divine judgement on the city and Temple in AD 70 and 135, and, to dismiss interest in Jerusalem as a characteristic of the Jews, not of the Christian Church. Christian identity was to be founded by contrast, not upon such a physical city, but upon the Living Christ and the future hope of the heavenly Jerusalem. Therefore, especially in his apologetical works against the Jews, Eusebius expressly linked the essence of Christian identity with an independence from the earthly Jerusalem. Jerusalem and its Temple had been eclipsed in importance by Christ, who was their typological fulfilment. The Old Testament, with its apparent teaching on the special nature of both Jerusalem and the Temple, could not therefore be read in a straightforward, monochrome manner, but instead needed very much to be read retrospectively, in the light of the coming of Christ and the calamity of AD 70.

For Eusebius these important events revealed two things. First, the Temple had indeed had a special and holy status in God's sight, but this was a temporary phenomenon that had now come to an end. Secondly, the Jews had been wrong to extend this special status to include the city as well; Jerusalem had never been a 'holy city'. For Eusebius, therefore, it was not just 'Jewish Jerusalem' that had been wrong; the problem went far deeper. It had been wrong to give Jerusalem a special status at all. The whole question of a 'holy city' was in and of itself wrong. Furthermore, with Jerusalem a now predominantly pagan city within a pagan empire, it was in any case quite impractical for Christians to foster any religious designs on the city of Jerusalem. The lessons of AD 70 were not easily forgotten.

With the coming of Constantine such views would need re-examination. For potentially the city of Jerusalem could now become a useful tool for the Christianization of the empire, its ideology and its institutions. The new imperial religion needed celebrations and symbols that would permeate the whole system with the new message. Jerusalem with its wealth of history and religious association was probably too potent a symbol for the Christian empire to ignore. Eusebius thus found himself in a dilemma. He was caught between his natural loyalty to the new emperor who was espousing the Christian cause and his equally natural commitment to his own life-long theological system. The emperor, and soon the Christian Church at large, were seemingly about to reintroduce notions that throughout his life Eusebius had dubbed as both Jewish and inherently misguided. The events of AD 325 therefore demanded a careful theological reappraisal of the whole issue.

The evidence to be adduced in our final chapter strongly suggests that it was his theology, not his need for political favour, which won the day. It will be shown that in the years after 325 Eusebius clearly gave this subject much attention and became increasingly clear on the issues at stake. Yet his ground shifts little: scripture still required this discerning Christ-centred exegesis, Christian identity still needed to be located not in Jerusalem but in the universal Church, and the concept of a present 'holy city' was evidently to be dismissed. Eusebius' integrity has often been doubted and he has been frequently cast as a maleable prelate in the hands of Constantine. On the question of Jerusalem, however, this now appears to be false. It was theological principle, not the imperial prince, that triumphed.

The new age was thus demanding a new theology. Cyril supplied it. As a young man, soon to become bishop of Jerusalem, Cyril was not labouring under the weight of a previous theology. Unlike Eusebius, he had no personal roots in the past which might prevent his moving briskly into radical, new patterns of thought. As a result he was free to offer a passionate, but considered, case for a positive Christian attitude to Jerusalem. The notions of judgement and rejection would be lifted from Jerusalem and be placed instead squarely upon the head of the Jews. Jerusalem would at last be set free from the stigma of divine judgement. Jewish Jerusalem might well have been judged in AD 70 for its treatment of Jesus, but the new Christian Jerusalem, which now 'worshipped Christ'[1] could rightly inherit with confidence the former biblical accolade of being a 'holy city' eternally special to God.

It will therefore be seen in the following that three factors were central to Cyril in his understanding of Jerusalem. First, although Christian Jerusalem was the legitimate inheritor of the best of biblical Jerusalem, it was to be thought of as quite distinct from Jewish Jerusalem: distinctiveness and continuity needed to be

---

[1] *Catech.*, 13.7.

carefully balanced. Secondly, it could rightly be designated 'holy', not only by virtue of its past associations but also because of its enduring specialness in God's sight; it had a continuing theological significance. Thirdly, it could claim a legitimate priority within the Church and indeed was the true centre of the entire world; Jerusalem had a primacy of place. Christian Jerusalem for Cyril was thus distinct, holy and pre-eminent.

Eusebius, by contrast, as has been suggested, would not view the city positively at all. For him Jerusalem was a place of judgement, no longer holy, and by no means pre-eminent. His response was strictly that of a historical and systematic theologian. Living in Caesarea he had the responsibility to contemplate these local phenomena within salvation history, but also the necessary distance for a more objective evaluation. His eventual elevation to the bishopric of that Church only strengthened this prior theological approach, for, as metropolitan of the whole province, he would have an extra, personal motivation for assessing Jerusalem in a more negative light. Yet the cause of that negative assessment really lay at a much deeper level, within a sincere and well-established framework of systematic theology. Cyril did not approach Jerusalem from a distance nor with an established theological system. He spoke and lived in its very centre and the fascination of a new Christian Jerusalem easily dictated his theology. The 'Jerusalem mystique'[2] was present and powerful, the potential of the city inviting, the presence of the pilgrims demanding and the possible increased status of the Jerusalem Church compelling. Cyril was himself convinced, and sought to instil within his catechumens a similar conviction, that indeed the 'prerogative of all good things was in Jerusalem'.[3]

Today three major world religions claim Jerusalem for their own, giving this city a special place within their life of faith. It is a situation always, but now especially, fraught with political consequences. With Cyril we mark the first explicit beginnings of this process in the second of those religions. It was the beginning of a process potent with future implications. It was also interestingly a process delayed within the history of Christianity for nearly three hundred years. For Christians, therefore, unlike Jews or Muslims,

---

[2] A phrase of Professor Chadwick: cf. (1960), 174.
[3] *Catech.*, 3.7 (*WCJ*, i, 112).

the issue of Jerusalem can never claim to be essential. Indeed Eusebius may have thought that such new thinking was itself a departure from, or at least a change within, the very essence of the Christianity which he knew. The issues were matters of great moment.

1. JERUSALEM, CONTINUOUS BUT DISTINCT

In all spheres of life the transfer of power is seldom a straightforward matter; with Jerusalem, any change in its ownership must inevitably verge on the dramatic. So important a city, such a precious jewel in the crown of any empire, is not easily yielded to another, nor do the new possessors find it simple to establish their rights over this ancient city. The new owners are inevitably confronted with a humbling and painful contrast: the novelty of their acquisition compared with the vast antiquity of that which they have acquired. In AD 325 the Christian Church found itself unwittingly the effective new possessor of Jerusalem. Unlike later 'takeovers' of the city, such as the Islamic conquest of the seventh century or the Israeli victory of recent years, on this occasion no show of force was required. In military terms it was the same Roman Empire in control. Yet, in religious terms, because of Constantine's conversion, Jerusalem now became Christian, not pagan. The civil administration of the city may have remained largely pagan and the Christian inhabitants still a minority, yet the Christian Church, as the local expression of the emperor's will, was effectively in control.

As Christians began to assume control they would, however, become acutely aware of this tension between novelty and antiquity. The city was new to them but by no means new in itself. Whilst rejoicing in the novelty of their new-found power, there would also be the desire to make Jerusalem's great history their own. Just as Muslims and Israelis in later years would assert that for religious reasons they were the now legitimate possessors of this ancient city, so too the Christians of the fourth century, conscious of this novel acquisition, desired to demonstrate their own long-established right to possess Jerusalem. Although only now for the first time were they in actual control of the city, they claimed to be its rightful occupants and indeed the true inheritors of the

Jerusalem symbol: Jerusalem had always, in a sense, belonged to them. It was a return to their original home, a *re*possession. In the ancient world, with its value of the past and ancient tradition, 'new things' were indeed 'often objected to because of the strangeness'.[4] In the midst of so much novelty there was thus a need for a proclaimed and visible continuity. The change in ownership was thus, they might claim, more apparent than real: Jerusalem had always really belonged to the Christian Church.

If continuity with regard to Jerusalem was important, so too was consistency within the Christian Church. For such interest in Jerusalem had until now, if anything, been an integral part of Judaism, not of Christianity. What was new for the Christian Church was in fact the well-established practice of the Jews—or at least, since AD 70, their much-cherished desire. With Christians now in control of Jerusalem one of the key elements of Christian self-definition over against Judaism was in danger of disappearing. Christians had formerly established their identity as those who, unlike the Jews, had little regard for the earthly Jerusalem. Now all of a sudden they were to emerge as its owners, and they could scarcely disregard it any longer. This new-found interest in Jerusalem, however, was an essentially alien factor within Christianity and brought them perilously close to the Jewish position which they had for so long vilified. Their claim for a historic right to be the possessors of Jerusalem, based on a continuity of interest in the city, was thus in itself a mark of some inconsistency.

Eusebius and Cyril were presumably both well aware of these developments, of the great novelty for the Christian Church in having religious control over Jerusalem, and of the proximity to Judaism which this engendered. How could the Church take on such a new phenomenon in a way that was consistent with the past? How could they distinguish their interest in Jerusalem from that shown by the Jews? Could Jerusalem be absorbed into the Christian bloodstream, or would it change something essential within the very nature of the Church? The responses of Cyril and Eusebius to these challenges would be.quite different. What was demanded was a delicate balance of continuity and distinction, of consistency and change; and it would appear that, with their

---

[4] Cyril's own words in *Catech.*, 10.11 (*WCJ*, i, 206). Eusebius similarly needed to demonstrate that Christianity was not really a new religion but dated back to the Patriarchs (in e.g., *Hist. Eccl.*, 1.4.1 ff.).

different understanding of these matters, the two of them sought their solutions in quite different ways.

Eusebius, with his expertise in the history of the pre-Constantinian Church, was clearly more likely than Cyril to be conscious of the need for consistency within the Church. Thus he would be anxious to show that the new Christian interest in Jerusalem was quite different and distinct from that of the Jews. Thus, for example, he saw the concept of a 'holy city' as an erroneous Jewish notion and gave Jerusalem instead a more universal and symbolic function.

Cyril, however, was happy to acknowledge that this Christian interest was very similar to that of the Jews; the Jews had recognized Jerusalem as a 'holy city' and so too now did the Church. The only difference was that the Jews had not received Christ. This alone was the mark of Christian self-definition; a spiritual attitude towards Jerusalem was no longer a necessary part of Christian identity. Thus Jewish aspirations for Jerusalem were wrong, in Cyril's understanding, not because it was wrong to give special significance to Jerusalem, but because it was wrong to be a non-Christian Jew. There could therefore be a legitimate Christian devotion to Jerusalem, however similar to that practised by the Jews, so long as it was practised by Christians.

Thus Cyril could state categorically: 'that Jerusalem crucified Christ, but that which now is worships him'.[5] Jewish Jerusalem was to be mourned because of its crime against Christ; a Christian Jerusalem was perfectly legitimate because Christians were those who worshipped Christ. Christians could thus do precisely as the Jews had done, in giving a special status to Jerusalem, and it would be quite justifiable purely because they were Christians; whatever Christians did was, in a sense, necessarily correct. Thus the concept of a 'holy city' could indeed be taken over by the Christian Church.

As a result, in stark contrast to Eusebius, Cyril never criticized the Jews for having had this concept of a 'holy city' and a prescribed interest in this one city, Jerusalem. Yes, like Eusebius, he compared the merits of Christian universalism with the limited, physical aspect of Judaism, but when he did so he spoke only of their narrow devotion to a 'certain land' ($\chi\acute{\omega}\rho\alpha\varsigma$ $\tau\iota\nu\acute{o}\varsigma$), not to the city of Jerusalem.[6]

---

[5] *Catech.*, 13.7.
[6] *Catech.*, 10.16; cf. also 18.25.

Meanwhile, his condemnation of the Jews was naturally never based on their devotion to Jerusalem, but instead almost always on their crime in crucifying Jesus.[7] In such references to the crucifixion he would never allow this one tragic episode in the otherwise glorious history of Jerusalem to deny the special nature of this city. God had indeed acted in judgement subsequently; but that judgement was expressed against the Temple, not against the city. 'The Temple of the Jews is fallen'[8] but the city of Jerusalem, formerly Jewish but now Christian, could certainly rise again.

In Cyril's understanding, therefore, Christian devotion to Jerusalem was essentially similar to its Jewish counterpart. Yes, as shall be seen, there were now extra Christian arguments which Cyril could muster for asserting the holiness of the city (such as the Incarnation and the Resurrection), but these arguments were seen as additional, not as replacements. They indeed provided the distinctive element, which differentiated Christian attitudes from those of the Jews, but underlying them there was a common core of devotion to this city, an unbroken and continuous recognition of its holiness, shared by both Jews and Christians. Moreover, if Cyril saw devotion to Jerusalem as a continuum, the same would be true of the city itself. The history of Jerusalem was a continuous entity and the Jerusalem of the fourth century no different from the Jerusalem of the biblical period. It was distinct from the Jewish Jerusalem inasmuch as some of its inhabitants now 'worshipped Christ', but otherwise it was essentially the same. Unlike Eusebius therefore, Cyril would not be at pains to emphasize the distinctive Christian approach to Jerusalem, nor would he draw attention to the novelty of this Christian interest in the city. His was an eye that was quick to see continuity and it was a perception that coloured his view both of Jerusalem's history and of the witness of scripture to Jerusalem. History and scripture were both perceived by Cyril in such a way as to emphasize the continuity of Jerusalem.

Yet in terms of history it was clear that the small Jerusalem of the fourth century was but a shadow of its former self. Eusebius, with his historical interests would have known just how calamitous had been the events of AD 70 in the history of Jerusalem. Jerusalem in his day (or Aelia Capitolina, as it was known officially) was

---

[7] For example, ibid., 13.7.
[8] Ibid., 10.11.

completely different from that spoken of in the Bible, and the contemporary Christian interest in the city was also something fundamentally new. It was no coincidence therefore that in his sole application of an Old Testament verse to a fourth-century entity (the church of the Holy Sepulchre), he emphasized that this was a *'new* Jerusalem';[9] the two Jerusalems were really quite different. Christian devotion had a different object, a new Jerusalem which was focused on the church of the Holy Sepulchre. Moreover, Christian interest in the city, so Eusebius might argue, was also quite different in its motivation from that of the Jews; for it was based on those unique events commemorated in that one basilica. As a result, Eusebius could more readily acknowledge that this devotion was a comparatively new phenomenon within the Church, for it was entirely consistent with the very origins and foundation of distinctive Christian belief in the Resurrection.

Cyril, however, stressed the underlying continuity and passed over the more violent and disruptive aspects of recent history. Thus, when it suited his exegesis, he hinted at the radical realignment of the city walls since Jesus' day (was the rock of Christ's tomb 'inside the ancient walls or inside the outer walls later constructed?'), yet he would do so in such a way as to suggest a city expanding peacefully for reasons of demography, not a city rebuilt from the ashes of war.[10] He would not refer explicitly to the dramatic changes of the previous three hundred years; he would not speak of the 'fall of Jerusalem', only of the destruction of the Jewish Temple;[11] and above all, unlike Eusebius, he would never call the city 'Aelia'. Instead, his eye for continuity singled out the many elements of biblical Jerusalem, such as the Mount of Olives, that still continued 'to this day' (μέχρι σήμερον).[12] Jerusalem was always Jerusalem; the history of Jerusalem was a continuum.

Moreover, as far as Cyril was concerned, Christian interest in Jerusalem was not essentially new; Jerusalem had always had a perennial attraction for pilgrims. Commenting on the crowds who witnessed the first Pentecost, Cyril claimed that 'the thronging of

---

[9] *V. Const.*, 3.33.
[10] *Catech.*, 14.9.
[11] Ibid., 10.11.
[12] Ibid., 14.23 (*WCJ*, ii, 47). For other references to this useful phrase, see above 8.1 at fn. 26.

multitudes of strangers from all parts is not something new in Jerusalem, but this was true in apostolic times.'[13] This very comment can only reflect his audience's assumption that Christian pilgrimage was indeed a recent and novel phenomenon. Yet Cyril sought to deny this novelty. Instead he implied that it had been a continuous phenomenon 'since apostolic times'. Christian interest in Jerusalem was not essentially novel.

Indeed, in this parallel between the Jewish pilgrimage to Jerusalem as recounted in Acts and that of Christians in the fourth century, Cyril reveals quite clearly his refusal to distinguish Jewish interest in Jerusalem from that shown by Christians. As argued above, Christian interest in Jerusalem was for Cyril no different from that of the Jews, except inasmuch as it was Christian. Jerusalem and its history were a continuity; so too was its religious significance.

However, this statement of Cyril's concerning the continuous nature of pilgrimage to Jerusalem had a further advantage: it showed the biblical support for pilgrimage. Citing a biblical precedent in any age is the ideal method for showing the real antiquity of an apparently novel phenomenon; for it also gives that activity a divine approval. Cyril thus had every incentive for restudying the text of scripture in order to find passages that endorsed the new interest of Christians in Jerusalem and legitimated their control over the city. In order to do this he would need to assert the continuity of the physical Jerusalem and its significance throughout scripture and beyond, and to suggest that references in both the Old and New Testaments could legitimately be taken as referring to the now Christian Jerusalem of the fourth century. Continuity was thus to be traced not just in recent history, but further back within the pages of scripture itself.

In so doing Cyril would naturally begin to apply to the earthly city of Jerusalem several texts which Christians had traditionally applied instead to the heavenly Jerusalem or to God's purposes in the worldwide Church. Assuming that the physical Jerusalem was no longer of any continuing significance, earlier Christian expositors had tended to spiritualize any reference to 'Jerusalem' within the biblical text. Cyril now sought to reintroduce the possiblity in exegesis of a reference to the physical Jerusalem. He was thus

<hr>

[13] Ibid., 17.16.

making a radical break with all previous Christian theology—
including, of course, that of Eusebius. A comparison of their quite
different interpretations of several biblical texts, which refer to
Jerusalem, will reveal quite clearly the radical new direction of
Cyril's thinking.

Eusebius had indeed been a champion of this traditional, spiritual
exegesis, and continued to be such until the very end of his days.
Only on that one occasion, when writing about the Holy Sepulchre,
had he ventured a more physical interpretation of some passages
in Isaiah which referred to a 'new Jerusalem'.[14] Yet this interpretation was very tentative and certainly most uncharacteristic.
Instead he had continued to employ the traditional methods of
interpretation throughout his very latest commentaries (Isaiah and
Psalms). Despite the temptation to forge a new interpretation in
the light of the new Christian possession of Jerusalem, Eusebius'
exegesis had remained resolutely the same. Scripture needed to
be read carefully and the spiritual reference of 'Jerusalem'
continuously kept to the fore.

Of all the scriptural verses which would meet with quite diverse
interpretations as a result of these two different approaches to
scripture, probably the most important would be St Matthew's
references to the 'holy city' (4.5, 27.53). As will be demonstrated
shortly, Cyril in contrast to Eusebius now had no reason to apply
these verses to anything other than his own Jerusalem.

Of less significance, but still of great interest, however, are the
following verses which Cyril relates specifically to fourth-century
Jerusalem, in contrast to Eusebius' more conventional usage:

(i) 'Cry out at the top of your voice, Jerusalem, herald of good
news' (Isa. 40.9). Cyril applied this to Peter standing in Jerusalem
on the day of Pentecost.[15]

By contrast, Eusebius had discussed this verse at least three
times but he had never particularized it in this way. In the *Proof
of the Gospel* he had quoted it as a prophecy of the preaching
done 'through the apostles' but offered no further explanation. He
only promised that his readers would 'know in what sense this is
to be taken when we have reached a further point on the road of
Gospel teaching'.[16] Clearly he was opposed to any easy, physical

[14] *V. Const.*, 3.33.
[15] *Catech.*, 17.21.
[16] *Dem. Ev.*, 3.1.5–6 (*FPG*, i, 103).

interpretation but the issue was not currently so important as to demand an immediate explanation. Later, in his commentary on Isaiah, this verse reminded him of 'the evangelists' and of the 'apostolic and evangelical chorus'.[17] Yet no particular occasion and certainly no particular apostle was in his mind. He was thinking of the Gospel being preached to the whole world.

Naturally this had been coupled with a non-physical understanding of Jerusalem. Eusebius pointed out quite unequivocally that 'Jerusalem' here refers not to a place but to a 'living community of people' (ἔμψυχον καὶ ζῶσαν); and, on this occasion, this expressly did *not* mean the inhabitants of the named physical city but rather the community on the 'heavenly Mt. Sion'.[18] Eusebius' exposition was perhaps slightly tortuous but the overriding message was clear. Cyril's meaning was equally clear but quite different.

(ii) 'Rejoice with Jerusalem, all you who love her' (Isa. 66.10). Cyril reworked this to refer to Jerusalem's joy in the Resurrection: 'Rejoice, O Jerusalem, and hold festival together, all you who love Jesus, for he is risen'.[19]

Eusebius, by contrast, in his *Commentary on Isaiah* had again quite naturally applied this verse to the 'new Jerusalem' which is constituted not of lifeless stones but of 'holy people'.[20]

Cyril would no doubt have accepted that 'Jerusalem' on such occasions was not to be understood merely of the physical city; he would have agreed with Eusebius' perhaps rather obvious insistence that the term was a 'personal' and communal one. Yet the 'community' to which he applied it was his own baptismal congregation in Jerusalem and he clearly desired these candidates to recognize the privilege of being in that selfsame physical city. Cyril's exegesis may well have been just 'imaginative',[21] but it could also have reflected a sincere belief that these verses could legitimately be applied to, and were prophetic of, his own fourth-century Jerusalem.

He is probably playing on the same ambiguity when he quotes the following scriptures in his final lecture, all of which he applies

[17] *Comm. in Is.* [58.1], 357.11, *idem* [40.9], 252.14, 19–20.
[18] Heb. 12.22 in *Comm. in Is.* [40.1], 247.19–23.
[19] *Catech.*, 14.1.
[20] *Comm. in Is.* [66.10], 403.30, cf. 404.10.
[21] Compare, e.g., Newman's opinion in (1842), p. xxi, that Cyril's use of scripture showed evident 'fancifulness and caprice'.

to 'this Jerusalem' and his catechumens shortly to be enlightened by baptism.[22]

(iii) 'Be enlightened, be enlightened, O New Jerusalem! Your light has come' (Isa. 60.1).

Commenting on this passage in the Isaiah commentary Eusebius had offered three possible expositions. 'Jerusalem' could refer to the Jews of the first century: in which case this invitation to be 'enlightened' was not heeded. Secondly, it could refer to the 'godly polity' ($\theta\epsilon o\sigma\epsilon\beta\grave{\epsilon}s$ $\pi o\lambda\acute{\iota}\tau\epsilon\upsilon\mu a$) of faithful people, formerly located in Israel but now found in the Church. Finally, moving in thought towards the Second Coming, it could be a reference to the 'New Jerusalem'.[23] This was the normal range of Eusebian possibilities, but he was unclear which to chose. His uncertainty contrasts markedly with Cyril's straightforward love of this 'fine passage', which he found such an apt encouragement for his candidates in Jerusalem.

(iv) 'After that you will be called city of justice, faithful city, Sion' (Isa. 1.26–7); 'for from Sion shall go forth instruction and the Word of the Lord from Jerusalem' (Isa. 2.3). Cyril used the latter (a verse taken to foretell the beginning of the Gospel message from Jerusalem) to justify his application of the favourable titles in the former passage to Christians in fourth-century Jerusalem.

In expounding the former passage Eusebius, by contrast, had denied that the physical Jerusalem had ever been worthy of these titles; this verse was instead a prophecy which was only to be fulfilled in the worldwide Church ($\theta\epsilon o\sigma\epsilon\beta\grave{\epsilon}s$ $\pi o\lambda\acute{\iota}\tau\epsilon\upsilon\mu a$), founded upon the apostles and the faithful succession of bishops.[24] Certainly the fact that the Gospel had begun from Jerusalem (or indeed from Palestine, as he stressed in his later years) had never induced him to use such glorious terms.

The verses of the second passage Eusebius needed to interpret in a highly spiritual way in order to draw a contrast with Jewish exegesis which, he supposed, would show great interest in the 'mountain of the Lord's house' (the physical Temple).[25] Hence, although, like Cyril, he saw the last clause of Isaiah 2.3 ('the Word of the Lord shall go forth from Jerusalem') as prophesying the

---

[22] *Catech.*, 18.34.
[23] *Comm. in Is.* [60.1], 368.27 and 369.24; 369.16–20; 370.10.
[24] *Comm. in Is.* [1.26], 12.23–8.
[25] See esp. *Comm. in Is.* [11.8–9], 85.5; cf. *idem* [2.1–4], 16.12.

universal spread of the Gospel, this had never been the occasion
to show any Christian interest in the physical Jerusalem.[26]

(v) 'I will rejoice in Jerusalem and exult in my people' (Isa.
65.18); 'Sion is scarcely in labour when she gives birth to her
children' (Isa. 66.8). Cyril used these verses to speak of God's
great delight in the baptismal candidates in Jerusalem.

The context in Isaiah for the former verse, with its reference to
the 'new earth', had naturally caused Eusebius instead to expound
this verse in heavenly and eschatological terms, describing God's
joy in His people in heaven and the pure worship of the 'New
Jerusalem'.[27] Meanwhile, the second verse Eusebius had naturally
applied to the almost instantaneous spread of the Church to 'most
of the inhabited world', which to him was deservedly a cause of
great wonder.[28]

To be sure, with several of these verses Cyril was merely playing
on the ambiguity of the word 'Jerusalem'. He was following the
traditional Christian interpretation, as represented by Eusebius,
which interpreted this concept in more 'personal' terms; yet, not
unnaturally, he also sought to show their even more poignant
fulfilment in his own catechumens who were shortly to be baptized
into the new Christian community in Jerusalem. However, in a
couple of instances he was relating an Old Testament verse specifically
to the physical Jerusalem in the first and fourth centuries AD.
St Peter in Jerusalem and now Cyril's catechumens actually fulfilled
the intention of Old Testament prophecy. This reveals a more
serious conviction. Jerusalem in scripture and in history was
evidently for Cyril a simple continuity. References to Jerusalem
written at an earlier time could therefore be applied automatically
to Jerusalem at a later date.

Canonical scripture was thus a potential 'gold-mine' of texts that
could be lifted from their original contexts and applied with great
advantage to the physical Jerusalem. Belief in the continuity of the
reference of 'Jerusalem' encouraged this way of expounding
scripture; scripture, thus expounded, then confirmed the continuity
of Jerusalem's special significance. It was a neat circular argument:
conviction coloured exegesis and exegesis then endorsed conviction.

---

[26] See *Dem. Ev.*, 1.4.8 (*FPG*, i, 24) and *Comm. in Is.* [2.1–4], 7.11–12; cf. also
Proph. Eclg., 4.1.
[27] *Comm. in Is.* [65.18], 397.16–17.
[28] Ibid. [66.8], 403.6–9.

As a result, Cyril could infer that God in his eternal purposes had a consistent and unchanging love for the unique city of Jerusalem. Texts which conveyed a positive picture of Jerusalem could rightly be appropriated by Christians, whilst the more negative ones could be omitted or applied exclusively to the Jews.

Thus Cyril asserted the continuity of Jerusalem in both history and scripture. As a result, he was able quite easily to introduce into the Christian Church the new concept of Jerusalem's special status. For, from his perspective, it was not new. It was the same God and the same city. The temporary aberration in Jerusalem's history, which had culminated in the crucifixion of God's Son outside the city wall, had been satisfactorily punished in the desolation of the Temple and was not to be allowed to disturb the underlying special status which God had given to Jerusalem. The Church for three hundred years had grown accustomed to a non-Christian Jerusalem. Now was the time to state anew the abiding significance of Jerusalem for Christians, and indeed for God himself.

2. HOLY JERUSALEM

With this understanding of scripture Cyril would then naturally have had little doubt about Jerusalem's special status: three times in his lectures he expressly referred to it as a 'holy city'.[29] His attitude to Jerusalem may indeed have coloured his interpretation of scripture; nevertheless that scripture, if taken quite straightforwardly, seemed manifestly to encourage Cyril's high estimate of Jerusalem. The text of scripture endorsed the holiness of the city. For not only, as just noted, had the Old Testament spoken on occasions so positively of Jerusalem but in the New Testament Jerusalem was twice spoken of as the 'holy city' by St Matthew.[30] Eusebius had attempted to spiritualize the meaning of these verses: the 'holy city' was 'clearly the heavenly one' (δηλαδὴ τὴν ἐπουράνιον).[31] Cyril's reply was quite emphatic: on the contrary, St Matthew was speaking quite clearly (δῆλον) of 'this city in which

[29] *Catech.*, 14.16, 17.22 and 17.31.
[30] Esp. Matt. 27.53; cf. *idem*, 4.5.
[31] *Comm. in Ps.* [87.11–13], 1064b.

we are now'.[32] It would not be the last time that two theologians would be able to claim scriptural support for their contradictory opinions. Cyril's straightforward approach, which saw the text in a more 'linear' fashion, led him to the affirmation of Jerusalem. Eusebius, however, equally committed to the authority of scripture but perhaps more aware of the need to balance its different teachings and more sensitive to the working of God's hand behind and beyond scripture, had come to a more negative conclusion.

If the text of scripture was a necessary first prerequisite for his affirmation of Jerusalem, Cyril could next appeal with some justification to all the major events within the New Testament that had occurred in Jerusalem. The *text* of scripture endorsed the holiness of Jerusalem; so too could the *events* of scripture. Although the New Testament writers themselves had not explicitly drawn this conclusion, surely the location within Jerusalem of the Incarnation, the Redemption, the Ascension and Pentecost (not to mention the Last Supper and the beginnings of the Church) conferred on that city, if it did not already reflect, a special status within God's sight? Surely the occurrence of these unique events within Jerusalem could be used as a valid additional argument to that based exclusively on the text of scripture alone?

This precise argument, it must be admitted, is not used by Cyril explicitly. Yet it would seem quite legitimate to infer that it did indeed feature in his thinking. For he used an exactly parallel form of argumentation on each of those three occasions when it was his concern to assert Jerusalem's special pre-eminence ($\dot{\alpha}\xi\acute{\iota}\omega\mu\alpha$).[33] Why was Jerusalem pre-eminent? Cyril asserted that it was because of the great events located in and around Jerusalem: the Incarnation, John's baptism and Pentecost. That practical pre-eminence, however, was itself a consequence of this more fundamental theological principle of Jerusalem as a 'holy city'. If Jerusalem's prestige in the present was bolstered by these major New Testament events, so too was its inherent and eternal holiness.

Eusebius predictably accepted neither this underlying concept of the 'holy city', nor the assumption that these major events increased the status of Jerusalem. Hence it will be useful to establish briefly from Cyril's own words those arguments that he would have used to present his alternative position.

---

[32] *Catech.*, 14.16.

[33] Ibid., 16.4, 3.7 and 17.13, all of which are discussed more fully below (10.3).

Cyril's contention that Jerusalem was a 'holy city' could be founded securely on the fact that it had been within God's eternal purpose to allow at least five major events of salvation history to occur within the immediate vicinity of this one city. First, Jerusalem was the city of the Incarnation itself: 'it was here that Christ descended from heaven; it was here that the Holy Spirit descended from heaven.'[34] Bethlehem's proximity meant that Cyril could speak without explanation of Christ's descending 'here' (ἐνταῦθα) in the same way as he spoke of the Spirit's descending 'here' (ἐνταῦθα) on Mt. Sion. His language of 'descent' was clearly influenced by his context, describing the descent of the Spirit at Pentecost; yet it also might well indicate, as we have suggested, that the condescending act of the Incarnation was in itself a more important theological event for Cyril than it was for Eusebius. For Eusebius Bethlehem had been in historical terms the place of Christ's *genesis*, while in more theological terms he considered it the place for the *theophaneia* of the *Logos*. For Cyril, however, it was the place where God himself had come down into the human realm in Christ. Moreover, this act of the Incarnation, which had begun in the Jerusalem area, was of course to be integrally involved with the city of Jerusalem throughout its course. This greater emphasis on the Incarnation in Cyril would thus naturally have its more practical consequences: Jerusalem, as indeed the whole Holy Land, would gain a greatly increased significance. Cyril had a heightened theology of the Incarnation and he purposely allowed that theology to heighten his valuation of Jerusalem; Eusebius, however, would question the legitimacy of both the theology and its consequences.

Secondly, this had been the scene of the Redemption. Cyril proceeds in this same passage to state that furthermore it was 'here' (ἐνταῦθα) that Jesus had been crucified.[35] Again our introductory examination of Cyril's thought revealed how his heightened theology of the Incarnation was matched by his heightened theology of Redemption. Cyril consistently gave to the Cross and Resurrection a greater theological weight than did Eusebius. He saw them as essentially salvific, effective for salvation and not merely revelatory, and he gave a special prominence to the Cross. Once again this theology would have its local consequences.

[34] Ibid., 16.4.
[35] Ibid.

At this point, however, there was a potential problem: when seen in more historical terms, the crucifixion, a cruel death engineered by the religious and political leaders within the city, was hardly to Jerusalem's credit. If Cyril wished to use the Cross and Resurrection as an argument in his case for Jerusalem's holiness, he needed to play down these negative aspects of the crucifixion, either through emphasizing the Resurrection at the expense of the Cross or through portraying the glory of the Cross. It is strong evidence for Cyril's wish to do precisely this that, as already noted, he consistently depicts the Cross in such glorious terms: the Cross is the 'glory of glories' of the worldwide Church; 'the Cross is a crown, not a dishonour'.[36] Cyril's desire to use the Cross and Resurrection as a means of increasing the glory of Jerusalem thus contributed to his promotion of the Cross in similarly glorious terms. The shame and the ignominy of the crucifixion were subsumed by the greater sense of the glory of the Cross.

Accidents of geography also played into Cyril's hand. Although these great events had occurred outside the Jerusalem of Jesus' day, their location was now appropriately in the very heart of the expanded city. Thus, whereas the former Jewish Jerusalem could be judged for its criminal part in the crucifixion which had occurred outside its gates, the Christian Jerusalem could be affirmed by the wonder and the glory of the Cross, which had occurred within its very centre. Convenient developments in both geography and theology could thus cause a paradoxical transformation: the city of the crucifixion could retain, and indeed increase, its right to be deemed the 'holy city'.

Next, of course, Jerusalem had been the privileged venue both for the Ascension and for Pentecost: 'he began in Bethlehem his struggles for men but here (ἐνταῦθα) on Olivet he was crowned for them'.[37] 'Here (ἐνταῦθα) the Spirit descended from heaven'.[38]

The list, however, is still not complete; for, as shall be seen shortly, Cyril could also claim that Jerusalem had been integrally

---

[36] Catech., 13.1, 22; full references above in 8.2 at fn. 67 ff. The alternative response would have been that employed by many Christians today, namely to emphasize the Resurrection at the expense of the cross and to give to Jerusalem the status of the 'city of the Resurrection'. It is interesting that Cyril's commitment to the centrality of the cross in theology and of Golgotha in Jerusalem prevented him from pursuing this attractive but perhaps ultimately misleading line of thought.

[37] Ibid., 14.23.

[38] Ibid., 16.4; cf. 17.13 ff. and 16.26.

involved with the institution of both dominical sacraments: 'all Jerusalem' had gone down to the Jordan for baptism and it was in Jerusalem on Mt. Sion that the 'mysteries of the New Covenant' had had their beginning.[39] For all these reasons Cyril might naturally assert that Jerusalem was undeniably unique in the Christian world.

Yet it was also more than that. For the Christian these great events were not historical accidents; they were undergirded by God's eternal will. These unique events were not matters of chance; they played an integral part in God's eternal purpose. Could not the same then be said of their unique location? Did not Jerusalem itself play an integral part in God's eternal purpose? As a result, could it not legitimately be called the 'holy city'? Surely, to call Jerusalem a 'holy city' was a convenient and legitimate way for Christians to affirm that this city had a special status in the sight of God?

The holiness of a city, however, is not an easy quality to define. It should not therefore surprise us if Cyril did not offer his own precise definition. It is one thing to talk of a 'holy city', it is quite another to enunciate exactly what that means in strict theological terms. Moreover, it may well have suited Cyril's purposes to leave the term deliberately unexplained. The 'holiness' of a city is a peculiarly religious term which somewhat loses its magnetic quality when scrutinized closely under the scientific microscope. Its power lies in its allusive suggestiveness. Nevertheless, Cyril's frequent use of the term and his whole concentration on the mesmeric power of Jerusalem in his own day strongly suggests that he had more in mind than a mere holiness of association, a holiness ascribed as a memorial to the past acts of God. What then did Cyril mean in his use of the term 'holy city'?

A 'holy city' for Cyril was not just a place in which God had occasionally been involved in the past: it was a place with a special quality in the present. Yet, at the other extreme, Cyril would probably have hesitated to state that God was in some sense especially present in the Jerusalem of the fourth century—in a fashion similar to that seemingly advocated for the city by some writers of the Old Testament.[40] The worldwide Church's experience

---

[39] Ibid., 3.7 and 18.33.
[40] See the royal Sion theology in, e.g., Pss. 46, 48.

of the risen Christ through his Spirit would not easily admit such
a concept, which once again confined the presence of God to a
prescribed and limited area. In between these two positions,
however, there was perhaps some room for the notion, outlined
above, that Jerusalem continued to have a special part to play
within God's purposes. Evidence for this position comes not just
from our foregoing analysis but also from Cyril's evident belief,
shown in his references to the Temple, that the appearance of the
Antichrist and the Lord's Second Coming would both occur in
Jerusalem, a view needless to say with which Eusebius would have
totally disagreed:

the Antichrist will come when in the Temple of the Jews not a stone
upon a stone will be left. For when the decay of time, or demolition with
a view to rebuilding, or other causes have overthrown all the stones both
of the outer circuit and the inner shrine, the Antichrist will appear . . .[41]

To Cyril's way of thinking, the Lord had clearly not finished with
Jerusalem. God's particular interest in this city was not a passing
phase confined to the biblical era before AD 70. It continued very
much into the present. As such it was a 'holy city'.

3. PRE-EMINENCE IN THE FOURTH CENTURY

From this inherent theological status that continued into the
present there then flowed, for Cyril, certain important practical
consequences. Such a city, if once 'holy' in God's consistent
purposes, necessarily had an elevated status which endured to the
present day. Theological priority should lead naturally to practical
pre-eminence. Holiness in the sight of God should lead at least to
a position of honour ($\dot{a}\xi\acute{\iota}\omega\mu a$) in the sight of men. It was this
logical corollary that Cyril was eager, as already noted, to impress
upon his audience and upon the wider world. Jerusalem was
pre-eminent and in many different ways.

(a) *In the life of faith*

As a pilgrim-pastor Cyril shows throughout his *Lectures* the unique
value which Jerusalem might have for the believer. As the scene

[41] *Catech.*, 15.15.

of the Incarnation and the other great events of the New Testament, Jerusalem could offer to the believer a veritable host of 'witnesses' to Christ, without parallel in the rest of the world. On three occasions Cyril gives an extended list of such 'witnesses':[42] some were people within the Bible, some generic species,[43] but the vast majority were physical places or objects to be seen only in Jerusalem. The value for the Christian of being in the very places where Christ had been himself permeates throughout every aspect of Cyril's thinking. He was well 'aware of the inspiration of the sacred sites and the privilege of his own church in possessing them'; thus 'again and again he pointedly refers to this unique circumstance of church life in Jerusalem.'[44]

Cyril alerted his catechumens to their privileged location in several ways. First, he reminded them that 'others merely hear but we see and touch'.[45] Christians in the rest of the world could only hear of the Gospel events; but Christians in Jerusalem could see, and even touch, the places where these events had occurred. Cyril indeed acknowledged in one passage that the privilege of being in Jerusalem in the fourth century was not as great as that of Thomas, who had been there only eight days after the first Easter; for Jesus himself was now absent and Thomas had had the last 'empirical' proof of the Resurrection. Thomas wanted to touch Jesus, something that Cyril says his catechumens 'who were not present would have sought', if only they could.[46] Nevertheless that very example of Thomas made respectable the natural desire of the Jerusalem Christians in Cyril's own day to see and to touch. 'It was for our sake that he touched so carefully'.[47] Thomas set a useful apostolic precedent; he was, in a sense, the 'proto-pilgrim', the 'patron saint' of pilgrims, who understood and validated the pilgrim's need for physical sight and touch. Three centuries later, in the absence of the human Christ, Cyril argued that only Jerusalem could begin to meet that need. Christ was no longer present but Jerusalem could offer some unique tangible and visible items that could bolster a Christian's faith in his absent Lord.

[42] Ibid., 10.19, 13.38–9, 14.22–3.
[43] For example, all 'rivers' potentially witness to Christ because of Christ's baptism in the Jordan (10.19).
[44] Dix (1945), 350.
[45] *Catech.*, 13.22.
[46] Ibid., 13.39.
[47] Loc. cit.

It is a measure of Cyril's deep concern to promote the cause of Jerusalem and to justify the development of pilgrimage that the lesson that he derived from this Thomas episode is most probably the exact reverse of that which the evangelist had originally intended in his portrayal of this unusual episode. For a careful reading of John's Gospel would suggest that Thomas, once presented with the risen Lord, did *not* in fact carry out his intended empirical test. Contrary to Cyril's teaching he did not 'touch so carefully'. Instead, sight rendered touch unnecessary. Moreover, in a paradoxical way, Jesus' apparent invitation to touch his wounds was quite probably a mild rebuke of Thomas' desire to touch.

Cyril naturally had good reason not to note this implied critique of touch as well as to miss the subtlety of St John's whole purpose in this passage. That purpose was to teach that the unique apostolic phase, when truly 'seeing was believing', had come to an end with the apostles. Hereafter there was instead a blessing precisely for those who would believe without this need for sight: 'Blessed are they who have not seen and yet have believed' (John 20.20). Cyril's situation in fourth-century Jerusalem, with his personal desire to assert the pre-eminence of Jerusalem and the pastoral need to sate the rising tide of pilgrims' desires, effectively caused him to turn upside down the central meaning of this passage. Thomas was not, as St John had implied, to be the last to 'see and touch' but the first of many. Thomas was to endorse the pre-eminence of Jerusalem in the life of faith.

A second way in which Cyril attempted to assert the value of Jerusalem for Christian believers was by using the phrase 'among us' ($\pi\alpha\rho$' $\dot{\eta}\mu\hat{\iota}\nu$). With this phrase past Gospel events could be portrayed by Cyril in such a way that Christians privileged to be now in Jerusalem could consider that they had themselves been present. Although Pentecost had occurred three hundred years previously, there was a sense in which it had occurred $\pi\alpha\rho$' $\dot{\eta}\mu\hat{\iota}\nu$, among those in fourth-century Jerusalem: 'The Spirit himself came down amongst us'.[48] Through this device Cyril could make the immovable 'boundaries of time' momentarily collapse.[49] His audience's privileged proximity, in place if not in time, could be

[48] *Catech.*, 16.26; cf. 12.16: 'the same Lord who ate with Abraham ate also amongst us'.

[49] The phrase of Strange and Meyers (1981), 171, quoted fully above in ch. 2 at fn. 11.

felt in terms of personal intimacy. The Gospel events had occurred here 'among us'.

Indeed, when referring to Pentecost once again, Cyril spoke brazenly 'not of the blessings of others but of those granted to us' (παρ' ἡμῖν).[50] This reference to 'those blessings granted to us' might reflect yet another argument that Cyril was tempted to use when stressing the great benefits for the Christian of being in Jerusalem: if God had chosen Jerusalem to be the scene of such blessings in the past, would not the same God be disposed to grant similar blessings in that same city now? The special blessings of the past 'among us' spilled over into the present. Jerusalem had been, and still was, the place of God's blessing.

Thirdly, Cyril drew an implicit contrast between his privileged audience and the poor Montanists. These 'charismatic' heretics of the late second century had 'seized upon Pepuza, a tiny village in Phrygia, and falsely named it Jerusalem'.[51] He does not condemn them for their understandable desire to be in the physical Jerusalem; he merely ridicules them for their unfortunate but desperate selection of such a 'tiny village' as Pepuza. It was a natural desire, one with which Cyril would have been most sympathetic, but it had only led them to absurdity; for Cyril and his audience were in the only true Jerusalem. Here alone could the desire to be in Jerusalem be satisfied; here alone could that desire lead not to futility but to increased faith.

Cyril thus emphasized again and again that the Gospel events had occurred 'here', 'in this Jerusalem',[52] the very one 'in which we are now'.[53] 'Here' (ἐνταῦθα) had occurred the Ascension,[54] the Incarnation, and Pentecost;[55] this was the place of the former Temple[56] and the location of the apostolic council.[57] Indeed he was speaking in the very location of the crucifixion[58] and in sight of the very rock of Golgotha.[59]

[50] Ibid., 17.13.
[51] Ibid., 16.8.
[52] Ibid., 17.13, 17.22, and 17.31.
[53] Ibid., 14.16.
[54] Ibid., 14.23.
[55] Ibid., 16.4.
[56] Ibid., 7.6; cf. 4.34.
[57] Ibid., 17.29.
[58] Ibid., 1.1, 5.10, 13.22, and 16.4.
[59] See esp. ibid., 13.22; cf. also 4.10, 10.19, and 13.3.

Cyril thus betrayed an acute consciousness of being able himself to speak in this privileged location and he consistently sought to instil this sense of privilege into his audience. His catechumens had a proximity to Christ—in place, if not in time—that was not shared by others. Jerusalem could be a great aid to their faith, indeed a source of blessing. Cyril was not asserting that presence in Jerusalem was 'necessary for salvation' but he was stressing its enormous benefits. Christians were not dependent as such on Jerusalem but the city could offer them something unique in their walk of faith. Here they could live not just 'by faith', but also 'by sight' (cf. 2 Cor. 5.7). That made Jerusalem different from anywhere else; it was pre-eminent in the life of faith.

(b) In the Church

Jerusalem's special role was not, however, to be felt only by individual believers but also in the corporate life of the Church. Its pre-eminent status was to be experienced, not only in the personal realm, but also in matters ecclesiastical. As already noted, the bishops assembled at Nicaea in 325 had sought in their seventh canon to give due recognition or 'honour' (τιμήν) to the bishop of Jerusalem, while being anxious to preserve the 'peculiar honour' or distinctive pre-eminence (τὸν οἰκεῖον ἀξίωμα) of the Caesarean metropolitan.[60] Just over twenty years later Cyril was now asserting instead the ἀξίωμα of Jerusalem. Moreover, on each of the three occasions when he did so, it was no coincidence that he based his argument upon a Gospel event which was integrally related to the future life of the Church. Jerusalem's ἀξίωμα, Cyril claimed, derives from her involvement in the institution of baptism and from the occurrence of Pentecost 'here in this city of Jerusalem'.[61] The city that had thus witnessed both the institution of the sacraments and the very foundation of the Church could surely not be denied an appropriate place of honour in the contemporary Church.

This connection between Jerusalem and the sacraments of the Church was quite deliberate, a most effective ploy for asserting the pre-eminence of Jerusalem in the life of the Church. Not

---

[60] Council of Nicaea, Canon 7; cf. *NE*, p. 360.
[61] Ibid., 3.7, 16.4, 17.13.

surprisingly the Eucharist is not often mentioned by Cyril in the *Catechetical Lectures*, for he was speaking to an audience as yet unbaptized. However, at the very end of his lectures he gives his catechumens a foretaste of this sacrament, and naturally reminds them of the fact it originated 'from here' (ἐντεῦθεν).[62] It was not to be missed that the first Eucharist had occurred in Jerusalem.

With baptism, however, the connection needed to be established somewhat more subtly. How could the first baptism in the Jordan be linked exclusively to Jerusalem? How could this act of confession redound to the greater honour of Jerusalem? Cyril's answer, as seen in his third lecture, was to play down the theme of confession as found in the Gospels, whilst omitting any reference to people being baptized other than those from Jerusalem. 'All Jerusalem' was baptized but no mention was made of the inhabitants of Judaea and the Jordan region (Mark 1.5; Matt. 3.5), and of course John's fierce attack on the religious leaders of Jerusalem (Matt. 3.7) was conveniently omitted. Thus Cyril could paint a nice, eirenic picture. 'There went out to him [John the Baptist] all Jerusalem to have the benefit of the first fruits of Baptism; for the prerogative [ἀξίωμα] of all good things is in Jerusalem.'[63] The confession of Jerusalem's citizens was thus converted from a rather uncomplimentary fact into an indication of Jerusalem's ἀξίωμα in 'all good things', both past and present. John's action did not indicate to Cyril any opposition to the city, but rather led to its affirmation. Thus John's baptism of sinners in the Jordan became paradoxically the glory of Jerusalem in the Judaean hills.

Once again, it may be noted, Cyril's perspective from Jerusalem caused him to see a Gospel event in quite a different way from Eusebius. In the *Proof of the Gospel* Eusebius suggests that a deep opposition to Jerusalem was integral to John's message and activity.[64] John's baptism for Eusebius effectively challenged and replaced Jerusalem as the place of supposed forgiveness and healing. '[God] has transferred the glory of Jerusalem to the desert of Jordan, since, from the time of John, the ritual of holiness began to be performed not at Jerusalem but in the desert . . . that they who needed the healing of their souls no longer hastened to Jerusalem but to that which was called the wilderness, because

---

[62] Ibid., 18.33.
[63] *Catech.*, 3.7.
[64] See esp. *Dem. Ev.*, 9.5–6 (*FPG*, ii, 161–5); *Proph. Eclg.*, 4.17–18.

there the forgiveness of sins was preached.'[65] Moreover, Eusebius' primary use of St Matthew's version, which attacked the prospective candidates as a 'brood of vipers', clearly indicated that the whole incident redounded not to Jerusalem's glory but, if anything, to its shame.[66] Eusebius later expounded the meaning of John's baptism in even more detail in his *Commentary on Isaiah*. Here again he underlines John's opposition to Jewish Jerusalem and with increased emphasis. John deliberately announced his baptism of repentance in the desert rather than in Jerusalem since this would signify the redundancy of Mosaic worship in Jerusalem and the emergence of true worship in the Gentile Church, the former 'desert'.[67] Since he was writing this after 325, the emphasis on John's opposition to Jerusalem might even have been Eusebius' way of opposing the emerging Christian Jerusalem. This much, however, is certain. Eusebius could never have claimed, as did Cyril, that John's baptism contributed to the pre-eminence of Jerusalem.

It was not only Jerusalem's involvement with the sacraments, however, which could bolster Cyril's case for its pre-eminence in the Church: Jerusalem was also the city of Pentecost, when the Spirit had been outpoured on the infant Church. Jerusalem was the 'first home' of the Church.

The ecclesiastical potential of such ideas was naturally enormous, a point evidently not lost on either Cyril or Eusebius. Thus, as was observed in our discussion of Mt. Sion, anxiety over the advancement of the Jerusalem Church perfectly explains why Eusebius' references to Pentecost and Mt. Sion are so scanty, indeed almost non-existent. By contrast, Cyril's desire for the Church's advancement led him to emphasize both Mt. Sion and Pentecost. His emphasis on Mt. Sion (with his references to the Last Supper and the Thomas episode)[68] was indeed coloured by some quite local considerations, but his emphasis on Pentecost clearly had an 'international' purpose. Mt. Sion as a place was indeed important for the pilgrims within Jerusalem; but Pentecost as an event was vital for Jerusalem within the worldwide Church.

---

[65] *Dem. Ev.*, 9.6.8 (*FPG*, ii, 164–5); cf. 9.5.8 (ii, 162).

[66] Matt. 3.7 in ibid., 9.5.3 (ii, 161). Only after this, in *idem*, 9.6.4 (ii, 164), did he quote the verse which Cyril seems to have preferred, 'there went out to him all the people of Jerusalem' (Mark 1.5); interestingly this verse is omitted in his later *Comm. in Is.* [40].

[67] *Comm. in Is.* [35.1–2], 227.4–228.14, [40.1–9], 249.11–17, and 250.11–251.3.

[68] *Catech.*, 18.33; see also 13.39, and 14.22.

Thus on this issue the contrast between the two bishops was marked. Indeed Eusebius' reticence concerning Pentecost may only have served to precipitate in later years Cyril's forceful response, for it is perhaps no accident that, of the three occasions when Cyril asserts the pre-eminence of Jerusalem in the present, two of these are linked to the prestigious occurence of Pentecost within the city. It is his teaching concerning the descent of the Holy Spirit at Pentecost that prompts him then to claim for Jerusalem the 'pre-eminence in all things'.[69] It his discussion of Acts 2 that draws forth his strong explanation, 'for this honour [ἀξίωμα] also is ours'.[70] The use of 'also' (καί) in this second passage could indeed be read as a rebuttal to those who shared the narrow focus of Eusebius and sought to limit Jerusalem's significance to a Triad of events in the life of Christ. Any attempts to limit Jerusalem's honours were not to be tolerated. Jerusalem had them 'all' (πάντων): Jerusalem was not only the scene of Christ's Incarnation, but also of the Spirit's descent and first beginnings of the Church.

Given his catechetical context and perhaps an appropriate portion of tactfulness, Cyril did not go on as yet to make explicit the further corollary, that the Jerusalem Church was in some sense the 'mother-church'. By the end of his life the worldwide Church would accept this as an appropriate title for the Church of Jerusalem.[71] For now, however, that lay in the future, a goal to be realized. Nevertheless, the necessary steps towards that goal were already being taken. The foundation of the worldwide Church in Jerusalem was not to be forgotten.

Cyril enhanced his argument for the pre-eminence of Jerusalem in the contemporary Church in three further ways. First, the 'diocese' of Jerusalem had none other than the Lord's own brother as its first bishop. The risen Lord had appeared to James, the 'first bishop of this diocese' (παροικία ταύτῃ).[72] Unfortunately the meaning of Cyril's subsequent sentence is unclear, with some textual uncertainty over the word πρωτοτύπος.[73] Cyril may just

---

[69] Ibid., 16.4.

[70] Ibid., 17.13.

[71] See the canons of Constantinople in 382 (according to Theodt., *Hist. Eccl.*, 5.9.17).

[72] *Catech.*, 14.21.

[73] See W. C. Reischl and J. Rupp, eds, *Sancti Cyrilli Opera*, ii (Munich, 1860), 136, fn. 11, where the preferred reading is the adverb πρωτοτύπως.

have been stressing James' fame;[74] but he may possibly have also been suggesting that James was the 'prototype' of all other bishops, the first that the worldwide Church had ever had.

Secondly, Cyril could use the narrative of the book of Acts to illustrate how Jerusalem had been the place of apostolic power and authority. Twice he interrupted his quotation of Luke's wording in order to draw attention to Jerusalem. Jesus told his disciples to wait for the promised power 'in the city'; Cyril specified that it was the city 'of Jerusalem'.[75] Luke spoke of crowds coming to the apostles from the neighbouring towns; Cyril added the words, 'to this holy Jerusalem'.[76] Jerusalem was clearly the place of the Spirit's power. Meanwhile the apostolic authority exercised in Jerusalem was seen clearly in the apostolic council of Acts 15: from 'here in Jerusalem' the apostles had issued a letter which 'freed the whole world'.[77] Jerusalem had also been the seat of apostolic authority.

Thirdly, Jerusalem was for Cyril the source-point of the Gospel. Jesus had begun his 'conquest of the world' from the moment of his Resurrection in this 'holy city'.[78] Paul had preached the Gospel 'from Jerusalem to Illyricum',[79] and most importantly this was where, in accordance with Isaiah's prophecy, 'the word of the Lord' had 'gone forth' to the world.[80]

This aspect of 'evangelical origin', as noted above, had been the only Gospel truth that Eusebius was prepared to use in order to draw contemporary attention to the physical region of Palestine. Unlike Cyril, he had not used the Incarnation and the Redemption to increase the status of contemporary Palestine, nor the foundation of the Church in Jerusalem at Pentecost, but Palestine might legitimately be termed the 'source' of the Gospel. Here at last then the two bishops might appear in some agreement: for who could deny that the Gospel had first been preached in Jerusalem?

Yet even here an intriguing difference can be discerned. For, as we have seen, in both his Constantinian speeches of 335/6 Eusebius had used the imagery of a 'spring' to describe the 'source' of the

---

[74] Hence the translation in *WCJ*, ii, 46.
[75] Luke 24.49 in *Catech.*, 16.9.
[76] Acts 5.16 in *Catech.*, 17.22.
[77] Ibid., 17.29.
[78] Ibid., 14.16.
[79] Rom. 15.19 in *Catech.*, 17.26.
[80] Isa. 2.3 in *Catech.*, 18.34.

Gospel. Yet in both he had clearly identified this source with Palestine as a whole, not with Jerusalem. In the former speech *On Christ's Sepulchre*, originally delivered in the Holy Sepulchre, he necessarily had to mention the city of Jerusalem. Yet he carefully reminded his audience first, with some local pride, that Palestine was his own homeland; only then did he refer to the city, and then not by name. 'But as for the thank-offerings dedicated to your God and Saviour in our personal hearth, I mean the province of Palestine, and in this city here, whence just as from a fount the saving *Logos* gushed forth for all men. . . .'[81] Thus, although 'whence' (ἔνθεν) indeed refers to the 'city' of Jerusalem, it also refers to 'Palestine' as a whole which was mentioned first. Eusebius betrayed an interesting order of priorities: himself, then Palestine, then Jerusalem!

When delivering his speech *In Praise of Constantine* the following summer in Constantinople, Eusebius could emphasize Palestine all the more. His situation was slightly different; he no longer needed to mention his own involvement in the locality and his own vested interests, nor did he need to mention the city at all. Instead he could state explicitly what was probably to have been inferred from *On Christ's Sepulchre*, 11: it was 'the Palestinian nation' which was 'that place' from which 'as from a fount gushed forth the life-bearing stream to all'.[82] No mention was made of Jerusalem. Instead it was Palestine as a whole that had been the source for the life-giving stream. On this issue Eusebius was indeed subtle; but his purposes were quite plain.

In the light of these repeated remarks made by Eusebius, it is intriguing to return to Cyril's references to the origins of the Gospel. 'The Word of the Lord shall go forth from Jerusalem'; from here it 'poured out upon the whole world'.[83] Cyril used almost exactly the same metaphor as had Eusebius (ἐξώμβρησεν compared with ἀνώμβρησεν) but now he applied it instead to Jerusalem alone. It was this city, not Palestine, that was the focal-point of God's purposes and the very source of the Gospel. In this way Eusebius' imagery was adopted, but his precise intention was neatly flouted; his methods were appropriated but his purposes opposed.

[81] *Sep. Chr.*, 11.2 (*DPC*, 103).
[82] *L. Const.*, 9.15 (*DPC*, 101).
[83] *Catech.*, 18.34.

Cyril's case for the ecclesiastical pre-eminence of Jerusalem was thus a carefully established construction, resting on certain sure, foundational arguments. This city alone was the place in which the sacraments had been instituted, the Church founded and the Gospel first proclaimed: here the Church had known its first bishop and experienced the new power and the liberating authority of the risen Christ. The implications for the Church at large were to be given a proper respect.

(c) In the 'Holy Land'

The message was equally plain within the 'Holy Land' itself: Caesarea needed to respect Jerusalem. For this more local contention Cyril had two further means of building his case. First, in referring to Caesarea, he could stress that of the two cities it was Jerusalem which was the 'holy city'. Secondly, on some occasions when discussing Gospel events that had not taken place in Jerusalem he could still show their integral connection with the city. Jerusalem thus had a central role within the Christian 'Holy Land'.

Cyril only refers to Caesarea twice, when following through the narrative of Acts in Lecture 17.[84] The two references come not far apart and it is in the second of these that Cyril makes his contention plain.

Cyril was relating the story (found in Acts 21 ff.) of St Paul's determination to go up to Jerusalem despite foreboding prophecies, and of his almost immediate expulsion and imprisonment in Caesarea. Although the unholy reception that St Paul received on his arrival in Jerusalem might have made this not the ideal moment for Cyril to assert the city's holiness, he did precisely that. 'Paul hastened to this holy city, Jerusalem' and then was taken before the 'judges' benches' at Caesarea.[85] The different function and status of the two cities thus became apparent: in the first century and in the fourth Caesarea may have been the political, administrative and legal centre but Jerusalem, both then and now, was the religious centre, the 'holy city'. The challenge to the metropolitan was reasonably obvious.

[84] *Catech.*, 17.27, 31.
[85] Ibid., 17.31.

Secondly, Cyril was concerned to connect his Jerusalem with Gospel events which had strictly occurred in other parts of the 'Holy Land'. This is seen most clearly in his third lecture when discussing John's baptism. Despite the original location of this event at least fifteen miles away across the Judaean desert, Cyril could claim, as was noted above, that contemporary Jerusalem had been integrally involved. 'All Jerusalem' had been baptized, thus proving that the city had the 'prerogative' or 'pre-eminence' (ἀξίωμα) 'in all good things'.⁸⁶ Yet there was a converse side to this. Although in the first century 'all Jerusalem' had indeed gone forth for baptism in the River Jordan, now, Cyril could assert, it was perhaps even more fitting to remain in Jerusalem because baptism was a baptism into Christ's Death and Resurrection.⁸⁷ What a privilege therefore for Cyril's catechumens to be baptized in the very building that now commemorated that salvific event! Their 'burial in water' repeated symbolically Christ's burial in the nearby 'rock' (πέτρα).⁸⁸ There was thus an even more fitting place for baptism than the Jordan, namely the place of Christ's death in Jerusalem. Moreover to be baptized in Jerusalem, according to Cyril, neatly fulfilled an Old Testament prophecy. Zephaniah's statement, 'Take heart, O Jerusalem, the Lord will take away your iniquities' was applied by Cyril to his catechumens' forthcoming baptism.⁸⁹ Of all possible locations for baptism, Jerusalem was therefore easily the most appropriate. Jerusalem offered it all.⁹⁰

A further connection between Jerusalem and other parts of the 'Holy Land' may perhaps be discerned in this same lecture. According to Cyril, the 'Master himself', in undergoing his temptation only *after* his baptism, had 'observed order and due season'; Cyril then urges his catechumens similarly not to 'disregard right order'.⁹¹ Was he drawing a parallel between Jesus' forty days in the wilderness after his baptism and the forty days of Easter after

⁸⁶ Ibid., 3.7.
⁸⁷ Rom. 6.3, used by Cyril in *Catech.*, 3.12.
⁸⁸ Ibid.
⁸⁹ Zeph. 3.14–15 in *Catech.*, 3.16.
⁹⁰ Interestingly, being baptized in the Jordan seems to have been one of the few activities of which Eusebius shows manifest approval in the *Onom*: 'several of the brethren . . . are honoured to receive their baptism in the Jordan' (Bethabara: 58.19). Quite possibly, in those days of the late third century, some baptismal candidates at Caesarea had opted to travel to the Jordan for this special occasion. Jerusalem, however, now claimed that she was yet more fitting.
⁹¹ *Catech.*, 3.14.

the catechumens' baptism on Easter Saturday? It is not clear. Nevertheless, though this was a season of great celebration in the liturgical year,[92] it is just possible that Cyril may have sensed an appropriate connection between these two periods of 'forty days' mentioned in the New Testament. These first forty days after baptism were after all a vital period for new Christians, just as the temptation had been a vitally important episode at the beginning of Jesus' ministry. In so saying, Cyril was in a way bringing another Gospel event into Jerusalem: the temptation in the desert became the first days after baptism in Jerusalem. The roads of sacred time and sacred place met in Jerusalem.

Then again, Cyril was also able to demonstrate the connection between Jerusalem and Galilee. For example, in his one reference to the Transfiguration on Mt. Tabor he was careful to quote Luke's account with its unique reference to Jerusalem: 'Moses and Elijah . . . appeared in glory and spoke of his departure, which he was to accomplish in Jerusalem'.[93] Luke's greater interest in Jesus' approach to Jerusalem from Galilee could thus be used by Cyril with advantage to show how the events in Jerusalem influenced even those days of the Galilean ministry. Not surprisingly, therefore, he later found an opportunity to quote Luke's famous verse on this theme: Jesus steadfastly 'set his face to go to Jerusalem'.[94] However, Jesus' determined approach to Jerusalem was for Cyril by no means an indication of that city's impending judgement. Hence Cyril made no reference to those more negative verses in Luke that described the ironical necessity of Jesus' death in Jerusalem ('for it cannot be that a prophet should perish away from Jerusalem. O Jerusalem, Jerusalem, killing the prophets and stoning those sent to you': 13.33–4) and Jesus' weeping over the city (19.41–4). Instead the Cross was portrayed by Cyril as Christ's most glorious work: it was the 'glory of Christ' and therefore naturally redounded to the glory of Jerusalem.[95] As a result, Galilee became in Cyril's understanding not so much a focus of opposition to Jerusalem but an outpost of its glory.

Moreover, Cyril was keen to show that, if Galilee had indeed

[92] As seen in, e.g., *Egeria*, 39.1 ff.; cf. also the last canon of Nicaea (reproduced in *NE*, p. 364).
[93] Luke 9.31 in *Catech.*, 12.16. See above 5.2(*b*).
[94] Luke 9.51 in *Catech.*, 13.6.
[95] *Catech.*, 13.1, 22; as suggested above in 10.2.

been the scene of important miracles, so too had Jerusalem. Thus in his one list of Jesus' miracles he ensured that the credits were equally distributed: two of the miracles he cited (the feeding of the five thousand and the releasing of the woman 'bound by Satan for eighteen years') had been located in Galilee, the other two (the healing of the blind man at Siloam and the raising of Lazarus) in the Jerusalem area (at Siloam and Bethany).[96] Similarly, if the events of Jesus' Galilean ministry revealed Christ's two-fold nature, so too did the raising of Lazarus and Jesus' own death in Jerusalem.[97] Jerusalem was rarely to be outshone.[98]

For the same reason Bethany, the Mount of Olives and Bethlehem were normally seen as integral parts of that great entity which was 'Jerusalem'. Egeria might need to explain to her absent readers that Bethany was 'about two miles from the city' but the local archdeacon in her day had spoken more simply and inclusively: 'let us all be ready at the Lazarium'.[99] Bethany was evidently considered an integral part of the Jerusalem liturgy. If Bethany was included within the city of Jerusalem, the Mount of Olives was yet more so: Christ's Ascension, Cyril claimed straightforwardly, had occurred 'here' ($\dot{\epsilon}\nu\tau\alpha\hat{\upsilon}\theta\alpha$) in Jerusalem.[100] In the same passage Cyril had temporarily needed, with his contrast between the beginning and the end of Christ's struggles, to speak of Bethlehem more distantly: Christ began his struggles 'from there' ($\dot{\epsilon}\kappa\epsilon\hat{\imath}\theta\epsilon\nu$). However, in another context Cyril eagerly showed that Christ's 'descent' in the Incarnation had also occurred 'here' ($\dot{\epsilon}\nu\tau\alpha\hat{\upsilon}\theta\alpha$) in Jerusalem.[101] These sites of major Gospel events were all part of Jerusalem's great heritage. The major events of salvation had all occurred in Cyril's Jerusalem.

A temporary distinction in geography between Jerusalem, Bethlehem, and the Mount of Olives respectively occurs in Cyril's imaginative discussion with the prophets Habakkuk and Zechariah, when he asked them for clear statement about Jesus' birth and the triumphal entry. The prophets replied that the Lord would come from the south (in his birth) and spoke of his triumphal entry

[96] Ibid., 13.1.
[97] Ibid., 4.9.
[98] Not coincidentally, Cyril's discussion of Jesus' calming the sea in 14.17 comes immediately after Cyril's open statement of Jerusalem's holiness (in 14.16).
[99] *Egeria*, 29.3; cf. 25.11.
[100] *Catech.*, 14.23.
[101] Ibid., 16.4.

into Jerusalem from the Mount of Olives.[102] However, these questions also reveal the centrality of Jerusalem within Cyril's thinking. Eusebius' exegesis of both the relevant verses had been quite different[103] and, in the former instance, unduly complex.[104] Cyril now unlocked those complexities with an attractively simple solution. All suddenly made sense if one interpreted these scriptures (as perhaps the authors themselves had written them) from the perspective of Jerusalem.

Jerusalem was thus the key to scripture. It was also the unrivalled centre within the 'Holy Land'. Jerusalem had played her part in all the events of Christ's life, whether in Galilee or the desert, on Mt. Tabor or by the Jordan. She it was who gave the true meaning both to the text and to the land, and not vice versa; she was the centre around which they had to revolve.[105]

(d) In the world

Cyril's vision of Jerusalem's pre-eminence extended, however, beyond the boundaries of Palestine. His eyes were fixed on the world. Thus, as already noted, the rock of Golgotha within Jerusalem was for him the 'very centre of the world'.[106] Previously, Christians such as Eusebius might have sensed that the universal spread of the Gospel had led necessarily to the eclipsed importance of that Gospel's source: the 'going forth' of the message only left

---

[102] *Catech.*, 12.20; 12.10–11.

[103] Hab. 3.3, and Zech. 14.4; for a discussion of the latter see above 7.1(*a*) and 7.2(*b*).

[104] Eusebius had only discussed Hab. 3.2–3 once, in *Dem. Ev.*, 6.15 (*FPG*, ii, 21–2). In the context of the argument, he was looking for prophecies of Christ's first coming. In this attempt he stated that 'Theman' was to be translated as συντέλεια ('consummation'): this was a prophecy of the Incarnation, which had occurred in 'these last days'. He clearly wanted to relate this verse to the Incarnation, but the result was somewhat forced. He therefore proceeded to offer a completely new interpretation, applying v. 3 instead to the Second Coming. He now conceded, without any hint of self-contradiction, that 'Theman' really meant 'south'. Meanwhile the 'shady mountains' refer to Eden or 'even the heavenly Jerusalem'. Despite his current desire for it to be otherwise, he thus agreed that this verse was more likely to be related to the Second Coming than to the first. However, he noticeably avoided any suggestion that 'south' might refer to Bethlehem to the south of Jerusalem.

[105] In *WCJ*, i, 115, the editors depict Jerusalem, in its relation to Caesarea before 325, as a 'second sun' rather than a 'satellite'; whatever the truth of this, Caesarea was now clearly to be the 'satellite' and Jerusalem the 'sun'.

[106] *Catech.*, 13.28.

the centre deserted.[107] That necessity for Cyril no longer pertained. Jerusalem, the centre from which the Gospel had first gone forth, had truly been restored.

Such notions of Jerusalem's centrality only increased its attraction for Christian pilgrims. Not surprisingly they were already in Cyril's day beginnning to come from the world over (παντοχόθεν).[108] But what for those who were less fortunate, who were separated perforce from this, their new but original centre? If they could not come to the centre, could the centre in any sense come to them?

A recent miraculous discovery, coupled with the generosity of the Jerusalem Church, ensured that it could. By the time he spoke in 348, Cyril could state confidently that the wood of the 'true cross' had been successfully distributed throughout almost the entire inhabited world; it had been 'given away' to the 'faithful' so that with it they might 'fill the whole world'.[109] This relic was the perfect way of establishing contact between the Church at home and the Church abroad, and could remind the latter of its rediscovered 'spiritual centre'. It could also bring absent Christians some proximity to Christ himself. The greater proximity, however, remained in Jerusalem. The 'wood of the cross' thus gave a tantalizing taste of the benefits that only Jerusalem enjoyed continuously. It was a gift that in no way weakened the giver; it only reminded the recipient of the donor's wealth and thereby increased the donor's prestige.

Thus Jerusalem could once again act as a source of the Christian message to the wider world. In Cyril's first list of 'witnesses'[110] the apostles were indeed named for their preaching; but Cyril commented first on the more recent dispersion of the 'true cross'. Once again the ripples of the Gospel went out to the expectant world. In the first century the apostles had carried the message of the Cross; in the fourth century pilgrims now carried its remains. This time, however, Jerusalem, the source in the centre, would not be replaced. Jerusalem remained pre-eminent.

Cyril's opinions were thus already forceful and programmatic. Within a decade of Eusebius' death, an aspiring bishop in the

---

[107] See, e.g., *Proph. Eclg.*, 4.1.
[108] *Catech.*, 17.16.
[109] Ibid., 4.10, 10.19 and 13.4.
[110] Ibid., 10.19.

Church at Jerusalem was asserting the pre-eminence of Jerusalem in every department of the Christian life—personal, local, ecclesiastical, and even global. Undergirding this argument for Jerusalem's primacy in practical matters lay an already well-established theological conviction: that Jerusalem was legitimately a 'holy city', and in some sense special to God. If the Jews had abused the concept of 'Jerusalem' this deeper truth was not affected; and even if Christians had only recently been able to express that truth in practice, Jerusalem had always been 'holy'. Any divine judgement rested on the Jews alone, symbolized in their destroyed Temple, and did not affect the city itself at all.

Christian Jerusalem was thus in some senses quite a distinct entity from the Jerusalem of the Jews. In other ways, however, it was for Cyril but a continuation. The Christian city could legitimately draw on the best elements in Jerusalem's long history as revealed in scripture. It could rightly claim always to have been a 'holy city' in God's sight; as a result, it could claim in the present a similar pre-eminence to that which it had enjoyed by divine right in the past. For Cyril, therefore, the case for Jerusalem's holiness and pre-eminence was reasonably straightforward. For Eusebius the matter was more complex.

11

EUSEBIUS' ATTITUDE TO
JERUSALEM

At long last we have reached the point in our enquiry when we can ask Eusebius himself for his thoughts about Jerusalem. As a Christian who had lived all his life in Palestine and not far from Jerusalem, how did he view that physical city situated in the central hills? Its history, both within the pages of scripture and subsequently, was evidently a source of great interest for him; but how did he view that city theologically? In what way had God been involved with this city in the past? If the Temple had been acknowledged by Jesus as truly his 'Father's house' (John 2.16), had a similarly special status been extended to the city as well? Had it ever been, in Eusebius' understanding, the 'city of God' or a 'holy city'? If it had, did such titles still pertain to this day, or had the new covenant superseded such aspects of the old, revealing the deeper, eternal will of God?

Such questions, which with their complexity pose a serious challenge to the Christian in any age who believes in the genuine involvement of a living God in this world, his self-consistency and his authorative revelation, were questions that could not be avoided by a historical and systematic theologian such as Eusebius who lived on the coast not sixty miles from the city. The events of 325 only brought them more urgently to the fore. How did Eusebius wrestle with these problems and what were his provisional conclusions at the very end of his life?

From the summaries of Eusebius' thinking that have already been provided, our conclusion will perhaps already be surmised. Eusebius had deep theological reasons, as well as more obviously personal ones, for denying (or at least minimizing) the significance of Jerusalem in the present. These convictions were well established before 325 and they would continue comparatively unchanged after that historic date. Before 325 Eusebius had consistently chided the Jews, both in his apologetics and in his exegesis, for their attachment to physical Jerusalem and had linked Christian identity instead to the spiritual realm; under the new covenant the *Logos* of God now beckoned us to leave such physical entities as the Temple or the city of Jerusalem and to contemplate instead the heavenly Jerusalem.[1] This spiritual emphasis had only been confirmed by the events of AD 70 and 135; God thereby revealed the redundancy of the physical Jerusalem. Jerusalem's exalted status was clearly a phenomenon of the past, not least because the primary function of this city had been simply to point forwards to the coming of Christ and the foundation of the universal Church. The great events of the New Testament fulfilled its typological function. The physical Jerusalem therefore had no continuing significance.

On this issue Eusebius the historian and Eusebius the theologian could clash violently. Just as today those who question the supposed religious significance of Jerusalem in the present often find themselves nevertheless intrigued by the magnetic quality of a city so steeped in meaning from the past, so too Eusebius, though no doubt attracted towards this enticing city with its unique religious history, would have wished at the same time to keep a discerning distance, being unwilling to give the city an allegiance beyond that which his theology permitted. In this way Eusebius could experience simultaneously a historian's fascination in the physical city and yet a theologian's desire to transcend that physical entity. Our question is this: did Eusebius retain this conviction, which asserted the need for such transcendence, or did he begin to soften his strict theological stance as a result of the great external changes of 325?

The contrasts which we have already noted between Eusebius and Cyril on this question of Jerusalem, when now combined with a close examination of his final writings, will indicate that Eusebius' theological convictions altered little. For example, since the Incarnation and the Redemption were not as important in his thinking as they were for Cyril, it has been observed how he did not begin to use these theological concepts as a' new justification for the holiness of the physical Jerusalem; of the New Testament events it would only be the outward movement of the Gospel message

---

[1] Cf. Gal. 4.26 and Heb. 12.22.

away from its 'source' that attracted his attention. As a result he could emphasize that the whole of Palestine, and not just Jerusalem, had been involved in the events of the Gospel and its spreading to the rest of the world. On one occasion he would indeed use the phrase, the 'New Jerusalem', but we noted how he applied it only in a narrow sense to the buildings around Christ's tomb, not to the city as a whole.[2] Thus the places of Christ might indeed gain a new significance as a result of Christian retrospective evaluation, but the significance of Jerusalem itself, as will be seen, was truly a thing of the past.

1. EUSEBIUS' REASONS

What, though, were his reasons? Why did Eusebius come to these predominantly negative conclusions? Before analysing his writings in some detail it will be valuable to have an overview of Eusebius' reasoning and of those key factors which influenced his approach to the subject of Jerusalem. There would seem to be at least four such major considerations.

First, there was the contentious matter of local church politics. If Eusebius' attitudes to Mt. Sion, to the Triad, and to the Jerusalem Church itself were all coloured by the ecclesiastical tension between Caesarea and Jerusalem, the same would inevitably be true of his theological attitude towards Jerusalem. His more negative approach was indeed grounded in a sincere adherence to his systematic theology, but he was bound to be influenced as well by his delicate role as metropolitan. Eusebius must have been acutely aware after 325 of the great anomaly in having Jerusalem under his jurisdiction as the bishop of Caesarea. There were good historical reasons for this, which he would no doubt ardently defend, but they led to a state of affairs that a Christian empire would soon wish to reverse. Thus, paradoxically and painfully, the very advent of a Christian empire, for which Eusebius had been hoping and which he so eagerly defended, was also the sure sign of the decline of his own bishopric. If Cyril's position in Jerusalem encouraged him to elevate the status of Jerusalem in theological and practical terms, then it was inevitable that Eusebius' position in Caesarea would have an

[2] *V. Const.*, 3.33.

equal and opposite effect. The rapid rise of the Jerusalem Church
in ecclesiastical status, that would reach its climax under Bishop
Juvenal in the following century, was naturally not something that
the aging metropolitan could be expected to relish.

Moreover, the little disguised aspirations of the Jerusalem Church
may have provided Eusebius with the perfect contemporary
example of how people in any age could abuse the concept of
'Jerusalem'. The city had a powerful function as a theological
symbol, deriving from the 'Sion theology' of the Old Testament
with its understanding of Jerusalem as a sign of God's presence.
Yet this vast potential for good could be corrupted to serve a great
evil: *corruptio optimorum pessima*. For by the time of Christ,
Eusebius might conclude, this symbol, which should have spoken
of God's dwelling among his people, had evidently become instead
a vehicle of opposition to God. Jerusalem of all places should have
welcomed God's new presence as revealed in the incarnate Christ;
but instead it was Jerusalem that rejected the Son of God and cast
him out to die. No wonder, for Eusebius, that God had now
destroyed the symbolic function of Jerusalem once and for all. Yet
were not now the Christians in Jerusalem, with all their enthusiasm,
running the risk of reintroducing what God had annulled? Would
they be able truly to harness such a symbol, or would they find
themselves in some sense controlled by it? An alert theologian
such as Eusebius, who did not have personal reasons for swiftly
adopting a wholehearted affirmation of Jerusalem, might find
plenty of grounds for severe anxieties and misgivings. Once again,
even though this time it was the Church in Jerusalem that would
be responsible, the religious power of Jerusalem was in danger of
being exploited, for political and personal gain.

However, this local tension between the sees of Caesarea and
Jerusalem, even though here mentioned first, must not be deemed
the sole or primary explanation for Eusebius' negative stance. His
thinking was too deep to be merely the result of petty politics. To
be sure, he had a personal motive for his opposition to Jerusalem,
but this was then undergirded and preceded by deep-seated
theological convictions. What were those convictions which checked
his enthusiasm for the physical Jerusalem?

A second major factor then, which probably influenced his
thinking far more than local Church politics, was his · great
experience in apologetics, the defence of the truth of Christianity

over against both paganism and Judaism. Although it was the *Preparation for the Gospel* and the *Proof of the Gospel* that most clearly illustrated Eusebius' great ability as an apologist, that apologetic outlook did not stop there; it spilt over into his exegetical works, especially the commentaries on Isaiah and the Psalms which were published at the very end of his life. Eusebius was an apologist to the end of his days.

In these two works, we may note how, for example, Eusebius needed frequently to explain the meaning of 'Jerusalem', as well as 'Sion' and 'Judaea'. These physical entities, referred to in the Old Testament, had to be given a distinctive, spiritual interpretation which contrasted with the supposedly physical interpretation of the Jews. In so doing he naturally came to speak of the 'true Sion', the 'true Judaea', and the 'true Jerusalem'.[3] These terms established an explicit contrast between the true, spiritual reference of these names and the false physical interpretation favoured by the Jews. It suited his apologetic arguments thus to draw a sharp distinction between Jewish and Christian attitudes to these entities; the Jews he caricatured as being exclusively concerned for these physical places, whilst Christians were idealized as being concerned only for the spiritual reality towards which those entities pointed.

It was not totally impossible for such emphases to be retained with the growth of Christian interest in the physical Jerusalem. Nevertheless there was something of an inconsistency here in the Christian position. In the past Christian exegesis had sought to transcend the earthly Jerusalem, but now Christians were reverting to an interest in this physical city. Moreover, Eusebius had frequently made this potential dilemma more acute by heightening the contrast between Judaism and Christianity in a surprising local way. He expressly ridiculed the Jews' interest in his own contemporary 'Palestine'. In introducing this contemporary name for the former land of the Bible, Eusebius was forced, in order to ridicule the Jews' misplaced spiritual desire, to caricature any such spiritual interest in Palestine. The true meaning and reference of

---

[3] See, e.g., *Comm. in Is.* [49.14–16], 313.32–314.24; *Comm. in Ps.* [64.2–3], 624c; cf. also *Dem. Ev.*, 4.12.4 (*FPG*, i, 186) and 4.17.15 (*FPG*, i, 219). The 'true Jerusalem', although a term not used in the New Testament, had clearly by Eusebius' day become an exegetical shorthand for the contrast between a Christian and Jewish interpretation: see, e.g., Origen, *Comm. in Jo.* [4.20], 13.13, 238.8; [4.46], 13.58, 288.29.

these biblical terms was not to be found 'here below or in the land of the Palestinians' but in the heavenly realm.[4] Furthermore he strengthened his case by appealing to the idolatrous nature of much of contemporary Palestine; as a result, interest in the physical and visible (αἰσθήτην) Jerusalem in Palestine was patently absurd.[5]

It might, however, be argued that such apologetic arguments had by Eusebius' day degenerated simply into a matter of convention, a stock in the apologetic trade. Even if this were the case, this would still nevertheless make it quite awkward for Christians now to attach a comparable spiritual significance to Jerusalem and Palestine. Yet, if we are correct in sensing that Eusebius was personally quite seriously committed to these apologetic arguments, that his convictions endorsed these conventions, then the problem went much deeper. For it is never an easy thing publicly to abandon one's former convictions, themselves so publicly stated. Moreover, Eusebius was making these statements throughout his life. Even in the later commentaries, when he would have been well aware of the new aspirations of other Christians, his thinking remained the same. Perhaps, then, his theology was merely 'compartmentalized' and internally contradictory? Perhaps he was quite happy to take one stance in apologetical and exegetical contexts but quite another in contemporary debate? But this seems unlikely. It is more probable to suggest that instead he felt quite uneasy with the activity and aspirations of his fellow Christians; for were they not now, though in a sincere and 'Christian' way, showing essentially the same attitude as that for which he had consistently criticized the Jews?

Eusebius' experience in apologetics, with the knowledge of Christian identity and the need for consistency which that fostered, thus gave him ample intellectual grounds for having at least some initial qualms over the emergence of a Christian Jerusalem.

A third influence on Eusebius' attitude to Jerusalem, and one interrelated with his experience of apologetics, was his understanding of the very nature of Christian spirituality. As we have sensed throughout our enquiry, the whole dynamic of Eusebius' spirituality was always from earth to heaven; the purpose of God was consistently to draw man upward from the physical to

---

[4] *Comm. in Is.* [49.14–16], 314.11.
[5] See, e.g., *Comm. in Ps.* [75.2–4], 876a–881b, and especially [86.3], 1044b–c quoted below at fn. 47.

the spiritual, from the seen to the unseen. Theologically for Eusebius the exaltation of Christ overshadowed the truth of the Incarnation, and the result, in terms of spirituality, was that a Christian's gaze was now to be fixed firmly on heaven; Christ's entry into the physical domain only served paradoxically to consume and to outmode the physical aspect of faith. Viewed in this light, it was precisely because Christ had visited the earthly Jerusalem and shown himself to transcend it that Christians could now be convinced of the greater, though invisible, reality of the 'true Jerusalem' above, the city of God in heaven. For example, Eusebius clearly delighted in the story of some Christians martyred in his own city of Caesarea who, when under interrogation before the governor, Firmilianus, had exhibited this essentially spiritual focus of the Christian life.[6] These Egyptian Christians, when asked as to their place of origin, claimed consistently that their only home-country was 'Jerusalem'. Firmilianus, not knowing where on earth this 'Jerusalem' might be, was clearly bewildered and exasperated. With our own modern interest in the physical Jerusalem we would tend to note the irony of the governor's ignorance of this former name for nearby Aelia Capitolina.[7] Eusebius' own concern as he related this story, however, had nothing to do with temporal Jerusalem. The irony for him was the governor's complete ignorance of the *spiritual* Jerusalem. Eusebius wished to highlight how, in contrast to the governor's thinking, which was 'resolutely earthbound',[8] the Christian martyrs had their sights fixed unwaveringly on the heavenly Jerusalem. This was the strength of Christian spirituality, indeed its essence. Furthermore, in this same passage he emphasized how the New Testament writers had explicitly contrasted this 'heavenly Jerusalem' with the physical Jerusalem. 'The present Jerusalem is in slavery with her children; but the Jerusalem above is free.'[9]

Christian interest in the physical Jerusalem thus touched on, and indeed threatened, something central within Eusebius' theological system. His spirituality was one that focused on the 'heavenly Jerusalem'. In so closely connecting Christian identity with the 'spiritual' Eusebius may indeed have been out of touch with more

---

[6] *Mart. Pal.*, 11.6–13.
[7] See Hunt (1982), 4–5, and Wilkinson (1981), 10.
[8] Hunt (1982), 5; cf. Eusebius' own words in *Mart. Pal.*, 11.19.
[9] Gal. 4.25–6; Eusebius also quotes Heb. 12.22 in *Mart. Pal.*, 11.9.

ordinary Christians, but that did not make it any the easier for
him to alter his thinking. Christians in the fourth century would
increasingly emphasize the role of the physical realm within the
life of faith, and would begin to emphasize the value of the
physical Jerusalem, but Eusebius could not; his spirituality belonged
essentially to a former generation. Perhaps Eusebius should have
foreseen this development, yet his guarded response to it was only
natural, for it was one that militated against the very dynamic of
his thought. Christian spirituality for Eusebius was essentially a
spiritual affair.

Fourthly (and finally), in all these areas Eusebius was influenced
and bound by an understandable need for consistency. The major
events of 325 challenged the essence of his own thinking and
indeed the essence, as he perceived it, of Christianity itself. In the
face of such a dramatic upheaval, there was a desperate need for
consistency. As a leading spokesman of the period Eusebius needed
to be seen to be consistent, but the same was true of the Church
at large, and indeed of God himself. For God had revealed his
eternal and unchanging truth to the Church. It was thus the task
of a theologian such as Eusebius to show that the new possibilities
of the future were in full accord with the revealed truth of the
past. As a result, his attitude towards Jerusalem, whatever it was
to be, would almost inevitably be an attitude marked by caution.

Radical change, such as that experienced by the Church in this
period, is never easily accommodated by the generation that has
lived so long in the former era. It is never easy to change one's
opinion, but it is especially difficult when one has been the most
prolific theological writer in the previous generation. Furthermore,
in the aftermath of Nicaea, as argued above, Eusebius had
additional, more personal motives for affirming the value of his
extensive earlier work. An elderly prelate under attack could not
surrender the validity of his own past, nor would such a theological
giant be able to make sudden changes.

However, with his historical interests, Eusebius would have had
a deep concern, not only for his own self-consistency, but also for
that of the Church as a whole. How could the Church of the
previous three hundred years enter into the new age of Constantine?
Would it be deflected from its true path in its sudden triumphalism?
How could Christianity absorb the new and powerful phenomenon
of Jerusalem into its system and retain its integrity? Not just for

his own sake, but for the sake of the Church, Eusebius was anxious to show the underlying continuity of Christian thought and not to introduce concepts which were manifestly novel.

Again, as a systematic and historical theologian, he would be eager to show the underlying continuity in the will of God. God was eternal and his purposes needed to be demonstrably consistent. If there had been some apparent changes in God's revealed will, Eusebius suggested that these changes were to be associated exclusively with the New Testament period when Christ had fulfilled and outmoded certain aspects of the Old Testament (such as sacrifices and the Temple). With the coming of Christ God had decisively revealed his definitive purposes for all time. No more changes were to be expected.

Moreover, for Eusebius, these changes observable in the New Testament were more apparent than real; they might appear as changes from a human perpsective, but they were not so from God's perspective. The divine will had been consistent all along. Because of his desire to emphasize the singleness of divine purpose, the continuity in God's ultimate will, Eusebius had come to see much of the Old Testament as a temporary parenthesis in God's dealings with man. God had always intended the Mosaic legislation (with its emphasis on Law, the Temple and Jerusalem) to be a mere passing phase in history; it was a concession to the Jews in their 'hardness of heart', before the *Logos* would come and restore to all mankind the spiritual worship practised of old by the patriarchs. This distinctive Eusebian argument, expanded most fully in the opening book of the *Proof of the Gospel*,[10] had, as we have seen, many useful functions. Yet for our present purposes we may note that one of its chief purposes was to demonstrate that the dramatic changes witnessed in the New Testament were not really changes at all; they were not a revolution so much as a reversion and a return to very first principles. Underlying the changes there was a vast continuity; God's will was eternally consistent.

This theological framework would therefore affect Eusebius' approach to Jerusalem after 325 in at least two ways. First, he was equipped in advance with a comprehensive system for interpreting and evaluating every part of scripture, a system in

---

[10] Especially *Dem. Ev.*, 1.3.

which he had already worked out the essential differences between
the old and new covenants and had established which entities
were to be understood as permanent and which as temporary. On
the whole it resulted in Eusebius having a marked tendency to
dismiss Old Testament themes as temporary and no longer
applicable. Even when compared with Origen, it has been observed
how Eusebius drew a 'far sharper and more insistent distinction
between the two Testaments, forever stressing the inferiority of
the Old'.[11]

Naturally within this system the Temple would be seen as a
temporary phenomenon, genuinely ordained by God in its day but
now fulfilled in Christ and his Church. Yet the same, we may note,
would also be true of Jerusalem. It would be easy for Jerusalem's
significance to be seen by Eusebius as equally temporary, never
truly a part of Gods eternal design.

Secondly, the existence of this theological framework before 325
clearly shows that already before that date Eusebius had been
anxious to discern and to defend the continuity of God's will;
apparent changes evidenced in the New Testament, he had argued,
were really not changes at all but were instead only the delayed
outworkings of God's original plan. To be able to show that God's
eternal purposes were consistent was thus already a matter of
great importance to Eusebius; this was an issue that he had already
faced.

Admittedly in his earlier works Eusebius had been defending
the continuity of God's will in relation only to the period of the
New Testament. Yet the same desires and convictions would
manifest themselves now as he turned to the more pressing and
immediate task of discerning what was to be God's will in his own
day. He had reduced all the complexities of the biblical revelation
into a manageable, simple and coherent system that reflected the
essential unity of God's purposes for mankind; not even the
dramatic event of a new Christian emperor would now cause
Eusebius to assert a change in those divine purposes. The coming
of Constantine could never offset the coming of Christ.

The contrast with Cyril is striking. As they assessed the
phenomenon of Jerusalem, Eusebius and Cyril were both concerned
with the same question of continuity. Yet they came to quite

---

[11] Barnes (1981), 101.

different conclusions. Eusebius took as his starting-point the negative strands towards Jerusalem in the New Testament and concluded that this revealed God's final will; the more positive aspects found in the Old Testament were to be read in this light and were to be deemed as a temporary phase now outmoded by the coming of Christ. Any significance for Jerusalem in times past was now eclipsed. God's ultimate will for the future did not include Jerusalem.

Cyril, however, began with a more linear and straightforward approach to scripture, accepted the positive references to Jerusalem at their face value, and then deemed the negative strands of the New Testament merely to be a judgement upon *Jewish* Jerusalem, which had rejected Christ. The significance of Jerusalem for Christians emerged unscathed; God's eternal will *did* include Jerusalem. Cyril and Eusebius thus espoused quite different theologies, the reasons for which should by now be well known.

Jerusalem, as now so then, was thus a two-sided phenomenon, which could call forth both positive and negative responses, both affirmation and denial. Eusebius himself could probably have sensed the many attractions of the kind of thinking so soon to be expressed by Cyril; but his own location in Caesarea, and more importantly his essential theology, ultimately pulled him in the opposite direction. Jerusalem was also an extremely complex phenomenon. The complexities noted below in Eusebius' approach to Jerusalem (as he sought to bring into a coherent synthesis an understanding of God's involvement with both the Temple and the city) contrast markedly with the simplicity of Cyril's position. Yet it would be well to see these complexities and minute qualifications, not as the deliberate confusion of a man eager to show his great learning, but as the sincere expression of a deep thinker facing an entity that could not easily be reduced into convenient and straightforward categories. For Jerusalem raised many questions, not one of which was easy to answer. Was Jerusalem a 'holy city', special to God? Had it ever been? Had it ever been truly the 'city of God'? What was the relationship between the city and the Temple in Old Testament days? How were Jesus' words of judgement against both the city and the Temple to be interpreted? What did the subsequent destruction of the Temple mean for the city which survived it? Could the phenomenon of Jerusalem re-emerge unscathed, and Jerusalem be

truly restored to her former status? It is our task now to analyse
Eusebius' answers to each of these major questions.

2. JERUSALEM, A 'HOLY CITY'?

Is Jerusalem a 'holy city'? In any age it is tempting to refer to
Jerusalem as such, but is it legitimate and what do we mean? At
the least the term 'holy city' can be used simply to highlight the
unique involvement of this city in the past religious experience of
man. Yet at a deeper level it can often be a means of claiming for
Jerusalem some special place within the purposes of God. On this
view the uniqueness of Jerusalem becomes, not just a factor in
human history, but a reality within the divine economy.

For the Christian who believes that major salvific events of
eternal significance occurred in Jerusalem this deeper meaning is,
of course, particularly attractive. To the eye of faith this was where
God met man. As a result, the historical Jerusalem has inevitably
a special place in the biography of faith; so too in the history of
grace. Seen in this light, Jerusalem becomes a 'holy city', not just
through religious association, nor through mere historical interest,
but through a sense of personal identification and indeed divine
involvement. It was clearly for some of these deeper reasons that
Cyril, as we have seen, insisted on Jerusalem being indeed a 'holy
city'. Yet it seems equally clear that Eusebius denied the validity
of this term altogether. Other aspects of our picture of Eusebius
may remain uncertain, but this much seems assured.

For Cyril the status of Jerusalem was enhanced by the great
Gospel events that had occurred there. Eusebius, however, considered the explicit teaching and the general dynamic of the New
Testament. Both of these were seemingly more negative towards
Jerusalem, emphasizing instead the outward thrust of the Gospel
away from Jerusalem. As a result, Eusebius stressed that Jerusalem
was no longer, and perhaps never had been, a 'holy city'.

Eusebius' thinking on this subject can best be gleaned by
analysing his exegesis of the two New Testament verses that at
first sight seem to contradict Eusebius' presentation and in which
the term 'holy city' seems to have been used as a straightforward
synonym for the physical Jerusalem. Not surprisingly both of these
occur in St Matthew's Gospel, the Gospel which makes the greatest

use of Jewish idiom. In St Matthew's account of the temptation the Devil took Jesus 'to the holy city and set him on the pinnacle of the Temple'.[12] In his Passion narrative, the evangelist includes the story of the earthquake at the time of Jesus' death, when 'many bodies of the saints were raised, and coming out of their tombs after his Resurrection they went into the holy city and appeared to many.'[13] For Cyril, as we have seen, these verses would be his major proof-texts; their reference to the physical Jerusalem was clear. Not so, however, for Eusebius.

Eusebius discusses these two verses, and especially the latter one, on several occasions, of which perhaps the most significant occurs in his *Commentary on Psalms*. In LXX Ps. 87 [88] the psalmist had feared the possibility of an imminent and futile death: 'dost thou work wonders for the dead?', he asks tauntingly; 'is thy steadfast love to be declared in the grave?' (vv. 11–13). Eusebius expounded the whole of this Psalm as a prophecy, spoken from Christ's perspective; it thus referred to Christ's death, his descent into Hades and his Resurrection. The result is fascinating for our purposes.

First, as already noted, it leads Eusebius to speak of the recent building work on the church of the Holy Sepulchre: these were truly 'wonders' that God had worked in the very place of death.[14] Then, secondly, just a few lines later, he uses Matthew 27.53 to illustrate Christ's descent into Hades; in so doing he emphasizes that the 'holy city' was *not* the physical Jerusalem but clearly the 'holy city of God, the heavenly one' (τὴν ἁγίαν πόλιν τοῦ θεοῦ, δηλαδὴ τὴν ἐπουράνιον).[15] Thus within the space of three sentences he both comments on the 'wonders' of the Holy Sepulchre and denies the 'holiness' of Jerusalem.

The precise date of these statements may be unclear (it could be a few years either side of the church's dedication in 335), but without doubt they come from the last years of Eusebius' life and well after 325 when the issue of Jerusalem's status came to the fore. It cannot therefore be claimed that Eusebius' denial of Jerusalem' holiness was a position that he held only in his earliest years before the Christian potential of Jerusalem was apparent.

---

12 Matt. 4.5; Luke 4.9 instead has 'Jerusalem'.
13 Matt. 27.52–3, unparalleled in the other Gospels.
14 *Comm. in Ps.* [87.11–13], 1064a; cf. above 4.3(*b*).
15 Ibid, 1064b.

On the contrary, his denying to the physical Jerusalem the status of a 'holy city' was made here in full cognizance of the emerging Christian Jerusalem.

Eusebius' exposition of Matthew 27.53 as a reference to a spiritual Resurrection and the heavenly Jerusalem was indeed nothing new. Origen too had consistently understood the verse in this way: the resurrected saints, he had asserted, entered the 'truly holy city, not the one over which Jesus wept' ('εἰς τὴν ἀληθῶς ἁγίαν πόλιν', τὴν μὴ κλαιομένην ὑπο τοῦ Ἰησοῦ Ἰερουσαλημ).[16] But what was the reason for this spiritualizing exegesis? After all, Matthew himself seems to have intended both these references to the 'holy city' to be understood in quite physical terms. Why did Origen and Eusebius insist instead on seeing it in purely spiritual terms?

It is not impossible that they were led to this position in part simply in response to the rather extraordinary nature of this Matthaean pericope; such a mass resurrection of corpses sounds rather macabre. Yet on the whole our authors would probably have been less questioning about such supernatural phenomena than ourselves. It is more likely, therefore, that their emphasis on the spiritual reference of the 'holy city' stemmed from their need to distinguish Christianity from Judaism and from their conviction, gained from other parts of the New Testament, that the concept of Jerusalem as a 'holy city' had really been outmoded or indeed repudiated by Christ. The concept of Jerusalem as a 'holy city' was a legacy of Judaism which Christianity was not to inherit.

Eusebius' insistence here that Matthew's 'holy city' was 'clearly the heavenly one' is almost pugnacious. Such vehemence probably reflects his earlier apologetic works and his need at that time to oppose quite forcefully what he believed to be the interpretation of the Jews. The focus of opposition, however, seems now to have changed. Perhaps Eusebius was no longer attacking his caricature of the Jews, but rather some Christians who were all too real. For the context is not manifestly anti-Jewish or strongly apologetic; instead this is a Christian exposition of a Gospel verse. What he was opposing is more likely, therefore, to have been any Christian attempt to reintroduce the idea of Jerusalem as a 'holy city'. Such

[16] *Comm. in Matt.* [17.1-2], 12.43, 169.5-7. For identical wording see the fragment in *idem* [17.6-8], Fr. 365b, 157.68-73; cf. also *idem* [27.53], CS 139, 288.4-6.

a concept, Eusebius maintained, was strictly a Jewish one, and not what Matthew had intended at all. Despite the fact, therefore, that it contained the 'wonders' of the Holy Sepulchre, fourth-century Jerusalem could not be called a 'holy city'. The individual place that commemorated Christ's Resurrection was indeed important; not so Jerusalem.

Although he was speaking in a different context within the new Christian empire, Eusebius' thinking here in the Psalms commentary at the very end of his life was thus fully in accord with his own earlier apologetics. For on two occasions in the *Proof of the Gospel* he had used this same verse to illustrate Christ's descent into Hades and in both of these he had again explicitly contradicted the notion of a 'holy' physical Jerusalem.

An examination of all these quotations by Eusebius of Matthew 27.53 will show how in each case Eusebius has slightly altered Matthew's text in order to endorse this spiritual interpretation.

Many bodies of the saints who had fallen asleep were raised, and coming out of their tombs after his resurrection they went into the holy city [εἰς τὴν ἁγίαν πόλιν] and appeared to many (Matt. 27.53).

Thus too his own body was raised up, and many bodies of the sleeping saints arose, and came together *with him* to the holy *and truly heavenly* city [εἰς τὴν ἁγίαν καὶ ὡς ἀληθῶς οὐρανο-πόλιν].[17]

Christ went thither for the salvation of the souls in Hades. . . . Which was indeed done, when many bodies of the saints that slept arose and entered *with him* the *truly* holy city *of God* [εἰς τὴν ἀληθῶς ἁγίαν τοῦ θεοῦ πόλιν].[18]

Many bodies of the saints who had fallen asleep were raised and *with the Saviour* entered the holy city *of God, clearly the heavenly one*.[19]

In all three passages Eusebius speaks of the saints entering the city *with* Jesus, something which is not implied necessarily in the Gospel text. More importantly, he inserts or adds words to qualify Matthew's straightforward 'holy city'. In both these ways he could colour the text to suit his spiritual interpretation.

The qualifying phrases that Eusebius uses vary; indeed, as we

[17] *Dem. Ev.*, 4.12.4 (*FPG*, i, 186; italics mine).
[18] Ibid., 10.8.64 (ii, 227; italics mine).
[19] *Comm. in Ps.* [87.11–13], 1064b; my trans. and italics.

shall demonstrate they may well reflect his increased awareness of the importance of the issue. Eusebius' intention, however, is the same throughout: the 'holy city' to which Matthew was referring was clearly the 'heavenly Jerusalem'. Moreover, Eusebius' phraseology on all three occasions reveals his awareness of other interpretations and indeed of an alternative 'holy city', even though this is never named as Jerusalem.

In the first passage 'truly' appears somewhat redundant; it surely has a greater meaning in the second passage when it qualifies 'holy' rather than 'heavenly'. For a 'false heavenly city' seems absurd but a 'false holy city' is very much a possibility. A little later in the same fourth book of the *Proof of the Gospel* Eusebius speaks of 'the heavenly city, the true Jerusalem' ($\tau\grave{\eta}\nu$ $o\vec{v}\rho\alpha\nu\acute{o}\pi o\lambda\iota\nu$, $\tau\grave{\eta}\nu$ $\dot{\alpha}\lambda\eta\theta\hat{\omega}s$ $'I\epsilon\rho o\upsilon\sigma\alpha\lambda\acute{\eta}\mu$)[20] and we should probably infer that this was his intended meaning in this earlier passage. However, this shift even within the *Proof of the Gospel* of his location of the adverb 'truly' may also have been influenced by an extended discussion yet later in that work in which the Jews' belief in Jerusalem as the 'holy city of God' was to be expressly deemed as 'false' and merely the product of human imagination.[21]

Thus even within this one work Eusebius was tightening his terminology and crystalizing his thinking. The issue of the status of Jerusalem in the present may already have been on his agenda. Just conceivably, since his recent elevation to the see of Caesarea around 311, he had become increasingly aware of the ecclesiastical consequences of the sentiments being brandished in the local Jerusalem Church. Be that as it may, Eusebius' thinking was becoming fixed. As was seen in our discussion of the *Proof of the Gospel*, 6.18, and his contrast between Jerusalem and the Mount of Olives, Eusebius was establishing, perhaps even unwittingly, an entrenched position that was quite definitely opposed to Jerusalem. Even if his supposed opponents at this earlier stage were the Jews, it would not be easy to renege on this issue; it would only be consistent to use the same argument later against Christians.

In the second and third passages Eusebius doctors Matthew's text by adding the phrase 'of God' ($\tau o\hat{v}$ $\theta\epsilon o\hat{v}$). The inclusion of these two words naturally determined that the 'holy city' must be

---

[20] *Dem. Ev.*, 4.17.15 (*FPG*, i, 219).
[21] Ibid., 8.2.9–16 (ii, 118–19), discussed below.

the heavenly one; for it was one thing to maintain that Jerusalem was a 'holy city', but it was quite another to believe that it could really be called God's own city, the 'city *of God*'. By linking these two concepts together, therefore, Eusebius could use the less feasible to dismiss the more feasible; the possible notion of a 'holy city' was jettisoned in the same breath as the less likely notion of the 'city of God'.

In the light of these two earlier passages Eusebius' wording in LXX Ps. 87 can now be seen to be quite consistent with his former thinking. Yet it was also more developed and forceful. His assertive phrase, 'clearly the heavenly one', which briskly dismisses all other possibilities, is indeed predictable but also more pointed. It is normal Eusebian theology but it is also more nuanced. The message here is more confident, hard-hitting and pugnacious than that conveyed in the earlier passages. As a result, it is tempting to suggest that the issue at stake was now no longer a dead one from the past, but rather contemporary and quite alive. Pragmatic reality was replacing theoretical apologetics; dull convention was being changed into deep conviction. The reason was the new possibility of a Christian Jerusalem.

Drawing on his developed theology in the days before 325 Eusebius thus continued to the end of his days, and indeed intensified, his opposition to the holiness of Jerusalem. Eusebius consistently applied Matthew 27.53, to the heavenly Jerusalem and quite deliberately took the opportunity in his expositions to contradict any notions that Jerusalem in Palestine was a 'holy city'.

Can the same be said, however, of Eusebius' interpretation of Matthew 4.5, the other New Testament verse which speaks of a 'holy city'? Although this verse occurs in the middle of the temptation narrative, which our modern minds might be disposed to view as not strictly historical, for Eusebius this was in many ways the more difficult verse to spiritualize. The reference to the 'pinnacle of the Temple' in the same verse was quite explicit and Eusebius in any case had theological reasons of his own for understanding the temptation as a historical event, a divine victory over evil which had truly occurred in this world. What, then, was Eusebius to do with this reference to the 'holy city'?

His tactic seems to have been one of careful avoidance. The two relevant passages which reveal this come again from the *Proof of the Gospel* and the Psalms commentary. In the former work, when discussing the temptation, Eusebius simply quoted Matthew without further explanation.[22] He offered no comment and made no attempt to identify this 'holy city' with either the earthly or the heavenly Jerusalem. The reference passed unexplained. Twenty years later, however, when he was expounding LXX Ps. 90 [91] as a prophecy of Christ's temptation, he chose to set the scene in his own words: the devil, according to Eusebius, simply led Jesus to the 'pinnacle of the Temple'.[23] In this way Matthew's reference to the 'holy city' was carefully omitted. As just noted, when expounding LXX Ps. 87 [88] he had insisted that St Matthew's 'holy city' was to be interpreted spiritually; now, just three Psalms later, in a context that prevented such a spiritual exegesis, he simply omitted St Matthew's reference altogether.

The proximity of these two psalms within the one commentary suggests that this omission was by no means accidental; that proximity would also tend to suggest a similar date of composition. Seen in this light this omission here of any reference to the 'holy city' takes on a new significance. It was probably a quite conscious and deliberate response on the part of the elderly Eusebius to recent local developments since 325.

Eusebius was caught in an awkward dilemma. This reference in St Matthew's temptation narrative to the 'holy city', unlike the later one in the Passion narrative, could not be spiritualized away. For Eusebius very much wanted Jesus' temptation to be a physical, historical event; thereby it could be both a real fulfilment of the prophecy in LXX Ps. 90 [91] and also a dramatic battle which Jesus truly faced for us 'by means of the body which he had assumed'.[24] As a result, Eusebius was unable to draw attention to this reference to the 'holy city', because his own exposition would force him to interpret this as the physical Jerusalem. He was effectively caught between two quite contradictory desires. On the one hand, he wished to portray the temptation as a physical event, on the other, to spiritualize the 'holy city'. Silence was therefore the only course.[25]

---

[22] *Dem. Ev.*, 9.7.23 (*FPG*, ii, 169).

[23] *Comm. in Ps.* [90.10–12], 1161b.

[24] *Dem. Ev.*, 9.7.7 (*FPG*, ii, 166–67); cf. *Theoph.*, 3.56.

[25] Moreover this silence was not unique in the years after 325. Eusebius' extended discussion of the temptation in the *Theophany* (3.55-9) also omits any reference to the 'holy city', a passage that he omitted entirely from the later speech *On Christ's Sepulchre*.

Cyril only discusses Jesus' temptation on one occasion[26] It would suit our purposes best if he had made a point of quoting Matthew 4.5, but unfortunately he did not. Yet there can be little doubt that he would have taken this as a direct reference to the physical Jerusalem, the city for which he had only a little earlier claimed the 'pre-eminence in all good things'.[27] For the Temple, the scene of this physical temptation, was clearly an important site for the Bordeaux Pilgrim in 333[28] and Cyril would be making his views sufficiently plain when discussing the 'holy city' of Matthew 27.53: despite what Eusebius had said, it was 'clearly this city in which we are now'.[29] Both these pericopes from Matthew's Gospel were dramatic and extraordinary but for Cyril, as we have seen, such colourful and dramatic episodes were only an attraction. For they showed how the supernatural had been at work in the 'holy city' of Jerusalem. Eusebius, however, refused to endorse such an interpretation of Matthew's verses. Writing his *Commentary on the Psalms* he either avoided the issue or came out firmly in favour of an exclusively spiritual interpretation. Matthew had not been referring to the physical Jerusalem of his own day and certainly not to that now known to Eusebius and Cyril in the fourth century.

The concept of the 'holy city', however, was not only raised in discussion of Matthew's Gospel. The term also occurs, of course, in the Old Testament. What did Eusebius make of this idea as it had been formulated in the Old Testament?

Eusebius was especially intrigued by the words of the angel Gabriel to the prophet Daniel: 'seventy weeks of years are decreed concerning your people and your holy city, to finish the transgression . . .' (Dan. 9.24). This gave Eusebius the perfect opportunity to bring out into the open the concept of Jerusalem as a 'holy city' and to criticize it explicitly. For the angel's use of the pronoun 'your' was taken by Eusebius to be an implied criticism of Daniel and his belief in the Jews as the people of God and in Jerusalem as the holy city of God. They were no longer God's, the angel had told Daniel, but 'yours':

The angel no longer calls them 'God's people', but Daniel's, saying 'thy people'. . . . It was that they might know that they were no longer worthy

---

[26] *Catech.*, 3.11–14; cf. also 10.10.
[27] Ibid., 3.7.
[28] *BP*, 590.1–2.
[29] *Catech.*, 14.16; cf. also 18.16.

to be called the people of God. And he adds 'and for thy holy city': where we hear again the unusual 'thy', for he says, 'for thy people, and for thy holy city', as much as to say, 'the city you think to be holy' [τὴν σοι νενομισμένην ἁγίαν]. . . . For since Daniel had often called . . . the place of the city 'the holy place of God', the One who answers in contrast says that neither people nor city are of God but 'thine'.[30]

Jerusalem might conceivably have been genuinely holy in the period preceding the time of Daniel (a point which Eusebius does not raise at this juncture), but it certainly was so no longer. Jerusalem did not have the status of a 'holy city'. Its holiness was now but a man-made concept, the result of human reasoning and fond imagining.

These were strong ideas, forcefully presented. Eusebius had found a useful text on which to build his case for the denial of Jerusalem as a holy city. Yet there was a cost. If he wished to attack this false notion in this way, he was forced to imply that a biblical writer, Daniel, had *himself* been party to this falsehood; Gabriel had need to correct Daniel for his erroneous use of this concept.

This was a fascinating argument, but it was also slightly risky. For it opened the door to the possibility that the genuine historical reference of the 'holy city', as it had originally been intended by the biblical authors, was indeed the physical Jerusalem. Strictly this did not contradict Eusebius' contention that Jerusalem was *now* no longer holy. Yet on the whole it was simplest to assert that Old Testament references to Jerusalem as 'holy' and special to God had always been intended by the original authors to refer to the heavenly Jerusalem. In this way the error of thinking in terms of the physical Jerusalem had only crept in at a subsequent stage, with the interpretation of scripture by the Jews; Christian interpretation, by contrast, rediscovered the author's original intention. Yet in admitting that Daniel was mistaken, Eusebius was in danger of admitting a more disturbing truth: references in the Bible to the 'holy city' (whether by Matthew, Daniel or Isaiah) had genuinely been meant to refer to the physical Jerusalem. Thus the very argument that Eusebius used to destroy the whole notion of the 'holy city' could eventually be used in its turn to undermine his own spiritualizing exegesis.

[30] *Dem. Ev.*, 8.2.9–15 (*FPG*, ii, 118).

Eusebius may well have realised this weakness in his exposition. For he does not use this argument again. Indeed, as we shall see, by the time he wrote his *Commentary on Isaiah* he made it quite clear that *this* biblical author had not been similarly deluded. The prophet obviously had used the term 'holy city' in a spiritual sense, never thinking of the physical Jerusalem. Quite probably Jerusalem, therefore, had never truly been a 'holy city'. Isaiah's words were then to be interpreted accordingly. The text of Isaiah had a couple of references to the 'holy city'. One of these references Eusebius did not discuss at all.[31] The other, however, he saw as being a reference to the 'spiritual soul' (λογικὴ ψυχή) and its desire to be holy, not admitting impurities;[32] the physical Jerusalem had been far from Isaiah's mind. The 'holy mountain' is also a frequent phrase in Isaiah, but only at the last occurrence is it explicitly identified with Jerusalem. Confronted with this slightly different possibility of a holy Jerusalem, Eusebius naturally appealed to the 'city of God, the heavenly Jerusalem';[33] again the physical Jerusalem was not to be considered.

Eusebius thus did not really focus on the physical entity of Jerusalem in the same way as he had done in the *Proof of the Gospel*. Partially this may have been determined by his exegetical context. However, the physical Jerusalem could in the meantime suddenly have become a bone of contention. Formerly Eusebius could attack it openly, whilst admitting that people like Daniel had held this physical understanding of the 'holy city'. Now the concept needed to be spiritualized entirely.

Finally, we may note how in this last passage in the commentary Eusebius urged that 'Jerusalem' should not be interpreted 'in a physical way such as the Jews would understand it' (σωματικῶς καταλλήλως ταῖς 'Ιουδαικοῖς ἀκοαῖς). This accusation of interpreting the text in a 'Jewish' fashion was one which he had always been able to level at other Christians.[34] Was he now subtly suggesting to his fellow-Christians that they should not introduce this false 'Jewish' concept of a 'holy Jerusalem'? Writing after 325, his opposition was again quite fierce but the issue was tackled less directly. If for reasons of tact he was indirect, he was not unclear:

---

[31] *Comm. in Is.* [48.2], 303.12 ff.
[32] Ibid. [52.1], 328.30.
[33] Ibid. [66.20], (407–8).
[34] See esp. *Proph. Eclg.*, 3.24.

the physical Jerusalem never had been, and certainly never would be, a 'holy city'.

3. JERUSALEM, THE 'CITY OF GOD'?

Another, and perhaps more common biblical phrase that Eusebius needed to discuss was the 'city of God'. Was Jerusalem the 'city of God'? Had it ever been?

In many ways this concept was very similar to that of the 'holy city' and frequently, as has just been seen in the interchange between Daniel and Gabriel, discussion of one often involved discussion of the other. However, it was also quite different in several ways. Whereas it was always possible to use the term 'holy city' in a weaker sense, which did not posit a special divine involvement with the city, the term 'city of God' necessarily had to be understood in a fuller sense. Moreover, the possessive genitive ('of God', $\tau o\hat{v}$ $\theta\epsilon o\hat{v}$) could be pushed in meaning to an extreme degree, such that the term spoke not just of God's possession and ownership of the city but of his actual *presence* in the city. If the latter meaning were insisted upon, as Eusebius appears to have done in several instances, it would be easy then to ridicule any idea of God's dwelling in an earthly city and to assert that only a spiritual reference to the heavenly city was appropriate. As such the 'city of God' became instead a common way of speaking of our ultimate home with God in heaven. Nevertheless, there was a sense in which Christians were keen then to relocate this in the physical realm by speaking of the Church as the 'city of God' on earth; in this way the Church militant and the Church triumphant could both claim this title. When Eusebius discussed 'the city of God' he thus had both an extra incentive and additional methods for denying its relevance to Jerusalem than when he discussed the phrase 'holy city'.

Yet Eusebius still needed to ask if the physical Jerusalem had ever been truly the 'city of God' in the past. For the validity and strength of the term in the present as a description of the Church both on earth and in heaven depended on the term having had a valid and viable reference in the Old Testament. Was the Old Testament precursor of the present 'city of God' (the Church) the place of Jerusalem or the people of God? Was its forbear a city or a community?

Naturally the very term 'city' and the extent of the biblical witness to the role of the physical Jerusalem suggested that it was indeed the city of Jerusalem which had truly been the city of God; if so, the legitimacy of now transferring this title from a place to a people would need to be defended and explained in terms of typology. As a result, it might be easier to opt for the other alternative, namely that the 'city of God' had always referred to the community of believers. This would indeed effectively reduce the status of the physical Jerusalem; yet unfortunately it might also weaken the very strength of the notion of a 'city'.

Perhaps not unreasonably, therefore, Eusebius seems to have vacillated between these two alternatives. However, the evidence adduced below also suggests that in the years after 325 Eusebius may increasingly have favoured the second, more communal, approach. If so, it would be yet another indication that he wished in those latter years to draw attention away from the city of Jerusalem in whatever way he could. Even if there were no Christians who were actually claiming that Jerusalem was the 'city of God', it would still weaken the prestige of that city if Eusebius could argue that in fact it *never* had been the 'city of God'.

Eusebius' fondness for this phrase as a description of our heavenly home with God can be seen in all his writings: the story of the martyrs executed under Firmilianus[35] and his own dedication speech at Tyre[36] are but two examples from the early 310's of a feature which can be seen in Eusebius at all times. He also frequently extended this concept to include the Church on earth.[37] 'The city of God is the Church' ($\dot{\eta}$ $\pi\acute{o}\lambda\iota s$ $\tau o\hat{v}$ $\theta\epsilon o\hat{v}$ $\dot{\eta}\mu\hat{\omega}\nu$ $\dot{\eta}$ $\dot{\epsilon}\kappa\kappa\lambda\eta\sigma\acute{\iota}a$).[38] Thus Eusebius exhibited the normal Christian position of using the 'city of God' as a description of the Church, both here on earth and in heaven.

Yet the original role of Jerusalem could not be forgotten altogether. There were thus, as Eusebius listed on several occasions,

[35] *Mart. Pal.*, 11.9.
[36] *Hist. Eccl.*, 10.4.2–72 (see esp. para. 70).
[37] For example, *Proph. Eclg.*, 3.24; *Dem. Ev.*, 5.26.2 and 6.17; *Comm. in Is.* [11.9], 85.3 ff.
[38] *Comm. in Ps.* [47.1–8], 419b; cf. his similar use of such psalms in his speech at Tyre in *Hist. Eccl.*, 10.4.2–9.

at least three different possible levels of meaning for any one reference to the 'city of God' in scripture: first, heaven itself; secondly, the worldwide Church of God; and thirdly, the Jewish city on earth.[39] Eusebius could then justify the shift from the third level of interpretation to the second by appealing to typology. What Jerusalem was under the old covenant, so the Church was under the new.

However, there was also a way of affirming the validity of the second level of interpretation which did not elevate the past role of Jerusalem in this way. This was to affirm, as indicated above, that the precursor of the Church was really the Old Testament people of God, that the true reference of the 'city' in the Old Testament was really the godly community.

Scholars have noted Eusebius' peculiar fondness for re-interpreting the 'city of God' as the 'godly polity' ($\tau\grave{o}$ $\theta\epsilon\sigma\sigma\epsilon\beta\grave{\epsilon}s$ $\pi\sigma\lambda\acute{\iota}\tau\epsilon\upsilon\mu\alpha$). Yet they have failed to discern the reason: 'the connotations of "city" ($\pi\acute{o}\lambda\iota s$) seem too limited and too material for his purposes; . . . hence he glosses it by "polity" ($\pi\sigma\lambda\acute{\iota}\tau\epsilon\upsilon\mu\alpha$)'.[40] All now becomes clear when it is recognized that the bad 'connotations' were those caused by the Jerusalem Church and others who sought to emphasize the physical Jerusalem. Eusebius emphasized that biblical references to the 'city of God' had truly referred to the 'godly polity' of that day precisely because this communal interpretation undermined any suggestion that instead it was the physical Jerusalem which in Old Testament days had been the true 'city of God'.

Eusebius sought thereby to make the notion of 'city' more abstract and communal, and to annul the distinctive role of Jerusalem in history. In this sense Eusebius would then be happy to admit that the 'godly polity' had indeed genuinely existed among the Jews of the Old Testament,[41] while arguing that this had now been transferred entirely to the Gentile Church. Although the Jews had once truly been the 'godly polity' they 'failed as citizens of such a polity, and . . . were banned from the heavenly Jerusalem'.[42]

---

[39] See, e.g., *Comm. in Is.* [49.11], 312. 31 ff., [51.16–17], 326.33 ff.; cf. also *idem* [35.10], 230.22, where he only distinguishes between the 'earthly and heavenly Sion'; and *Dem. Ev.*, 6.24.5–7 (*FPG*, ii, 45–6).

[40] Cranz (1952), 60, who cites also ibid., 9.6.6 (*FPG*, ii, 164) and *Comm. in Ps.* [45.4], 408d, to endorse Eusebius' 'marked preference' for this term (p. 62).

[41] *Dem. Ev.* 6.24.6 (*FPG*, ii, 45), and *Comm. in Is.* [1.26–7], 12.20 ff.

[42] Cranz (1952), 60.

Eusebius had used this concept once in the *Proof of the Gospel*[43] but it is of particular interest within our own enquiry to discover that he used it more keenly and far more frequently in the later Isaiah commentary.[44] Did this increasing emphasis on the personal and corporate meaning of the word 'city' reflect an increased desire in Eusebius to transcend any interest in the physical city of Jerusalem? This seems more than likely. Attention was thereby taken away from the Jerusalem of the past, and therefore from the Jerusalem of the present. The 'city of God' thus became in Eusebius' later years increasingly identified with the worldwide Church, which indeed had played such a large part in his thinking throughout his life. The physical Jerusalem was only to be considered within the context of the universal Church; indeed the worldwide Church had truly replaced the physical Jerusalem.

Eusebius' chief attack on Jerusalem as the 'city of God' occurs in his exposition of LXX Ps. 86.3 [87.3]: 'Glorious things of thee are spoken, O city of God'.[45] Once again this commentary can almost certainly be dated to the last years of Eusebius' life in the light of his reference to the 'wonders' of the Holy Sepulchre in his exposition of the following psalm.[46] Eusebius must therefore have been fully aware of the growing potential of a Christian Jerusalem. His stark and virulent language is therefore all the more remarkable.

To think that the formerly established metropolis of the Jews in Palestine is the city of God is not only base [ταπεῖνον], but even impious [δυσσεβές], the mark of exceedingly base and petty thinking [σφόδρα ταπεινῆς καὶ μικροπρεποῦς διανοίας]. . . . Its gates are now deserted and destroyed [ἐρήμους καὶ ἠφανισμένας] . . . and Greeks, foreigners and idolaters live there. . . . The city of God is clearly . . . the godly polity throughout the world. It is the Church of God which is the greatest city fit for God.[47]

Naturally in context he is chiefly criticizing the Jews; for only by the Jews would the city's current inhabitants be reckoned as 'foreigners' (ἀλλοφύλοι). Yet he could also have been using this exposition to call into question any renewed Christian interest in

[43] *Dem. Ev.*, 6.24 (*FPG*, ii, 45).
[44] See *Comm. in Is.* [22.1], 144.2, [32.16–18], 212.18, [45.13], 293.21, [51.17], 326.36–7, [60.3], 370.22; cf. *Comm. in Ps.* [51.7–9], 449c.
[45] *Comm. in Ps.* [86.3], 1040b–1048a.
[46] Ibid. [87.11–13], 1064a.
[47] Ibid. [86.3], 1044b–c; my translation.

the city and the validity of believing it to have been the 'city of God' in the past. He did so in three ways.

The derelict nature of Jerusalem's gates was a favourite Eusebian taunt:[48] any so-called 'city of God' should be able to claim God's special protection and therefore have a better track record for safety and peace than had poor Jerusalem.[49] Even in the Old Testament it had suffered some terrible attacks; perhaps, Eusebius suggested, it had never been the 'city of God'.

Then again, his argument concerning 'idolatry', while aimed primarily at the Jews, might well have had a secondary purpose, calling into question any Christian claims that Jerusalem could possibly be special to God when so many of its inhabitants continued to be pagan. Cyril might attempt to blur the issue by claiming optimistically that 'this Jerusalem worships him',[50] but in moments of criticism other Christians took exception to Jerusalem's claims for just such reasons;[51] it was a pagan city and far from 'holy'. Indeed Eusebius himself not many years before had commented more than once on the idolatry now prevalent in Jerusalem.[52] Unless therefore Eusebius was totally hypocritical, using this argument against the Jews but not against himself as a Christian, he must have questioned the legitimacy of Christians claiming a similarly exalted status for a still largely pagan Jerusalem. An unholy, godless Jerusalem could not be the 'city of God'.

Finally, the way he stressed in this passage the importance of the worldwide Church reflected his perennial wish to make this the central aspect of Christian identity and the overarching context for all Christian approaches to Jerusalem. In each of these three ways, then, the elderly Eusebius continued to pour scorn on any interest in the physical Jerusalem.

Eusebius' attacks on Jerusalem in his later years seem to become more intense. Once again it was the Jews who were ostensibly the

[48] This might appear to warrant an earlier date. However, even Christian Jerusalem must have continued in a sorry state for some time and even then some remains of the earlier walls and gates will have been left in visible ruins (see Tsafrir (1978), 551–9); cf. Cyril's remarks concerning Sion in *Catech.*, 16.18.

[49] Cf. ibid. [75.2–3], 879b and also *Comm. in Is.* [32.17–18], 212.18, where the 'city of peace' must be some 'other city'.

[50] *Catech.*, 13.7.

[51] Most noticeably Gregory of Nyssa in his celebrated attack on pilgrimage in *Ep.*, 2 (PG, xlvi, 1009–16), discussed in Telfer (1955a), 27–8 and Kotting (1959); cf. also Jerome, *Ep.* 58 (PL, xxii, 579–86).

[52] *Dem. Ev.*, 7.1.79, 7.1.91, 8.3.10–12 (*FPG*, ii, 63, 65, 141 respectively).

chief object of these attacks, but it is not impossible that he also had in mind some new Christian tendencies as well, which militated against his more 'spiritual' exegesis. The passage quoted above from the *Commentary on the Psalms* was a major attack on all those who ascribed a special significance to Jerusalem. If he had desired gently to change his mind on this matter, all he would have needed to do was lessen his apologetic clamour. Instead Eusebius' insistence that the physical Jerusalem was irrelevant only grew stronger. The very intensity of this passage suggests instead a man using the context of his apologetics to make some vital points about a Jerusalem under Christian control. If committed at all to the truth of his apologetics, he would surely then have had qualms about an over-enthusiastic Christian appropriation of such a 'Jerusalem concept'. To be sure, Christians were not expressly claiming that Jerusalem was still the 'city of God'; but many of the arguments he used to attack this supposedly Jewish notion would equally well have applied to Christians seeking to introduce a Christian 'holy city' in some form.

Ostensibly, however, Eusebius' chief concern was simply to deny that contemporary Jerusalem was the 'city of God'. This much was comparatively simple. More complex, however, was an assessment of Jerusalem in the past. Had it ever in any sense been truly the 'city of God'? Had God ever given his divine backing to this city or was this totally a human invention?

Two points have already been observed. First, some of his arguments against the present Jerusalem as the city of God would equally well have applied to Jerusalem in the past; secondly, he promoted increasingly not the city of Jerusalem, but the 'godly polity' of Old Testament believers as the genuine precursor of the Church, the new 'city of God' on earth. Both these arguments suggested that the physical Jerusalem had not truly been the 'city of God' in the past. Did he then go the whole way and assert that Jerusalem had *never* in any true sense been the 'city of God'? The evidence suggests that he was certainly moving in that direction, but that he may never have reached a final conclusion, perhaps never being able quite to deny Jerusalem's past status altogether.

We might have expected Eusebius to discuss this question of the *former* status of Jerusalem in that passage in the *Proof of the Gospel* where he had analysed Gabriel's words to Daniel concerning the 'holy city'. For, according to Eusebius' interpretation, Gabriel was also questioning the prophet's description of Jerusalem as the 'city of God'.

The prophet then clearly called the city not a city pure and simple but the 'city of God' [τοῦ θεοῦ πολιν]. . . . But Gabriel . . . on the contrary says, 'for thy people' and 'for thy holy city', showing in so many words that city, people and sanctuary were unworthy to be called God's.[53]

Had these three entities *never* been 'of God', or had they been genuinely 'of God' in time past but were so no longer?

Concerning the 'people' he was clear; Daniel's fellow Jews genuinely had been the 'people of God' but they were so *'no longer'*.[54] However, concerning the Temple and the city he was silent. Admittedly, the genuine special status of the former Temple he was to make clear later in this same book[55] and perhaps we should assume that the same was true of the city. Yet that assumption may well pass over a distinction that Eusebius was beginning to draw between the city and the Temple. In this particular passage he was not able to draw this distinction, since Gabriel seemingly treated both entities in an equal fashion. His opportunity, as we shall see shortly, would come ten years later in the *Theophany* when he could use an exactly parallel argument to question the validity of the city ever truly having had a special status; on that occasion, however, the words under consideration were not Gabriel's, but those of Jesus himself.[56]

That Eusebius wished at least to cast some doubt on the special status of Jerusalem in the past is made clear from as early a work as the *Prophetic Eclogues*, in which he spoke of Jerusalem as the 'city once *thought* to be holy' (ἡ πρότερον νενομισμένη πόλις ἁγία).[57] This early scepticism about Jerusalem's former claim to be a 'holy city' was now matched in Eusebius' later years by his questioning of its former status as the 'city of God'; Jerusalem was the city which the Jews had formerly honoured as the 'city of God' (ἡ πάλαι τετιμημένη ὡς θεοῦ πόλις),[58] but who was to say if this had ever really been sanctioned by God himself? Such passages in Eusebius, when combined with his greater use of the concept of

---

[53] Ibid., 8.2.16 (ii, 119).
[54] Ibid., 8.2.10 (ii, 118).
[55] Ibid., 8.2.111–20 (ii, 136–7).
[56] See below 11.4 at fn. 83.
[57] *Proph. Eclg.*, 3.18 (italics mine).
[58] *Comm. in Is.* [54.1], 339.28.

the 'godly polity', might well suggest that he was becoming
increasingly sceptical of Jerusalem's past status as the 'city of God'.

On the other hand there are a couple of later references that
tell in the opposite direction. In the *Commentary on Isaiah*, when
discussing the Assyrians' attack on Jerusalem in the eighth century,
he extracted the principle: 'it is not fitting to despise the city of
God' (οὐ προσήκει καταφρονεῖν τὴν τοῦ θεοῦ πόλις).[59] In its context
this would appear to be his description of the physical Jerusalem
of that day; Jerusalem had thus truly been the 'city of God' at
that time. However, he immediately proceeds to speak of the
Church and this may have been the real grounds for this apparent
identification. Moreover, not long before, he had given the first of
his many definitions of the 'city of God' as the 'godly polity' of
devout and faithful people; this meaning may therefore have been
automatically assumed.[60]

More puzzling for our purposes is Eusebius' single statement in
the Psalms commentary that Jerusalem was *'no longer* the city of
God'.[61] This use of 'no longer' would seem to indicate that at an
earlier time Jerusalem had truly held this status. At the time of
expounding this particular passage, Eusebius clearly found himself
unable to deny completely the special status of Jerusalem in the
past.

The reason for this ambiguity in Eusebius' position has already
been suggested. On the one hand, his desire to play down the
significance of Jerusalem in the present gave him good reason to
play down its true significance in the past. On the other hand, the
biblical image of the 'city of God' (which was so important in
Eusebius' thinking about the Church) depended for its vitality on
its having had a visible and concrete reality in the Old Testament,
namely the physical Jerusalem. The metaphorical imagery drew
strength from being grounded in a real historical place. Old
Testament Jerusalem thus needed to be affirmed as the 'city of
God' in contexts that pointed away to its typological fulfilment in
the Church, but denied in those contexts that pointed only to
Jerusalem of the present day.

Strictly, within Eusebius' own neat framework, there need have
been no problem. Given his understanding of the temporary and

---

[59] Ibid. [31.9], 205.18–19.
[60] Ibid. [26.1], 166.10–11.
[61] *Comm. in Ps.* [68.26], 753c.

typological function of the Old Testament, he would presumably himself have been quite able both to affirm the unique role of Jerusalem in the past and to deny its continuing significance in the present. But not everyone shared that framework. Those who wished to assert the significance of Jerusalem in the present (such as the Jerusalem Church and, for quite different reasons, the Jews) naturally would dismiss this sharp distinction between the Old and New Testaments.

In these circumstances Eusebius needed to play down, and even on occasions to deny, the special status of Jerusalem in the past. His increasing use of the concept of the 'godly polity' (τὸ θεοσεβὲς πολίτευμα) fitted this need exactly. It was really to this community that the Old Testament writers had been referring when using the term 'city of God'. In this way Eusebius could affirm that the Bible gave priority to people over places and that the 'city of God' was primarily a communal term. The 'city of God' thus retained its vitality and potency, while Jerusalem in Palestine was robbed of its status. The victory of the Church through the coming of Christ thus spelt the defeat of Jerusalem. For Cyril, by contrast, the victory of the Church through the coming of Constantine spelt the restoration of Jerusalem.

4. THE CITY AND THE TEMPLE BEFORE THE COMING OF CHRIST

So far Eusebius' understanding of Jerusalem has been assessed solely through an analysis of the two terms, the 'holy city' and the 'city of God'. He was clear that these could not be applied to Jerusalem in the present and was beginning to question whether they had been truly applicable even in the Old Testament period. Further light on his theological approach to Jerusalem, can, however, be gained through analysing his references to the Temple. What were Eusebius' attitudes towards this and how did they contrast with those that he had towards the city? It is through noting his clear-cut understanding of the Temple's status, both past and present, that his ambiguity concerning the city comes to light. Moreover, an analysis of those passages where he is discussing both city and Temple helps us to discern the way in which he increasingly drew a distinction between these two entities. In the

Old Testament a special status had indeed been given to the Temple, but Eusebius questioned whether, strictly this had ever been true of the city.

This distinction between the city and the Temple was, of course, far from being a radical new discovery, suddenly brought to light after 325. Eusebius had employed the distinction in more general terms throughout his writing career. What was new was the purpose that it now served. Thus he had naturally on many occasions spoken of 'Jerusalem and its Temple' purely by way of description.[62] Moreover, when listing the fates of the Jews, the separation of the two terms was a useful way of 'doubling' their calamity: thus they were deprived of both 'their royal city and their worship',[63] 'their city' and their 'whole system of worship',[64] their 'royal place' ($\beta a \sigma \iota \lambda \iota \kappa \grave{o} \nu$ $\tau \acute{o} \pi o \nu$) and their Temple ($i \epsilon \rho \acute{o} \nu$).[65] Although for obvious grammatical and geographical reasons the Temple was mentioned second in these references, its importance was not thereby to be deemed secondary. On the contrary, the Temple was the heart of the city which gave to the latter its significance. Jerusalem could rightly be termed 'Libanus', Eusebius explained in a characteristic typological exposition, only 'because of the holy altar within it'.[66] Hence, as in Josephus' description of Jerusalem the Temple was the crowning glory of the city,[67] so too the destruction of the Temple was the climax of Eusebius' narrative concerning the fall of the city in AD 70.[68] It would thus be quite easy, when it became necessary, to claim that the status of the city was essentially secondary, deriving solely from the location of the Temple within its walls.

The distinction between the city and the Temple was thus already well established in Eusebius' thought. Eusebius' past theology acted as a useful preparation. After 325, however, he needed a greater clarity. What really was the relation between these two entities? What was God's attitude to them both in scripture? Were they similar or quite different? All these questions

---

[62] See, e.g., *Chron.*, §1, 11.1, 1276b, and §2, 506d; *Onom.*, 210.10-11; *Proph. Eclg.*, 3.45; *Dem. Ev.*, 6.18.23 (*FPG*, ii, 29).

[63] *Dem. Ev.*, 6.13.27 (*FPG*, ii, 18).

[64] Ibid., 6.18.12 (ii, 27).

[65] *Sep. Chr.*, 17.8.

[66] *Dem. Ev.*, 7.3.26 (*FPG*, ii, 90).

[67] *BJ*, 5.4-5.

[68] *Hist. Eccl.*, 3.5.4.

had important practical consequences in the Palestine of the fourth century. It was therefore an old distinction, but now invested with a new meaning and great significance.

Eusebius thus had before him the major task of establishing what was God's will in the fourth century both for the city and for the destroyed Temple. What were Christians to do with these two entities? It was not possible, however, to answer these pressing practical questions without wrestling at least to some degree with the question of the Old Testament period. The status of the city and the Temple in the present were necessarily linked, even if by way of contrast, with their status in the past under the old covenant. Before we ask for Eusebius' thoughts concerning his own day we therefore need first to examine briefly his thoughts about the past. The evidence for Eusebius' attitude to the Old Testament Temple comes in several places, but again especially in the passage of the *Proof of the Gospel* to which we have already referred; concerning the Old Testament city there is also one intriguing sentence in the *Theophany*.

Of the two questions, that relating to the Temple was by far the simplest. The testimony of scripture was manifold and explicit; Jesus' actions and words, even if condemnatory for the future, also clearly affirmed for Eusebius the unique status of the Temple in the past.

The veil of the Temple was torn . . . and the 'abomination of desolation' stood in the holy place, inasmuch as the Being had left them desolate, Who had from time immemorial till that day been the guardian and protector of that place. For it is fitting to believe that up to the Saviour's Passion there was some Divine Power guarding the Temple and the Holy of Holies.[69]

Eusebius' meaning was explicit and unequivocal. However, there are for us several interesting factors to note, both in this passage and in others that refer to the Temple in the Old Testament period. For example, though the context does not require a reference to the city of Jerusalem, it is not insignificant that this most positive description of the Old Testament Temple, the most affirming to be found in any of Eusebius' references, occurs in a context which excludes any reference to the city whatsoever.

[69] *Dem. Ev.*, 8.2.112–13 (*FPG*, ii, 136).

Eusebius was free to affirm the special status of the Temple without raising the less clear-cut issue of the city.

Just two chapters later in the *Proof of the Gospel*, however, Eusebius came close, it seemed, to undermining this clearly stated position. For he referred to the Temple as the 'place reckoned by the Jews to be holy and sacred' (ὁ νενομισμένος αὐτοῖς ἅγιος καὶ ἱερὸς τόπος).[70] Was the whole notion of a holy Temple, after all, only a figment of Jewish imagination (νενομισμένος)? On closer inspection, however, this passage only confirms his recently stated principle. For he is speaking of the events of AD 70, the years after the death of Christ and the rending of the veil; by that time, as far as Eusebius was conerned, the Temple had indeed lost its holiness. His statement therefore did not deny that the Temple had had such a holiness before the coming of Christ. Furthermore, the consistency of Eusebius' thought on this matter is not denied by his occasional derogatory references to the 'Temple of the Jews' or '*their* Temple'; this only indicated that Jewish hopes after the coming of Christ were *now* false.[71]

Eusebius thus seems to have been consistent throughout his life on this point; the Temple had truly been special to God before the coming of Christ. In his earlier works he was clearly moved, indeed outraged, by the desecration of the Temple by Antiochus and the Romans;[72] the 'Temple of God' was 'ancient and famous' (πάλαι περιβόητος)[73] and worthy to be described as 'venerable' (σεμνός);[74] it was therefore particularly tragic that the stones of the 'Temple itself and its ancient precincts' had been reused for pagan buildings.[75] After 325 Eusebius continued with this same positive approach, despite the new Christian interest in the Temple's present state of desolation and judgement. Apart from a couple of references in the Isaiah commentary where Eusebius was anxious to show that the Lord Himself was the true source of holiness (ἁγίασμα),[76] Eusebius was not tempted to portray the

[70] Ibid., 8.4.22 (ii, 146).
[71] See, e.g., ibid., 1.1.7, 5.23, 7.1.91 (i, 4, 267; ii, 65 respectively); *Comm. in Ps.* [108], 1340d.
[72] *Chron.*, §2, 506d, 518c and 519d; for Pompey, cf. *Dem. Ev.*, 8.2.75 (*FPG*, ii, 129).
[73] *Hist. Eccl.*, 3.5.4.
[74] *Dem. Ev.*, 8.2.104, 9.3.9 (*FPG*, ii, 134, 158).
[75] Ibid., 8.3.12 (ii, 141).
[76] *Comm. in Is.* [5.2-7], 30.30, and [8.14], 58.29.

Old Testament Temple in a negative light. Instead his genuine admiration and approval of the Temple continued: it had been an object 'worthy of wonder (θαύματος)',[77] deservedly famous (διαβόητον),[78] and indeed the choicest part of the city (ἐξαιρετόν).[79] Even though destroyed, the Temple continued to be regarded by Eusebius as having once been genuinely holy and special in God's sight.

This is confirmed by two especially interesting references from his *Commentary on the Psalms*, which also introduce us to the contrast that Eusebius drew between the Temple and the city of the Old Testament period. First, it was the Temple alone, Eusebius claimed, and not the earthly Jerusalem, which served as a 'type' or 'icon' (εἰκών) for the heavenly Jerusalem; when King David spoke of 'his holy Temple' he was referring to 'the Jerusalem above, of which the earthly Temple was to be a type'.[80] The Old Testament Temple had a theological and typological function which the city did not share. Similarly, he then taunted the Jews that they could now see the 'destruction of *their* tents' (a reference to Jerusalem) and the 'desolation of *the* holy place' (the Temple).[81] Even though the Temple was now destroyed, he did not always have to castigate the Jews for belief in *their* supposed 'holy place'. Unlike the city this genuinely had been holy until the coming of Christ; it had truly been *the* holy place, not just *theirs*.

The vital question, however, was this: had that special status extended to the Old Testament city? From these last references, as well as our analysis of the 'holy city' and the 'city of God', the probable answer may already be surmised. That special status was *not* to be extended to the city. Eusebius' exalted language concerning the Temple was not paralleled in a similar exalted description of the city. Indeed the presence of the one only reveals the absence of the other. Eusebius' praise for the Temple only highlights his lack of praise for the city. In the *Proof of the Gospel*, as we have just seen, he had spoken of God's protection and oversight (ἐπισκοπή) with regard to the Temple; however, there

---

[77] Ibid. [54.2], 340.17.
[78] *Comm. in Ps.* [55.17–20], 485c.
[79] Ibid. [67.29], 713c.
[80] Ibid. [17.5–7], 170a.
[81] Ibid. [68.26–9] 753d.

had been not the slightest suggestion that this divine oversight extended to the city.[82]

In this light an intriguing statement made by Eusebius in the *Theophany* now takes on a new significance.

When Jesus saw the city, he wept over it and said, 'If only you had known the things that belong to your peace' [Luke 19.41 f.]. The things prior to these were predicted respecting the Temple; these, which are now before us, respecting the city itself, which the Jews named the 'city of God' [τὴν τοῦ θεοῦ πόλιν], because of the Temple of God that had been built within it [διὰ τὸν ἐν αὐτῇ τοῦ θεοῦ ἱδρυμένον νεών].[83]

The clear implication was that, while the Temple had been genuinely 'of God', the idea that the city of Jerusalem had any special status in God's sight, that it was even the 'city of God', was a false notion, wrongly extrapolated by the Jews. They had been wrong to take it upon themselves to extend such a divine status to the city.

It is important to note that this observation about the 'city of God' was not in any way required of Eusebius by the passage in Luke which he was discussing. Evidently, therefore, Eusebius had his own reason for introducing this distinction, for it showed that this important difference between the city and the Temple in God's sight was to underpin all contemporary discussion about them. Eusebius was concerned in this passage not only to demarcate clearly which Gospel passages related to the Temple and which to the city, but also to alert his readers to the fact that these two entities needed carefully to be distinguished for reasons of theology. It was no good to confuse the two and to assume simplistically that what was true for one was true for the other; for their status in God's sight was by no means equal and their functions in his purposes were quite different. The contemporary situation in Palestine required a closer examination of the biblical text and deeper understanding of God's purposes. For Christians in their exegesis were not to make the same mistake as the Jews by blurring the distinction between these two entities.

Moreover, Eusebius' indication here that the Jews were wrong to have called Jerusalem the 'city of God' would affect his attitude to the Fall of Jerusalem in AD 70. If Jerusalem had truly been the

---

82 *Dem, Ev.*, 8.2.111–20 (*FPG*, ii, 136–7).
83 *Theoph.*, 4.19 (*LET*, 248).

'city of God', then the calamity of AD 70 clearly revealed the end
of this special divine status. If, on the other hand, it had been
falsely so called by the Jews, then the events of AD 70 were to be
seen instead as a condemnation of this people, a humiliation of
their pride in claiming such grandiose titles for their mother city.
It was their pride which went before the city's fall. As suggested
above, Eusebius never totally abandoned the former of these two
models and never totally denied the ancient Jerusalem the status
of the 'city of God'; but in this passage he was clearly deciding in
favour of the second approach. It was the Jews, and not God
himself, who had called Jerusalem the 'city of God'.

This critique of Judaism had, however, a contemporary application. Eusebius was alerting his Christian readers to the mistakes
of the Jews in the past precisely in order that they might not
repeat them in the excitement of the present. His references to
'the Jews' in passages such as this showed that for Eusebius, in
contrast to Cyril, Jewish thinking about Jerusalem had been not
just a failure, which *Christians* could now rectify, but a mistake in
its own right, which Christians must not repeat. The Jews had
tried to call Jerusalem the 'city of God' and look how God had
responded! This attack on the Jewish understanding of Jerusalem
thus logically would have led him to be critical of any Christians
who sought now to establish a special status for the city. In the
euphoria of the new Christian empire Christians needed more than
ever to heed the lessons of history.

Moreover, the very reason that Eusebius discerned as the cause
of this Jewish attitude also spelt an immediate warning to Eusebius'
readers. The Jews had named Jerusalem 'the city of God, because
of the Temple of God that had been built within it'. Christians
therefore needed to be wary of making a similar mistake concerning
the church of the Holy Sepulchre, or any other 'holy place' in
Jerusalem. The presence of these unique locations within the walls
of Jerusalem did not increase the status of the city in which they
stood. Parts did not thus affect the whole. Eusebius himself seems
to have employed quite carefully this distinction between the part
and the whole, the 'holy place' and the 'holy city'. Thus in later
years he praised the Holy Sepulchre as the 'New Jerusalem'[84] and
commented on other Gospel sites, but their location in Jerusalem

---

[84] *V. Const.*, 3.33.

would not make that city a 'holy' one—no more than the Temple had done in Old Testament times. This important distinction, as already noted, would be seen most clearly in his commentary on LXX Ps. 87 [88], where he emphasized that the new Holy Sepulchre as a single entity was indeed a 'wonder' but denied that the physical Jerusalem was in any sense a 'holy city'.[85]

Eusebius' wording here in the *Theophany*, his first thoughts on the issue after 325, was thus to be indicative of his future stance. As he wrote these words and examined in detail these prophecies of Jesus, he was clearly thinking of the contemporary city of Jerusalem after 325. Yet it was precisely in that context that he had so clearly denied the special status of the city before the coming of Christ. This was therefore a clear and effective veto on any re-emergence of such a special status in his own day. It was indeed a significant and timely denial, to which we shall return; it was a statement made after careful consideration of both the immediate present and the ancient past.

Meanwhile, he had clearly stated in that same context the opposite truth for the Temple before the coming of Christ: unlike the city, in Old Testament days this had indeed been genuinely 'of God' (τοῦ θεοῦ). The status of the city in the Old Testament period before the coming of Christ had therefore been quite different from that of the Temple. The Temple had been truly 'holy', the object of God's careful oversight; not so the city.

5. THE CITY AND THE TEMPLE SINCE THE COMING OF CHRIST

The question of the status of Jerusalem and the Temple in the Old Testament naturally brings us to the question of the status of the city and the Temple in the New Testament period; what was changed through the coming of Christ and the catastrophic events of AD 70? This is hardly surprising since Eusebius' own discussion of this issue in the Old Testament period (as indeed our own analysis of that discussion) was prompted by a very present need, to discover what was to be the status of the city and the Temple in his own day. How were Christians with the new powers of

---

[85] *Comm. in Ps.* [87.11–13], 1064b.

Empire to treat these two local phenomena? In order to answer this question Eusebius needed first to outline the Old Testament picture and then to discern in what way the coming of Christ and the fall of Jerusalem had modified or altered that picture. What especially had been Jesus' attitude to both the Temple and the city? In the light of these, Eusebius, the historian and systematic theologian, could then begin to ask the important question of his own day: how could Christians in the present act in a way which was consistent with God's revelation and activity in the past? The present situation had thus sent Eusebius back to a renewed study of the past: that past then gave a secure foundation for the present.

The first focus of his study was understandably Jesus himself, and his prophetic words against both the city and the Temple. Thus, in three fascinating chapters of the *Theophany* he analysed Jesus' teaching on this subject in detail,[86] an analysis that would then colour his thinking for the rest of his life.

Eusebius' conclusions were as follows. Although the Temple had indeed been holy, it must now remain desolate forever. The city, however, precisely because it had never been holy in God's sight, would never have any special status in the future—though it could, of course, be reinhabited. The destruction of the Temple therefore was eternal, but the desolation of the city was only temporary. The Temple, which had once been so holy was now to be accursed and abandoned; the city, however, which had always been only 'neutral', could continue to be inhabited but theologically should remain strictly neutral.

Evidence for Eusebius' increased clarity on these issues after 325 can be found in both late commentaries; there is a marked tightening of Eusebius' terminology in these works in order to show this difference between the temporary desolation of the city and the permanent desolation of the Temple. When talking of the city, he now spoke not of its destruction but of its being 'besieged'; for a siege is a once-off event which leaves only a temporary desolation.[87] By contrast, the Temple, in these two passages was respectively 'razed to its foundations' and had experienced a final destruction (ἐσχάτον ἀφανισμόν).[88]

---

[86] *Theoph.*, 4.18–20.

[87] See esp. *Comm. in Is.* [40.2], 249.15, and *Comm. in Ps.*, [78.1], 941b.

[88] See also *Comm. in Ps.* [73.1–10], 851a–d. Similarly, 'besieged' in *Comm. in Is.* [35] compares with the more final καθαίρεσις of *Dem. Ev.*, 9.5.8 (*FPG*, ii, 162).

This clear-cut distinction might indeed seem natural enough but it contrasts with Eusebius' looser language before 325, in the days when the issues were less urgent. Thus, although he had spoken of the 'final desolation' (ἐσχάτη ἐρημία) of the Temple alone[89] he also used this phrase for the 'places' (τόπους) in Jerusalem.[90] Most strange of all, in his early *Commentary on Luke*, he had spoken of 'the desolation of the city and the besieging of the Temple' (ἡ ἐρημία τῆς πόλεως, ἡ πολιορκία τοῦ ἱεροῦ).[91] This was precisely the opposite of his usage after 325. At that time the necessity for precision had clearly not presented itself.

Such a necessity came in 325, when Christians needed to have an informed policy concerning the Temple and the city. Eusebius' response was swift. In book 4 of the *Theophany* he responded to the issues directly, and the foundation of his response was the drawing of this distinction between the city and the Temple. The Temple, once so special in God's sight, was to remain perfectly desolate; the city, however, precisely because it had never been and never could be of any real theological significance, was quite free to be reinhabited.

Eusebius clearly believed that he had dominical support for this distinction. For, in the passage already quoted, he asserted that Jesus' previous statements, which Eusebius had been discussing in the preceding chapter, had been concerned simply with the Temple (περὶ τοῦ νεώ), while Jesus' present statement concerned only the city (περὶ τῆς πόλεως).[92] Eusebius was making a tight distinction which he believed was inherent in the Gospels themselves. Jesus himself, he believed, had been speaking 'with special care and great precision' (σφόδρα ἀκριβῶς)[93] and, as a result, Eusebius would now be extracting the maximum amount of significance from those careful words uttered by the Lord himself. It is now our task, beginning with *Theophany* 4.18, to examine the words of Eusebius (not those of Jesus), noting his *own* careful clarity of expression, in order to assess his attitude to Jerusalem.

'Jerusalem, Jerusalem, you have killed the prophets and stoned those who are sent to you. . . . Behold, your house is forsaken and desolate . . .'

---

89 *Dem. Ev.*, 1.1.7 (*FPG*, i, 4).
90 Ibid., 8.3.10 (*FPG*, ii, 140); cf. *idem*, 6.13.17, 6.18.23 (ii, 15, 29).
91 *Comm. in Luc.* [13.20], 569b.
92 *Theoph.*, 4.19, quoted above at fn. 83.
93 Ibid., 4.18

[Matt. 23.37–8]. Impurity and pollution afterwards marked their doings; and this was the sin in which they dared to persist against our Saviour. And it was right, not only that the inhabitants of the city, but also the land itself, in which they so greatly boasted, should be made to suffer the things which the deeds of the inhabitants deserved. And these they did suffer! For it was not long before the Romans . . .* burned down the Temple, 'their house',* and reduced it to utter desolation.

It was with special care that he spoke* not of the city being desolate but only* the 'house' with in it, that is the Temple; which he was unwilling should again be called 'his', or yet the 'house of God', but 'theirs' only.

He prophesied too that it should be desolate in no other way than as deprived of that providential care [πρότερον ἐπισκοπούσης προνοίας] which was formerly exerted over it. Hence he said, 'Behold, your house is left desolate'.

And it is right that we should wonder at the fulfilment of this prediction, since at no time did this place undergo such an entire desolation as this was. Not at the time when it was rased to its foundations by the Babylonians. . . . For the whole period of the desolation of the place in those times was seventy years; because it was not fully said to them at that time, 'Behold, your house is left desolate.' Nor was it then so forsaken; . . . soon after it was dignified with a renewal [ἀνανέωσις] much more illustrious than its former state, as one of the prophets had foretold: 'the glory of this latter house shall be greater than that of the former' [Hag. 2.9]. After the enouncement therefore of the Saviour, that they should be *left*, and their house come by the judgement of God to utter desolation, to those who visit these places, the sight affords the most complete fulfilment of the prediction.

The period too has been that of many years, and so long as not only to be double the desolation of seventy years (which was that in the time of the Babylonians) but even to surpass four times its duration; and thus confirming the judgement pronounced by our Saviour.[94]

---

[94] *Theoph.*, 4.18 (*LET*, 245–7, except for two corrections marked within asterisks). Fortunately a Greek fragment exists for this section of the *Theophany* (GCS, 26–32) which allows us to improve on, and sometimes to correct, Lee's translation of the Syriac manuscript. Here the Greek in both instances supports our interpretation of Eusebius' distinction between the city and the Temple. Thus it was only the 'Temple, 'their house'' (τὸν οἶκον αὐτῶν καὶ τὸν νεών), that was reduced to utter desolation, not the 'captive city and Temple' (as in *LET*, 245). Similarly, Jesus' words suggested that it was not the city but the Temple that would be desolate, (οὐ τὴν πόλιν ἐρῆμον . . . ἀλλὰ τὸν ἐν αὐτῇ οἶκον), whereas in Lee (p. 246) this reads 'not only the city itself should be desolate but the house that was within it'. Admittedly Lee brackets the word 'only', thus acknowledging that this was not in the original, but its inclusion completely destroys Eusebius' whole point. Note also in this and the following chapter how he confusingly translates πολιορκία as 'utter destruction' or 'reduction' (*Theoph.*, 4.18, 19, in GCS, iii, 29.4, 23; 30.8); this blurs the distinction noted above in fn. 87.

It was no coincidence that each of Eusebius' four points here had some contemporary significance in the years after 325. First, Eusebius noted that Jesus had not said that the *city* would be 'desolate', but only its 'house', 'namely the Temple'. Eusebius was quick to introduce his distinction between the city and the Temple. What this meant for the city he would be outlining in the next chapter; until then, however, Eusebius would himself be talking exclusively about the Temple. Jesus' words encouraged and endorsed this distinction which was now of such value in the fourth century.

Secondly, Jesus' use of 'your' meant that the Temple was *no longer* the house of God (τοῦ θεοῦ). This reiterated precisely Eusebius' argument in the *Proof of the Gospel* concerning Gabriel's words to Daniel.[95] There, however, the precise *former* status of the city, the people, and the sanctuary had been left unspecified. Here, however, since he had made it abundantly clear that he was speaking only of the Temple, he was able to use οὐκέτι ('no longer') to signify that the Temple had indeed formerly been the 'house of God'. As noted above, this would be in marked contrast to the city, which even in Old Testament times had never truly been the 'city of God'. Thus, even in the middle of this prophecy against the Temple, Eusebius was at pains to show that the Temple had genuinely been 'of God' under the Old Covenant.

This was endorsed by his third point. The Temple's 'desolation' in AD 70 was caused by the cessation of that 'providential care which was formerly exerted over it'. Again this briefly stated the conclusion of a passage in the *Proof of the Gospel*;[96] before the coming of Christ the Temple had enjoyed a genuine divine 'oversight' and protection. But now God was abandoning the Temple. Neverthelss this underlying *personal* dereliction or abandonment was to be manifested in a *physical* desolation. The destroyed Temple was meant to be a visible and physical symbol of something profoundly personal.

Finally, he commented on the length of this present desolation, pointing out how it exceeded that which the Temple had experienced in the sixth century BC. At that time the Temple had been restored after 70 years and God had renewed his promise of

---

[95] *Dem. Ev.*, 8.2.9–16 (*FPG*, ii, 118–19).

[96] Ibid., 8.2.111–20 (ii, 136–7) quoted in part at fn. 69 above.

divine 'oversight'; but that was only because Jesus had not yet pronounced this powerful prophetic dictum. Eusebius interpreted Jesus' words as a prophecy that the Jews would be abandoned (ἀφείθησαν) and 'their house' come to utter desolation (εἰς ἔσχατον ἐρημίας). The Gospel word for the Temple being 'forsaken' (ἀφίεται) was thus to be understood in the strongest possible sense. The Temple had thus not simply been destroyed; it had been forsaken, jettisoned, abandoned. Admittedly Eusebius did not state here explicitly that this destruction should be forever. However, his next comment (on the time that had already lapsed since AD 70) raised the issue of duration and certainly indicated that Eusebius was wishing this situation to continue in the present day and indeed indefinitely. Eusebius' meaning and intentions were quite clear. The Temple was to be abandoned for all time.

The contemporary context of Eusebius' discussion is yet more clearly focused in the next section: he repeats his claim that anyone who cares to visit the city as it now is can see for himself the truth of Jesus' words.

'Truly, I say to you, there will not be left here one stone upon another, that will not be thrown down' [Matt. 24.2]. The scriptures moreover show that the whole building and the extreme ornamenting of the Temple there were indeed thus worthy of being considered miraculous; and, for proof of this, there are preserved even to this time some remaining vestiges of these its ancient decorations.

But of these ancient things the greatest miracle of all is the Divine word, the foreknowledge of our Saviour, which fully announced to those, who were wondering at the buildings of the Temple, the judgement that there should not be left in the place at which they were wondering 'one stone upon another that would not be thrown down'. For it was right that this place should undergo an entire destruction and desolation, on account of the audacity of its inhabitants, since it was the residence of impious men.

And, just as the prediction was, are the results in fact remaining: the whole Temple and its walls, as well as those ornamented and beautiful buildings which were within it and which exceeded all description, have suffered desolation from that time to this. With time too this increases; and so has the power of the Word gone on destroying, that in many places no vestige of their foundations is now visible—which any one who desires it may see with his own eyes.[97]

[97] *Theoph.*, 4.18 (*LET*, 247).

This passage is clearly of great interest to modern readers with concerns in either archaeology or prophecy,[98] but for our purposes one point is especially significant: according to Eusebius, the Temple was punished for the sins of the *city*. Thus even though the city and not the Temple was strictly the 'residence of impious men' (οἰκητήριον ἀσεβῶν ἀνδρῶν) it was not the city itself which had to undergo the 'entire destruction and desolation' (τὴν παντελῆ φθορὰν καὶ ἐρημίαν), but rather just the 'place' (τόπος).

The precise reference of τόπος was conveniently obscure and thereby lessened the paradox of the Temple being punished for the evil of the city's inhabitants. Yet it clearly referred, as did all this chapter, to the Temple and Eusebius was quick to restate this single-minded emphasis on the Temple in the next sentence: 'the whole Temple and its walls . . . have suffered desolation from that time to this.' The Temple was thus to be made paradoxically the *locus* for God's visible judgement on both the Temple *and* the city. 'It was right that this place [the Temple] should undergo an entire destruction and desolation, on account of the audacity of its [the city's] inhabitants.' Only the deliberate lack of precision in grammar allowed this lack of logic to pass unchecked.

In the next chapter, however, when talking of the city on its own, Eusebius began to argue in the opposite direction. Whereas

[98] Eusebius himself thus seems to have been satisfied that Jesus' prophecy (that 'no stone' would be 'left upon another') had been adequately fulfilled. However, in his next paragraph he proceeds to acknowledge that the literalist might be more doubtful. In response he notes that some Christians have taken these words of Jesus as applying only to that particular portion of the building that had been pointed out by the disciples. He himself, however, suggests that, with the passing of time, natural decay, perhaps aided by a special divine power, will ensure a complete fulfilment of Jesus' words.

Christian concern over this particular prophecy of Jesus can be seen again in Cyril (*Catech.*, 15.15) who acknowledges that it is as yet unfulfilled: it will only be fulfilled now at the time of the Antichrist. In the light of such words the Jews' attempt to rebuild the Temple fifteen years later in 363 was not surprisingly an episode fraught with eschatological overtones. For a probably inauthentic letter of Cyril concerning this, see Brock (1977), who emphasizes how this one Gospel verse became a focal point for 'propaganda' (p. 282).

Eusebius' words show that the issue had already been felt for some time. However, he noticeably responds to the problem without any reference to the Second Coming. Unlike Cyril he did not link the physical Jerusalem to the return of Christ in any way (see above, esp. 3.1(*b*)). For a similar avoidance of such an eschatological connection, note his refusal to admit that the cessation of Gentile inhabitation (in the light of Luke 21.24) would ever in the future usher in the return of Christ, in *Comm in Luc.* [21.28–33], 597b-604a; cf. also below in *Theoph.*, 4.20.

the Temple was indeed, according to Eusebius, to suffer in physical
terms for the personal disobedience of the city's inhabitants, this
was not, paradoxically, true for the city itself. Jesus indeed 'wept
over the city'; yet 'it was not that he had so much pity on the
buildings, nor indeed upon the land, as he had first upon the souls
of its inhabitants and then the prospect of their destruction'.[99]
Eusebius thus suggested that with the city Jesus had been focusing
on the people, not the physical buildings; with the Temple the
reverse was the case. Eusebius could not claim that the city's
buildings would experience no destruction at all, but he could
assert that the chief focus of God's judgement (and therefore
paradoxically of his compassion in Christ) was upon the inhabitants.
Even if it had to suffer in AD 70, the city would not therefore have
to experience destruction for evermore. That fell upon the Temple
alone. Any apparent judgement on the city therefore would *not*
be eternally binding.

But what did that mean for the Jerusalem of the fourth century?
In his discussion of the fate of the city, Eusebius then came to
some more verses in Luke's Gospel, this time from the apocalyptic
discourse.

'When you see Jerusalem surrounded by armies, then know that its
desolation has come near. Then let those who are in Judaea flee to the
mountains; . . . and Jerusalem will be trodden down by the Gentiles,
until the times of the Gentiles are fulfilled' [Luke 21.20–24]. Previous to
this he said, 'Behold your house is forsaken and desolate.' He now gives
by the words before us the signs of the times of the final destruction [τῆς
παντελοῦς ἐρημίας] of the place [τοῦ τόπου]. . . .

Now, let no one imagine that, after the besieging of the place [τὴν
πολιορκίαν τοῦ τόπου] and the desolation that would be in it, another
renewal [ἀνανέωσις] of it shall take place, as it was in the times of
Cyrus, . . . Antiochus Epiphanes . . . and Pompey. For many times did
this place suffer the effects of a siege and was afterwards dignified by a
more excellent restoration. But when you shall see it [αὐτήν] besieged
by armies, know that which comes upon it to be the final and full
desolation and destruction [τὴν ἐσχάτην τῆς πόλεως ἐρημίαν καὶ τὸν παντελῆ
ἀφανισμόν]. He designates the 'desolation of Jerusalem' by the destruction
of the Temple and the laying aside of those services which were formerly
performed within it according to the law of Moses. You are not to suppose

---

[99] Luke 19.41, as expounded in *Theoph.*, 4.19 (*LET*, 248); cf. *Dem. Ev.*, 8.2.103
(*FPG*, ii, 134) where again the city really stands for its inhabitants.

that the desolation of the city, mentioned in these words, was to be such that no one should any more reside in it. For he says after this that the city shall be inhabited, not by the Jews, but by the Gentiles: 'Jerusalem will be trodded down by the Gentiles.' It was known therefore to him that it would be inhabited by the Gentiles. But he styled this its 'desolation' because it should no more be inhabited by its own children, nor would the service of law be established within it.[100]

In this prophecy about Jerusalem, Jesus had made no mention of the Temple. Yet Eusebius evidently wished that he had! Jesus' prophecy of Jerusalem's 'final destruction' (παντελοῦς ἐρημίας) did not fit neatly into Eusebius' system; he would much rather that somehow this prophecy could have applied to the Temple. It was for this reason that Eusebius then immediately quoted again his favoured verse, 'your house is forsaken and desolate'.[101] In this way he could alter the reader's focus and deflect some of the force of Jesus' prophecy away from the city onto the Temple. Once again his use of τόπος for the destruction of the 'place' would help to obscure this gap in his argument.

He then confronted one contemporary false notion by asserting that there will be no 'restoration' or 'renewal' of the 'place' (ἀνανέωσις τοῦ τόπου). In the context that Eusebius was seeking to establish, this was probably meant to refer exclusively to the Temple. As such it would endorse his earlier usage of this word ἀνανέωσις ('renewal');[102] it would also conform exactly to the argument which we expect him to be developing, namely that the Temple alone, and not the city, was doomed never to be 'restored'.

However, at just this point, Eusebius blurs the whole issue by twice using the word πολιορκία, a word naturally related more to the siege of a city (πόλις), and by speaking of the 'final and full desolation and destruction' (τὴν ἐσχάτην ἐρημίαν καὶ τὸν παντελῆ ἀφανισμόν) of the *city* (τῆς πόλεως), words which in other works after 325 were used only for the Temple. Was he in fact referring to the city as well?

Most probably Eusebius was dislodged temporarily from his tight

---

100 *Theoph.*, 4.20, based on the translation in *LET*, 250-52, but with emendments. Lee omits the important reference to the 'final destruction' of the *city* and consistently uses 'reduction' for πολιορκία which suggests something more final than Eusebius' original and loses the implied reference to the wider city (πόλις); again cf. above fn. 87.

101 Matt. 23.37 (= Luke 13.35).

102 *Theoph.*, 4.18. See above at fn. 94.

city/Temple distinction by this particular Gospel passage. For, despite Eusebius' pretensions to the contrary, Luke was really speaking of the city, not of the Temple. Eusebius was thus reaping the rewards for having falsely imposed this restrictive distinction upon the text. As a result, conscious of this problem, he immediately tried to argue that Jesus' 'Jerusalem' was not a reference to the city (as it had been in only the previous chapter), but only to its 'Temple and Mosaic worship'. He also reinterpreted the 'desolation' so that it referred not to the physical destruction of the city, but rather to the extended absence of the Jews from Jerusalem, or perhaps to the extended desertion of the Temple. No longer did Eusebius receive his distinctions from the scriptural text; instead he imposed them upon it.

Nevertheless, he could have made this 'special pleading' *before* his discussion of any 'restoration' (ἀνανέωσις). The 'restoration' in question would then have been expressly that of the Temple alone. As it is, Eusebius' imprecision occurs precisely at the moment when he is discussing the possibility of a future 'restoration' or ἀνανέωσις and is not clarified till afterwards. In Eusebius' text as it stands, therefore, the 'restoration' seems to refers to the city: it was the city that would not experience a renewal like it had known in the past.

Of the many cases in Eusebius' writings where his language is imprecise, we have discovered perhaps the majority are the result of deliberate choice, not mere confusion. Could it be, then, that here too this apparent muddle at just this point betrays something deeper, an uncertainty or an anxiety (whether conscious or unconscious) about the restoration of Jerusalem? Yes, he did wish God's act of 'final destruction' to be understood to have been directed primarily towards the Temple, but was there not something about the biblical *city* of Jerusalem which also had been judged, something that was lost for ever and would never be reintroduced?

A few lines later he assures us that this denial of a future restoration of Jerusalem does not mean that the city should be left totally uninhabited. In accordance with Jesus' words Gentiles could indeed occupy it. Was Eusebius therefore drawing another distinction? It was quite legitimate, he might be suggesting, for Gentiles to continue inhabiting Jerusalem in the fourth century; but it was not legitimate for Christians to revive Jerusalem to its former glory. His use of the city/Temple distinction, whereby judgement was located exclusively on the Temple, had thus been intended as a means of justifying the continued inhabitation of the city (and indeed its Gentile occupation), but not as a means of establishing the theological legitimacy for creating a new Christian Jerusalem, restored to its biblical pre-eminence. Inhabitation was one thing, ἀνανέωσις or a 'renaissance' quite another.

If this reading is correct, then Eusebius had no qualms about Christian reinhabitation of the city; after all the city had continued to exist since AD 70, and there was no reason to suppose that it should remain deserted as a result of God's judgement. However, this removal of judgement from the city (and its transference to the Temple) was *not* to be equated with the reintroduction of any special concept of 'Jerusalem'. Eusebius may have been setting Jerusalem free from future divine judgement, but he was not setting it free so that Christians could make the same mistakes as the Jews before them. Christians should indeed inhabit the city, but they should not reintroduce the notion that 'Jerusalem' was somehow special in God's sight.

Such qualms about the restoration of Jerusalem, if this is what this text reveals, might conceivably have been allayed if Eusebius had drawn the distinction here between Jerusalem *per se* and the *Jewish* Jerusalem. Eusebius might then only have been questioning the restoration of a *Jewish* Jerusalem. A Christian Jerusalem was something quite different. This is an attractive and simple explanation of his meaning. Yet it would have been just as simple for Eusebius himself to make this distinction explicit. He only needed to define the 'Jerusalem' in question as the *Jewish* one ('Ιουδαϊκή or τῶν 'Ιουδαίων) and his meaning would have become quite clear. His failure to do so can be explained in three quite different ways: First, Eusebius may indeed have come to value this distinction, but as yet the issues of contemporary Jerusalem and its status were still quite new to him and he had not yet made this distinction. Alternatively, it is possible that he already valued this distinction and wanted to employ it in this discussion. However, he did not do so because he was conscious that this would bring into the open the apparent hypocrisy of Christians desiring Jerusalem after having attacked the Jews for that desire. A third solution, however, is that this was not after all a distinction which Eusebius deemed to be valid. He had genuine qualms himself about this hypocrisy and, worried by the aspirations of the

Jerusalem Church, sought to show that there was something about Jerusalem that had been lost forever and could not be re-established, even under Christian auspices. Gentile inhabitation of Jerusalem was a fulfilment of Jesus' prophecy and prevented people from thinking that the Jews' exclusion from Jerusalem was simply due to the city no longer being inhabited;[103] apart from that, however, the city had no special function in the present and no longer any special status in God's sight. Cyril would soon state quite explicitly this distinction between the two cities, between the Jewish Jerusalem which had crucified Jesus and the Christian one which 'now worshipped him',[104] but that was the brazen touch of the Jerusalem Church twenty years later. Our abiding question, however, is this: was Eusebius himself moving towards that position later adopted by Cyril or was he still shying away from it? All our analysis of Eusebius' attitude to Jerusalem indicates the latter, that he was by no means a secret admirer of the position soon to be espoused by Cyril; instead he was decisively opposed to it.

An intriguing phrase later in this same chapter in the *Theophany* offers some corroborative evidence for this position and confirms that the third interpretation above is most likely to have been correct. The present city of Jerusalem was not to look for any 'restoration', for it was not apparently even to be called 'Jerusalem'!

Not many words are required to show how these things have been fulfilled, since we can easily see with our own eyes how the Jews are dispersed to all nations and how the inhabitants of that which was formerly Jerusalem, but is now named Aelia Capitolina [τῆς πάλαι μεν Ἱερουσαλήμ, νῦν δε . . . ᾿Αιλίας] are foreigners.[105]

If he had so wished, Eusebius could have used slightly different language to indicate that 'Aelia' was only a temporary name and that the use of 'Jerusalem' was now legitimate. Instead, however, his wording only emphasized the redundancy of the former name 'Jerusalem'. Jerusalem was now 'Aelia Capitolina'. There was perhaps no clearer way of denying the possibility of a restored Jerusalem and the validity of a special concept of 'Jerusalem' than this denial that the city should even be called 'Jerusalem'! The

---

[103] As Eusebius argued a few lines later in ibid., 4.20.
[104] *Catech.*, 13.7.
[105] *Theoph.*, 4.20 (*LET*, 252).

'Jerusalem' of the Bible for Eusebius was in effect no longer in existence.

Not surprisingly Cyril never used the name 'Aelia' for the city. He preferred not to highlight the paganism of the second and third centuries and the upheavals which this era represented in Jerusalem's history; for him Jerusalem was a continuous entity. Cyril's constant use of the name 'Jerusalem' was also adopted by other Christians after 325. The Bordeaux Pilgrim, for example, visiting in 333, never referred to the city by its pagan name; he had travelled from Bordeaux not to see Aelia but Jerusalem! Even if the city continued to be known as 'Aelia' in the world of imperial administration,[106] in the Christian world after 325, almost without exception, the city once more became 'Jerusalem'.[107] Eusebius' usage here in the *Theophany*, written in the first years after 325, is thus all the more striking. Despite the great potential that evidently existed for a now Christian Jerusalem, he stressed the continuing validity of the name 'Aelia'.

Eusebius had his own reasons after 325 for continuing the practice of using the name 'Aelia'. Two centuries earlier 'Aelia' had been coined as a deliberately anti-Jewish term, and no doubt Eusebius' use of the term here in the *Theophany* is just part of his exegetical polemic against the Jews. Yet this pagan name could also now be used by Eusebius as a timely means of making two important points, one ecclesiastical, the other theological. By calling Jerusalem 'Aelia' Eusebius could on the one hand play down the city's potential for increased ecclesiastical status, while simultaneously preventing the hasty reintroduction of any theological concept of a special 'Jerusalem'.

The former ecclesiastical point can be discerned quite clearly in the seventh canon made at Nicaea, where 'Aelia' was used to dampen the aspirations of the Jerusalem bishop. Bishop Macarius was to be 'honoured', but he was still to be referred to as the 'bishop of Aelia'.[108] This use of 'Aelia' was a forlorn attempt to

---

[106] For references in the official byzantine lists, see Hunt (1982), 149, fn. 106.

[107] Egeria's one reference early in her diary (9.7) to 'Aelia, that is Jerusalem' occurs in a context of routes and *mansiones* and is therefore coloured by the usage of the imperial administration. Meanwhile Jerome's use of 'Aelia' in his translation of Eusebius' *Onomasticon* was only an accurate rendition of the original and therefore must have been consciously anachronistic—though 'Aelia' could also have been an attractive option because of his antagonism towards contemporary Jerusalem.

[108] Council of Nicaea, canon 7; see *NE*, p. 360.

maintain the pre-Constantinian *status quo* and to strike a con-
ciliatory balance. For Eusebius the term would then be a necessary
safeguard against future advances. For the Jerusalem Church,
however, it would be quite unacceptable. What had previously
been a term used against the Jews was now being used against
the Jerusalem Church. In the context of this ecclesiastical tension,
it is hardly surprising that in his next published work Eusebius
attempted, even if only within the safety of an apparently apologetic
context, to insist upon the continuance of this name. 'Aelia' was
his means of keeping Jerusalem in check. Cyril and others would
have none of it.

However, our overall argument shows that Eusebius' reasons
here were not purely those of a threatened metropolitan. He had
prior theological grounds for questioning the recultivation at all of
a Jerusalem mystique under Christian auspices. Eusebius was thus
using 'Aelia' in the *Theophany* to make a theological point, not
just an ecclesiastical one. It was no coincidence that he introduced
this term at the end of his detailed investigation into the present
status of the Temple and the city within God's purposes. He had
been coming to the conclusion that the city, unlike the Temple,
had never been special to God in times past; although it was not
now under judgement and therefore could be reinhabited, it was
never to be elevated once more to that false status which the Jews
had ascribed to it. His use of 'Aelia' now neatly confirmed the
point. The events of AD 70 and 135 had brought to an end all that
was biblically 'Jerusalem', both its name and its ideology. One way
of preventing the return of that ideology was to prevent, if possible,
the reintroduction of the name. 'Jerusalem' had too many lively
associations.

Eusebius' discussion was therefore not dictated purely by
ecclesiastical politics but rather by the urgent necessity for Christian
practice to be based in true theology. If he would soon abandon
any attempt to insist on the continued use of the name 'Aelia',[109]
he would not, however, be reintroducing the ideology of a special
Jerusalem. His opposition to such a concept lay at a much deeper
level, close to the heart of the man and his theology.

---

[109] See below at fn. 117 for details of the caution which Eusebius still exercised
in his terminology for 'Jerusalem' after this date.

6. CONCLUSION

Eusebius' imprecision noted above over ἀνανέωσις ('renewal') has touched on the most important question underlying all our enquiry. Eusebius was increasingly clear in his distinction between the city and the Temple. He made the Temple in its continued desolation the recipient for all God's judgement upon the former Jewish city; the Temple was therefore not to be 'renewed'. But did the same apply to the city? Was he deliberately removing divine judgement from the surviving city of Jerusalem in order that Christians should then be able to Christianize it themselves? Or was he showing that the whole Jewish concept had been wrong and judged by God and that therefore Christians should be wary of making the same mistake? Was he opposing the city or seeking gradually to accommodate it?

Putting the same question another way, when he attacked the Jews for their love of *their* city and *their* metropolis,[110] was he using that adjective to show that their exalted understanding of Jerusalem was purely their own invention, a product of *their* human imagination, not divine will? Or was he opposing their city only in order that Christians might establish *their* city?

Eusebius had been increasingly keen to argue that only the Temple had ever been truly 'holy' and that this had never been true of the city; the Jews had wrongly sought to extend this status to Jerusalem as a whole. Could he now argue in all honesty that it was fair for Christians to reintroduce a special status for Jerusalem? Had the Jews' special loyalty to Jerusalem been repudiated in order for it to be appropriated or rather that it might be opposed?

The cumulative evidence adduced above indicates that Eusebius was most probably opposing all such attempts to make Jerusalem special, whether by Jews or by Christians. For the overall picture, which has emerged progressively throughout this chapter, is of a man with severe qualms over the reintroduction of the 'Jerusalem' idea. Thus in his apologetic writing against the Jews he consistently attacked their religious dependency on Jerusalem and even their interest in the physical Palestine. He acknowledged the temporary

---

[110] For example, in *Dem. Ev.*, 2.1.2, 6.18.12, 8.4.23 (*FPG*, i, 64; ii, 27, 146 respectively) and *Theoph.*, 4.3.

special status of the Temple, but questioned whether such a status had ever been extended to the city. The physical city of Jerusalem was probably never truly the 'city of God' and certainly had never been a 'holy city'. Jerusalem could not therefore be a 'holy city' in the present and no ἀνανέωσις of Jerusalem in this sense was to be envisaged for the future. Jerusalem's only significance was a paradoxical and negative one; in theological terms, if not in name, it was simply 'Aelia', a testimony to God's judgement of Jerusalem in the past.

It may be objected, however, that much of this picture has been derived from the *Theophany*. Would Eusebius really have come to the same conclusions a decade later at the very end of his life? Almost certainly, yes. For, as argued above, Eusebius had strong personal reasons for being seen to be as consistent as possible, and his attitude was based on the convictions of a lifetime. Moreover, although the *Theophany* (with its explicit discussion of precisely these issues) has indeed provided much of the evidence, our analysis has also drawn quite extensively upon Eusebius' latest commentaries, on Isaiah and the Psalms. In these two books he clearly continued his opposition to such Jewish attitudes[111] and towards the concept of Jerusalem as a 'holy city';[112] it was also in the Isaiah commentary that he began to emphasize the more personal meaning of the 'city of God', as the 'godly polity'. Meanwhile, at no point in either of these commentaries did Eusebius ever hint at any renewed Christian interest in Jerusalem.

That Eusebius persisted in such thinking to the end of his life is confirmed by what we have learned of his three Constantinian works. In his speech *On Christ's Sepulchre*, for example, he discreetly avoided any reference to the 'city',[113] while in his speech *In Praise of Constantine* he brought out quite clearly his emphasis on Palestine, rather than Jerusalem, as having been the source of the 'life-bearing stream to all'.[114] In this latter work, as also in the *Life of Constantine*, his description of the Triad was not related to the city of Jerusalem.[115] Instead, just as in his discussion of LXX

[111] See, e.g., *Comm. in Is.* [49.14–16], 313.32–314.24; *Comm. in Ps.* [75.2–4], 876b–81a, [86.3], 1040b–48a.

[112] See *Comm. in Ps.* [87.11–13], 1064b.

[113] See above 4.5 at fn. 112 for the way he substituted 'heavenly place' (*Sep. Chr.*, 14.12) for the earlier 'heavenly city' (*Theoph.*, 3.39).

[114] *L. Const.*, 9.15 (*DPC*, 101); cf. *Sep. Chr.*, 11.2. See above 10.3(*b*).

[115] *L. Const.*, 9.15–17; *V. Const.*, 3.41–43. See above 6.2(*a*)–(*b*).

Ps. 87, his concentration was on the particular places of Christ, not on the city of Jerusalem. These were what consumed his attention. As a result, it was only of the Holy Sepulchre as a single building, not of the city, that he once used his colourful description, the 'new Jerusalem'.[116] The issue of 'Jerusalem' as such was never addressed.

It is interesting to note that Eusebius' use here of the form, Ἰερουσαλήμ, as opposed to Ἱεροσόλυμα, is unique within the *Life of Constantine*. At all other times, in this work and elsewhere, when referring to the physical city on earth, he consistently used only Ἱεροσόλυμα;[117] this alternative form Ἰερουσαλήμ, was reserved for references to the heavenly Jerusalem, a usage which reflected that of the New Testament.[118] By employing this distinction Eusebius mave been trying to preserve an important distinction between the heavenly Jerusalem and the physical city on earth which happened to share an almost identical name; he was able to acknowledge the use of Ἱεροσόλυμα for the fourth-century city, whilst avoiding the need ever to give to that city the theological significance which for him lay only in Ἰερουσαλήμ. The two needed to be kept quite distinct. As a result, this exceptional reference to the νέα Ἰερουσαλήμ was far from being a reference to the contemporary city of Jerusalem; Eusebius was quite clearly not giving this glorious title to the Palestinian city of Ἱεροσόλυμα. Rather he was suggesting quite tentatively (τάχα που) that, just as earlier he had seen the Mount of Olives as a possible symbol of the universal Church,[119] so too now the Constantinian buildings over the tomb might be seen similarly as such a universal symbol. The 'true Jerusalem' was ever and only the Church of God, both 'militant' and 'triumphant'; but these new buildings could proclaim uniquely the victory of that Church in the world and in eternity.

For Eusebius, therefore, that city in the Judaean hills was not the 'new Jerusalem'. It was not the 'true Jerusalem'. It never had been truly the 'city of God'. It was by no means a 'holy city'. He would never be able to share the warm and positive approach to Jerusalem of his younger contemporary, Cyril. Even the great

---

[116] *V. Const.*, 3.33.

[117] See, e.g., *V. Const.*, 3.25, 29.2; 4.40.2, 43.1, 43.2, 47; *Comm. in Is.* [16.5], 109.23, [17.5], 116–20, [38.4–8], 242.21.

[118] Gal. 4.25–6; Heb. 12.22; Rev. 3.12, 21.2.

[119] *Dem. Ev.*, 6.18.26 (*FPG*, ii, 30–31); see above 7.2(*b*)–(*c*).

upheavals of 325 and the exciting possibilities for Christians in Palestine were insufficient to sway him from these convictions; if anything, they only strengthened them because they sent him back into his own theological system, to think more deeply, and to emerge with even greater clarity and stronger convictions than before. Eusebius was not unprepared to modify his opinions on occasions, but underlying any such changes there lay a strong strand of continuity; and it was strong because it was deep.

To those who have assumed that Eusebius would naturally have fully endorsed a new Christian Jerusalem upon the arrival of Constantine, the above picture may be slightly surprising. Yet, even if some of our observations prove to be incorrect, the accumulative picture is striking and compelling: Eusebius' attitudes to Jerusalem were certainly more complex and probably more negative than have previously been supposed.

Eusebius had a lifetime's reputation in theology behind him; he had constantly advocated the spiritual nature of Christianity and he had thought deeply upon the working of God in his own land of Palestine. That was indeed a complex task and his entire corpus reflects the complexity of the issues with which he was dealing. He was also a man of a lifetime's conviction: if he retained an ultimate detachment from Jerusalem and an overall approach that was negative, he was doing so only because of the positive strengths that he sensed in his own emphases. For he was not obdurately puritanical, with nothing positive to offer in its place; he belonged instead to a strong tradition which emphasized the essentially spiritual nature of the Christian faith. His past, of which he was justly proud, thus gave him good reason for moving only slowly and for retaining a necessary detachment and objectivity.

That detachment was, of course, partially caused by his living in Caesarea. Eusebius was near enough to see the importance of the issues of Jerusalem and the places of Christ, but distant enough to transcend them; Cyril, by contrast, lived in the very midst of them. However, Cyril also came to those issues afresh; he was not an elderly metropolitan with a lengthy reputation behind him but a young presbyter with a promising future. The confidence of youth met the caution of the aged. Thus, for example, whereas Eusebius would have sought to distinguish Christianity from Judaism by *contradicting* Jewish beliefs (as he perceived them),

Cyril would more easily *appropriate* those beliefs: Christian opposition to Jerusalem could give way to a Christian re-appropriation of Jerusalem, for Christians no longer had to be the very opposite of the Jews.

Eusebius may have begun in his final years to modify some of his opinions, to relax his stance towards a more acceptable mean: Cyril, and others in the Jerusalem Church, starting at that mid-point would carry Eusebius' thought further than had ever been intended. Thus, for example, Eusebius had carefully made the distinction between the Temple and the city, but in his own mind this did not give the city a renewed status. Cyril, grateful for Eusebius' perspicacious distinction, could then use it to undergird his own elevated view of Jerusalem—quite the opposite of Eusebius' own original intention. Eusebius thus cleared the city of present judgement but still saw the 'city' judged in the destroyed Temple. Cyril did not see this judgement of the city, only the judgement of the Jews and *their* Temple.[120] Christians could now adopt the apparently 'Jewish' attitude towards Jerusalem precisely because 'this Jerusalem now worshipped him'.[121] Eusebius himself, how-ever, could not make this brazen distinction, nor was he paving the way for a Christian Jerusalem—though subsequent Christians in all ages could claim that he did. The attitudes of Cyril might at first sight seem close to Eusebius' but ultimately they were quite different. It was not just that two sees were in conflict with one another: more truly there was a clash between two theologies and indeed two different eras.

For too long the words of Cyril (concerning the places of Christ and the 'true cross', but also concerning Jerusalem) have been allowed to speak on Eusebius' behalf; and Eusebius himself has been judged by his few statements in his Constantinian writings. The above portrait has shown him instead to be a man with much thinking worthy of analysis in its own right, a man who wrestled with the significance of the places of Christ and the city of Jerusalem in his very changing times. Cyril's voice has also been heard, but not in order to obscure that of Eusebius; rather that we may hear, by contrast, Eusebius' finer and more subtle tones.

---

[120] *Catech.*, 15.15.
[121] Ibid., 13.7.

EPILOGUE

We live in times far removed from those of Eusebius and Cyril; yet the places of Christ and the city of Jerusalem still remain. Pilgrims in every subsequent generation have come to see for themselves those unique locations where Jesus once lived. Often today it is not Jerusalem but Galilee (or the 'land of the Bible' as a whole) that evokes a deeper response from the Christian visitor: for the city of Jerusalem, changed so radically since the days of Christ, is in itself perplexing, for some even bewildering. Its teeming life, its combination of the unique and the very ordinary, its beauty and ugliness, confront one at every corner; and over its streets hangs an invisible question mark that will not go away. What is the meaning of Jerusalem, what its significance?

Some are tempted to avoid this question but others know that they must attempt an answer, however tentative. Jesus 'set his face to go to Jerusalem' (Luke 9.51), fully aware of the city's power, its heights and its depths. Christian pilgrims *in situ*, just as the author or theologian *in absentia*, must similarly face up to that question of Jerusalem. The places of Christ lead inevitably to, and cannot be separated from, the entity of Jerusalem.

For the last twenty years the modern city has posed a question yet more pressing. Although supposedly a 'unified' city, its division is quite apparent to all. 'East Jerusalem' and 'West Jerusalem' stand for two different peoples, the Arabs and the Jews: within the space of a mile two completely separate worlds can be encountered. What a difference there is between the response of a visitor who goes up to Jerusalem ('Yerushalayim') from Tel Aviv through terrain which is characteristically Mediterranean and that of the person approaching Jerusalem ('Al Quds') from Jericho through the Judaean desert and arriving over the crest of the Mount of Olives!

Christians resident on either side not unnaturally tend to identify with the aspirations of their respective neighbours: Christians in West Jerusalem elevate the status of Jerusalem in empathy with the Jews; those in East Jerusalem, able to claim a far more ancient tradition within the Christian Church, likewise share with both Muslim and Christian Arabs a belief in Jerusalem as a 'holy city', though for quite different reasons. Christians in the West may be tempted to look to the Old Testament; those in the East most certainly to the New.

Jews, Muslims and Christians thus live side by side and their aspirations for Jerusalem frighteningly coincide. They each consider the city to be of great religious importance; more alarmingly still, the fate of Jerusalem can be made a vital part of their religious (and also political) identity. Thus the people of all three religions give to the single city a significance and then derive from that city a foundation for their identity. The contemporary situation thus heightens the importance of the question of Jerusalem; but it also increases our qualms over the potential dangers of giving so great a significance to such an entity. Is there a Christian solution?

In the light of our historical analysis, we might well be tempted to ask (while fully aware of the dangers of over-simplification in such retrospective questioning) where Eusebius and Cyril would have fitted into modern Jerusalem. The problems of their day now seem slight, when compared with today's tangled complexity. But could their example help us in any way?

Cyril, we suggest, would certainly have found his 'home' in East Jerusalem and its 'old city'. Here is celebrated the truth of the Incarnation and the Redemption; here the faithful are blessed by their proximity to the particular places of Christ; here there is the colour and the drama of rich liturgical celebration. Here there is, above all, a Christian 'holy city' in both belief and practice. Its attractiveness would have been felt not only by ourselves but also by Cyril; he would have instinctively recognized it. Indeed he might with some justice claim to have been the mind behind its inception, its founding father.

Eusebius, however, would not have come to terms so easily with the 'holy city' of East Jerusalem. Naturally his living sixty-five years in the pre-Constantinian era would explain in part any such unfamiliarity; so too his more academic and cerebral approach. Yet the deepest cause would be his past theology. In that theology he had centred upon such concepts as theophany and revelation, the universal and the spiritual, but not so much upon Incarnation or on the particular. Moreover, his emphasis on the Word of God as text gave less room for the physical and the active; while his emphasis on the *Logos* of God gave less room for the personal and for the Spirit. The 'holy places' in East Jerusalem, however, depend for their vitality on the lively meeting between the Person of Christ and his faithful people enacted in a particular physical place of the Incarnation. If Eusebius would have been unprepared for such practice, he would also have been little prepared for the natural corollary, that this Jerusalem was a 'holy city'. The beckoning attraction of East Jerusalem would in Eusebius have been met with some resistance.

Yet by no means would Eusebius have then found West Jerusalem to be more appealing. He had spent his entire life opposing the significance ascribed to Jerusalem by the Jews: naive endorsement of such notions would have been anathema to him. His whole exegesis of Scripture was designed to prevent such a false reading of the Old Testament. Would Eusebius thus have found himself caught between the two approaches of today, located perhaps in the theological equivalent of 'no man's land', the remains of which can still be seen between East and West Jerusalem?

Cyril would quickly re-appropriate the theology of Jerusalem's significance, but would undergird it principally with distinctive Christian reasons, culled from the events of the New Testament. Our question is this: would Eusebius have done the same, or would he have questioned the significance of Jerusalem in its entirety? Would he wish Christians to distinguish themselves from Judaism by appropriating the concepts of the former religion (while resting them on quite distinct Christian bases) or would he wish them to oppose those concepts in their very essence? Our analysis suggests that Eusebius would, at least initially, have favoured the latter course, which was more consistent with his earlier theology. Christians were not to ascribe a renewed significance to 'Jerusalem' as such.

Ultimately, of course, one cannot speak for Eusebius. However, in the complex, intractable situation of the present day, it is tempting to see in Eusebius' more detached approach to Jerusalem, and in his emphasis on the spiritual roots of the Christian Church, a more hopeful prospect for the future. The city's problems are largely caused by different religions giving a special significance to the same city. Could Christians diffuse that tension by relinquishing *their* attachment to the city, by transcending that significance for the sake of Christ, by denying the inherent holiness of Jerusalem?

Such a stance might initially seem like escapism or surrender. Yet history suggests that those who conquer Jerusalem often lose as much as they gain: their conquest is but a Pyrrhic victory. Moreover, it could be a distinctively Christian response, affirming that Christ's victory may only be achieved through Christian surrender, that life only comes through death. For Jerusalem was, and for ever will be, the city of the crucifixion. If the Cross challenges people the world over to 'die to self', it does so all the more strongly in Jerusalem: it beseeches us to die with our own notions of Jerusalem and for 'Jerusalem' itself to die. Only so can the city of the crucifixion become also the city of the Resurrection. The salvific events in Jerusalem have a message that Jerusalem itself, above all, needs to heed.

Those who try to approach Jerusalem or to use it without first confronting the Cross may be destined to failure; those who love it too simplistically may be destined to cause yet more pain for the future. Its true lovers refuse to give it any ultimate loyalty. They deny its appeals for self-glorification. In their love for it they remain ultimately detached—for the sake of Jerusalem itself, but also for the sake of Christ. The city of the crucifixion can never be glorified.

Contemporary need only increases the need for historical enquiry: the issues are too immense and Jerusalem too potent for hasty assumptions, apparently innocuous but eventually disastrous. Our own enquiry into the thinking of Eusebius and Cyril has deliberately focused on that pivotal period in the history of Jerusalem and the 'Holy Land', when Christians were first confronted with the need for responsible thought and practice. A Christian in Jerusalem today lives at the end of a continuum which chiefly owes its beginning to these two men. Cyril manifests an obvious, perhaps hasty, enthusiasm: Eusebius a more cautious and historical approach. If at times Eusebius' complexity contrasts unfavourably with Cyril's straightforward simplicity, we would do well to be patient. For, though we would very much wish it otherwise, Eusebius' struggle, indeed his predicament, has become our own.

APPENDIX

QUESTIONS OF AUTHENTICITY AND DATING

EUSEBIUS

On the host of questions that have naturally been raised concerning the dating and authenticity of Eusebius' works, it has been simplest to accept in outline the overall conclusions of Timothy Barnes (1981), though for some of the Constantinian works the proposals of Hal Drake (1976) have been preferred.

The precise dating of several of Eusebius' works is either little contested or of no great consequence for our present purposes. To Eusebius' earliest period (to 303) can be confidently assigned the first edition of the *Chronicle*, his treatise *Against Hierocles* and his *Canons* on the synoptic Gospels; while to his middle period (303–325) belong his *Prophetic Eclogues*, his *Commentary on Luke* (sometime after 313), the *Martyrs of Palestine* (the long rescension of which was written in 311, the shorter in ?313),[1] the *Preparation for the Gospel* (c.314–18), and the *Proof of the Gospel* (c.318–23); his *Gospel Questions and Solutions*, addressed to Marinus and Stephanus, might belong to either period. Finally, it is clear that his treatise *On the Paschal Festival* and his letters to the Church in Caesarea and to Constantia Augusta were all written soon after the council of Nicaea in 325, and that his polemical work *Against Marcellus* and the *Ecclesiastical Theology* were both written at the very end of his life (?338).

There are, however, some works, the dating of which has been a matter of much controversy and affects an author's presentation of Eusebius. Our conclusions on these matters are stated briefly below:

1. The *Onomasticon* was not one of Eusebius' latest works, as was

[1] See Barnes (1981), 148–158, 278.

argued by Wallace-Hadrill,[2] but rather was written around 293; for, as Barnes argues, there are no references to Constantine's building works in Palestine and, more importantly, Eusebius describes Petra both as a 'city of Arabia' and as a 'city of Palestine',[3] a reflection of the way the boundaries of Palestine were altered during the 290s.[4]

2. The first seven books of the *Ecclesiastical History*, even though evidently revised later,[5] were published as a unit before the outbreak of the persecution in 303.[6] However, it seems that by 325, in the light of the important political events of those intervening years, Eusebius revised this work perhaps as many as four times, adding books 8 to 10 and incorporating a revised version of the *Martyrs of Palestine*.[7]

3. The *Theophany*, which incorporates parts of Eusebius' earlier works (especially the *Proof of the Gospel*), has been dated by some to the last years of Eusebius' life.[8] However, the reference to the sacred prostitution still being practised at Heliopolis in Phoenicia[9] evidently suggests a date 'shortly after 324',[10] because this pagan practice was soon discontinued by Constantine.[11] The *Theophany* thus precedes by a decade Eusebius' reworking of it for his speech *On Christ's Sepulchre*.

4. Both the *Commentary on the Psalms* and the *Commentary on Isaiah* were produced after 325. For, though they must surely be indeed the 'final reflections' of a *lifetime's* meditation,[12] nevertheless they both make explicit references to the years after the arrival of Constantine. In the Isaiah commentary Eusebius refers to the downfall of the persecutors, to the appointment of Christian governors and indeed to the existence of a Christian emperor,[13]

---

[2] Wallace-Hadrill (1960), 55-7, following Thomsen (1906), 131 and Schwartz (1907), 1434.

[3] *Onom.*, 36.13-14, 142.7-8, 144.7-9.

[4] Barnes (1981), 110-11, following his (1975), 111-14.

[5] Cf. Grant (1980), 15 and 33 ff.

[6] See Barnes (1981), 128-9, whose opinion is contrary to those cited in 346, fn. 10; cf. also his article (1980).

[7] See Barnes (1981), 156-63, 191-2; Grant (1980), 10-21; Lawlor and Oulton edn. of *Hist. Eccl.* (1928), ii, 2-11.

[8] Wallace-Hadrill (1960), 52-5 and Lightfoot (1880), 333.

[9] *Theoph.*, 2.14.

[10] Barnes (1981), 186 and 367, fn. 176.

[11] *V. Const.*, 3.57.

[12] Barnes (1981), 97.

[13] Refs in ibid., 391, fnn. 39-41.

and in the Psalms work there is a clear reference to the Constantinian building work over the Holy Sepulchre (even if not yet fully completed).[14]

5. Eusebius' speech *On Christ's Sepulchre* was first delivered at the dedication of the Holy Sepulchre on 17 September 335. This has been identified as chapters 11–18 of what has come down to us as *de Laudibus Constantini*.[15] On that occasion the speech would probably also have included a discourse on the physical appearance of the basilica, which Eusebius may subsequently have reused in the *Life of Constantine*.[16] It is highly probable that Eusebius then reused this same speech when addressing the emperor in Constantinople two months later:[17] with the heated controversy over Athanasius at the council of Tyre and his need to hasten from Palestine to Constantinople, Eusebius would have had little time to prepare a new speech.

6. Eusebius' tricennalian oration *In Praise of Constantine* was delivered on 25 July 336; it is preserved in chapters 1–10 of *de Laudibus Constantini*.[18] Eusebius most probably began work on the *Life of Constantine* before Constantine's death,[19] perhaps even while resident in Constantinople during 336.[20] It is possible that book 4 (with its contemporary information) was drafted first, before work was begun on books 1–3. However, it seems clear that Eusebius himself died before it could be properly revised and that it was therefore published posthumously.[21]

Most works attributed to Eusebius, including the *Life of Constantine*, are now accepted as authentic. The authenticity of his

[14] *Comm. in Ps.* [87.11–13], 1064a.

[15] As demonstrated especially by Drake (1976), 35–45; cf. also Barnes (1981), 187, and (1977).

[16] *V. Const.*, 3.25–28, 33–40. The presence of this physical description of the buildings in book 3 may explain the absence of such a description in the *Sep. Chr.*, when it came to be appended to the *V. Const.*; the fact that this contradicts Eusebius' promise in *V. Const.*, 4.46 suggests that book 4 had not been properly revised at the time of Eusebius' death.

[17] Drake (1981), 38–45, arguing from Eusebius' apparently conflicting remarks in *V. Const.*, 4.33, 45–6. Barnes, however, suggests that there may have been two different speeches and that a later editor mistakenly appended the wrong one: see (1977) and (1981), 271.

[18] Barnes (1981), 253 ff.; Drake (1976), 31–8, and 81.

[19] Barnes (1981), 265 and Meyer (1882), 23 ff.

[20] Drake (1988).

[21] Barnes (1981), 265; Pasquali (1910), 369, 386; Winkelmann (GCS, lix, 59, 1975), p. liii ff. For a survey of the immense modern bibliography on the *V. Const.* (including its authenticity), see Winkelmann (1962), 187 ff.

Letter to Constantia was questioned by Murray (1977); her arguments, however, were convincingly countered by Gero (1981). It seems most unlikely that later iconoclasts would have forged this letter in the name of the Arian-tainted Eusebius; on the contrary, the letter accords perfectly both with Eusebius' theology in general and also with the known interest of the imperial family in Palestinian matters.

In the light of the manuscript tradition, questions are inevitably raised concerning the authenticity of much of Eusebius' *Commentary on the Psalms*. As a result it has been simplest to confine our quotations from this work to the 'indubitably Eusebian section', reproduced in PG, xxiii, 441-1221.[22]

Chronological Table

The following outline chronology may therefore be proposed for Eusebius' works:

Before AD 303
  Chronicle
  Onomasticon
  Ecclesiastical History (bks. 1-7)
  Against Hierocles
  Canons

AD 303-325
  Prophetic Eclogues
  Commentary on Luke
  Martyrs of Palestine
  Ecclesiastical History (bks. 8-10)
  Preparation for the Gospel
  Proof of the Gospel
  Gospel Questions and Solutions

AD 325-339
  Letter to the Church of Caesarea
  On the Paschal Festival

[22] As does Barnes (1981), 334, fn. 135. For a more detailed discussion of this question, see Geerard (1974), ii, 263-4; and for a useful assessment of the authenticity of each section of the commentary, see BibPat, iv, 23-7. For the reconstruction of other parts of Eusebius' commentary, see, e.g., Devreesse (1924) and Richard (1956), 88 ff.

(AD 325–339 *cont.*)

Theophany
Letter to Constantia Augusta
Commentary on Isaiah
Commentary on the Psalms
On Christ's Sepulchre
In Praise of Constantine
Against Marcellus
Ecclesiastical Theology
Life of Constantine

CYRIL

1. The precise date of Cyril's *Catechetical Lectures* can safely be narrowed down to either 348 or 350.[23] Jerome states that Cyril composed these lectures when he was very young ('in adolescentia').[24] As a result many scholars favour the early date, even though this may entail Cyril still having been a presbyter at the time (in the last years of Bishop Maximus' episcopate).[25] Others think this unlikely and favour the later date of 350.[26] For our purposes the exact date is of little consequence; for convenience a date of 348 has been assumed throughout the above.[27]

2. The *Letter to Constantius* was clearly written immediately after the appearance of the *parhelion* in the Jerusalem sky on 7 May 351. The date of his *Homily on the Paralytic* remains unclear.

3. Although the authenticity of the five *Mystagogic Lectures* traditionally attributed to Cyril has recently been well defended by Yarnold,[28] it is commonly supposed that they are more likely to date from the years of Cyril's successor, Bishop John.[29] In either

---

[23] *de Vir. Illust.*, 112 (PL, xxiii, 707a).

[24] See Telfer (1955a), 36–8.

[25] See Dix (1945), 347–8, Wilkinson (1981), 9, and Rubin (1982a), 101, fn. 23.

[26] See Telfer, (1955a) 38, and Hunt (1982), 39.

[27] On the problem of how these *Lectures* are to be placed within the days of Lent, see Cabrol (1895), 143–63 and Telfer (1955a), 34–6.

[28] Yarnold (1978).

[29] See Swaans (1942), Cross (1951), pp. xx–xxi, Telfer (1955a), 39–40, *WCJ*, ii, 143–9, and Piedagnel in his introduction to SC, 126 (Paris, 1966), 18–40. For a general discussion, see Quasten, iii (1960), 363–7.

case, they evidently belong to a period much later than the *Catechetical Lectures*. As a result, it has been simplest in our concentration on Cyril's earliest thought to exclude them from our analysis.

BIBLIOGRAPHICAL ABBREVIATIONS

For the bibliographical details of the modern editions of patristic and ancient texts referred to throughout this volume see Bibliography, § I.

AJ	Josephus, *Antiquities of the Jews*
AJA	*American Journal of Archaeology*
AJT	*American Journal of Theology*
AL	*Armenian Lectionary*, ed. Renoux, PO, 35–6 (1969–71)
AnBoll	*Analecta Bollandiana*
BA	*Biblical Archaeologist*
BAR	*Biblical Archaeological Review*
BASOR	*Bulletin of the American Schools of Oriental Research*
BibPat	Biblica Patristica (4 vols., CNRS, Paris, 1975–)
BZ	*Biblische Zeitschrift*
BJ	Josephus, *Bellum Judaicum*
BLE	*Bulletin de littérature ecclésiastique*
BSOAS	*Bulletin of the School of Oriental and African Studies*
CCC	*Creeds, Councils and Controversies* (ed. J. Stevenson, London, 1966)
CCSL	Corpus Christianorum: Series Latina
CHR	*Catholic Historical Review*
CSCO	Corpus scriptorum Christianorum orientalium
CSEL	Corpus scriptorum ecclesiasticorum Latinorum
DB	*Dictionary of the Bible* (ed. J. Hastings, Edinburgh, 1898–1902, rev. 1963)
DBS	Dictionnaire de la Bible: Supplément (ed. L. Pirot, Paris, 1928–)
DCB	*Dictionary of Christian biography, literature, sects and doctrines* (ed. W. Smith and H. Wace, London, 1877–87)
DOP	*Dumbarton Oaks Papers*
DS	Dictionnaire de spiritualité, ascétique et mystique (Paris, 1932–)
DT	Justin Martyr, *Dialogue with Trypho*

EI	*Eretz-Israel*
GCS	Die griechischen christlichen Schriftsteller der ersten drei Jahrhunderte (Berlin 1897–)
GL	*Georgian Lectionary*, ed. Tarchnišvili, CSCO, 189 (1959)
GP	Abel, F. M., *Géographie de la Palestine* (Paris, 1933–8)
GRBS	*Greek, Roman and Byzantine Studies*
HJ	*Heythrop Journal*
HTR	*Harvard Theological Review*
HUCA	*Hebrew Union College Annual*
IEJ	*Israel Exploration Journal*
IES	Israel Exploration Society
JEH	*Journal of Ecclesiastical History*
JN	Vincent, L. H. and Abel, F. M., *Jérusalem Nouvelle* (Paris, 1914)
JPOS	*Journal of the Palestine Oriental Society*
JTS	*Journal of Theological Studies*
LCC	Library of Christian Classics
Lex	*A Greek-English Lexicon* (ed. H. G. Liddell and R. Scott; new edn., Oxford, 1968)
NE	*A New Eusebius* (ed. J. Stevenson, London, 1957)
NPNF	A Select Library of the Nicene and Post-Nicene Fathers of the Christian Church (Oxford, 1887–92; new ser. 1890–)
OCP	*Orientalia Christiana Periodica*
PBSR	*Papers of the British School at Rome*
PEFQS	*Quarterly Statement: Palestine Exploration Fund*
PEQ	*Palestine Exploration Quarterly*
PG	Patrologia Graeca (ed. J. P. Migne, Paris, 1857–)
PGL	*A Patristic Greek Lexicon* (ed. G. W. H. Lampe, Oxford, 1961)
PL	Patrologia Latina (ed. J. P. Migne, Paris, 1841–)
PO	Patrologia Orientalis (Paris, 1907–)
RB	*Revue biblique*
RBK	Reallexikon zur byzantinischen Kunst (ed. K. Wessel and M. Restle, Stuttgart, 1966–)
RE	*Real-Encyclopädie fur classischen Altertumswissen- schaft* (Pauly/ Wissowa; Stuttgart, 1894–Munich, 1976)
RHE	*Revue d'histoire ecclésiastique*
RHR	*Revue de l'histoire des religions*
RSLR	*Rivista di storia e letteratura religiosa*

RSR	*Recherches de science religieuse*
SBFLA	*Studii biblici Franciscani liber annuus*
SC	Sources chrétiennes (Paris, 1941–)
SE	*Studia evangelica*
SP	*Studia patristica*
TU	Texte und Untersuchungen zur Geschichte der altchrist-lichen Literatur (Leipzig/Berlin, 1882–)
VigChr	*Vigiliae Christianae*
ZDPV	*Zeitschrift des deutschen Palästina-Vereins*
ZNW	*Zeitschrift fur die neutestamentliche Wissenschaft*

BIBLIOGRAPHY

I. PATRISTIC AUTHORS
(EDITIONS AND TRANSLATIONS)

(a) Eusebius

Eusebius' works are listed in alphabetical order of their English titles (with their standard abbreviation in brackets). The edition is then cited, to which all references in footnotes refer. Finally, the standard English translation is listed where available.

Against Marcellus [*Adv. Marc.*]: GCS iv (ed. E. Klostermann, 1906; revised G. C. Hansen, 1972), 1–58.

Chronicle [*Chron.*]: GCS vii, 1–2 (revised ed. R. Helm, 1956).

Commentary on Luke [*Comm. in Luc.*]: PG xxiv, 529–606.

Commentary on Isaiah [*Comm. in Is.*]: GCS ix (ed. J. Ziegler, 1975).

Commentary on the Psalms [*Comm. in Ps.*]: PG xxiii, 441–1221.

Ecclesiastical History [*Hist. Eccl.*]: GCS ii, 1–3 (ed. E. Schwartz, 1903–9); Lawlor, H. J. and Oulton, J. E. L., *Eusebius: the Ecclesiastical History and the Martyrs of Palestine* (London, 1928), i, 1–325.

Ecclesiastical Theology [*Theol. Eccl.*]: GCS iv (ed. E. Klostermann, 1906; revised G. C. Hansen, 1972), 59–182.

Gospel Questions and Solutions [*QM, QS, QMS*]: PG xxii, 879–1016.

In Praise of Constantine [*L. Const.*]: GCS i, 195–223.22 (ed. I. A. Heikel, 1911); Drake, H. A., *In Praise of Constantine* (Berkeley, 1976), 83–102.

Letter to the Church of Caesarea [*Ep. Caes.*]: PG xx, 1535–44.

Letter to Constantia Augusta [*Ep. Const.*]: PG xx, 1545–50; Mango, C. A., *The Art of the Byzantine Empire: 312–1453* (New Jersey, 1972), 16–18.

Life of Constantine [*V. Const.*]: GCS i (2) (ed. F. Winkelmann, 1975); not Heikel's earlier edition; Richardson, E. C., *The Life of Constantine*, NPNF, i (Oxford and New York, 1890), 481–559.

Martyrs of Palestine [*Mart. Pal.*]: GCS ii (ed. E. Schwartz, 1908), 907–950; Lawlor, H. J. and Oulton, J. E. L., *Eusebius: the Ecclesiastical History and the Martyrs of Palestine* (London, 1928), i, 327–400.

Onomasticon [Onom.]: GCS iii¹ (ed. E. Klostermann, 1904).

On Christ's Sepulchre [*Sep. Chr.*]: GCS i, 223.23–259 (ed. I. A. Heikel, 1911); Drake, H. A., *In Praise of Constantine: Historical Study and New Translation of Eusebius' 'Tricennial Orations'* (Berkeley, 1976), 103–127.

On the Paschal Festival [*Pasch.*]: PG xxiv, 693–706.

Preparation for the Gospel [*Praep. Ev.*]: GCS viii, 1–2 (ed. K. Mras, 1954 and 1956); Gifford, E. H., *Eusebii Praeparatio Evangelica* (Oxford, 1903).

Proof of the Gospel [*Dem. Ev.*]: GCS vi (ed. I. A. Heikel, 1913); Ferrar, W. J., *The Proof of the Gospel* (2 vols., London, 1920).

Prophetic Eclogues [*Proph. Eclg.*]: PG xxii, 1017–1262.

Theophany [*Theoph.*]: GCS iii,[2] (ed. H. Gressmann, 1904); Lee, S., *Eusebius on the Theophaneia* (Cambridge, 1843).

For further information see Geerard M., *Clavis Patrum Graecorum* (Turnhout, 1974), ii, 262–75.

(*b*) *Cyril*

All the extant works of Cyril (including the probably inauthentic *Mystagogic Lectures*) are found in the following edition:

Reischl, W. K., and Rupp, J. eds., *Sancti Cyrilli Opera* (Munich, 1848–60); McCauley, L. P., and Stephenson, A. A., *The Works of Saint Cyril of Jerusalem* (2 vols., Washington, 1969–70).

Earlier English translations of Cyril's *Lectures* include those by E. H. Gifford, following Newman (1842), in NPNF, vii (Oxford, 1894) and Telfer (a selection) in LCC, iv (London, 1965), both of which have useful introductions on Cyril's life and thought.

(*c*) *Origen*

The edition of Origen's work that has been used throughout is that in the Berlin corpus (GCS, Origen, i–xii), unless otherwise specified.

(*d*) *Other authors*

The Bordeaux Pilgrim [*BP*]: Geyer, P., and Cuntz, O., eds., CCSL, 175, 1–26 (Turnhout, 1965); Wilkinson, J., *Egeria's Travels* (rev. edn., Jerusalem, 1981), 153–63.

Egeria: Franceschini, A., and Weber, R., eds., CCSL 175, 29–103 (Turnhout, 1965): Wilkinson, J., op. cit., 89–147.

II. MODERN AUTHORS

ABEL, F. M. (1918). 'Mont des Oliviers: Ruine de la grotte de l'Eléona', *RB*, 27, 55–8.

—— (1927). 'Koursi', *JPOS*, 7, 112–121.

—— (1933–8). *Géographie de la Palestine* (2 vols, Paris).

AHARONI, Y. (1966). *The Land of the Bible* (Eng. transl., London).

ARMSTRONG, G. T. (1979). 'The Cross in the Old Testament according to Athanasius, Cyril of Jersalem and the Cappadocian Fathers', *Theologia Crucis—Signum Crucis* (Tubingen), 17–38.

AVI-YONAH, M. (1940). *Map of Roman Palestine* (Jerusalem).

—— (1950–51). 'The Foundation of Tiberias', *IEJ*, 1, 160–69.

—— (1954). *The Madaba Mosaic Map* (Jerusalem).

—— (1957). 'Jerusalem and Caesarea', *Judah and Jerusalem* (IES, Jerusalem), 79–85.

—— (1966). *The Holy Land from the Persian to the Arab Conquests (536 BC–AD 640): a historical geography* (Grand Rapids).

—— (1974). *Carta Atlas of the History of the Land of Israel* (Jerusalem).

—— (1976). *The Jews of Palestine: a political history from the Bar Kokba War to the Arab Conquest* (Oxford).

—— (1976). *Gazetteer of Roman Palestine* (Qedem, 5; Jerusalem).

BAGATTI, B. (1952). *Gli antichi edifici sacri di Betlemme* (Jerusalem).

—— (1964). 'Origini dei luoghi santi in Palastina', *SBFLA*, 14, 32–64.

—— (1965). 'Le antichità di Kh. Qana e di Kefer Kenna in Galilea', *SBFLA*, 15, 251–92.

—— (1968). 'Recenti scavi a Betlemme', *SBFLA*, 18, 181–237.

—— (1969). *Excavations in Nazareth* (Eng. transl., Jerusalem).

—— (1971). *The Church from the Circumcision: History and Archaeology of the Judaeo-Christians* (Eng. transl., Jerusalem).

BAGATTI, B. and TESTA, E. (1978). *Il Golgota e la Croce* (Jerusalem).

BALDI, D. (1955). *Enchiridion Locorum Sanctorum* (rev. edn., Jerusalem).

—— (1960). 'Il problema del sito di Bethsaida e delle Motipliazioni dei Pani', *SBFLA*, 10, 120–46.

BARDY, G. (1948). *La question des langues dans l'Église anciennne* (Paris).

BARNABÉ, B. (1901). *Tabor: La Montagne de la Galilee* (Jerusalem).

BARNES, T. D. (1975). 'The Composition of Eusebius' *Onomasticon*', *JTS*, n.s. 26, 412–15.

—— (1977). 'Two Speeches by Eusebius', *GRBS*, 18, 341–5.

—— (1980). 'The editions of Eusebius' "Ecclesiastical History"', *GRBS*, 21, 191–201.

—— (1981). *Constantine and Eusebius* (Cambridge, MA).

—— (1984). 'Some inconsistencies in Eusebius', *JTS*, n.s. 35, 470–75.

BAUS, K. (1965). *From the Apostolic Community to Constantine* (Eng. transl., Freiburg).

BAYNES, N. H. (1972). *Constantine the Great and the Christian Church* (British Academy Raleigh Lecture on History, 1929; 2nd. edn., London).

BENOIT, P. (1975). 'L'emplacement de Bethléem au temps de Jesus', *Dossiers de l' Archéologie*, 10/3, 58–63.

BERKHOF, H. (1939). *Die Theologie des Eusebius von Caesarea* (Amsterdam).

BIHAIN, E. (1973). 'L'épître de Cyrille de Jérusalem à Constance sur la vision de la croix', *Byzantion*, 43, 264–96.

BINDLEY, T. H. (1917). 'On some points, doctrinal and practical, in the Catechetical Lectures of St Cyril of Jerusalem', *AJT*, 21, 598–607.

BISSOLI, G. (1981). 'S. Ciriollo di Gerusalemme: Omelia Sul Paralitico della piscina probatica', *SBFLA*, 31, 177–90.

BONNET, M. and LIPSIUS, R. A. (1891-1903). *Acta Apostolorum Apocrypha* (3 vols., Leipzig).

BOTTE, B. (1932). *Les origines de la Noël et de l'Épiphanie* (Louvain).

BRIAND, J. (1973). *Sion* (Jerusalem).

BROCK, S. P. (1976). 'The rebuilding of the Temple under Julian, a new source', *PEQ*, 108, 103–7.

—— (1977). 'A Letter attributed to Cyril of Jerusalem on the rebuilding of the Temple', *BSOAS*, 40, 267–86.

BROSHI, M. (1977). 'Recent Excavations in the Church of the Holy Sepulchre', *Qadmoniot*, 10/1, 30–32. For an Eng. version, see *BAR* (Dec. 1977), 4–13.

BROWN, J. (1984). 'Holy Places in the Holy Land', *Christian* (Spring), 12–17.

BROWN, R. E. (1966). *The Gospel according to John* (London).

BRUEGGEMANN, W. (1977). *The Land: place as gift, promise and challenge in biblical faith* (Philadelphia).

CABROL, F. (1895). *Étude sur la 'Peregrinatio Silviae': Les églises de Jerusalem: la discipline et la liturgie au ive siècle* (Paris).

—— (1906). *Les Origines Liturgiques* (Paris).

CADIOU. R. (1936). *Commentaires inédits des Psaumes: étude sur les textes d'Origène contenus dans le manuscrit Vindobonensis 8* (Paris).

CAMERON, A. (1983). 'Eusebius of Caesarea and the Rethinking of History', in E. Gabba, ed., *Tria Corda: scritti in onore di Arnaldo Momigliano* (Como), 71–88.

CARDMAN, F. (1979). 'The Rhetoric of Holy Places', *Eighth Patristic Studies Conference: Oxford 1979*, 18–25. See Livingstone, E. A. (1982).

—— (1984). 'Jerusalem and the Sanctification of Place: Christian Holy Places in the Fourth and Fifth Centuries', in P. Henry, ed., *Schools of Thought in the Christian Tradition* (Philadelphia), 49–64.

CHADWICK, H. (1948). 'The Fall of Eustathius of Antioch', *JTS*, 49, 27–35.

—— (1958). 'Ossius of Cordova and the Presidency of the Council of Antioch, 325', *JTS*, n.s. 9, 292–304.

—— (1959). 'The Circle and the Ellipse: Rival Concepts of Authority in the Early Church' (Inaugural Lecture, Oxford); repubd. in *Variorum Reprints* (1982).

—— (1960). 'Faith and Order at the Council of Nicaea', *HTR*, 53, 171–95.

CHESNUT, G. F. (1978). *The first Christian histories: Eusebius, Socrates, Sozomen, Theodoret and Evagrius* (Paris; 2nd edn., Macon, GA, 1986).

CHITTY, D. (1966). *The Desert a City* (Oxford).

CONANT, J. (1956). 'The Original Buildings at the Holy Sepulchre in Jerusalem', *Speculum*, 31, 1–48.

CORBO, V. C. (1965). *Ricerche archeologiche al monte degli Ulivi* (Jerusalem).

—— (1969). *The House of St Peter at Capharnaum* (Jerusalem).

—— (1970). *The Synagogue at Capharnaum* (Jerusalem).

—— (1975). *Cafarnao. 1. Gli edifici della città* (Jerusalem).

—— (1981). *Il Santo Sepolchro di Gerusalemme* (Jerusalem).

CORBO, V., LOFFREDA, S., and SPIJKERMAN, A. (1970). *La sinagoga de Cafarnao dopo gli scavi del 1969* (Jerusalem).

COÜASNON, C. (1974). *The Church of the Holy Sepulchre in Jerusalem* (British Academy Shweich Lecture, London).

CRANZ, F. E. (1952). 'Kingdom and Polity in Eusebius of Caesarea', *HTR*, 45, 47–66.

CROSS, F. L. (1951). *St Cyril of Jerusalem's Lectures on the Christian Sacraments: the Procatechesis and the Five Mystagogic Catecheses* (London).

CROUZEL, H. (1985). *Origène* (Paris).

CROWFOOT, J. W. (1941). *Early Churches in Palestine* (British Academy Shweich Lecture, London).

CULLMANN, O. (1953). *Early Christian Worship* (London).

CURTIS, J. B. (1957). 'The Mount of Olives in Judaeo-Christian tradition', *HUCA*, 28, 137–80.

DALMAN, G. (1935). *Sacred Sites and Ways* (Eng. transl., London).

DANBY, H. (1933). *The Mishnah* (Oxford).

DANIÉLOU, J. (1963). 'Histoire des origines chrétiennes', *RSR*, 51, 112–63.

DAVIES, J. G. (1954). 'The *Peregrinatio Egeriae* and the Ascension', *VigChr*, 8, 93–100.

—— (1957). 'Eusebius' Description of the Martyrium at Jerusalem', *AJA*, 61, 171–3.

DAVIES, W. D. (1974). *The Gospel and the Land: early Christianity and Jewish territorial doctrine* (Berkeley).

DE LANGE, N. R. M. (1976). *Origen and the Jews: studies in Jewish-Christian relations in third century Palestine* (Cambridge).

DESJARDINS, R. (1972). 'Les vestiges du Seigneur au mont des Oliviers', *BLE*, 73, 51–72.

DEVOS, P. (1967). 'La date du voyage d'Égerié', *AnBoll*, 85, 165–94.

—— (1968). 'Égerié a Bethléem', *AnBoll*, 86, 87–108.

—— (1969). 'La "Servante de Dieu" Poemenia', *AnBoll*, 87, 189–212.

DEVREESSE, R. (1924). 'La chaîne sur les Psaumes de Daniele Barbaro', *RB*, 33, 65–81.

—— (1928). 'Chaînes exegetiques grecques', DBS i (Paris), 1119–1233.

DIX, G. (1945). *The Shape of the Liturgy* (London).

DONNER, H. (1979). *Pilgerfahrt ins Heilige Land* (Stuttgart).

DORIVAL, G. (1975). 'La reconstitution du "Commentaire sur les Psaumes" d'Eusèbe de Césarée', *SP*, 15, (= TU, 28), 170–76.

DRAKE, H. A. (1975). 'When was the "de Laudibus Constantini" delivered?', *Historia*, 24, 345–56.

—— (1976). *In Praise of Constantine* (transl. with extended intro.; Berkeley).

—— (1984). 'The Return of the Holy Sepulchre', *CHR*, 70, 263–7.

—— (1985). 'Eusebius on the True Cross', *JEH*, 36, 1–22.

—— (1986). 'Athanasius' First Exile', *GRBS*, 27, 193–204.

—— (1988). 'What Eusebius Knew: The Genesis of the *Vita Constantini*', *Classical Philology*, 83, 20–38.

DUCKWORTH, H. T. F. (1922). *The Church of the Holy Sepulchre* (London).

DUNN, J. D. G. (1975). *Jesus and the Spirit* (London).

—— (1977). *Unity and Diversity in the New Testament* (London).

DYGGVE, E. (1950). 'La question du Saint-Sepulchre a l'époque Constantinienne', *Sixth International Congress of Byzantine Studies: Paris*, 111–23.

ELIADE, M. (1968). *The Sacred and the Profane: the nature of religion* (Eng. transl., New York).

ELLIOTT-BINNS, L. E. (1956). *Galilean Christianity* (London).

ELLUL, J. (1970). *The Meaning of the City* (Eng. transl., Grand Rapids, MI).

FINEGAN, J., (1969). *Archaeology of the New Testament: the Life of Jesus and the Beginning of the Early Church* (Princeton, MA).

FOAKES-JACKSON, F. J. (1933). *Eusebius Pamphili: First Christian Historian—a study of the man and his writings* (Cambridge).

FOERSTER, G. (1971). 'Recent Excavations at Capernaum', *Qadmoniot*, 16, 126–31.

FREND, W. H. C. (1971). 'Ecclesiastical Histoy: its growth and relevance', *The Philosophical Journal* (Glasgow), 8, 38–51.

—— (1984). *The Rise of Christianity* (London).

FREYNE, S. (1980). *Galilee from Alexander the Great to Hadrian: 323 BCE to 135 CE* (Wilmington,).

GARITTE, G. (1958). *Le calendrier Palestino-Géorgien du Sinaiticus 24 (Xe siècle)* (Brussels).

GEERARD, M. (1974). *Clavis Patrum Graecorum* (Turnhout).

GERO, S. (1981). 'The True Image of Christ: Eusebius' "Letter to Constantia" Reconsidered', *JTS*, n.s. 32, 460–70.

GIFFORD, E. H. (1894). *Cyril of Jerusalem*, NPNF, vii (Oxford).

—— (1903). *Eusebii Praeparatio Evangelica* (Oxford).

GOODMAN, M. (1983). *State and Society in Roman Galilee*, AD 132–212 (New Jersey).

GRABAR, A. (1946). *Martyrium: recherches sur le culte des reliques et l'art chrétien antique* (2 vols, Paris).

GRAHAM, S. (1913). *With the Russian Pilgrims to Jerusalem* (London).

GRANT, R. M. (1967). 'Early Episcopal Succession', *SP*, 7 (=TU, 108), 179–84.

—— (1971). 'The Case against Eusebius or "Did the Father of Church History write History?" ', *SP*, 12, (=TU, 115), 413–21.

—— (1980). *Eusebius as Church Historian* (Oxford).

GRAY, J. (1969). *A History of Jerusalem* (London).

GREENLEE, J. H. (1955). *The Gospel text of Cyril of Jerusalem* (Copenhagen).

GRESSMANN, H. (1903). 'Studien zu Eusebs Theophanie', TU, 23.3.

GROH, D. E. (1983). 'The Onomastikon of Eusebius and the Rise of Christian Palestine', *Ninth Patristic Studies Conference: Oxford 1983*, 23–32. See Livingstone, E. A. (1985).

HAMILTON, R. W. (1947). *The Church of the Nativity, Bethlehem: a guide* (Jerusalem).

—— (1952). 'Jerusalem in the Fourth Century', *PEQ*, 83–90.

—— (1978). 'Patterns of Holiness', in *Archaeology in the Levant* (Warminster), 194–201.

HAMRICK, E. W. (1977). 'The Third Wall of Agrippa I', *BA*, 40, 18–23.

HANSON, R. P. C. (1959). *Allegory and Event: a study of the sources and significance of Origen's interpretation of Scripture* (London).

HARL, M. (1958). *Origène et la fonction révélatrice du Verbe Incarné* (Paris).

HARNACK, A. and PREUSCHEN, E. (1893–1904). *Geschichte der altchristlichen Literatur bis Eusebius* (Leipzig).

HARNACK, A. (1908). *The Mission and Expansion of Christianity in the First Three Centuries* (Eng. transl., New York).

HARVEY, A. E. (1966). 'Melito and Jerusalem', *JTS*, n.s. 17, 401–4.

HARVEY, W. (1935a). *The Church of the Holy Sepulchre, Jerusalem; structural survey final report* (London); with an introduction by E. T. Richmond.

——— (1935b). *Structural Survey of the Church of the Nativity, Bethlehem* (London).

HEISENBERG, A. (1908). *Grabeskirche und Apostelkirche. Zwei Basiliken Konstantins* (Leipzig).

HENNECKE, E., ed. (1963–5). *New Testament Apocrypha* (2 vols; Eng. transl., London).

HERFORD, R. T. (1903). *Christianity in Talmud and Midrash* (London).

HEYER, F. (1984). *Kirchengeschichte des Heiligen Landes* (Kohlhammer).

HOLLIS, C., and BROWNRIGG, R. (1969). *Holy Places: Jewish, Christian and Muslim monuments in the 'Holy Land'* (London).

HONIGMANN, E. (1950). 'Juvenal of Jerusalem', *DOP*, 5, 209–79.

HUNT, E. D. (1982). *Holy Land Pilgrimage in the later Roman Empire AD 312–460* (Oxford).

JAMES, M. R. (1953). *The Apocryphal New Testament* (rev. edn., Oxford).

JEREMIAS, J. (1926). 'Wo lag Golgotha und das Heilige Grab?', Ἄγγελος, 1 (Leipzig), 141–73.

——— (1958). *Heiligengräber in Jesu Umwelt* (Gottingen).

——— (1969). *Jerusalem in the Time of Jesus* (Eng. transl., London).

KEE, A. (1982). *Constantine versus Christ: the Triumph of Ideology* (London).

KELLY, J. N. D. (1972). *Early Christian Creeds* (3rd edn., London).

——— (1975). *Jerome: his life, writings, and controversies* (London).

——— (1977). *Early Christian Doctrines* (5th edn., London).

KENYON, K. M. (1979). *Archaeology in the Holy Land* (4th edn., London).

KLOSTERMANN, E. (1902). 'Eusebius Schrift περὶ τῶν τοπικῶν ὀνομάτων', *TU*, 23.2, 1–28.

KOPP, K. (1963). *The Holy Places of the Gospels* (Eng. transl., Freiburg).

KOTTING, B. J. (1950). *Peregrinatio Religiosa: Wallfahrten in der Antike und das Pilgerwesen in der alten Kirche* (Munster).

——— (1959). 'Gregor von Nyssa's Wallfahrtskritik', *SP*, 5 (= TU, 80), 360–7.

KRAUTHEIMER, R. (1975). *Early Christian and Byzantine Architecture* (3rd edn., Harmondsworth).

KRETSCHMAR, G. (1971). 'Festkalender und Memorialstätten Jerusalems in altkirchlicher Zeit', *ZDPV*, 87, 167–205.

——— (1988). *Jerusalemer Heiligtumstraditionen in altkirchlicher und fruhislamischer Zeit* (Wiesbaden).

KUHNEL, B. (1987). *From the earthly. to the heavenly Jerusalem: representations of the Holy City in Christian Art of the First Millenium* (Rome).

LAGRANGE, M. J. (1895). 'Origène, la critique textuelle et la tradition topographique', *RB*, 4, 501–24.

LAMPE, G. W. H. (1984). 'AD 70 in Christian Reflection' in E. Bammel and C. F. D. Moule, eds., *Jesus and the Palestine of his day* (Cambridge), 153-72.

LASSUS, J. (1967). 'L'Empereur Constantin, Eusèbe et les Lieux Saints', *RHR*, 171, 135-44.

LAWLOR, H. J. (1912). *Eusebiana* (Oxford).

LEBON, P. J. (1924). 'Saint Cyrille de Jérusalem et sa position doctrinale dans les luttes provoquées par l'arianisme', *RHE*, 20, 181-210, 357-86.

LEVINE, L. I. (1975a). *Caesarea under Roman Rule* (Leiden).

—— (1975b). *Roman Caesarea: An Archaeological-Topographical Study* (Jerusalem).

LIGHTFOOT, J. B. (1880). 'Eusebius', *DCB*, ii, 308-48.

LIGHTFOOT, R. H. (1938). *Locality and Doctrine in the Gospels* (London).

LIMOR, O. (1978). *Christian Traditions on the Mount of Olives in the Byzantine and Arab Periods* (diss., Hebrew U., Jerusalem).

LINDER, A. (1985). 'Jerusalem as a focus of Confrontation between Judaism and Christianity' in R. I. Cohen, ed., *Vision and conflicts in the Holy Land* (Jerusalem).

LIVINGSTONE, E. A., ed. (1982). *SP*, 17 (Oxford) [1979 Oxford Conference].

—— (1985). *SP*, 18 (Michigan) [1983 Oxford Conference].

—— (1989). *SP*, 19-22 (Louvain) [1987 Oxford Conference].

LOFFREDA, S. (1969). 'Scavi a Kafr Kanna', *SBFLA*, 19, 328-48.

—— (1972). 'The Synagogue at Capharnaum. Archaeological Evidence for its Late Chronology', *SBFLA*, 22, 204-35.

—— (1975). *The Sanctuaries of Tabgha* (Eng. transl., Jerusalem).

LOHMEYER, E. T. (1936). *Galiläa und Jerusalem* (Gottingen).

LUIBHEID, C. (1978). *Eusebius of Caesarea and the Arian Crisis* (Dublin).

MACKOWSKI, R. M. (1979). 'Scholar's Qanah', *BZ*, 23, 278-84.

MADER, E. (1957). *Mambre* (2 vols., Freiburg).

MANGO, C. A. (1972). *The Art of the Byzantine Empire, 312-1453* (New Jersey).

MARAVAL, P. (1982). 'La Transfiguration au Mt. Tabor?', *La Monde de la Bible*, 23, 24.

MARCHET, X. (1924). *Le veritable emplacement du Palais de Caïaphe* (Paris).

MARXSEN, W. (1969). *Mark the Evangelist* (Eng. transl., Nashville, TN).

McBIRNIE, W. S. (1975). *The Search for the Authentic Tomb of Jesus* (CA).

McGUCKIN, J. A. (1983). 'The Patristic Exegesis of the Transfiguration', *Ninth Patristic Studies Conference: Oxford 1983*, 335-41. *See* Livingstone, E. A. (1985).

MEISTERMANN, B. (1921). *Capharnaüm et Bethsaide* (Paris).

—— (1920). *Gethsemani* (Paris).

MILIK, J. T. (1959 and 1960). 'Notes d'épigraphie et de topographie Palestiniennes', *RB*, 66 (1959), 550–75; *RB*, 67 (1960), 354–67 and 550–91.

MOMIGLIANO, A. (1963). 'Pagan and Christian Historiography in the fourth century AD.' in *The Conflict between Paganism and Christianity* (Oxford), 79–99.

MOSSHAMMER, A. A. (1979). *The Chronicle of Eusebius and Greek chronographic tradition* (Lewisburg).

MURPHY-O'CONNOR, J. (1988). *The Holy Land: an Archaeological Guide from Earliest Times to 1700* (rev. edn., Oxford).

MURRAY, C. (1977). 'Art and the Early Church', *JTS*, n.s. 28, 303–45.

NAUTIN, P. (1977). *Origène, sa vie et son oeuvre* (Paris).

NEVILLE, G. (1971). *The City of our God: God's presence amongst his people* (London).

NEWMAN, J. H. (1842). *The Catechetical Lectures of Saint Cyril*, Library of the Fathers (Oxford).

OPITZ, H. G. (1935). 'Euseb von Caesarea als Theologe', *ZNW*, 34, 1–19.

ORFALI, G. (1922). *Capharnaüm et ses ruines* (Paris).

—— (1924). *Gethsemani* (Paris).

OTTO, R. (1923). *The Idea of the Holy* (Eng. transl., Oxford).

OVADIAH, A. (1970). *Corpus of the Byzantine Churches in the Holy Land* (Eng. transl., Bonn); suppl. in *Levant*, 14 (1982), 122–70.

PARKES, J. (1934). *The Conflict of the Church and the Synagogue* (London).

PARROT, A. (1957). *Golgotha and the Church of the Holy Sepulchre* (Eng. transl., London).

PASQUALI, G. (1910). 'Die Composition der Vita Constantini des Eusebius', *Hermes*, 46, 369–86.

PAULIN, A. (1959). *Saint Cyrille de Jérusalem Catéchète* (Paris).

PEROWNE, S. (1965). Jerusalem and Bethlehem (London).

—— (1976). *Holy Places of Christendom* (London).

PINKERFELD, J. (1960). 'David's Tomb', *Rabinovitz Fund Bulletin*, 3, 41–3.

PITRA, J. B., ed. (1876–91). *Analecta Sacra* (8 vols., Paris).

PIXNER, B. (1979). 'Nea Sion', *Heilige Land*, 3. 2/3, 2–13.

—— (1985). 'Le synagogue de Capharnaum', *Le Monde de la Bible*, 38, 23–26.

POLLARD, T. E. (1970). *Johannine Christology and the Early Church* (Cambridge).

PRITZ, R. A. (1988). Nazarene Jewish Christianity: from the end of the

New Testament period until its disappearance in the fourth century (Jerusalem and Leiden).

QUASTEN, J. (1950–60). *Patrology* (3 vols; Utrecht).

RABAN, A. (1985). *Harbour Archeology: Proceedings of the First International Workshop on Ancient Mediterranean Harbours* ([*BAR*] Oxford).

RAHLFS, A., ed. (1935). *Septuaginta* (Stuttgart).

RENARD, H. (1900). 'Die Marienkirchen auf dem Berge Sion in ihrem Zusammenhang mit dem Abendmahlssaale, *Das Heilige Land*, 44, 3–23.

RENOUX, A. (1969–71). *Le codex arménien Jérusalem 121* (2 vols: PO, 35.1, 36.2; Turnhout).

RICHARD, M. (1956). 'Les premières chaînes sur le psautier', *Bulletin d'information de l'institut de recherche et d'histoire des textes*, 87–98.

RICHARDSON, E. C. (1890). *Eusebius*, NPNF, i (Oxford and New York).

RICKEN, F. (1967). 'Die Logoslehre des Eusebios von Caesarea und der Mittelplatonismus', *Theologie und philosophie*, 42, 341–58.

ROKEAH, D. (1985). *Jews, Christians and Pagans in Conflict* (Jerusalem).

ROMANOFF, P. (1937). *Onomasticon of Palestine* (New York).

RONDEAU, M. (1961). 'Eusèbe de Césarée', DS, 4 (Paris).

RUBIN, Z. (1982a). 'The Church of the Holy Sepulchre and the conflict between the sees of Caesarea and Jerusalem' in L. I. Levine, ed., *Jerusalem Cathedra*, 2 (Jerusalem and Detroit), 79–105.

—— (1982b). 'Joseph the Comes and the attempts to convert the Galilee to Christianity in the fourth century CE.', *Cathedra*, 26, 105–16.

—— (1984). 'The tenure of Maximus, Bishop of Jerusalem, and the conflict between Caesarea and Jerusalem during the fourth century', *Cathedra*, 31, 31–42.

SAFRAI, S. (1973). 'The Holy Congregation in Jerusalem', *Scripta Hierosolymitana*, 62–78.

SALLER, S. J. (1957). *Excavations at Bethany* (Jerusalem).

SALLER, S. J. and TESTA, E (1961). *The Archaeological Setting of the Shrine of Bethphage* (Jerusalem).

SCHWARTZ, E. (1907). 'Eusebios von Caesarea', *RE*, 6, 1370–1439.

—— (1913). *Kaiser Constantin und die christliche Kirche* (Leipzig and Berlin).

SIMON, M. (1972). *La Civilisation de l'antiquité et le Christianisme* (Paris).

SIMONETTI, M. (1983). 'Esegesi e ideologia nel Commento a Isaia di Eusebio', *RSLR*, 19.1.

SIRINELLI, J. (1961). *Les vues historiques d'Eusèbe de Césarée durant la periode prenicéenne* (Dakar).

SMALLWOOD, E. M. (1976). *The Jews under Roman Rule* (Leiden).

SMITH, G. A. (1931). *The Historical Geography of the Holy Land* (25th edn., London).

SPERBER, D. (1978). *Roman Palestine 200–400, the Land* (Ramat-Gan).

STANLEY, A. P. (1883). *Lectures on the History of the Eastern Church* (new edn., London).

STEAD, G. C. (1973). 'Eusebius and the Council of Nicaea', *JTS*, n.s. 24, 85–100.

STEMBERGER, G. (1974). 'Galilee—Land of Salvation', in *The Gospel and the Land*, see W. D. Davies (1974), 409–38.

STEPHENSON, A. A. (1955). 'St Cyril of Jerusalem and the Alexandrian Christian Gnosis', *SP*, 1 (=TU, 63), 147–56.

STEVENSON, J. (1929). *Studies in Eusebius* (Cambridge).

—— (1957). *A New Eusebius* (London).

—— (1966). *Creeds, Councils and Controversies* (London).

STORCH, R. (1971). 'The "Eusebian Constantine"', *Church History*, 40, 145–55.

STORME, A. (1969). *Bethany* (Jerusalem).

—— (1971). *Le Mont des Oliviers* (Jerusalem).

—— (1982). 'La grotte et la crèche de Bethléem dans les textes primitifs', *La Terre Sainte* (Nov.), 266–74.

STRANGE, J. F. (1977). 'The Capernaum and Herodium Publications' [review of Corbo. 1975], *BASOR*, 226 (April), 67–73.

STRANGE, J. F. and MEYERS, E. (1981). *Archaeology, the Rabbis and Early Christianity* (London).

STRANGE, J. F. and SHANKS, H. (1982). 'Has the house where Jesus stayed in Capernaum been found?', *BAR*, (Dec.), 26–37.

—— (1983). 'The Synagogue where Jesus preached found at Capernaum', *BAR*, (Dec.), 24.

SWAANS, W. J. (1942). 'À propos des "Catécheses mystagogiques" attribuées à S. Cyrille de Jérusalem', *Muséon*, 55, 1–43.

SWETE, H. B. (1912). *The Holy Spirit in the Ancient Church* (London).

TARCHNIŠVILI, M., ed., (1959). 'Le Grand Lectionnaire de l'Église de Jérusalem (V–VIIIe)', CSCO, 189, 205 (Louvain, 1959).

TELFER, W. (1955a). *Cyril of Jerusalem and Nemesius of Emesa*, LCC, iv (London).

—— (1955b). 'Constantine's Holy Land Plan', *SP*, 1 (=TU, 63), 696–700.

TESTA, E. (1964). 'Le Grotte dei misteri Giudeo-Cristiane', *SBFLA*, 65–144.

—— (1972). 'La Nuova Sion', *SBFLA*, 48–72.

THOMSEN, P. (1902). 'Palästina nach dem Onomasticon des Eusebius', *ZDPV*, 26, 97–188.

—— (1906). 'Untersuchungen zur älteren Palästinaliteratur', *ZDPV*, 29, 101–32.

—— (1907). *Loca Santa* (Halle).

TODD, J. (1983). 'Wither Pilgrimage?', *Publications of Notre Dame of Jerusalem*, 20–54.

TRAKATELLIS, D. C. (1976). *The Pre-existence of Christ in the writings of Justin Martyr* (Missoula).

TRIGG, J. W. (1983). *Origen: the Bible and Philosophy in the third-century Church* (London).

TSAFRIR, Y. (1967). 'The Conflict between Jews and Christians in the Tiberias region', *Kol Eretz Naphtali* (Jerusalem), 79–90.

—— (1975). *Zion: the Southwestern Hill of Jerusalem and its Place in the Urban Development of Jerusalem during the Byzantine period* (diss., Hebrew U., Jerusalem).

—— (1977). 'Muqaddasi's Gates of Jerusalem: a new identification based on Byzantine sources', *IEJ*, 27, 152–62.

—— (1978). 'Jerusalem', in RBK, iii, 525–615.

—— (1984). *Archeology and Art: Eretz Israel from the Destruction of the Second Temple to the Moslim Conquest*, ii (Jerusalem).

TURNER, C. H. (1900). 'Early Episcopal Lists', *JTS*, 1, 529–53.

TURNER, H. W. (1965). 'The Christian Version of the Sacred Place', *SE*, 5 (=TU, 103), 141–5.

VILNAY, Z. (1973). *Legends of Jerusalem* (Philadelphia).

VINCENT, L. H. (1957). 'L'Eléona, sanctuaire primitif de l'Ascension', *RB*, 64, 48–71.

WALKER, P. W. L. (1987). 'Eusebius, Cyril and the Holy Places', *Tenth Patristic Studies Conference: Oxford 1987*, 20, 306–314. See Livingstone, E. A. (1989).

WALLACE-HADRILL, D. S. (1960). *Eusebius of Caesarea* (London).

WARD-PERKINS, J. B. (1954). 'Constantine and the Origins of the Christian Basilica', *PBSR*, 22, 69–90.

—— (1966). 'Memoria, Martyr's Tomb and Martyr's Church', *JTS*, n.s. 17, 20–37.

WARMINTON, B. H. (1983). 'The Sources of Some Constantinian Documents in Eusebius' "Ecclesiastical History" and "Life of Constantine"', *Ninth Patristic Studies Conference: Oxford 1983*, 93–8. See Livingstone, E. A. (1985).

WAUGH, E. (1950). *Helena* (London).

WEBER, A. (1965). 'ΑΡΧΗ: *Ein Beitrag zur Christologie des Eusebius von Cäsarea* (Rome).

WERBLOWSKY, R. J. Z. (1973–4). 'Jerusalem: "holy city" of three religions', *Jaarbericht ex Oriente Lux*, 23, 423–39.

WILKEN, R. L. (1986). 'Early Christian Chiliasm, Jewish Messianism, and the idea of the Holy Land', *HTR*, 79, 298–307.

WILKINSON, J. (1972). 'The Tomb of Christ', *Levant*, 4, 83–97.

428   *Bibliography*

—— (1974). 'L'apport de Saint Jérome à la topographie', *RB*, 81, 245–57.

—— (1976). 'Christian Pilgrims in Jerusalem during the Byzantine Period', *PEQ*, 108, 75–101.

—— (1977). *Jerusalem Pilgrims before the Crusades* (Warminster).

—— (1978). *Jerusalem as Jesus knew it: Archaeology as Evidence* (London).

—— (1979). 'Jewish influences on the early Christian rite of Jerusalem', *Muséon*, 92, 347–59.

—— (1981). *Egeria's Travels* (rev. edn., Jerusalem).

WILLIAMS, G. H. (1951a). 'Christology and Church-State Relations in the Fourth Century', *Church History*, 20/3 (Sept.), 3–33; 20/4 (Dec., 1951b), 3–26.

WILSON, C. W. (1902). 'Sion', *DB*, iv, 982–4.

WINDISCH, H. (1925). 'Die ältesten christlichen Palästinapilger', *ZDPV*, 48, 145–58.

WINKELMANN, F. (1962). 'Zur Geschichte des Authentizatsproblems der Vita Constantini', *Klio*, 40, 187–243.

WISTRAND, E. K. H. (1952). *Konstantins Kirche am heiligen Grab in Jerusalem nach den ältesten literarischen Zeugnissen* (Gothenburg).

WOLF, C. U. (1964). 'Eusebius of Caesarea and the Onomastikon', *BA*, 27, 66–96.

WOLFSON, H. A. (1957). 'Philosophical implications of the theology of Cyril of Jerusalem', *DOP*, 11, 1–19.

WRIGHT, C. J. H. (1983). *Living as the People of God: the relevance of Old Testament Ethics* (Leicester).

WRIGHT, W. (1866). 'Eusebius of Caesarea on the Star', *Journal of Sacred Literature*, 4th ser. 9, 117–36; 10 (1867), 150–64.

YARNOLD, E. (1978). 'The authorship of the Mystagogic Catecheses attributed to Cyril of Jerusalem', *HJ*, 19, 143–61.

—— (1983). 'Who planned the churches at the Christian Holy Places in the Holy Land?', *Ninth Patristic Studies Conference: Oxford 1983*, 105–9. *See* Livingstone, E. A. (1985).

ZIEGLER, J. (1931). 'Die Peregrinatio Aetheriae und das Onomastikon des Eusebius', *Biblica*, 12, 70–84.

INDEX OF SCRIPTURE REFERENCES

Old Testament

New Testament

INDEX OF TEXTS

References in **bold** indicate a major discussion.

(*a*) Eusebius

(*b*) Cyril

GENERAL INDEX

References in **bold** indicate a major discussion.